Writing and Reading Across the Curriculum

Writing and Reading Across the Curriculum

Brief Edition

Second Edition

Laurence Behrens
University of California
Santa Barbara

Leonard J. Rosen
Bentley College

PEARSON
Longman

New York • San Francisco • Boston
London • Toronto • Sydney • Tokyo • Singapore • Madrid
Mexico City • Munich • Paris • Cape Town • Hong Kong • Montreal

To Bonnie, Michael, Amy, and Keiko—
and to L.C.R., Jonathan, and Matthew

Senior Sponsoring Editor: Virginia L. Blanford
Executive Marketing Manager: Megan Galvin-Fak
Senior Supplements Editor: Donna Campion
Production Manager: Eric Jorgensen
Project Coordination, Text Design, and Electronic Page Makeup: Elm Street Publishing Services, Inc.
Cover Designer/Manager: John Callahan
Photo Researcher: Julie Tesser
Manufacturing Buyer: Lucy Hebard
Printer and Binder: Courier Corporation
Cover Printer: Courier Corporation

For permission to use copyrighted material, grateful acknowledgment is made to the copyright holders on pp. 507–510, which are hereby made part of this copyright page.

Library of Congress Cataloging-in-Publication Data
Behrens, Laurence.
        Writing and reading across the curriculum/Laurence Behrens, Leonard J. Rosen.—Brief ed., 2nd ed.
            p. cm.
        Includes index.
        ISBN 0-321-39581-6
            1. College readers. 2. Interdisciplinary approach in education—Problems, exercises, etc.
        3. English language—Rhetoric—Problems, exercises, etc. 4. Academic writing—Problems, exercises, etc. I. Rosen, Leonard J. II. Title.

PE1417.B396 2006
808'.0427—dc22

                                                                                                2005055228

Please visit us at www.ablongman.com/behrens

ISBN 0-321-39581-6

3 4 5 6 7 8 9 10—CRS—08 07

Detailed Contents

Chapter 2
Critical Reading and Critique   24

Chapter 3
Synthesis   45

What Is a Synthesis?   45

Purpose   45

PART II
AN ANTHOLOGY OF READINGS   105

AMERICAN STUDIES
Chapter 7
What's Happening at the Mall?   245

BUSINESS
Chapter 9
New and Improved: Six Decades of Advertising   409

Preface

Writing and Reading Across the Curriculum: Brief Edition was created for those who find the standard edition appealing and useful but who also find its length impractical. The present text, for the most part, represents a selection from, rather than a condensation of, the longer edition. Rather than reducing the number of selections in each of the seven chapters of the anthology section (a problematic strategy because the chapters have been designed as wholes, rather than as assemblages of parts), we have retained five of the chapters from the standard edition in their entirety. This approach offers teachers and students considerable flexibility in selecting source material for discussion and writing on a given disciplinary topic while still providing a sufficient variety of topics for a ten- to fifteen-week academic term.

The rhetoric section preceding the anthology of readings has been abbreviated to cover those writing types for which *Writing and Reading Across the Curriculum (WRAC)* is best known: the *summary*, the *critique*, and the *synthesis*. In this second brief edition, we add the skill of *analysis*. The *Brief Edition* does not include the longer text's chapters on introductions, conclusions, and theses, and on research. Many instructors, however, already supplement their course reader with a handbook that provides ample coverage of these topics.

STRUCTURE

Like the longer text, *Writing and Reading Across the Curriculum: Brief Edition* is divided into two parts. The first part introduces the strategies of summary, critique, synthesis, and analysis. We take students step-by-step through the process of writing papers based on source material, explaining and demonstrating how summaries, critiques, syntheses, and analyses can be generated from the kinds of readings students will encounter later in the book—and throughout their academic careers. The second part of the text consists of five subject chapters drawn from both academic and professional disciplines. Each subject is not only interesting in its own right but is representative of the kinds of topics typically studied during the course of an undergraduate education. We also believe that students and teachers will discover connections among the thematic chapters of this edition that further enhance opportunities for writing, discussion, and inquiry.

FOCUS ON ARGUMENTATION

Part I of *Writing and Reading Across the Curriculum: Brief Edition* is designed to prepare students for college-level assignments across the disciplines. This edition continues the standard edition's strengthened emphasis on the writing process and on argument, in particular. We emphasize the following:

- **The Elements of Argument: Claim, Support, Assumption.** This section adapts the Toulmin approach to argument to the kinds of readings that students will encounter in Part II of the text.

- **Developing and Organizing the Support for Your Arguments.** This section helps students to mine source materials for facts, expert opinions, and examples that will support their arguments.
- **Annotated Student Argument Paper.** A sample student paper highlights and discusses argumentative strategies that a student writer uses in drafting and developing a paper.

PART I: NEW APPARATUS, TOPICS, READINGS, AND STUDENT PAPERS

New Apparatus, Chapters 1–4

New Boxes and Exercises

Throughout Part I, we have added boxed material that emphasizes the practical applications of writing summaries, syntheses, and critiques. We have also provided brief exercises so that students can practice reading and writing critically in a controlled environment, with specially chosen selections, as they work through the instructional materials.

Chapter 1: Summary

A New Model for Marriage

Students are taken through the process of writing a summary of Barbara Graham's "The Future of Love: Kiss Romance Goodbye, It's Time for the Real Thing." We demonstrate how to annotate a source and divide it into sections, how to develop a thesis, and how to write and smoothly join section summaries.

Chapter 2: Critical Reading and Critique

A model essay, based on Greg Critser's "Too Much of a Good Thing" (in the "Weight Debate" chapter), has been written to demonstrate the process of critique.

Chapter 3: Synthesis

Volunteering in America

We offer a new argument synthesis, "Keeping Volunteering Voluntary," along with summaries and excerpts of several source materials for that paper. The argument synthesizes (among other sources) the work of William James, Plato's "Crito," and opinion pieces by various advocates and detractors of national service. While conceding that the government has a constitutional right to raise armies, the writer argues that an analogous right to compel young people to national, nonmilitary service has no basis either logically or morally.

Chapter 4: Analysis

We are pleased and excited to offer a major new chapter to Part I on writing analyses. The chapter opens with brief, competing analyses of *The Wizard of Oz* that demonstrate how, employing different analytical principles (one psychoanalytic and the other political), two writers can read very different meanings into the classic movie. Following an example analysis by Marie Winn that examines excessive television viewing as an addiction ("The Plug-in Drug"), we present a student example of analysis: an application of a theory by sociologist Randall Collins to living conditions in a college dormitory. We explain how to locate principles useful for conducting analyses, and we show how to write analyses themselves. Throughout Part II in the anthology, students will find ample occasions to practice this essential skill.

PART II: THEMATIC CHAPTERS

Part II of *Writing and Reading Across the Curriculum: Brief Edition* provides students with opportunities to practice the skills of summary, synthesis, critique, and analysis they have learned in Part I.

Chapter 5: Cyberspace and Identity

E-mail and other forms of cybercommunication have so thoroughly insinuated themselves into our lives that we can hardly imagine life without them—an extraordinary development given that little more than a decade ago, the technology was not widely known beyond the scientific and engineering communities. That cybercommunication enhances—and distracts us from—our daily business is a given. Less clear though is the extent to which the technology has begun to alter our sense of self—an alteration that we explore in this chapter. Is the stockbroker who enters an online space to play one of the endless variants of *Dungeons and Dragons* the same starched professional she projects to her colleagues and clients at the office? When e-mailing a prospective date in an online club, how does a young man represent himself, knowing that he cannot be seen? In this edition, we add new selections on the phenomena of instant messaging and blogging, as well as a new version of Michael Lewis's astounding story about a fifteen-year-old high school student who became a top legal expert on a major online information site.

Chapter 6: Obedience to Authority

The chapter that focuses on obedience continues to build on the profoundly disturbing Milgram experiments. Other selections in this chapter, such as Philip K. Zimbardo's account of his Stanford prison experiment and Solomon E. Asch's "Opinions and Social Pressure," have provided additional perspectives on the significance of the obedience phenomenon. This edition adds three articles: The chapter now opens with a selection on the Abu Ghraib (Iraq) prison scandal. Crispin

Sartwell suggests that under certain circumstances we are all capable of committing acts of unspeakable evil. And Theodore Dalrymple maintains that blind disobedience to authority can be just as dangerous as blind obedience.

Chapter 7: What's Happening at the Mall?

In this chapter we gather the work of a historian, an urban planner, a geographer, a sociologist, and scholars in American studies and comparative religion to investigate a fixture on the American landscape: the shopping mall. Malls are not only ubiquitous (45,000 of them as of 2003); they stand at the confluence of streams in American myth, race, class, business, gender, law, and design. As James Farrell, one of the authors in this chapter, puts it: Malls are "a place where we answer important questions: What does it mean to be human? What are people for? What is the meaning of things? Why do we work? What do we work for?" What's happening at the mall, it turns out, is important sociologically and culturally—but it is far from obvious. The selections gathered here will challenge students' commonplace views of malls. With this chapter we have tried to make the ordinary a bit strange (malls as religious centers?) and in the process provide ample occasion for thoughtful writing.

Chapter 8: Weight Debate

Four years ago, when this chapter first appeared, the nation was just waking up to what the medical community was describing as an "epidemic" of obesity. Since that time the problem of unwanted weight gain has only intensified; we have, accordingly, retained the topic, cycling out three selections and adding three: an overview of America's problems with weight from *U.S. News and World Report*; updated statistics from the Centers for Disease Control; and an editorial from the journal *Science* on the ironies of our government's assigning one agency both to promote the interests of the food industry and to advise Americans on how to lose weight. This chapter offers students an opportunity to explore the place of food and weight, both in their own lives and in the broader cultural landscape.

Chapter 9: New and Improved: Six Decades of Advertising

The centerpiece of this new chapter is a portfolio of forty-two full-page advertisements for cigarettes, liquor and beer, automobiles, food, and beauty and cleaning products that have appeared in popular American and British magazines since the mid-1940s. Advertisements are key indicators not only of our consumerism but also of our changing cultural values and our less variable human psychology. Students will find the new advertising chapter ideal for practicing their analysis skills. Prior to the portfolio, we offer several analytic tools that students can use to discern how advertisements operate: how they attempt to manipulate us, how they reveal our values and our sometimes hidden drives. The first article identifies the fifteen basic appeals of advertising; the next two consider the textual and graphic elements of the marketer's craft. Another summarizes the charges commonly leveled against advertising. A fascinating view of how marketers have presented five product categories over sixty years, this chapter will help students see themselves, culturally speaking, as products of a particular time and place.

ANCILLARIES

Student Supplements

- The *Writing and Reading Across the Curriculum* **Companion Website (www.ablongman.com/behrens)** includes additional exercises, links, model papers, and many more student resources.

- **MyCompLab** (www.mycomplab.com) offers a wide array of resources for composition students. Available packaged free with most Longman titles.

- *The New American Webster Handy College Dictionary*, Third Edition, is available as a free supplement for students, when bundled with the text. ISBN 0-451-18166-2.

Instructor Supplements

- The *Instructor's Manual* for *Writing and Reading Across the Curriculum*, Ninth Edition, which can be used with this Brief Edition, provides sample syllabi and course calendars, chapter summaries, classroom ideas for writing assignments, introductions to each set of readings, and answers to review questions. Included as well are tips on how to incorporate the textbook's Companion Website into the course material. ISBN 0-321-17959-5.

- The **Companion Website (www.ablongman.com/behrens)** links to the full *Instructor's Manual* in a password-protected instructor section. The site includes additional exercises, links, model papers, and many more student resources. Instructors, please contact your Longman representative for further details.

ACKNOWLEDGMENTS

We have benefited over the years from the suggestions and insights of many teachers—and students—across the country. We would especially like to thank: James Allen, *College of DuPage*; Chris Anson, *North Carolina State University*; Phillip Arrington, *Eastern Michigan University*; Anne Bailey, *Southeastern Louisiana University*; Carolyn Baker, *San Antonio College*; Joy Bashore, *Central Virginia Community College*; Nancy Blattner, *Southeast Missouri State University*; Mary Bly, *University of California, Davis*; Bob Brannan, *Johnson County Community College*; Paul Buczkowski, *Eastern Michigan University*; Jennifer Bullis, *Whatcom Community College*; Paige Byam, *Northern Kentucky University*; Susan Callendar, *Sinclair Community College*; Anne Carr, *Southeast Community College*; Jeff Carroll, *University of Hawaii*; Joseph Rocky Colavito, *Northwestern State University*; Michael Colonnese, *Methodist College*; James A. Cornette, *Christopher Newport University*; Timothy Corrigan, *Temple University*; Kathryn J. Dawson, *Ball State University*; Cathy Powers Dice, *University of Memphis*;

Kathleen Dooley, *Tidewater Community College;* Judith Eastman, *Orange Coast College;* David Elias, *Eastern Kentucky University;* Susan Boyd English, *Kirkwood Community College;* Kathy Evertz, *University of Wyoming;* Bill Gholson, *Southern Oregon University;* Karen Gordon, *Elgin Community College;* Deborah Gutschera, *College of DuPage;* Lila M. Harper, *Central Washington University;* M. Todd Harper, *University of Louisville;* Kip Harvigsen, *Ricks College;* Michael Hogan, *Southeast Missouri State University;* Sandra M. Jensen, *Lane Community College;* Anita Johnson, *Whatcom Community College;* Mark Jones, *University of Florida;* Jane Kaufman, *University of Akron;* Rodney Keller, *Ricks College;* Walt Klarner, *Johnson County Community College;* Jeffery Klausman, *Whatcom Community College;* Alison Kuehner, *Ohlone College;* William B. Lalicker, *West Chester University;* Dawn Leonard, *Charleston Southern University;* Clifford L. Lewis, *U Mass Lowell;* Signee Lynch, *Whatcom Community College;* Krista L. May, *Texas A&M University;* Roark Mulligan, *Christopher Newport University;* Joan Mullin, *University of Toledo;* Stella Nesanovich, *McNeese State University;* Susie Paul, *Auburn University at Montgomery;* Aaron Race, *Southern Illinois University–Carbondale;* Nancy Redmond, *Long Beach City College;* Deborah Reese, *University of Texas at Arlington;* Priscilla Riggle, *Bowling Green State University;* Jeanette Riley, *University of New Mexico;* Robert Rongner, *Whatcom Community College;* Sarah C. Ross, *Southeastern Louisiana University;* Raul Sanchez, *University of Utah;* Rebecca Shapiro, *Westminster College;* Mary Sheldon, *Washburn University;* Philip Sipiora, *University of Southern Florida;* Joyce Smoot, *Virginia Tech;* Bonnie A. Spears, *Chaffey College;* Bonnie Startt, *Tidewater Community College;* R. E. Stratton, *University of Alaska–Fairbanks;* Katherine M. Thomas, *Southeast Community College;* Victor Villanueva, *Washington State University;* Jackie Wheeler, *Arizona State University;* Pat Stephens Williams, *Southern Illinois University at Carbondale;* and Kristin Woolever, *Northeastern University.*

We extend our gratitude to the following reviewers for their help in the preparation of this edition: Mark Brosamer, *Ohlone College;* Virginia Dumont-Poston, *Lander University;* Lynnell Edwards, *Concordia University;* Nikolai Endres, *Western Kentucky University;* Barbara Gross, *Rutgers NCAS;* Vicki Hill, *Brewton-Parker College;* Kacie Jossart, *University of North Dakota;* Jim Kenkel, *Eastern Kentucky University;* Malcolm Kiniry, *Rutgers University;* RoseAnn Morgan, *Middlesex County College;* David Moton, *Bakersfield College;* Taunya Paul, *York Technical College;* Robert Francis Peltier, *Trinity College;* and Jan Thompson, *Landmark College.*

A special thanks to our resourceful sponsoring editor, Ginny Blanford, along with Rebecca Gilpin and Eric Jorgensen of Longman, for helping shepherd the manuscript through the editorial and production process. For the able work of Martha Beyerlein of Elm Street Publishing Services, our photo researcher Julie Tesser, and Sheila Varela (for her expert help in securing permissions), we are most appreciative. Finally, a continued, heartfelt expression of gratitude to Joe Opiela, our longtime friend, supporter, and publisher.

LAURENCE BEHRENS
LEONARD J. ROSEN

A Note to the Student

Your sociology professor asks you to write a paper on attitudes toward the homeless population of an urban area near your campus. You are expected to consult books, articles, websites and other online sources on the subject, and you are also encouraged to conduct surveys and interviews.

Your professor is making a number of assumptions about your capabilities. Among them:

- that you can research and assess the value of relevant sources;
- that you can comprehend college-level material, both print and electronic;
- that you can synthesize separate but related sources;
- that you can intelligently respond to such material.

In fact, these same assumptions underlie practically all college writing assignments. Your professors will expect you to demonstrate that you can read and understand not only textbooks but also critical articles and books, primary sources, Internet sources, online academic databases, CD-ROMs, and other material related to a particular subject of study. For example: for a paper on the progress of the Human Genome Project, you would probably look to articles and Internet sources for the most recent information. Using an online database, you would find articles on the subject in such print journals as *Nature, Journal of the American Medical Association,* and *Bioscience,* as well as leading newspapers and magazines. A Web search engine might lead you to a useful site called "A New Gene Map of the Human Genome" <http://www.ncbi.nlm.nih.gov/genemap99/> and the site of the "Human Genome Sequencing Department" at the Lawrence Berkeley National Laboratory <http://www-hgc.lbl.gov/>. You would be expected to assess the relevance of such sources to your topic and to draw from them the information and ideas you need. It's even possible that the final product of your research and reading may not be a conventional paper at all, but rather a website that you create which explains the science behind the Human Genome Project, explores a particular controversy about the project, or describes the future benefits geneticists hope to derive from the project.

You might, for a different class, be assigned a research paper on the films of director Martin Scorsese. To get started, you might consult your film studies textbook, biographical sources on Scorsese, and anthologies of criticism. Instructor and peer feedback on a first draft might lead you to articles in both popular magazines (such as *Time*) and scholarly journals (such as *Literature/Film Quarterly*), a CD-ROM database, *Film Index International,* and relevant websites (such as the "Internet Movie Database" <http://us.imdb.com>).

These two example assignments are very different, of course; but the skills you need to work with them are the same. You must be able to research relevant sources. You must be able to read and comprehend these sources. You must be able to perceive the relationships among several pieces of source material. And you must be able to apply your own critical judgments to these various materials.

Writing and Reading Across the Curriculum: Brief Edition provides you with the opportunity to practice the essential college-level skills we have just outlined and the forms of writing associated with them, namely:

- the *summary*
- the *critique*
- the *synthesis*
- the *analysis*

Each chapter of Part II of this text represents a subject from a particular area of the academic curriculum: Technology/Communication, Psychology, Sociology, Health Sciences, and Business. These chapters, dealing with such topics as "Cyberspace and Identity," "Obedience to Authority," and "Weight Debate," illustrate the types of material you will study in your other courses.

Questions following the readings will allow you to practice typical college writing assignments. Review Questions help you recall key points of content. Discussion and Writing Suggestions ask you for personal, sometimes imaginative responses to the readings. Synthesis Activities at the end of each chapter allow you to practice assignments of the type that are covered in detail in Part I of this book. For instance, you may be asked to *describe* the Milgram experiment, and the reactions to it, or to *compare and contrast* a controlled experiment to a real-life (or fictional) situation. Finally, Research Activities ask you to go beyond the readings in this text in order to conduct your own independent research on these subjects.

In this book, you'll find articles and essays written by physicians, literary critics, sociologists, psychologists, lawyers, political scientists, journalists, and specialists from other fields. Our aim is that you become familiar with the various subjects and styles of academic writing and that you come to appreciate the interrelatedness of knowledge. Biologists, sociologists, and historians have different ways of contributing to our understanding of weight gain. Human activity and human behavior are classified into separate subjects primarily for convenience. The novel you read in your literature course may be able to shed some light upon an assigned article from your economics course—and vice versa.

We hope, therefore, that your writing course will serve as a kind of bridge to your other courses and that as a result of this work you can become more skillful at perceiving relationships among diverse topics. Because it involves such critical and widely applicable skills, your writing course may well turn out to be one of the most valuable—and one of the most interesting—of your academic career.

LAURENCE BEHRENS
LEONARD J. ROSEN

How to Write Summaries, Critiques, Syntheses, and Analyses

Summary

1

WHAT IS A SUMMARY?

The best way to demonstrate that you understand the information and the ideas in any piece of writing is to compose an accurate and clearly written summary of that piece. By a *summary* we mean a *brief restatement, in your own words, of the content of a passage* (a group of paragraphs, a chapter, an article, a book). This restatement should focus on the *central idea* of the passage. The briefest of all summaries (one or two sentences) will do no more than this. A longer, more complete summary will indicate, in condensed form, the main points in the passage that support or explain the central idea. It will reflect the order in which these points are presented and the emphasis given to them. It may even include some important examples from the passage. But it will not include minor details. It will not repeat points simply for the purpose of emphasis. And it will not contain any of your own opinions or conclusions. A good summary, therefore, has three central qualities: *brevity, completeness,* and *objectivity.*

CAN A SUMMARY BE OBJECTIVE?

Of course, the last quality mentioned above, objectivity, might be difficult to achieve in a summary. By definition, writing a summary requires you to select some aspects of the original and leave out others. Since deciding what to select and what to leave out calls for your personal judgment, your summary really is a work of interpretation. And, certainly, your interpretation of a passage may differ from another person's. One factor affecting the nature and quality of your interpretation is your *prior knowledge* of the subject. For example, if you're attempting to summarize an anthropological article and you're a novice in that field, then your summary of the article will likely differ from that of your professor, who has spent twenty years studying this particular area and whose judgment about what is more or less significant is undoubtedly more reliable than your own. By the same token, your personal or professional *frame of reference* may also affect your interpretation. A union representative and a management representative attempting to summarize the latest management offer would probably come up with two very different accounts. Still, we believe that in most cases it's possible to produce a reasonably objective summary of a passage if you make a conscious, good-faith effort to be unbiased and to prevent your own feelings on the subject from distorting your account of the text.

USING THE SUMMARY

In some quarters, the summary has a bad reputation—and with reason. Summaries often are provided by writers as substitutes for analyses. As students, many of us have summarized books that we were supposed to *review critically*. All the same, the summary does have a place in respectable college work. First, writing a summary is an excellent way to understand what you read. This in itself is an important goal of academic study. If you don't understand your source material, chances are you won't be able to refer to it usefully in an essay or research paper. Summaries help you understand what you read because they force you to put the text into your own words. Practice with writing summaries also develops your general writing habits, since a good summary, like any other piece of good writing, is clear, coherent, and accurate.

WHERE DO WE FIND WRITTEN SUMMARIES?

Here are a few types of writing that involve summary:

Academic Writing

- **Critique papers.** Summarize material in order to critique it.
- **Synthesis papers.** Summarize to show relationships between sources.
- **Analysis papers.** Summarize theoretical perspectives before applying them.
- **Research papers.** Take notes and report on research through summary.
- **Literature reviews.** Analyze work through brief summaries.
- **Argument papers.** Summarize evidence and opposing arguments.
- **Essay exams.** Demonstrate understanding of course materials through summary.

Workplace Writing

- **Policy briefs.** Condense complex public policy.
- **Business plans.** Summarize costs, relevant environmental impacts, and other important matters.
- **Memos, letters, and reports.** Summarize procedures, meetings, product assessments, expenditures, and more.
- **Medical charts.** Record patient data in summarized form.
- **Legal briefs.** Summarize relevant facts of cases.

Second, summaries are useful to your readers. Let's say you're writing a paper about the McCarthy era in the United States, and in part of that paper you want to discuss Arthur Miller's *The Crucible* as a dramatic treatment of the subject. A summary of the plot would be helpful to a reader who hasn't seen or read—or who doesn't remember—the play. Or perhaps you're writing a paper about the politics of recent humanitarian aid missions. If your reader isn't likely to be familiar with such groups as Doctors Without Borders, it would be a good idea to summarize the objectives and activities of such organizations at some early point in the paper. In many cases (an exam, for instance), you can use a summary to demonstrate your knowledge of what your professor already knows; when writing a paper, you can use a summary to inform your professor about some relatively unfamiliar source.

Third, summaries are required frequently in college-level writing. For example, on a psychology midterm, you may be asked to explain Carl Jung's theory of the collective unconscious and to show how it differs from Sigmund Freud's theory of the personal unconscious. You may have read about this theory in your textbook or in a supplementary article, or your instructor may have outlined it in his or her lecture. You can best demonstrate your understanding of Jung's theory by summarizing it. Then you'll proceed to contrast it with Freud's theory—which, of course, you must also summarize.

THE READING PROCESS

It may seem to you that being able to tell (or retell) in summary form exactly what a passage says is a skill that ought to be taken for granted in anyone who can read at high school level. Unfortunately, this is not so: For all kinds of reasons, people don't always read carefully. In fact, it's probably safe to say that usually they don't. Either they read so inattentively that they skip over words, phrases, or even whole sentences, or, if they do see the words in front of them, they see them without registering their significance.

When a reader fails to pick up the meaning and implications of a sentence or two, usually there's no real harm done. (An exception: You could lose credit on an exam or paper because you failed to read or to realize the significance of a crucial direction by your instructor.) But over longer stretches—the paragraph, the section, the article, or the chapter—inattentive or haphazard reading interferes with your goals as a reader: to perceive the shape of the argument, to grasp the central idea, to determine the main points that compose it, to relate the parts of the whole, and to note key examples. This kind of reading takes a lot more energy and determination than casual reading. But, in the long run, it's an energy-saving method because it enables you to retain the content of the material and to use that content as a basis for your own responses. In other words, it allows you to develop an accurate and coherent written discussion that goes beyond summary.

CRITICAL READING FOR SUMMARY

- *Examine the context.* Note the credentials, occupation, and publications of the author. Identify the source in which the piece originally appeared. This information helps illuminate the author's perspective on the topic he or she is addressing.
- *Note the title and subtitle.* Some titles are straightforward, whereas the meanings of others become clearer as you read. In either case, titles typically identify the topic being addressed and often reveal the author's attitude toward that topic.
- *Identify the main point.* Whether a piece of writing contains a thesis statement in the first few paragraphs or builds its main point without stating it up front, look at the entire piece to arrive at an understanding of the overall point being made.
- *Identify the subordinate points.* Notice the smaller subpoints that make up the main point, and make sure you understand how they relate to the main point. If a particular subpoint doesn't clearly relate to the main point you've identified, you may need to modify your understanding of the main point.
- *Break the reading into sections.* Notice which paragraph(s) make up the introduction, body, and conclusion of a piece. Break up the body paragraphs into sections that address the writer's various subpoints.
- *Distinguish between points, examples, and counterarguments.* Critical reading requires careful attention to what writers are *doing* as well as what they are *saying.* When a writer quotes someone else, or relays an example of something, ask yourself why this is being done. What point is the example supporting? Is another source being quoted as support for a point, or as a counterargument that the writer sets out to address?
- *Watch for transitions within and between paragraphs.* In order to follow the logic of a piece of writing, as well as to distinguish between points, examples, and counterarguments, pay attention to the transitional words and phrases writers use. Transitions function like road signs, preparing the reader for what's next.
- *Read actively and recursively.* Don't treat reading as a passive, linear progression through a text. Instead, read as though you are engaged in a dialogue with the writer: Ask questions of the text as you read, make notes in the margin, underline key ideas in pencil, put question or exclamation marks next to passages that confuse or excite you. Go back to earlier points once you finish a reading, stop during your reading to recap what's been presented so far, and move back and forth through a text.

HOW TO WRITE SUMMARIES

Every article you read will present a unique challenge as you work to summarize it. As you'll discover, saying in a few words what has taken someone else a great many can be difficult. But like any other skill, the ability to summarize

---

GUIDELINES FOR WRITING SUMMARIES

- *Read the passage carefully.* Determine its structure. Identify the author's purpose in writing. (This will help you distinguish between more important and less important information.) Make a note in the margin when you get confused or when you think something is important; highlight or underline points sparingly, if at all.
- *Reread the passage.* This time divide the passage into sections or stages of thought. The author's use of paragraphing will often be a useful guide. On the passage itself, *label* each section or stage of thought. *Underline* key ideas and terms. Write notes in the margin.
- *Write one-sentence summaries,* on a separate sheet of paper, of each stage of thought.
- *Write a thesis—a one- or two-sentence summary of the entire passage.* The thesis should express the central idea of the passage, as you have determined it from the preceding steps. You may find it useful to follow the approach of most newspaper stories—naming the *what, who, why, where, when,* and *how* of the matter. For persuasive passages, summarize in a sentence the author's conclusion. For descriptive passages, indicate the subject of the description and its key feature(s). (Note: In some cases, *a suitable thesis may already be in the original passage.* If so, you may want to quote it directly in your summary.)
- *Write the first draft of your summary* by (1) combining the thesis with your list of one-sentence summaries or (2) combining the thesis with one-sentence summaries *plus* significant details from the passage. In either case, eliminate repetition and less important information. Disregard minor details or generalize them (e.g., George H. W. Bush and Bill Clinton might be generalized as "recent presidents"). Use as few words as possible to convey the main ideas.
- *Check your summary against the original passage* and make whatever adjustments are necessary for accuracy and completeness.
- *Revise your summary,* inserting transitional words and phrases where necessary to ensure coherence. Check for style. *Avoid a series of short, choppy sentences.* Combine sentences for a smooth, logical flow of ideas. Check for grammatical correctness, punctuation, and spelling.

improves with practice. Here are a few pointers to get you started. They represent possible stages, or steps, in the process of writing a summary. These pointers are not meant to be ironclad rules; rather, they are designed to encourage habits of thinking that will allow you to vary your technique as the situation demands.

DEMONSTRATION: SUMMARY

To demonstrate these points at work, let's go through the process of summarizing a passage of expository material—that is, writing that is meant to inform and/or persuade. Read the following selection carefully. Try to identify its parts and understand how they work together to create an overall point.

The Future of Love: Kiss Romance Goodbye, It's Time for the Real Thing
Barbara Graham

Author of the satire Women Who Run with Poodles: Myths and Tips for Honoring Your Mood Swings *(Avon, 1994), Barbara Graham has written articles for* Vogue, Self, Common Boundary, *and other publications. She regularly contributes articles to the* Utne Reader, *from which this essay was taken.*

1   Freud and his psychoanalytic descendants are no doubt correct in their assessment that the search for ideal love—for that one perfect soulmate—is the futile wish of not fully developed selves. But it also seems true that the longing for a profound, all-consuming erotic connection (and the heightened state of awareness that goes with it) is in our very wiring. The yearning for fulfillment through love seems to be to our psychic structure what food and water are to our cells.

2   Just consider the stories and myths that have shaped our consciousness: Beauty and the Beast, Snow White and her handsome prince, Cinderella and Prince Charming, Fred and Ginger, Barbie and Ken. (Note that, with the exception of the last two couples, all of these lovers are said to have lived happily ever after—even though we never get details of their lives after the weddings, after children and gravity and loss have exacted their price.) Still, it's not just these lucky fairy tale characters who have captured our collective imagination. The tragic twosomes we cut our teeth on—Romeo and Juliet, Tristan and Iseult, Launcelot and Guinevere, Heathcliff and Cathy, Rhett and Scarlett—are even more compelling role models. Their love is simply too powerful and anarchic,

Barbara Graham, "The Future of Love: Kiss Romance Goodbye, It's Time for the Real Thing," *Utne Reader* Jan.–Feb. 1997: 20–23.

too shattering and exquisite, to be bound by anything so conventional as marriage or a long-term domestic arrangement.

3   If recent divorce and remarriage statistics are any indication, we're not as astute as the doomed lovers. Instead of drinking poison and putting an end to our love affairs while the heat is still turned up full blast, we expect our marriages and relationships to be long-running fairy tales. When they're not, instead of examining our expectations, we switch partners and reinvent the fantasy, hoping that this time we'll get it right. It's easy to see why: Despite all the talk of family values, we're constantly bombarded by visions of perfect romance. All you have to do is turn on the radio or TV or open any magazine and check out the perfume and lingerie ads. "Our culture is deeply regressed," says Florence Falk, a New York City psychotherapist. "Everywhere we turn, we're faced with glamorized, idealized versions of love. It's as if the culture wants us to stay trapped in the fantasy and does everything possible to encourage and expand that fantasy." Trying to forge an authentic relationship amidst all the romantic hype, she adds, makes what is already a tough proposition even harder.

4   What's most unusual about our culture is our feverish devotion to the belief that romantic love and marriage should be synonymous. Starting with George and Martha, continuing through Ozzie and Harriet right up to the present day, we have tirelessly tried to formalize, rationalize, legalize, legitimize, politicize, and sanitize rapture. This may have something to do with our puritanical roots, as well as our tendency toward oversimplification. In any event, this attempt to satisfy all of our contradictory desires under the marital umbrella must be put in historical context in order to be properly understood.

5   "Personal intimacy is actually quite a new idea in human history and was never part of the marriage ideal before the 20th century," says John Welwood, a Northern California–based psychologist and author, most recently, of Love and Awakening. "Most couples throughout history managed to live together their whole lives without ever having a conversation about what was going on within or between them. As long as family and society prescribed the rules of marriage, individuals never had to develop any consciousness in this area."

6   In short, marriage was designed to serve the economic and social needs of families, communities, and religious institutions, and had little or nothing to do with love. Nor was it expected to satisfy lust.

7   In Myths to Live By, Joseph Campbell explains how the sages of ancient India viewed the relationship between marriage and passion. They concluded that there are five degrees of love, he writes, "through which a worshiper is increased in the service and knowledge of his God." The first degree has to do with the relationship of the worshiper to the divine. The next three degrees of love, in order of importance, are friendship, the parent/child relationship, and marriage. The fifth and highest form is passionate, illicit love. "In marriage, it is declared, one is still possessed of reason," Campbell adds. "The seizure of passionate love can be, in such a context, only illicit, breaking in upon the order of one's dutiful life in virtue as a devastating storm."

8   No wonder we're having problems. The pressures we place on our tender unions are unprecedented. Even our biochemistry seems to militate against

long-term sexual relationships. Dr. Helen Fisher, an anthropologist at Rutgers University and author of *Anatomy of Love,* believes that human pair-bonds originally evolved according to "the ancient blueprint of serial monogamy and clandestine adultery" and are originally meant to last around four years—at least long enough to raise a single dependent child through toddlerhood. The so-called seven-year-itch may be the remains of a four-year reproductive cycle, Fisher suggests.

9   Increasingly, Fisher and other researchers are coming to view what we call love as a series of complex biochemical events governed by hormones and enzymes. "People cling to the idea that romantic love is a mystery, but it's also a chemical experience," Fisher says, explaining that there are three distinct mating emotions and each is supported in the brain by the release of different chemicals. Lust, an emotion triggered by changing levels of testosterone in men and women, is associated with our basic sexual drive. Infatuation depends on the changing levels of dopamine, norepinephrine, and phenylethylamine (PEA), also called the "chemicals of love." They are natural—addictive—amphetaminelike chemicals that stimulate euphoria and make us want to stay up all night sharing our secrets. After infatuation and the dizzying highs associated with it have peaked—usually within a year or two—this brain chemistry reduces, and a new chemical system made up of oxytocin, vasopressin, and maybe the endorphins kicks in and supports a steadier, quieter, more nurturing intimacy. In the end, regardless of whether biochemistry accounts for cause or effect in love, it may help to explain why some people—those most responsive to the release of the attachment chemicals—are able to sustain a long-term partnership, while thrillseekers who feel depressed without regular hits of dopamine and PEA are likely to jump from one liaison to the next in order to maintain a buzz.

10   But even if our biochemistry suggests that there should be term limits on love, the heart is a stubborn muscle and, for better or worse, most of us continue to yearn for a relationship that will endure. As a group, Generation Xers—many of whom are children of divorce—are more determined than any other demographic group to have a different kind of marriage than their parents and to avoid divorce, says Howard Markman, author of *Fighting for Your Marriage.* What's more, lesbians and gay men who once opposed marriage and all of its heterosexual, patriarchal implications now seek to reframe marriage as a more flexible, less repressive arrangement. And, according to the U.S. National Center for Health Statistics, in one out of an estimated seven weddings, either the bride or the groom—or both—are tying the knot for at least the third time—nearly twice as many as in 1970. There are many reasons for this, from the surge in the divorce rate that began in the '70s, to our ever-increasing life span. Even so, the fact that we're still trying to get love right—knowing all we know about the ephemeral nature of passion, in a time when the stigmas once associated with being divorced or single have all but disappeared—says something about our powerful need to connect.

11   And, judging from the army of psychologists, therapists, clergy, and other experts who can be found dispensing guidance on the subject, the effort to save—or reinvent, depending on who's doing the talking—love and marriage has

become a multimillion dollar industry. The advice spans the spectrum. There's everything from *Rules,* by Ellen Fein and Sherrie Schneider, a popular new book which gives 90's women 50's-style tips on how to catch and keep their man, to Harville Hendrix's *Getting the Love You Want,* and other guides to "conscious love." But regardless of perspective, this much is clear: Never before have our most intimate thoughts and actions been so thoroughly dissected, analyzed, scrutinized, and medicalized. Now, people who fall madly in love over and over are called romance addicts. Their disease, modeled on alcoholism and other chemical dependencies, is considered "progressive and fatal."

12   Not everyone believes the attempt to deconstruct love is a good thing. The late philosopher Christopher Lasch wrote in his final (and newly released) book, *Women and the Common Life:* "The exposure of sexual life to scientific scrutiny contributed to the rationalization, not the liberation, of emotional life." His daughter, Elisabeth Lasch-Quinn, an historian at Syracuse University and the editor of the book, agrees. She contends that the progressive demystification of passionate life since Freud has promoted an asexual, dispassionate, and utilitarian form of love. Moreover, like her father, she believes that the national malaise about romance can be attributed to insidious therapeutic modes of social control—a series of mechanisms that have reduced the citizen to a consumer of expertise. "We have fragmented life in such a way," she says, "as to take passion out of our experience."

13   Admittedly, it's a stretch to picture a lovesick 12th-century French troubadour in a 12-step program for romance addicts. Still, we can't overlook the fact that our society's past efforts to fuse together those historically odd bedfellows— passionate love and marriage—have failed miserably. And though it's impossible to know whether all the attention currently being showered on relationships is the last gasp of a dying social order—marriage—or the first glimmer of a new paradigm for relating to one another, it's obvious that something radically different is needed.

Read, Reread, Highlight

Let's consider our recommended pointers for writing a summary.

As you reread the passage, note in the margins of the essay important points, shifts in thought, and questions you may have. Consider the essay's significance as a whole and its stages of thought. What does it say? How is it organized? How does each part of the passage fit into the whole? What do all these points add up to?

Here is how the first few paragraphs of Graham's article might look after you had marked the main ideas, by highlighting and by marginal notations.

psychic
importance
of love

Freud and his psychoanalytic descendants are no doubt correct in their assessment that the search for ideal love—for that one perfect soulmate— is the futile wish of not fully developed selves. But it also seems true that the longing for a profound, all-consuming erotic connection (and the heightened state of awareness that goes with it) is in our very wiring. The yearning for fulfillment through love seems to be to our psychic structure what food and water are to our cells.

fictional, sometimes tragic examples of ideal love

Just consider the stories and myths that have shaped our consciousness: Beauty and the Beast, Snow White and her handsome prince, Cinderella and Prince Charming, Fred and Ginger, Barbie and Ken. (Note that, with the exception of the last two couples, all of these lovers are said to have lived happily ever after—even though we never get details of their lives after the weddings, after children and gravity and loss have exacted their price.) Still, it's not just these lucky fairy tale characters who have captured our collective imagination. The tragic twosomes we cut our teeth on—Romeo and Juliet, Tristan and Iseult, Launcelot and Guinevere, Heathcliff and Cathy, Rhett and Scarlett—are even more compelling role models. Their love is simply too powerful and anarchic, too shattering and exquisite, to be bound by anything so conventional as marriage or a long-term domestic arrangement.

difficulty of having a real relationship in a culture that glamorizes ideal love

If recent divorce and remarriage statistics are any indication, we're not as astute as the doomed lovers. Instead of drinking poison and putting an end to our love affairs while the heat is still turned up full blast, we expect our marriages and relationships to be long-running fairy tales. When they're not, instead of examining our expectations, we switch partners and reinvent the fantasy, hoping that this time we'll get it right. It's easy to see why: Despite all the talk of family values, we're constantly bombarded by visions of perfect romance. All you have to do is turn on the radio or TV or open any magazine and check out the perfume and lingerie ads. "Our culture is deeply regressed," says Florence Falk, a New York City psychotherapist. "Everywhere we turn, we're faced with glamorized, idealized versions of love. It's as if the culture wants us to stay trapped in the fantasy and does everything possible to encourage and expand that fantasy." Trying to forge an authentic relationship amidst all the romantic hype, she adds, makes what is already a tough proposition even harder.

contradictions of ideal love and marriage

What's most unusual about our culture is our feverish devotion to the belief that romantic love and marriage should be synonymous. Starting with George and Martha, continuing through Ozzie and Harriet right up to the present day, we have tirelessly tried to formalize, rationalize, legalize, legitimize, politicize, and sanitize rapture. This may have something to do with our puritanical roots, as well as our tendency toward oversimplification. In any event, this attempt to satisfy all of our contradictory desires under the marital umbrella must be put in historical context in order to be properly understood.

"personal intimacy" never considered part of marriage before 20th century

"Personal intimacy is actually quite a new idea in human history and was never part of the marriage ideal before the 20th century," says John Welwood, a Northern California–based psychologist and author, most recently, of *Love and Awakening*. "Most couples throughout history managed to live together their whole lives without ever having a conversation about what was going on within or between them. As long as family and society prescribed the rules of marriage, individuals never had to develop any consciousness in this area."

In short, marriage was designed to serve the economic and social needs of families, communities, and religious institutions, and had little or nothing to do with love. Nor was it expected to satisfy lust.

Divide Selection into Stages of Thought

When a selection doesn't contain sections with thematic headings, as is the case with "The Future of Love," how do you determine where one stage of thought ends and the next one begins? Assuming that what you have read is coherent and unified, this should not be difficult. (When a selection is unified, all of its parts pertain to the main subject; when a selection is coherent, the parts follow one another in logical order.) Look, particularly, for transitional sentences at the beginning of paragraphs. Such sentences generally work in one or both of the following ways: (1) they summarize what has come before; (2) they set the stage for what is to follow.

For example, look at the sentence that opens paragraph 10: "But even if our biochemistry suggests that there should be term limits on love, the heart is a stubborn muscle and, for better or worse, most of us continue to yearn for a relationship that will endure." Notice how the first part of this sentence restates the main idea of the preceding section. The second part of the transitional sentence announces the topic of the upcoming section: three paragraphs devoted to the efforts people make to attain, save, or reinvent romantic relationships.

Each section of an article generally takes several paragraphs to develop. Between paragraphs, and almost certainly between sections of an article, you will usually find transitions that help you understand what you have just read and what you are about to read. For articles that have no subheadings, try writing your own section headings in the margins as you take notes. Then proceed with your summary.

The sections of Graham's article may be described as follows:

> **Section 1:** *Introduction*—a yearning for "fulfillment through love" pervades our culture, and that yearning is shaped by myths and romantic fantasies (paragraphs 1–3).

> **Section 2:** *Marriage and love*—we expect passionate love to lead to happy, lifelong marriage. This is a relatively new and unique practice in human history (paragraphs 4–7).

> **Section 3:** *Biochemistry and love*—love has a biochemical component, which complicates our abilities to sustain long-term relationships (paragraphs 8–9).

Section 4: *Marriage and love revisited*—many people are currently trying to preserve and/or reinvent marriage and love (paragraphs 10–12).

Section 5: *Conclusion*—the fusion of passionate love with the institution of marriage hasn't worked very well, and we need something "radically different" to replace it (paragraph 13).

Write a One- or Two-Sentence Summary of Each Stage of Thought

The purpose of this step is to wean you from the language of the original passage, so that you are not tied to it when writing the summary. Here are one-sentence summaries for each stage of thought in the five sections of "The Future of Love":

Section 1: Introduction—a yearning for "fulfillment through love" pervades our culture, and that yearning is shaped by myths and romantic fantasies (paragraphs 1–3).

> As Americans, we crave romantic love; but we have unreal expectations based upon idealized images of love we learn from fantasies and fairy tales.

Section 2: Marriage and love—we expect passionate love to lead to happy, lifelong marriage. This is a relatively new and unique practice in human history (paragraphs 4–7).

> We expect the passionate love of fairy tales to lead to "happily ever after" in the institution of marriage, and when this fails, we move on and try it again. Ironically, the idea that marriage should be based on love—rather than upon social and economic concerns—is a relatively recent practice in Western history.

Section 3: Biochemistry and love—love has a biochemical component, which complicates our abilities to sustain long-term relationships (paragraphs 8–9).

> Biochemists are discovering that love and lust have hormonal causes, and their evidence suggests that our biological makeup predisposes us to seek the excitement of short-term relationships.

Section 4: Marriage and love revisited—many people are currently trying to preserve and/or reinvent marriage and love (paragraphs 10–12).

> Despite all the difficulties, we spend a lot of
> time analyzing the elements of relationships in
> order to preserve or perhaps reinvent marriage.
> We clearly want to make it work.

Section 5: Conclusion—the fusion of passionate love with the institution of marriage hasn't worked very well, and we need something "radically different" to replace it (paragraph 13).

> Because confining passionate love to the institu-
> tion of marriage hasn't worked very well, we need
> to revise our model for human relationships.

Write a Thesis: A One- or Two-Sentence Summary of the Entire Passage

The thesis is the most general statement of a summary (or any other type of academic writing). It is the statement that announces the paper's subject and the claim that you or—in the case of a summary—another author will be making about that subject. Every paragraph of a paper illuminates the thesis by providing supporting details or explanations. The relationship of these paragraphs to the thesis is analogous to the relationship of the sentences within a paragraph to the topic sentence. Both the thesis and the topic sentences are general statements (the thesis being the more general) that are followed by systematically arranged details.

To ensure clarity for the reader, *the first sentence of a summary should begin with the author's thesis, regardless of where it appears in the article itself.* Authors may locate their thesis at the beginning of their work, in which case the thesis operates as a general principle from which details of the presentation follow. This is called a *deductive* organization: thesis first, supporting details second. Alternatively, authors may locate their thesis at the end of the work, in which case they begin with specific details and build toward a more general conclusion, or thesis. This is called an *inductive* organization—an example of which you see in "The Future of Love."

A thesis consists of a subject and an assertion about that subject. How can we go about fashioning an adequate thesis for a summary of "The Future of Love"? Probably no two proposed thesis statements for this article would be worded identically, but it is fair to say that any reasonable thesis will indicate that the subject is the current state of love and marriage in American society. How does Graham view the topic? What *is* the current state of love and marriage, in her view? Looking back over our section summaries, Graham's focus on the illusions of fairy tales and myths, the difference between marriage in the present day and its earlier incarnations, and the problems of divorce and "romance addiction" suggest she does not view the current state of affairs in an altogether positive light. Does she make a statement anywhere that pulls all this together? Her conclusion, in paragraph 13, contains her main idea:

"our society's past efforts to fuse together those historically odd bedfellows—passionate love and marriage—have failed miserably." Moreover, in the next sentence, she says "it's obvious that something radically different is needed." Further evidence of Graham's main point can be found in the complete title of the essay: "The Future of Love: Kiss Romance Goodbye, It's Time for the Real Thing." Mindful of Graham's subject and the assertion she makes about it, we can write a thesis statement *in our own words* and arrive at the following:

> The contemporary institution of marriage is in trouble, and this may be due to our unrealistic expectations that passionate love leads to lasting union; it may be time to develop a new model for love and relationships.

To clarify for our readers the fact that this idea is Graham's and not ours, we'll qualify the thesis as follows:

> In her article "The Future of Love: Kiss Romance Goodbye, It's Time for the Real Thing," Barbara Graham describes how our unrealistic expectations that passionate love leads to lasting union may be partly causing the troubled state of marriage today; thus she suggests we develop a new model for love and relationships.

The first sentence of a summary is crucially important, for it orients readers by letting them know what to expect in the coming paragraphs. In the example above, the sentence refers directly to an article, its author, and the thesis for the upcoming summary. The author and title reference also could be indicated in the summary's title (if this were a freestanding summary), in which case their mention could be dropped from the thesis. And lest you become frustrated too quickly, keep in mind that writing an acceptable thesis for a summary takes time—in this case, it took the three drafts, shown below, or roughly seven minutes to compose one sentence and another few minutes of fine-tuning after a draft of the entire summary was completed. The thesis needed revision because the first draft was too vague and incomplete; the second draft was more specific and complete, but left out the author's point about correcting the problem; the third draft was more complete, but it was cumbersome.

> **Draft 1:** Barbara Graham argues that our attempts to confine passionate love to the institution of marriage have failed.
> *(Too vague—the problem isn't clear enough)*

Draft 2: Barbara Graham ~~argues that our attempts to confine passionate love to the institution of marriage have failed.~~ describes how the contemporary institution of marriage is in trouble, and this may be due, she thinks, to our unrealistic expectations that passionate love will lead to lasting union. *(Incomplete—what about her call for a change?)*

Draft 3: In her article "The Future of Love: Kiss Romance Goodbye, It's Time for the Real Thing," Barbara Graham describes how ~~the contemporary institution of marriage is in trouble, and this may be due, she thinks, to~~ our unrealistic expectations that passionate love will lead to lasting union may be causing the troubles in the contemporary institution of marriage today, so she argues that perhaps it's time to develop a new model for love and relationships. *(Wordy)*

Final: In her article "The Future of Love: Kiss Romance Goodbye, It's Time for the Real Thing," Barbara Graham suggests that because unrealistic expectations for romantic love may undermine marriage, we should develop a new model for love and relationships.

Write the First Draft of the Summary

Let's consider two possible summaries of the example passage: (1) a short summary, combining a thesis with one-sentence section summaries, and (2) a longer summary, combining a thesis, one-sentence section summaries, and some carefully chosen details. Again, realize that you are reading final versions; each of the following summaries is the result of at least two full drafts.

Summary 1: Combine Thesis Sentence with One-Sentence Section Summaries

In her article "The Future of Love: Kiss Romance Goodbye, It's Time for the Real Thing," Barbara Graham suggests that because unrealistic expectations for romantic love may undermine marriage, we should develop a new model for love and relationships. The existing model, and our craving for romantic love, is based heavily upon idealized images of love we learn from fantasies and fairy tales.

We expect the passionate love of fairy tales to lead to "happily ever after" in the institution of marriage, and when this fails, we move on and try it again. Ironically, the idea that marriage should be based on love—rather than upon social and economic concerns—is a relatively recent practice in Western history. While the romantic marriage ideal doesn't fit with tradition, biological evidence is mounting against it as well. Biochemists are discovering that love and lust have hormonal causes, and their evidence suggests that our biological makeup predisposes us to seek the excitement of short-term relationships.

Nonetheless, despite all the difficulties, we spend a lot of time analyzing the elements of relationships in order to preserve or perhaps reinvent marriage. We clearly want to make it work. Because confining passionate love to the institution of marriage hasn't worked very well, Graham ends by suggesting that we ought to revise our model for human relationships.

Discussion

This summary consists essentially of a restatement of Graham's thesis plus the section summaries, altered or expanded a little for stylistic purposes. The first sentence encompasses the summary of Section 1 and is followed by the summaries of Sections 2, 3, 4, and 5. Notice the insertion of a transitional sentence (highlighted) between the summaries of Sections 2 and 3, helping to link the ideas more coherently.

Summary 2: Combine Thesis Sentence, Section Summaries, and Carefully Chosen Details

The thesis and one-sentence section summaries can also be used as the outline for a more detailed summary. Most of the details in the passage, however, won't be necessary in a summary. It isn't necessary even in a longer summary of this passage to discuss all of Graham's examples—specific romantic fairy tales, ancient Indian views of love and passion, the specific hormones involved with love and lust, or the examples of experts who examine and write about contemporary relationships. It would be appropriate, though, to mention one example of fairy tale romance, to refer to the historical information on marriage as an economic institution, and to explain some of the biological findings about love's chemical basis.

None of these details appeared in the first summary, but in a longer summary, a few carefully selected details might be desirable for clarity. How do you decide which details to include? First, since the idea that love and marriage are not necessarily compatible is the main point of the essay, it makes sense to cite some of the most persuasive evidence supporting this idea. For example, you could mention that for most of Western history, marriage was meant "to serve the economic and social needs of families, communities, and religious institutions," not the emotional and sexual needs of individuals. Further, you might explain the biochemists' argument that serial monogamy based on mutual interests and clandestine adultery—not lifelong, love-based marriage—are the forms of relationships best serving human evolution.

You won't always know which details to include and which to exclude. Developing good judgment in comprehending and summarizing texts is largely a matter of reading skill and prior knowledge (see page 3). Consider the analogy of the seasoned mechanic who can pinpoint an engine problem by simply listening to a characteristic sound that to a less experienced person is just noise. Or consider the chess player who can plot three separate winning strategies from a board position that to a novice looks like a hopeless jumble. In the same way, the more practiced a reader you are, the more knowledgeable you become about the subject, and the better able you will be to make critical distinctions between elements of greater and lesser importance. In the meantime, read as carefully as you can and use your own best judgment as to how to present your material.

Here's one version of a completed summary, with carefully chosen details. Note that we have highlighted phrases and sentences added to the original, briefer summary.

(Thesis)

> In her article "The Future of Love: Kiss Romance Goodbye, It's Time for the Real Thing," Barbara Graham suggests that because unrealistic expectations for romantic love may undermine marriage, we should develop a new model for love and relationships.

(Section 1, ¶s 1–3)

> As Americans, we crave romantic love; but we have unreal expectations based upon idealized images of love we learn from fantasies and fairy tales such as "Beauty and the Beast" and "Cinderella." Tragedies such as Romeo and Juliet teach us about the all-consuming nature of "true love," and these stories are tragic precisely because the lovers never get to fulfill what we've been taught is the ideal: living happily ever after, in wedded bliss. The idea that romantic love should be confined to marriage is perhaps the biggest fantasy to which we subscribe. When we are unable to make this fantasy real—and it seems that this is often the case—we end that marriage and move on to the next one. The twentieth century is actually the first century in

(Section 2, ¶s 4–7)

Western history in which so much was asked of marriage. In earlier eras, marriage was designed to meet social and economic purposes, rather than fulfill individual emotional and sexual desires.

Casting further doubt on the effectiveness of the current model of marriage, biochemists are discovering how hormones and enzymes influence feelings of love and lust. It turns out that the "chemistry" a person newly in love often feels for another has a basis in fact, as those early feelings of excitement and contentment are bio-chemical in nature. When people jump from one relationship to the next, they may be seeking that chemical "rush." Further, these biochemical discoveries fit with principles of evolutionary survival, because short-term relationships—and even adulterous affairs—help to more quickly propagate the species.

(Section 3, ¶s 8–9)

Nonetheless, despite such historical and biological imperatives, we don't seem interested in abandoning the pursuit of love and marriage. In order to preserve or perhaps reinvent marriage, we spend a lot of time scrutinizing and dissecting the dynamics of relationships. Self-help books on the subject of love and relationships fill book-store shelves and top best-seller lists.

(Section 4, ¶s 10–12)

While some argue that such scrutiny ruins rather than reinvigorates love, perhaps our efforts to understand relationships can help us to invent some kind of revised model for human relationships—since trying to confine passionate love to the institution of marriage clearly hasn't worked very well.

(Section 5, ¶ 13)

Discussion

Our final two suggested steps for writing summaries have two goals: (1) to check your summary against the original passage, making sure that you have included all the important ideas, and (2) to revise so that the summary reads smoothly and coherently.

The structure of this summary generally reflects the structure of the original—with one notable departure. As we noted earlier, Graham uses an inductive approach, stating her thesis at the end of the essay. The summary, however, states the thesis right away, then proceeds deductively to develop that thesis.

Compared to the first, briefer summary, this effort mentions fairy tales and tragedy; develops the point about traditional versus contemporary versions of marriage; explains the biochemical/evolutionary point; and refers specifically to self-help books and their role in the issue.

How long should a summary be? This depends on the length of the original passage. A good rule of thumb is that a summary should be no longer than one-fourth of the original passage. Of course, if you were summarizing an entire chapter or even an entire book, it would have to be much shorter than that. The summary above is about one-fourth the length of the original passage. Although it shouldn't be very much longer, you have seen (pages 17–18) that it could be quite a bit shorter.

The length as well as the content of the summary also depends on its *purpose*. Let's suppose you decided to use Graham's piece in a paper that dealt with the biochemical processes of love and lust. In this case, you might summarize *only* Graham's discussion of Fisher's findings, and perhaps the point Graham makes about how biochemical discoveries complicate marriage. If, instead, you were writing a paper in which you argued against attempts to redefine marriage, you would likely give less attention to the material on biochemistry. To help support your view, you might summarize Graham's points in paragraph 10 about the persistent desire for lasting union found among members of Generation X and evidenced in the high numbers of marriages and remarriages. Thus, depending on your purpose, you would summarize either selected portions of a source or an entire source, as we will see more fully in the chapters on syntheses.

EXERCISE 1.1

Individual and Collaborative Summary Practice

Turn to Chapter 6 and read Solomon A. Asch's article "Opinions and Social Pressure" (pages 176–82). Follow the steps for writing summaries outlined above—read, underline, and divide into stages of thought. Write down a one- or two-sentence summary of each stage of thought in Asch's article. Then, gather in groups of three or four classmates, and compare your summary sentences. Discuss the differences in your sentences, and come to some consensus about the divisions in Asch's stages of thought—and the ways in which to best sum these up.

As a group, write a one- or two-sentence thesis statement summing up the entire passage. You could go even further, and, using your individual summary sentences—or the versions of these your group revised—put together a brief summary of Asch's article, modeled upon the brief summary of Graham's essay on pages 17–18.

AVOIDING PLAGIARISM

Plagiarism is generally defined as the attempt to pass off the work of another as one's own. Whether born out of calculation or desperation, plagiarism is the least tolerated offense in the academic world. The fact that most plagiarism is unintentional—arising from ignorance of conventions rather than deceitfulness—makes no difference to many professors.

The ease of cutting and pasting whole blocks of text from Web sources into one's own paper makes it tempting for some to take the easy way out and avoid doing their own research and writing. But apart from the serious ethical issues involved, the same technology that makes such acts possible also makes it possible for instructors to detect them. Software marketed to instructors allows them to conduct Web searches, using suspicious phrases as keywords. The results often provide irrefutable evidence of plagiarism.

Of course, plagiarism is not confined to students. Recent years have seen a number of high-profile cases—some of them reaching the front pages of newspapers—of well-known scholars who were shown to have copied passages from sources into their own book manuscripts, without proper attribution. In some cases, the scholars maintained that these appropriations were simply a matter of carelessness, and that in the press and volume of work, they had lost track of which words were theirs and which were the words of their sources. But such excuses sounded hollow: These careless acts inevitably embarrassed the scholars professionally, disappointed their many admirers, and tarnished their otherwise fine work and reputations.

You can avoid plagiarism and charges of plagiarism by following the basic rules provided on page 23.

The following is an excerpt from an article by Richard Rovere on Senator Joseph P. McCarthy, along with several student versions of the ideas represented:

> McCarthy never seemed to believe in himself or in anything he had said. He knew that Communists were not in charge of American foreign policy. He knew that they weren't running the United States Army. He knew that he had spent five years looking for Communists in the government and that—although some must certainly have been there, since Communists had turned up in practically every other major government in the world—he hadn't come up with even one.*

One student wrote the following version of this passage:

> McCarthy never believed in himself or in anything he had said. He knew that Communists were not in charge of American foreign policy and weren't running the United States Army. He knew that he had spent five years looking for Communists in the government, and although there must certainly have been some there, since Communists were in practically every other major government in the world, he hadn't come up with even one.

Clearly, this is intentional plagiarism. The student has copied the original passage almost word for word.

---

* Richard Rovere, "The Most Gifted and Successful Demagogue This Country Has Ever Known," *New York Times Magazine* 30 Apr. 1967: 192+.

Here is another version of the same passage:

> McCarthy knew that Communists were not running for-
> eign policy or the Army. He also knew that although
> there must have been some Communists in the gov-
> ernment, he hadn't found a single one, even though
> he had spent five years looking.

This student has attempted to put the ideas into her own words, but both the wording and the sentence structure still are so heavily dependent on the original passage that even if it *were* cited, most professors would consider it plagiarism.

In the following version, the student has sufficiently changed the wording and sentence structure, and she uses a signal phrase (a phrase used to introduce a quotation or paraphrase, signaling to the reader that the words to follow come from someone else) to properly credit the information to Rovere, so that there is no question of plagiarism:

> According to Richard Rovere, McCarthy was fully
> aware that Communists were running neither the gov-
> ernment nor the Army. He also knew that he hadn't
> found a single Communist in government, even after
> a lengthy search (192).

And although this is not a matter of plagiarism, as noted above, it's essential to quote accurately. You are not permitted to change any part of a quotation or to omit any part of it without using brackets or ellipses.

RULES FOR AVOIDING PLAGIARISM

- Cite *all* quoted material and *all* summarized and paraphrased material, unless the information is common knowledge (e.g., the Civil War was fought from 1861 to 1865).
- Make sure that both the *wording* and the *sentence structure* of your summaries and paraphrases are substantially your own.

2 Critical Reading and Critique

CRITICAL READING

When writing papers in college, you are often called on to respond critically to source materials. Critical reading requires the abilities to both summarize and evaluate a presentation. As you have seen in Chapter 1, a *summary* is a brief restatement in your own words of the content of a passage. An *evaluation*, however, is a more difficult matter.

In your college work, you read to gain and *use* new information; but as sources are not equally valid or equally useful, you must learn to distinguish critically among them by evaluating them.

There is no ready-made formula for determining validity. Critical reading and its written equivalent—the *critique*—require discernment, sensitivity, imagination, knowledge of the subject, and above all, willingness to become involved in what you read. These skills cannot be taken for granted and are developed only through repeated practice. You must begin somewhere, though, and we recommend that you start by posing two broad categories of questions about passages, articles, and books that you read: (1) What is the author's purpose in writing? Does he or she succeed in this purpose? (2) To what extent do you agree with the author?

Question Category 1: What Is the Author's Purpose in Writing? Does the Author Succeed in This Purpose?

All critical reading *begins with an accurate summary.* Thus before attempting an evaluation, you must be able to locate an author's thesis and identify the selection's content and structure. You must understand the author's *purpose.* Authors write to inform, to persuade, and to entertain. A given piece may be primarily *informative* (a summary of the research on cloning), primarily *persuasive* (an argument on why the government must do something to alleviate homelessness), or primarily *entertaining* (a play about the frustrations of young lovers). Or it may be all three (as in John Steinbeck's novel *The Grapes of Wrath,* which revolves around migrant workers during the Great Depression). Sometimes, authors are not fully conscious of their purpose. Sometimes their purpose changes as they write. Also, more than one purpose can overlap: An essay may need to inform the reader about an issue in order to make a persuasive point. But if the finished piece is coherent, it will have a primary reason for having been written, and it should be apparent that the author is attempting primarily to inform, persuade, or entertain a particular audience. To identify this primary reason—this purpose—is your first job as a critical reader. Your

---

> ### WHERE DO WE FIND WRITTEN CRITIQUES?
>
> *Here are a few types of writing that involve critique:*
>
> ### Academic Writing
>
> - **Research papers.** Critique sources in order to establish their usefulness.
> - **Position papers.** Stake out a position by critiquing other positions.
> - **Book reviews.** Combine summary with critique.
> - **Essay exams.** Demonstrate understanding of course material by critiquing it.
>
> ### Workplace Writing
>
> - **Legal briefs and legal arguments.** Critique previous rulings or arguments made by opposing counsel.
> - **Business plans and proposals.** Critique other, less cost-effective approaches.
> - **Policy briefs.** Communicate failings of policies and legislation through critique.

next job is to determine how successful the author has been. As a critical reader, you bring different criteria, or standards of judgment, to bear when you read pieces intended to inform, persuade, or entertain.

Writing to Inform

A piece intended to inform will provide definitions, describe or report on a process, recount a story, give historical background, and/or provide facts and figures. An informational piece responds to questions such as the following:

What (or who) is _____?

How does _____ work?

What is the controversy or problem about?

What happened?

How and why did it happen?

What were the results?

What are the arguments for and against _____?

To the extent that an author answers these and related questions and the answers are a matter of verifiable record (you could check for accuracy if you had the time and inclination), the selection is intended to inform. Having determined this, you can organize your response by considering three other criteria: accuracy, significance, and fair interpretation of information.

Evaluating Informative Writing

Accuracy of Information. If you are going to use any of the information presented, you must be satisfied that it is trustworthy. One of your responsibilities as a critical reader, then, is to find out if it is accurate. This means you should check facts against other sources. Government publications are often good resources for verifying facts about political legislation, population data, crime statistics, and the like. You can also search key terms in library databases and on the Web. Since material on the Web is essentially "self-published," however, you must be especially vigilant in assessing its legitimacy. A wealth of useful information is now available on the Internet—but there is also a tremendous amount of misinformation, distorted "facts," and unsupported opinion.

Significance of Information. One useful question that you can ask about a reading is "So what?" In the case of selections that attempt to inform, you may reasonably wonder whether the information makes a difference. What can the person who is reading gain from this information? How is knowledge advanced by the publication of this material? Is the information of importance to you or to others in a particular audience? Why or why not?

Fair Interpretation of Information. At times you will read reports, the sole function of which is to relate raw data or information. In these cases, you will build your response on the two questions in category 1, introduced on page 24: What is the author's purpose in writing? Does she or he succeed in this purpose? More frequently, once an author has presented information, he or she will attempt to evaluate or interpret it—which is only reasonable, since information that has not been evaluated or interpreted is of little use. One of your tasks as a critical reader is to make a distinction between the author's presentation of facts and figures and his or her attempts to evaluate them. Watch for shifts from straightforward descriptions of factual information ("20 percent of the population") to assertions about what this information means ("*a mere* 20 percent of the population"), what its implications are, and so on. Pay attention to whether the logic with which the author connects interpretation with facts is sound. You may find that the information is valuable but the interpretation is not. Perhaps the author's conclusions are not justified. Could you offer a contrary explanation for the same facts? Does more information need to be gathered before firm conclusions can be drawn? Why?

Writing to Persuade

Writing is frequently intended to persuade—that is, to influence the reader's thinking. To make a persuasive case, the writer must begin with an assertion that is arguable, some statement about which reasonable people could disagree. Such an assertion, when it serves as the essential organizing principle of the article or book, is called a *thesis*. Here are two examples:

> Because they do not speak English, many children in this affluent land are being denied their fundamental right to equal educational opportunity.

> Bilingual education, which has been stridently promoted by a small group of activists with their own agenda, is detrimental to the very students it is supposed to serve.

Thesis statements such as these—and the subsequent assertions used to help support them—represent conclusions that authors have drawn as a result of researching and thinking about an issue. You go through the same process yourself when you write persuasive papers or critiques. And just as you are entitled to critically evaluate the assertions of authors you read, so your professors—and other students—are entitled to evaluate *your* assertions, whether they be encountered as written arguments or as comments made in class discussion.

Keep in mind that writers organize arguments by arranging evidence to support one conclusion and oppose (or dismiss) another. You can assess the validity of the argument and the conclusion by determining whether the author has (1) clearly defined key terms, (2) used information fairly, (3) argued logically and not fallaciously (see pages 28–53).

EXERCISE 2.1

Informative and Persuasive Thesis Statements

With a partner from your class, write one informative and one persuasive thesis statement for *three* of the following topics:

School prayer

Gun control

Sex education in schools

Grammar instruction in English class

Violent lyrics in music

Teaching computer skills in primary schools

Curfews in college dormitories

Course registration procedures

For example, for the topic *school prayer,* your informative thesis statement might read this way:

> Both advocates and opponents of school prayer frame their position as a matter of freedom.

Your persuasive thesis statement might be worded as follows:

> As long as schools don't dictate what kinds of prayers students should say, then school prayer should be allowed and even encouraged.

Don't worry about taking a position that you agree with or feel you could support. The exercise doesn't require that you write an essay at this point.

Evaluating Persuasive Writing

Read on pages 354–57 the argument "Too Much of a Good Thing," by Greg Critser, a recommendation to curtail the steep, recent rise in childhood obesity. We will illustrate our discussion on defining terms, using information fairly, and arguing logically by referring to Critser's argument. The example critique that follows these illustrations will be based on this same argument.

EXERCISE 2.2

Critical Reading Practice

Before continuing with the chapter's reading, look back at the Critical Reading for Summary box on page 6 of Chapter 1. Use each of the guidelines listed there to examine the essay by Greg Critser on pages 354–57. Note in the margins of the selection, or on a separate sheet of paper, the essay's main point, subpoints, and use of examples.

Persuasive Strategies

Clearly Defined Terms. The validity of an argument depends to some degree on how carefully an author has defined key terms. Take the assertion, for example, that American society must be grounded in "family values." Just what do people who use this phrase mean by it? The validity of their argument depends on whether they and their readers agree on a definition of "family values"—as well as what it means to be "grounded in" family values. If an author writes that in the recent past, "America's elites accepted as a matter of course that a free society can sustain itself only through virtue and temperance in the people" (Charles Murray, "The Coming White Underclass," *Wall Street Journal*, 20 Oct. 1993), readers need to know what, exactly, the author means by "elites" and by "virtue and temperance" before they can assess the validity of the argument. In such cases, the success of the argument—its ability to persuade—hinges on the definition of a term. So, in responding to an argument, be sure you (and the author) are clear on what exactly is being argued. Only then can you respond to the logic of the argument, to the author's use of evidence, and to the author's conclusions.

Critser supports his argument for launching a campaign to end overconsumption by stating that efforts to stigmatize "unhealthful behaviors . . . conform with what we know about effective health messages." While Critser does provide examples of what he considers "effective health messages," his definition of *effective* is open to debate. By what measures have "the campaign against unsafe sex and the campaign against smoking" been effective? The reader might well point to level HIV infection rates in the United States and continuing billion-dollar profits by tobacco companies and challenge Critser's definition of *effective.*

Fair Use of Information. Information is used as evidence in support of arguments. When you encounter such evidence, ask yourself two questions: (1) Is the information accurate and up-to-date? At least a portion of an argument becomes invalid if the information used to support it is inaccurate or out-of-date. (2) Has the author cited *representative* information? The evidence used in an argument must be presented in a spirit of fair play. An author is less than ethical who presents only evidence favoring his views when he is well aware that contrary evidence exists. For instance, it would be dishonest to argue that an economic recession is imminent and to cite only indicators of economic downturn while ignoring and failing to cite contrary (positive) evidence.

Critser uses the information he cites fairly and accurately: He presents statistics in paragraph 2 on the rise of childhood obesity; he refers to a published study in paragraph 6 to refute the assertion that "kids know when they are full"; and he cites studies again in paragraphs 8 and 9. However, Critser chooses not to use, let alone mention, other information that bears on the topic of weight gain. For example, he argues that we should create an anti-obesity campaign that stigmatizes the behavior of those who lack the willpower to stop eating. The assumption: A lack of willpower is the primary reason people are obese. Whether or not this view is correct, a great deal of information (scientific studies included) suggests that other causes may be implicated in obesity. By not raising the possibility that genes or hormones, for instance, might play a role, information about which Critser is undoubtedly aware, he fails to present full and representative information on his chosen topic. True, the op-ed piece is a brief form, leaving not much room to develop an argument. Still, Critser leaves the impression that he has cited the most pertinent information on combating obesity when, in fact, he has disregarded a great deal of information.

Logical Argumentation: Avoiding Logical Fallacies

At some point, you will need to respond to the logic of the argument itself. To be convincing, an argument should be governed by principles of *logic*—clear and orderly thinking. This does *not* mean that an argument should not be biased. A biased argument—that is, an argument weighted toward one point of view and against others, which is in fact the nature of argument—may be valid as long as it is logically sound.

Several examples of faulty thinking and logical fallacies to watch for follow.

Emotionally Loaded Terms. Writers sometimes attempt to sway readers by using emotionally charged words—words with positive connotations to sway readers to their own point of view (e.g., "family values") or words with negative connotations to sway readers away from the opposing point of view. The fact that an author uses emotionally loaded terms does not necessarily invalidate the argument. Emotional appeals are perfectly legitimate and time-honored modes of persuasion. But in academic writing, which is grounded in logical argumentation, they should not be the *only* means of persuasion. You should be sensitive to *how* emotionally loaded terms are being used. In particular, are they being used deceptively or to hide the essential facts?

Critser's use of the word *gluttony* inserts an emotionally charged, moralizing tone into his argument. Gluttony is one of the "seven deadly sins" that, for centuries, people have been warned against committing, so destructive are they of character. Critser takes pains to say that he is no moralist ("no one should be stigmatized for being overweight"), but that claim is made false by his introduction of a "sin" into a discussion about public health. Critser operates with a value judgment that he does not fully want to own. Critical readers might legitimately object to the notion that overeating is a "sin" that ought to be stigmatized.

***Ad Hominem* Argument.** In an *ad hominem* argument, the writer rejects opposing views by attacking the person who holds them. By calling opponents names, an author avoids the issue. Consider this excerpt from a political speech:

> I could more easily accept my opponent's plan to increase revenues by collecting on delinquent tax bills if he had paid more than a hundred dollars in state taxes in each of the past three years. But the fact is, he's a millionaire with a millionaire's tax shelters. This man hasn't paid a wooden nickel for the state services he and his family depend on. So I ask you: Is *he* the one to be talking about taxes to *us?*

It could well be that the opponent has paid virtually no state taxes for three years; but this fact has nothing to do with, and is a ploy to divert attention from, the merits of a specific proposal for increasing revenues. The proposal is lost in the attack against the man himself, an attack that violates the principles of logic. Writers (and speakers) must make their points by citing evidence in support of their views and by challenging contrary evidence.

Faulty Cause and Effect. The fact that one event precedes another in time does not mean that the first event has caused the second. An example: Fish begin dying by the thousands in a lake near your hometown. An environmental group immediately cites chemical dumping by several manufacturing plants as the cause. But other causes are possible: A disease might have affected the fish; the growth of algae might have contributed to the deaths; or acid rain might be a factor. The origins of an event are usually complex and are not always traceable to a single cause. So you must carefully examine cause-and-effect reasoning when you find a writer using it. In Latin, this fallacy is known as *post hoc, ergo propter hoc* ("after this, therefore because of this").

TON

Tone refers to the overall emotional effect produced by the wri
choice of language. Writers might use especially emphatic words to
create a tone: A film reviewer might refer to a "magnificent performance" or a columnist might criticize "sleazeball politics."

These are extreme examples of tone; but tone can be more subtle,
particularly if the writer makes a special effort *not* to inject emotion
into the writing. As we've indicated above in the section on emotionally loaded terms, the fact that a writer's tone is highly emotional does
not necessarily mean that the writer's argument is invalid. Conversely,
a neutral tone does not ensure an argument's validity.

Note that many instructors discourage student writing that projects
a highly emotional tone, considering it inappropriate for academic or
preprofessional work. (One sure sign of emotion: the exclamation
mark, which should be used sparingly.)

Critser claims in this argument that dietary restraint will help reduce childhood obesity. Readers familiar with the literature on obesity know that a
debate exists concerning the causes of the condition. For instance, some obese
people may eat as little as their thin friends do but still lose no weight. For
them, it is clear, lack of willpower does not contribute to their weight problems. Genes and body chemistry may play causal roles, but Critser mentions
no causes other than lack of willpower. Asserting that one cause leads to an
effect—or failing to assert that multiple causes do—gives readers the right
to question the logic of an argument.

Either/Or Reasoning. Either/or reasoning also results from an unwillingness
to recognize complexity. If an author analyzes a problem and offers only two
courses of action, one of which he or she refutes, then you are entitled to
object that the other is not thereby true. Usually, several other options (at the
very least) are possible. For whatever reason, the author has chosen to overlook them. As an example, suppose you are reading a selection on genetic
engineering and the author builds an argument on the basis of the following:

> Research in gene splicing is at a crossroads: Either scientists will be
> carefully monitored by civil authorities and their efforts limited to
> acceptable applications, such as disease control; or, lacking regulato-
> ry guidelines, scientists will set their own ethical standards and begin
> programs in embryonic manipulation that, however well intended,
> exceed the proper limits of human knowledge.

Certainly, other possibilities for genetic engineering exist beyond the two
mentioned here. But the author limits debate by establishing an either/or

choice. Such limitation is artificial and does not allow for complexity. As a critical reader, be on the alert for either/or reasoning.

Hasty Generalization. Writers are guilty of hasty generalization when they draw their conclusions from too little evidence or from unrepresentative evidence. To argue that scientists should not proceed with the human genome project because a recent editorial urged that the project be abandoned is to make a hasty generalization. This lone editorial may be unrepresentative of the views of most individuals—both scientists and laypeople—who have studied and written about the matter. To argue that one should never obey authority because Stanley Milgram's Yale University experiments in the 1960s show the dangers of obedience is to ignore the fact that Milgram's experiment was concerned primarily with obedience to *immoral* authority. Thus, the experimental situation was unrepresentative of most routine demands for obedience—for example, to obey a parental rule or to comply with a summons for jury duty—and a conclusion about the malevolence of all authority would be a hasty generalization.

False Analogy. Comparing one person, event, or issue to another may be illuminating, but it may also be confusing or misleading. Differences between the two may be more significant than the similarities, and conclusions drawn from one may not necessarily apply to the other. A writer who argues that it is reasonable to quarantine people with AIDS because quarantine has been effective in preventing the spread of smallpox is assuming an analogy between AIDS and smallpox that (because of the differences between the two diseases) is not valid.

A false analogy can also be found in Critser's comparison between a proposed campaign to stigmatize obesity and "highly effective" campaigns that stigmatize unsafe sex and smoking (paragraph 4), which suggests that obesity is fundamentally similar to unsafe sex and smoking. Critser assumes that all three damaging behaviors have similar causes (i.e., lack of self-restraint) that can be addressed using similar means (campaigns to stigmatize). But if the analogy between obesity and smoking or unsafe sex breaks down because we find that their causes differ (and research is far from conclusive on the matter), then readers have no reason to agree with Critser that campaigns that reduce smoking and unsafe sex will help to reduce obesity.

Begging the Question. To beg the question is to assume as a proven fact the very thesis being argued. To assert, for example, that America is not in decline because it is as strong and prosperous as ever is not to prove anything: It is merely to repeat the claim in different words. This fallacy is also known as *circular reasoning.*

In one sense, when Critser advocates restraint to lower the incidence of obesity, he is doing an admirable job. He raises and rebuts two arguments against urging restraint on those who weigh too much (in paragraphs 3–7) and then argues directly that restraint is a successful strategy in combating obesity (in paragraphs 8–9). But Critser also assumes that lack of restraint alone is primarily the cause of obesity. Given the volume of compelling evidence (which he does not mention) that genes and other factors may play a role in weight gain, he would do well to argue—and not assume—that lack of restraint is a primary reason people gain weight. But he assumes the validity of this important point instead of proving it. He also assumes the validity of two lesser points: (1) that the campaigns against unsafe sex and smoking have been effective; and (2) that obesity is a condition comparable to unsafe sex and smoking and, thus, a condition that would benefit from campaigns to stigmatize unhealthy behaviors.

Non Sequitur. *Non sequitur* is Latin for "it does not follow"; the term is used to describe a conclusion that does not logically follow from a premise. "Since minorities have made such great strides in the past few decades," a writer may argue, "we no longer need affirmative action programs." Aside from the fact that the premise itself is arguable (*have* minorities made such great strides?), it does not follow that because minorities *may* have made great strides, there is no further need for affirmative action programs.

Oversimplification. Be alert for writers who offer easy solutions to complicated problems. "America's economy will be strong again if we all 'buy American,'" a politician may argue. But the problems of America's economy are complex and cannot be solved by a slogan or a simple change in buying habits. Likewise, a writer who argues that we should ban genetic engineering assumes that simple solutions ("just say 'no'") will be sufficient to deal with the complex moral dilemmas raised by this new technology.

For example, Critser does consider how causes other than lack of willpower may contribute to obesity. This is not to say that a lack of restraint plays no valid or even major role in weight gain. People can and should learn to say "no" to supersized fries. But to the extent Critser does not acknowledge other causes of obesity, he leaves himself open to the charge of oversimplification. His proposed "campaign against over-consumption" is one solution. It will not alone solve the obesity problem.

EXERCISE **2.3**

Understanding Logical Fallacies

Make a list of the nine logical fallacies discussed in the last section. Briefly define each one in your own words. Then, in a group of three or four classmates, refer to your definitions and the examples we've provided for each logical fallacy. Collaborate with your group to find or invent examples for each of the fallacies. Compare your examples with those generated by the other groups in your class.

Writing to Entertain

Authors write not only to inform and persuade but also to entertain. One response to entertainment is a hearty laugh, but it is possible to entertain without laughter: A good book or play or poem may prompt you to reflect, grow wistful, become elated, get angry. Laughter is only one of many possible reactions. As with a response to an informative piece or an argument, your response to an essay, poem, story, play, novel, or film should be precisely stated and carefully developed. Ask yourself some of the following questions (you won't have space to explore all of them, but try to consider some of the most important): Did I care for the portrayal of a certain character? Did that character (or a group of characters united by occupation, age, ethnicity, etc.) seem overly sentimental, for example, or heroic? Did his adversaries seem too villainous or stupid? Were the situations believable? Was the action interesting or merely formulaic? Was the theme developed subtly or powerfully, or did the work come across as preachy or shrill? Did the action at the end of the work follow plausibly from what had come before? Was the language fresh and incisive or stale and predictable? Explain as specifically as possible what elements of the work seemed effective or ineffective and why. Offer an overall assessment, elaborating on your views.

Question Category 2: To What Extent Do You Agree or Disagree with the Author?

When formulating a critical response to a source, try to distinguish your evaluation of the author's purpose and success at achieving that purpose from your agreement or disagreement with the author's views. The distinction allows you to respond to a piece of writing on its merits. As an unbiased, evenhanded critic, you evaluate an author's clarity of presentation, use of evidence, and adherence to principles of logic. To what extent has the author succeeded in achieving his or her purpose? Still withholding judgment, offer your assessment and give the author (in effect) a grade. Significantly, your assessment of the presentation may not coincide with your views of the author's conclusions: You may agree with an author entirely but feel that the presentation is superficial; you may find the author's logic and use of evidence to be rock solid but at the same time may resist certain conclusions. A critical evaluation works well when it is conducted in two parts. After evaluating the author's purpose and design for achieving that purpose, respond to the author's main assertions. In doing so, you'll want to identify points of agreement and disagreement and also evaluate assumptions.

Identify Points of Agreement and Disagreement

Be precise in identifying points of agreement and disagreement with an author. You should state as clearly as possible what *you* believe, and an effective way of doing this is to define your position in relation to that presented in the piece. Whether you agree enthusiastically, disagree, or agree with reservations, you can organize your reactions in two parts: (1) summarize the author's position; and (2) state your own position and elaborate on your reasons for holding it. The elaboration, in effect, becomes an argument itself, and this is true regardless of the position you take. An opinion is effective when you support it by supplying evidence. Without such evidence, opinions cannot be authoritative. "I thought the article on inflation was lousy." Why?

"I just thought so, that's all." This opinion is worthless because the criticism is imprecise: The critic has taken neither the time to read the article carefully nor the time to explore his or her own reactions carefully.

<hr>

Exploring Your Viewpoints—in Three Paragraphs

Go to a Web site that presents short persuasive essays on current social issues, such as reason.com, opinion-pages.org, drudgereport.com, or Speakout.com. Or go to an Internet search engine and type in a social issue together with the word "articles," "editorials," or "opinion," and see what you find. Locate a selection on a topic of interest that takes a clear, argumentative position. Write one paragraph summarizing the author's key ~~~ Write two paragraphs articulating your agreement or disagreem ent . .he author. (Devote each paragraph to a *single* point of agreement or disagree ment.) Be sure to explain why you think or feel the way you do an , wher ever possible, cite relevant evidence—from your reading, experience, or observation.

<hr>

Explore the Reasons for Agreement and Disagreement: Evaluate Assumptions

One way of elaborating your reactions to a reading is to explore the underlying *reasons* for agreement and disagreement. Your reactions are based largely on assumptions that you hold and how these assumptions compare with the author's. An *assumption* is a fundamental statement about the world and its operations that you take to be true. A writer's assumptions may be explicitly stated; but just as often assumptions are implicit and you will have to "ferret them out"—that is, to infer them. Consider an example:

> *In vitro* fertilization and embryo transfer are brought about outside the bodies of the couple through actions of third parties whose compe tence and technical activity determine the success of the procedure. Such fertilization entrusts the life and identity of the embryo into the power of doctors and biologists and establishes the domination of technology over the origin and destiny of the human person. Such a relationship of domination is in itself contrary to the dignity and equality that must be common to parents and children.*

This paragraph is quoted from the February 1987 Vatican document on artificial procreation. Cardinal Joseph Ratzinger, principal author of the document and installed as Pope Benedictus XVI in April, 2005, makes an implicit

---

* From the Vatican document *Instruction on Respect for Human Life in Its Origin and on the Dignity of Procreation*, given at Rome, from the Congregation for the Doctrine of the Faith, 22 Feb. 1987, as presented in *Origins: N.C. Documentary Service* 16.40 (19 Mar. 1987): 707.

assumption in this paragraph: No good can come of the domination of technology over conception. The use of technology to bring about conception is morally wrong. Yet thousands of childless couples, Roman Catholics included, have rejected this assumption in favor of its opposite: Conception technology is an aid to the barren couple; far from creating a relationship of unequals, the technology brings children into the world who will be welcomed with joy and love.

Assumptions provide the foundation on which entire presentations are built. If you find an author's assumptions invalid—that is, not supported by factual evidence—or if you disagree with value-based assumptions underlying an author's positions, you may well disagree with conclusions that follow from these assumptions. The author of a book on developing nations may include a section outlining the resources and time that will be required to industrialize a particular country and so upgrade its general welfare. Her assumption—that industrialization in that particular country will ensure or even affect the general welfare—may or may not be valid. If you do not share the assumption, in your eyes the rationale for the entire book may be undermined.

How do you determine the validity of assumptions once you have identified them? In the absence of more scientific criteria, you may determine validity by how well the author's assumptions stack up against your own experience, observations, reading, and values. A caution, however: The overall value of an article or book may depend only to a small degree on the validity of the author's assumptions. For instance, a sociologist may do a fine job of gathering statistical data about the incidence of crime in urban areas along the eastern seaboard. The sociologist also might be a Marxist, and you may disagree with the subsequent analysis of the data. Yet you may still find the data extremely valuable for your own work.

Readers will want to examine two assumptions at the heart of Critser's proposal to launch a campaign against overeating. The first is that lack of willpower alone causes, or primarily causes, obesity. While Critser does not directly assert this cause-and-effect relationship, he implies it by failing to mention other possible causes of obesity. If, for instance, genes or hormones are involved in the weight gain of some people, then it seems cruel to argue that their lack of willpower is somehow responsible—that if only they "tried harder" they could shed those unwanted pounds. Readers may also want to examine another of Critser's assumptions, that a moralizing tone is appropriate to a discussion of public health. Readers might take a different view, based on a very different assumption: that in combating problems in public health, we must deal with behaviors, not with attitudes and values associated with behaviors. Thus, in campaigns to reduce HIV infections, we would not speak of "sin" (as "gluttony" is a sin) but would instead focus strictly on reducing behaviors that spread infection. Readers are entitled to meet each of an author's assumptions with assumptions of their own; to evaluate the validity of those assumptions; and to begin formulating a critique, based on their agreement or disagreement.

CRITIQUE

In Chapter 1 we focused on summary—the condensed presentation of ideas from another source. Summary is key to much of academic writing because it relies so heavily on the works of others for support of claims. It's not going too far to say that summarizing is the critical thinking skill from which a majority of academic writing builds. However, most academic thinking and writing do not stop at summary; usually we use summary to restate our understanding of things we see or read. Then we put that summary to use. In academic writing, one typical use of summary is as a prelude to *critique—a formalized, critical reading of a passage.* It also is a personal response, but writing a critique is considerably more rigorous than saying that a movie is "great," or a book is "fascinating," or "I didn't like it." These are all responses, and, as such, they're a valid, even essential, part of your understanding of what you see and read. But such responses don't illuminate the subject for anyone—even you—if you haven't explained how you arrived at your conclusions.

Your task in writing a critique is to turn your critical reading of a passage into a systematic evaluation in order to deepen your reader's (and your own) understanding of that passage. Among other things, you're interested in determining what an author says, how well the points are made, what assumptions underlie the argument, what issues are overlooked, and what implications can be drawn from such an analysis. Critiques, positive or negative, should include a fair and accurate summary of the passage; they should also include a statement of your own assumptions. It is important to remember that you bring to bear an entire set of assumptions about the world. Stated or not, these assumptions underlie every evaluative comment you make; you therefore have an obligation, both to the reader and to yourself, to clarify your standards by making your assumptions explicit. Not only do your readers stand to gain by your forthrightness, but you do as well: In the process of writing a critical assessment, you are forced to examine your own knowledge, beliefs, and assumptions. Ultimately, the critique is a way of learning about yourself—yet another example of the ways in which writing is useful as a tool for critical thinking.

How to Write Critiques

You may find it useful to organize your critiques in five sections: (1) introduction, (2) summary, (3) assessment of the presentation (on its own terms), (4) your response to the presentation, and (5) conclusion.

The box opposite offers some guidelines for writing critiques. Note that they are guidelines, not a rigid formula. Thousands of authors write critiques that do not follow the structure outlined here. Until you are more confident and practiced in writing critiques, however, we suggest you follow these guidelines. They are meant not to restrict you, but rather to provide a workable sequence for writing critiques.

> ## GUIDELINES FOR WRITING CRITIQUES
>
> - ***Introduce.*** Introduce both the passage under analysis and the author. State the author's main argument and the point(s) you intend to make about it.
>
>   Provide background material to help your readers understand the relevance or appeal of the passage. This background material might include one or more of the following: an explanation of why the subject is of current interest; a reference to a possible controversy surrounding the subject of the passage or the passage itself; biographical information about the author; an account of the circumstances under which the passage was written; or a reference to the intended audience of the passage.
> - ***Summarize.*** Summarize the author's main points, making sure to state the author's purpose for writing.
> - ***Assess the presentation.*** Evaluate the validity of the author's presentation, as distinct from your points of agreement or disagreement. Comment on the author's success in achieving his or her purpose by reviewing three or four specific points. You might base your review on one (or more) of the following criteria:
>
>   Is the information accurate?
>
>   Is the information significant?
>
>   Has the author defined terms clearly?
>
>   Has the author used and interpreted information fairly?
>
>   Has the author argued logically?
>
> - ***Respond to the presentation.*** Now it is your turn to respond to the author's views. With which views do you agree? With which do you disagree? Discuss your reasons for agreement and disagreement, when possible, tying these reasons to assumptions—both the author's and your own.
> - ***Conclude.*** State your conclusions about the overall validity of the piece—your assessment of the author's success at achieving his or her aims and your reactions to the author's views. Remind the reader of the weaknesses and strengths of the passage.

DEMONSTRATION: CRITIQUE

The critique that follows is based on Greg Critser's "Too Much of a Good Thing," which appeared in the *Los Angeles Times* as an op-ed piece on July 22, 2001 (see pages 354–57) and which we have to some extent already begun to examine. In this formal critique, you will see that it is possible to agree with an author's main point or proposal, at least provisionally, but disagree with his or her method of demonstration, or argument. Critiquing a different selection, you could just as easily accept the author's facts and figures but reject the conclusion he or she draws from them. As long as you carefully articulate the author's assumptions and your own, explaining in some detail your agreement and disagreement, the critique is yours to take in whatever direction you see fit.

Let's summarize the preceding sections by returning to the core questions that guide critical reading. You will see how, when applied to Critser's argument, they help to set up a critique.

What Is the Author's Purpose in Writing?

As is the case with most editorials, Greg Critser's "Too Much of a Good Thing" is an argument. He wants readers to accept his proposal for resolving the obesity epidemic among children. Parents, Critser argues, should supervise what and how much their kids eat. Those who learn lessons of dietary restraint early on can avoid weight problems later in life.

Does the Author Succeed in This Purpose?

Critser takes a behavioral approach to the problem of obesity. To the extent that obesity is caused by undisciplined eating habits, his proposal is logical and convincing. But other studies show that not all causes of obesity are rooted in poor eating habits. Genetic makeup and hormone imbalances may also be at work. Critser makes no mention of these, and his analysis and proposed solution therefore seem limited. In addition, he adopts an antifat, judgmental tone in the essay that will likely offend people who are trying to lose weight. In sum, Critser is only partially successful in his argument.

To What Extent Do You Agree or Disagree with the Author?

Because Critser's analysis and proposed solution are based on the assumption that obesity has a single cause (poor eating habits), he opens himself to the objection that he has oversimplified the problem. Still, common sense suggests that overweight and obese people do contribute to their conditions by making unhealthy dietary choices. So Critser's suggestion that we teach children to eat moderately before they become obese is worth supporting—provided care is taken to acknowledge the nonbehavioral causes of obesity. Critser's moralistic tone gets in the way of an otherwise reasonable (if limited) argument. Of course, we might object to his tone but continue to find merit in his proposal.

The selections you will be likely to critique are those, like Critser's, that argue a specific position. Indeed, every argument you read is an invitation to agreement or disagreement. It remains only for you to speak up and justify your position.

Model Critique*

A Critique of Greg Critser's
"Too Much of a Good Thing"

1   Citing statistics on the alarming increase in the
rates of childhood obesity, especially in the industrialized West, Greg Critser (<u>L.A. Times</u> Op-Ed, 22
July 2001) argues that parents can help avert obesity
in their own homes by more closely supervising the
diets of their children, serving reasonably sized
portions, and limiting snacks. Critser, who has
extensively researched obesity in his book <u>Fat Land:</u>
<u>How Americans Became the Fattest People in the World</u>
(Houghton Mifflin 2003), argues that through education we can create a leaner cultural norm, much as
the French did earlier in the century when faced with
a similar problem.

2   The stakes for maintaining a healthy body weight
couldn't be higher. Fully one-quarter of American
children through the age of eighteen "are overweight
or obese"—an "epidemic," according to the United
States Surgeon General (485). Not only are obese
individuals at increased risk for a wide range of
medical problems, but the nation as a whole will
absorb enormous costs for their obesity, "eventually
mak[ing] the battle against HIV/AIDS seem inexpensive" (485). Clearly we have good reason to fight the
rise of obesity, and Critser's suggestion that individual families become a battleground for that fight
makes perfect sense, as long as we realize that there
will be other battlegrounds (for example, the hospital, the pharmacy, and the genetics lab). We should
also take care that in "stigmatizing the unhealthful
behaviors that cause obesity" (485) we do not turn a
public health campaign into a moral crusade.

3   It takes no advanced degree in nutrition to
accept the claim that children (indeed, all of us)
should learn to eat in moderation. Apparently,
before the age of five the lesson isn't even needed.
Younger children, entirely on their own, will limit
how much food they eat at a meal regardless of the
amounts served. By five, however, they will eat

---

* References to Critser are to his article as reprinted in *Writing and Reading Across the Curriculum.*

whatever is put before them. In a culture of the
"supersized," high-fat, sugar-loaded, fast-food
meal, such lack of restraint can lead to obesity. If
we can teach children before their fifth birthday
what counts as a reasonable portion, they might
learn—for life—to eat in moderation. Critser cites
other research to show that simple and yet profound
dietary lessons, learned early, can make all the
difference in averting a life spent battling the
scale. He wisely gives parents an important role in
teaching these lessons because parents, after all,
teach all sorts of lessons. However, with statistics
showing that roughly half of the adult population in
this country is overweight or obese, Critser may
want to urge parents to learn lessons about moderation themselves before attempting to become teachers
for their children.

4   Critser's plan for combating the rise of childhood obesity through education is certainly reasonable, as far as it goes. But he focuses almost
exclusively on behavioral factors when scientists
have discovered that obesity has other, nonbehavioral
causes (Gibbs). In labs across the world, researchers
are identifying genes and hormones that influence
weight gain. No one fully understands all the mechanisms by which overweight people, who may eat as
little as their skinnier counterparts, gain or shed
pounds. But it is clear that being fat is not simply
about lacking willpower—that is, about "unhealthful
behaviors" (485)—around food. Thus, we should not
expect Critser's approach of teaching dietary moderation to work in every case. For many people, solutions to weight gain will be found both in new
dietary behaviors and in medicines that come from
labs where researchers study how the body burns and
stores fat. To the extent that obesity is the result
of a child's inability to say "no" to a supersized
meal, we should teach restraint just as Critser
advises. But his behavioral fix will not work for
everyone, and parents should be instructed on what to
do when teaching restraint alone fails to keep their
children reasonably trim.

5   A more serious problem with Critser's argument is
his use (twice) of the word "gluttony" and the judgmental attitude it implies. Early in the essay
Critser argues that American parents need "to promulgate . . . dietary restraint, something our ancestors

knew simply as avoiding gluttony" (485). Gluttony was one of the seven deadly sins (along with pride, greed, envy, anger, lust, and sloth), which Christian theologians have been denouncing for nearly 1,500 years (University) to little effect. While Critser insists that "no one should be stigmatized for being overweight," he advocates "stigmatizing the unhealthful behaviors that cause obesity" (485), assuming that people distinguish between the sin and the sinner. In practice, people rarely do. Critser does little to distance himself from anti-fat bias after introducing the bias-heavy term "gluttony" into the essay—which is a mistake: The overweight and obese have a hard enough time losing weight. They should not have to suffer the judgments of those who suggest "that thinness signals self-discipline and self-respect, whereas fatness signals self-contempt and lack of resolve" (Worley).

6   Given a proposal that is otherwise so sensible, Critser doesn't need to complicate matters by inviting moral judgments. He is at his most convincing when he makes a straightforward recommendation to change the behavior of children based on sound scientific research. Effective dietary strategies can be taught, and parents are the best teachers in this case as long as they realize that teaching restraint will be only one of several approaches and that judgments equating thinness with virtue should have no place in our efforts. We face a difficult challenge in meeting the growing problem of childhood obesity, and for the most part Greg Critser suggests a reasonable and workable place to begin.

Works Cited

Critser, Greg. "Too Much of a Good Thing." Editorial. <u>Los Angeles Times</u> 22 July 2001: B12

Gibbs, W. Wayt. "Gaining on Fat." <u>Scientific American</u> Aug. 1996: 46–52.

University of Leicester History of Art Department. "Seven Deadly Sins." University of Leicester Web site 20 Dec. 2001. 2 Aug. 2002 <http://www.le.ac.uk/arthistory/seedcorn/faq-sds.html>.

Worley, Mary. "Fat and Happy: In Defense of Fat Acceptance." National Association to Advance Fat Acceptance 22 Aug. 2002 <http://www.naafa.org>.

CRITICAL READING FOR CRITIQUE

- *Use the tips from Critical Reading for Summary on page 6:* Remember to examine the context; note the title and subtitle; identify the main point; identify the subpoints; break the reading into sections; distinguish between points, examples, and counterarguments; watch for transitions within and between paragraphs; and read actively.
- *Establish the writer's primary purpose in writing:* Is the piece primarily meant to inform, persuade, or entertain?
- *Evaluate informative writing. Use these criteria (among others):*

  Accuracy of information

  Significance of information

  Fair interpretation of information

- *Evaluate persuasive writing. Use these criteria (among others):*

  Clear definition of terms

  Fair use and interpretation of information

  Logical reasoning

- *Evaluate writing that entertains. Use these criteria (among others):*

  Interesting characters

  Believable action, plot, and situations

  Communication of theme

  Use of language

- *Decide whether you agree or disagree with the writer's ideas, position, or message:* Once you have determined the extent to which an author has achieved his or her purpose, clarify your position in relation to the writer's.

EXERCISE 2.5

Informal Critique of Sample Essay

Before reading the discussion of this model critique, write your own informal response to the critique. What are its strengths and weaknesses? To what extent does the critique follow the general guidelines for writing critiques that we outlined on page 38? To the extent it varies from the guidelines, speculate on why. Jot down some ideas for a critique that take a different approach to Critser's essay.

Discussion

- Paragraph 1 of the model critique introduces the selection to be reviewed, along with the author, and summarizes the author's main claim.

- Paragraph 2 provides brief background information. It sets a context that explains why the topic of obesity is important. The paragraph ends with the writer's thesis, offering qualified support for the proposal that parents should teach children to eat moderately.

- Paragraph 3 summarizes the argument of Critser's editorial. Note that the topic sentence expresses approval of the editorial's main (argumentative) thesis: Children should learn to eat in moderation.

- Paragraph 4 raises the first objection to Critser's argument, that he misrepresents the complexity of obesity by discussing only behavioral causes and solutions. The paragraph expresses qualified support for his position, but suggests that other, nonbehavioral ways of viewing the problem and other, nonbehavioral solutions should be explored.

- Paragraph 5 raises a significant disagreement with Critser's moralistic tone. The paragraph lays out the ways in which Critser is inappropriately judgmental.

- Paragraph 6, the conclusion, summarizes the overall position of the critique—to accept Critser's basic recommendation that parents teach dietary restraint to children, but to reject the moral judgments that make obese people feel inadequate.

Practice Critique

Select either of the following articles in Part II of this book:

"The Genocidal Killer in the Mirror," Crispin Sartwell (pages 232–33)

"Fat and Happy: A Defense of Fat Acceptance," Mary Ray Worley (pages 362–66)

Write a critique of the selected article, following the directions in this chapter for determining the author's purpose in writing the piece and for assessing the author's success in achieving that purpose.

For a somewhat more challenging assignment, try writing a critique of one of the following articles:

"Disobedience as a Psychological and Moral Problem," Erich Fromm (pages 226–31)

Before writing your critique, consider the earlier discussions of evaluating writing in this chapter. Examine the author's use of information and persuasive strategies. Review the logical fallacies and identify any of these in the selection you've chosen to critique. First work out your ideas informally, perhaps producing a working outline. Then write a rough draft of your critique. Review the article—the subject of your critique—and revise your rough draft at least once before considering it finished.

Synthesis

WHAT IS A SYNTHESIS?

A *synthesis* is a written discussion that draws on two or more sources. It follows that your ability to write syntheses depends on your ability to infer relationships among sources—essays, articles, and fiction as well as nonwritten sources such as lectures, interviews, and observations. This process is nothing new for you, since you infer relationships all the time—say, between something you've read in the newspaper and something you've seen for yourself, or between the teaching styles of your favorite and least favorite instructors. In fact, if you've written research papers, you've already written syntheses. In an *academic synthesis,* you make explicit the relationships that you have inferred among separate sources.

The skills you've already learned and practiced in the previous two chapters will be vital in writing syntheses. Clearly, before you're in a position to draw relationships between two or more sources, you must understand what those sources say; in other words, you must be able to *summarize* those sources. Readers will frequently benefit from at least partial summaries of sources in your synthesis essays. At the same time, you must go beyond summary to make judgments—judgments based, of course, on your *critical reading* of your sources: what conclusions you've drawn about the quality and validity of these sources, whether you agree or disagree with the points made in your sources, and why you agree or disagree.

Further, you must go beyond the critique of individual sources to determine the relationships among them. Is the information in source B, for example, an extended illustration of the generalizations in source A? Would it be useful to compare and contrast source C with source B? Having read and considered sources A, B, and C, can you infer something else—D (not a source, but your own idea)?

Because a synthesis is based on two or more sources, you will need to be selective when choosing information from each. It would be neither possible nor desirable, for instance, to discuss in a ten-page paper on the American Civil War every point that the authors of two books make about their subject. What you as a writer must do is select from each source the ideas and information that best allow you to achieve your purpose.

PURPOSE

Your purpose in reading source materials and then in drawing on them to write your own material is often reflected in the wording of an assignment. For instance, consider the following assignments on the Civil War:

45

WHERE DO WE FIND WRITTEN SYNTHESES?

Here are just a few of the types of writing that involve synthesis:

Academic Writing

- **Analysis papers.** Synthesize and apply several related theoretical approaches.
- **Research papers.** Synthesize multiple sources.
- **Argument papers.** Synthesize different points into a coherent claim or position.
- **Essay exams.** Demonstrate understanding of course material through comparing and contrasting theories, viewpoints, or approaches in a particular field.

Workplace Writing

- **Newspaper and magazine articles.** Synthesize primary and secondary sources.
- **Position papers and policy briefs.** Compare and contrast solutions for solving problems.
- **Business plans.** Synthesize ideas and proposals into one coherent plan.
- **Memos and letters.** Synthesize multiple ideas, events, and proposals into concise form.
- **Web sites.** Synthesize information from various sources to present in Web pages and related links.

American history: Evaluate the author's treatment of the origins of the Civil War.

Economics: Argue the following proposition, in light of your readings: "The Civil War was fought not for reasons of moral principle but for reasons of economic necessity."

Government: Prepare a report on the effects of the Civil War on Southern politics at the state level between 1870 and 1917.

Mass communications: Discuss how the use of photography during the Civil War may have affected the perceptions of the war by Northerners living in industrial cities.

Literature: Select two twentieth-century Southern writers whose work you believe was influenced by the divisive effects of the Civil War. Discuss the ways this influence is apparent in a novel or a group of

short stories written by each author. The works
should not be *about* the Civil War.

Applied technology: Compare and contrast the technology of warfare
available in the 1860s with the technology available
a century earlier.

Each of these assignments creates for you a particular purpose for writing. Having located sources relevant to your topic, you would then select, for possible use in a paper, only those parts that helped you in fulfilling this purpose. And how you used those parts, how you related them to other material from other sources, would also depend on your purpose. For instance, if you were working on the government assignment, you might possibly draw on the same source as another student working on the literature assignment by referring to Robert Penn Warren's novel *All the King's Men*, about Louisiana politics in the early part of the twentieth century. But because the purposes of these assignments are different, you and the other student would make different uses of this source. Those same parts or aspects of the novel that you find worthy of detailed analysis might be mentioned only in passing by the other student.

USING YOUR SOURCES

Your purpose determines not only what parts of your sources you will use but also how you will relate them to one another. Since the very essence of synthesis is the combining of information and ideas, you must have some basis on which to combine them. *Some relationships among the material in your sources must make them worth synthesizing.* It follows that the better able you are to discover such relationships, the better able you will be to use your sources in writing syntheses. Notice that the mass communications assignment requires you to draw a *cause-and-effect* relationship between photographs of the war and Northerners' perceptions of the war. The applied technology assignment requires you to *compare* and *contrast* state-of-the-art weapons technology in the eighteenth and nineteenth centuries. The economics assignment requires you to *argue* a proposition. In each case, *your purpose will determine how you relate your source materials to one another.*

Consider some other examples. You may be asked on an exam question or in instructions for a paper to *describe* two or three approaches to prison reform during the past decade. You may be asked to *compare and contrast* one country's approach to imprisonment with another's. You may be asked to *develop an argument* of your own on this subject, based on your reading. Sometimes (when you are not given a specific assignment) you determine your own purpose: You are interested in exploring a particular subject; you are interested in making a case for one approach or another. In any event, your purpose shapes your essay. Your purpose determines which sources you research, which ones you use, which parts of them you use, at which points in your essay you use them, and in what manner you relate them to one another.

TYPES OF SYNTHESES: ARGUMENT AND EXPLANATORY

In this chapter we categorize syntheses into two main types: *argument* and *explanatory*. The easiest way to recognize the difference between these two types may be to consider the difference between a newspaper article and an editorial on the same subject. Most likely, we'd say that the main purpose of the newspaper article is to convey *information*, and the main purpose of the editorial is to convey *opinion* or *interpretation*. Of course, this distinction is much too simplified: Newspaper articles often convey opinion or bias, sometimes subtly, sometimes openly; and editorials often convey unbiased information, along with opinion. But as a practical matter, we can generally agree on the distinction between a newspaper article that primarily conveys information and an editorial that primarily conveys opinion.

We'll say, for the sake of convenience, that the newspaper article provides an explanation and that the editorial provides an argument. This is essentially the distinction we make between explanatory and argument syntheses.

As an example of the distinction, read the following paragraph:

> Researchers now use recombinant DNA technology to analyze genetic changes. With this technology, they cut and splice DNA from different species, then insert the modified molecules into bacteria or other types of cells that engage in rapid replication and cell division. The cells copy the foreign DNA right along with their own. In short order, huge populations produce useful quantities of recombinant DNA molecules. The new technology also is the basis of genetic engineering, by which genes are isolated, modified, and inserted back into the same organism or into a different one.*

Now read this paragraph:

> Many in the life sciences field would have us believe that the new gene splicing technologies are irrepressible and irreversible and that any attempt to oppose their introduction is both futile and retrogressive. They never stop to even consider the possibility that the new genetic science might be used in a wholly different manner than is currently being proposed. The fact is, the corporate agenda is only one of two potential paths into the Biotech Century. It is possible that the growing number of anti-eugenic activists around the world might be able to ignite a global debate around alternative uses of the new science—approaches that are less invasive, more sustainable and humane and that conserve and protect the genetic rights of future generations.†

---

* Cecie Starr and Ralph Taggart, "Recombinant DNA and Genetic Engineering," *Biology: The Unity and Diversity of Life* (New York: Wadsworth, 1998).

† Jeremy Rifkin, "The Ultimate Therapy: Commercial Eugenics on the Eve of the Biotech Century," *Tikkun* May–June 1998: 35.

Both of these passages deal with the topic of biotechnology, but the two take quite different approaches. The first passage came from a biology textbook, while the second appeared in a magazine article. As we might expect from a textbook on the broad subject of biology, the first passage is explanatory and informative; it defines and explains some of the key concepts of biotechnology without taking a position or providing commentary about the implications of the technology. Magazine articles often present information in the same ways; however, many magazine articles take specific positions, as we see in the second passage. This passage is argumentative or persuasive. Its primary purpose is to convey a point of view regarding the topic of biotechnology.

While each of these excerpts presents a clear instance of writing that is either explanatory or argumentative, it is important to note that the sources for these excerpts—the textbook chapter and the magazine article—contain elements of both explanation and argument. The textbook writers, while they refrain from taking a particular position, do note the controversies surrounding biotechnology and genetic engineering. They might even subtly reveal a certain bias in favor of one side of the issue, through their word choice, tone, and perhaps through devoting more space and attention to one point of view. Explanatory and argumentative writing are not mutually exclusive. The overlap in the categories of explanation and argument is also found in the magazine article: In order to make his case against genetic engineering, the writer has to explain certain elements of the issue. Yet, even while these categories overlap to a certain extent, the second passage clearly has argument as its primary purpose, whereas the first passage is primarily explanatory.

In Chapter 2 we noted that the primary purpose in a piece of writing is either informative, persuasive, or entertaining (or some combination of the three). Some scholars of writing argue that all writing is essentially persuasive, and even without entering into that complex argument, we've just seen how the varying purposes in writing do overlap. In order to persuade others of a particular position, we typically must also inform them about it; conversely, a primarily informative piece of writing must also work to persuade the reader that its claims are truthful. Both informative and persuasive writing often include entertaining elements, and writing intended primarily to entertain also typically contains information and persuasion. For practical purposes, however, it is possible—and useful—to identify the *primary* purpose in a piece of writing as informative/explanatory, persuasive/argumentative, or entertaining. Entertainment as a primary purpose is the one least often practiced in purely academic writing—perhaps to your disappointment!—but information and persuasion are ubiquitous. Thus, while recognizing the overlap between these categories, we distinguish in this chapter between two types of synthesis writing: argument (or persuasive) and explanatory (or informative). Just as distinguishing the primary purpose in a piece of writing helps you to critically read and evaluate it, distinguishing the primary purpose in your own writing helps you to make the appropriate choices regarding your approach.

We'll first present some guidelines for writing syntheses in general and then focus on the argument synthesis. Toward the end of the chapter, we'll discuss the explanatory synthesis.

HOW TO WRITE SYNTHESES

Although writing syntheses can't be reduced to a lockstep method, it should help you to follow the guidelines listed in the box below.

GUIDELINES FOR WRITING SYNTHESES

- *Consider your purpose in writing.* What are you trying to accomplish in your essay? How will this purpose shape the way you approach your sources?
- *Select and carefully read your sources,* according to your purpose. Then reread the passages, mentally summarizing each. Identify those aspects or parts of your sources that will help you fulfill your purpose. When rereading, *label* or *underline* the sources for main ideas, key terms, and any details you want to use in the synthesis.
- *Take notes on your reading.* In addition to labeling or underlining key points in the readings, you might write brief one- or two-sentence summaries of each source. This will help you in formulating your thesis statement and in choosing and organizing your sources later.
- *Formulate a thesis.* Your thesis is the main idea that you want to present in your synthesis. It should be expressed as a complete sentence. You might do some predrafting about the ideas discussed in the readings in order to help you work out a thesis. If you've written one-sentence summaries of the readings, looking these over will help you to brainstorm connections between readings and to devise a thesis.

  When you write your essay drafts, you will need to consider where your thesis fits in your paper. Sometimes the thesis is the first sentence, but more often it is *the final sentence of the first paragraph.* If you are writing an *inductively arranged* synthesis (see page 63), the thesis sentence may not appear until the final paragraphs.
- *Decide how you will use your source material.* How will the information and the ideas in the passages help you fulfill your purpose?
- *Develop an organizational plan,* according to your thesis. How will you arrange your material? It is not necessary to prepare a formal outline. But you should have some plan that will indicate the order

---

(handwritten margin note: Shopping is the American way of life)

THE ARGUMENT SYNTHESIS

It's likely that most of the papers you'll be writing in the next few years will be focused on developing support for particular positions or claims, so we'll consider the argument synthesis first and in more detail. An argument synthesis is *persuasive* in purpose. An example: *Welfare reform has largely succeeded* (or *failed*). Writers working with the same source material might conceive of and support other, opposite theses. So the thesis for an argument synthesis is a claim about which reasonable people could disagree. It is a claim with

---

in which you will present your material and that will indicate the relationships among your sources.

- *Draft the topic sentences for the main sections.* This is an optional step, but you may find it a helpful transition from organizational plan to first draft.
- *Write the first draft of your synthesis*, following your organizational plan. Be flexible with your plan, however. Frequently, you will use an outline to get started. As you write, you may discover new ideas and make room for them by adjusting the outline. When this happens, reread your work frequently, making sure that your thesis still accounts for what follows and that what follows still logically supports your thesis.
- *Document your sources.* You must do this by crediting them within the body of the synthesis—citing the author's last name and page number from which the point was taken and by providing full citation information in a list of "Works Cited" at the end. Don't open yourself to charges of plagiarism! (See pages 21–23.)
- *Revise your synthesis*, inserting transitional words and phrases where necessary. Make sure that the synthesis reads smoothly, logically, and clearly from beginning to end. Check for grammatical correctness, punctuation, and spelling.

Note: The writing of syntheses is a recursive process, and you should accept a certain amount of backtracking and reformulating as inevitable. For instance, in developing an organizational plan (point 6 of the procedure), you may discover a gap in your presentation that will send you scrambling for another source—back to point 2. You may find that formulating a thesis and making inferences among sources occur simultaneously; indeed, inferences are often made before a thesis is formulated. Our recommendations for writing syntheses will give you a structure; they will get you started. But be flexible in your approach; expect discontinuity and, if possible, be comforted that through backtracking and reformulating you will eventually produce a coherent, well-crafted essay.

which—given the right arguments—your audience might be persuaded to agree. The strategy of your argument synthesis is therefore to find and use convincing *support* for your *claim*.

The Elements of Argument: Claim, Support, and Assumption

One way of looking at an argument is to see it as an interplay of three essential elements: claim, support, and assumption. A *claim* is a proposition or conclusion that you are trying to prove. You prove this claim by using *support* in the form of fact or expert opinion. Linking your supporting evidence to your claim is your *assumption* about the subject. This assumption—also called a *warrant*—is an underlying belief or principle about some aspect of the world and how it operates, as we discussed in Chapter 2. By nature, assumptions (which are often unstated) tend to be more general than either claims or supporting evidence.

For example, here are the essential elements of an argument advocating parental restriction of television viewing for their high school children:

> Claim
> High school students should be restricted to no more than two hours of TV viewing per day.
>
> Support
> An important new study and the testimony of educational specialists reveal that students who watch more than two hours of TV a night have, on average, lower grades than those who watch less TV.
>
> Assumption
> Excessive TV viewing adversely affects academic performance.

As another example, here's a claim concerning computer-mediated communication.

> E-mail, instant messaging, blogging, and other forms of Web-based communication threaten to undermine human intimacy, connection, and ultimately community.

Here are the other elements of this argument:

Support

- While the Internet presents us with increased opportunities to meet people, these meetings are limited by geographical distance.

- People are spending increasing amounts of time in cyberspace: In 1998, the average Internet user spent over four hours per week online, a figure that has nearly doubled recently.

- College health officials report that excessive Internet usage threatens many college students' academic and psychological well-being.

- New kinds of relationships fostered on the Internet often pose challenges to preexisting relationships.

Assumptions

- The communication skills used and the connections formed during Internet contact fundamentally differ from those used and formed during face-to-face contact.

- "Real" connection and a sense of community are sustained by face-to-face contact, not by Internet interactions.

Arguments should be constructed logically, or rationally, so that assumptions link evidence (supporting facts and expert opinions) to claims. As we'll see, however, logic is only one component of effective arguments.

EXERCISE 3.1

Practicing Claim, Support, and Assumption

Devise two sets of claims with support and assumptions for each. First, devise a one-sentence claim addressing the positive impact (or potentially positive impact) of computer-mediated communication on relationships—whether you personally agree with the claim or not. Then list the supports on which such a claim might rest and the assumptions that underlie these. Second, write a claim that states your own position on any debatable topic you choose. Again, devise statements of support and relevant assumptions.

DEMONSTRATION: DEVELOPING A SOURCE-BASED ARGUMENT SYNTHESIS— VOLUNTEERING IN AMERICA

To demonstrate how to plan and draft an argument synthesis, let's consider another subject. If you were taking an economics or sociology course, you might at some point consider the extent to which Americans volunteer— that is, give away their time freely—for causes they deem worthy. In a market economy, why would people agree to forgo wages in exchange for their labor? Are there other kinds of compensation for people who volunteer? Is peer pressure involved? Can a spirit of volunteerism be taught or encouraged? And, in light of the articles that follow and the example argument based on them, can the government—which has the constitutional right to compel military service—*compel* citizens to serve their communities (rendering their service something other than voluntary)?

Suppose, in preparing to write a short paper on volunteering, you located the following sources:

- "A New Start for National Service," John McCain and Evan Bayh
- "A Time to Heed the Call," David Gergen
- "Volunteering in the United States, 2003" Bureau of Labor Statistics, U.S. Department of Labor
- "AmeriCorps Mission Statement"
- "National Service, Political Socialization, and Citizenship," Eric B. Gorham
- "Calls for National Service," Roger Landrum, Donald J. Eberly, and Michael W. Sherraden
- "The Moral Equivalent of War," William James
- "Crito," Plato
- "Keeping Alive the Spirit of National Service," Richard North Patterson
- "Rumsfeld: No Need for Draft; 'Disadvantages Notable,'" Kathleen T. Rhem
- "Politics and National Service: A Virus Attacks the Volunteer Sector," Bruce Chapman

We've provided excerpts for a few of these sources in the pages that follow and a summary of the others. As you read, carefully note the kinds of information and ideas you could draw upon to develop an *argument synthesis*. In preparing your papers, naturally you will draw upon entire articles and book chapters, not brief excerpts. (The discussion of how these passages can form the basis of an argument synthesis resumes on page 63.)

A New Start for National Service
John McCain and Evan Bayh

John McCain (R-AZ) and Evan Bayh (D-IN) are U.S. senators. This op-ed piece appeared in the New York Times *on 6 November 2001, a few weeks after the terrorist attacks of September 11.**

1   Since Sept. 11, Americans have found a new spirit of national unity and purpose. Forty years ago, at the height of the cold war, President John F. Kennedy challenged Americans to enter into public service. Today, confronted with a challenge no less daunting than the cold war, Americans again are eager for ways to serve at home and abroad. Government should make it easier for them to do so.

2   That is why we are introducing legislation to revamp national service programs and dramatically expand opportunities for public service.

3   Many tasks lie ahead, both new and old. On the home front, there are new security and civil defense requirements, like increased police and border patrol needs. We will charge the Corporation for National Service, the federal office that oversees national volunteer programs, with the task of assembling a plan that would put civilians to work to assist the Office of Homeland Security. The military will need new recruits to confront the challenges abroad, so our bill will also improve benefits for our service members.

4   At the same time, because the society we defend needs increased services, from promoting literacy to caring for the elderly, we [should] expand AmeriCorps and senior service programs to enlarge our national army of volunteers.

5   AmeriCorps' achievements have been impressive: thousands of homes have been built, hundreds of thousands of seniors given the care they need to live independently and millions of children tutored.

6   Since its inception in 1993, nearly 250,000 Americans have served stints of one or two years in AmeriCorps. But for all its concrete achievements, AmeriCorps has been too small to rouse the nation's imagination. Under our bill, 250,000 volunteers each year would be able to answer the call—with half of them assisting in civil defense needs and half continuing the good work of AmeriCorps.

7   We must also ask our nation's colleges to promote service more aggressively. Currently, many colleges devote only a small fraction of federal work-study funds to community service, while the majority of federal resources are used to fill low-skill positions. This was not Congress's vision when it passed the Higher Education Act of 1965. Under our bill, universities will be required to promote student involvement in community activities more vigorously. . . .

8   Public service is a virtue, and national service should one day be a rite of passage for young Americans. This is the right moment to issue a new call to service and give a new generation a way to claim the rewards and responsibilities of active citizenship.

---

* John McCain and Evan Bayh, "A New Start for National Service," Op-Ed, *New York Times*, 6 Nov. 2001.

A Time to Heed the Call
David Gergen

David Gergen is an editor-at-large for U.S. News & World Report, *in which this essay appeared on 24 December 2001. He has served as an advisor to Presidents Nixon, Ford, Reagan, and Clinton and currently directs the Center for Public Leadership at the John F. Kennedy School of Government.**

1   How do we transform [our country's] new love of nation [following the events of September 11] into a lasting mission? How do we keep the flame alive? With imagination, we could do just that if we boldly call millions of young Americans to give at least a year of service to the nation. Remember FDR's Civilian Conservation Corps and the magnificent parks all those young people built in the wilderness? There are many parallel responsibilities today. Beefing up border operations, teaching kids in poor schools, helping out in hospitals—those are just a few. Add three months of physical training, with kids from Brooklyn mixing in with kids from Berkeley, and the results would be eye popping.

2   Giving something back. Voluntary service when young often changes people for life. They learn to give their fair share. Some 60 percent of alumni from Teach for America, a marvelous program, now work full time in education, and many others remain deeply involved in social change. Mark Levine, for example, has started two community-owned credit unions in Washington Heights, N.Y., for recent immigrants. Alumni of City Year, another terrific program, vote at twice the rates of their peers. Or think of the Peace Corps alumni. Six now serve in the House of Representatives, one (Christopher Dodd) in the Senate.

3   A culture of service might also help reverse the trend among many young people to shun politics and public affairs. Presidential voting among 18-to-29-year-olds has fallen over the past three decades from half to less than a third. In a famous poll of a year ago, some 47 percent said their regular source of political news was the late-night comedy shows. If the young were to sign up for national service, as scholar Bill Galston argues, that could lead to greater civic engagement. . . .

4   The best plan on offer today is one advanced by Sens. John McCain of Arizona, a Republican, and Democrat Evan Bayh of Indiana and given strong support by the Democratic Leadership Council. It would build on AmeriCorps, the volunteer program started by President Clinton, at first opposed and now embraced by many Republicans. AmeriCorps has achieved significant results but remains modest in size with about 50,000 volunteers. It has never enjoyed the panache of the Peace Corps—as many as 2 out of 3 Americans say they have never heard of the program. McCain and Bayh would expand AmeriCorps fivefold, to 250,000 volunteers a year, and channel half the new recruits into homeland-security efforts. The program would also open up more chances for seniors to serve—another important contribution. . . .

---

* David Gergen, "A Time to Heed the Call," *U.S. News & World Report*, 24 Dec. 2001, 60–61.

5   September 11 was a seminal moment for America. Everyone who lived through it will remember exactly where he or she was when the terrible news came. But the moment will pass unless we seize it and give it more permanent meaning. Fortunately, some already hear the call.

Volunteering in the United States, 2003
Bureau of Labor Statistics, U.S. Department of Labor

Every year, the Bureau of Labor Statistics (BLS) collects and analyzes patterns of volunteering in the United States. On page 58, in tabular form, is a summary of data collected from September 2002 to September 2003. According to the BLS, "Volunteers are defined as persons who did unpaid work (except for expenses) through or for an organization. [These data are based on] a monthly survey of about 60,000 households that obtains information on employment and unemployment among the nation's civilian noninstitutional population age 16 and over."*

AmeriCorps Mission Statement

"AmeriCorps is a network of national service programs that engage more than 50,000 Americans each year in intensive service to meet critical needs in education, public safety, health, and the environment. AmeriCorps members serve through more than 2,100 non-profits, public agencies, and faith-based organizations. They tutor and mentor youth, build affordable housing, teach computer skills, clean parks and streams, run after-school programs, and help communities respond to disasters. Created in 1993, AmeriCorps is part of the Corporation for National and Community Service, which also oversees Senior Corps and Learn and Serve America. Together these programs engage more than 2 million Americans of all ages and backgrounds in service each year."† AmeriCorps' four-part mission involves "Getting Things Done," "Strengthening Communities," "Encouraging Responsibility," and "Expanding Opportunity."

---

* Bureau of Labor Statistics, "Volunteering in the United States, 2003" (Washington, DC: U.S. Department of Labor, 2003).

† Institute for Future Work Force Development. "National AmeriCorps History." *Youth in Action AmeriCorps*. Northern Arizona University. 10 July 2003. 20 July 2003 <http://www4.nau.edu> Path: americorps; AmeriCorps History.

TABLE 3.A Volunteers by selected characteristics, September 2002 and 2003

(Numbers in thousands)

Characteristic	September 2002r			September 2003		
	Number	Percent of population	Median annual hours	Number	Percent of population	Median annual hours
Sex						
Total, both sexes	59,783	27.4	52	63,791	28.8	52
Men	24,706	23.6	52	26,805	25.1	52
Women	35,076	31.0	50	36,987	32.2	52
Age						
Total, 16 years and over	59,783	27.4	52	63,791	28.8	52
16 to 24 years	7,742	21.9	40	8,671	24.1	40
25 to 34 years	9,574	24.8	33	10,337	26.5	36
35 to 44 years	14,971	34.1	52	15,165	34.7	50
45 to 54 years	12,477	31.3	52	13,302	32.7	52
55 to 64 years	7,331	27.5	60	8,170	29.2	60
65 years and over	7,687	22.7	96	8,146	23.7	88
Educational attainment (1)						
Less than a high school diploma	2,806	10.1	48	2,793	9.9	48
High school graduate, no college (2)	12,542	21.2	49	12,882	21.7	48
Less than a bachelor's degree (3)	15,066	32.8	52	15,966	34.1	52
College graduates	21,627	43.3	60	23,481	45.6	60

(1) Data refer to persons 25 years and over.
(2) Includes high school diploma or equivalent.
(3) Includes the categories some college, no degree; and associate degree.
r = revised. Estimates for 2002 have been revised to reflect the use of Census 2000-based population controls.

National Service, Political Socialization, and Citizenship
Eric B. Gorham

This first chapter of Eric B. Gorham's National Service, Citizenship, and Political Education *(1992) defines national service "as a nation-wide program of community work that citizens, mostly young people, enter for one or two years. It is either voluntary or coercive, and employs participants in public sector or 'voluntary' sector jobs at subminimum wages. In the process, participants serve the needs of the nation, acquire job and life skills, and learn the essentials of American citizenship." Gorham goes on to trace the history of America's national service in the twentieth century, referring to William James's famous "Moral Equivalent of War"; the initiatives of various presidents, beginning with Roosevelt; and various local initiatives like Seattle's Program for Local Service. According to Gorham, "Proponents [of national service] maintain that young people must learn citizenship, and either they argue that such programs inculcate this generally, or they have attached particular programs designed to increase the civic competence of young adults. Indeed, the rhetoric of citizenship . . . defends national service on moral and political grounds." In his book, Gorham argues that the language government uses to promote programs for national service betrays an effort to "reproduce a postindustrial, capitalist economy in the name of good citizenship." Eric Gorham is associate professor of political science at Loyola University, New Orleans.**

Calls for National Service
Roger Landrum, Donald J. Eberly, and Michael W. Sherraden

The passage introduces the work of William James, who in a famous speech in 1906 essentially began America's conversation about national service in the twentieth century. The authors suggest that "James was clearly thinking only of young men and the image of Ivy League undergraduates. . . . He didn't consider the issue of constitutional limits on involuntary servitude. His recommendation of conscription was softened only by the concepts of collectivity and social sanctions. . . . Still, James succeeded in embedding a phrase, 'the moral equivalent of war,' in the national consciousness; he raised the fundamental issue of proper socialization of youth in the context of a democracy at peace; and he planted the idea of national service." The essay appears in a collection of scholarly commentaries on national service, edited by Sherraden and Eberly.†

---

* For credit information on Gorham, see the "Works Cited" list on p. 72.

† For credit information on Landrum, *et al.*, see the "Works Cited" list on p. 72.

The Moral Equivalent of War
William James

William James (1842–1910), an influential philosopher, psychologist, and professor at Harvard University, is best known for his works The Varieties of Religious Experience *(1902) and* The Principles of Psychology *(1890). "The Moral Equivalent of War," first delivered in 1906 as a speech at Stanford University and later published in 1910, became a seminal document in the national service movement. In the speech, James argues that the qualities of character that distinguish soldiers (for instance, self-discipline and regard for the common good) are important to developing and maintaining a civil society. James believes these qualities "can be bred without war" and lays out a "moral equivalent of war" for doing so. The essay, which is central to any understanding of the national service movement in the twentieth century, can be found at <http://www.des.emory.edu/mfp/moral.html>.*

Crito
Plato

Socrates (c. 470 BCE–c. 399 BCE) was condemned to die by the authorities of Athens for "corrupting" its youth through his teachings. In a famous dialogue of Plato, Crito wishes to convince his friend and teacher to escape before the sentence (death by the drinking of hemlock, a poison) is to be carried out. Instead of running, Socrates explains to Crito the obligations of a citizen to the state. His reference to "the laws" and to "we" and "us" is to the authorities of Athens—and, by extension, to any governing body to which people freely give their allegiance. The excerpt here provides a flavor for Socrates' logic. The entire dialogue can be found at the Classic Literature Online Library, <http://www.greece.com/library/plato/crito_04.html>.

Socrates:

Then the laws will say: "Consider, Socrates, if this is true, that in your present attempt you are going to do us wrong. For, after having brought you into the world, and nurtured and educated you, and given you and every other citizen a share in every good that we had to give, we further proclaim and give the right to every Athenian, that if he does not like us when he has come of age and has seen the ways of the city, and made our acquaintance, he may go where he pleases and take his goods with him; and none of us laws will forbid him or interfere with him. Any of you who does not like us and the city, and who wants to go to a colony or to any other city, may go where he likes, and take his goods with him. But he who has experience of the manner in which we order justice and administer the State, and still remains, has entered into an implied contract that he will do as we command him. And he who disobeys us is . . . wrong."*

---

* Plato, "Crito." *Classic Greek Literature Online*, 28 June 2004 <http://www.greece.com/library/plato/crito_04.html>.

Keeping Alive the Spirit of National Service
Richard North Patterson

Richard North Patterson is a prolific novelist who lives in San Francisco and Martha's Vineyard. His books include Protect and Defend *(2001) and* Balance of Power *(2003). In an op-ed essay on national service appearing in the* Boston Globe *on 1 August 1999, he argues for congressional re-authorization of the AmeriCorps program as a way of restoring to American youth what he thinks was lost over the past several decades: "a common experience, a chance to serve, which cuts across the barriers of race, class, and education." In national service, Patterson sees "the chance for our young to make their best contribution to a stronger country and a better society."*

Rumsfeld: No Need for Draft; "Disadvantages Notable"
Kathleen T. Rhem

Kathleen Rhem writes for the American Forces Press Service. In an article posted on the DefenseLINK Web site on 7 January 2003, she cites senior Pentagon officials in reporting that the United States has no need for, and no plans to implement, a national military draft. The all-volunteer army, says the Chairman of the Joint Chiefs of Staff, is "efficient; it's effective; it's given the United States of America . . . a military that is second to none." The Pentagon intends to keep its forces voluntary to maintain morale and readiness. In fact, forced military service, say the officials, has "notable disadvantages."

Politics and National Service: A Virus Attacks the Volunteer Sector
Bruce Chapman

Bruce Chapman, former U.S. Ambassador to the U.N. organizations in Vienna and former senior fellow at the Hudson Institute, currently serves as president of the Discovery Institute of Seattle, Washington, a public policy center for studying national and international affairs. An early proponent of the all-volunteer army who dedicated many years to public service (as secretary of state for the State of Washington, former director of the U.S. Census Bureau, and as an aide to President Reagan), Chapman opposes all government involvement in volunteer programs, likening proposals for government-sponsored national service to the influenza virus. The excerpted selection that follows appears in a collection of essays, National Service: Pro & Con *(1990).**

---

* Bruce Chapman, "Politics and National Service: A Virus Attacks the Volunteer Sector," Williamson M. Evers, ed. *National Service: Pro & Con* (Stanford: Hoover Institution Press, 1990) 133–44.

1 Why does the national service virus keep coming back? Perhaps because its romance is so easy to catch, commanding a nostalgic imagination and evoking times when Americans were eager to sacrifice for their country. Claiming to derive inspiration from both military experience and the social gospel—if we could only get America's wastrel youth into at least a psychic uniform we might be able to teach self-discipline again and revive the spirit of giving—it hearkens back to William James's call for a "moral equivalent of war." But at the end of the twentieth century should we be looking to war for moral guidance?

2   True service is one of the glories of our civilization in the West, especially in the great independent (or volunteer) sector of American society. Inspiration for service in the West comes from the Bible in parable and admonition and is constantly restated in the long historical tradition of Judeo-Christian faith. Personal service is a freewill offering to God. This is very different from performance of an obligation to government, which is a tax on time or money.

3   True service, then, has a spiritual basis, even for some outside the Judeo-Christian tradition per se. Fulfillment of an obligation to government, in contrast, has a contractual basis unless it is founded on an outright commitment to a coercive utopianism. Either way, it is not true service. Nor can enrollment in a government-funded self-improvement project or acceptance of a government job be called true service. Indeed, when coercion or inducements are provided, as in the various national service schemes, the spirit of service is to that degree corrupted.

Consider Your Purpose

Your specific purpose in writing an argument synthesis is crucial. What, exactly, you want to do will affect your claim, the evidence you select to support your claim, and the way you organize the evidence. Your purpose may be clear to you before you begin research, may emerge during the course of research, or may not emerge until after you have completed your research. (Of course, the sooner your purpose is clear to you, the fewer wasted motions you will make. On the other hand, the more you approach research as an exploratory process, the likelier that your conclusions will emerge from the sources themselves, rather than from preconceived ideas.)

Let's say that while reading these sources, your own encounters with a service organization (perhaps you help schoolchildren improve their literacy skills) have influenced your thinking on the subject. You find yourself impressed that so many people at the literacy center volunteer without being compelled to do so. You observe that giving time freely adds to the pleasures of volunteering, and to its significance as well. Meanwhile, perhaps your school is considering a service "requirement"—that is, a mandate that all students perform a given number of community service hours in order to graduate. The juxtaposition of "compelled" service with freely given service sparks in you an idea for a source-based paper.

You can understand and even sympathize with the viewpoints of educators who believe that while they have students in their clutches (so to speak), they have an opportunity to pass on an ethic of service. To students who would not volunteer time on their own, setting a graduation requirement makes sense. Yet you might regard "forced" volunteerism as a contradiction in terms that defeats the essential quality of volunteering: freely donated time. Perhaps you believe that time given freely to meet the needs of others is an act of selflessness that brings profound satisfaction. Your purpose in writing, then, emerges from these kinds of responses to the source material.

Make a Claim: Formulate a Thesis

As we indicated in the introduction to argument synthesis, one useful way of approaching an argument is to see it as making a *claim*. A claim is a proposition, a conclusion that you are trying to prove or demonstrate. If your purpose is to demonstrate that the state should not compel people to serve their communities, then that is the claim at the heart of your argument. The claim is generally expressed in one-sentence form as a *thesis*. You draw *support* from your sources as you argue logically for your claim.

Of course, not every piece of information in a source is useful for supporting a claim. By the same token, you may draw support for your claim from sources that make entirely different claims. You may use as support for your own claim, for example, a sentiment expressed in William James's "The Moral Equivalent of War," that values such as selfless concern for the common good, learned through service, "are absolute and permanent human goods." Yet while James called for "a conscription of the whole youthful population" to nonmilitary service projects, you may believe that service should be voluntary. Still, you could cite James and comment, where you think appropriate, on where you and he diverge.

Similarly, you might use one source as part of a *counterargument*—an argument opposite to your own—so that you can demonstrate its weaknesses and, in the process, strengthen your own claim. On the other hand, the author of one of your sources may be so convincing in supporting a claim that you adopt it yourself, either partially or entirely. The point is that *the argument is in your hands*: You must devise it yourself and must use your sources in ways that will support the claim expressed in your thesis.

You may not want to divulge your thesis until the end of the paper, to draw the reader along toward your conclusion, allowing the thesis to flow naturally out of the argument and the evidence on which it is based. If you do this, you are working *inductively*. Or you may wish to be more direct and *begin* with your thesis, following the thesis statement with evidence to support it. If you do this, you are working *deductively*. In academic papers, deductive arguments are far more common than inductive arguments.

Based on your own experience and reactions to reading sources, you may find yourself agreeing with Bruce Chapman's argument that compelled or monetarily induced service "corrupts" the experience of service. At the same time, you may find yourself unwilling to take Chapman's extreme stance that even modest stipends such as the ones earned while working for AmeriCorps and other government programs constitute "corruption." While you believe that government programs encouraging service are beneficial, you certainly don't want to see the federal government create a nonmilitary version of compulsory national service. After a few tries, you develop the following thesis:

> The impulse to expand service through volunteer programs like AmeriCorps, VISTA, and the Peace Corps is understandable, even praiseworthy. But as volunteerism grows and gains public support, we should resist letting its successes become an argument for *compulsory* national service.

Decide How You Will Use Your Source Material

Your claim commits you to (1) discussing the benefits of service in government-sponsored programs like AmeriCorps and VISTA, and (2) arguing that, benefits notwithstanding, there are good reasons not to make national service compulsory. The sources provide plenty of information and ideas—that is, evidence—that will allow you to support your claim. (You might draw on one universally available source, the U.S. Constitution, not included in the materials here.) William James and Plato, backed by contemporary commentators Eric Gorham and Roger Landrum, Donald Eberly, and Michael Sherraden, provide a philosophical and historical foundation for the paper. The statistics generated by the Department of Labor offer current, accurate information on volunteerism in America. The selections by David Gergen, Richard North Patterson, and Senators McCain and Bayh provide pro-service arguments, while the essay by Bruce Chapman provides a negative one.

Develop an Organizational Plan

Having established your overall purpose and your claim, having developed a thesis (which may change as you write and revise the paper), and having decided how to use your source materials, how do you logically organize your essay? In many cases, including this one, a well-written thesis will suggest an overall organization. Thus, the first part of your argument synthesis will define volunteerism and set a broad historical context, along with mention of a possible early attempt to make national service compulsory. The second part will argue that national service should *not* be made compulsory. Sorting through your material and categorizing it by topic and subtopic, you might arrive at the following outline:

I. Introduction. Pervasiveness of volunteerism in America. Use Bureau of Labor Statistics data.

II. The desire to "make more of a good thing." The McCain/Bayh "Call to Service Act." *Thesis*.

III. Intellectual history of service:

    A. Recent history. Refer to William James. State that service need not be military.

    B. Ancient history. Refer to Plato. State that citizens owe the State an obligation.

IV. Can the U.S. government compel citizens to service?

    A. Military service. Yes. Right granted by U.S. Constitution.

    B. Transition: military vs. civilian.

    C. Civilian service: No.
       1. Logical reason: public service is not analogous to military service.
       2. Moral reason: compelled or induced service (that is, with money) "corrupts" spirit of service.
          a. Concede point that "less pure" forms of service that pay stipends, such as AmeriCorps and VISTA, are beneficial.
          b. But state forcefully that compulsory (as opposed to minimally compensated) service does corrupt the spirit of service.

V. Conclusion:

    A. Government should expand opportunities to serve *voluntarily* (even with pay).

    B. It should resist the impulse to compel young people to serve.

Formulate an Argument Strategy

The argument represented by this outline will build not only on evidence drawn from sources but also on the writer's assumptions. Consider the barebones logic of the argument:

Voluntary service, paid or unpaid, promotes good citizenship and benefits the community. (*assumption*)

People who have worked in volunteer programs have made significant contributions to community and public life. (*support*)

We should support programs that foster volunteerism. (*claim*)

The crucial point about which reasonable people will disagree is the *assumption* that unpaid *and* paid volunteer service promote good citizenship. One source author, Bruce Chapman, makes a partial and extreme form of this assumption when he writes that financially rewarded service is "corrupted" (see page 62). A less-extreme assumption—the one guiding the model paper—is possible: Citizenship can be learned in a minimally paid environment such as AmeriCorps. The writer of the model paper agrees with Chapman, however, about another assumption: that nonmilitary service should never be forced on anyone.

Writers can accept or partially accept an opposing assumption by making a *concession*, in the process establishing themselves as reasonable and willing to compromise. In our example, the writer does exactly this (see paragraph 10 in the sample synthesis that follows) and uses as *supporting evidence* facts from David Gergen's report that many paid veterans of government-sponsored teaching programs learn about citizenship and continue to teach after their contracted time is up. By raising potential objections and making concessions, the writer blunts the effectiveness of *counterarguments*.

The *claim* of the example argument about service is primarily a claim about *policy*, about actions that should (or should not) be taken. An argument can also concern a claim about *facts* (Does X exist? Does X lead to Y? How can we define X?) or a claim about *value* (What is X worth?). You have seen that the present argument rests on an assumed definition of "service." Depending on how you define the term, you will agree—or not—with the writer. Among the source authors, Bruce Chapman defines service one way (it is neither rewarded with money nor compelled), while David Gergen and Senators McCain and Bayh define it another (as work done with or without minimal pay to help others and reinforce core values). As you read the following paper, watch how the writer weaves these opposing views into the argument.

A well-reasoned argument will involve a claim primarily about fact, value, *or* policy. Secondary arguments are sometimes needed, as in the present example, to help make a case.

Draft and Revise Your Synthesis

The final draft of a completed synthesis, based on the above outline, follows. Thesis, transitions, and topic sentences are highlighted; Modern Language Association (MLA) documentation style is used throughout. Note that for the sake of clarity, references in the following synthesis are to pages in the standard edition of *Writing and Reading Across the Curriculum*.

A cautionary note: When writing syntheses, it is all too easy to become careless in properly crediting your sources. Before drafting your paper, please review the section on avoiding plagiarism in Chapter 1 (pages 21–23).

Model Synthesis

Keeping Volunteering Voluntary

1 The spirit of volunteerism is alive and well in America. In 2002–2003, 28.8 percent of Americans, 16 and older, some 63.8 million, freely gave time to their communities (Bureau 140). Moved by a desire to serve others, more than one-quarter of us donate 52 hours a year, more than one full work-week, to building shelters, coaching Little League, caring for the elderly, teaching literacy, and countless other community minded pursuits (Bureau 140). Experts tell us that volunteerism builds character, teaches citizenship, and addresses unfulfilled national needs (Gorham 141).

2　Saying that nearly one in three Americans volunteer is another way of saying that just more than two in three do not. Given volunteering's benefits both to the individual and the community, it is little wonder that from time to time politicians propose to make more of a good thing. In this spirit, in November 2001 Senators John McCain (R-AZ) and Evan Bayh (D-IN) introduced Bill S1274, the "Call to Service Act," which would dramatically increase the opportunities to serve in government-sponsored volunteer programs. "Public service is a virtue," write the senators in a *New York Times* op-ed piece not quite two months after the horrors of September 11, 2001. They believe that this "is the right moment to issue a new call to service and give a new generation a way to claim the rewards and responsibilities of active citizenship." The impulse to expand service through volunteer programs like AmeriCorps, VISTA, and the Peace Corps is understandable, even praiseworthy. But as volunteerism grows and gains public support, we should resist letting its successes become an argument for compulsory national service.

3   Senators McCain and Bayh do not call for compulsory service. Nonetheless, one can hear an echo of the word "compulsory" in their claim that "national service should one day be a rite of passage for young Americans." The word "should" suggests obligation, and the word "all" is clearly implied. It's not a stretch to imagine the senators and others at some point endorsing a program of compulsory service, an idea that has been around for nearly a century. In 1906, the philosopher William James called for "a conscription of the whole youthful population" to nonmilitary projects that would improve character (142). James, whom many consider the intellectual father of national service, admired the discipline and sacrifice of soldiers but thought it absurd that such "[m]artial virtues" as "intrepidity, contempt of softness, surrender of private interest, [and] obedience to command" should be developed only in the service of war. He imagined a "reign of peace" in which these qualities would "remain the rock upon which" peaceful states might be built (142).

4   In the early twentieth century, there were not nearly as many young people as today, both in the general public and in college (Landrum, Eberly, and Sherraden 142), and so the details of implementing a plan for national service may have seemed manageable. A hundred years later we might regard James's proposal as impractical or even illegal, but at the time he struck an important chord. His vision of learning what Senators McCain and Bayh call "the rewards and responsibilities of active citizenship" (138) through nonmilitary service in peace time (a "moral equivalent of war") entered our national vocabulary and remains a part of it today (Landrum, Eberly, and Sherraden 142).

5   The question of what sort of service, or obligation, citizens owe a country is as old as civilization. In one of his famous dialogues, Plato records a conversation between Socrates, whom Athens had imprisoned and condemned to death for corrupting the city's youth with his teachings, and a friend who urges that he escape and save himself. Socrates argues that if he has accepted and enjoyed the privileges of citizenship, then he must also accept the judgment of the State. This is his obligation. According to Socrates, citizens obligate themselves to the State when they accept its benefits (143). But how is that obligation to be paid? Some twenty-four

hundred years after Socrates accepted what he thought was his duty and drank a cup of hemlock, Americans pay their obligations to the government differently (thank goodness!): through taxes, jury duty, and obedience to laws passed by elected officials.

6   Can the government compel us to do more? Can it compel us, for instance, to military or nonmilitary service? The U.S. Constitution grants Congress the right to raise armies (Article 1, Section 8, Clause 14). The way Congress chooses to do this, however, reflects the needs of a particular time. During World War II and the Vietnam War, the government implemented a military draft. Today, for reasons of professionalism and morale, the Department of Defense prefers an all-volunteer army to an army of conscripts. The Chairman of the Joint Chiefs of Staff was recently reported to have said that the "country doesn't need a draft because the all-volunteer force works—in fact, the United States has the most effective military in the world precisely because it is all-volunteer" (Rhem 143–44).

7   The State has a constitutional right to draft young people into military service in times of military need, whether it chooses to exercise that right through an all-volunteer or a conscripted army. But does the State also have the right to require citizens to perform nonmilitary service? For example, because our libraries are understaffed, our parks overgrown, and many of our schoolchildren reading below grade level, should the State be able to require citizens to serve the unmet needs of the larger community? No—for both logical and moral reasons.

8   Military need is not logically equivalent to nonmilitary need, mostly because we fulfill nonmilitary needs through the normal operations of government. When the State identifies work to be done for the common good, it taxes citizens and directs its employees to perform that work. The State might also put out bids and pay contractors to perform the work. This is how we build highways and libraries. If the State performs these basic functions poorly, it fails in its responsibilities. The remedy to this failure should not be the drafting of America's youth into national service for one or two years. The State could not honestly or reasonably call for national service as a means of improving the moral character of youth when its real need is to find cheap labor

for cleaning streets and teaching third graders how to read. If the State lacks the money or competence to do its work well, then citizens should overhaul the system by electing new, more effective representatives. If necessary, the legislature could raise taxes. But it should not use its own failures to justify public service.

9   Nor could the State compel young people to national, nonmilitary service on moral grounds. We know that volunteerism promotes selflessness, a concern for community, and an appreciation of country (McCain and Bayh; Gergen; James; Patterson). Still, the essential quality of volunteerism is that it is time given freely. "True service," writes Bruce Chapman, "has a spiritual basis [rooted in the Judeo-Christian tradition]. . . . Fulfillment of an obligation to government, in contrast, has a contractual basis." Chapman argues that "performance of an obligation to government . . . is a tax on time or money." The spirit of service is "corrupted" when it is either forced or rewarded with money (144).

10   Chapman makes the extreme argument that volunteer programs that pay youth in room and board, health care, and tuition vouchers corrupt the spirit of giving. He ignores the financial realities of young people, many of whom, if they received no money for their service, would refuse to serve. And then they would lose the possibility of learning from programs that encourage civic participation and patriotism. That would be a shame, for the members of AmeriCorps, the Peace Corps, and VISTA, for instance, all receive a small stipend. They grow as individuals and as citizens, learning lifelong lessons. Former presidential advisor and journalist David Gergen describes this growth:

> Voluntary service when young often changes people for life. They learn to give their fair share. Some 60 percent of alumni from Teach for America, a marvelous program, now work full time in education, and many others remain deeply involved in social change. . . . Alumni of City Year, another terrific program, vote at twice the rates of their peers. Or think of the Peace Corps alumni. Six now serve in the House of Representatives, one (Christopher Dodd) in the Senate. (139)

Unquestionably, national programs for volunteers can benefit both the individuals serving and the communities served—even if those individuals receive a small stipend. So we don't have to accept Chapman's extreme position that even a hint of money "corrupts" the volunteer's spirit.

11   Still, as Chapman points out, volunteerism that is forced in any way, that turns the impulse to serve into an obligation, would corrupt. If the State required nonmilitary service for the "good" of the individual (and recall that it could not reasonably or honestly do so), the act of service would no longer be rooted in generosity. And it is the spirit of generosity, of one person's freely giving to another, that underlies all the good that volunteering achieves. Convert the essential generous impulse to an obligation, and the very logic for compelling service—to teach civic values—disappears. The State could no more expect those forced into service to have learned good citizenship or patriotism than we could expect a child whose parents order him to "make friends with Johnny" to have learned anything useful about friendship or to feel a special kinship with Johnny. Affection, citizenship, and patriotism don't work that way. They are freely given, or they are coerced. And if coerced, they are corrupt.

12   Without any incentive other than the good it would do their communities and their own hearts, 63.8 million Americans—more than one quarter of the country—volunteer. Could more people volunteer, specifically more young people? Yes, especially in light of the finding that young people in their early twenties volunteer the least, relative to all other age groups (Bureau 140). The McCain/Bayh "Call to Service Act." deserves enthusiastic support, as does any effort to encourage service by people younger than 25. Those who serve while young turn out to be more involved with their communities over the course of their lives (Gergen; Corporation), and such involvement can only benefit us all. Reasonable rewards such as tuition vouchers, minimal pay, health care, and room and board can give young people the safety net they need to experiment with serving others and in that way discover their own wellsprings of generosity.

13   So let's support McCain/Bayh and every such effort to encourage service. Ideally, enough programs will be in place one day to offer all high school and college graduates the option of serving their communities. "[T]oo often," writes Richard

North Patterson, "we offer young people a vision of community which extends to the nearest shopping mall" (143). Government-sponsored programs for service can make us better than that, and we should promote volunteerism wherever and whenever we can. But we must guard against using the success of these programs as a pretext for establishing mandatory national or community service.

Works Cited

Bureau of Labor Statistics. "Volunteering in the United States, 2003." 18 Dec. 2003. 17 Jan. 2004 <http://www.bls.gov/news.release/volun.nr0.htm>.

Chapman, Bruce. "Politics and National Service: A Virus Attacks the Volunteer Sector." National Service: Pro & Con. Ed. Williamson M. Evers. Stanford, CA: Hoover Institution P, 1990. 133—44.

Constitution of the United States of America. The New York Public Library Desk Reference. New York: Webster's New World, 1989.

Corporation for National and Community Service. "AmeriCorps Mission." AmeriCorps: Getting Things Done. Program Directory, Spring/Summer 1995. Microfiche Y2N.21/29 10AM3. Washington, DC: GPO, 1995.

Gergen, David. "A Time to Heed the Call." U.S. News & World Report 24 Dec. 2001: 60—61.

Gorham, Eric B. "National Service, Political Socialization, and Citizenship." National Service, Citizenship, and Political Education. Albany: SUNY P, 1992. 5—30.

James, William. "The Moral Equivalent of War." International Conciliation 27 (Washington, DC: Carnegie Endowment for International Peace, 1910): 8-20.

Landrum, Roger, Donald J. Eberly, and Michael W. Sherraden. "Calls for National Service." National Service: Social, Economic and Military Impacts. Ed. Michael W. Sherraden and Donald J. Eberly. New York: Pergamon, 1982. 21—38.

McCain, John, and Evan Bayh. "A New Start for National Service." New York Times 6 Nov. 2001: A25.

Patterson, Richard North. "Keeping Alive the Spirit of National Service." Boston Globe 1 Aug. 1999: A19.

Plato, "Crito." Classic Literature Online Library. Trans. Benjamin Jowett. 17 July 2003 <http://www.greece.com/library/plato/crito_04.html>.

Rhem, Kathleen T. "Rumsfeld: No Need for Draft; 'Disadvantages Notable.'" American Forces Information Service 7 Jan. 2003. 17 July 2003 <http://www.dod.gov/news/Jan2003/n01072003_200301074.html>.

Discussion

The writer of this argument synthesis on compulsory national service attempts to support a *claim*—one that favors national service but insists on keeping it voluntary—by offering *support* in the form of facts (rates of volunteerism from the Bureau of Labor Statistics) and opinions (testimony of experts). However, since the writer's claim rests on a definition of "true service," its effectiveness depends partially upon the extent to which we, as readers, agree with the *assumptions* underlying that definition. (See our discussion of assumptions in Chapter 2, pages 35–36.) An assumption (sometimes called a *warrant*) is a generalization or principle about how the world works or should work—a fundamental statement of belief about facts or values. In this particular case, the underlying assumption is that "true service" to a community must be voluntary, never required. The writer makes this assumption explicit. Though you are under no obligation to do so, stating assumptions explicitly will clarify your arguments to readers.

Assumptions often are deeply rooted in people's psyches, sometimes deriving from lifelong experiences and observations and not easily changed, even by the most logical of arguments. People who learned the spirit of volunteerism early in life, perhaps through "required" activities in religious or public school, might not accept the support offered for the claim that required service would be illogical or "corrupted." But others might well be persuaded and might agree that programs to expand opportunities for national service should be supported, though service itself should never be compelled. A discussion of the model argument's paragraphs, along with the argument strategy for each, follows. Note that the writer avoids plagiarism by carefully attributing and quoting sources.

- **Paragraph 1:** The writer uses statistics to establish that a culture of volunteerism is alive and well in America.

  Argument strategy: In this opening paragraph, the writer sets up the general topic—volunteerism in America—and establishes that Americans volunteer in impressive numbers. The writer uses information from the Bureau of Labor Statistics to anticipate and deflect possible criticism from those who might say: "So few of us volunteer that we should require national service in order to promote citizenship and to build character."

- **Paragraph 2:** Here the writer sets a context for and introduces the McCain/Bayh proposal to expand national service. The writer then presents the thesis.

  Argument strategy: This paragraph moves in one direction with an inspiring call to service by Senators McCain and Bayh and then takes a sharp, contrasting turn to the thesis. The first part of the thesis, "as volunteerism grows and gains public support," clearly follows from (and summarizes) the first part of paragraph 2. The transition "But" signals the contrast, which sets up the warning. A contrast generates interest by creating tension, in this case prompting readers to wonder: "Why *should* we resist compulsory service?"

- **Paragraphs 3–5:** In these paragraphs, the writer discusses the intellectual history of service: first, the writing of William James in the early years of the past century, and next, Plato's account of a dialogue between Socrates and a student. The writer discusses their relevance to the issue at the center of this essay: service to the greater community.

  Argument strategy: At this point, the writer is *preparing* to offer reasons for accepting the claim that we must resist compulsory service. The goal of paragraphs 3–5 is to set a historical context for the essay by establishing service as a significant cultural norm in America and, more broadly, by showing that the notion of obligation to the State is fundamental to civil societies. The end of paragraph 5 makes a transition to modern-day America and begins to move from the preparation for argument to the argument.

- **Paragraph 6:** This paragraph opens with two questions and sets up a key distinction in the essay between military and nonmilitary service. After raising the distinction, the writer devotes the paragraph to establishing the right of the American government to draft citizens into the army. A high-ranking military administrator is quoted to the effect that the all-volunteer army is a better fighting force than earlier, conscripted armies.

  Argument strategy: This paragraph begins moving the reader into the argument by introducing and discussing the first part of the distinction just presented: military service. The writer establishes that compulsory military service is constitutional and in keeping with the historical obligations that citizens owe the State. But even here, in a case in which the State has the clear authority to conscript people, the writer quotes a military official as saying that voluntary service is superior to compulsory service. The reader will find this strong preference for volunteerism continued in the second part of the essay devoted to nonmilitary service.

- **Paragraph 7:** This transitional paragraph raises the core question on which the argument hangs: Does the State have the right, as it does in military matters, to press citizens into nonmilitary, national service? The writer answers the question in the final sentence of this paragraph and, in so doing, forecasts the discussion that follows.

  Argument strategy: Here the writer sets up the second part of the paper, where reasons for accepting the claim will be presented. Up until this point, the writer has established that (1) volunteers can build character through service, (2) citizens owe a debt to the State, and (3) the State can legally collect on that debt by drafting citizens into the army in time of war. In this transition paragraph, the writer poses the question that will take the rest of the paper to answer. The question becomes an invitation to read.

- **Paragraphs 8–9:** In these two paragraphs, the writer answers—in the negative—the question posed in paragraph 7. The State does *not* have the right to press citizens into national service. Paragraph 8 offers a logical reason: that military and nonmilitary service are not equivalent. Paragraph 9 offers a moral reason: that coerced or compulsory service is "corrupted."

    Argument strategy: These paragraphs lay out the main reasons for accepting the claim that we should resist letting the successes of volunteerism become an argument for compulsory national service. The writer argues on two grounds—logical and moral—in an effort to build a strong case.

- **Paragraph 10:** Here the writer concedes a problem with the view (expressed by Chapman) in paragraph 9 that service that is either compelled or financially rewarded is corrupted. Allowing that this extreme position does not take into account the financial needs of young people, the writer endorses an alternate view, that minimal payment for service is legitimate. To support this more moderate position, the writer quotes David Gergen.

    Argument strategy: With this concession, the writer backs off an extreme view. The tactic makes the writer look both reasonable and realistic just prior to arguing very firmly, in the next paragraph, against compulsory service.

- **Paragraph 11:** Here the writer endorses one of Chapman's strongly held positions: forced service corrupts the spirit of volunteerism.

    Argument strategy: Here is the emotional core of the argument. The writer has previously argued that for logical reasons (paragraph 8) compulsory service must be rejected. The writer devotes three paragraphs to developing moral reasons, in the end endorsing Chapman's view. In paragraph 11, the writer uses an analogy for the first time: compelling service is equivalent to compelling a child to like someone. Neither works. The value of service rests on the offering of oneself freely to those in need.

- **Paragraphs 12–13:** The writer concludes by re-stating the claim—in two paragraphs.

    Argument strategy: These concluding paragraphs parallel the two-part structure of the thesis: Part 1 (paragraph 12), that volunteerism has many benefits and deserves support; Part 2 (paragraph 13), that we must resist any effort to make service compulsory.

Other approaches to an argument synthesis would be possible, based on the sources provided here. One could agree with Bruce Chapman and adopt the extreme view against both compulsory and paid service. Such an argument would make no concessions of the sort found in paragraph 10 of the model synthesis. Another approach would be to argue that young people must be taught the value of service before they take these values on themselves, and that the best way to teach an ethic of service is to require a year or two of "compulsory volunteering." That which is required, goes the logic of this argument, eventually becomes second nature. We might make a parallel case about teaching kids to read. Kids may not enjoy practicing thirty minutes every night, but eventually they come to realize the joys and benefits of reading, which last a lifetime. Still another argument might be to focus on the extent to which Americans meet (or fail to meet) their obligations to the larger community. This would be a glass-half-full/half-empty argument, beginning with the statistic that one-quarter of Americans regularly volunteer. The half-full argument would praise current efforts and, perhaps, suggest policies for ensuring continued success. The half-empty argument would cite the statistic with alarm, claim that we have a problem of shockingly low volunteer rates, and then propose a solution. Whatever your approach to the subject, in first *critically examining* the various sources and then *synthesizing* them to support a position about which you feel strongly, you are engaging in the kind of critical thinking that is essential to success in a good deal of academic and professional work.

DEVELOPING AND ORGANIZING THE SUPPORT FOR YOUR ARGUMENTS

Experienced writers seem to have an intuitive sense of how to develop and present supporting evidence for their claims. This sense is developed through much hard work and practice. Less experienced writers wonder what to say first, and having decided on that, wonder what to say next. There is no single method of presentation. But the techniques of even the most experienced writers often boil down to a few tried-and-tested arrangements.

As we've seen in the model synthesis in this chapter, the key to devising effective arguments is to find and use those kinds of support that most persuasively strengthen your claim. Some writers categorize support into two broad types: *evidence* and *motivational appeals*. Evidence, in the form of facts, statistics, and expert testimony, helps make the appeal to *logos* or reason. Motivational appeals—appeals to *pathos* and *ethos*—are employed to get people to change their minds, to agree with the writer or speaker, or to decide upon a plan of activity.

Let's now look at some of the most common principles for using and organizing support for your claims.

Summarize, Paraphrase, and Quote Supporting Evidence

In most of the papers and reports you will write in college and the professional world, evidence and motivational appeals derive from summarizing, paraphrasing, and quoting material in the sources that either have been provided to you or that you have independently researched. (See Chapter 1 on when to summarize and paraphrase material from sources.) For example, in paragraph 10 of the model argument synthesis, you will find a block quotation from David Gergen used to make the point that minimally paid volunteer programs can provide lifelong lessons. You will also find several brief quotations woven into sentences throughout. In addition, you will find summaries and a paraphrase. In each case, the writer is careful to cite sources.

Provide Various Types of Evidence and Motivational Appeals

Keep in mind the appeals to both *logos* and *pathos*. As we've discussed, the appeal to *logos* is based on evidence that consists of a combination of *facts, statistics, and expert testimony*. In the model synthesis, the writer uses all of these varieties of evidence: facts (from David Gergen's article on how "[v]oluntary service . . . often changes people for life"); statistics (the incidence of volunteering in the United States); and testimony (from Eric Gorham, Bruce Chapman, David Gergen, Roger Landrum, Donald Rumsfeld, and William James). The model synthesis makes an appeal to *pathos* by engaging the reader's self interest: Certainly if the federal government were to institute compulsory national service, the lives of many readers would be touched. More explicitly, paragraph 11 makes a moral argument against compulsory service. Through analogy (compelling citizens to service is equivalent to ordering a child to like someone), the writer attempts to claim the reader's sympathy and respect for common sense. In effect, the writer says, responsible parents would never do such a thing; responsible governments shouldn't either. (Of course, readers could reject the analogy and the assumption about good parenting on which it rests. Some parents might very well push their children into friendships and believe themselves justified for doing so.)

Use Climactic Order

Organize by climactic order when you plan to offer a number of categories or elements of support for your claim. Recognize that some elements will be more important—and likely more persuasive—than others. The basic principle here is that you should *save the most important evidence for the end,* since whatever you have said last is what readers are likely to most remember. A secondary principle is that whatever you say first is what they are *next* most likely to remember. Therefore, when you have several reasons to support your claim, an effective argument strategy is to present the second most important, then one or more additional reasons, saving the most important reason for last. Paragraphs 8–11 of the model synthesis do exactly this.

Use Logical or Conventional Order

Using logical or conventional order means that you use as a template a preestablished pattern or plan for arguing your case.

One common pattern is describing or arguing a *problem/solution*. Using this pattern, you begin with an introduction in which you typically define the problem, then perhaps explain its origins, then offer one or more solutions followed by a conclusion.

Another common pattern is presenting *two sides of a controversy*. Using this pattern, you introduce the controversy and your own point of view or claim, then explain the other side's arguments, providing reasons why your point of view should prevail.

A third common pattern is *comparison-contrast*, discussed shortly.

The order in which you present elements of an argument is sometimes dictated by the conventions of the discipline in which you are writing. For example, lab reports and experiments in the sciences and social sciences often follow this pattern: *Opening* or *Introduction*, *Methods and Materials* [of the experiment or study], *Results, Discussion*. Legal arguments often follow the so-called IRAC format: *Issue, Rule, Application, Conclusion*.

Present and Respond to Counterarguments

When developing arguments on a controversial topic, you can effectively use *counterargument* to help support your claims. When you use counterargument, you present an argument *against* your claim, but then show that this argument is weak or flawed. The advantage of this technique is that you demonstrate that you are aware of the other side of the argument and that you are prepared to answer it.

Here is how a counterargument typically is developed:

I. Introduction and claim

II. Main opposing argument

III. Refutation of opposing argument

IV. Main positive argument

Use Concession

Concession is a variation of counterargument. As in counterargument, you present the opposing (or otherwise objectionable) viewpoint, but instead of demolishing that argument, you concede that it does have some validity and even some appeal, although your own argument is the stronger one. This concession bolsters your own standing—your own *ethos*—as a fair-minded person who is not blind to the virtues of the other side. (See paragraph 10 of the example synthesis for a variation of the concession argument.) You'll find that instead of making an *opposing* argument, the writer produces a supporting argument but views one part of it as flawed. The writer rejects that section (the extreme position that *any* form of compensation corrupts the spirit of volunteerism) and endorses the remaining sections. In terms of overall argument strategy, the result—the reader sees the writer as being reasonable—is the same as it would be if the writer used the more standard concession in which an opposing argument is viewed as having some merit. Here is an outline for a more typical concession argument:

I. Introduction and claim

II. Important opposing argument

III. Concession that this argument has some validity

IV. Positive argument(s)

Sometimes, when you are developing a counterargument or concession argument, you may become convinced of the validity of the opposing point of view and change your own views. Don't be afraid of this happening. Writing is a tool for learning. To change your mind because of new evidence is a sign of flexibility and maturity, and your writing can only be the better for it.

Use Comparison and Contrast Synthesis

A particularly important type of synthesis is built on patterns of comparison and contrast. Techniques of comparison and contrast enable you to examine two subjects (or sources) in terms of one another. When you compare, you consider *similarities*. When you contrast, you consider *differences*. By comparing and contrasting, you perform a multifaceted analysis that often suggests subtleties that otherwise might not have come to your (or your reader's) attention.

To organize a comparison-and-contrast synthesis, you must carefully read sources in order to discover *significant criteria for analysis*. A *criterion* is a specific point to which both of your authors refer and about which they may agree or disagree. (For example, in a comparative report on compact cars, criteria for *comparison and contrast* might be road handling, fuel economy, and comfort of ride.) The best criteria are those that allow you not only to account for obvious similarities and differences—those concerning the main aspects of your sources or subjects—but also to plumb deeper, exploring subtle yet significant comparisons and contrasts among details or subcomponents, which you can then relate to your overall thesis.

Organizing Comparison-and-Contrast Syntheses

Two basic approaches to organizing a comparison-and-contrast argument synthesis are available: organization by *source or subject* and organization by *criteria*.

Organizing by Source or Subject

You can organize a comparative synthesis by first summarizing each of your sources or subjects and then discussing significant similarities and differences between them. Having read the summaries and become familiar with the distinguishing features of each source, your readers will most likely be able to appreciate the more obvious similarities and differences. In the discussion, your task is to focus on both the obvious and subtle comparisons and contrasts—that is, on those that most clearly support your thesis.

Organization by source or subject is best saved for passages that can be briefly summarized. If the summary of your source or subject becomes too long, your readers might forget the points you made in the first summary as they are reading the second. A comparison-and-contrast synthesis organized by source or subject might proceed like this:

  I. Introduce the paper; lead to thesis.

 II. Summarize source/subject A by discussing its significant features.

III. Summarize source/subject B by discussing its significant features.

IV. Write a paragraph (or two) in which you discuss the significant points of comparison and contrast between sources or subjects A and B. Alternatively, begin comparison-contrast in section III upon introducing source or subject B.

End with a conclusion in which you summarize your points and, perhaps, raise and respond to pertinent questions.

Organizing by Criteria

Instead of summarizing entire sources one at a time with the intention of comparing them later, you could discuss two sources simultaneously, examining the views of each author point by point (criterion by criterion), comparing and contrasting these views in the process. The criterion approach is best used when you have a number of points to discuss or when passages or subjects are long and/or complex. A comparison-and-contrast synthesis organized by criteria might look like this:

  I. Introduce the paper; lead to thesis.

 II. Criterion 1
    a. Discuss what author A says about this point.
    b. Discuss what author B says about this point, comparing and contrasting B's treatment of the point with A's.

III. Criterion 2
    a. Discuss what author A says about this point.
    b. Discuss what author B says about this point, comparing and contrasting B's treatment of the point with A's.

And so on. Proceed criterion by criterion until you have completed your discussion. Be sure to arrange criteria with a clear method; knowing how the discussion of one criterion leads to the next will ensure smooth transitions throughout your paper. End by summarizing your key points and, perhaps, raising and responding to pertinent questions.

However you organize your comparison-and-contrast synthesis, keep in mind that comparing and contrasting are not ends in themselves. Your discussion should point somewhere: to a conclusion, an answer to "So what—why bother to compare and contrast in the first place?" If your discussion is part of a larger synthesis, point to and support the larger claim. If you write a stand-alone comparison-and-contrast, though, you must by the final paragraph answer the "why bother?" question.

EXERCISE **3.2**

Comparing and Contrasting

Refer back to the readings on the compulsory national service controversy. Select two that take opposing sides, such as David Gergen's "A Time to Heed the Call" (page 56) and Bruce Chapman's "Politics and National Service: A Virus Attacks the Volunteer Sector" (pages 61–62). Identify at least two significant criteria for analysis—two specific points to which both authors refer and about which they agree or disagree. Then imagine you are preparing to write a short comparison-and-contrast paper and devise two outlines: the first organized by source and the second organized by criteria.

Avoid Common Fallacies in Developing and Using Support

In the section on critical reading in Chapter 2, we considered some of the criteria that, as a reader, you might use for evaluating informative and persuasive writing (see pages 25–33). We discussed how you might assess the accuracy, the significance, and the author's interpretation of the information presented. We also considered the importance in good argument of clearly defined key terms and the pitfalls of emotionally loaded language. Finally, we saw how to recognize such logical fallacies as either/or reasoning, faulty cause-and-effect reasoning, hasty generalization, and false analogy. As a writer, no less than as a critical reader, be aware of these common problems and try to avoid them.

Be aware, also, of your responsibility to cite source materials appropriately. When you quote a source, double- and triple-check that you have done so accurately. When you summarize or paraphrase, take care to use your own language and sentence structures (though you can, of course, also quote within these forms). When you refer to someone else's idea—even if you are not quoting, summarizing, or paraphrasing—give the source credit. By maintaining an ethical stance with regard to the use of sources, you take your place in and perpetuate the highest traditions of the academic community.

THE EXPLANATORY SYNTHESIS

Some of the papers you write in college will be more or less explanatory (as opposed to argumentative) in nature. An explanation helps readers understand a topic. Writers explain when they divide a subject into its component parts and present them to the reader in a clear and orderly fashion. Explanations may entail descriptions that re-create in words some object, place, emotion, event, sequence of events, or state of affairs. As a student reporter, you may need to explain an event—to relate when, where, and how it took place. In a science lab, you would observe the conditions and results of an experiment and record them for review by others. In a political science course, you might review research on a particular subject—say, the complexities underlying the debate over gay marriage—and then present the results of your research to your professor and the members of your class.

Your job in writing an explanatory synthesis—or in writing the explanatory portion of an argument synthesis—is not to argue a particular point, but rather *to present the facts in a reasonably objective manner.* Of course, explanatory papers, like other academic papers, should be based on a thesis. But the purpose of a thesis in an explanatory paper is less to advance a particular opinion than to focus the various facts contained in the paper.

The explanatory synthesis is fairly modest in purpose. It emphasizes the materials in the sources themselves, not the writer's interpretation of them. Because your reader is not always in a position to read your sources, this kind of synthesis, if done well, can be very informative. But the main characteristic of the explanatory synthesis is that it is designed more to *inform* than to *persuade.* As the writer of an explanatory synthesis, you remain, for the most part, a detached observer.

Practice Explanatory Synthesis

Write an explanatory synthesis on volunteerism using the sources presented earlier in this chapter (pages 55–62). Use the following guidelines:

- **Consider your purpose.** Your purpose in this paper is to present the relevant facts about volunteerism in a reasonably objective manner. You yourself should not take a position on which types of volunteer efforts are most worthy of support; your responsibility, rather, is to report objectively on the opposing sides of the debate (as represented in your sources) as well as on the essential facts about the state of volunteering in America today.

- **Select and carefully read your sources.** Draw upon the same sources that the writer of the argument synthesis used. You may use some or all of these sources; feel free to enhance your discussion by discovering additional sources through research.

- **Formulate a thesis.** Design your thesis primarily to *inform* rather than to *persuade*. Example: "A tradition of volunteering runs deep in American history and informs the wide variety of volunteer efforts one finds on the local and national levels today."

- **Decide how you will use your source material.** Locate facts and ideas from the readings that will help you to support your thesis.

- **Develop an organizational plan.** Devise an outline that will enable you to present your material effectively. A thesis will often imply an organizational plan. For example, the sample thesis above commits you to (1) recounting the history of volunteerism in America, (2) categorizing the types of volunteer efforts one finds today, and (3) drawing a relation between efforts today (both locally and nationally) and efforts undertaken earlier in American history. This order might offer the most logical structure for your discussion; but during the composing process, you might decide on a different order—which may require you to modify your original thesis.

- **Draft clear, organizing statements for the main sections.** Expand each major point of your outline into a statement that distills the main idea(s) of the paragraph(s) it will organize. Give every paragraph within a section a clear topic sentence.

- **Write and revise your synthesis; document your sources.** See the model argument paper on volunteerism for an example synthesis with carefully documented sources.

SUMMARY

In this chapter, we've considered two main types of synthesis: the *argument synthesis* and the *explanatory synthesis*. Although for ease of comprehension we've placed them into separate categories, these types are not, of course, mutually exclusive. Both argument syntheses and explanatory syntheses often involve elements of one another. Which format you choose will depend upon your *purpose* and the method that you decide is best suited to achieve this purpose.

If your main purpose is to help your audience understand a particular subject, and in particular to help them understand the essential elements or significance of this subject, then you will be composing an explanatory synthesis. If your main purpose, on the other hand, is to persuade your audience to agree with your viewpoint on a subject, or to change their minds, or to decide upon a particular course of action, then you will be composing an argument synthesis. If one effective technique for making your case is to establish similarities or differences between your subject and another one, then you will compose a comparison-contrast synthesis—which may well be just *part* of a larger synthesis.

In planning and drafting these syntheses, you can draw upon a variety of strategies: supporting your claims by summarizing, paraphrasing, and quoting from your sources; and choosing from among formats such as climactic or conventional order, counterargument, and concession that will best help you achieve your purpose.

The strategies of synthesis you've practiced in these chapters so far will be important in composing a research paper, the successful execution of which involves all of the skills in summary, critique, and synthesis that we've discussed so far.

Analysis

WHAT IS AN ANALYSIS?

An *analysis* is an argument in which you study the parts of something to understand how it works, what it means, or why it might be significant. The writer of an analysis uses an analytical tool: a *principle* or *definition* on the basis of which an object, an event, or a behavior can be divided into parts and examined. Here are excerpts from two analyses of L. Frank Baum's *The Wizard of Oz:*

> At the dawn of adolescence, the very time she should start to distance herself from Aunt Em and Uncle Henry, the surrogate parents who raised her on their Kansas farm, Dorothy Gale experiences a hurtful reawakening of her fear that these loved ones will be rudely ripped from her, especially her Aunt (Em—M for Mother!).*

> [*The Wizard of Oz*] was originally written as a political allegory about grassroots protest. It may seem harder to believe than Emerald City, but the Tin Woodsman is the industrial worker, the Scarecrow [is] the struggling farmer, and the Wizard is the president, who is powerful only as long as he succeeds in deceiving the people.†

As these paragraphs suggest, what you discover through an analysis depends entirely on the principle or definition you use to make your insights. Is *The Wizard of Oz* the story of a girl's psychological development, or is it a story about politics? The answer is *both.* In the first example, psychiatrist Harvey Greenberg applies the principles of his profession and, not surprisingly, sees *The Wizard of Oz* in psychological terms. In the second example, a newspaper reporter applies the political theories of Karl Marx and, again not surprisingly, discovers a story about politics.

Different as they are, these analyses share an important quality: Each is the result of a specific principle or definition used as a tool to divide an object into parts to see what it means and how it works. The writer's choice of analytical tool simultaneously creates and limits the possibilities for analysis. Thus, working with the principles of Freud, Harvey Greenberg sees *The Wizard of Oz* in psychological, not political, terms; working with the theories of Karl Marx, Peter Dreier understands the movie in terms of the economic relationships among characters. It's as if the writer of an analysis who adopts one analytical tool puts on a pair of glasses and sees an object in a specific way. Another writer, using a different tool (and a different pair of glasses), sees the object differently.

---

* Harvey Greenberg, *The Movies on Your Mind* (New York: Dutton, 1975) 16.

† Peter Dreier, "Oz Was Almost Reality," *Cleveland Plain Dealer* 3 Sept. 1989.

WHERE DO WE FIND WRITTEN ANALYSES?

Here are just a few types of writing that involve analysis:

Academic Writing

- **Experimental and lab reports.** Analyze the meaning or implications of the study results in your Discussion section.
- **Research papers.** Analyze information in sources; apply theories to material being reported.
- **Process analysis.** Break down the steps or stages involved in completing a process.
- **Literary analysis.** Analyze characterization, plot, imagery, or other elements in works of literature.
- **Essay exams.** Demonstrate understanding of course material by analyzing data using course concepts.

Workplace Writing

- **Grant proposals.** Analyze the issues you seek funding for in order to address them.
- **Reviews of the arts.** Employ dramatic or literary analysis to assess artistic works.
- **Business plans.** Break down and analyze capital outlays, expenditures, profits, materials, and the like.
- **Medical charts.** Review patient symptoms and explore treatment options.
- **Legal briefs.** Break down and analyze facts of cases and elements of legal precedents; apply legal rulings and precedents to new situations.
- **Case studies.** Describe and analyze the particulars of a specific medical, social service, advertising, or business case.

At this point, you may be a bit skeptical. Are there as many analyses of *The Wizard of Oz* as there are people to read it? Yes, or at least as many analyses as there are analytical tools. This does not mean that all analyses are equally valid or useful. The writer must convince the reader. In creating an essay of analysis, the writer must organize a series of related insights, using the analytical tool to examine first one part and then another of the object being studied. To read Harvey Greenberg's essay on *The Wizard of Oz* is to find paragraph after paragraph of related insights—first about Aunt Em, then the Wicked Witch, then Toto, and then the Wizard. All these insights point to Greenberg's single conclusion that "Dorothy's 'trip' is a marvelous metaphor for the psychological journey every adolescent must make."* Without Greenberg's analysis, we prob-

---

* Harvey Greenberg, *The Movies on Your Mind* (New York: Dutton, 1975) 16.

ably would not have thought about the movie as a psychological journey. This is precisely the power of an analysis: its ability to reveal objects or events in ways we would not otherwise have considered.

The writer's challenge is to convince readers that (1) the analytical tool being applied is legitimate and well matched to the object being studied; and (2) the analytical tool is being used systematically to divide the object into parts and to make a coherent, meaningful statement about these parts and the object as a whole.

DEMONSTRATION OF ANALYSIS

The first example of analysis that follows was written by a professional writer; the second was written by a student in response to an assignment in his sociology class. Each example illustrates the two defining features of analysis just discussed: (1) a statement of an analytical principle or definition and (2) the use of that principle or definition in closely examining an object, behavior, or event. As you read, try to identify these features. An exercise with questions for discussion follows each example.

The Plug-In Drug
Marie Winn

Writer and media critic Marie Winn has been interested in the effect of television on both individuals and the larger culture. The following analysis of television viewing as an addictive behavior originally appeared in her book, The Plug-In Drug: Television, Computers, and Family Life *(2002). In this passage, she carefully defines the term* addiction *and then applies it systematically to the behavior under study.*

1   The word "addiction" is often used loosely and wryly in conversation. People will refer to themselves as "mystery-book addicts" or "cookie addicts." E. B. White wrote of his annual surge of interest in gardening: "We are hooked and are making an attempt to kick the habit." Yet nobody really believes that reading mysteries or ordering seeds by catalogue is serious enough to be compared with addictions to heroin or alcohol. In these cases the word "addiction" is used jokingly to denote a tendency to overindulge in some pleasurable activity.

2   People often refer to being "hooked on TV." Does this, too, fall into the light-hearted category of cookie eating and other pleasures that people pursue with unusual intensity? Or is there a kind of television viewing that falls into the more serious category of destructive addiction?

3   Not unlike drugs or alcohol, the television experience allows the participant to blot out the real world and enter into a pleasurable and passive mental state. To be sure, other experiences, notably reading, also provide a temporary respite

Marie Winn, *The Plug-In Drug: Television, Computers, and Family Life* (New York: Penguin, 2002).

from reality. But it's much easier to stop reading and return to reality than to stop watching television. The entry into another world offered by reading includes an easily accessible return ticket. The entry via television does not. In this way television viewing, for those vulnerable to addiction, is more like drinking or taking drugs—once you start it's hard to stop.

4   Just as alcoholics are only vaguely aware of their addiction, feeling that they control their drinking more than they really do ("I can cut it out any time I want—I just like to have three or four drinks before dinner"), many people overestimate their control over television watching. Even as they put off other activities to spend hour after hour watching television, they feel they could easily resume living in a different, less passive style. But somehow or other while the television set is present in their homes, it just stays on. With television's easy gratifications available, those other activities seem to take too much effort.

5   A heavy viewer (a college English instructor) observes:

> I find television almost irresistible. When the set is on, I cannot ignore it. I can't turn it off. I feel sapped, will-less, enervated. As I reach out to turn off the set, the strength goes out of my arms. So I sit there for hours and hours.

6   Self-confessed television addicts often feel they "ought" to do other things—but the fact that they don't read and don't plant their garden or sew or crochet or play games or have conversations means that those activities are no longer as desirable as television viewing. In a way, the lives of heavy viewers are as unbalanced by their television "habit" as drug addicts' or alcoholics' lives. They are living in a holding pattern, as it were, passing up the activities that lead to growth or development or a sense of accomplishment. This is one reason people talk about their television viewing so ruefully, so apologetically. They are aware that it is an unproductive experience, that by any human measure almost any other endeavor is more worthwhile.

7   It is the adverse effect of television viewing on the lives of so many people that makes it feel like a serious addiction. The television habit distorts the sense of time. It renders other experiences vague and curiously unreal while taking on a greater reality for itself. It weakens relationships by reducing and sometimes eliminating normal opportunities for talking, for communicating.

8   And yet television does not satisfy, else why would the viewer continue to watch hour after hour, day after day? "The measure of health," wrote the psychiatrist Lawrence Kubie, "is flexibility . . . and especially the freedom to cease when sated." But heavy television viewers can never be sated with their television experiences. These do not provide the true nourishment that satiation requires, and thus they find that they cannot stop watching.

EXERCISE 4.1

Reading Critically: Winn

Typically in analyses, authors first present their analytical principle in full and then systematically apply parts of the principle to the object or phenomenon under study. In her brief analysis of television viewing, Marie Winn pursues an alternate, though equally effective, strategy by *distributing* parts of her ana-lytical principle across the essay. Locate where Winn defines key elements of addiction. Locate where she uses each element as an analytical lens to exam-ine television viewing as a form of addiction.

In the first two paragraphs, how does Winn create a funnel-like effect that draws readers into the heart of her analysis?

Recall a few television programs that genuinely moved or stirred you to worthwhile reflection or action. To what extent does Winn's analysis describe your positive experiences as a television viewer? (Consider how Winn might argue that from within an addicted state, a person may feel "humored, moved or educated" but is in fact—from a sober outsider's point of view—deluded.) If Winn's analysis of television viewing as an addiction does *not* account for your experience, does it follow that her analysis is flawed? Explain.

The Coming Apart of a Dorm Society
Edward Peselman

Edward Peselman wrote the following paper as a first-semester sophomore, in response to the following assignment from his sociology professor:

Read Chapter 3, "The Paradoxes of Power," in Randall Collins's Sociological Insight: An Introduction to Non-Obvious Sociology *(2nd ed., 1992). Use any of Collins's observations to examine the sociology of power in a group with which you are familiar. Write for readers much like yourself: freshmen or sophomores who have taken one course in sociology. Use Collins as a way of learning something "non-obvious" about a group to which you belong or have belonged.*

The citations in this paper follow American Psychological Association (APA) format.

The Coming Apart of a Dorm Society
Edward Peselman

1 During my first year of college, I lived in a dormi-tory, like most freshmen on campus. We inhabitants of the dorm came from different cultural and economic backgrounds. Not surprisingly, we brought with us many of the traits found in people outside of col-lege. Like many on the outside, we in the dorm sought personal power at the expense of others. The gaining and maintaining of power can be an ugly business, and I saw people hurt and in turn hurt others all for the sake of securing a place in the dorm's prized social order. Not until one of us challenged that order did I realize how fragile it was.

2   Randall Collins, a sociologist at the University of California, Riverside, defines the exercise of power as the attempt "to make something happen in society" (1992, p. 61). A society can be understood as something as large and complex as "American society"; something more sharply defined—such as a corporate or organizational society; or something smaller still—a dorm society like my own, consisting of six 18-year-old men who lived at one end of a dormitory floor in an all-male dorm.

3   In my freshman year, my society was a tiny but distinctive social group in which people exercised power. I lived with two roommates, Dozer and Reggie. Dozer was an emotionally unstable, excitable individual who vented his energy through anger. His insecurity and moodiness contributed to his difficulty in making friends. Reggie was a friendly, happy-go-lucky sort who seldom displayed emotions other than contentedness. He was shy when encountering new people, but when placed in a socially comfortable situation he would talk for hours.

4   Eric and Marc lived across the hall from us and therefore spent a considerable amount of time in our room. Eric could be cynical and was often blunt: He seldom hesitated when sharing his frank and sometimes unflattering opinions. He commanded a grudging respect in the dorm. Marc could be very moody and, sometimes, was violent. His temper and stubborn streak made him particularly susceptible to conflict. The final member of our miniature society was Benjamin, cheerful yet insecure. Benjamin had certain characteristics which many considered effeminate, and he was often teased about his sexuality—which in turn made him insecure. He was naturally friendly but, because of the abuse he took, he largely kept to himself. He would join us occasionally for a pizza or late-night television.

5   Together, we formed an independent social structure. Going out to parties together, playing cards, watching television, playing ball: These were the activities through which we got to know each other and through which we established the basic pecking order of our community. Much like a colony of baboons, we established a hierarchy based on power relationships. According to Collins, what a powerful person wishes to happen must be achieved by controlling others. Collins's observation can help to define

who had how much power in our social group. In the
dorm, Marc and Eric clearly had the most power.
Everyone feared them and agreed to do pretty much
what they wanted. Through violent words or threats of
violence, they got their way. I was next in line: I
wouldn't dare to manipulate Marc or Eric, but the
others I could manage through occasional quips.
Reggie, then Dozer, and finally Benjamin.

6   Up and down the pecking order, we exercised control through macho taunts and challenges. Collins
writes that "individuals who manage to be powerful
and get their own way must do so by going along with
the laws of social organization, not by contradicting
them" (p. 61). Until mid-year, our dorm motto could
have read: "You win through rudeness and intimidation." Eric gained power with his frequent and brutal
assessments of everyone's behavior. Marc gained power
with his temper—which, when lost, made everyone run
for cover. Those who were not rude and intimidating
drifted to the bottom of our social world. Reggie was
quiet and unemotional, which allowed us to take
advantage of him because we knew he would back down
if pressed in an argument. Yet Reggie understood that
on a "power scale" he stood above Dozer and often
shared in the group's tactics to get Dozer's food
(his parents were forever sending him care packages).
Dozer, in turn, seldom missed opportunities to take
swipes at Benjamin, with references to his sexuality.
From the very first week of school, Benjamin could
never—and never wanted to—compete against Eric's
bluntness or Marc's temper. Still, Benjamin hung out
with us. He lived in our corner of the dorm, and he
wanted to be friendly. But everyone, including
Benjamin, understood that he occupied the lowest spot
in the order.

7   That is, until he left mid-semester. According to
Collins, "any social arrangement works because people
avoid questioning it most of the time" (p. 74). The
inverse of this principle is as follows: When a
social arrangement is questioned, that arrangement
can fall apart. The more fragile the arrangement (the
flimsier the values on which it is based), the more
quickly it will crumble. For the entire first semester, no one questioned our rude, macho rules and
because of them we pigeonholed Benjamin as a wimp. In
our dorm society, gentle men had no power. To say the
least, ours was not a compassionate community. From a

distance of one year, I am shocked to have been a
member of it. Nonetheless, we had created a mini-
society that somehow served our needs.

8   At the beginning of the second semester, we found
Benjamin packing up his room. Marc, who was walking
down the hall, stopped by and said something like:
"Hey buddy, the kitchen get too hot for you?" I was
there, and I saw Benjamin turn around and say: "Do
you practice at being such a _____, or does it come
naturally? I've never met anybody who felt so good
about making other people feel lousy. You'd better
get yourself a job in the army or in the prison
system, because no one else is going to put up with
your _____." Marc said something in a raised voice.
I stepped between them, and Benjamin said: "Get out."
I was cheering.

9   Benjamin moved into an off-campus apartment with
his girlfriend. This astonished us, first because of
his effeminate manner (we didn't know he had a girlfriend) and second because none of the rest of us had
been seeing girls much (though we talked about it
constantly). Here was Benjamin, the gentlest among
us, and he blew a hole in our macho society. Our
social order never really recovered, which suggests
its flimsy values. People in the dorm mostly went
their own ways during the second semester. I'm not
surprised, and I was more than a little grateful.
Like most people in the dorm, save for Eric and Marc,
I both got my lumps and I gave them, and I never felt
good about either. Like Benjamin, I wanted to fit in
with my new social surroundings. Unlike him, I didn't
have the courage to challenge the unfairness of what
I saw.

10   By chance, six of us were thrown together into a
dorm and were expected, on the basis of proximity
alone, to develop a friendship. What we did was sink
to the lowest possible denominator. Lacking any real
basis for friendship, we allowed the forceful, macho
personalities of Marc and Eric to set the rules,
which for one semester we all subscribed to—even
those who suffered.

11   The macho rudeness couldn't last, and I'm glad it
was Benjamin who brought us down. By leaving, he
showed a different and a superior kind of power. I
doubt he was reading Randall Collins at the time, but
he somehow had come to Collins's same insight: As
long as he played by the rules of our group, he suffered because those rules placed him far down in the

dorm's pecking order. Even by participating in pleasant activities, like going out for pizza, Benjamin supported a social system that ridiculed him. Some systems are so oppressive and small-minded that they can't be changed from the inside. They've got to be torn down. Benjamin had to move, and in moving he made me (at least) question the basis of my dorm friendships.

Reference

Collins, R. (1992). *Sociological insight: An introduction to non-obvious sociology* (2nd ed.). New York: Oxford University Press.

EXERCISE 4.2

Reading Critically: Peselman

What is the function of paragraph 1? Though Peselman does not use the word *sociology,* what signals does he give that this will be a paper that examines the social interactions of a group? Peselman introduces Collins in paragraph 2. Why? What does Peselman accomplish in paragraphs 3–4? How does his use of Collins in paragraph 5 logically follow the presentation in paragraphs 3–4? The actual analysis in this paper takes place in paragraphs 5–11. Point to where Peselman draws on the work of Randall Collins, and explain how he uses Collins to gain insight into dorm life.

HOW TO WRITE AN ANALYSIS

Consider Your Purpose

Whether you are assigned a topic to write on or are left to your own devices, you inevitably face this question: What is my main idea? Like every paper, an analysis has at its heart an idea you want to convey. For Edward Peselman, it was the idea that a social order based on flimsy values is not strong enough to sustain a direct challenge to its power, and thus will fall apart eventually. From beginning to end, Peselman advances this one idea: first, by introducing readers to the dorm society he will analyze; next, by introducing principles of analysis (from Randall Collins); and finally, by examining his dorm relationships in light of these principles. The entire set of analytical insights coheres as a paper because the insights are *related* and point to Peselman's single idea.

Peselman's paper offers a good example of the personal uses to which analysis can be put. Notice that Peselman gravitated toward events in his life that confused him and about which he wanted some clarity. Personal topics can be especially fruitful for analysis when you know the particulars well and can provide readers with details. You view the topic with some puzzlement, and, through the application of your analytical tool, you may come to understand it. When you select topics to analyze from your experience, you provide yourself with a motivation to write and learn. When you are motivated in this way, you spark the interest of readers.

Using Randall Collins as a guide, Edward Peselman returns again and again to the events of his freshman year in the dormitory. We sense that Peselman himself wants to know what happened in that dorm. He writes, "I saw people hurt and in turn hurt others all for the sake of securing a place in the dorm's prized social order." Peselman does not approve of what happened, and the analysis he launches is meant to help him understand.

Locate an Analytical Principle

When you are given an assignment that asks for analysis, use two specific reading strategies to identify principles and definitions in source materials.

- **Look for a sentence that makes a general statement about the way something works.** The statement may strike you as a rule or a law. The line that Edward Peselman quotes from Randall Collins has this quality: "[A]ny social arrangement works because people avoid questioning it most of the time." Such statements are generalizations, conclusions to sometimes complicated and extensive arguments. You can use these conclusions to guide your own analyses as long as you are aware that for some audiences, you will need to re-create and defend the arguments that resulted in these conclusions.

- **Look for statements that take this form: "X" can be defined as (or "X" consists of) the following: A, B, and C.** The specific elements of the definition—A, B, and C—are what you use to identify and analyze parts of the object being studied. You've seen an example of this approach in Marie Winn's multipart definition of addiction (pages 87–88), which she uses to analyze television viewing. As a reader looking for definitions suitable for conducting an analysis, you might come across Winn's definition of addiction and then use it for your own purposes, perhaps to analyze the playing of video games as an addiction.

Essential to any analysis is the validity of the principle or definition being applied, the analytical tool. Make yourself aware, both as writer and reader, of a tool's strengths and limitations. Pose these questions of the analytical principles and definitions you use: Are they accurate? Are they well accepted? Do *you* accept them? What are the arguments against them? What are their limitations? Since every principle or definition used in an analysis is the end product of an argument, you are entitled—even obligated—to challenge it. If the analytical tool is flawed, then the analysis that follows from it will be flawed also.

The following excerpt is from *Sociological Insight* by Randall Collins; Edward Peselman uses a key sentence from this material as an analytical tool in his paper on power relations in his dorm (see page 91). The sentence that Peselman will use in his paper has been underlined.

1 Try this experiment some time. When you are talking to someone, make them explain everything they say that isn't completely clear. The result, you will discover, is a series of uninterrupted interruptions:

A: Hi, how are you doing?
B: What do you mean when you say "how"?
A: You know. What's happening with you?
B: What do you mean, "happening"?
A: Happening, you know, what's going on.
B: I'm sorry. Could you explain what you mean by "what"?
A: What do you mean, what do I mean? Do you want to talk to me or not?

2   It is obvious that this sort of questioning could go on endlessly, at any rate if the listener doesn't get very angry and punch you in the mouth. But it illustrates two important points. First, virtually everything can be called into question. We are able to get along with other people not because everything is clearly spelled out, but because we are willing to take most things people say without explanation. Harold Garfinkel, who actually performed this sort of experiment, points out that there is an infinite regress of assumptions that go into any act of social communication. Moreover, some expressions are simply not explainable in words at all. A word like "you," or "here," or "now" is what Garfinkel calls "indexical." You have to know what it means already; it can't be explained.

3   "What do you mean by 'you'?"

4   "I mean *you, you!*" About all that can be done here is point your finger.

5   The second point is that people get mad when they are pressed to explain things that they ordinarily take for granted. This is because they very quickly see that explanations could go on forever and the questions will never be answered. If you really demanded a full explanation of everything you hear, you could stop the conversation from ever getting past its first sentence. The real significance of this for a sociological understanding of the way the world is put together is not the anger, however. It is the fact that people try to avoid these sorts of situations. They tacitly recognize that we have to avoid these endless lines of questioning. Sometimes small children will start asking an endless series of "whys," but adults discourage this.

6   <u>In sum, any social arrangement works because people avoid questioning it most of the time.</u> That does not mean that people do not get into arguments or disputes about just what ought to be done from time to time. But to have a dispute already implies there is a considerable area of agreement. An office manager may dispute with a clerk over just how to take care of some business letter, but they at any rate know more or

less what they are disputing about. They do not get off into a . . . series of questions over just what is meant by everything that is said. You could very quickly dissolve the organization into nothingness if you followed that route: There would be no communication at all, even about what the disagreement is over.

7   Social organization is possible because people maintain a certain level of focus. If they focus on one thing, even if only to disagree about it, they are taking many other things for granted, thereby reinforcing their social reality.

The statement that Peselman has underlined—"any social arrangement works because people avoid questioning it most of the time"—is the conclusion of an argument that takes Collins, using the example of repeated questioning of terms, several paragraphs to develop. Peselman agrees with the conclusion and uses it in paragraph 7 of his paper. Observe that for his own purposes Peselman does *not* reconstruct Collins's argument. He selects *only* Collins's conclusion and then imports that into his paper. Once he identifies in Collins a principle he can use in his analysis, he converts the principle into questions that he then directs to his topic: life in his freshman dorm. Two questions follow directly from Collins's insight:

1. What was the social arrangement in the dorm?
2. How was this social arrangement questioned?

Peselman clearly defines his dormitory's social arrangement in paragraphs 3–6 (with the help of another principle borrowed from Collins). Beginning with paragraph 7, he explores how one member of his dorm questioned that arrangement:

> That is, until he left mid-semester. According to Collins, "any social arrangement works because people avoid questioning it most of the time" (p. 74). The inverse of this principle is as follows: when a social arrangement is questioned, that arrangement can fall apart. The more fragile the arrangement (the flimsier the values on which it is based), the more quickly it will crumble. For the entire first semester, no one questioned our rude, macho rules and because of them we pigeonholed Benjamin as a wimp. In our dorm society, gentle men had no power. To say the least, ours was not a compassionate community. From a distance of one year, I am shocked to have been a member of it. Nonetheless, we had created a mini-society that somehow served our needs.

Formulate the Argument

An analysis is an argument with two components. The first component states and establishes the writer's agreement with a certain principle or definition.

Part 1 of the Argument

This component of the argument essentially takes the following form:

> **Claim 1:** Principle X (or definition X) is valuable.

Principle X can be a theory as encompassing and abstract as the statement that *myths are the enemy of truth.* Principle X can be as modest as the definition of a term—for instance, "addiction" or "comfort." As you move from one subject area to another, the principles and definitions you use for analysis will change, as these assignments illustrate:

Sociology: Write a paper in which you place yourself in American society by locating both your absolute position and relative rank on each single criterion of social stratification used by Lenski and Lenski. For each criterion, state whether you have attained your social position by yourself or if you have "inherited" that status from your parents.

Literature: Apply principles of Jungian psychology to Hawthorne's "Young Goodman Brown." In your reading of the story, apply Jung's principles of the *shadow, persona,* and *anima.*

Physics: Use Newton's second law ($F = ma$) to analyze the acceleration of a fixed pulley, from which two weights hang: m_1 (.45 kg) and m_2 (.90 kg). Explain in a paragraph the principle of Newton's law and your method of applying it to solve the problem. Assume that your reader is not comfortable with mathematical explanations: do not use equations in your paragraph.

Finance: Using Guidford C. Babcock's "Concept of Sustainable Growth" [*Financial Analysis* 26 (May–June 1970): 108–14], analyze the stock price appreciation of the XYZ Corporation, figures for which are attached.

The analytical tools to be applied in these assignments change from discipline to discipline. Writing in response to the sociology assignment, you would use sociological principles developed by Lenski and Lenski. In your literature class, you would use principles of Jungian psychology; in physics, Newton's second law; and in finance, a particular writer's concept of "sustainable growth." But whatever discipline you are working in, the first part of your analysis will clearly state which (and whose) principles and definitions you are applying. For audiences unfamiliar with these principles, you will need to explain them; if you anticipate objections, you will need to argue that they are legitimate principles capable of helping you as you conduct an analysis.

Part 2 of the Argument

In the second component of your argument, you *apply* specific parts of your principle or definition to the topic at hand. Regardless of how it is worded, this second argument in an analysis can be rephrased to take the following form:

Claim 2: By applying Principle (or definition) X, we can understand
   (topic) as *(conclusion based on analysis).*

This is your thesis, the main idea of your analytical essay. Fill in the first blank with the specific object, event, or behavior you are examining. Fill in the second blank with your conclusion about the meaning or significance of this object, based on the insights made during your analysis. The second claim of Marie Winn's analysis can be rephrased as follows:

GUIDELINES FOR WRITING ANALYSIS

Unless you are asked to follow a specialized format, especially in the sciences or the social sciences, you can present your analysis as a paper by following the guidelines below. As you move from one class to another, from discipline to discipline, the principles and definitions you use as the basis for your analyses will change, but the following basic steps will remain the same:

- *Create a context for your analysis.* Introduce and summarize for readers the object, event, or behavior to be analyzed. Present a strong case about why an analysis is needed: Give yourself a motivation to write, and give readers a motivation to read. Consider setting out a problem, puzzle, or question to be investigated.
- *Introduce and summarize the key definition or principle that will form the basis of your analysis.* Plan to devote the first part of your analysis to arguing for the validity of this principle or definition *if* your audience is not likely to understand it or if they are likely to think that the principle or definition is *not* valuable.
- *Analyze your topic.* Systematically apply elements of this definition or principle to parts of the activity or object under study. You can do this by posing specific questions, based on your analytic principle or definition, about the object. Discuss what you find part by part (organized perhaps by question), in clearly defined sections of the essay.
- *Conclude by stating clearly what is significant about your analysis.* When considering your essay as a whole, what new or interesting insights have you made concerning the object under study? To what extent has your application of the definition or principle helped you to explain how the object works, what it might mean, or why it is significant?

By applying a multipart definition, we can understand *television viewing* as *an addiction.*

Develop an Organizational Plan

The writing of a first draft will benefit enormously if you plan out the logic of your analysis. Turn key elements of your analytical principle or definition into questions and then develop the paragraph-by-paragraph logic of the paper.

Turn Key Elements of a Principle or Definition into Questions

Prepare for an analysis by developing questions based on the definition or principle you are going to apply, and then by directing these questions to the activity or object to be studied. The method is straightforward: State as clearly as possible the principle or definition to be applied. Divide the principle or definition into its parts and, using each part, develop a question. For example, Marie Winn develops a multipart definition of addiction, each part of which is readily turned into a question that she directs at a specific behavior: television viewing. Her analysis of television viewing can be understood as *responses* to each of her analytical questions. Note that in her brief analysis, Winn does not first define addiction and then analyze television viewing. Rather, *as* she defines aspects of addiction, she analyzes television viewing.

Develop the Paragraph-by-Paragraph Logic of Your Paper

The following paragraph from Edward Peselman's essay illustrates the typical logic of a paragraph in an analytical essay:

> Up and down the pecking order, we exercised control through macho taunts and challenges. Collins writes that "individuals who manage to be powerful and get their own way must do so by going along with the laws of social organization, not by contradicting them" (p. 61). Until mid-year, our dorm motto could have read: "You win through rudeness and intimidation." Eric gained power with his frequent and brutal assessments of everyone's behavior. Marc gained power with his temper—which, when lost, made everyone run for cover. Those who were not rude and intimidating drifted to the bottom of our social world. Reggie was quiet and unemotional, which allowed us to take advantage of him because we knew he would back down if pressed in an argument. Yet Reggie understood that on a "power scale" he stood above Dozer and often shared in the group's tactics to get Dozer's food

> (his parents were forever sending him care packages). Dozer, in turn, seldom missed opportunities to take swipes at Benjamin, with references to his sexuality. From the very first week of school, Benjamin could never—and never wanted to—compete against Eric's bluntness or Marc's temper. Still, Benjamin hung out with us. He lived in our corner of the dorm, and he wanted to be friendly. But everyone, including Benjamin, understood that he occupied the lowest spot in the order.

We see in this example paragraph the typical logic of analysis:

- *The writer introduces a specific analytical tool.* Peselman quotes a line from Randall Collins:

  > "[I]ndividuals who manage to be powerful and get their own way must do so by going along with the laws of social organization, not by contradicting them."

- *The writer applies this analytical tool to the object being examined.* Peselman states *his* dorm's law of social organization:

  > Until mid-year, our dorm motto could have read: "You win through rudeness and intimidation."

- *The writer uses the tool to identify and then examine the meaning of parts of the object.* Peselman shows how each member (the "parts") of his dorm society conforms to the laws of "social organization":

  > Eric gained power with his frequent and brutal assessments of everyone's behavior. Marc gained power with his temper—which, when lost, made everyone run for cover. Those who were not rude and intimidating drifted to the bottom of our social world. . . .

An analytical paper takes shape when a writer creates a series of such paragraphs and then links them with an overall logic. Here is the logical organization of Edward Peselman's paper:

- Paragraph 1: Introduction states a problem—provides a motivation to write and to read.
- Paragraph 2: Randall Collins is introduced—the author whose work will provide principles for analysis.
- Paragraphs 3–4: Background information is provided—the cast of characters in the dorm.
- Paragraphs 5–9: The analysis proceeds—specific parts of dorm life are identified and found significant, using principles from Collins.

CRITICAL READING FOR ANALYSIS

- *Read to get a sense of the whole in relation to its parts.* Whether you are clarifying for yourself a principle or definition to be used in an analysis, or reading a text that you will analyze, understand how parts function to create the whole. If a definition or principle consists of parts, use these to organize sections of your analysis. If your goal is to analyze a text, be aware of its structure: note the title and subtitle; identify the main point and subordinate points and where they are located; break the material into sections.
- *Read to discover relationships within the object being analyzed.* Watch for patterns. When you find them, be alert—for you create an occasion to analyze, to use a principle or definition as a guide in discussing what the pattern may mean:

    In fiction, a pattern might involve responses of characters to events or to each other, recurrence of certain words or phrasings, images, themes, or turns of plot, to name a few.

    In poetry, a pattern might involve rhyme schemes, rhythm, imagery, figurative or literal language, and more.

  Your challenge as a reader is first to see a pattern (perhaps using a guiding principle or definition to do so) and then to locate other instances of that pattern. By reading carefully in this way, you prepare yourself to conduct an analysis.

- Paragraphs 10–11: Summary and conclusion are provided—the freshman dorm society disintegrated for reasons set out in the analysis. A larger point is made: Some oppressive systems must be torn down.

Draft and Revise Your Analysis

You will usually need at least two drafts to produce a paper that presents your idea clearly. The biggest changes in your paper will typically come between your first and second drafts. No paper that you write, including an analysis, will be complete until you revise and refine your single compelling idea: your analytical conclusion about what the object, event, or behavior being examined means or how it is significant. You revise and refine by evaluating your first draft, bringing to it many of the same questions you pose when evaluating any piece of writing, including these:

- Are the facts accurate?
- Are my opinions supported by evidence?

- Are the opinions of others authoritative?
- Are my assumptions clearly stated?
- Are key terms clearly defined?
- Is the presentation logical?
- Are all parts of the presentation well developed?
- Are dissenting points of view presented?

Address these same questions on the first draft of your analysis, and you will have solid information to guide your revision.

Write an Analysis, Not a Summary

The most common error made in writing analyses—which is *fatal* to the form—is to present readers with a summary only. For analyses to succeed, you must *apply* a principle or definition and reach a conclusion about the object, event, or behavior you are examining. By definition, a summary (see Chapter 1) includes none of your own conclusions. Summary is naturally a part of analysis; you will need to summarize the object or activity being examined and, depending on the audience's needs, summarize the principle or definition being applied. But in an analysis, you must take the next step and share insights that suggest the meaning or significance of some object, event, or behavior.

Make Your Analysis Systematic

Analyses should give the reader the sense of a systematic, purposeful examination. Marie Winn's analysis illustrates the point: She sets out specific elements of addictive behavior in separate paragraphs and then uses each, within its paragraph, to analyze television viewing. Winn is systematic in her method, and we are never in doubt about her purpose.

Imagine another analysis in which a writer lays out four elements of a definition but then applies only two, without explaining the logic for omitting the others. Or imagine an analysis in which the writer offers a principle for analysis but directs it to only a half or a third of the object being discussed, without providing a rationale for doing so. In both cases, the writer would be failing to deliver on a promise basic to analyses: Once a principle or definition is presented, it should be thoroughly and systematically applied.

Answer the "So What?" Question

An analysis should make readers *want* to read. It should give readers a sense of getting to the heart of the matter, that what is important in the object or activity under analysis is being laid bare and discussed in revealing ways. If when rereading the first draft of your essay, you cannot imagine readers saying, "I never thought of _____ this way," then something may be seriously wrong. Reread closely to determine why the paper might leave readers flat and exhausted, as opposed to feeling that they have gained new and important insights. Closely reexamine your own motivations for writing. Have *you* learned anything significant through the analysis? If not, neither will readers, and they will turn away. If you have gained important insights through your analysis, communicate them clearly. At some point, pull together your related insights and say, in effect: "Here's how it all adds up."

Attribute Sources Appropriately

In an analysis the nature of the form dictates that you work with one or two sources and apply insights from those to some object or phenomenon you want to understand more thoroughly. The strength of an analysis derives mostly from *your* application of a principle or definition. You will have fewer sources to cite in an analysis than in a synthesis. Nevertheless, take special care to cite and quote, as necessary, the one or two sources you use throughout the analysis.

ANALYSIS: A TOOL FOR UNDERSTANDING

As this chapter has demonstrated, analysis involves applying principles as a way to probe and understand. With incisive principles guiding your analysis, you will be able to pose questions, observe patterns and relationships, and derive meaning. Do not forget that this meaning will be only one of several possible meanings. Someone else, possibly you, using different analytical tools could observe the same phenomena and arrive at very different conclusions regarding meaning or significance. We end the chapter, therefore, as we began it: with the two brief analyses of *The Wizard of Oz*. The conclusions expressed in one look nothing like the conclusions expressed in the other, save for the fact that both seek to interpret the same movie. And yet we can say that both are useful, both reveal meaning:

> At the dawn of adolescence, the very time she should start to distance herself from Aunt Em and Uncle Henry, the surrogate parents who raised her on their Kansas farm, Dorothy Gale experiences a hurtful reawakening of her fear that these loved ones will be rudely ripped from her, especially her Aunt (Em—M for Mother!).*

> [*The Wizard of Oz*] was originally written as a political allegory about grass-roots protest. It may seem harder to believe than Emerald City, but the Tin Woodsman is the industrial worker, the Scarecrow [is] the struggling farmer, and the Wizard is the president, who is powerful only as long as he succeeds in deceiving the people.†

---

* Harvey Greenberg, *The Movies on Your Mind* (New York: Dutton, 1975) 16.

† Peter Dreier, "Oz Was Almost Reality," *Cleveland Plain Dealer* 3 Sept. 1989.

You have seen in this chapter how it is possible for two writers, analyzing the same object or phenomenon but applying different analytical principles, to reach vastly different conclusions about what the object or phenomenon may mean or why it is significant. *The Wizard of Oz* is both an inquiry into the psychology of adolescence and a political allegory. What else the classic film may be awaits revealing with the systematic application of other analytical tools. In the same way, the insights you gain as a writer of analyses depend entirely on your choice of tool and the subtlety with which you apply it.

An Anthology
of Readings

Cyberspace and Identity

A cartoon in the *New Yorker* a few years ago showed two dogs sitting near a computer. One dog says to the other, "On the Internet, nobody knows you're a dog." That's as succinct a statement as one can make about the benefits and the drawbacks of electronic communication. On the one hand, the Internet is a great democratizer: everyone is equal because anyone can publish anything. On the other hand, if anyone can publish anything, then for all we know, some of the material we read online might be written by "dogs."

The speed with which the Internet has become an essential medium of personal, business, and professional communication is truly breathtaking. Virtually unknown to the general public little more than a decade ago, e-mail and instant messaging are now so ubiquitous that it's hard to imagine how we ever got along without them. (Quite well, thank you, skeptics will respond.) Many people obsessively check their e-mail ten or more times a day. We appear to measure our worth and status according to how many people (and canines) are sending us messages. We are daily bombarded with megabytes of spam and other useless communications. On the other hand, the Internet provides many with lifelines to family and friends. In Times Square, New York, an all-night Internet café provides immigrants with inexpensive means of staying in touch with loved ones in their home countries. On the AskMe.com Web site, people who need answers to questions in any of hundreds of categories can get free advice from "experts." (Let the buyer beware, however: as an article reprinted at the end of this chapter demonstrates, experts are not always what they appear to be.)

Is the Internet a truly new mode of communication, or is it just an electronic hybrid of the conventional letter and the telephone conversation? The 1999 movie *You've Got Mail* delighted audiences with the very contemporary situation of a couple enjoying an e-mail relationship that was more intense than the relationships they were simultaneously experiencing with their live-in lovers. The comic mileage was generated by the fact that in real life they actually knew and detested each other. Is this kind of situation only possible because of the distinctive nature of e-mail? Significantly, *You've Got Mail* was a remake of a 1940 Ernst Lubitsch film called *The Shop Around the Corner*. The latter film was also remade in 1949 as an MGM musical, *In the Good Old Summertime*, and in the 1960s as a Broadway show, *She Loves Me*. In the first three versions, the lovers are pen pals who work side by side in the same shop but don't know the identities of their correspondents. More recently, of course, when few people write personal letters, the same situation calls for a new mode of communication—though one sharing certain essential features of the old mode of communication.

As some of the writers in this chapter point out, cybercommunication is a mixed blessing—if not an actual curse. Increasingly, employers monitor their employees' e-mail, or install software to block instant messaging; and they sometimes impose penalties (even to the point of firing people) for inappropriate use of company e-mail facilities. A spouse going through a divorce or custody proceeding may obtain a warrant to search the e-mail of the other spouse, in an attempt to find incriminating evidence. The veil of anonymity provided by the Internet can expose people to vicious "flaming" attacks—abusive, sometimes threatening messages. And because "nobody knows you're a dog," people can pretend to be what they are not. For some, assuming alternate identities can be a healthy form of play and self-development; for others, it can be a mode of perpetrating deception or even criminal fraud.

A fascinating recent case of such e-deception involved the online magazine *Slate*. In February 2002 an individual named Robert Klingler, who claimed to be the North American head of BMW, sent an e-mail to one of the magazine's editors, proposing to write a series of five diary entries for *Slate* about his activities as a top-level executive of a major automobile manufacturer. *Slate* took Klingler up on his offer and the first two entries appeared in the magazine. Deputy editor Jack Shafer recounts what happened next:

> When *Slate* readers pointed out to the editors that neither Google.com nor Nexis searchers produced any hits for a "Robert Klingler and the automobile industry," we assumed the worst and took the entries down from the site. A phone call to the European auto company in question confirmed that no "Robert Klingler" worked for them.*

Subsequent efforts to track down and contact "Robert Klingler" proved unsuccessful. Meanwhile, *Slate*, with egg on its face, ruefully admitted that it had been duped, apologized to its readers, candidly posted all of the evidence on its site, and promised "greater vigilance in the future."[†]

In this chapter, we will explore the interrelationship between cybercommunication (both in its private and its public forums, including e-mail and "blog" sites) and identity—what we generally think of as our essential self, that unique core of personhood and personality that makes each person dif-

---

* Jack Shafer, "*Slate* Gets Duped," *Slate* 5 March 2002. <http://slate.msn.com/?id=2062867>.

[†] See the above selection by Shafer for additional links to the "Klingler" affair, including Shafer's subsequent (12 March 2002) investigative article, "Who Is 'Robert Klingler'?: On the Trail of the Man Who Duped *Slate*," as well as Klingler's diary entries and readers' responses to the imbroglio.

ferent from anyone else. But what is a "true" identity? Is it the self that we create for ourselves over the years and project to the world at large—our families, our friends, our coworkers, the general public? Is it the self to which we retreat when we are alone, perhaps fantasizing about operating in some alternate universe? Is it some combination of these? Under what circumstances is our "true" identity (assuming there is such a thing) most likely to emerge? And, to pose one of the central questions of this chapter: How has the Internet, with its new modes of communication, allowed us to develop new ways of creating—or obliterating—identity?

Some writers think that the Internet offers fertile fields of play for experimenting with our identities. Even so simple an act as choosing a screen name for ourselves—BadBarry, Icequeen, Coolsurferdude, Beachbunny—attaches a label to a particular aspect of our identity (or one that may not previously have existed); and when we create alternate screen names, we create alternate identities, each of which may have a distinctive personality, each of which we may explore and develop in e-mail, instant messages, electronic bulletin boards, chat rooms, online gaming, and other arenas of the Internet.

In "We've Got Mail—Always," Andrew Leonard surveys the revolution wrought by e-mail and considers some of its benefits and drawbacks. The technical aspects of e-mail—just how does a message get from sender to recipient?—are engagingly outlined by John Dyson in "Journey of an E-Mail." In "The End of History" Fred Kaplan reports on many historians' concern that the ephemeral nature of e-mail, combined with the decline of letters, will leave their future colleagues with precious few records to draw upon when reporting key events of the twenty-first century.

The next several pieces explore relatively new and popular phenomena in cyberspace: instant messaging and blogging. In "I Think, Therefore IM," Jennifer Lee explains how teachers are often baffled by the abbreviated *lingua franca* students began using in their e-mails and instant messages and are now transferring to their academic papers. Another new cyberphenomenon, the Weblog, is introduced by John C. Dvorak in "The Blog Phenomenon." And in "The Intimacy of Blogs," Michael Snider takes note of several of the more interesting blog sites.

"A Shared Sadness," by Russ Parsons, shows the coming together of a small online community when one of their members faces major surgery. The next piece explores the phenomenon of online romances; in "Virtual Love," Meghan Daum writes of her own experience with a passionate e-mail affair. Next, sociologist Sherry Turkle explains how creating and experimenting with multiple identities on the Internet can be psychologically healthy. Two examples of this kind of identity-creation follow. In "Boy, You Fight Like a Girl," Alex Pham discusses why gender-switching is so popular among online gamers. And in "The 15-Year-Old Legal Whiz," Michael Lewis recounts how a teenager with no legal training became the top legal expert on a widely used information Web site.

We've Got Mail—Always
Andrew Leonard

We begin this chapter with a broad survey of the e-mail revolution. Andrew Leonard's first sentence introduces his basic approach: "Is e-mail a blessing or a curse?" He goes on to illustrate areas in which it is one or the other—or both at once. Leonard begins and ends with his own experiences, but in the course of the article, he covers many areas of contemporary life in which e-mail has changed the way that we communicate with one another. This article first appeared as part of a special issue of Newsweek *devoted to computers, dated 20 September 1999. Leonard is a contributing editor for* Newsweek *and a senior technology correspondent of the online magazine* Salon.com.

1   Is e-mail a blessing or a curse? Last month, after a week's vacation, I discovered 1,218 unread e-mail messages waiting in my IN box. I pretended to be dismayed, but secretly I was pleased. This is how we measure our wired worth in the late 1990s—if you aren't overwhelmed by e-mail, you must be doing something wrong.

2   Never mind that after subtracting the stale office chitchat, spam, flame wars, dumb jokes forwarded by friends who should have known better and other e-mail detritus, there were perhaps seven messages actually worth reading. I was doomed to spend half my workday just deleting junk. E-mail sucks.

3   But wait—what about those seven? A close friend in Taipei I haven't seen in five years tells me he's planning to start a family. A complete stranger in Belgium sends me a hot story tip. Another stranger offers me a job. I'd rather lose an eye than lose my e-mail account. E-mail rocks!

4   E-mail. Can't live with it, can't live without it. Con artists and real artists, advertisers and freedom fighters, lovers and sworn enemies—they've all flocked to e-mail as they would to any new medium of expression. E-mail is convenient, saves time, brings us closer to one another, helps us manage our ever-more-complex lives. Books are written, campaigns conducted, crimes committed—all via e-mail. But it is also inconvenient, wastes our time, isolates us in front of our computers and introduces more complexity into our already too-harried lives. To skeptics, e-mail is just the latest chapter in the evolving history of human communication. A snooping husband now discovers his wife's affair by reading her private e-mail—but he could have uncovered the same sin by finding letters a generation ago.

5   Yet e-mail—and all online communication—is in fact something truly different; it captures the essence of life at the close of the 20th century with an authority that few other products of digital technology can claim. Does the pace of life seem ever faster? E-mail simultaneously allows us to cope with that acceleration and contributes to it. Are our attention spans shriveling under barrages of new, improved forms of stimulation? The quick and dirty e-mail is made to order for those whose ability to concentrate is measured in nanoseconds. If we accept that the creation of the globe-spanning Internet is one of the most important technological innovations of the last half of this century, then we must

give e-mail—the living embodiment of human connection across the Net—pride of place. The way we interact with each other is changing; e-mail is both the catalyst and the instrument of that change.

6   The scope of the phenomenon is mind-boggling. Worldwide, 225 million people can send and receive e-mail. Forget about the Web or e-commerce or even online pornography: e-mail is the Internet's true killer app—the software application that we simply must have, even if it means buying a $2,000 computer and plunking down $20 a month to America Online. According to Donna Hoffman, a professor of marketing at Vanderbilt University, one survey after another finds that when online users are asked what they do on the Net, "e-mail is always No. 1."

7   Oddly enough, no one planned it, and no one predicted it. When research scientists first began cooking up the Internet's predecessor, the Arpanet, in 1968, their primary goal was to enable disparate computing centers to share resources. "But it didn't take very long before they discovered that the most important thing was the ability to send mail around, which they had not anticipated at all," says Eric Allman, chief technical officer of Sendmail, Inc., and the primary author of a 20-year-old program—Sendmail—that still transports the vast majority of the world's e-mail across the Internet. It seems that what all those top computer scientists really wanted to use the Internet for was as a place to debate, via e-mail, such crucially important topics as the best science-fiction novel of all time. Even though Allman is now quite proud that his software helps hundreds of millions of people communicate, he says he didn't set out originally to change the world. As a systems administrator at UC Berkeley in the late '70s, he was constantly hassled by computer-science researchers in one building who wanted to get their e-mail from machines in another location. "I just wanted to make my life easier," says Allman.

8   Don't we all? When my first child was born in 1994, e-mail seemed to me some kind of Promethean gift perfectly designed to help me cope with the irreconcilable pressures of new-fatherhood and full-time freelance writing. It saved me time and money without ever requiring me to leave the house; it salvaged my social life, allowed me to conduct interviews as a reporter and kept a lifeline open to my far-flung extended family. Indeed, I finally knew for sure that the digital world was viscerally potent when I found myself in the middle of a bitter fight with my mother—on e-mail. Again, new medium, old story.

9   My mother had given me an e-mail head start. In 1988, she bought me a modem so I could create a CompuServe account. The reason? Her younger brother had contracted a rapidly worsening case of Parkinson's disease. He wasn't able to talk clearly, and could hardly scrawl his name with a pen or pencil. But he had a computer, and could peck out words on a keyboard. My mom figured that if the family all had CompuServe accounts, we could send him e-mail. She grasped, long before the Internet became a household word, how online communication offered new possibilities for transcending physical limitations, how as simple a thing as e-mail could bring us closer to those whom we love.

10   It may even help us find those whom we want to love in the first place. Jenn Shreve is a freelance writer in the San Francisco Bay Area who keeps a close eye on the emerging culture of the new online generation. For the last couple

of years, she's seen what she considers to be a positive change in online dating habits. E-mail, she argues, encourages the shy. "It offers a semi-risk-free environment to initiate romance," says Shreve. "Because it lacks the immediate threat of physical rejection, people who are perhaps shy or had painful romantic failures in the past can use the Internet as a way to build a relationship in the early romantic stages."

11   But it's not just about lust. E-mail also flattens hierarchies within the bounds of an office. It is far easier, Shreve notes, to make a suggestion to your superiors and colleagues via e-mail than it is to do so in a pressure-filled meeting room. "Any time when you have something that is difficult to say, e-mail can make it easier," she says. "It serves as a buffer zone."

12   Of course, e-mail's uses as a social lubricant can be taken to extremes. There is little point in denying the obvious dark side to the lack of self-constraint encouraged by e-mail. Purveyors of pornography rarely call us on the phone and suggest out loud that we check out some "hot teen action." But they don't think twice about jamming our e-mail boxes full of outrageously prurient advertisements. People who would never insult us face to face will spew the vilest, most objectionable, most appalling rhetoric imaginable via e-mail or an instant message, or in the no-holds-barred confines of a chat room.

13   Cyberspace's lapses in gentility underscores a central contradiction inherent in online communication. If it is true that hours spent on the Net are often hours subtracted from watching television, one could argue that the digital era has raised the curtains on a new age of literacy—more people are writing more words than ever before! But what kind of words are we writing? Are we really more literate, or are we sliding ever faster into a quicksand of meaningless irrelevance, of pop-cultural triviality—expressed, usually, in lowercase letters—run amok? E-mail is actually too easy, too casual. Gone are the days when one would worry over a letter to a lover or a relative or a colleague. Now there's just time for that quick e-mail, a few hastily cobbled together thoughts written in a colloquial style that usually borders on unedited stream of consciousness. The danger is obvious: snippy comments to a friend, overly sharp retorts to one's boss, insults mistakenly sent to the target, not the intended audience. E-mail allows us to act before we can think—the perfect tool for a culture of hyperstimulation.

14   So instead of creating something new, we forward something old. Instead of crafting the perfect phrase, we use a brain-dead abbreviation: IMHO for In My Humble Opinion, or ROTFLMAO, for Rolling On The Floor Laughing My A— Off. Got a rumor? E-mail it to 50 people! Instant messaging and chat rooms just accentuate the casual negative. If e-mail requires little thought, then instant messaging—flashing a message directly onto a recipient's computer monitor—is so insubstantial as to be practically nonexistent.

15   E-mail, ultimately, is a fragile thing, easy to forge, easy to corrupt, easy to destroy. A few weeks ago a coworker of mine accidentally and irretrievably wiped out 1,500 of his own saved messages. For a person who conducts the bulk of his life online, such a digital tragedy is akin to erasing part of your own memory. Suddenly, nothing's left. It is comforting to think that, if preserved

in a retrievable way, all the notes the world is passing back and forth today constitute a vast historical archive, but the opposite may also be true. Earlier this summer, I visited some curators at the Stanford University Library who are hard at work compiling a digital archive of Silicon Valley history. They bemoaned a new, fast-spreading corporate policy that requires the deletion of all corporate e-mails after every 60 or 90 days. As Microsoft and Netscape have learned to their dismay, old e-mails, however trivial they seem when they are written, can and will come back to haunt you. It is best, say the lawyers, to just wipe them all out.

16   Still, e-mail is enabling radically new forms of worldwide human collaboration. Those 225 million people who can send and receive it represent a network of potentially cooperating individuals dwarfing anything that even the mightiest corporation or government can muster. Mailing-list discussion groups and online conferencing allow us to gather together to work on a multitude of projects that are interesting or helpful to us—to pool our collective efforts in a fashion never before possible. The most obvious place to see this collaboration right now is in the world of software. For decades, programmers have used e-mail to collaborate on projects. With increasing frequency, this collaboration is occurring across company lines, and often without even the spur of commercial incentives. It's happening largely because it can—it's relatively easy for a thousand programmers to collectively contribute to a project using e-mail and the Internet. Perhaps each individual contribution is small, but the scale of the Internet multiplies all efforts dramatically.

17   Meanwhile, now that we are all connected, day and night, across time zones and oceans and corporate firewalls, we are beginning to lose sight of the distinction between what is work and what is play.

18   Six years after I logged onto CompuServe for the first time, I went to Australia for three weeks. Midway through my visit, I ended up in Alice Springs, a fraying-at-the-edges frontier town about a thousand miles away from anywhere in the middle of the great Australian outback. An exotic place, nestled among the oldest mountain remnants of the world, where flocks of parrots swoop and flutter through the downtown shopping district. But instead of wandering through the desert seeking out wallabies and feral camels, I found myself dialing long distance to a friend's University of Melbourne Internet account, and transferring from there via a telnet program to my own account at the Well in San Francisco. Once on the Well, I checked my mail to see if a fact checker for *Wired* magazine had any fresh queries for me concerning a story I had recently submitted.

19   I was on the job—in large part because I had an e-mail address and had made the Devil's bargain with the wired world. As I listened for the sound of the modem connecting in Alice Springs, I felt in the pit of my stomach that I had lost control over some valuable part of my life. Your employer will refrain from calling you at 11:30 at night, but not from sending an inquiring, hectoring, must-be-promptly-answered-as-soon-as-you-log-on e-mail. E-mail doesn't just collapse distance, it demolishes all boundaries. And that can be, depending on the moment, either a blessing or a curse.

Review Questions

1. Summarize some of the ways that e-mail can be, as Leonard puts it, either a "blessing or a curse."
2. What was the original purpose of the people who invented e-mail?
3. How does Leonard inject himself into his discussion of e-mail?

Discussion and Writing Suggestions

1. What part does e-mail play in your own life? Explain how you have experienced some of the e-mail "blessings" and "curses" to which Leonard refers, illustrating your account with relevant anecdotes.

2. Many people bemoan the e-mail revolution, complaining that it has replaced letter-writing, which they see as a superior form of communication. Consider the advantages and disadvantages of e-mail communication versus those of communication by letter and by telephone. Begin by creating a table, with rows for e-mail, letter-writing, and telephone calls, and with columns for advantages and disadvantages. Develop this table into a short paper. In your discussion consider particular situations that illustrate the benefits and drawbacks of each form of communication.

3. According to freelance writer Jenn Shreve, e-mail "offers a semi-risk-free environment to initiate romance." To what extent have you found this to be true, either in your own experience or the experience of others you know? Why "semi-risk-free," as opposed to "risk-free"?

4. Leonard notes that "E-mail allows us to act before we can think." Recount an occasion when you have written an e-mail message in the heat of anger (or passion), pushed the "Send" button "in haste" and then "at leisure" regretted sending your words. What was the aftermath? Did the incident change how you wrote and sent e-mail in the future?

5. One of the ways that e-mail changes its users, according to Leonard, is to reduce their "gentility" when communicating with others, particularly others they don't know personally. To what extent has e-mail changed the way you think about yourself, changed your concept of your own identity? For example, when you send e-mail messages to particular individuals, do you, in effect, redefine yourself or reconstruct yourself according to the type of person you would like to be, to those individuals? By the same token, do the e-mail messages you receive from certain people imply a certain "you"—one who may be somewhat different from the "you" that exists apart from e-mail? Why do you think e-mail is a good tool for bringing about these redefinitions and reconstructions of your self?

Journey of an E-Mail
John Dyson

Every day, we operate and depend upon a multitude of technical devices without having the foggiest idea how they work. Forget high-tech computers: how many of us could explain the operation of a radio, a telephone, a light bulb, the electric motor that powers our fan? How many of us could give an accurate and coherent account of the internal workings of a low-tech device like a flush toilet?

The main job of a science writer is to explain to nontechnically inclined people how the technology that we take for granted works. In the following selection, freelance writer John Dyson explains just what happens when we click "Send" on our e-mail screen.

1   Doug and Julie Young raise Dandie Dinmont terriers. They also publish a newsletter for fellow lovers of the breed. Not too long ago they wanted a picture of Mr. D, our family pet.

2   I could have sent the photo by ordinary mail, but that would have taken at least four days. Instead, sitting down at the computer in my den overlooking London's River Thames, I sent an e-mail. I typed in an address, young@montizard.com, composed a short message, then attached a photograph I'd scanned into my PC. Finally I clicked Send. Mr. D instantly vanished from my screen— headed to a farmhouse in rural Ohio.

3   Along with more than 150 million others around the world, I use e-mail all the time and can't imagine living without it. How it actually works, of course, was a mystery. So one day I decided to find out. Mounting my bicycle, I pedaled off to follow my dog through cyberspace.

4   The first stop was a brick office plaza between a canal and an elevated highway in Brentford, west London. This was one of the homes of Cable & Wireless, the company that connects my computer to the Internet by telephone lines.

5   Escorted through security checks and card-swipe doors, I entered a brightly lit, windowless room with rows of fridge-size metal cabinets called racks, containing computers the size of TV sets, each costing as much as a car. In an adjoining control room, engineers, some of whom were wearing earrings, were monitoring rows of complicated numbers on video screens. As the racks tend to look the same, engineers give them names. "This is Marvin," said Jason Semple, pointing to one. "He's your postbox."

6   A burly 27-year-old, Semple hooked a finger over the spine of what looked like one of scores of videocassettes on a shelf. He slid out a circuit board glittering with tiny gold wires and silver connectors.

7   "When your PC dials our number, it's answered by one of these modems," Semple explained. "It checks your name and password with another computer, then asks what you want."

8   My computer had replied, "I've got mail."

9   Next, Mr. D was fed into a "mail server"—a bunch of computers filling five racks. One read my e-mail's destination and checked another, which stored Internet addresses like a gigantic phone directory.

10   The Cable & Wireless directory could do ten look-ups a second. It didn't find montizard.com, so it asked a bigger directory, storing ten million addresses in Europe and Africa. That didn't work either, so it asked one of 13 core directories (ten in the United States, two in Europe, one in Japan) holding every Internet address in the world.

11   Back came the answer: "Send mail to BuckeyeNet." This is the company connecting the Youngs to the Internet. BuckeyeNet's Internet address—209.41.2.152—was clipped like a dog tag to Mr. D's collar.

12   Next, something bizarre happened. Imagine a postal clerk who chops your letter into little bits and puts them in separate envelopes. This is done to every e-mail. All the bits and bytes representing Mr. D were instantly divided among about 120 packets. Every one was stamped with BuckeyeNet's address, plus my own address, so the jigsaw puzzle could be reassembled at the other end.

13   But they didn't go all at once. Instead, a single packet was sent off like a scout car, to knock on the door of BuckeyeNet, say hello and make a connection. The first stop was a gateway router, which would help the scout car find the way.

14   Picture the Internet as 65,000 interstate highways crisscrossing the globe and connected to smaller roads and streets. Like a cop with a walkie-talkie on every crossroad, the router learns the fastest way to get an e-mail to its destination. It knows all the routes and, by talking with other "cops" down the road every half-minute, it discovers where the delays are—say, heavy telephone traffic or a cut cable.

15   A Cable & Wireless router sent Mr. D's hello packet across London to the company's transmission center in Docklands, where another router fed it into the stream of e-mail packets heading for the westerly tip of Cornwall, the nearest part of England to America.

16   All this happened in four milliseconds—like a lightning flash.

17   I took a decidedly slower train to Cornwall and went to Porthcurno, a cliff-top village. There, in a barn-size room, is the base station of the transatlantic Gemini cable.

18   Take a hair-thin fiber of glass, wrap it in a protective jacket, then incorporate it with others in a rubbery protective tube. This is fiber-optic cable, known in the trade as pipe.

19   A flashing laser at one end fires digital on/off signals along the fiber. At about 120,000 miles a second—more than half the speed of light—they zip to the other end.

20   "It's the high-tech equivalent of two kids signaling each other with flashlights," explained Dave Shirt, operations director. With pretty quick fingers, I'd say: the lasers flash ten billion times a second.

21   Mr. D's packet next jostled for elbowroom with a torrent of transatlantic electronic traffic—equivalent to 100,000 closely typed pages every second, or

400,000 simultaneous phone calls. Think that's a lot? At present six parallel lanes of traffic hurtle along every glass fiber. Newly laid cables will soon have 128 lanes, preparing for the explosion of Internet traffic when every movie ever made could be available online.

22   I returned to London, hopped a plane to New York and rented a car, then picked up Mr. D's trail again on a long, flat beach in Manasquan, N.J., where the Gemini cable comes ashore. Next the e-mail zipped along poles and beside rail-road tracks before flashing into 60 Hudson Street, in downtown Manhattan. Time taken from London: approximately 40 milliseconds, or one-tenth of a blink of the eye.

23   This 22-floor art-deco building is a "telco hotel" where telephone compa-nies own or rent space for equipment so they can connect to one another more easily. The scout packet was switched into high-capacity "fat pipes" crossing the continent. It also hit what engineers call ATM—asynchronous transfer mode.

24   Now Mr. D was diced yet again into dozens of identically sized cells which flashed through the back of a telephone exchange in West Orange, N.J., just west of New York.

25   But from there the cells had a really wild ride, zipping through pipe beside railroad tracks, into and out of Philadelphia, up the Ohio Valley, through Cleveland and into another telephone exchange at Willow Springs, outside Chicago. Here the bits came together, and the original packet was restored. It all took a fraction of a second.

26   Barely pausing for a breath, so to speak, the scout packet next raced through Chicago and Detroit, before landing in a building in Columbus, Ohio—head-quarters of Fiber Network Solutions. There I met the company's co-founder, Kyle Bacon, a laid-back 27-year-old wearing two gold earrings.

27   Bacon, who used to duck classes to work on his university's computer system, helped set up a network that controls Internet pipes so businesses and industry have to pay the company to open the tap. That was three years ago. Now the company employs 45 people, and Bacon drives a silver BMW whose license plate reads FAT PIPE.

28   A router in the company switched Mr. D into a skinny pipe running direct to the home of BuckeyeNet—then a two-room office with a dirt parking lot, some five miles from rural Lancaster. BuckeyeNet has over a thousand clients and 13 computers. By way of comparison, the biggest Internet-access provider in the world, America Online, has some 19 million subscribers and servers covering football fields of floor space.

29   Dressed in shorts and, naturally, sporting a gold earring, Jonathan Sheline, 27, told me he'd set up the company after leaving the Army, where he'd served hitches in the infantry and counterintelligence. In just 18 months his net was one of the largest in the town. Our friends the Youngs are among its $17.95-a-month clients.

30   BuckeyeNet's mail server unwrapped Mr. D's scout packet, which carried a message. "Helo," it said. "I am j.dyson at cwcom.net." "Helo" means *hello* in a computer language called Simple Mail Transfer Protocol (SMTP).

31   BuckeyeNet's mail server sent an acknowledgment to London, which took one-tenth of a second to arrive. Next the two computers negotiated the connection. Their conversation, using codes as well as plain text, went like this.

32   Ohio: Okay, I'm listening. SMTP is spoken here.

33   London: I have mail from j.dyson at cwcom.net.

34   Ohio: Pleased to meet you.

35   London: I've got mail for montizard.com.

36   Ohio (checking list of clients): Okay, I can handle that.

37   London: I'm ready to send data.

38   Ohio: Start mail input.

39   From London, five packets hit the road. If any crashed or failed to arrive, the Ohio dispatcher would let London know and they'd be sent again. When this bunch arrived, Ohio said: "I got the first five, give me five more."

40   Despite all the messages Ping-Ponging across the Atlantic, the last bit of Mr. D straggled into BuckeyeNet's server less than half a minute after I had originally clicked Send. For me it had been nine hours in the air, four hours waiting for a connection and an hour and a half in cars. And my luggage was left behind. But Mr. D still had to go the last five miles.

41   When I arrived in their old farmhouse on nearly five acres outside Rushville, Doug and Julie Young were making breakfast for 35 dogs, 30 ferrets, two llamas and a parrot. Julie had an armful of cans, bowls and milk cartons, difficult to carry because they were all different sizes.

42   Meanwhile, from a big paper bag, Doug filled a container with pellets of dog food—the perfect metaphor for understanding why e-mails are minced and shredded into packets and cells. Like pellets, they pour more easily and therefore travel much faster.

43   A big, jovial man of 51, Doug uses e-mail to talk with breeders all over the world. When he clicked Get Mail, the BuckeyeNet server checked his mailbox and forwarded its contents down the phone line. The stream of bits materialized into Mr. D gazing imperially out of the screen from his kitchen chair, not a bit ruffled after his 4000-mile dash.

Review Questions

1. How did Dyson's own server computer in West London know where to send his message?

2. Why are e-mail messages chopped into numerous electronic pieces (or "packets") before they are transmitted?

3. What is SMTP?

Discussion and Writing Suggestions

1. Write a summary (one or two paragraphs) of the process Dyson describes without using any of the specifics: personal or place

names. Your summary should represent a general description of how a piece of e-mail makes its way from sender to recipient.

2. Discuss the ways in which Dyson attempts to make what is essentially a complex process intelligible and interesting to his readers. To what extent do you think he succeeds?

3. To what extent were you surprised by the mechanics of e-mail routing, as explained by Dyson? Before you read this article, what did you imagine happened when you hit the "send" button to transmit your e-mail message to its intended recipient(s)?

4. Think of a technical or scientific process that you understand reasonably well, but that many other people don't. Using Dyson's article as a model, describe what happens in a way that removes some of the mystery from the process, without unduly simplifying it. Examples: What happens when you turn the ignition key in your car? What happens when rain or snow starts falling? How do insects pollinate plants? How is beer or wine made? What happens when you push down the flush lever of a toilet?

The End of History
Fred Kaplan

One of the most basic qualities of digital communication is its impermanence. It's true, as many caution, that the average user can't permanently delete compromising or potentially embarrassing messages by simply hitting the Delete key. Lawyers, armed with subpoenas and aided by technical experts, can recover supposedly deleted messages documenting illicit romances and other unethical or unwise activities, to the consternation of the indiscreet sender. Still, such recovery is not an easy or common practice, and it remains the case that multitudes of messages that previously helped to form the historical record—letters, memos, reports, and so on—no longer exist because of the medium on which they were created.

The short shelf life of electronic documents poses a serious problem for historians, who, years later, attempt to locate documents through which they can construct historical narratives. These historical narratives can be viewed as a collective identity: We discover or rediscover who we are by studying and reflecting on what we did. We define ourselves as a people or as a culture ("America is a generous country," "The U.S. too often tries to impose its will on other countries," etc.) by referring to the historical record—a record constructed out of perishable documents. In the following article, Fred Kaplan addresses the problem of digital deletion of what may become the historical record.

Kaplan is a columnist and jazz critic for the online magazine Slate. *His work has also appeared in such magazines and newspapers as the* New Yorker, Atlantic Monthly, Harper's, New York Times, Boston Globe, Guardian (London), *and* Ottawa Citizen. *This piece was first posted in the 4 June 2003 issue of* Slate.

1 When tomorrow's historians go to write the chronicles of decision-making that led to Gulf War II [2003], they may be startled to find there's not much history to be written. The same is true of Clinton's war over Kosovo, Bush Sr.'s Desert Storm, and a host of other major episodes of U.S. national security policy. Many of the kinds of documents that historians of prior wars, and of the Cold War, have taken for granted—memoranda, minutes, and the routine back-and-forth among assistant secretaries of state and defense or among colonels and generals in the Joint Chiefs of Staff—simply no longer exist.

2 The problem is not some deliberate plot to conceal or destroy evidence. The problem—and it may seem churlish to say so in an online publication—is the advent of e-mail.

3 In the old days, before the mid-to-late 1980s, Cabinet officials and their assistants and deputy assistants wrote memos on paper, then handed them to a secretary in a typing pool. The secretary would type it on a sheet of paper backed by two or three carbon sheets, then file the carbons. Periodically, someone from the national archive would stop by with a cart and haul away the carbons for posterity.

4 Nobody does this today. There are no typing pools to speak of. There are few written memos.

5 Eduard Mark, a Cold War historian who has worked for 15 years in the U.S. Air Force historian's office, has launched a one-man crusade to highlight, and repair, this situation. He remembers an incident from the early '90s, when he was researching the official Air Force history of the Panama invasion, which had taken place only a few years earlier. "I went to the Air Force operations center," Mark says. "They had a little Mac computer on which they'd saved all the briefings. They were getting ready to dump the computer. I stopped them just in time, and printed out all the briefings. Those printouts I made are the only copies in existence."

6 That was a decade ago, when computers were not yet pervasive in the Pentagon and many offices still printed important documents on paper. The situation now, Mark says, is much worse.

7 Almost all Air Force documents today, for example, are presented as PowerPoint briefings.* They are almost never printed and rarely stored. When they are saved, they are often unaccompanied by any text. As a result, in many cases, the briefings are incomprehensible.

8 The new, paperless world has encouraged a general carelessness in official record-keeping. Mark says that J5, the planning department of the Joint Chiefs of Staff, does not, as a rule, save anything. When I talked with Mark on the phone Tuesday, he said he had before him an unclassified document, signed by the Air Force chief of staff and the secretary of the Air Force, ordering the creation of a senior steering group on "transformation" (the new buzzword for making military operations more agile and more inter-service in nature). The document was not dated.

9 Mark has personal knowledge of the situation with the Air Force. However, officials and historians in other branches of the national-security bureaucracy say, on background, that the pattern is pretty much the same across the board.

---

* PowerPoint is a software program used to prepare presentations. It allows for the creation and display—generally projected—of textual and graphic information.

10   Certain high-level documents are usually (but, even then, not always) saved—memos that cross the desks of the president, Cabinet secretaries, and military chiefs (the Air Force and Army chiefs of staff, and the chief of naval operations). But beneath that level, it's hit and miss, more often miss.

11   An enterprising historian writing about World Wars I or II can draw on the vast military records at the National Archive, as well as letters from Churchill, Roosevelt, de Gaulle, and others. (Who writes letters anymore?) Those chronicling the Cold War or the Vietnam War can plumb the presidential libraries of Truman, Eisenhower, Kennedy, Johnson, and Ford (less so of Nixon because it's a privately funded library), and find plenty of illuminating memos written to and from not just Cabinet officers, such as John Foster Dulles, Robert McNamara, and Dean Rusk, but the crucial sub-Cabinet officials and security advisers, such as Andrew Goodpaster, Walt Rostow, John McNaughton, McGeorge Bundy, and George Ball.

12   Twenty years from now, if someone went looking for similar memos by Paul Wolfowitz, Richard Perle, Richard Armitage, and Elliott Abrams on, say, the Bush administration's Middle East policies, not many memos would be found because they don't exist. Officials today e-mail their thoughts and proposals. Perhaps some individuals have been fastidious about printing and saving their e-mails, but there is no system in place for automatically doing so.

13   Robert Caro, author of the revealingly massive and detailed biographies of Lyndon Johnson and Robert Moses, often advises aspiring historians, "Turn every page." What to do, though, if there aren't any pages to turn?

Review Questions

1. Why, according to Kaplan, is "e-mail wrecking our national archive"?

2. In what area of activity does Kaplan find most of his examples?

3. Upon what kind of documents did historians of the past—for example, those studying World War I or II—rely in researching their books and articles?

Discussion and Writing Suggestions

1. To what extent do you consider what Kaplan describes to be a serious problem? What do you foresee as some of the consequences of not having a relatively complete written record of military, government, business, and other activities, as a result of the ephemeral nature of e-mail communication?

2. Examine one or more of your history textbooks, focusing on a particular subject—for example, the Civil War, the Russian Revolution, the Great Depression. On what kinds of documentary and other evidence does the historical narrative appear to be based? (See if

the narrative is footnoted and check the footnote references.) What parts of this narrative might be missing if the documents on which they were based had been destroyed or were not available? How might the loss of such documentary evidence have affected the way that we view the event today?

3. Describe an instance in your own life when the loss or premature deletion of an e-mail message has caused you inconvenience, or worse.

I Think, Therefore IM
Jennifer Lee

From time immemorial teachers have been distressed over violations of standard English form in student papers. But student e-mail can generate an entirely new level of dismay. Many writers (and not just students) assume that it is unnecessary, in e-mail messages, to capitalize words such as "I" (or any other words, for that matter), to punctuate, or—the subject of the following article—even to use complete words. In her article on "Teens' Instant-Messaging Lingo," Stephanie Dunnewind quotes the following sentence: "I wz gtin2d@ & now gota type it agen b patient!" Increasingly, such lingo is employed not only in e-mail but also in papers. Like screen names, cyberlingo is a way of expressing identity, both individually ("How creative can I be in devising abbreviations and new words?") and collectively ("I am part of a community that uses such language as a matter of course"). In the following selection Jennifer Lee, a New York Times *staff writer, considers this phenomenon. Lee's piece first appeared in the 19 September 2002 issue of the* Times.

1   Each September Jacqueline Harding prepares a classroom presentation on the common writing mistakes she sees in her students' work.

2   Ms. Harding, an eighth-grade English teacher at Viking Middle School in Gurnee, Ill., scribbles the words that have plagued generations of schoolchildren across her whiteboard:

There. Their. They're.

Your. You're.

To. Too. Two.

Its. It's.

This September, she has added a new list: u, r, ur, b4, wuz, cuz, 2.

3   When she asked her students how many of them used shortcuts like these in their writing, Ms. Harding said, she was not surprised when most of them raised their hands. This, after all, is their online lingua franca: English adapted for the spitfire conversational style of Internet instant messaging.

Jennifer Lee, "I Think, Therefore IM," *New York Times*, 19 September 2002.

4   Ms. Harding, who has seen such shortcuts creep into student papers over the last two years, said she gave her students a warning: "If I see this in your assignments, I will take points off."

5   "Kids should know the difference," said Ms. Harding, who decided to address this issue head-on this year. "They should know where to draw the line between formal writing and conversational writing."

6   As more and more teenagers socialize online, middle school and high school teachers like Ms. Harding are increasingly seeing a breezy form of Internet English jump from e-mail into schoolwork. To their dismay, teachers say that papers are being written with shortened words, improper capitalization and punctuation, and characters like &, $ and @.

7   Teachers have deducted points, drawn red circles and tsk-tsked at their classes. Yet the errant forms continue. "It stops being funny after you repeat yourself a couple of times," Ms. Harding said.

8   But teenagers, whose social life can rely as much these days on text communication as the spoken word, say that they use instant-messaging shorthand without thinking about it. They write to one another as much as they write in school, or more.

9   "You are so used to abbreviating things, you just start doing it unconsciously on schoolwork and reports and other things," said Eve Brecker, 15, a student at Montclair High School in New Jersey.

10   Ms. Brecker once handed in a midterm exam riddled with instant-messaging shorthand. "I had an hour to write an essay on *Romeo and Juliet*," she said. "I just wanted to finish before my time was up. I was writing fast and carelessly. I spelled 'you' 'u.' " She got a C.

11   Even terms that cannot be expressed verbally are making their way into papers. Melanie Weaver was stunned by some of the term papers she received from a 10th grade class she recently taught as part of an internship. "They would be trying to make a point in a paper, they would put a smiley face in the end," said Ms. Weaver, who teaches at Alvernia College in Reading, PA. "If they were presenting an argument and they needed to present an opposite view, they would put a frown."

12   As Trisha Fogarty, a sixth-grade teacher at Houlton Southside School in Houlton, Maine, puts it, today's students are "Generation Text."

13   Almost 60 percent of the online population under age 17 uses instant messaging, according to Nielsen/NetRatings. In addition to cellphone text messaging, Weblogs and e-mail, it has become a popular means of flirting, setting up dates, asking for help with homework and keeping in contact with distant friends. The abbreviations are a natural outgrowth of this rapid-fire style of communication.

14   "They have a social life that centers around typed communication," said Judith S. Donath, a professor at the Massachusetts Institute of Technology's Media Lab who has studied electronic communication. "They have a writing style that has been nurtured in a teenage social milieu."

15   Some teachers see the creeping abbreviations as part of a continuing assault of technology on formal written English. Others take it more lightly, saying that it is just part of the larger arc of language evolution.

16   "To them it's not wrong," said Ms. Harding, who is 28. "It's acceptable because it's in their culture. It's hard enough to teach them the art of formal writing. Now we've got to overcome this new instant-messaging language."

17   Ms. Harding noted that in some cases the shorthand isn't even shorter. "I understand 'cuz,' but what's with the 'wuz'? It's the same amount of letters as 'was,' so what's the point?" she said.

18   Deborah Bova, who teaches eighth-grade English at Raymond Park Middle School in Indianapolis, thought her eyesight was failing several years ago when she saw the sentence "B4 we perform, ppl have 2 practice" on a student assignment.

19   "I thought, 'My God, what is this?'" Ms. Bova said. "Have they lost their minds?"

20   The student was summoned to the board to translate the sentence into standard English: "Before we perform, people have to practice." She realized that the students thought she was out of touch. "It was like 'Get with it, Bova,'" she said. Ms. Bova had a student type up a reference list of translations for common instant-messaging expressions. She posted a copy on the bulletin board by her desk and took another one home to use while grading.

21   Students are sometimes unrepentant.

22   "They were astonished when I began to point these things out to them," said Henry Assetto, a social studies teacher at Twin Valley High School in Elverson, Pa. "Because I am a history teacher, they did not think a history teacher would be checking up on their grammar or their spelling," said Mr. Assetto, who has been teaching for 34 years.

23   But Montana Hodgen, 16, another Montclair student, said she was so accustomed to instant-messaging abbreviations that she often read right past them. She proofread a paper last year only to get it returned with the messaging abbreviations circled in red.

24   "I was so used to reading what my friends wrote to me on Instant Messenger that I didn't even realize that there was something wrong," she said. She said her ability to separate formal and informal English declined the more she used instant messages. "Three years ago, if I had seen that, I would have been 'What is that?'"

25   The spelling checker doesn't always help either, students say. For one, Microsoft Word's squiggly red spell-check lines don't appear beneath single letters and numbers such as u, r, c, 2 and 4. Nor do they catch words which have numbers in them such as "l8r" and "b4" by default.

26   Teenagers have essentially developed an unconscious "accent" in their typing, Professor Donath said. "They have gotten facile at typing and they are not paying attention."

27   Teenagers have long pushed the boundaries of spoken language, introducing words that then become passe with adult adoption. Now teenagers are taking charge and pushing the boundaries of written language. For them, expressions like "oic" (oh I see), "nm" (not much), "jk" (just kidding) and "lol" (laughing out loud), "brb" (be right back), "ttyl" (talk to you later) are as standard as conventional English.

28   "There is no official English language," said Jesse Sheidlower, the North American editor of the *Oxford English Dictionary.* "Language is spread not

because anyone dictates any one thing to happen. The decisions are made by the language and the people who use the language."

29   Some teachers find the new writing style alarming. "First of all, it's very rude, and it's very careless," said Lois Moran, a middle school English teacher at St. Nicholas School in Jersey City.

30   "They should be careful to write properly and not to put these little codes in that they are in such a habit of writing to each other," said Ms. Moran, who has lectured her eighth-grade class on such mistakes.

31   Others say that the instant-messaging style might simply be a fad, something that students will grow out of. Or they see it as an opportunity to teach students about the evolution of language.

32   "I turn it into a very positive teachable moment for kids in the class," said Erika V. Karres, an assistant professor at the University of North Carolina at Chapel Hill who trains student teachers. She shows students how English has evolved since Shakespeare's time. "Imagine Langston Hughes's writing in quick texting instead of 'Langston writing,' " she said. "It makes teaching and learning so exciting."

33   Other teachers encourage students to use messaging shorthand to spark their thinking processes. "When my children are writing first drafts, I don't care how they spell anything, as long as they are writing," said Ms. Fogarty, the sixth-grade teacher from Houlton, Maine. "If this lingo gets their thoughts and ideas onto paper quicker, the more power to them." But during editing and revising, she expects her students to switch to standard English.

34   Ms. Bova shares the view that instant-messaging language can help free up their creativity. With the help of students, she does not even need the cheat sheet to read the shorthand anymore.

35   "I think it's a plus," she said. "And I would say that with a + sign."

Review Questions

1. What are the main features of "instant-messaging language"?
2. What reasons are most frequently offered for the ever-more-frequent use of this language?
3. What objections do some teachers (and others) have to instant-messaging language?

Discussion and Writing Suggestions

1. Do you engage in what teacher Jacqueline Harding calls "this new instant-messaging language" in e-mail communications with your friends and family? Have you used such language in your school-work or in e-mails to teachers? If so, what has been the reaction? How do you think teachers should handle the use of such language? To what extent do you view instant-messaging lingo—or instant-messaging itself—as an expression of your identity? Lee quotes several people in her article: With whom do you most agree? Why?

2. MIT professor Judith S. Donath says (paragraph 14) that students "have a social life that centers around typed communication." To what extent do you agree with this comment?

3. Several people quoted for this article point to a difference between formal and informal uses of language. To what extent do you recognize such a distinction? Which types of written communications are best expressed in informal language? In formal language? What do you see as the main advantages and disadvantages of each type of language?

The Blog Phenomenon
John C. Dvorak

Blogs, or Weblogs—public online diaries—are only the most recent examples of proliferating cyberspace phenomena. That is to say, blogging is the latest way that people, in their infinite resourcefulness and ingenuity, have devised to communicate with one another. Blog sites are the latest way of announcing to the world: "I am here. My thoughts and my doings are interesting to the rest of the world." In the following selection, computer guru John C. Dvorak explains and offers reasons for this new online development. Dvorak writes on technology and software issues for PC Magazine, *and he is the author of numerous books on personal computing and software, including* Hypergrowth: The Rise and Fall of Osborne Computer Corporation *(1984, with Adam Osborne) and* Dvorak's Guide to Desktop Telecommunications *(1992, with Nick Anis). This article first appeared in* PC Magazine *on 26 February 2002.*

1   A recent overlooked Web trend—overlooked by the mainstream media, at least—is the proliferation of public diaries, generically referred to as Blogs. The term originated from "WeB log" and was further promoted by pyra.com as a Blog at its www.blogger.com site, although www.pita.com is considered the original source of easy-to-use Web logging. People who "Blog" are called Bloggers, and right now there are hundreds, thousands of Blogs on the Net.

2   The vanity page is dead; long live the Blog. The vanity Web page has lost momentum. People who posted one have already done so, and the growth has slowed. Most are uninteresting and uninspired. Cat pictures dominate too many of them. A Blog is the next iteration, and most vanity site mavens have gravitated toward these things. Serious vanity site developers have gone into posting hobby or special-interest sites, having learned by experience how to make an attractive Web page. This is, indeed, progress.

3   And the universe of these diaries can even be searched at various specialty search sites, such as www.blogfinder.com.

4   Generally speaking, these postings are fascinating, since they often have serious elements of Hyde Park corner blather, besides blatant exhibitionism and obvious self-indulgence. And whatever you think of them, you'll admit that they are much more interesting than the static vanity site from years ago.

5   One of the best examples you'll find on the Web of a homebrew special-interest site is the stunning Jacob's Bugatti Pages at www.homestead.mac.com/

bugatti/jacob. If you have a hobby and want to make the Web part of that hobby, then look no further than Jacob's for inspiration. But if you just want to pontificate and talk about yourself, start a Blog.

6   Blogging goes beyond software posting and uses an entire system that allows for easy creation. With a Blog there is no coding to do. The Blog is usually more attractive than sloppy HTML* done by an amateur, and by nature it demands updating so that the material is kept current. People can't resist updating the diary and apologize if they don't do it—as if anyone really cares. You have to be dedicated to a Web site to keep it current. Not so the Blog; it's more addictive. And hobbyist Blogs have emerged. For example, some people like to watch a lot of movies and review them. They see a movie and immediately post their comments. Some of these homebrew reviewers are better than the pros.

7   Still, with the few hobbyist exceptions, Blogs are mostly personal diaries. Here's where the sociology comes in. Why, exactly, do people want to have other people read these ramblings? Many are incriminating! Ask a Web log addict why he or she does it and you'll get a range of answers that tend towards the "because it's easy" or "because it's fun!" bromides. I think there are deeper reasons. Here are a few obvious possibilities:

- *Ego gratification.* Some people need to be the center of attention. It makes them feel good about themselves to tell the world what important things they've been doing and what profound thoughts they've been having. Curiously, while this looks like the most obvious reason for a Web log, I think it's probably the least likely reason, since it's too trite and shallow.
- *Antidepersonalization.* When people begin to think that they are nothing more than a cog in the wheel of society, they look for any way to differentiate themselves. The Web log proves they are different. Just read it. You'll see.
- *Elimination of frustration.* Day-to-day life, especially in the city, is wrought with frustration, and the Web log gives people the ability to complain to the world. You get to read a lot of complaining in these logs. If you think I'm a complainer, oh boy!
- *Societal need to share.* As a cynic who gets paid to write, I have a hard time with this explanation. But it seems some people genuinely like to "share," and this is one way.
- *Wanna-be writers.* A lot of people want to be published writers. Blogs make it happen without the hassle of getting someone else to do it or having to write well—although there is good writing to be found. Some is shockingly good. Most of it is miserable. I expect to see those Open Learning classes around the country offering courses in Blog writing.

8   Whatever the reason for the Blog phenomenon, it's not going to go away anytime soon. The main positive change: far fewer cat pictures!

---

* HyperText Mark-Up Language is a system of "tags" (rather than a computer "language") that instructs the Web browser how to format and display text and graphics.

Review Questions

1. What is a "blog"?

2. Why are blogs tending to replace personal ("vanity") Web pages, according to Dvorak?

3. What are the main reasons cited by Dvorak for the rise and proliferation of blogs?

Discussion and Writing Suggestions

1. Examine some blogs (e.g., <www.blogfinder.com>, <www.blogtree.com>). Locate and review some of the blogs referenced both in this article and in Michael Snider's article, which follows next. To what extent do you find such sites interesting and worth posting? To what extent to you regard them as mere "vanity" or "ego gratification" projects? Cite specific examples to support your conclusions.

2. To what extent do you agree that blogs are "not going to go away anytime soon"? Have you read—or did you regularly read—blogs before reading this article? Have you posted your own? Which (if any) of the reasons for creating blogs discussed by Dvorak toward the end of his article do you find most persuasive?

3. Examine some blog sites from the perspective of how the writers present themselves to the world. What kind of people are they, based upon not only their words but also on their choice of subjects, their distinctive "voices," and the appearance of their sites? To what extent do you like their attitude about the things they write about? To what extent do you agree with their opinions? To what extent would you like to meet them or even have dinner with them? To what extent do you detect indications that their personas are created, that they are hiding behind masks?

4. In a subsequent article written for *PC Magazine* almost two years after this one, Dvorak, in a more pessimistic mood, noted two significant developments since he wrote "The Blog Phenomenon." One was the "wholesale abandonment of blog sites" by writers who could not be bothered to keep them up. The other was the "casual co-opting of the blog universe by Big Media." In the latter category he noted the emergence of numerous professional blog sites created by large firms such as the *Washington Post* and MSNBC. To what extent do you agree that the early enthusiasm for blogs may have been overheated? To what extend will personal blogs continue to play a significant role in the cyberspace universe of e-mail, instant messages, and the Web?

| The Intimacy of Blogs |
| Michael Snider |

In the previous selection, John C. Dvorak explains the phenomenon of blogs. In the follow-ing article, Michael Snider, a columnist for Macleans, *a Canadian (print) magazine, focuses on some of the people who have created Weblogs and discusses why they felt impelled to create their sites. Plain Layne, Rambling Rhodes, and Gudy Two Shoes: these are only three of the thousands of individuals who, through their Web sites, attract a new kind of audience. Call it ego gratification, call it therapy, call it identity creation, call it literature, Web logs are in (for now). This article first appeared in the 15 September 2003 issue of* Macleans.

1 When Plain Layne suddenly pulled her site down in early June, a little corner of the blogosphere went nuts. Instead of the 26-year-old Minnesotan's poignant daily entries on her Weblog, an on-line journal, a blunt one-line message greet-ed visitors: "Take very good care of you." No more honestly introspective nar-ratives of her life. No more unbridled entries detailing the search for her birth parents, sessions with her therapist or her disappointing love affair with Violet, the stubby-tongued Dragon Lady. Comments flooded cyberspace. "Her sur-prising, unannounced departure is sending me and my overactive imagination into a frenzy of worry," wrote Gudy Two Shoes on his own Weblog. "If she's gone then I wish her well," posted Intellectual Poison. "She got me started with this whole blogging thing, something that I am truly grateful for." And Daintily Dirty asked, "Are the relationships we create by our blogging of any value?"

2 That's a good question. It turned out that Plaine Layne, aka Layne Johnson, wasn't gone for good. She'd just had a week during which she moved into a new house and witnessed the birth of her surrogate little sister's baby before getting her site back up (*http://plainlayne.dreamhost.com*). But the reaction from her readers was genuine. One of the prime reasons people blog is to make connections with others, and when Plain Layne went missing, it was like a neighbour had just up and moved in the middle of the night, with no for-warding address.

3 Weblogs are independent Web sites usually operated by a single person or by a small group of people. They serve as frequently updated forums to discuss whatever the blogger wants to discuss. Unmonitored, each blogger is author, editor and publisher, beholden solely to his or her own whims and desires. There are political blogs, media blogs, gay blogs, sports blogs, war blogs, anti-war blogs, tech blogs, photo blogs—hundreds of thousands of blogs, actually (estimates are as high as two million). "Blogging is not people wasting other people's time talking about the minutiae of their lives," says Joe Clark, 38, a Toronto author who operates several blogs. "The thing that's attractive about reading Weblogs is that you know there is one human being or a group of human beings behind them."

4 Free and easy-to-use publishing programs with names like Blogger, Movable Type and Live Journal spurred the phenomenon. Now, anyone with a computer

and an Internet connection can set up their own blog with relative ease. Paul Martin blogs, journalists blog, pundits, critics and social misfits blog. And what can you find there? Well, imagine standing in front of a library of gargantuan magazine racks loaded with glossy covers with everything from newsweeklies to girlie mags.

5   Blogs break down into two very general groups: linking blogs and personal online journals. Political blogs like Glenn Reynolds' *Instapundit.com*, media blogs like Jim Romenesko's Poynter Online (*www.poynter.org/medianews*), or tech blogs like *slashdot.com* are of the former kind. They're link-driven sites that connect readers to theme-related news stories and sometimes add a little commentary along with it. A personal blog is more like a diary entry or column in a daily newspaper, *a la* Rebecca Eckler of the *National Post* or Leah McLaren of the *Globe and Mail*—all about "me and what I think." Writers recount events in their lives—sometimes very private ones—and air their thoughts to a public audience.

6   Reasons vary. Sometimes, the practice is therapeutic. For some, like Ryan Rhodes, who runs Rambling Rhodes (*http://ramblingrhodes.blogspot.com*), blogging has some functional purposes. Rhodes, from Rochester, Minn., is news editor for an IBM publication called *eServer Magazine* but also writes humour columns for some local newspapers. He figured blogging would be a good writing exercise that might offer him instant feedback from readers. "I like knowing the stuff I write is being read," says Rhodes, "and I like it when it hits someone in a positive way and they tell me, so I can use it later for my column."

7   Personal blogs are famous for breaking usual standards of disclosure, revealing details considered by some to be very private. Dan Gudy, a 29-year-old Berliner, kept a diary when he was a teenager but gave it up, unhappy with the results. "My first experience was a total failure," says Gudy. "It was only myself talking about myself and I do that enough." But last year, when he created his site, Gudy Two Shoes (*http://gudy.blogspot.com*), the self-described introvert discovered that blogging opened a release valve. "I had to deal with some problems at the time and somehow needed to let it out. Part of me asked, why not use a blog for that?" Now, Gudy blogs about the books he reads and bike-riding through the German countryside. He also blogs about his sex life with his wife. "People can talk about what a nice bike ride they had or what a nice meal they had, but why can't they talk about what a nice f— they had last night?"

8   For many, that very willingness to discuss intimate details is one of the most alluring facets of blogging. "Your Weblog becomes an exterior part of you," says Clark, "so you can have some distance from your feelings, even though you're putting them out for everyone to read. But then all your readers are right up close and they know you because you're writing directly to them." In turn, readers can offer their own feedback: personal blogs frequently allow them to comment after each post, with something as easy as clicking a link that opens a pop-up box where they can add their own two cents' worth. "When I first started blogging," writes Daintily Dirty (*http://www.blogdreams.blogspot.com*), an anonymous 32-year-old blogger who chatted with *Macleans* via instant messenger, "I had no idea what I was getting into with the personal nature of the interactions. But the connections you find are what keep you coming back."

9   Layne Johnson's readers can attest to that. An excellent narrative writer who opens her soul to her readers, Plain Layne's daily entries regularly receive dozens of comments. "I hopped from one blog to the next and somewhere found Plain Layne," says Gudy. "What made me stay was her brutal honesty and intimacy of sharing, her very beautiful way of writing." Rhodes echoes the sentiment. "Layne is digital crack," he says. "Hands down, as far as I've read, she's got the best personal blog. I have to read her every day."

10   Johnson politely turned down a request for an interview, explaining her blogging is a personal exercise that's meant to be cathartic. And somehow, that's the way it should be. Plain Layne does her talking, or typing, on her blog. "I think the hardest thing about sharing your life on-line is that at some point you discover people know you," Johnson wrote in a June post. "They know you from the inside out, the way your mind works, what makes you laugh or cry, your hopes and fears." It's clear to see she uses her blog as an outlet, a place to dump her anxiety and frustration in a search for identity and understanding. It's also a place of amusement and mirth, with stories of stupefying office meetings and uproarious golf outings, all told with a flair and talent that would make some "me" columnists envious.

11   Blogs might seem too revealing for people who prefer their diaries to remain private. But more and more strangers are inviting millions of other strangers into their lives, with a willingness to share just about anything, finding their own shelf space on the world's most accessible magazine rack, open to anyone who cares to pick up a copy. Welcome to the blogosphere.

Review Questions

1. What is the rhetorical function of Snider's opening anecdote about Plain Layne?

2. How does Snider categorize the two general groups of blogs?

3. What are the main uses of blogging, according to Snider?

Discussion and Writing Suggestions

1. Have you or someone you know created a blog? If so, describe its contents and its format.

2. Check out Plain Layne <http://plainlayne.dreamhost.com>, Rambling Rhodes <ramblingrhodes.blogspot.com>, Gudy Two Shoes <gudy.blogspot.com>, or another site mentioned by Snider. Write a one- to two-page report on what you find, describing the site. What kind of personality appears to be authoring the site?

3. Examine a particular blog site and assess it, providing analysis and evaluation, and offering suggestions for its improvement.

A Shared Sadness
Russ Parsons

Most e-mail messages are private communications between a sender and one or more specifically designated recipients. Increasingly popular, however, are public electronic forums, such as chat groups, bulletin boards, newsgroups, the Usenet, and "Multi-User Domains" (MUDs). These groups, or electronic communities, are generally organized around particular personal or professional interests—e.g., Shakespeare studies, cancer survival, environmental issues, online romance. In these forums, to which users generally register or subscribe, senders post messages that can be read by all members of the group, and to which any member can respond. New and old members can also read discussion "threads" that transpired among members of the group days or even months ago.

In the following article, Los Angeles Times *staff writer Russ Parsons recounts one such discussion thread concerning a person he had never met, but whose fate touched him, and many others, deeply. Parsons's article offers another perspective on how electronic communication has helped foster new ways of relating to one another, has helped create new communities of like-minded individuals. "A Shared Sadness" first appeared in the* Los Angeles Times *on 7 August 1998.*

1   People who haven't spent much time there seem to imagine cyberspace as their own private nightmare brought to life. To some people it is a scary place, full of predators of one stripe or another. To some it is a virtual Gomorrah, a RAM-charged peep show catering to unimaginable perversions.

2   Others fear it as a cold place, a place of separation peopled only by the lonely, locked in their own little worlds. Though they may talk to one another, do they communicate?

3   "What about a sense of community?" asked a friend of mine the other day. "What about things like communication on shared subjects other than the narrow topics at hand, those things that provide the glue that transforms a group of people into a community?" (He is a professor, and he does talk that way.)

4   So I told him about Gary Holleman. Gary helped start one of the Internet discussion groups, or chat lists, I belong to. A chat list, for the uninitiated, is kind of like an ongoing letter dedicated to a specific topic. If you have something to say about that topic, you e-mail your comment to a central computer, which then forwards it to everyone else on the list. If they have something to add, they can either respond to you privately or send another message back to the central computer.

5   You can find a chat list for just about any special interest imaginable. I belong to five: one devoted to mysteries, one for wine, one for the organization Slow Food, one for cookbooks and another—the one Holleman started—for chefs and cooks.

6   There are a couple of hundred people who are on the list: not all of them are chefs and cooks. Some are culinary students or work in related fields. Some are merely curious eavesdroppers (called lurkers).

7   Conversations—that is the only way to describe them—cover everything from practical matters like Alto-Sham slow cookers (from context, I gather that this is a kind of steam oven used in production kitchens) to a rather heated philosophical argument about whether cooking is an art or a craft. At any one time, several of these topics (called threads) are happening at the same time.

8   One day early last October, in the midst of these workaday discussions, there was a note titled "Gary Holleman's Broken Heart." In it, with surprising wit and panache (we're talking chefs, remember?), Gary, a corporate chef who did product research and development, informed us that he had suddenly learned he needed some heart surgery.

9   *As you may or may not know, I recently found out that I need some spare parts for my heart—an operation that my doctors perform every day and is analogous to a medical "slam-dunk." However, for my friends, family and especially me, the prospects are somewhat more intimidating.*

10   The problem, he wrote, began at lunch at a food conference in Portland, Ore.:

11   *"The mean age of the population is gradually moving upward, and with it a new concern for fat-free, heart-healthy foods," the luncheon speaker from Noble Assn. said as he discussed food trends for the late 1990s. The woman next to me was full of questions for me about the Internet. I heard neither the speaker nor my lunch partner. My heart felt as if it were jumping through my chest. I was sure I had taken on a cartoonish figure [and that] everyone in the room could see my heart beating two feet in front of my body. In fact, I was worried my heart had invaded the personal space of the gentleman across the table.*

12   The problem recurred the next morning. He called his doctor back home in Minnesota and was told to go immediately to a cardiologist. There he learned that he had a leaky heart valve and would need to have open-heart surgery within a couple of weeks. Since the nearest major medical center was in Fargo, N.D., that's where he headed.

13   *I was stunned. The doctor says I have a four-plus aortic insufficiency (on a scale of one to four, four being the worst). While over the past year I had been unable to keep up my 15–20-miles-a-week jogging schedule, I had no idea that the problem was a lack of oxygen due to a broken heart. I thought I was just getting old.*

14   After a couple of days of tests, he was told there was a complication: He also had an enlarged aortic artery that might have to be replaced as well.

15   *"While not technically difficult, this would be a much more complex operation," Dr. Damle said with his beautiful East Indian accent. Complex means longer. And slightly more risk, I assume.*

16   To keep everyone updated on his progress, Gary created a small mailing list that he would post to regularly. If we sent him a note, he'd add our names.

17   I didn't know Gary and, to be perfectly honest, his name hadn't registered from his postings in the past. His was a face in the crowd of postings that comes through my computer every day—someone I saw every day but never thought much about.

18   But I was touched by the hopeful, funny tone of the note. It was a nice piece of writing. I sent him a note, telling him so and suggested that when it was all over, he should collect these essays for a book. That got me on the list.

19   The next day another missive arrived.

20   *Can a heartbroken man in Minnesota find happiness in a Fargo operating room? Read on.*

21   *"Allergic to any foods?" the intake nurse asked as she diligently filled out the proper forms.*

22   *"No, but I am a vegetarian. Ovolacto," I replied.*

23   *"A chef AND a vegetarian?"*

24   *An hour later the food arrived. A splendid vegetarian feast—sort of. One cup of hot, canned, diced beets. Another cup of hot, canned, diced beets. One scoop of instant mashed potatoes (I recognize the flavor: NIFDA Red Label). Another scoop of instant mashed potatoes.*

25   There was worse news than lunch, though.

26   *The CT scan is in, and the results are clear. I have an aortic aneurysm. "The walls of the aortic artery are weak and enlarged. I am sure that is what is causing the failure of the valve," said Dr. Damle.*

27   *The word "aneurysm" was not what I wanted to hear. It means, in Damle's words, that "we have increased the magnitude of the operation significantly." This means more risk, and, as I think it, he says it.*

28   Gary sounded more upbeat after the weekend.

29   *The "rose-colored glasses" in pill form prescribed by my surgeon, also known as antianxiety medicine, are working well. I know this for several reasons:*

30   *(1) I just traveled 500 miles round-trip over 24 hours with three of my teens and my wife, and I still think I have had an absolutely marvelous weekend. We went to visit my four grandkids. Yes, at 42 years old I am too young for either heart surgery or grandkids, but I am blessed with both. However, I don't think there is a correlation.*

31   *(2) I also know the antianxiety medicine is working because I have forgotten what I had anxiety about in the first place.*

32   Well, not entirely. He told of talking with one of his kids over lunch.

33   *"So, did your mother tell you there has been a change in plans for the operation? I need more extensive surgery."*

34   *"Yeah, I guess I heard. But it's still routine surgery, right?"*

35   *It's always a hard thing to know, much less tell someone else, just how risky an operation is. There is always balance—honesty and plain talk countered by hope, comfort and matter-of-factness.*

36   *"Well, yes, routine . . . I guess." How routine can open-heart surgery get, I wonder?*

37   *"Oh, that's good."*

38   *"But you know when we talked before, I said it was a slam-dunk medical procedure? Well, now it's more like a three-point shot."*

39   *I see the panic in his eyes. He is remembering how well I play basketball. In fact, I am remembering how well I play basketball. Thinking quickly, I add, "But, uh, Michael Jordan is taking the three-point shot!" The concern fades from his face, and we eat our salads in silence.*

40   The next post was full of news of the next day's surgery. It turns out that because of the location of the aneurysm, the surgery was going to be even more complex to avoid starving the brain of blood.

41   *The risk here is substantial. It's starting to feel more like a half-court shot by a random spectator trying to win a million dollars. I exaggerate. The doctor I have chosen is the finest doctor in North Dakota for this type of operation. (OK, I admit it. There aren't that many doctors in N.D., but Damle is excellent.)*

42   Getting ready for the surgery, he and his wife, Lois, rented a suite in a hotel across the street from the hospital. Since there was a kitchen, why not fix dinner? It had to be better than hospital food.

43   *My only disappointment making dinner was a result of the apparent dearth of fresh basil in Fargo, N.D. We went to Hornbacher's grocery store—the biggest in town—only to find REALLY shabby looking herbs, none of which resembled basil. I inquired at the checkout counter.*

44   *"Where is the best produce section in town?" I asked the checkout person. She thought for a moment, as if it were a trick question. "Uh, here?"*

45   *"Excuse me, I don't THINK so. Not in a MILLION YEARS! Your herbs look like they are left over from the floods of '97! They look like they went THROUGH the floods!" I could feel my blood pressure rising. And then I remember that I forgot to take my midday antianxiety pill.*

46   *And that brings me to the night before the dawn that has consumed my thoughts for the last two weeks. The blood tests are in. The doctor is ready. My family is by my side. I have my Ambien sleeping pills. And from reading the flood of e-mail I have received, I know my friends are thinking of me and praying for me. It is not generally my nature to try and attract attention (in the grocery store, from my friends or God for that matter), but I am indeed comforted and joyful over the love and affection that has been uploaded to my little port on the Net. Thank you, God bless you all. I'll key you soon.*

47   The next day, in order to keep calls to the family at a minimum, a member of the chat list was designated to act as go-between. I checked in every hour to see how Gary was doing.

48   There were constant updates. First:

49   *The surgery is taking longer than expected, but that's not necessarily a bad sign.*

50   Then:

51   *I have just spoken with the nurse's station, and Gary has been returned to surgery. I am hoping things are going well, but this may be the time to start praying.*

52   It got worse.

53   *Gary is in very, very critical condition. Please stop what you are doing for just a moment and pray however and to whomever you do it.*

54   By 4, it seemed a corner had been turned.

55   *Gary is out of surgery. His heart is being supported by a left ventricular assist device. He is much improved. He is currently in intensive care and will be in the recovery room soon.*

56   But at 5:

57   *I just spoke with Lois. Gary has been taken back into surgery for the third time. She does not know for what. We all continue to hope and pray.*

58   A couple of minutes later:

59   *I just spoke to Gary's brother Michael, and Gary's condition has taken an unforeseen turn toward critical.*

60   After that, a maddening silence. I found things to straighten up around my desk, staying late and doing busy work in between logging on to check for news. Finally, just after 7:

61   *Gary Holleman left us half an hour ago. We all loved him.*

62   Messages flew back and forth as the news spread. It seemed everyone had been doing just what I had been doing—staying close to the computer to check in. The next day—Oct. 22, 1997—was declared a day of silence in Gary's honor. We took up a collection for his children and—this being cyberspace, again—someone added a tribute section to his home page where anyone who wanted could write a note about Gary.

63   Just like anyplace else, we grieved for a friend we'd lost and knew that our little community had been changed forever.

Review Questions

1. What is a chat list?

2. Summarize "A Shared Sadness." Avoid direct quotations, but try to convey the sense of the changing circumstances of Holleman's condition, particularly once he undergoes surgery.

Discussion and Writing Suggestions

1. Discuss the significance of the title "A Shared Sadness." In your discussion consider how Parsons uses the word "community." What kind of community developed in the wake of Holleman's illness and surgery? How was this virtual community different from what we generally think of as a "community"? How would you characterize the distinctive identity of the members of the community that followed the news of Holleman's changing condition?

2. Many people who have read this article have found it unusually touching. Given that thousands of people die of heart disease every year, which aspects of "A Shared Sadness" make the story of this particular death so moving?

3. The Web site on Gary Holleman referred to in this article no longer exists, but other sites devoted to Holleman do. (You can conduct a search to find them on Google.com.) Read some of the postings by those who knew Holleman, either in person, or through the chat list, and write a short account of what you find.

4. Have you ever been in the waiting room or been waiting at home while someone you know underwent major surgery? Describe your reactions and the reactions of others around you, or others you were in contact with, as the surgery approached, and as news of its progress filtered out. To what extent were your reactions similar to those of Parsons and his virtual community?

Virtual Love
Meghan Daum

Star vehicles like You've Got Mail *aside, the popular media abounds with stories—some inspirational, some cautionary—about online romances. In a typical pattern, couples first meet one another in public chat rooms, then retire to private spaces for one-on-one e-mail conversations, then at some point, perhaps, "progress" to cybersex. (In no small number of cases, one or both parties are already married, and the discovery of the online romance by the outraged spouse leads to divorce. Question: Does engaging in an online, entirely text-based romance constitute infidelity to one's spouse or significant other?) Many of these relationships remain at a virtual level; in other cases, couples begin communicating by telephone, and then, perhaps, decide to meet one other in person. Some of these stories have happy endings; most don't. Disappointment seems almost a given: even in those cases not involving outright fraud or misrepresentation (a male representing himself as female, a 50-year-old married woman representing herself as a 30-year-old single, a request by one party to the other for "travel expenses"), the reality is seldom able to match the expectation raised by the intoxication of an idealized cyberromance.*

Online dating originates not only in special-interest chat rooms but also in numerous matchmaking sites on the Web, like Matchmaker.com, AmericanSingles.com, Altmatch.com, CatholicSingles.com, and ThirdAge.com. One site, Match.com, takes credit for about a thousand weddings that have resulted from couples meeting at its site. In the following article, the author describes how she met her partner in yet another way: when he unexpectedly e-mailed her after reading some of her published work. The progress of this relationship is detailed in "Virtual Love." Meghan Daum is a freelance writer whose articles have appeared in such magazines as Harper's, Vogue, *and the* New Yorker. *This article first appeared in the 25 August–1 September 1997 issue of the* New Yorker.

1   It was last November; fall was drifting away into an intolerable chill. I was at the end of my twenty-sixth year, and was living in New York City, trying to support myself as a writer, and taking part in the kind of urban life that might be construed as glamorous were it to appear in a memoir in the distant future. At the time, however, my days felt more like a grind than like an adventure: hours of work strung between the motions of waking up, getting the mail, watching TV with my roommates, and going to bed. One morning, I logged on to my America Online account to find a message under the heading "is this the real meghan daum?" It came from someone with the screen name PFSlider. The body of the message consisted of five sentences, written entirely in lowercase letters, of perfectly turned flattery: something about PFSlider's admiration of

some newspaper and magazine articles I had published over the last year and a half, something about his resulting infatuation with me, and something about his being a sportswriter in California.

2   I was engaged for the thirty seconds that it took me to read the message and fashion a reply. Though it felt strange to be in the position of confirming that I was indeed "the real meghan daum," I managed to say, "Yes, it's me. Thank you for writing." I clicked the "Send Now" icon, shot my words into the void, and forgot about PFSlider until the next day, when I received another message, this one headed "eureka."

3   "wow, it is you," he wrote, still in lowercase. He chronicled the various conditions under which he'd read my few-and-far-between articles—a boardwalk in Laguna Beach, the spring-training pressroom for a baseball team that he covered for a Los Angeles newspaper. He confessed to having a crush on me. He referred to me as "princess daum." He said he wanted to have lunch with me during one of his two annual trips to New York.

4   The letter was outrageous and endearingly pathetic, possibly the practical joke of a friend trying to rouse me out of a temporary writer's block. But the kindness pouring forth from my computer screen was bizarrely exhilarating, and I logged off and thought about it for a few hours before writing back to express how flattered and "touched"—this was probably the first time I had ever used that word in earnest—I was by his message.

5   I am not what most people would call a computer person. I have no interest in chat rooms, newsgroups, or most Web sites. I derive a palpable thrill from sticking a letter in the United States mail. But I have a constant low-grade fear of the telephone, and I often call people with the intention of getting their answering machines. There is something about the live voice that I have come to find unnervingly organic, as volatile as live television. E-mail provides a useful antidote for my particular communication anxieties. Though I generally send and receive only a few messages a week, I take comfort in their silence and their boundaries.

6   PFSlider and I tossed a few innocuous, smart-assed notes back and forth over the week following his first message. Let's say his name was Pete. He was twenty-nine, and single. I revealed very little about myself, relying instead on the ironic commentary and forced witticisms that are the conceit of so many E-mail messages. But I quickly developed an oblique affection for PFSlider. I was excited when there was a message from him, mildly depressed when there wasn't. After a few weeks, he gave me his phone number. I did not give him mine, but he looked it up and called me one Friday night. I was home. I picked up the phone. His voice was jarring, yet not unpleasant. He held up more than his end of the conversation for an hour, and when he asked permission to call me again I granted it, as though we were of an earlier era.

7   Pete—I could never wrap my mind around his name, privately thinking of him as PFSlider, "E-mail guy," or even "baseball boy"—began phoning me two or three times a week. He asked if he could meet me, and I said that that would be O.K. Christmas was a few weeks away, and he told me that he would be coming back East to see his family. From there, he would take a short flight to

New York and have lunch with me.

8   "It is my off-season mission to meet you," he said.

9   "There will probably be a snowstorm," I said.

10   "I'll take a team of sled dogs," he answered.

11   We talked about our work and our families, about baseball and Bill Clinton and Howard Stern and sex, about his hatred for Los Angeles and how much he wanted a new job. Sometimes we'd find each other logged on simultaneously and type back and forth for hours.

12   I had previously considered cyber-communication an oxymoron, a fast road to the breakdown of humanity. But, curiously, the Internet—at least in the limited form in which I was using it—felt anything but dehumanizing. My interaction with PFSlider seemed more authentic than much of what I experienced in the daylight realm of living beings. I was certainly putting more energy into the relationship than I had put into many others. I also was giving Pete attention that was by definition undivided, and relishing the safety of the distance between us by opting to be truthful instead of doling out the white lies that have become the staple of real life. The outside world—the place where I walked around avoiding people I didn't want to deal with, peppering my casual conversations with half-truths, and applying my motto "Let the machine take it" to almost any scenario—was sliding into the periphery of my mind.

13   For me, the time on-line with Pete was far superior to the phone. There were no background noises, no interruptions from "call waiting," no long-distance charges. Through typos and misspellings, he flirted maniacally. "I have an absurd crush on you," he said. "If I like you in person, you must promise to marry me." I was coy and conceited, telling him to get a life, baiting him into complimenting me further, teasing him in a way I would never have dared to do in person, or even on the phone. I would stay up until 3 A.M. typing with him, smiling at the screen, getting so giddy that when I quit I couldn't fall asleep. I was having difficulty recalling what I used to do at night. It was as if he and I lived together in our own quiet space—a space made all the more intimate because of our conscious decision to block everyone else out. My phone was tied up for hours at a time. No one in the real world could reach me, and I didn't really care.

14   Since my last serious relationship, I'd had the requisite number of false starts and five-night stands, dates that I wasn't sure were dates, and emphatically casual affairs that buckled under their own inertia. With PFSlider, on the other hand, I may not have known my suitor, but, for the first time in my life, I knew the deal: I was a desired person, the object of a blind man's gaze. He called not only when he said he would call but unexpectedly, just to say hello. He was protected by the shield of the Internet; his guard was not merely down but nonexistent. He let his phone bill grow to towering proportions. He told me that he thought about me all the time, though we both knew that the "me" in his mind consisted largely of himself. He talked about me to his friends, and admitted it. He arranged his holiday schedule around our impending date. He managed to charm me with sports analogies. He didn't hesitate. He was unblinking and unapologetic, all nerviness and balls to the wall.

15   And so PFSlider became my everyday life. All the tangible stuff fell away. My body did not exist. I had no skin, no hair, no bones. All desire had convert- ed itself into a cerebral current that reached nothing but my frontal lobe. There was no outdoors, no social life, no weather. There was only the computer screen and the phone, my chair, and maybe a glass of water. Most mornings, I would wake up to find a message from PFSlider, composed in Pacific time while I slept in the wee hours. "I had a date last night," he wrote. "And I am not ashamed to say it was doomed from the start because I couldn't stop thinking about you."

16   I fired back a message slapping his hand. "We must be careful where we tread," I said. This was true but not sincere. I wanted it, all of it. I wanted unfet- tered affection, soul-mating, true romance. In the weeks that had elapsed since I picked up "is this the real meghan daum?" the real me had undergone some kind of meltdown—a systemic rejection of all the savvy and independence I had worn for years, like a grownup Girl Scout badge.

17   Pete knew nothing of my scattered, juvenile self, and I did my best to keep it that way. Even though I was heading into my late twenties, I was still a child, ignorant of dance steps and health insurance, a prisoner of credit-card debt and student loans and the nagging feeling that I didn't want anyone to find me until I had pulled myself into some semblance of an adult. The fact that Pete had literally seemed to discover me, as if by turning over a rock, lent us an aura of fate which I actually took half-seriously. Though skepticism seemed like the obvious choice in this strange situation, I discarded it precisely because it was the obvious choice, because I wanted a more interesting nar- rative than cynicism would ever allow. I was a true believer in the urban dream: the dream of years of struggle, of getting a break, of making it. Like most of my friends, I wanted someone to love me, but I wasn't supposed to need it. To admit to loneliness was to smack the face of progress, to betray the times in which we lived. But PFSlider derailed me. He gave me all of what I'd never even realized I wanted.

18   My addiction to PFSlider's messages indicated a monstrous narcissism, but it also revealed a subtler desire, which I didn't fully understand at the time. My need to experience an old-fashioned kind of courtship was stronger than I had ever imagined. And the fact that technology was providing an avenue for such archaic discourse was a paradox that both fascinated and repelled me. Our rela- tionship had an epistolary quality that put our communication closer to the eigh- teenth century than to the impending millennium. Thanks to the computer, I was involved in a well-defined courtship, a neat little space in which he and I were both safe to express the panic and the fascination of our mutual affection. Our interaction was refreshingly orderly, noble in its vigor, dignified despite its shamelessness. It was far removed from the randomness of real-life relation- ships. We had an intimacy that seemed custom-made for our strange, lonely times. It seemed custom-made for me.

19   The day of our date, a week before Christmas, was frigid and sunny. Pete was sitting at the bar of the restaurant when I arrived. We shook hands. For a split second, he leaned toward me with his chin, as if to kiss me. He was shorter than I had pictured, though he was not short. He struck me as clean-cut. He had

very nice hands. He wore a very nice shirt. We were seated at a very nice table. I scanned the restaurant for people I knew, saw none, and couldn't decide how I felt about that.

20   He talked, and I heard nothing he said. I stared at his profile and tried to figure out whether I liked him. He seemed to be saying nothing in particular, but he went on forever. Later, we went to the Museum of Natural History and watched a science film about storm chasers. We walked around looking for the dinosaurs, and he talked so much that I wanted to cry. Outside, walking along Central Park West at dusk, through the leaves, past the yellow cabs and the splendid lights of Manhattan at Christmas, he grabbed my hand to kiss me and I didn't let him. I felt as if my brain had been stuffed with cotton. Then, for some reason, I invited him back to my apartment. I gave him a few beers and finally let him kiss me on the lumpy futon in my bedroom. The radiator clanked. The phone rang and the machine picked up. A car alarm blared outside. A key turned in the door as one of my roommates came home. I had no sensation at all—only a clear conviction that I wanted Pete out of my apartment. I wanted to hand him his coat, close the door behind him, and fight the ensuing empti- ness by turning on the computer and taking comfort in PFSlider.

21   When Pete finally did leave, I berated myself from every angle: for not kiss- ing him on Central Park West, for letting him kiss me at all, for not liking him, for wanting to like him more than I had wanted anything in such a long time. I was horrified by the realization that I had invested so heavily in a made-up charac- ter—a character in whose creation I'd had a greater hand than even Pete him- self. How could I, a person so self-congratulatingly reasonable, have been sucked into a scenario that was more akin to a television talk show than to the relatively full and sophisticated life I was so convinced I led? How could I have received a fan letter and allowed it to go this far?

22   The next day, a huge bouquet of FTD flowers arrived from him. No one had ever sent me flowers before. I forgave him. As human beings with actual flesh and hand gestures and Gap clothing, Pete and I were utterly incompatible, but I decided to pretend otherwise. He returned home and we fell back into the computer and the phone, and I continued to keep the real world safely away from the desk that held them. Instead of blaming him for my disappointment, I blamed the earth itself, the invasion of roommates and ringing phones into the immaculate communication that PFSlider and I had created.

23   When I pictured him in the weeks that followed, I saw the image of a plane lifting off over an overcast city. PFSlider was otherworldly, more a concept than a person. His romance lay in the notion of flight, the physics of gravity defiance. So when he offered to send me a plane ticket to spend the weekend with him in Los Angeles I took it as an extension of our blissful remoteness, a three- dimensional E-mail message lasting an entire weekend.

24   The temperature on the runway at J.F.K. was seven degrees Fahrenheit. Our DC-10 sat for three hours waiting for deicing. Finally, it took off over the frozen city, and the ground below shrank into a drawing of itself. Phone calls were made, laptop computers were plopped onto tray tables. The recirculating air dried out my contact lenses. I watched movies without the sound and told myself that they were probably better that way. Something about the plastic

interior of the fuselage and the plastic forks and the din of the air and the engines was soothing and strangely sexy.

25   Then we descended into LAX. We hit the tarmac, and the seat-belt signs blinked off. I hadn't moved my body in eight hours, and now I was walking through the tunnel to the gate, my clothes wrinkled, my hair matted, my hands shaking. When I saw Pete in the terminal, his face seemed to me just as blank and easy to miss as it had the first time I'd met him. He kissed me chastely. On the way out to the parking lot, he told me that he was being seriously considered for a job in New York. He was flying back there next week. If he got the job, he'd be moving within the month. I looked at him in astonishment. Something silent and invisible seemed to fall on us. Outside, the wind was warm, and the Avis and Hertz buses ambled alongside the curb of Terminal 5. The palm trees shook, and the air seemed as heavy and palpable as Pete's hand, which held mine for a few seconds before dropping it to get his car keys out of his pocket. He stood before me, all flesh and preoccupation, and for this I could not forgive him.

26   Gone were the computer, the erotic darkness of the telephone, the clean, single dimension of Pete's voice at 1 A.M. It was nighttime, yet the combination of sight and sound was blinding. It scared me. It turned me off. We went to a restaurant and ate outside on the sidewalk. We strained for conversation, and I tried not to care that we had to. We drove to his apartment and stood under the ceiling light not really looking at each other. Something was happening that we needed to snap out of. Any moment now, I thought. Any moment and we'll be all right. These moments were crowded with elements, with carpet fibers and automobiles and the smells of everything that had a smell. It was all wrong. The physical world had invaded our space.

27   For three days, we crawled along the ground and tried to pull ourselves up. We talked about things that I can no longer remember. We read the Los Angeles *Times* over breakfast. We drove north past Santa Barbara to tour the wine country. I felt like an object that could not be lifted, something that secretly weighed more than the world itself. Everything and everyone around us seemed imbued with a California lightness. I stomped around the countryside, an idiot New Yorker in my clunky shoes and black leather jacket. Not until I studied myself in the bathroom mirror of a highway rest stop did I fully realize the preposterousness of my uniform. I was dressed for war. I was dressed for my regular life.

28   That night, in a tiny town called Solvang, we ate an expensive dinner. We checked into a Marriott and watched television. Pete talked at me and through me and past me. I tried to listen. I tried to talk. But I bored myself and irritated him. Our conversation was a needle that could not be threaded. Still, we played nice. We tried to care, and pretended to keep trying long after we had given up. In the car on the way home, he told me that I was cynical, and I didn't have the presence of mind to ask him just how many cynics he had met who would travel three thousand miles to see someone they barely knew.

29   Pete drove me to the airport at 7 A.M. so I could make my eight-o'clock flight home. He kissed me goodbye—another chaste peck that I recognized from countless dinner parties and dud dates. He said that he'd call me in a few days when he got to New York for his job interview, which we had discussed only

in passing and with no reference to the fact that New York was where I happened to live. I returned home to frozen January. A few days later, he came to New York, and we didn't see each other. He called me from the plane taking him back to Los Angeles to tell me, through the static, that he had got the job. He was moving to my city.

30   PFSlider was dead. There would be no meeting him in distant hotel lobbies during the baseball season. There would be no more phone calls or E-mail messages. In a single moment, Pete had completed his journey out of our mating dance and officially stepped into the regular world—the world that gnawed at me daily, the world that fostered those five-night stands, the world where romance could not be sustained, because so many of us simply did not know how to do it. Instead, we were all chitchat and leather jackets, bold proclaimers of all that we did not need. But what struck me most about this affair was the unpredictable nature of our demise. Unlike most cyber-romances, which seem to come fully equipped with the inevitable set of misrepresentations and false expectations, PFSlider and I had played it fairly straight. Neither of us had lied. We'd done the best we could. Our affair had died from natural causes rather than virtual ones.

31   Within a two-week period after I returned from Los Angeles, at least seven people confessed to me the vagaries of their own E-mail affairs. This topic arose, unprompted, in the course of normal conversation. I heard most of these stories in the close confines of smoky bars and crowded restaurants, and we all shook our heads in bewilderment as we told our tales, our eyes focused on some point in the distance. Four of these people had met their correspondents, by traveling from New Haven to Baltimore, from New York to Montana, from Texas to Virginia, and from New York to Johannesburg. These were normal people, writers and lawyers and scientists. They were all smart, attractive, and more than a little sheepish about admitting just how deeply they had been sucked in. Mostly, it was the courtship ritual that had seduced us. E-mail had become an electronic epistle, a yearned-for rule book. It allowed us to do what was necessary to experience love. The Internet was not responsible for our remote, fragmented lives. The problem was life itself.

32   The story of PFSlider still makes me sad, not so much because we no longer have anything to do with each other but because it forces me to see the limits and the perils of daily life with more clarity than I used to. After I realized that our relationship would never transcend the screen and the phone—that, in fact, our face-to-face knowledge of each other had permanently contaminated the screen and the phone—I hit the pavement again, went through the motions of everyday life, said hello and goodbye to people in the regular way. If Pete and I had met at a party, we probably wouldn't have spoken to each other for more than ten minutes, and that would have made life easier but also less interesting. At the same time, it terrifies me to admit to a firsthand understanding of the way the heart and the ego are snarled and entwined like diseased trees that have folded in on each other. Our need to worship somehow fuses with our need to be worshipped. It upsets me still further to see how inaccessibility can make this entanglement so much more intoxicating. But I'm also thankful that

I was forced to unpack the raw truth of my need and stare at it for a while. It was a dare I wouldn't have taken in three dimensions.

33   The last time I saw Pete, he was in New York, three thousand miles away from what had been his home, and a million miles away from PFSlider. In a final gesture of decency, in what I later realized was the most ordinary kind of closure, he took me out to dinner. As the few remaining traces of affection turned into embarrassed regret, we talked about nothing. He paid the bill. He drove me home in a rental car that felt as arbitrary and impersonal as what we now were to each other.

34   Pete had known how to get me where I lived until he came to where I lived: then he became as unmysterious as anyone next door. The world had proved to be too cluttered and too fast for us, too polluted to allow the thing we'd attempted through technology ever to grow in the earth. PFSlider and I had joined the angry and exhausted living. Even if we met on the street, we wouldn't recognize each other, our particular version of intimacy now obscured by the branches and bodies and falling debris that make up the physical world.

Discussion and Writing Suggestions

1. Daum remarks that, contrary to what she had previously assumed about cybercommunication, her e-mail correspondence with Pete was "anything but dehumanizing. My interaction with PFSlider seemed more authentic than much of what I experienced in the daylight realm of living beings. I was certainly putting more energy into the relationship than I had put into many others" (paragraph 12). To what extent have you experienced this same reaction to virtual correspondence (if not virtual romance)? How do you account for this phenomenon?

2. To what extent do you see the problems that developed between Daum and PFSlider a result of the new identities that each had created for the other in an effort to nurture and sustain their relationship? To what extent did the Internet make the creation of such identities possible—in a way that, for example, phone conversations, letters, or earlier face-to-face meetings, might have made less easy?

3. Daum writes that PFSlider told her that "he thought about me all the time, though we both knew that the 'me' in his mind consisted largely of himself" (paragraph 14). What do you think she means? In what sense did they "both" know this? Do you think that this statement would have been less true had Pete and she first encountered one another face-to-face? Or if they had first made contact by letter and telephone rather than by e-mail?

4. Daum notes that as her virtual relationship developed, "the real me had undergone some kind of meltdown—a systematic rejection of

all the savvy and independence I had worn for years, like a grownup Girl Scout badge" (paragraph 16). Why do you think this happened? To what extent do your own experiences or those of others you know bear out this phenomenon? To what extent is the Internet (as opposed to the power of new romance, virtual or old-fashioned) the key factor in causing such a "meltdown"?

5. How do you account for the particular way in which Daum's relationship developed, both before and after she and Pete physically met? Consider, in particular, Daum's reflections to herself (paragraph 21) immediately after their first date. Was the relationship doomed from the start, because of the unrealistic expectations that each had developed, or might people different from these particular two have been able to sustain their relationship over the long term? To what extent does Daum's case provide a general lesson about online romances?

6. Daum remarks (paragraph 30) that her affair with Pete "died from natural causes rather than virtual ones." And she concludes (paragraph 34) that her and Pete's "particular version of intimacy [was] now obscured by the branches and bodies and falling debris that make up the physical world." What do you think she means by these statements? What were the "natural causes"? What are the "branches and bodies and falling debris"?

Cyberspace and Identity
Sherry Turkle

What we think of as our identity is generally our unique inner self—that core personality that makes us different from our friends, our brothers or sisters, even our identical twin. Not only do we like to think of our identity as unique, but we also see it as unified and whole. People who have multiple personalities, like those we read about in the cases of The Three Faces of Eve or Sybil, are clinical aberrations. Increasingly, however, this view of the unitary self is being challenged. We have long known that personalities can fragment; but it is only recently that the concept of fragmented or "decentered" selves has been seen not only as normal but actually as psychologically healthy. Certainly, in some extreme cases, the personality can fragment to the point where the individual cannot function normally (particularly if one personality is not aware of the existence of the others). But if Superman and his alternate identity Clark Kent can healthfully coexist in the same body, then why not DrJane and Hellraiser as two different screen names of a single Internet subscriber? It is not that one side of the self excludes the other; it is rather that both (or in fact several) sides are aspects of the same individual, and there is no reason why one cannot "cycle through" the various sides of oneself while remaining a balanced, functioning member of society.

In the following article, sociologist Sherry Turkle explores this concept of multiple identity, as it has been fostered by the development of cyberspace communication. Turkle did her undergraduate work at Radcliffe College and earned a joint doctorate in sociology and personality psychology from Harvard University in 1976. A licensed clinical psychologist, Turkle is Professor of the Sociology of Science in the Program in Science, Technology, and Society at the Massachusetts Institute of Technology. One of the most highly regarded authorities in the field, Turkle has written numerous articles on computer technologies and virtual communities in such periodicals as the Utne Reader, Sociological Inquiry, Social Research, Sciences, American Prospect, Signs, *and* Daedalus. *Her books include* Psychoanalytic Politics: Jacques Lacan and Freud's French Revolution *(1981),* The Second Self: Computers and the Human Spirit *(1984), and* Life on the Screen: Identity in the Age of the Internet *(1995). In 1995 she was selected by* Newsweek *as one of the "50 For the Future: the Most Influential People to Watch in Cyberspace." Turkle has been featured on the cover of* Wired *(April 1996) and* Technology Review *(February/March 1996). She has also been profiled in* Scientific American *(April 1998) and the* New York Times *(18 June 1998). This article, originally entitled "Looking Toward Cyberspace: Beyond Grounded Sociology: Cyberspace and Identity," first appeared in* Contemporary Sociology *in November 1999.*

1   We come to see ourselves differently as we catch sight of our images in the mirror of the machine. Over a decade ago, when I first called the computer a "second self" (1984), these identity-transforming relationships were most usually one-on-one, a person alone with a machine. This is no longer the case. A rapidly expanding system of networks, collectively known as the Internet, links millions of people together in new spaces that are changing the way we think, the nature of our sexuality, the form of our communities, our very identities. In cyberspace, we are learning to live in virtual worlds. We may find ourselves alone as we navigate virtual oceans, unravel virtual mysteries, and engineer virtual skyscrapers. But increasingly, when we step through the looking glass, other people are there as well.

2   Over the past decade, I have been engaged in the ethnographic and clinical study of how people negotiate the virtual and the "real" as they represent themselves on computer screens linked through the Internet. For many people, such experiences challenge what they have traditionally called "identity," which they are moved to recast in terms of multiple windows and parallel lives. Online life is not the only factor that is pushing them in this direction; there is no simple sense in which computers are causing a shift in notions of identity. It is, rather, that today's life on the screen dramatizes and concretizes a range of cultural trends that encourage us to think of identity in terms of multiplicity and flexibility.

Virtual Personae

3   In this essay, I focus on one key element of online life and its impact on identity: the creation and projection of constructed personae into virtual space. In cyberspace, it is well known, one's body can be represented by one's own textual description: The obese can be slender, the beautiful plain. The fact that self-presentation is written in text means that there is time to reflect upon and edit one's "composition," which makes it easier for the shy to be outgoing, the "nerdy" sophisticated. The relative anonymity of life on the screen—one has the choice of being known only by one's chosen "handle" or online name—gives people the chance to express often unexplored aspects of the self. Additionally, multiple aspects of self can be explored in parallel. Online services offer their

users the opportunity to be known by several different names. For example, it is not unusual for someone to be BroncoBill in one online community, ArmaniBoy in another, and MrSensitive in a third.

4   The online exercise of playing with identity and trying out new identities is perhaps most explicit in "role playing" virtual communities (such as Multi-User Domains, or MUDs) where participation literally begins with the creation of a persona (or several); but it is by no means confined to these somewhat exotic locations. In bulletin boards, newsgroups, and chat rooms, the creation of personae may be less explicit than on MUDs, but it is no less psychologically real. One IRC (Internet Relay Chat) participant describes her experience of online talk: "I go from channel to channel depending on my mood. . . . I actually feel a part of several of the channels, several conversations . . . I'm different in the different chats. They bring out different things in me." Identity play can happen by changing names and by changing places.

5   For many people, joining online communities means crossing a boundary into highly charged territory. Some feel an uncomfortable sense of fragmentation, some a sense of relief. Some sense the possibilities for self-discovery. A 26-year-old graduate student in history says, "When I log on to a new community and I create a character and know I have to start typing my description, I always feel a sense of panic. Like I could find out something I don't want to know." A woman in her late thirties who just got an account with America Online used the fact that she could create five "names" for herself on her account as a chance to "lay out all the moods I'm in—all the ways I want to be in different places on the system."

6   The creation of site-specific online personae depends not only on adopting a new name. Shifting of personae happens with a change of virtual place. Cycling through virtual environments is made possible by the existence of what have come to be called "windows" in modern computing environments. Windows are a way to work with a computer that makes it possible for the machine to place you in several contexts at the same time. As a user, you are attentive to just one of windows on your screen at any given moment, but in a certain sense, you are a presence in all of them at all times. You might be writing a paper in bacteriology and using your computer in several ways to help you: You are "present" to a word processing program on which you are taking notes and collecting thoughts, you are "present" to communications software that is in touch with a distant computer for collecting reference materials, you are "present" to a simulation program that is charting the growth of bacterial colonies when a new organism enters their ecology, and you are "present" to an online chat session where participants are discussing recent research in the field. Each of these activities takes place in a "window," and your identity on the computer is the sum of your distributed presence.

7   The development of the windows metaphor for computer interfaces was a technical innovation motivated by the desire to get people working more efficiently by "cycling through" different applications, much as time-sharing computers cycle through the computing needs of different people. But in practice, windows have become a potent metaphor for thinking about the self as a multiple, distributed, "time-sharing" system.

8   The self no longer simply plays different roles in different settings—something that people experience when, for example, one wakes up as a lover; makes breakfast as a mother; and drives to work as a lawyer. The windows metaphor suggests a distributed self that exists in many worlds and plays many roles at the same time. The "windows" enabled by a computer operating system support the metaphor, and cyberspace raises the experience to a higher power by translating the metaphor into a life experience of "cycling through."

Identity, Moratoria, and Play

9 Cyberspace, like all complex phenomena, has a range of psychological effects. For some people, it is a place to "act out" unresolved conflicts, to play and replay characterological difficulties on a new and exotic stage. For others, it provides an opportunity to "work through" significant personal issues, to use the new materials of cybersociality to reach for new resolutions. These more positive identity effects follow from the fact that for some, cyberspace provides what Erik Erikson ([1950]1963) would have called a "psychosocial moratorium," a central element in how he thought about identity development in adolescence. Although the term moratorium implies a "time out," what Erikson had in mind was not withdrawal. On the contrary, the adolescent moratorium is a time of intense interaction with people and ideas. It is a time of passionate friendships and experimentation. The adolescent falls in and out of love with people and ideas. Erikson's notion of the moratorium was not a "hold" on significant experiences but on their consequences. It is a time during which one's actions are, in a certain sense, not counted as they will be later in life. They are not given as much weight, not given the force of full judgment. In this context, experimentation can become the norm rather than a brave departure. Relatively consequence-free experimentation facilitates the development of a "core self," a personal sense of what gives life meaning that Erikson called "identity."

10   Erikson developed these ideas about the importance of a moratorium during the late 1950s and early 1960s. At that time, the notion corresponded to a common understanding of what "the college years" were about. Today, 30 years later, the idea of the college years as a consequence-free "time out" seems of another era. College is pre-professional, and AIDS has made consequence-free sexual experimentation an impossibility. The years associated with adolescence no longer seem a "time out." But if our culture no longer offers an adolescent moratorium, virtual communities often do. It is part of what makes them seem so attractive.

11   Erikson's ideas about stages did not suggest rigid sequences. His stages describe what people need to achieve before they can move ahead easily to another developmental task. For example, Erikson pointed out that successful intimacy in young adulthood is difficult if one does not come to it with a sense of who one is, the challenge of adolescent identity building. In real life, however, people frequently move on with serious deficits. With incompletely resolved "stages," they simply do the best they can. They use whatever materials they have at hand to get as much as they can of what they have missed.

Now virtual social life can play a role in these dramas of self-reparation. Time in cyberspace reworks the notion of the moratorium because it may now exist on an always-available "window."

Expanding One's Range in the Real

12 Case, a 34-year-old industrial designer happily married to a female co-worker, describes his real-life (RL) persona as a "nice guy," a "Jimmy Stewart type like my father." He describes his outgoing, assertive mother as a "Katharine Hepburn type." For Case, who views assertiveness through the prism of this Jimmy Stewart/Katharine Hepburn dichotomy, an assertive man is quickly perceived as "being a bastard." An assertive woman, in contrast, is perceived as being "modern and together." Case says that although he is comfortable with his temperament and loves and respects his father, he feels he pays a high price for his own low-key ways. In particular, he feels at a loss when it comes to confrontation, both at home and at work. Online, in a wide range of virtual communities, Case presents himself as females whom he calls his "Katharine Hepburn types." These are strong, dynamic, "out there" women who remind Case of his mother, who "says exactly what's on her mind." He tells me that presenting himself as a woman online has brought him to a point where he is more comfortable with confrontation in his RL as a man.

13   Case describes his Katharine Hepburn personae as "externalizations of a part of myself." In one interview with him, I used the expression "aspects of the self," and he picked it up eagerly, for his online life reminds him of how Hindu gods could have different aspects or subpersonalities, all the while being a whole self. In response to my question "Do you feel that you call upon your personae in real life?" Case responded:

> Yes, an aspect sort of clears its throat and says, "I can do this. You are being so amazingly conflicted over this and I know exactly what to do. Why don't you just let me do it?" . . . In real life, I tend to be extremely diplomatic, non-confrontational. I don't like to ram my ideas down anyone's throat. [Online] I can be, "Take it or leave it." All of my Hepburn characters are that way. That's probably why I play them. Because they are smart-mouthed, they will not sugarcoat their words.

In some ways, Case's description of his inner world of actors who address him and are able to take over negotiations is reminiscent of the language of people with multiple-personality disorder. But the contrast is significant: Case's inner actors are not split off from each other or from his sense of "himself." He experiences himself very much as a collective self, not feeling that he must goad or repress this or that aspect of himself into conformity. He is at ease, cycling through from Katharine Hepburn to Jimmy Stewart. To use analyst Philip Bromberg's language (1994), online life has helped Case learn how to "stand in the spaces between selves and still feel one, to see the multiplicity and still feel a unity." To use computer scientist Marvin Minsky's (1987) phrase, Case feels at ease cycling through his "society of mind," a notion of identity as distributed and heterogeneous. Identity, from the Latin *idem*, has been used habitually to refer to the sameness between two qualities. On the Internet, however, one can be many, and one usually is.

An Object to Think with for Thinking About Identity

14 In the late 1960s and early 1970s, I was first exposed to notions of identity and multiplicity. These ideas—most notably that there is no such thing as "the ego," that each of us is a multiplicity of parts, fragments, and desiring connections—surfaced in the intellectual hothouse of Paris; they presented the world according to such authors as Jacques Lacan, Gilles Deleuze, and Felix Guattari. But despite such ideal conditions for absorbing theory, my "French lessons" remained abstract exercises. These theorists of poststructuralism spoke words that addressed the relationship between mind and body, but from my point of view had little to do with my own.

15   In my lack of personal connection with these ideas, I was not alone. To take one example, for many people it is hard to accept any challenge to the idea of an autonomous ego. While in recent years, many psychologists, social theorists, psychoanalysts, and philosophers have argued that the self should be thought of as essentially decentered, the normal requirements of everyday life exert strong pressure on people to take responsibility for their actions and to see themselves as unitary actors. This disjuncture between theory (the unitary self is an illusion) and lived experience (the unitary self is the most basic reality) is one of the main reasons why multiple and decentered theories have been slow to catch on—or when they do, why we tend to settle back quickly into older, centralized ways of looking at things.

16   When, 20 years later, I used my personal computer and modem to join online communities, I had an experience of this theoretical perspective which brought it shockingly down to earth. I used language to create several characters. My textual actions are my actions—my words make things happen. I created selves that were made and transformed by language. And different personae were exploring different aspects of the self. The notion of a decentered identity was concretized by experiences on a computer screen. In this way, cyberspace becomes an object to think with for thinking about identity—an element of cultural bricolage.

17   Appropriable theories—ideas that capture the imagination of the culture at large—tend to be those with which people can become actively involved. They tend to be theories that can be "played" with. So one way to think about the social appropriability of a given theory is to ask whether it is accompanied by its own objects-to-think-with that can help it move out beyond intellectual circles.

18   For example, the popular appropriation of Freudian ideas had little to do with scientific demonstrations of their validity. Freudian ideas passed into the popular culture because they offered robust and down-to-earth objects to think with. The objects were not physical but almost-tangible ideas, such as dreams and slips of the tongue. People were able to play with such Freudian "objects." They became used to looking for them and manipulating them, both seriously and

not so seriously. And as they did so, the idea that slips and dreams betray an unconscious began to feel natural.

19   In Freud's work, dreams and slips of the tongue carried the theory. Today, life on the computer screen carries theory. People decide that they want to interact with others on a computer network. They get an account on a commercial service. They think that this will provide them with new access to people and information, and of course it does. But it does more. When they log on, they may find themselves playing multiple roles; they may find themselves playing characters of the opposite sex. In this way, they are swept up by experiences that enable them to explore previously unexamined aspects of their sexuality or that challenge their ideas about a unitary self. The instrumental computer, the computer that does things for us, has revealed another side: a subjective computer that does things *to* us as people, to our view of ourselves and our relationships, to our ways of looking at our minds. In simulation, identity can be fluid and multiple, a signifier no longer clearly points to a thing that is signified, and understanding is less likely to proceed through analysis than by navigation through virtual space.

20   Within the psychoanalytic tradition, many "schools" have departed from a unitary view of identity, among these the Jungian, object-relations, and Lacanian. In different ways, each of these groups of analysts was banished from the ranks of orthodox Freudians for such suggestions, or somehow relegated to the margins. As the United States became the center of psychoanalytic politics in the mid-twentieth century, ideas about a robust executive ego began to constitute the psychoanalytic mainstream.

21   But today, the pendulum has swung away from that complacent view of a unitary self. Through the fragmented selves presented by patients and through theories that stress the decentered subject, contemporary social and psychological thinkers are confronting what has been left out of theories of the unitary self. It is asking such questions as, What is the self when it functions as a society? What is the self when it divides its labors among its constituent "alters"? Those burdened by posttraumatic dissociative disorders suffer these questions; I am suggesting that inhabitants of virtual communities play with them. In our lives on the screen, people are developing ideas about identity as multiplicity through new social *practices* of identity as multiplicity.

22   With these remarks, I am not implying that chat rooms or MUDs or the option to declare multiple user names on America Online are causally implicated in the dramatic increase of people who exhibit symptoms of multiple-personality disorder (MPD), or that people on MUDs have MPD, or that MUDding (or online chatting) is like having MPD. I am saying that the many manifestations of multiplicity in our culture, including the adoption of online personae, are contributing to a general reconsideration of traditional, unitary notions of identity. Online experiences with "parallel lives" are part of the significant cultural context that supports new theorizing about nonpathological, indeed healthy, multiple selves.

23   In thinking about the self, *multiplicity* is a term that carries with it several centuries of negative associations, but such authors as Kenneth Gergen (1991), Emily Martin (1994), and Robert Jay Lifton (1993) speak in positive

terms of an adaptive, "flexible" self. The flexible self is not unitary, nor are its parts stable entities. A person cycles through its aspects, and these are themselves ever-changing and in constant communication with each other. Daniel Dennett (1991) speaks of the flexible self by using the metaphor of consciousness as multiple drafts, analogous to the experience of several versions of a document open on a computer screen, where the user is able to move between them at will. For Dennett, knowledge of these drafts encourages a respect for the many different versions, while it imposes a certain distance from them. Donna Haraway (1991), picking up on this theme of how a distance between self states may be salutary, equates a "split and contradictory self" with a "knowing self." She is optimistic about its possibilities: "The knowing self is partial in all its guises, never finished, whole, simply there and original; it is always constricted and stitched together imperfectly; and therefore able to join with another, to see together without claiming to be another." What most characterizes Haraway's and Dennett's models of a knowing self is that the lines of communication between its various aspects are open. The open communication encourages an attitude of respect for the many within us and the many within others.

24   Increasingly, social theorists and philosophers are being joined by psychoanalytic theorists in efforts to think about healthy selves whose resilience and capacity for joy comes from having access to their many aspects. For example, Philip Bromberg (1994) insists that our ways of describing "good parenting" must now shift away from an emphasis on confirming a child in a "core self" and onto helping a child develop the capacity to negotiate fluid transitions between self states. The healthy individual knows how to be many but to smooth out the moments of transition between states of self. Bromberg says: "Health is when you are multiple but feel a unity. Health is when different aspects of self can get to know each other and reflect upon each other." Here, within the psychoanalytic tradition, is a model of multiplicity as a state of easy traffic across selves, a conscious, highly articulated "cycling through."

From a Psychoanalytic to a Computer Culture?

25 Having literally written our online personae into existence, they can be a kind of Rorschach test. We can use them to become more aware of what we project into everyday life. We can use the virtual to reflect constructively on the real. Cyberspace opens the possibility for identity play, but it is very serious play. People who cultivate an awareness of what stands behind their screen personae are the ones most likely to succeed in using virtual experience for personal and social transformation. And the people who make the most of their lives on the screen are those who are able to approach it in a spirit of self-reflection. What does my behavior in cyberspace tell me about what I want, who I am, what I may not be getting in the rest of my life?

26   As a culture, we are at the end of the Freudian century. Freud, after all, was a child of the nineteenth century; of course, he was carrying the baggage of a very different scientific sensibility than our own. But faced with the challenges

of cyberspace, our need for a practical philosophy of self-knowledge, one that does not shy away from issues of multiplicity, complexity, and ambivalence, that does not shy away from the power of symbolism, from the power of the word, from the power of identity play, has never been greater as we struggle to make meaning from our lives on the screen. It is fashionable to think that we have passed from a psychoanalytic culture to a computer culture—that we no longer need to think in terms of Freudian slips but rather of information processing errors. But the reality is more complex. It is time to rethink our relationship to the computer culture and psychoanalytic culture as a proudly held joint citizenship.

References

Bromberg, Philip. 1994. "Speak that I May See You: Some Reflections on Dissociation, Reality, and Psychoanalytic Listening." *Psychoanalytic Dialogues* 4 (4): 517–47.

Dennett, Daniel. 1991. *Consciousness Explained.* Boston: Little, Brown.

Erikson, Erik. [1950] 1963. *Childhood and Society,* 2nd ed. New York: Norton.

Gergen, Kenneth. 1991. *The Saturated Self-Dilemmas of Identity in Contemporary Life.* New York: Basic Books.

Haraway, Donna. 1991. "The Actors are Cyborg, Nature Is Coyote, and the Geography Is Elsewhere: Postscript to 'Cyborgs at Large!'" In *Technoculture,* edited by Constance Penley and Andrew Ross. Minneapolis: University of Minnesota Press.

Lifton, Robert Jay. 1993. *The Protean Self: Human Resilience in an Age of Fragmentation.* New York: Basic Books.

Martin, Emily. 1994. *Flexible Bodies: Tracking Immunity in American Culture from the Days of Polio to the Days of AIDS.* Boston: Beacon Press.

Minsky, Martin. 1987. *The Society of Mind.* New York: Simon & Schuster.

Turkle, Sherry. [1978] 1990. *Psychoanalytic Politics: Jacques Lacan and Freud's French Revolution.* 2nd ed. New York: Guilford Press.

———1984. *The Second Self: Computers and the Human Spirit.* New York: Simon & Schuster.

———1995. *Life on the Screen: Identity in the Age of the Internet.* New York: Simon & Schuster.

Review Questions

1. As she draws upon the ideas of psychologist Erik Erikson, how does Turkle examine the implications of creating multiple cyber-personalities on the Internet?

2. For Turkle, how did the Internet help support the theory that the "unitary self" is an illusion?

3. What is the basis of the analogy between Freud's theories about dreams and slips of the tongue and people assuming multiple identities on the Internet?

Discussion and Writing Suggestions

1. For Turkle, one of the most exciting—and healthy—aspects of the Internet is that it allows us to create and explore multiple personas and personalities for ourselves. To what extent have you experienced this sense of creation and re-creation of yourself as you communicate with individuals and groups in various cybercontexts?

2. Turkle discusses Case, the man who cycles between his "Katherine Hepburn" and "Jimmy Stewart" personas. What is the significance of this phenomenon? Turkle argues that this "collective self" phenomenon is different from multiple personality disorder, in that there is unity in multiplicity. To what extent do you agree?

3. Turkle writes, "In our lives on the screen, people are developing ideas about identity as multiplicity through new social *practices* of identity as multiplicity" (paragraph 21). Write a paper using this sentence as a thesis. Develop specific examples from your own experience or the experiences of people you know.

4. Turkle argues that there is a difference between people who have multiple personality disorder (MPD) and people who assume multiple personalities or who explore multiple aspects of themselves on the Internet. What is the difference? To what extent do you agree with Turkle's ideas on this point?

5. Turkle contends that we need "a practical philosophy of self-knowledge, one that does not shy away from issues of multiplicity, complexity, and ambivalence, that does not shy away from the power of symbolism, from the power of the word, from the power of identity play" (paragraph 26). Assuming that you agree, how should a philosophy of such self-knowledge be fostered? Do schools have a role here? Or do adolescents need to develop such awareness on their own?

Boy, You Fight Like a Girl
Alex Pham

In the previous article, Sherry Turkle discusses how people on the Net are able to "cycle" through multiple personas. This phenomenon is exemplified in a particular Internet subculture: online gaming. In "Boy, You Fight Like a Girl," Los Angeles Times staff writer Alex Pham discusses the penchant of many online gamers for gender-switching—and the reactions they encounter. This article first appeared in the Los Angeles Times on 17 May 2001.

1 In her flowing crimson cape, thigh-high leather boots and metal-studded red leather bustier, Cardinal is a bow-and-arrow-toting *femme fatale*.

2   But not only is Cardinal not real—she's a character in the popular computer game "Ultima Online"—she's not really female. Cardinal is the alter-ego of Kenn Gold, a 33-year-old former Army sergeant with thorny green-and-black tattoos covering both of his muscular arms.

3   As one of the thousands of online gamers who play characters of the opposite gender, Gold created Cardinal as a tactical move: Female characters generally get treated better in the male-dominated world of virtual adventuring. Yet he was unprepared for the shock of seeing the world through a woman's eyes.

4   "I can't even begin to tell you how funny it is to watch guys trip all over themselves and be dumb," Gold said. "It's very amusing to see them try to be really sophisticated and cool, when they're turning out to be just the opposite."

5   Changing genders has long been a piece of online role-playing games—part juvenile mischievousness, part theatrical posing and part psychological release. But as the genre explodes—online games now attract hundreds of thousands of players—it's prompted a blossoming of cross-gender experimentation and created sexually amorphous virtual worlds that some revel in and others curse.

6   Men find they must constantly brush off unwanted advances, and their female characters are not taken as seriously. But they also find it easier to chat with other players and escape the relentless competition among male characters.

7   The story is the same for women who play men to avoid cheesy pick-up lines. They discover that moving among predominantly male groups involves participating in constant one-upmanship. And as their male characters move up the ranks, they fear losing the respect of other players if their true gender is discovered.

8   Online adventures are one of the fastest-growing segments of the computer game market, with titles such as "EverQuest," "Asheron's Call" and "Ultima Online." And it's not just kids with nothing better to do. Teachers, nurses, construction workers and accountants create alter-egos and join with others to explore virtual realms and slay imaginary beasts.

9   In "EverQuest," the most popular of the games with more than 360,000 subscribers, players spend an average of 20 hours a week online. Players call it "EverCrack" because it's so addictive. Much of the allure is the ability to put mundane daily life aside and pretend to be something they're not—an elf, a woodsman, a knight.

10   The ultimate challenge: to be another gender. Although some gamers swap genders to explore their own sexuality—a tiny fraction are cross-dressers in real life—the vast majority do it as a test of skill.

11   "There's a long history of this as a performance genre," said Henry Jenkins, director of comparative media studies at the Massachusetts Institute of Technology. "There is Glenda Jackson who plays Hamlet. Dustin Hoffman played Tootsie. It's a great challenge, a way to show virtuosity."

Virtual Experience Can Have Real Ramifications

12 Encouraging the make-believe are online avatars—the graphic representation of a player's character. Scantily clad females are impossibly thin and full-bosomed. Males are muscular and rendered in heroic proportions. As a result, the contrast

between avatar and player can be striking, even when gamers are playing their own gender.

13   In "EverQuest," only 20% of subscribers are female, but 40% of avatars are. Even accounting for the number of women who play male characters, that amounts to roughly half the female characters in "EverQuest" being played by men such as Gold.

14   This might be fun and games, but as any serious player of such adventures will attest, online experiences—with their power to make people laugh, cry or become angry—can have real-life consequences.

15   "It certainly makes you more aware of how men treat women," said Ralph Koster, 29, who has played a female character for years in an early online text-based game, "LegendMUD." "You're more aware that there are a lot of gendered interactions that we don't recognize as such. It makes you think more about what you're saying and how you're sending subtle messages without being aware of it."

16   For instance, "if you're a female character, just something as innocent as smiling might get read wrong." And if a male character tries to help a female character, it's assumed he wants something. Often, he does.

17   Mark Wight, a 28-year-old heavy-equipment operator from Ramona, Calif., said he wanted to hook his female character, Cytarack, into a hunting group so she could gain experience and advance in the game.

18   "There was this one guy who traveled halfway across the game's virtual continent to hunt with her, but it seemed he was more interested in other things," Wight said, explaining that some players engage in online "cybersex" with each other—basically a modern twist on phone sex in which acts are described in real-time chat. "I don't play her anymore because people get other ideas. Many adults play because they're looking for somebody on the other side."

19   In his Mission Viejo apartment, Gold jockeys two computers as he maneuvers Cardinal around "Ultima Online's" virtual realm. He chain smokes Camels, surrounded by stacks of "X-Men" comic books and an exhaustive collection of "Star Trek" video tapes.

20   In the Army, Gold commanded a Black Hawk helicopter maintenance crew. These days, he's a graduate student in English at Cal State Fullerton, where he teaches freshman composition.

21   At this moment, however, he is Cardinal, a spell-casting huntress on horseback with a mane of pink hair, leather gloves and black tights.

22   Gold confesses that he has another female character—this one in "EverQuest"—whom he declines to name because no one knows she is played by a man. His character is a longtime member of a "guild," a band of players who agree to play together.

23   Many of his band would be upset, explained Gold, who spends about 35 hours each week playing "EverQuest" and "Ultima Online." "They'd feel they couldn't trust me anymore. I'd be ostracized. These are guys who think they're worldly, and it scares them to think that there are women they're interested in who may actually be guys."

24   The deception cuts both ways. Louise, a 44-year-old Sacramento house painter who declined to give her last name, plays a male character and is the

leader of her "EverQuest" guild. She said she fears that if the members of her guild were to discover not only her gender but her age, she would lose their respect.

25   "Some of them are teenage boys," Louise said. "I don't think they'd take it too well. There's a belief that women can't be aggressive. But that's not true at all. I love to be aggressive. It gives me a real adrenaline rush."

26   In daily life, though, she is shy. It is only when she slips into a role-playing mode that Louise says she can fully express her aggressive nature without fear of being belittled.

27   But because online relationships can be as intense as their real-world counterparts, there is the potential to wreak psychological havoc.

Emboldened Under Veil of Online Anonymity

28 Gold five years ago attended an online wedding involving two characters in a game called "Meridian 59." Once the vows were exchanged, the bride declared that she was actually a man and that the two had had cybersex, humiliating the groom in front of their virtual guests. It was all a revenge plot the "bride" had devised because the groom had killed another of the player's characters months earlier in the game.

29   What makes such behavior possible, of course, is the anonymous nature of the Web. Online players are less accountable for their words and, therefore, less inhibited with their expressions.

30   "The Internet makes you bolder," said Rick Hall, a game producer at Origin Systems, the company that created "Ultima Online." "If you're the type of guy who wouldn't approach a girl in real life, you can do it online. And if you get shot down, who cares."

31   Similarly, anonymity gives people the freedom to emphasize a particular personality trait or mood they would stifle in real life. Many players maintain a stable of characters they can pull out to match their mood.

32   Geoffrey Zatkin, a senior game designer for the company that wrote "EverQuest," rotates between three characters—a male fencer, a male rogue and a female druid. Each represents a facet of his identity. The fencer is witty, the rogue aloof and the druid outgoing. Zatkin plays the female character when feeling chatty.

33   For Ramin Shokrizade, playing female characters allows him to escape the competitiveness that pervades the male culture.

34   "Among power gamers, it gets to be very competitive," said Shokrizade, 35, an exercise trainer and math and science tutor in Palm Desert who says he plays online role-playing games an average of 80 hours a week. "If you're female, they don't do that with you. I enjoy chatting with other players and helping people out. I've been a track coach for 15 years, so I'm used to helping people. This is just a way of practicing what I know."

35   Still, Shokrizade was surprised at how differently he was treated as a female character.

36   "It was strange," he said. "If you don't mind being in a supportive role, life is a lot easier for you. You're not expected to be in a leadership role."

37   Players who wish to escape gender constraints online ironically find themselves in a medium that, if anything, reinforces sexual stereotypes.

38   "Females tend to get in groups faster, but we get harassed," said Aaron Harvey, a 26-year-old freelance Web designer from Ventura who plays a female gnome in "EverQuest." "People are constantly trying to pick us up. I've been offered [more powerful weaponry] for cybersex, which I turn down rather quickly."

39   Often, players who gender-swap online are reluctant to talk about their reasons.

40   "It's not something you would talk about or be proud of," said Pavel Curtis, who developed a well-known text-based online community called LambdaMOO when he was a researcher at Xerox's Palo Alto Research Center. "Society doesn't see it as a healthy form of experimentation. At best, it's seen as duplicitous. At worst, it's sick and perverted."

41   Such strongly held views underscore how important gender identity is to people—even online, where physical appearances are not supposed to matter.

42   "We tailor our actions based on who we think we're talking to," said Amy Bruckman, assistant professor in the College of Computing at Georgia Tech in Atlanta. "Because these factors shape our interactions, we're often uncomfortable when we don't know these cues on age, race and gender."

43   As a result, much effort goes into spotting fakes. The clues cited by players are telling indications of how people perceive gender. Bruckman recalled a time when she tried to pass as a male character but was instantly pegged as an impostor. How? "It was just my style of speaking. I used long sentences with lots of adjectives, which is seen as stereotypic of females," Bruckman said.

44   "Everybody, it seems, needs to know," Koster said. "It's like a void that needs to be filled, and it's deeply ingrained in our culture. There's this notion that the Internet will give us this utopia where gender, age and race don't matter. The idea that we'll all be disembodied floating lights just ain't gonna happen."

Discussion and Writing Suggestions

1. Do you or anyone you know engage in online gaming? To what extent can you confirm the kinds of behavior Pham discusses in "Boy, You Fight Like a Girl"—particularly, gender switching and the reaction to gender switching? What is your take on this phenomenon?

2. What kind of gender stereotypes are revealed in the experiences of people who engage in gender-switching while participating in online games? To what extent do you think such gender stereotyping is aggravated by the very experience of participating in such games? That is, to what extent might the anonymity of the Internet make sexists of people who, in their "real world" interpersonal relations, generally behave with more tolerance and sensitivity? To what extent (on the other hand) might online gaming attract people with sexist mindsets?

3. How does the type of online behavior discussed in Pham's article tie into Dyson's observations on Internet anonymity and Turkle's discussion of multiple personas? To what extent are Dyson, on the one hand, and Turkle, on the other, likely to regard gender-switching during online gaming as psychologically healthy?

4. Amy Bruckman recalls that she tried to pass as a male while playing online games, but was immediately spotted because of her "style of speaking." In general, do you believe that males and females have different styles of speaking (or writing)? If so, what characterizes these different styles? Do you think you are likely to be successful in passing yourself off as a member of the opposite sex?

   You might try an experiment along these lines: divide a group of people into an equal number of males and females. Have some in each group adopt personas in which they switch genders. Have people write an anonymous series of notes to one another, asking and answering questions, devising a system by which the notes are transmitted from one person to another. (E-mailing would work only if anonymity can be maintained; otherwise, notes would have to be written on paper.) Have writers attempt to determine the actual genders of their anonymous correspondents. Ask those people who successfully determined the gender of their correspondents (as opposed to just guessed correctly) what were the "giveaways."

The 15-Year-Old Legal Whiz
Michael Lewis

The last few selections have focused on how people create new identities for themselves on the Internet—or perhaps more accurately, how they create new aspects of themselves as they communicate online. In particular, Sherry Turkle focused on the creation of new selves as an exploration of different personas. And in the introduction to this chapter, we described the "Robert Klingler" affair, in which an individual claiming to be the North American head of a major European automobile manufacturer succeeded in getting a couple of his "Diary" entries published in the online magazine Slate *before the editors realized that they had been taken in by a skillful con artist.*

In the following article, Michael Lewis, a contributing editor for the New York Times Magazine, *details the fascinating account of how a 15-year-old with no legal training posed as an expert attorney on the Web—and not only got away with it but was confirmed in his expert status, both by his "clients" and by actual, practicing attorneys! That this is possible raises questions not only about the special status of the law as an elite profession, but also about how the Internet tends to make anyone with a little knowledge into an authority. This article first appeared in the* New York Times Magazine *on 15 July 2001 and, as adapted below, appears in Lewis's book* Next: The Future Just Happened *(2001).*

1   In the summer of 2000, in a desert town called Perris, halfway between Los Angeles and Palm Springs, lived a 15-year-old boy named Marcus Arnold. His parents had immigrated to Perris from Belize, by way of South-Central L.A. Why anyone would move to Perris from anywhere was not immediately clear. Perris was one of those non-places that America specializes in creating. One day it was a flat hazy stretch of sand and white rock beneath an endless blue sky; the next some developer had laid out a tract of 25,000 identical homes; and the day after that it was teeming with people who were there, mainly, because it was not someplace else.

2   Marcus lived with his parents and his twin brother in a small brick house. A great big bear of a boy, Marcus was six feet tall and weighed maybe 200 pounds. He did not walk but lumbered from the computer to the front door, then back again. The computer squatted on a faux antique desk in the alcove between the dining room and the living room, which were as immaculately kept as showrooms in a model home. It was the only computer in the house, he said. In theory, the family shared it; in practice, it belonged to him. He now needed as much time on it as he could get, as he was a leading expert on AskMe.com. His field was the law.

3   The blue screen displayed the beginning of an answer to a question on AskMe.com Marcus had bashed out before I arrived:

> Your son should not be in jail or on trial. According to Miranda versus Arizona the person to be arrested must be read his rights before he was asked any questions. If your son was asked any questions before the reading of his rights he should not be in prison. If you want me to help you further write me back on this board privately.

4   The keyboard vanished beneath Marcus's jumbo hands and another page on AskMe.com popped up on the screen. Marcus wanted to show me the appallingly weak answer to a question that had been offered by one of the real lawyers on the site. "I can always spot a crummy attorney," he said. "There are people on the Web site who have no clue what they're talking about, they are just there to get rankings and to sell their services and to get paid." Down went his paws, out of sight went the keyboard, and up popped one of Marcus's favourite Web sites. This one listed the menus on death row in Texas. Photographs of men put to death by the state appeared next to hideous lists of the junk food they'd ordered for their last meals.

5   Marcus had stumbled upon AskMe.com late in the spring of 2000. He was studying for his biology exam and looking for an answer to a question. He noticed that someone had asked a question about the law to which he knew the answer. Then another. A thought occurred: why not answer them himself? To become an official expert he only needed to fill in a form, which asked him, among other things, his age. He did this on June 5—a day enshrined in Marcus's mind. "I always wanted to be an attorney since I was, like, 12," he said, "but I couldn't do it because everyone is going to be, 'like, what? Some 12-year-old kid is going to give me legal advice?'"

6   "They'd feel happier with a 15-year-old?"

7   He drew a deep breath and made a face that indicated that he took this to be a complicated question. "So when I first went on AskMe," he said, "I told everybody I was 20, roughly about 20, and everyone believed me." Actually, he claimed to be 25. To further that impression he adopted the handle "LawGuy 1975."

8   Once he became an expert, Marcus's career took on a life of its own. The AskMe rankings were driven by the number of questions the expert answered, the speed of his replies, and the quality of those replies, as judged by the recipients, who bestowed on them a rating of between one and five stars. By July 1 Marcus was ranked number 10 out of 150 or so experts in AskMe.com's criminal law division, many of whom were actual lawyers. As he tells it, that's when he decided to go for the gold. "When I hit the top 10 I got some people who were like, 'Congratulations, blah blah blah.' So my adrenaline was pumping to answer more questions. I was just, like, 'You know what, let me show these people I know what I'm doing'." He needed to inspire even more people to ask him questions, and to reply to them quickly, and in a way that prompted them to reward him with lots of stars. To that end he updated the page that advertised his services. When he was done it said:

9   I am a law expert with two years of formal training in the law. I will help anyone I can! I been involved in trials, legal studies and certain forms of jurisprudence. I am not accredited by the state bar association yet to practise law . . . sincerely, Justin Anthony Wyrick, Jr.

10   "Justin was the name I always wanted—besides mine," Marcus said. Justin Anthony Wyrick Jr. had a more authoritative ring to it, in Marcus's opinion, and in a lot of other people's, too. On one day Marcus received and answered 110 questions.

11   The more questions Marcus answered, the more people who logged onto the boards looking for legal advice wanted to speak only to him. In one two-week stretch he received 943 legal questions and answered 939. When I asked him why he hadn't answered the other four, a look of profound exasperation crossed his broad face. "Traffic law," he said. "I'm sorry, I don't know traffic law." By the end of July he was the No. 3 rated expert in criminal law on AskMe.com. Beneath him in the rankings were 125 licensed attorneys and a wild assortment of ex-cops and ex-cons. The next youngest person on the board was 31.

12   In a few weeks Marcus had created a new identity for himself: legal wizard. School he now viewed not so much as preparation for a future legal career as material for an active one. He investigated a boondoggle taken by the local school board and discovered it had passed off on the taxpayer what to him appeared to be the expenses for a private party. He brought that, and a lot more, up at a public hearing. Why grown-up people with grown-up legal problems took him seriously was the great mystery Marcus didn't much dwell on—except to admit that it had nothing to do with his legal training. He'd had no legal training, formal or informal. On the top of the Arnold family desk was a thin dictionary, plus stacks and stacks of court cases people from AskMe who had come to rely on Marcus's advice had mimeographed and sent to him, for his review. (The clients sent him the paperwork and he wrote motions, which the clients then passed on to licensed attorneys for submission to a court.) But there was nothing on the desk, or in the house, even faintly resembling a book

about the law. The only potential sources of legal information were the family computer and the big-screen TV.

13 "Where do you find books about the law?" I asked.

14 "I don't," he said, tap-tap-tapping away on his keyboard. "Books are boring. I don't like reading."

15 "So you go on legal Web sites?"

16 "No."

17 "Well, when you got one of these questions did you research your answer?

18 "No, never. I just know it."

19 "You just know it."

20 "Exactly."

21 The distinct whiff of an alternate reality lingered in the air. It was just then that Marcus's mother, Priscilla, came through the front door. She was a big lady, teetering and grunting beneath jumbo-sized sacks of groceries. A long box of donuts jutted out of the top of one.

22 "Hi Marcus, what you doing?" she said, gasping for breath.

23 "Just answering questions," he said.

24 "What were you answering?" she asked, with real pleasure. She radiated pride.

25 "I got one about an appellate bond—how to get one," he said. "Another one about the Supreme Court. A petition to dismiss something."

26 "We got some chili cheese dogs here."

27 "That's cool."

28 "Where did you acquire your expertise?" I asked.

29 "Marcus was born with it!" shouted Priscilla. Having no idea how to respond, I ignored her.

30 "What do you mean?" Marcus asked me. He was genuinely puzzled by my question.

31 "Where does your information come from?"

32 "I don't know," he said. "Like, I really just don't know."

33 "How can you not know where knowledge comes from?" I asked.

34 "After, like, watching so many TV shows about the law," he said, "it's just like you know everything you need to know." He gave a little mock shiver. "It's scary. I just know these things."

35 Again Priscilla shouted from the kitchen. "Marcus has got a gift!"

36 She shouted from the kitchen: "Marcus had his gift in the womb. I could feel it."

37 "What do you think these people would have done if you weren't there to answer their questions?" I asked Marcus.

38 "They would have paid an attorney," he said. But as he said it his big grin vanished and a cloud shadowed his broad, open face. It may well have been that he was recalling the public relations fiasco that followed the discovery by a hundred or so licensed attorneys on AskMe.com the true identity of the new expert moving up their ranks. In any case, he lifted his giant palms toward me in the manner of the Virgin Mary resisting the entreaties of the Holy Spirit, and said, "Look, I'm not out there to take business from other people. That's not my job."

39 "But you think that legal expertise is overrated?"

40   "Completely."

41   Once Marcus attained his high rankings on AskMe.com, a lot of people he didn't really know began to ask for his phone number and his fee structure. For the first time, his conscience began to trouble him. He decided it was time to come clean with his age. To do this he changed his expert profile. Where it had read "legal expert," it now read "15-year-old intern attorney expert." A few hours after he posted his confession, hostile messages came hurtling toward him. A few of them came from his "clients," but most came from the lawyers and others who competed with him for rankings and prizes and publicity. A small war broke out on the message boards, with Marcus accusing the lawyers of ganging up on him to undermine his number three ranking and the lawyers accusing Marcus of not knowing what he was talking about. The lawyers began to pull up Marcus's old answers and bestow on them lowly one-star ratings—thus dragging down his average. (At the time, third parties could score expert answers; after the incident AskMe.com changed its policy.) Then they did something even worse: asked him detailed questions about the finer points of the law. When he couldn't supply similarly detailed answers, they laid into him. Marcus's replies to the e-mail lashings read less like the work of a defense attorney than of a man trying to talk his torturers into untying him:

42   "I am reporting your abusive response, for it hurts my reputation and my dignity as an expert on this board."

43   "Please don't e-mail me threats."

44   "You really are picking on me."

45   "Leave me alone! I am not even a practising attorney!"

46   "Please, I beg of you, stop sending me letters saying that you'll be watching me, because you are scaring my parents."

47   "I really just want to be friends."

48   "Can't we just be friends?"

49   To which Marcus's wittiest assailant replied, "In your last two posts you've ended by asking that I be your friend. That's like the mortally wounded gladiator asking to be friends with the lion."

50   On the one hand, the whole episode was absurd—Marcus Arnold was a threat to no one but himself and, perhaps, the people who sought his advice. To practice law you still needed a license, and no 15-year-old boy was going to be granted one. At the same time, Marcus had wandered into an arena live with combustible particles. The Internet had arrived at an embarrassing moment for the law. The knowledge gap between lawyers and non-lawyers had been shrinking for some time, and the Internet was closing it further.

51   Legal advice was being supplied over the Internet, often for free—and it wasn't just lawyers doing the supplying. Students, cops, dicks, even ex-cons went onto message boards to help people with their questions and cases. At the bottom of this phenomenon was a corrosively democratic attitude toward legal knowledge. "If you think about the law," the past chairman of the American Bar Association, Richard S. Granat, told the *New York Times,* in an attempt to explain the boom in do-it-yourself Internet legal services, "a large component is just information. Information itself can go a long way to help solve legal problems."

52   Marcus had been publicly humiliated by the real lawyers, but it didn't stop him from offering more advice. Then the clients began to speak. With pretty much one voice they said: Leave the kid alone! A lot of people seemed to believe that any 15-year-old who had risen so high in the ranks of AskMe.com legal experts must be some kind of wizard. They began to seek him out more than ever before; they wanted his, and only his, advice. In days Marcus's confidence was fully restored. "You always have your critics," he said. "I mean, with the real lawyers, it's a pride issue. They can't let someone who could be their son beat them. Plus they have a lot more time than I do. I'm always stretched for time. Six hours a day of school, four hours of homework, sometimes I can't get on line to answer the questions until after dinner."

53   Marcus's ranking rebounded. Two weeks after he disclosed his age, he was on the rise; two weeks later he hit No. 1. The legal advice he gave to a thousand or so people along the way might not have withstood the scrutiny of the finest legal minds. Some of it was the sort of stuff you could glean directly from Judge Judy; more of it was a simple restating of the obvious in a friendly tone. Marcus didn't have much truck with the details; he didn't handle complexity terribly well. But that was the whole the point of him—he didn't need to. A lot of what a real lawyer did was hand out simple information in a way that made the client feel served, and this Marcus did well. He may have had only the vaguest idea of what he was talking about and a bizarre way of putting what he did know. But out there in the void, they loved him.

Review Questions

1. How did Marcus Arnold's legal career start, according to Lewis?
2. How did Marcus rapidly climb in the AskMe rankings?
3. From what sources did Marcus get the answers he was providing to people who asked him questions about the law?
4. What, for Lewis, is the chief lesson of Marcus's success as a legal expert?
5. How did Marcus Arnold fall—and then rise again?

Discussion and Writing Suggestions

1. In an earlier version of this article, Lewis wrote that role theorists claim that "we have no 'self' as such. Our selves are merely the masks we wear in response to the social situations in which we find ourselves. The Internet had offered up a new set of social situations, to which people had responded by grabbing for a new set of masks." To what extent do you agree with this assertion? Support

your response with illustrations from your own experience or the experiences of people you know. Relate your comments at some point to Lewis's discussion of Marcus Arnold.

2. To what extent do you approve of what Marcus Arnold did? Do you think that he is a healthy or an unhealthy symptom of what is happening on the Internet? To what extent would you be prepared to seek legal advice from Arnold?

3. In an earlier version of this article, Lewis argued that Marcus "was using the Internet the way adults often use their pasts." But since young people like Marcus do not have much of a past, they turn to the future and "imagine themselves into some future adult world." To what extent do you think that this theory accounts for the fascination of many young people for the Internet—i.e., that it provides a means of fantasizing about their lives in the future?

4. Go to <www.AskMe.com>, find a category and subcategory with which you are reasonably familiar, and browse through the answers to questions that some of the experts have provided. How good are their answers? Could you have provided better ones? (Try a few.) Do the more reliable and complete answers appear to come from experts who—according to their own description of their qualifications and credentials—have had the most training and experience?

SYNTHESIS ACTIVITIES

1. Write an article for a newsmagazine exploring the various facets of the Internet revolution. Use the selection by Leonard as a model for survey articles of this type, but avoid using more than one or two of Leonard's own examples. Draw upon not only Leonard but also Lee, Dvorak, Snider, Parsons, Turkle, Pham, and Lewis. Focus in particular on how the Internet provides a means of exploring and defining aspects of our identity. Keep the article relatively objective—that is, it should essentially take the form of an *explanatory* synthesis—but don't be afraid of venturing mildly argumentative assessments of the e-mail phenomenon or the directions in which our Internet culture is headed.

2. Argue that the net effects of the cyberrevolution are positive—*or that* they are negative. In formulating your argument, acknowledge and explain that e-mail has both positive and negative aspects, but assert that on balance, the positive outweighs the negative (or vice versa) in terms of how e-mail has affected both private and public discourse. Draw upon as many articles and selections in this chapter as will be helpful in supporting your case.

3. How has the Internet changed the way we think about identity? Draw upon the selections in the latter part of the chapter—Daum, Dyson, Lee, Dvorak, Snider, Turkle, Pham, and Lewis—to explore this topic. Consider such matters as (1) the identity or identities we create when we send messages; (2) the implied identities of those who send us messages; (3) the relationship or conflict between our actual identity and our implied identity or identities (see, especially, Turkle on this subject); (4) the relationship between our physical selves and our implied selves.

4. In her article "Cyberspace and Identity," Sherry Turkle points out that starting in the 1960s, many people who studied identity concluded that "there is no such thing as 'the ego,' that each of us is a multiplicity of parts, fragments, and desiring connections" (paragraph 14). Similarly, in an earlier version of his article on 15-year-old legal expert Marcus Arnold, Michael Lewis noted some recent ideas about the self promulgated by role theorists, who argue that "we have no 'self' as such. Our selves are merely the masks we wear in response to the social situations in which we find ourselves. The Internet had offered up a new set of social situations, to which people had responded by grabbing up a new set of masks."

   Using either the statement by Turkle or the statement by Lewis as an analytical principle, discuss particular anecdotes and events recounted in some of the selections in this chapter. Most of the authors represented in the chapter have something to say on this matter; but focus, in particular, on Leonard, Lee, Snider, Parsons, Daum, Pham, and Lewis.

5. Daum's experience with online romance is common, if not universal. While some lucky souls do indeed find their future mates over the Internet, most who attempt online romance find that the relationships burn brightly for awhile and then smolder and die—particularly, once the parties actually meet.

   Why should this be so? What accounts for the eventual failure of so many online romances? Aren't we expressing our "true" selves in e-mail messages? Or are the selves we project simply idealized versions of our selves that cannot survive in the "real world"? To what extent is there an inherent conflict, a tension, between our physical selves and our cyberselves? In your response, draw not only upon Daum and other selections in this chapter.

6. Reread the final paragraph (paragraph 34) of Daum's article, "Virtual Love." Reflecting on the course of her relationship with PFSlider, she writes, "The world had proved to be too cluttered and fast for us, too polluted to allow the thing we'd attempted through technology ever to grow in the earth." Consider this thought, and extract an analytical principle that can be applied in other contexts. For example, what is she saying about romance? What is she saying

about technology? What does she mean by "cluttered and fast" and "polluted"? (Note also the "branches and bodies and falling debris that make up the physical world" in the paragraph's final sentence.) Write an analysis of some situation or set of situations outside of this article, using the principle you infer from Daum's paragraph. You might want to bring in particular examples from other articles in the chapter, such as those by Leonard, Dvorak, Snider, Turkle, Pham, and Lewis.

7. The e-mail revolution appears to have changed some of the rules of communication, often for the worse. One of the more unpleasant developments of the new medium is "flaming"—the sending of abusive, insulting, sometimes vicious messages, or even threats, to another with whom one may have a minor disagreement. Considerably less serious, but still annoying to many e-mail recipients, is the tendency of some writers not to use punctuation or capital letters, indeed not to bother proofreading (or even signing) their messages at all. While some believe that e-mail messages do not require strict adherence to stylistic conventions, others take issue. In *The Elements of E-Mail Style*, authors David Angell and Brent Heslop assert, "Using all lower-case letters is annoying for the recipient and can result in your message being misunderstood or not read at all."*

   Do you regard such disregard of conventions, intentional or not, as breaches of communication etiquette or are they simply part of the distinctive nature of e-mail culture? Attempt to explain these and perhaps other negative features of Internet communication, drawing upon some of the selections that you have read in this chapter.

8. In a piece entitled "The Return of the Word," Adam Gopnik writes, "E-mail has succeeded brilliantly for the same reason that the videophone failed miserably: what we actually want from our exchanges is the minimum human contact commensurate with the need to connect with other people. 'Only connect.' Yes, but *only* connect."† What do you think Gopnik means? Why "*only* connect"? Just what kind of contact do we crave, do we need from our Internet correspondents? In your response, draw upon some of the following selections: Leonard, Dvorak, Snider, Parsons, Daum, Turkle, Pham, and Lewis.

---

* David Angell and Brent Heslop, *The Elements of E-Mail Style: Communicate Effectively via Electronic Mail* (Reading, MA: Addison-Wesley, 1994).

† Adam Gopnik, "The Return of the Word," *New Yorker*, 6 December 1999. The quotation "Only connect" is from *Howards End* (1910) by E. M. Forster.

RESEARCH ACTIVITIES

1. Explore some aspect of online romance. What services are available for people who want to find love on the Internet? What are the benefits and drawbacks of using such services? What are the special thrills and the hazards of seeking love online? How is online romance similar to and different from the old-fashioned kind? What happens when two people who have met and fallen in love (or lust) online meet in person? Begin your research by reviewing some of the selections in this chapter that focus on these matters, and then pursue the matter further by seeking additional sources. (Note in particular an article by Jennifer Egan, "Love in the Time of No Time," which appeared in the 23 November 2003 issue of the *New York Times Magazine*.)

2. One of the most popular offshoots of e-mailing is "instant messaging," a process that allows people to have e-mail exchanges in real time, one that represents a kind of hybrid between the letter (in that messages are written) and the telephone (in that an exchange takes place over a relatively brief, unbroken period of time). Write an article for a newsmagazine exploring the phenomenon of instant messaging—how it got started, why it has become so popular, how it became a legal issue (when America Online initially refused to license its instant-messaging software), where it seems headed.

3. As Andrew Leonard explains in "We've Got Mail—Always," e-mail was invented in the late 1960s when scientists in different locations who used the Arpanet, the predecessor of the Internet, sought to develop a way of sharing resources and information with one another. Write a report on the early history of e-mail, focusing on the period before 1990 when it became a mass phenomenon. Who were the main players? What were the key moments? What were the technical challenges? At what point did it become apparent that e-mail was going to have far broader applications than was originally conceived?

4. Like anything else, e-mail has a significant legal dimension. Of increasing concern to employees is the privacy of their e-mail and the extent to which employers can monitor their e-mail and use it against them. Employers have been known to send fake e-mails to employees pretending to be other employers offering more lucrative or prestigious jobs. Employees who responded favorably were deemed disloyal and subsequently denied promotion. In 2000, civil libertarians became alarmed when the FBI revealed that it was using a software program called Carnivore to monitor all e-mail passing through a particular Internet Service Provider (ISP), ostensibly in an attempt to catch terrorists, drug dealers, and child pornographers. During a divorce proceeding, one spouse may obtain a court order to search the e-mail records of the other spouse

for incriminating information about extramarital affairs. Explore some of the ways that e-mail monitoring and searching has been used against people, along with some of the ways that civil libertarians and others have been resisting activities in court.

5. Visit some chat rooms or electronic bulletin boards and "lurk" over the ongoing electronic communications—that is, read what others are writing without announcing your own presence. Visit forums on a variety of subjects. For example, if you are a member of America Online, you'll find chat rooms available on numerous subjects. If you read electronic publications like Slate.com or Salon.com, you can trace discussion threads in which readers react to articles that have been published. Report on what you find. What tentative conclusions can you draw about the types of communication that occur in such places? Categorize the types of comments made. What appear to be the effects of anonymity? To what extent do you detect that writers are creating personas for themselves, identities that may be different from what they are like in person?

6. Conduct a survey about e-mail use. Try to keep the group you survey relatively homogenous (e.g., undergraduates) and organize that group by subcategories (e.g., class standing, major, gender, whether an individual has her or his own computer or must use college equipment). Develop a questionnaire, as well as a set of interview questions, exploring such issues as the main purposes of sending e-mail messages, the average length of messages, how often e-mail is checked, and the use of chat rooms and electronic bulletin boards. Write a report based on your findings. Use tables and graphs or charts to summarize your data. Use standard social science format for developing your report: an *introduction*, a section on *methods* of gathering data, a section on *results*, a *discussion* of the results, and a *conclusion*.

7. Visit AskMe.com and browse through the questions and answers by various "experts" in one of the numerous categories listed. It's best to select a category—whether movies, computer software, or refinishing cabinets—with which you have some "expert" knowledge, yourself. Notice how many of the responses have been rated (on a scale of one to five stars) by the questioner and by other experts. Assess the quality of the responses, based on your own knowledge of the subject, and compare them with the ratings posted. Write a report, possibly for a magazine like *Consumer Reports*, assessing the quality of information provided by particular experts in this area on AskMe.com.

6

Obedience to Authority

Would you obey an order to inflict pain on another person? Most of us, if confronted with this question, would probably be quick to answer: "Never!" Yet if the conclusions of researchers are to be trusted, it is not psychopaths who kill noncombatant civilians in wartime and torture victims in prisons around the world but rather ordinary people following orders. People obey. This is a basic, necessary fact of human society. As psychologist Stanley Milgram has written, "Obedience is as basic an element in the structure of social life as one can point to. Some system of authority is a requirement of all communal living."

The question, then, is not, "Should we obey the orders of an authority figure?" but rather, "To what *extent* should we obey?" Each generation seems to give new meaning to these questions. During the Vietnam War, a number of American soldiers followed a commander's orders and murdered civilians in the hamlet of My Lai. In 1987 former White House military aide Oliver North was prosecuted for illegally diverting money raised by selling arms to Iran—considered by the U.S. government to be a terrorist state—to fund the anticommunist Contra (resistance) fighters in Nicaragua. North's attorneys claimed that he was following the orders of his superiors. And, although North was found guilty,* the judge who sentenced him to perform community service (there was no prison sentence) largely agreed with this defense when he called North a pawn in a larger game played by senior officials in the Reagan administration. In the 1990s the world was horrified by genocidal violence in Rwanda and in the former nation of Yugoslavia. These were civil wars, in which people who had been living for generations as neighbors suddenly, upon the instigation and orders of their leaders, turned upon and slaughtered one another.

Finally, in April 2004, the world (particularly, the Muslim world) was horrified by accounts—and graphic photographs—of the degrading torture and humiliation of Iraqi prisoners at the hands of American soldiers in a Baghdad prison. Among the questions raised by this incident: Were these soldiers obeying orders to "soften up" the prisoners for interrogation? Were they fulfilling the roles of prison guards they thought were expected of them? Were they abusing others because, given the circumstances, they could? President Bush asserted that this kind of abuse "does not reflect the nature of the American people." But as the Milgram and Zimbardo experiments in this chapter demonstrate, we are likely to be unpleasantly surprised by revelations of just what our "nature" really is—not only as Americans but, more fundamentally, as human beings.

---

* In July 1990, North's conviction was overturned on appeal.

   In less dramatic ways, conflicts over the extent to which we obey orders surface in everyday life. At one point or another, you may face a moral dilemma at
work. Perhaps it will take this form: The boss tells you to overlook File X in
preparing a report for a certain client. But you're sure that File X pertains directly to the report and contains information that will alarm the client. What should
you do? The dilemmas of obedience also emerge on some campuses with the
rite of fraternity or sports-related hazing. Psychologists Janice Gibson and Mika
Haritos-Fatouros have made the startling observation that whether the obedience in question involves a pledge's joining a fraternity or a torturer's joining
an elite military corps, the *process* by which one acquiesces to a superior's order
(and thereby becomes a member of the group) is remarkably the same:

> There are several ways to teach people to do the unthinkable, and we
> have developed a model to explain how they are used. We have also
> found that college fraternities, although they are far removed from the
> grim world of torture and violent combat, use similar methods for ini-
> tiating new members, to ensure their faithfulness to the fraternity's
> rules and values. However, this unthinking loyalty can sometimes lead
> to dangerous actions: Over the past 10 years, there have been countless
> injuries during fraternity initiations and 39 deaths. These training tech-
> niques are designed to instill obedience in people, but they can easily
> be a guide for an intensive course in torture.

   1. *Screening to find the best prospects:*
      - Normal, well-adjusted people with the physical, intellectual,
        and, in some cases, political attributes necessary for the task.
   2. *Techniques to increase binding among these prospects:*
      - Initiation rites to isolate people from society and introduce
        them to a new social order, with different rules and values.
      - Elitist attitudes and "in-group" language, which highlight the
        differences between the group and the rest of society.
   3. *Techniques to reduce the strain of obedience:*
      - Blaming and dehumanizing the victims, so it is less disturb-
        ing to harm them.
      - Harassment, the constant physical and psychological intimi-
        dation that prevents logical thinking and promotes the instinc-
        tive responses needed for acts of inhuman cruelty.
      - Rewards for obedience and punishments for not cooperating.
      - Social modeling by watching other group members commit
        violent acts and then receive rewards.
      - Systematic desensitization to repugnant acts by gradual expo-
        sure to them, so they appear routine and normal despite con-
        flicts with previous moral standards.*

---

* Janice T. Gibson and Mika Haritos-Fatouros, "The Education of a Torturer," *Psychology Today*
November 1986. Reprinted with permission from *Psychology Today Magazine.* Copyright 1986
Sussex Publishers, Inc.

Many of these processes appear to have been at work in the Iraqi prison scandal.

In this chapter, you will explore the dilemmas inherent in obeying the orders of an authority. First, you will learn more about the Abu Ghraib prison scandal from a *U.S. News & World Report* article in which Marianne Szegedy-Maszak asks: "Was it conditions at [the Iraqi prison] or perverse human nature that led to these atrocities?" Next, psychologist Solomon E. Asch describes an experiment he devised to demonstrate the powerful influence of group pressure upon individual judgment. Psychologist Stanley Milgram then reports on his own landmark study in which he set out to determine the extent to which ordinary individuals would obey the clearly immoral orders of an authority figure. The results were shocking, not only to the psychiatrists who predicted that few people would follow such orders but also to many other social scientists and people—some of whom applauded Milgram for his fiendishly ingenious design, some of whom bitterly attacked him for unethical procedures. We include one of these attacks, a scathing review by psychologist Diana Baumrind. Another, and later, perspective on the reaction to Milgram's experiment is provided by British writer Ian Parker in his essay "Obedience."

Next, Philip K. Zimbardo reports on his famous (and controversial) Stanford Prison experiment, which eerily anticipates the brutality of young American soldiers at the Abu Ghraib prison. In Zimbardo's experiment, volunteers exhibited astonishingly convincing and obedient attitudes as they play-acted at being prisoners and guards. Three essays conclude the chapter. In "Disobedience as a Psychological and Moral Problem," psychoanalyst and philosopher Erich Fromm discusses the comforts of obedient behavior. In "The Genocidal Killer in the Mirror," Crispin Sartwell draws on the recent history of genocide to shake our belief that under similar circumstances we would behave honorably. Finally, in "Just Do What the Pilot Tells You," British physician Theodore Dalrymple reminds us that obedience to authority is not always a bad thing; in fact, routine *dis*obedience to authority can be just as dangerous as unthinking obedience.

The Abu Ghraib Prison Scandal:
Sources of Sadism
Marianne Szegedy-Maszak

In January 2004, a military investigator in Baghdad found on his cot a disk containing images of horrific physical abuse and humiliation committed by American military guards against Iraqi detainees at Abu Ghraib prison. A whistleblower, who (along with his family) was subsequently placed in protective custody because of death threats, found the images so disturbingly at odds with standards of military conduct and basic decency that he reported the abuse, which quickly grew into an international scandal. President Bush strongly condemned the "disgraceful conduct by a few American troops who dishonored our country and disregarded our values." Others, recalling abuses in Vietnam and Nazi Germany, wondered whether the military's culture of obedience and the extreme circumstances of war can turn otherwise decent people into agents of terror. At stake are the questions at the heart of this chapter: What if these "few" American soldiers weren't monsters? What if they were typical men and women who, caught in the wrong circumstances, found themselves committing atrocities? Faced with similar pressures, might the most ordinary person (of any nation) be capable of heinous acts?

Criminal charges were brought against seven enlisted soldiers from the 372nd Military Police Company. Specialist Jeremy C. Sivits pleaded guilty, was sentenced to a year in prison, and subsequently cooperated with authorities in building the case against the other defendants. Pfc. Lynndie England, prominent in many of the photos (including one that shows her dragging a naked Iraqi man on a leash), was sentenced to three years. Attorneys for the other five indicated that they would employ a "following orders" defense. An investigative report by a panel chaired by Maj. Gen. George Fay (which some critics have labeled a "whitewash"), released in August 2005, named some officers from the 205th Military Intelligence Brigade as bearing culpability for what happened. The commander of this unit, Col. Thomas Pappas, was reprimanded for failing to assure that his officers followed the Geneva Conventions at Abu Ghraib. Additionally, a separate Pentagon investigation chaired by former CIA director James Schlesinger, criticized Secretary of Defense Donald Rumsfeld and his senior aides, though the Schlesinger report was prohibited from entering into "matters of personal responsibility."

In "Sources of Sadism," which first appeared in the 24 May 2004 edition of U.S. News & World Report, Marianne Szegedy-Maszak explores some of the reasons psychologists have offered to explain how American soldiers (at least one of whom was college-aged at the time of the abuses) could have knowingly degraded and tortured Iraqi detainees. The author refers directly to two experiments you will read about at some length in this chapter: Philip Zimbardo's Stanford Prison Experiment and Stanley Milgram's experiments in obedience.

If you have not yet seen the Abu Ghraib photos and wish to do so (be warned—they are disturbing), you can readily find them on the Internet.

1   Those hoping to see a flicker of anger or remorse or conscience on the faces of the American soldiers photographed tormenting Iraqi prisoners in Abu Ghraib are likely to be disappointed. Evidence of how these young recruits apparently became gleeful sadists can be found in neither their faces nor their biographies.

2   While many theories have been advanced about the forces that tragically came together at Abu Ghraib—inadequate training, overzealous intelligence gathering, failure of leadership—none can adequately account for the hardening of heart necessary for such sadism. So the question is: Are there particular conditions in Iraq today that might shed light on why these soldiers committed these unconscionable acts?

3   The usual points of reference in psychology are two classic studies that attempted to explore the capacity for evil residing in "normal" people. In 1971, Stanford psychologist Philip Zimbardo created a simulated prison and randomly assigned students to be either guards or prisoners. With astonishing speed,

the "guards" indulged in forms of torture and humiliation not unlike those horrifying us today. This followed on earlier experiments by Yale psychologist Stanley Milgram on obedience to authority. Milgram recruited volunteers to participate in what he described as a study on learning. An actor sat in a chair that students believed was wired with electricity. Each time this actor would give an incorrect answer, the students would be directed by Milgram to deliver a larger shock. As the subject in the electric chair seemed to suffer more and more, 2 out of 3 of the unwitting students administered shocks that would have been lethal in real life.

These experiments demonstrate that Everyman is a potential torturer. But what relevance does that have to Baghdad today? Robert Okin, a professor of psychiatry at the University of California-San Francisco who has worked with victims of torture, says that while there are lessons to be learned from these studies, the particulars of the soldiers' life in Abu Ghraib also need to be taken into account. In Iraq, Okin says, the abuse became "an inexcusable way of working off their rage, anxiety about their own safety, and their sense of helplessness."

5   The anxiety and helplessness are exacerbated by difficult living conditions and constant danger—including the unfavorable odds of 450 military guards overseeing 7,000 often hostile prisoners. Then there is the issue of sex: One of the least discussed aspects of the occupation in Iraq has been the lack of a reliable local brothel where male soldiers are able to unwind. Experts have long appreciated the fact that sexual activity can often be a way of relieving the anxiety of war.

6   Abu Ghraib also has three traits that psychologist Herbert Kelman has described as necessary for torture: authorization, routinization, and dehumanization. To translate the jargon, authorization means that someone with power needs to say that extreme measures are acceptable. (Pfc. Lynndie England said in an interview last week that her superiors said, "Hey, you're doing great; keep it up.")

7   Authorization leads to routinization, a kind of division of labor. In Nazi Germany, for example, one person had responsibility for writing the orders to deport the Jews, someone else for shaving their heads, and so on. The guards at Abu Ghraib were told they were merely "softening up" the prisoners for interrogation. Such parceling out of responsibility, says Boston psychiatrist Jonathan Shay, "seems to tantalize someone's moral compass, making it possible to do things that might be personally distasteful."

8   Dehumanization follows. In Vietnam the enemy became "slopes," and in Iraq they're "towel heads." Covering prisoners' faces with hoods, Okin adds, makes it possible for the soldiers to sever any empathic human connection with them."

9   The protected walls of Abu Ghraib made it an island where conventional morality no longer applied. When these soldiers testify at court-martial, perhaps their testimony will contribute to the psychological theories on blind obedience to authority. However, Okin says, "The ethical questions just don't go away; horror doesn't go away by being able to explain it." And indeed, as the explanations always fall short, the horror continues to loom large.

Review Questions

1. What are the "usual points of reference in psychology" for abuses like those that occurred at Abu Ghraib?

2. According to Herbert Kelman, what conditions are necessary for a person to commit acts of torture?

3. How might the circumstances that soldiers faced in Iraq have contributed to the events at Abu Ghraib?

4. What are the limits of psychological explanations of torture, according to Szegedy-Maszak?

Discussion and Writing Suggestions

1. How did you respond when the Abu Ghraib prison scandal broke? (If you were not aware of the scandal, consider the factors that may have kept the news from reaching you.)

2. A former commander of the Army Reserve unit implicated in the Abu Ghraib abuse (the 372nd MP Company) and now an attorney with the federal government, James D. Villa, wrote the following in an op-ed essay for the *Washington Post* on 12 May 2004: "Various people, including the families of some of the soldiers in question, have said that the soldiers were not given appropriate training to run a detention facility and had inadequate support to do their jobs. While these statements may be true, in what Army field manual can one locate the section about stacking naked prisoners like cordwood, or affixing collars to their necks? Is special training needed to show a soldier that this sort of thing is contemptible and contrary to any standards of decency?" Your comments?

3. To what extent do you feel that the harsh conditions soldiers faced in Iraq either excuse the abuse of Iraqi prisoners or make you more understanding of that abuse?

4. Szegedy-Maszak writes that the "protected walls of Abu Ghraib made it an island where conventional morality no longer applied." What is it about being on a metaphorical island (that is, being cut off from the influence of others) that invites people to abandon conventional morality? In your own experience, can you identify "island-like" moments in which conventional morality seemed no longer to apply?

5. At least several of those involved in the Abu Ghraib abuse were of college age. Do you regard them as moral monsters—as isolated bad apples? How different are they from ordinary Americans, particularly ordinary Americans in stressful conditions?

Opinions and Social Pressure
Solomon E. Asch

In the early 1950s, Solomon Asch (b. 1907), a social psychologist at Rutgers University, conducted a series of simple but ingenious experiments on the influence of group pressure upon the individual. Essentially, he discovered, individuals can be influenced by groups to deny the evidence of their own senses. Together with the Milgram experiments of the next decade (see the selections that follow here), these studies provide powerful evidence of the degree to which individuals can surrender their own judgment to others, even when those others are clearly in the wrong. The results of these experiments have implications far beyond the laboratory: they can explain a good deal of the normal human behavior we see every day—at school, at work, at home.

1   That social influences shape every person's practices, judgments, and beliefs is a truism to which anyone will readily assent. A child masters his "native" dialect down to the finest nuances; a member of a tribe of cannibals accepts cannibalism as altogether fitting and proper. All the social sciences take their departure from the observation of the profound effects that groups exert on their members. For psychologists, group pressure upon the mind of the individual raises a host of questions they would like to investigate in detail.

2   How, and to what extent, do social forces constrain people's opinions and attitudes? This question is especially pertinent in our day. The same epoch that has witnessed the unprecedented technical extension of communication has also brought into existence the deliberate manipulation of opinion and the "engineering of consent." There are many good reasons why, as citizens and as scientists, we should be concerned with studying the ways in which human beings form their opinions and the role that social conditions play.

3   Studies of these questions began with the interest in hypnosis aroused by the French physician Jean Martin Charcot (a teacher of Sigmund Freud) toward the end of the 19th century. Charcot believed that only hysterical patients could be fully hypnotized, but this view was soon challenged by two other physicians, Hyppolyte Bernheim and A. A. Liébault, who demonstrated that they could put most people under hypnotic spell. Bernheim proposed that hypnosis was but an extreme form of a normal psychological process which became known as "suggestibility." It was shown that monotonous reiteration of instructions could induce in normal persons in the waking state involuntary bodily changes such as swaying or rigidity of the arms, and sensations such as warmth and odor.

4   It was not long before social thinkers seized upon these discoveries as a basis for explaining numerous social phenomena, from the spread of opinion to the formation of crowds and the following of leaders. The sociologist Gabriel Tarde summed it all up in the aphorism: "Social man is a somnambulist."

5   When the new discipline of social psychology was born at the beginning of this century, its first experiments were essentially adaptations of the sugges-

tion demonstration. The technique generally followed a simple plan. The subjects, usually college students, were asked to give their opinions or preferences concerning various matters; some time later they were again asked to state their choices, but now they were also informed of the opinions held by authorities or large groups of their peers on the same matters. (Often the alleged consensus was fictitious.) Most of these studies had substantially the same result: confronted with opinions contrary to their own, many subjects apparently shifted their judgments in the direction of the views of the majorities or the experts. The late psychologist Edward L. Thorndike reported that he had succeeded in modifying the esthetic preferences of adults by this procedure. Other psychologists reported that people's evaluations of the merit of a literary passage could be raised or lowered by ascribing the passage to different authors. Apparently the sheer weight of numbers or authority sufficed to change opinions, even when no arguments for the opinions themselves were provided.

6   Now the very ease of success in these experiments arouses suspicion. Did the subjects actually change their opinions, or were the experimental victories scored only on paper? On grounds of common sense, one must question whether opinions are generally as watery as these studies indicate. There is some reason to wonder whether it was not the investigators who, in their enthusiasm for a theory, were suggestible, and whether the ostensibly gullible subjects were not providing answers which they thought good subjects were expected to give.

7   The investigations were guided by certain underlying assumptions, which today are common currency and account for much that is thought and said about the operations of propaganda and public opinion. The assumptions are that people submit uncritically and painlessly to external manipulation by suggestion or prestige, and that any given idea or value can be "sold" or "unsold" without reference to its merits. We should be skeptical, however, of the supposition that the power of social pressure necessarily implies uncritical submission to it: independence and the capacity to rise above group passion are also open to human beings. Further, one may question on psychological grounds whether it is possible as a rule to change a person's judgment of a situation or an object without first changing his knowledge or assumptions about it.

8   In what follows I shall describe some experiments in an investigation of the effects of group pressure which was carried out recently with the help of a number of my associates. The tests not only demonstrate the operations of group pressure upon individuals but also illustrate a new kind of attack on the problem and some of the more subtle questions that it raises.

9   A group of seven to nine young men, all college students, are assembled in a classroom for a "psychological experiment" in visual judgment. The experimenter informs them that they will be comparing the lengths of lines. He shows two large white cards [see Figure 1]. On one is a single vertical black line—the standard whose length is to be matched. On the other card are three

vertical lines of various lengths. The subjects are to choose the one that is of the same length as the line on the other card. One of the three actually is of the same length; the other two are substantially different, the difference ranging from three quarters of an inch to an inch and three quarters.

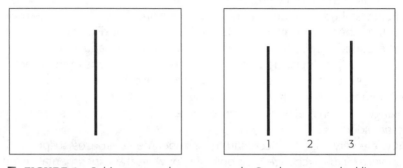

FIGURE 1   Subjects were shown two cards. One bore a standard line. The other bore three lines, one of which was the same length as the standard. The subjects were asked to choose this line.

10   The experiment opens uneventfully. The subjects announce their answers in the order in which they have been seated in the room, and on the first round every person chooses the same matching line. Then a second set of cards is exposed; again the group is unanimous. The members appear ready to endure politely another boring experiment. On the third trial there is an unexpected disturbance. One person near the end of the group disagrees with all the others in his selection of the matching line. He looks surprised, indeed incredulous, about the disagreement. On the following trial he disagrees again, while the others remain unanimous in their choice. The dissenter becomes more and more worried and hesitant as the disagreement continues in succeeding trials; he may pause before announcing his answer and speak in a low voice, or he may smile in an embarrassed way.

11   What the dissenter does not know is that all the other members of the group were instructed by the experimenter beforehand to give incorrect answers in unanimity at certain points. The single individual who is not a party to this pre-arrangement is the focal subject of our experiment. He is placed in a position in which, while he is actually giving the correct answers, he finds himself unexpectedly in a minority of one, opposed by a unanimous and arbitrary majority with respect to a clear and simple fact. Upon him we have brought to bear two opposed forces: the evidence of his senses and the unanimous opinion of a group of his peers. Also, he must declare his judgments in public, before a majority which has also stated its position publicly.

12   The instructed majority occasionally reports correctly in order to reduce the possibility that the naive subject will suspect collusion against him. (In only a

few cases did the subject actually show suspicion; when this happened, the experiment was stopped and the results were not counted.) There are 18 trials in each series, and on 12 of these the majority responds erroneously.

13   How do people respond to group pressure in this situation? I shall report first the statistical results of a series in which a total of 123 subjects from three institutions of higher learning (not including my own Swarthmore College) were placed in the minority situation described above.

14   Two alternatives were open to the subject: he could act independently, repudiating the majority, or he could go along with the majority, repudiating the evidence of his senses. Of the 123 put to the test, a considerable percentage yielded to the majority. Whereas in ordinary circumstances individuals matching the lines will make mistakes less than 1 per cent of the time, under group pressure the minority subjects swung to acceptance of the misleading majority's wrong judgments in 36.8 per cent of the selections.

15   Of course individuals differed in response. At one extreme, about one quarter of the subjects were completely independent and never agreed with the erroneous judgments of the majority. At the other extreme, some individuals went with the majority nearly all the time. The performances of individuals in this experiment tend to be highly consistent. Those who strike out on the path of independence do not, as a rule, succumb to the majority even over an extended series of trials, while those who choose the path of compliance are unable to free themselves as the ordeal is prolonged.

16   The reasons for the startling individual differences have not yet been investigated in detail. At this point we can only report some tentative generalizations from talks with the subjects, each of whom was interviewed at the end of the experiment. Among the independent individuals were many who held fast because of staunch confidence in their own judgment. The most significant fact about them was not absence of responsiveness to the majority but a capacity to recover from doubt and to reestablish their equilibrium. Others who acted independently came to believe that the majority was correct in its answers, but they continued their dissent on the simple ground that it was their obligation to call the play as they saw it.

17   Among the extremely yielding persons we found a group who quickly reached the conclusion: "I am wrong, they are right." Others yielded in order "not to spoil your results." Many of the individuals who went along suspected that the majority were "sheep" following the first responder, or that the majority were victims of an optical illusion; nevertheless, these suspicions failed to free them at the moment of decision. More disquieting were the reactions of subjects who construed their difference from the majority as a sign of some general deficiency in themselves, which at all costs they must hide. On this basis they desperately tried to merge with the majority, not realizing the longer-range consequences to themselves. All the yielding subjects underestimated the frequency with which they conformed.

18   Which aspect of the influence of a majority is more important—the size of the majority or its unanimity? The experiment was modified to examine this question. In one series the size of the opposition was varied from one to 15

persons. The results showed a clear trend. When a subject was confronted with only a single individual who contradicted his answers, he was swayed little: he continued to answer independently and correctly in nearly all trials. When the opposition was increased to two, the pressure became substantial: minority subjects now accepted the wrong answer 13.6 per cent of the time. Under the pressure of a majority of three, the subjects' errors jumped to 31.8 per cent. But further increases in the size of the majority apparently did not increase the weight of the pressure substantially. Clearly the size of the opposition is important only up to a point.

19   Disturbance of the majority's unanimity had a striking effect. In this experiment the subject was given the support of a truthful partner—either another individual who did not know of the prearranged agreement among the rest of the group, or a person who was instructed to give correct answers throughout.

20   The presence of a supporting partner depleted the majority of much of its power. Its pressure on the dissenting individual was reduced to one fourth: that is, subjects answered incorrectly only one fourth as often as under the pressure of a unanimous majority. The weakest persons did not yield as readily. Most interesting were the reactions to the partner. Generally the feeling toward him was one of warmth and closeness; he was credited with inspiring confidence. However, the subjects repudiated the suggestion that the partner decided them to be independent.

21   Was the partner's effect a consequence of his dissent, or was it related to his accuracy? We now introduced into the experimental group a person who was instructed to dissent from the majority but also to disagree with the subject. In some experiments the majority was always to choose the worst of the comparison lines and the instructed dissenter to pick the line that was closer to the length of the standard one; in others the majority was consistently intermediate and the dissenter most in error. In this manner we were able to study the relative influence of "compromising" and "extremist" dissenters.

22   Again the results are clear. When a moderate dissenter is present the effect of the majority on the subject decreases by approximately one third, and extremes of yielding disappear. Moreover, most of the errors the subjects do make are moderate, rather than flagrant. In short, the dissenter largely controls the choice of errors. To this extent the subjects broke away from the majority even while bending to it.

23   On the other hand, when the dissenter always chose the line that was more flagrantly different from the standard, the results were of quite a different kind. The extremist dissenter produced a remarkable freeing of the subjects; their errors dropped to only 9 percent. Furthermore, all the errors were of the moderate variety. We were able to conclude that dissents *per se* increased independence and moderated the errors that occurred, and that the direction of dissent exerted consistent effects.

24   In all the foregoing experiments each subject was observed only in a single setting. We now turned to studying the effects upon a given individual of a change in the situation to which he was exposed. The first experiment examined the consequences of losing or gaining a partner. The instructed partner

began by answering correctly on the first six trials. With his support the subject usually resisted pressure from the majority: 18 of 27 subjects were completely independent. But after six trials the partner joined the majority. As soon as he did so, there was an abrupt rise in the subjects' errors. Their submission to the majority was just about as frequent as when the minority subject was opposed by a unanimous majority throughout.

25   It was surprising to find that the experience of having had a partner and of having braved the majority opposition with him had failed to strengthen the individuals' independence. Questioning at the conclusion of the experiment suggested that we had overlooked an important circumstance; namely, the strong specific effect of "desertion" by the partner to the other side. We therefore changed the conditions so that the partner would simply leave the group at the proper point. (To allay suspicion it was announced in advance that he had an appointment with the dean.) In this form of the experiment, the partner's effect outlasted his presence. The errors increased after his departure, but less markedly than after a partner switched to the majority.

26   In a variant of this procedure the trials began with the majority unanimously giving correct answers. Then they gradually broke away until on the sixth trial the naive subject was alone and the group unanimously against him. As long as the subject had anyone on his side, he was almost invariably independent, but as soon as he found himself alone, the tendency to conform to the majority rose abruptly.

27   As might be expected, an individual's resistance to group pressure in these experiments depends to a considerable degree on how wrong the majority was. We varied the discrepancy between the standard line and the other lines systematically, with the hope of reaching a point where the error of the majority would be so glaring that every subject would repudiate it and choose independently. In this we regretfully did not succeed. Even when the difference between the lines was seven inches, there were still some who yielded to the error of the majority.

28   The study provides clear answers to a few relatively simple questions, and it raises many others that await investigation. We would like to know the degree of consistency of persons in situations which differ in content and structure. If consistency of independence or conformity in behavior is shown to be a fact, how is it functionally related to qualities of character and personality? In what ways is independence related to sociological or cultural conditions? Are leaders more independent than other people, or are they adept at following their followers? These and many other questions may perhaps be answerable by investigations of the type described here.

29   Life in society requires consensus as an indispensable condition. But consensus, to be productive, requires that each individual contribute independently out of his experience and insight. When consensus comes under the dominance of conformity, the social process is polluted and the individual at the same time surrenders the powers on which his functioning as a feeling and thinking being depends. That we have found the tendency to conformity in our society so strong that reasonably intelligent and well-meaning young people are

willing to call white black is a matter of concern. It raises questions about our ways of education and about the values that guide our conduct.

30   Yet anyone inclined to draw too pessimistic conclusions from this report would do well to remind himself that the capacities for independence are not to be underestimated. He may also draw some consolation from a further observation: those who participated in this challenging experiment agreed nearly without exception that independence was preferable to conformity.

Review Questions

1. What is "suggestibility"? How is this phenomenon related to social pressure?

2. Summarize the procedure and results of the Asch experiment. What conclusions does Asch draw from these results?

3. To what extent did varying the size of the majority and its unanimity affect the experimental results?

4. What distinction does Asch draw between consensus and conformity?

Discussion and Writing Suggestions

1. Before discussing the experiment, Asch considers how easily people's opinions or attitudes may be shaped by social pressure. To what extent do you agree with this conclusion? Write a short paper on this subject, drawing upon examples from your own experience or observation or from your reading.

2. Do the results of this experiment surprise you? Or do they confirm facts about human behavior that you had already suspected, observed, or experienced? Explain, in two or three paragraphs. Provide examples, relating these examples to features of the Asch experiment.

3. Frequently, the conclusions drawn from a researcher's experimental results are challenged on the basis that laboratory conditions do not accurately reflect the complexity of human behavior. Asch draws certain conclusions about the degree to which individuals are affected by group pressures based on an experiment involving subjects choosing matching line lengths. To what extent, if any, do you believe that these conclusions lack validity because the behavior at the heart of the experiment is too dissimilar to real-life situations of group pressure on the individual? Support your opinions with examples.

4. We are all familiar with the phenomenon of "peer pressure." To what extent do Asch's experiments demonstrate the power of peer pressure? To what extent do you think that other factors may be at work? Explain, providing examples.

5. Asch's experiments, conducted in the early 1950s, involved groups of "seven to nine young men, all college students." To what extent do you believe that the results of a similar experiment would be different today? To what extent might they be different if the subjects had included women, as well, and subjects of various ages, from children, to middle-aged people, to older people? To what extent do you believe that the social class or culture of the subjects might have an impact upon the experimental results? Support your opinions with examples and logical reasoning. (Beware, however, of overgeneralizing, based upon insufficient evidence.)

The Perils of Obedience
Stanley Milgram

In 1963, a Yale psychologist conducted one of the classic studies on obedience. Stanley Milgram designed an experiment that forced participants either to violate their conscience by obeying the immoral demands of an authority figure or to refuse those demands. Surprisingly, Milgram found that few participants could resist the authority's orders, even when the participants knew that following these orders would result in another person's pain. Were the participants in these experiments incipient mass murderers? No, said Milgram. They were "ordinary people, simply doing their jobs." The implications of Milgram's conclusions are immense.

Consider these questions: Where does evil reside? What sort of people were responsible for the Holocaust, and for the long list of other atrocities that seem to blight the human record in every generation? Is it a lunatic fringe, a few sick but powerful people who are responsible for atrocities? If so, then we decent folk needn't ever look inside ourselves to understand evil since (by our definition) evil lurks out there, in "those sick ones." Milgram's study suggested otherwise: that under a special set of circumstances the obedience we naturally show authority figures can transform us into agents of terror.

The article that follows is one of the longest in this book, and it may help you to know in advance the author's organization. In paragraphs 1–11, Milgram discusses the larger significance and the history of dilemmas involving obedience to authority; he then summarizes his basic experimental design and follows with a report of one experiment. Milgram organizes the remainder of his article into sections, which he has subtitled "An Unexpected Outcome," "Peculiar Reactions," "The Etiquette of Submission," and "Duty Without Conflict." He begins his conclusion in paragraph 108. If you find the article too long or complex to complete in a single sitting, then plan to read sections at a time, taking notes on each until you're done. Anticipate the article that immediately follows this one: It reviews Milgram's work and largely concerns the ethics of his experimental design. Consider these ethics as you read so that you, in turn, can respond to Milgram's critics.

Stanley Milgram (1933–1984) taught and conducted research at Yale and Harvard universities and at the Graduate Center, City University of New York. He was named Guggenheim Fellow in 1972–1973 and a year later was nominated for the National Book Award for Obedience to Authority. *His other books include* Television and Antisocial Behavior *(1973),* The City and the Self *(1974),* Human Aggression *(1976), and* The Individual in the Social World *(1977).*

1   Obedience is as basic an element in the structure of social life as one can point to. Some system of authority is a requirement of all communal living, and it is only the person dwelling in isolation who is not forced to respond, with defiance or submission, to the commands of others. For many people, obedience is a deeply ingrained behavior tendency, indeed a potent impulse overriding training in ethics, sympathy, and moral conduct.

2   The dilemma inherent in submission to authority is ancient, as old as the story of Abraham, and the question of whether one should obey when commands conflict with conscience has been argued by Plato, dramatized in *Antigone,* and treated to philosophic analysis in almost every historical epoch. Conservative philosophers argue that the very fabric of society is threatened by disobedience, while humanists stress the primacy of the individual conscience.

3   The legal and philosophic aspects of obedience are of enormous import, but they say very little about how most people behave in concrete situations. I set up a simple experiment at Yale University to test how much pain an ordinary citizen would inflict on another person simply because he was ordered to by an experimental scientist. Stark authority was pitted against the subjects' strongest moral imperatives against hurting others, and with the subjects' ears ringing with the screams of the victims, authority won more often than not. The extreme willingness of adults to go to almost any lengths on the command of an authority constitutes the chief finding of the study and the fact most urgently demanding explanation.

4   In the basic experimental design, two people come to a psychology laboratory to take part in a study of memory and learning. One of them is designated as a "teacher" and the other a "learner." The experimenter explains that the study is concerned with the effects of punishment on learning. The learner is conducted into a room, seated in a kind of miniature electric chair; his arms are strapped to prevent excessive movement, and an electrode is attached to his wrist. He is told that he will be read lists of simple word pairs, and that he will then be tested on his ability to remember the second word of a pair when he hears the first one again. Whenever he makes an error, he will receive electric shocks of increasing intensity.

5   The real focus of the experiment is the teacher. After watching the learner being strapped into place, he is seated before an impressive shock generator. The instrument panel consists of thirty level switches set in a horizontal line. Each switch is clearly labeled with a voltage designation ranging from 15 to 450 volts. The following designations are clearly indicated for groups of four switches, going from left to right: Slight Shock, Moderate Shock, Strong Shock, Very Strong Shock, Intense Shock, Extreme Intensity Shock, Danger: Severe Shock. (Two switches after this last designation are simply marked XXX.)

6   When a switch is depressed, a pilot light corresponding to each switch is illuminated in bright red; an electric buzzing is heard; a blue light, labeled "voltage energizer," flashes; the dial on the voltage meter swings to the right; and various relay clicks sound off.

7   The upper left-hand corner of the generator is labeled SHOCK GENERATOR, TYPE ZLB, DYSON INSTRUMENT COMPANY, WALTHAM, MASS. OUTPUT 15 VOLTS—450 VOLTS.

8   Each subject is given a sample 45-volt shock from the generator before his run as teacher, and the jolt strengthens his belief in the authenticity of the machine.

9   The teacher is a genuinely naive subject who has come to the laboratory for the experiment. The learner, or victim, is actually an actor who receives no shock at all. The point of the experiment is to see how far a person will proceed in a concrete and measurable situation in which he is ordered to inflict increasing pain on a protesting victim.

10   Conflict arises when the man receiving the shock begins to show that he is experiencing discomfort. At 75 volts, he grunts; at 120 volts, he complains loudly; at 150, he demands to be released from the experiment. As the voltage increases, his protests become more vehement and emotional. At 285 volts, his response can be described only as an agonized scream. Soon thereafter, he makes no sound at all.

11   For the teacher, the situation quickly becomes one of gripping tension. It is not a game for him; conflict is intense and obvious. The manifest suffering of the learner presses him to quit; but each time he hesitates to administer a shock, the experimenter orders him to continue. To extricate himself from this plight, the subject must make a clear break with authority.*

12   The subject, Gretchen Brandt,† is an attractive thirty-one-year-old medical technician who works at the Yale Medical School. She had emigrated from Germany five years before.

13   On several occasions when the learner complains, she turns to the experimenter coolly and inquires, "Shall I continue?" She promptly returns to her task when the experimenter asks her to do so. At the administration of 210 volts, she turns to the experimenter, remarking firmly, "Well, I'm sorry, I don't think we should continue."

14   EXPERIMENTER: The experiment requires that you go on until he has learned all the word pairs correctly.

15   BRANDT: He has a heart condition. I'm sorry. He told you that before.

16   EXPERIMENTER: The shocks may be painful but they are not dangerous.

17   BRANDT: Well, I'm sorry, I think when shocks continue like this, they *are* dangerous. You ask him if he wants to get out. It's his free will.

18   EXPERIMENTER: It is absolutely essential that we continue. . . .

---

* The ethical problems of carrying out an experiment of this sort are too complex to be dealt with here, but they receive extended treatment in the book from which this article is adapted.

† Names of subjects described in this piece have been changed.

19   BRANDT: I'd like you to ask him. We came here of our free will. If he wants to continue I'll go ahead. He told you he had a heart condition. I'm sorry. I don't want to be responsible for anything happening to him. I wouldn't like it for me either.

20   EXPERIMENTER: You have no other choice.

21   BRANDT: I think we are here on our own free will. I don't want to be responsible if anything happens to him. Please understand that.

22   She refuses to go further and the experiment is terminated.

23   The woman is firm and resolute throughout. She indicates in the interview that she was in no way tense or nervous, and this corresponds to her controlled appearance during the experiment. She feels that the last shock she administered to the learner was extremely painful and reiterates that she "did not want to be responsible for any harm to him."

24   The woman's straightforward, courteous behavior in the experiment, lack of tension, and total control of her own action seem to make disobedience a simple and rational deed. Her behavior is the very embodiment of what I envisioned would be true for almost all subjects.

An Unexpected Outcome

25   Before the experiments, I sought predictions about the outcome from various kinds of people—psychiatrists, college sophomores, middle-class adults, graduate students, and faculty in the behavioral sciences. With remarkable similarity, they predicted that virtually all subjects would refuse to obey the experimenter. The psychiatrists, specifically, predicted that most subjects would not go beyond 150 volts, when the victim makes his first explicit demand to be freed. They expected that only 4 percent would reach 300 volts, and that only a pathological fringe of about one in a thousand would administer the highest shock on the board.

26   These predictions were unequivocally wrong. Of the forty subjects in the first experiment, twenty-five obeyed the orders of the experimenter to the end, punishing the victim until they reached the most potent shock available on the generator. After 450 volts were administered three times, the experimenter called a halt to the session. Many obedient subjects then heaved sighs of relief, mopped their brows, rubbed their fingers over their eyes, or nervously fumbled cigarettes. Others displayed only minimal signs of tension from beginning to end.

27   When the very first experiments were carried out, Yale undergraduates were used as subjects, and about 60 percent of them were fully obedient. A colleague of mine immediately dismissed these findings as having no relevance to "ordinary" people, asserting that Yale undergraduates are a highly aggressive, competitive bunch who step on each other's necks on the slightest provocation. He assured me that when "ordinary" people were tested, the results would be quite different. As we moved from the pilot studies to the regular experimental series, people drawn from every stratum of New Haven life came to be employed in the experiment: professionals, white-collar workers, unemployed persons, and industrial workers. *The experiment's total outcome was the same as we had observed among the students.*

28   Moreover, when the experiments were repeated in Princeton, Munich, Rome, South Africa, and Australia, the level of obedience was invariably somewhat *higher* than found in the investigation reported in this article. Thus one scientist in Munich found 85 percent of his subjects to be obedient.

29   Fred Prozi's reactions, if more dramatic than most, illuminate the conflicts experienced by others in less visible form. About fifty years old and unemployed at the time of the experiment, he has a good-natured, if slightly dissolute, appearance, and he strikes people as a rather ordinary fellow. He begins the session calmly but becomes tense as it proceeds. After delivering the 180-volt shock, he pivots around in his chair and, shaking his head, addresses the experimenter in agitated tones:

30   PROZI: I can't stand it. I'm not going to kill that man in there. You hear him hollering?

31   EXPERIMENTER: As I told you before, the shocks may be painful, but . . .

32   PROZI: But he's hollering. He can't stand it. What's going to happen to him?

33   EXPERIMENTER (*his voice patient, matter-of-fact*): The experiment requires that you continue, Teacher.

34   PROZI: Aaah, but unh, I'm not going to get that man sick in there—know what I mean?

35   EXPERIMENTER: Whether the learner likes it or not, we must go on, through all the word pairs.

36   PROZI: I refuse to take the responsibility. He's in there hollering!

37   EXPERIMENTER: It's absolutely essential that you continue, Prozi.

38   PROZI (*indicating the unused questions*): There's too many left here. I mean, Jeez, if he gets them wrong, there's too many of them left. I mean, who's going to take the responsibility if anything happens to that gentleman?

39   EXPERIMENTER: I'm responsible for anything that happens to him. Continue, please.

40   PROZI: All right. (*Consults list of words.*) The next one's "Slow—walk, truck, dance, music." Answer, please (*A buzzing sound indicates the learner has signaled his answer.*) Wrong. A hundred and ninety-five volts. "Dance." (*Zzumph!*)

41   LEARNER (*yelling*): Let me out of here! My heart's bothering me! (*Teacher looks at experimenter.*)

42   EXPERIMENTER: Continue, please.

43   LEARNER (*screaming*): Let me out of here! You have no right to keep me here! Let me out of here, my heart's bothering me, let me out!

44   PROZI (*shakes head, pats the table nervously*): You see, he's hollering. Hear that? Gee, I don't know.

45   EXPERIMENTER: The experiment requires . . .

46   PROZI (*interrupting*): I know it does, sir, but I mean—hunh! He don't know what he's getting in for. He's up to 195 volts! (*Experiment continues, through 210 volts, 225 volts, 240 volts, 255 volts, 270 volts, at which point Prozi, with evident relief, runs out of word-pair questions.*)

47   EXPERIMENTER: You'll have to go back to the beginning of that page and go through them again until he's learned them all correctly.

48   PROZI: Aw, no. I'm not going to kill that man. You mean I've got to keep going up with the scale? No sir. He's hollering in there. I'm not going to give him 450 volts.

49   EXPERIMENTER: The experiment requires that you go on.

50   LEARNER: Ohhh. I absolutely refuse to answer anymore. (*Shouting urgently now.*) Let me out of here! You can't hold me here! Get me out. Get-me-out-of-here!

51   EXPERIMENTER: Continue. The next word is "Green," please.

52   PROZI: "Green—grass, hat, ink, apple." (*Nothing happens. No answering buzz. Just gloomy silence.*)

53   PROZI: I don't think he is going to answer.

54   EXPERIMENTER: If the learner doesn't answer in a reasonable time, about four or five seconds, consider the answer wrong. And follow the same procedures you have been doing for wrong answers. Say, "Wrong," tell him the number of volts, give him the punishment, read him the correct answer. Continue, please.

55   PROZI: "Green—grass, hat, ink, apple." Answer, please. (*More silence. Subject just sits there.*)

56   EXPERIMENTER: Go on with the procedure, please.

57   PROZI: Three hundred and fifteen volts. The answer is "ink." (*Zzumph!*)

58   LEARNER: Ohh. Ooohh.

59   PROZI (*relieved to hear response*): Next one . . .

60   LEARNER: I absolutely refuse to answer.

61   PROZI: You got to. You get a shock if you don't answer. (*Experiment continues with learner refusing to answer, and finally, failing even to grunt or groan. At 375 volts, the subject stands up.*)

62   PROZI: I think something's happened to that fellow in there. I don't get no answer. He was hollering at less voltage. Can't you check in and see if he's all right, please?

63   EXPERIMENTER: (*with same detached calm*): Not once we've started. Please continue, Teacher.

64   PROZI (*sits down, sighs deeply*): "Cool—day, shade, water, paint." Answer, please. Are you all right in there? Are you all right?

65   EXPERIMENTER: Please continue, Teacher. Continue, please. (*Subject pushes lever. Zzumph!*)

66   PROZI (*swiveling around in his chair*): Something's happened to that man in there. (*Swiveling back.*) Next one. "Low—dollar, necklace, moon, paint." (*Turning around again.*) Something's happened to that man in there. You better check on him, sir. He won't answer or nothing.

67   EXPERIMENTER: Continue. Go on, please.

68   PROZI: You accept all responsibility?

69   EXPERIMENTER: The responsibility is mine. Correct. Please go on. (*Subject returns to his list, starts running through words as rapidly as he can read them, works through to 450 volts.*)

70   PROZI: That's that.

71   EXPERIMENTER: Continue using the 450 switch for each wrong answer. Continue, please.

72   PROZI: But I don't get anything!

73   EXPERIMENTER: Please continue. The next word is "white."

74   PROZI: Don't you think you should look in on him, please?

75   EXPERIMENTER: Not once we've started the experiment.

76   PROZI: What if he's dead in there? (*Gestures toward the room with the electric chair.*) I mean, he told me he can't stand the shock, sir. I don't mean to be rude, but I think you should look in on him. All you have to do is look in on him. All you have to do is look in the door. I don't get no answer, no noise. Something might have happened to the gentleman in there, sir.

77   EXPERIMENTER: We must continue. Go on, please.

78   PROZI: You mean keep giving him what? Four-hundred-fifty volts, what he's got now?

79   EXPERIMENTER: That's correct. Continue. The next word is "white."

80   PROZI (*now at a furious pace*): "White—cloud, horse, rock, house." Answer, please. The answer is "horse." Four hundred and fifty volts. (*Zzumph!*) Next word, "Bag—paint, music, clown, girl." The answer is "paint." Four hundred and fifty volts. (*Zzumph!*) Next word is "Short—sentence, movie . . ."

81   EXPERIMENTER: Excuse me, Teacher. We'll have to discontinue the experiment.

Peculiar Reactions

82   Morris Braverman, another subject, is a thirty-nine-year-old social worker. He looks older than his years because of his bald head and serious demeanor. His brow is furrowed, as if all the world's burdens were carried on his face. He appears intelligent and concerned.

83   When the learner refuses to answer and the experimenter instructs Braverman to treat the absence of an answer as equivalent to a wrong answer, he takes his instruction to heart. Before administering 300 volts he asserts officiously to the victim, "Mr. Wallace, your silence has to be considered as a wrong answer." Then he administers the shock. He offers half-heartedly to change places with the learner, then asks the experimenter, "Do I have to follow these instructions literally?" He is satisfied with the experimenter's answer that he does. His very refined and authoritative manner of speaking is increasingly broken up by wheezing laughter.

84   The experimenter's notes on Mr. Braverman at the last few shocks are:

> Almost breaking up now each time gives shock. Rubbing face to hide laughter. Squinting, trying to hide face with hand, still laughing. Cannot control his laughter at this point no matter what he does. Clenching fist, pushing it onto table.

85   In an interview after the session, Mr. Braverman summarizes the experiment with impressive fluency and intelligence. He feels the experiment may have been designed also to "test the effects on the teacher of being in an essentially sadistic role, as well as the reactions of a student to a learning situation that was authoritative and punitive." When asked how painful the last few shocks administered to the learner were, he indicates that the most extreme category on the scale is not adequate (it read EXTREMELY PAINFUL) and places his mark at the edge of the scale with an arrow carrying it beyond the scale.

86   It is almost impossible to convey the greatly relaxed, sedate quality of his conversation in the interview. In the most relaxed terms, he speaks about his severe inner tension.

87   EXPERIMENTER: At what point were you most tense or nervous?

88   MR. BRAVERMAN: Well, when he first began to cry out in pain, and I realized this was hurting him. This got worse when he just blocked and refused to answer. There was I. I'm a nice person, I think, hurting somebody, and caught up in what seemed a mad situation . . . and in the interest of science, one goes through with it.

89   When the interviewer pursues the general question of tension, Mr. Braverman spontaneously mentions his laughter.

90   "My reactions were awfully peculiar. I don't know if you were watching me, but my reactions were giggly, and trying to stifle laughter. This isn't the way I usually am. This was a sheer reaction to a totally impossible situation. And my reaction was to the situation of having to hurt somebody. And being totally helpless and caught up in a set of circumstances where I just couldn't deviate and I couldn't try to help. This is what got me."

91   Mr. Braverman, like all subjects, was told the actual nature and purpose of the experiment, and a year later he affirmed in a questionnaire that he had learned something of personal importance: "What appalled me was that I could possess this capacity for obedience and compliance to a central idea, i.e., the value of a memory experiment, even after it became clear that continued adherence to this value was at the expense of violation of another value, i.e., don't hurt someone who is helpless and not hurting you. As my wife said, 'You can call yourself Eichmann.'* I hope I deal more effectively with any future conflicts of values I encounter."

The Etiquette of Submission

92   One theoretical interpretation of this behavior holds that all people harbor deeply aggressive instincts continually pressing for expression, and that the experiment provides institutional justification for the release of these impulses. According to this view, if a person is placed in a situation in which he has complete power over another individual, whom he may punish as much as he likes, all that is sadistic and bestial in man comes to the fore. The impulse to shock the victim is seen to flow from the potent aggressive tendencies, which are part of the motivational life of the individual, and the experiment, because it provides social legitimacy, simply opens the door to their expression.

93   It becomes vital, therefore, to compare the subject's performance when he is under orders and when he is allowed to choose the shock level.

94   The procedure was identical to our standard experiment, except that the teacher was told that he was free to select any shock level on any of the trials. (The experimenter took pains to point out that the teacher could use the high-

---

* *Adolf Eichmann* (1906–1962), the Nazi official responsible for implementing Hitler's "Final Solution" to exterminate the Jews, escaped to Argentina after World War II. In 1960, Israeli agents captured him and brought him to Israel, where he was tried as a war criminal and sentenced to death. At his trial, Eichmann maintained that he was merely following orders in arranging murders of his victims.

est levels on the generator, the lowest, any in between, or any combination of levels.) Each subject proceeded for thirty critical trials. The learner's protests were coordinated to standard shock levels, his first grunt coming at 75 volts, his first vehement protest at 150 volts.

95   The average shock used during the thirty critical trials was less than 60 volts—lower than the point at which the victim showed the first signs of discomfort. Three of the forty subjects did not go beyond the very lowest level on the board, twenty-eight went no higher than 75 volts, and thirty-eight did not go beyond the first loud protest at 150 volts. Two subjects provided the exception, administering up to 325 and 450 volts, but the overall result was that the great majority of people delivered very low, usually painless, shocks when the choice was explicitly up to them.

96   This condition of the experiment undermines another commonly offered explanation of the subjects' behavior—that those who shocked the victim at the most severe levels came only from the sadistic fringe of society. If one considers that almost two-thirds of the participants fall into the category of "obedient" subjects, and that they represented ordinary people drawn from working, managerial, and professional classes, the argument becomes very shaky. Indeed, it is highly reminiscent of the issue that arose in connection with Hannah Arendt's 1963 book, *Eichmann in Jerusalem*. Arendt contended that the prosecution's efforts to depict Eichmann as a sadistic monster was fundamentally wrong, that he came closer to being an uninspired bureaucrat who simply sat at his desk and did his job. For asserting her views, Arendt became the object of considerable scorn, even calumny. Somehow, it was felt that the monstrous deeds carried out by Eichmann required a brutal, twisted personality, evil incarnate. After witnessing hundreds of ordinary persons submit to the authority in our own experiments, I must conclude that Arendt's conception of the banality of evil comes closer to the truth than one might dare imagine. The ordinary person who shocked the victim did so out of a sense of obligation—an impression of his duties as a subject—and not from any peculiarly aggressive tendencies.

97   This is, perhaps, the most fundamental lesson of our study: ordinary people, simply doing their jobs, and without any particular hostility on their part, can become agents in a terrible destructive process. Moreover, even when the destructive effects of their work become patently clear, and they are asked to carry out actions incompatible with fundamental standards of morality, relatively few people have the resources needed to resist authority.

98   Many of the people were in some sense against what they did to the learner, and many protested even while they obeyed. Some were totally convinced of the wrongness of their actions but could not bring themselves to make an open break with authority. They often derived satisfaction from their thoughts and felt that—within themselves, at least—they had been on the side of the angels. They tried to reduce strain by obeying the experimenter but "only slightly," encouraging the learner, touching the generator switches gingerly. When interviewed, such a subject would stress that he had "asserted my humanity" by administering the briefest shock possible. Handling the conflict in this manner was easier than defiance.

99   The situation is constructed so that there is no way the subject can stop shocking the learner without violating the experimenter's definitions of his own competence. The subject fears that he will appear arrogant, untoward, and rude if he breaks off. Although these inhibiting emotions appear small in scope alongside the violence being done to the learner, they suffuse the mind and feelings of the subject, who is miserable at the prospect of having to repudiate the authority to his face. (When the experiment was altered so that the experimenter gave his instructions by telephone instead of in person, only a third as many people were fully obedient through 450 volts.) It is a curious thing that a measure of compassion on the part of the subject—an unwillingness to "hurt" the experimenter's feelings—is part of those binding forces inhibiting his disobedience. The withdrawal of such deference may be as painful to the subject as to the authority he defies.

Duty Without Conflict

100   The subjects do not derive satisfaction from inflicting pain, but they often like the feeling they get from pleasing the experimenter. They are proud of doing a good job, obeying the experimenter under difficult circumstances. While the subjects administered only mild shocks on their own initiative, one experimental variation showed that, under orders, 30 percent of them were willing to deliver 450 volts even when they had to forcibly push the learner's hand down on the electrode.

101   Bruno Batta is a thirty-seven-year-old welder who took part in the variation requiring the use of force. He was born in New Haven, his parents in Italy. He has a rough-hewn face that conveys a conspicuous lack of alertness. He has some difficulty in mastering the experimental procedure and needs to be corrected by the experimenter several times. He shows appreciation for the help and willingness to do what is required. After the 150-volt level, Batta has to force the learner's hand down on the shock plate, since the learner himself refuses to touch it.

102   When the learner first complains, Mr. Batta pays no attention to him. His face remains impassive, as if to dissociate himself from the learner's disruptive behavior. When the experimenter instructs him to force the learner's hand down, he adopts a rigid, mechanical procedure. He tests the generator switch. When it fails to function, he immediately forces the learner's hand onto the shock plate. All the while he maintains the same rigid mask. The learner, seated alongside him, begs him to stop, but with robotic impassivity he continues the procedure.

103   What is extraordinary is his apparent total indifference to the learner; he hardly takes cognizance of him as a human being. Meanwhile, he relates to the experimenter in a submissive and courteous fashion.

104   At the 330-volt level, the learner refuses not only to touch the shock plate but also to provide any answers. Annoyed, Batta turns to him, and chastises him: "You better answer and get it over with. We can't stay here all night." These are the only words he directs to the learner in the course of an hour. Never again does he speak to him. The scene is brutal and depressing, his hard, impassive face showing total indifference as he subdues the screaming learner and gives him shocks. He seems to derive no pleasure from the act itself, only quiet satisfaction at doing his job properly.

105 When he administers 450 volts, he turns to the experimenter and asks, "Where do we go from here, Professor?" His tone is deferential and expresses his willingness to be a cooperative subject, in contrast to the learner's obstinacy.

106 At the end of the session he tells the experimenter how honored he has been to help him, and in a moment of contrition, remarks, "Sir, sorry it couldn't have been a full experiment."

107 He has done his honest best. It is only the deficient behavior of the learner that has denied the experimenter full satisfaction.

108 The essence of obedience is that a person comes to view himself as the instrument for carrying out another person's wishes, and he therefore no longer regards himself as responsible for his actions. Once this critical shift of viewpoint has occurred, all of the essential features of obedience follow. The most far-reaching consequence is that the person feels responsible *to* the authority directing him but feels no responsibility *for* the content of the actions that the authority prescribes. Morality does not disappear—it acquires a radically different focus: the subordinate person feels shame or pride depending on how adequately he has performed the actions called for by authority.

109 Language provides numerous terms to pinpoint this type of morality: *loyalty, duty, discipline* all are terms heavily saturated with moral meaning and refer to the degree to which a person fulfills his obligations to authority. They refer not to the "goodness" of the person per se but to the adequacy with which a subordinate fulfills his socially defined role. The most frequent defense of the individual who has performed a heinous act under command of authority is that he has simply done his duty. In asserting this defense, the individual is not introducing an alibi concocted for the moment but is reporting honestly on the psychological attitude induced by submission to authority.

110 For a person to feel responsible for his actions, he must sense that the behavior has flowed from "the self." In the situation we have studied, subjects have precisely the opposite view of their actions—namely, they see them as originating in the motives of some other person. Subjects in the experiment frequently said, "If it were up to me, I would not have administered shocks to the learner."

111 Once authority has been isolated as the cause of the subject's behavior, it is legitimate to inquire into the necessary elements of authority and how it must be perceived in order to gain compliance. We conducted some investigations into the kinds of changes that would cause the experimenter to lose his power and to be disobeyed by the subject. Some of the variations revealed that:

- *The experimenter's physical presence has a marked impact on his authority.* As cited earlier, obedience dropped off sharply when orders were given by telephone. The experimenter could often induce a disobedient subject to go on by returning to the laboratory.

- *Conflicting authority severely paralyzes action.* When two experimenters of equal status, both seated at the command desk, gave incompatible orders, no shocks were delivered past the point of their disagreement.

- *The rebellious action of others severely undermines authority.* In one variation, three teachers (two actors and a real subject) administered a test and shocks. When the two actors disobeyed the experimenter and refused to go beyond a certain shock level, thirty-six of the forty subjects joined their disobedient peers and refused as well.

112   Although the experimenter's authority was fragile in some respects, it is also true that he had almost none of the tools used in ordinary command structures. For example, the experimenter did not threaten the subjects with punishment—such as loss of income, community ostracism, or jail—for failure to obey. Neither could he offer incentives. Indeed, we should expect the experimenter's authority to be much less than that of someone like a general, since the experimenter has no power to enforce his imperatives, and since participation in a psychological experiment scarcely evokes the sense of urgency and dedication found in warfare. Despite these limitations, he still managed to command a dismaying degree of obedience.

113   I will cite one final variation of the experiment that depicts a dilemma that is more common in everyday life. The subject was not ordered to pull the lever that shocked the victim, but merely to perform a subsidiary task (administering the word-pair test) while another person administered the shock. In this situation, thirty-seven of forty adults continued to the highest level on the shock generator. Predictably, they excused their behavior by saying that the responsibility belonged to the man who actually pulled the switch. This may illustrate a dangerously typical arrangement in a complex society: it is easy to ignore responsibility when one is only an intermediate link in a chain of action.

114   The problem of obedience is not wholly psychological. The form and shape of society and the way it is developing have much to do with it. There was a time, perhaps, when people were able to give a fully human response to any situation because they were fully absorbed in it as human beings. But as soon as there was a division of labor things changed. Beyond a certain point, the breaking up of society into people carrying out narrow and very special jobs takes away from the human quality of work and life. A person does not get to see the whole situation but only a small part of it, and is thus unable to act without some kind of overall direction. He yields to authority but in doing so is alienated from his own actions.

115   Even Eichmann was sickened when he toured the concentration camps, but he had only to sit at a desk and shuffle papers. At the same time the man in the camp who actually dropped Cyclon-b into the gas chambers was able to justify *his* behavior on the ground that he was only following orders from above. Thus there is a fragmentation of the total human act; no one is confronted with the consequences of his decision to carry out the evil act. The person who assumes responsibility has evaporated. Perhaps this is the most common characteristic of socially organized evil in modern society.

Review Questions

1. Milgram states that obedience is a basic element in the structure of social life. How so?

2. What is the dilemma inherent in obedience to authority?

3. Summarize the obedience experiments.

4. What predictions did experts and laypeople make about the experiments before they were conducted? How did these predictions compare with the experimental results?

5. What are Milgram's views regarding the two assumptions bearing on his experiment that (1) people are naturally aggressive and (2) a lunatic, sadistic fringe is responsible for shocking learners to the maximum limit?

6. How do Milgram's findings corroborate Hannah Arendt's thesis about the "banality of evil"?

7. What, according to Milgram, is the "essence of obedience"?

8. How did being an intermediate link in a chain of action affect a subject's willingness to continue with the experiment?

9. In the article's final two paragraphs, Milgram speaks of a "fragmentation of the total human act." To what is he referring?

Discussion and Writing Suggestions

1. Milgram writes (paragraph 2): "Conservative philosophers argue that the very fabric of society is threatened by disobedience, while humanists stress the primacy of the individual conscience." Develop the arguments of both the conservative and the humanist regarding obedience to authority. Be prepared to debate the ethics of obedience by defending one position or the other.

2. Would you have been glad to have participated in the Milgram experiments? Why or why not?

3. The ethics of Milgram's experimental design came under sharp attack. Diana Baumrind's review of the experiment typifies the criticism; but before you read her work, try to anticipate the objections she raises.

4. Given the general outcome of the experiments, why do you suppose Milgram gives as his first example of a subject's response the German émigré's refusal to continue the electrical shocks?

5. Does the outcome of the experiment upset you in any way? Do you feel the experiment teaches us anything new about human nature?

6. Comment on Milgram's skill as a writer of description. How effectively does he portray his subjects when introducing them? When re-creating their tension in the experiment?

7. Mrs. Braverman said to her husband: "You can call yourself Eichmann." Do you agree with her? Explain.

8. Reread paragraphs 29 through 81, the transcript of the experiment in which Mr. Prozi participated. Appreciating that Prozi was debriefed—that is, was assured that no harm came to the learner— imagine what Prozi might have been thinking as he drove home after the experiment. Develop your thoughts into a monologue, written in the first person, with Prozi at the wheel of his car.

Review of Stanley Milgram's Experiments on Obedience
Diana Baumrind

Many of Milgram's colleagues saluted him for providing that "hard information" about human nature. Others attacked him for violating the rights of his subjects. Still others fault- ed his experimental design and claimed he could not, with any validity, speculate on life out- side the laboratory based on the behavior of his subjects within.

In the following excerpted review, psychologist Diana Baumrind excoriates Milgram for "entrapping" his subjects and potentially harming their "self-image or ability to trust adult authorities in the future." In a footnote at the end of this selection (page 201), we summa- rize Milgram's response to Baumrind's critique.

Diana Baumrind is a psychologist who, when writing this review, worked at the Institute of Human Development, University of California, Berkeley. The review appeared in American Psychologist *shortly after Milgram published the results of his first experiments in 1963.*

1   . . . The dependent, obedient attitude assumed by most subjects in the experi- mental setting is appropriate to that situation. The "game" is defined by the experimenter and he makes the rules. By volunteering, the subject agrees implicitly to assume a posture of trust and obedience. While the experimental conditions leave him exposed, the subject has the right to assume that his secu- rity and self-esteem will be protected.

2   There are other professional situations in which one member—the patient or client—expects help and protection from the other—the physician or psycholo- gist. But the interpersonal relationship between experimenter and subject addi- tionally has unique features which are likely to provoke initial anxiety in the subject. The laboratory is unfamiliar as a setting and the rules of behavior ambiguous compared to a clinician's office. Because of the anxiety and passiv- ity generated by the setting, the subject is more prone to behave in an obedi- ent, suggestible manner in the laboratory than elsewhere. Therefore, the laboratory is not the place to study degree of obedience or suggestibility, as a function of a particular experimental condition, since the base line for these phenomena as found in the laboratory is probably much higher than in most

other settings. Thus experiments in which the relationship to the experimenter as an authority is used as an independent condition are imperfectly designed for the same reason that they are prone to injure the subjects involved. They disregard the special quality of trust and obedience with which the subject appropriately regards the experimenter.

3   Other phenomena which present ethical decisions, unlike those mentioned above, *can* be reproduced successfully in the laboratory. Failure experience, conformity to peer judgment, and isolation are among such phenomena. In these cases we can expect the experimenter to take whatever measures are necessary to prevent the subject from leaving the laboratory more humiliated, insecure, alienated, or hostile than when he arrived. To guarantee that an especially sensitive subject leaves a stressful experimental experience in the proper state sometimes requires special clinical training. But usually an attitude of compassion, respect, gratitude, and common sense will suffice, and no amount of clinical training will substitute. The subject has the right to expect that the psychologist with whom he is interacting has some concern for his welfare, and the personal attributes and professional skill to express his good will effectively.

4   Unfortunately, the subject is not always treated with the respect he deserves. It has become more commonplace in sociopsychological laboratory studies to manipulate, embarrass, and discomfort subjects. At times the insult to the subject's sensibilities extends to the journal reader when the results are reported. Milgram's (1963) study is a case in point. The following is Milgram's abstract of his experiment:

> This article describes a procedure for the study of destructive obedience in the laboratory. It consists of ordering a naive S to administer increasingly more severe punishment to a victim in the context of a learning experiment.* Punishment is administered by means of a shock generator with 30 graded switches ranging from Slight Shock to Danger: Severe Shock. The victim is a confederate of E. The primary dependent variable is the maximum shock the S is willing to administer before he refuses to continue further.† 26 Ss obeyed the experimental commands fully, and administered the highest shock on the generator. 14 Ss broke off the experiment at some point after the victim protested and refused to provide further answers. The procedure created extreme levels of nervous tension in some Ss. Profuse sweating, trembling, and stuttering were typical expressions of this emotional disturbance. One unexpected sign of tension—yet to be explained— was the regular occurrence of nervous laughter, which in some Ss developed into uncontrollable seizures. The variety of interesting behavioral

---

* In psychological experiments, *S* is an abbreviation for *subject;* *E* is an abbreviation for *experimenter*.

† In the context of a psychological experiment, a *dependent variable* is a behavior that is expected to change as a result of changes in the experimental procedure.

dynamics observed in the experiment, the reality of the situation for the S, and the possibility of parametric variations* within the framework of the procedure point to the fruitfulness of further study [p. 371].

5   The detached, objective manner in which Milgram reports the emotional disturbance suffered by his subjects contrasts sharply with his graphic account of that disturbance. Following are two other quotes describing the effects on his subjects of the experimental conditions:

> I observed a mature and initially poised businessman enter the laboratory smiling and confident. Within 20 minutes he was reduced to a twitching, stuttering wreck, who was rapidly approaching a point of nervous collapse. He constantly pulled on his earlobe, and twisted his hands. At one point he pushed his fist into his forehead and muttered: "Oh God, let's stop it." And yet he continued to respond to every word of the experimenter, and obeyed to the end [p. 377].

> In a large number of cases the degree of tension reached extremes that are rarely seen in sociopsychological laboratory studies. Subjects were observed to sweat, tremble, stutter, bite their lips, groan, and dig their fingernails into their flesh. These were characteristic rather than exceptional responses to the experiment.
>   One sign of tension was the regular occurrence of nervous laughing fits. Fourteen of the 40 subjects showed definite signs of nervous laughter and smiling. The laughter seemed entirely out of place, even bizarre. Full-blown, uncontrollable seizures were observed for 3 subjects. On one occasion we observed a seizure so violently convulsive that it was necessary to call a halt to the experiment... [p. 375].

Milgram does state that,

> After the interview, procedures were undertaken to assure that the subject would leave the laboratory in a state of well being. A friendly reconciliation was arranged between the subject and the victim, and an effort was made to reduce any tensions that arose as a result of the experiment [p. 374].

It would be interesting to know what sort of procedures could dissipate the type of emotional disturbance just described. In view of the effects on subjects, traumatic to a degree which Milgram himself considers nearly unprecedented in sociopsychological experiments, his casual assurance that these tensions were dissipated before the subject left the laboratory is unconvincing.

6   What could be the rational basis for such a posture of indifference? Perhaps Milgram supplies the answer himself when he partially explains the subject's destructive obedience as follows, "Thus they assume that the discomfort caused the victim is momentary, while the scientific gains resulting from the experiment

---

* *Parametric variation* is a statistical term that describes the degree to which information based on data for one experiment can be applied to data for a slightly different experiment.

are enduring" [p. 378]. Indeed such a rationale might suffice to justify the means used to achieve his end if that end were of inestimable value to humanity or were not itself transformed by the means by which it was attained.

7   The behavioral psychologist is not in as good a position to objectify his faith in the significance of his work as medical colleagues at points of breakthrough. His experimental situations are not sufficiently accurate models of real-life experience; his sampling techniques are seldom of a scope which would justify the meaning with which he would like to endow his results; and these results are hard to reproduce by colleagues with opposing theoretical views. Unlike the Sabin vaccine,* for example, the concrete benefit to humanity of his particular piece of work, no matter how competently handled, cannot justify the risk that real harm will be done to the subject. I am not speaking of physical discomfort, inconvenience, or experimental deception per se, but of permanent harm, however slight. I do regard the emotional disturbance described by Milgram as potentially harmful because it could easily effect an alteration in the subject's self-image or ability to trust adult authorities in the future. It is potentially harmful to a subject to commit, in the course of an experiment, acts which he himself considers unworthy, particularly when he has been entrapped into committing such acts by an individual he has reason to trust. The subject's personal responsibility for his actions is not erased because the experimenter reveals to him the means which he used to stimulate these actions. The subject realizes that he would have hurt the victim if the current were on. The realization that he also made a fool of himself by accepting the experimental set results in additional loss of self-esteem. Moreover, the subject finds it difficult to express his anger outwardly after the experimenter in a self-acceptant but friendly manner reveals the hoax.

8   A fairly intense corrective interpersonal experience is indicated wherein the subject admits and accepts his responsibility for his own actions, and at the same time gives vent to his hurt and anger at being fooled. Perhaps an experience as distressing as the one described by Milgram can be integrated by the subject, provided that careful thought is given to the matter. The propriety of such experimentation is still in question even if such a reparational experience were forthcoming. Without it I would expect a naive, sensitive subject to remain deeply hurt and anxious for some time, and a sophisticated, cynical subject to become even more alienated and distrustful.

9   In addition the experimental procedure used by Milgram does not appear suited to the objectives of the study because it does not take into account the special quality of the set which the subject has in the experimental situation. Milgram is concerned with a very important problem, namely, the social consequences of destructive obedience. He says,

> Gas chambers were built, death camps were guarded, daily quotas of corpses were produced with the same efficiency as the manufacture of appliances. These inhumane policies may have originated in the mind of a single person,

---

* The Sabin vaccine provides immunization against polio.

> but they could only be carried out on a massive scale if a very large number
> of persons obeyed orders [p. 371].

But the parallel between authority-subordinate relationships in Hitler's Germany and in Milgram's laboratory is unclear. In the former situation the SS man or member of the German Officer Corps, when obeying orders to slaughter, had no reason to think of his superior officer as benignly disposed towards himself or their victims. The victims were perceived as subhuman and not worthy of consideration. The subordinate officer was an agent in a great cause. He did not need to feel guilt or conflict because within his frame of reference he was acting rightly.

10   It is obvious from Milgram's own description that most of his subjects were concerned about their victims and did trust the experimenter, and that their distressful conflict was generated in part by the consequences of these two disparate but appropriate attitudes. Their distress may have resulted from shock at what the experimenter was doing to them as well as from what they thought they were doing to their victims. In any case there is not a convincing parallel between the phenomena studied by Milgram and destructive obedience as the concept would apply to the subordinate-authority relationship demonstrated in Hitler's Germany. If the experiments were conducted "outside of New Haven and without any visible ties to the university," I would still question their validity on similar although not identical grounds. In addition, I would question the representativeness of a sample of subjects who would voluntarily participate within a noninstitutional setting.

11   In summary, the experimental objectives of the psychologist are seldom incompatible with the subject's ongoing state of well being, provided that the experimenter is willing to take the subject's motives and interests into consideration when planning his methods and correctives. Section 4b in *Ethical Standards of Psychologists* (APA, undated) reads in part:

> Only when a problem is significant and can be investigated in no other way is the psychologist justified in exposing human subjects to emotional stress or other possible harm. In conducting such research, the psychologist must seriously consider the possibility of harmful aftereffects, and should be prepared to remove them as soon as permitted by the design of the experiment. Where the danger of serious aftereffects exists, research should be conducted only when the subjects or their responsible agents are fully informed of this possibility and volunteer nevertheless [p. 12].

From the subject's point of view procedures which involve loss of dignity, self-esteem and trust in rational authority are probably most harmful in the long run and require the most thoughtfully planned reparations, if engaged in at all. The public image of psychology as a profession is highly related to our own actions, and some of these actions are changeworthy. It is important that as research psychologists we protect our ethical sensibilities rather than adapt our personal standards to include as appropriate the kind of indignities to which Milgram's subjects were exposed. I would not like to see experiments such as Milgram's proceed unless the subjects were fully informed of the dangers of serious aftereffects and his correctives were clearly shown to be effective in restoring their state of well being.*

References

American Psychological Association (n.d.). *Ethical standards of psychologists: A summary of ethical principles.* Washington, DC: APA.

Milgram, S. (1963). Behavioral study of obedience. *Journal of Abnormal and Social Psychology. 67,* 371–378.

---

* Stanley Milgram replied to Baumrind's critique in a lengthy critique of his own [From Stanley Milgram, "Issues in the Study of Obedience: A Reply to Baumrind," *American Psychologist* 19, 1964, pp. 848–851]. Following are his principal points:

• Milgram believed that the experimental findings were in large part responsible for Baumrind's criticism. He writes:

Is not Baumrind's criticism based as much on the unanticipated findings as on the method? The findings were that some subjects performed in what appeared to be a shockingly immoral way. If, instead, every one of the subjects had broken off at "slight shock," or at the first sign of the learner's discomfort, the results would have been pleasant, and reassuring, and who would protest?

• Milgram objected to Baumrind's assertion that those who participated in the experiment would have trouble justifying their behavior. Milgram conducted follow-up questionnaires. The results, summarized in Table 1, indicate that 84 percent of the subjects claimed they were pleased to have been a part of the experiment.

TABLE 1   Excerpt from Questionnaire Used in a Follow-up Study of the Obedience Research

Now That I Have Read the Report, and All Things Considered . . .	Defiant	Obedient	All
1. I am very glad to have been in the experiment	40.0%	47.8%	43.5%
2. I am glad to have been in the experiment	43.8%	35.7%	40.2%
3. I am neither sorry nor glad to have been in the experiment	15.3%	14.8%	15.1%
4. I am sorry to have been in the experiment	0.8%	0.7%	0.8%
5. I am very sorry to have been in the experiment	0.0%	1.0%	0.5%

Note—Ninety-two percent of the subjects returned the questionnaire. The characteristics of the nonrespondents were checked against the respondents. They differed from the respondents only with regard to age; younger people were overrepresented in the nonresponding group.

• Baumrind objected that studies of obedience cannot meaningfully be carried out in a laboratory setting, since the obedience occurred in a context where it was appropriate. Milgram's response: "I reject Baumrind's argument that the observed obedience does not count because it occurred where it is appropriate. That is precisely why it *does* count. A soldier's obedience is no less meaningful because it occurs in a pertinent military context."

• Milgram concludes his critique in this way: "If there is a moral to be learned from the obedience study, it is that every man must be responsible for his own actions. This author accepts full responsibility for the design and execution of the study. Some people may feel it should not have been done. I disagree and accept the burden of their judgment."

Review Questions

1. Why might a subject volunteer for an experiment? Why do subjects typically assume a dependent, obedient attitude?
2. Why is a laboratory not a suitable setting for a study of obedience?
3. For what reasons does Baumrind feel that the Milgram experiment was potentially harmful?
4. For what reasons does Baumrind question the relationship between Milgram's findings and the obedient behavior of subordinates in Nazi Germany?

Discussion and Writing Suggestions

1. Baumrind contends that the Milgram experiment is imperfectly designed for two reasons: (1) The laboratory is not the place to test obedience; (2) Milgram disregarded the trust that subjects usually show an experimenter. To what extent do you agree with Baumrind's objections? Do you find them all equally valid?

2. Baumrind states that the ethical procedures of the experiment keep it from having significant value. Do you agree?

3. Do you agree with Baumrind that the subjects were "entrapped" into committing unworthy acts?

4. Assume the identity of a participant in Milgram's experiment who obeyed the experimenter by shocking the learner with the maximum voltage. You have just returned from the lab, and your spouse asks you about your day. Compose the conversation that follows.

Obedience
Ian Parker

As Ian Parker points out, Milgram's experiment became "the most cited, celebrated—and reviled—experiment in the history of social psychology." Parker also explains, however, that for Milgram himself the experiment was a mixed blessing: it would both "make his name and destroy his reputation."

Milgram was fascinated by the Asch experiment, but when all was said and done, this experiment was only about lines. He wondered if it were possible "to make Asch's conformity experiment more humanely significant." Milgram's breakthrough, his "incandescent moment," came when he asked himself "Just how far would a person go under the experimenter's orders?" We have seen the results in the experiment he describes and discusses in an earlier selection.

In the following selection, Ian Parker, a British writer who lives in New York, focuses on both the immediate and the long-term reaction to Milgram's experiments among both the general public and Milgram's professional colleagues and also of the effect of the experiment upon the experimenter himself. This selection is excerpted from an article that Parker wrote for the Autumn 2000 issue of Granta. *Parker writes regularly for the* New Yorker *and has also written for* Human Sciences, History of the Human Sciences, Political Studies, *and* Human Relations.

1   Milgram had a world exclusive. He had caught evil on film. He had invented a kind of torture machine. But it was not immediately clear what he should do with his discovery. When he began the study, he had no theory, nor was he planning to test another man's theory. His idea had sprung from contemplation of Solomon Asch, but the "incandescent" moment at Princeton was a shift away from theory into experimental practice. He had had an idea for an experiment. Now, he was in an odd situation: he had caused something extraordinary to happen, but, technically, his central observation counted for nothing. With no provocation, a New Haven man had hit a fellow citizen with 450 volts. To the general observer, this will come as a surprise, but it is not a social scientific discovery, as Edward E. Jones, the distinguished editor of the *Journal of Personality,* made clear to Milgram when he declined the invitation to publish Milgram's first paper. "The major problem," Jones wrote to Milgram, "is that this is really the report of some pilot research on a method for inducing stress or conflict . . . your data indicate a kind of triumph of social engineering . . . we are led to no conclusions about obedience, really, but rather are exhorted to be impressed with the power of your situation as an influence context." The *Journal of Abnormal and Social Psychology* also rejected the paper on its first submission, calling it a "demonstration" rather than an experiment.

2   Milgram had described only one experimental situation. When he resubmitted the paper to the same journal, he now included experimental variables, and it was publishable. In the rewrite, Milgram put the emphasis on the way in which differences in situation had caused differences in degrees of obedience: the closer the learner to the teacher, the greater the disobedience, and so on. These details were later lost as the experiment moved out of social psychology into the larger world. But it could hardly have happened otherwise. The thought that people were zapping each other in a Yale laboratory is bound to be more striking than the thought that zapping occurs a little less often when one is looking one's victim in the eye. The unscientific truth, perhaps, is that the central comparison in Milgram's study is not between any two experimental variables: it is between what happened in the laboratory, and what we thought would happen. The experimental control in Milgram's model is our hopelessly flawed intuition.

3   "Somehow," Milgram told a friend in 1962, "I don't write as fast or as easily as I run experiments. I have done about all the experiments I plan to do on Obedience, am duly impressed with the results, and now find myself acutely constipated." Milgram found it hard to knock the experiment into social scientific shape. It would be another decade before he incorporated his findings into a serious theory of the sources of human obedience. When he did so, in the

otherwise absorbing and beautifully written book *Obedience to Authority* (1974), his thoughts about an "agentic state"—a psychological zone of abandoned autonomy—were not widely admired or developed by his peers, not least because they were so evidently retrospective. Most readers of *Obedience to Authority* are more likely to take interest in the nods of acknowledgment made to Arthur Koestler's *The Ghost in the Machine,* and to Alex Comfort, the English anarchist poet, novelist, and author of *The Joy of Sex.* Most readers will take more pleasure—and feel Milgram took more pleasure—in the novelistic and strikingly unscientific descriptions of his experimental subjects. ("Mrs Dontz," he wrote, "has an unusually casual, slow-paced way of speaking, and her tone expresses constant humility; it is as if every assertion carries the emotional message: 'I'm just a very ordinary person, don't expect a lot from me.' Physically, she resembles Shirley Booth in the film *Come Back, Little Sheba.*")

4   But while Milgram was struggling to place his findings in a proper scientific context, they seemed to have found a natural home elsewhere. Stanley Milgram—a young social psychology professor at the start of his career—appeared to be in a position to contribute to one of the late twentieth century's most pressing intellectual activities: making sense of the Holocaust. Milgram always placed the experiments in this context, and the figure of Adolf Eichmann, who was seized in Buenos Aires in the spring of 1960, and whose trial in Jerusalem began a year later, loomed over his proceedings. (In a letter that urged Alan Elms to keep up the supply of experimental volunteers, Milgram noted that this role bore "some resemblance to Mr. Eichmann's position.") The trial, as Peter Novick has recently written in *The Holocaust in American Life,* marked "the first time that what we now call the Holocaust was presented to the American public as an entity in its own right, distinct from Nazi barbarism in general." When Milgram published his first paper on the obedience studies in 1963, Hannah Arendt's articles about the trial had just appeared in the *New Yorker,* and in her book, *Eichmann in Jerusalem,* and they had given widespread currency to her perception about "the banality of evil." Milgram put Eichmann's name in the first paragraph of his first obedience paper, and so claimed a place in a pivotal contemporary debate. His argument was this: his study showed how ordinary people are surprisingly prone to destructive obedience; the crimes of the Holocaust had been committed by people obeying orders; those people, therefore, could now be thought ordinary. The argument had its terrifying element and its consoling element: according to Milgram, Americans had to see themselves as potential murderers; at the same time we could understand Nazis to be no more unusual than any New Haven guy in a check shirt.

5   It may seem bizarre now: Milgram returned to ordinary Nazis their Nuremberg defense, nicely polished in an American laboratory. But the idea struck a chord, and news quickly spread of Milgram's well-meaning, all-American torturers. "Once the [Holocaust] connection was in place," said Arthur G. Miller, a leading Milgram scholar, "then the experiments took on a kind of a larger-than-life quality." Milgram's work was reported in the *New York Times* (65% IN TEST BLINDLY OBEY ORDER TO INFLICT PAIN), and the story was quickly picked up by *Life, Esquire,* ABC television, UPI, and the British press. The fame of the experiments

spread, and as the Sixties acquired their defining spirit, Holocaust references were joined by thoughts of My Lai; this was a good moment in history to have things to say about taking orders. By the time Milgram had published his book and released a short film of the experiment, his findings had spread into popular culture, and into theological, medical, and legal discussions. Thomas Blass, a social psychologist at the University of Maryland, Baltimore County, who is preparing a Milgram biography, has a large collection of academic references, including a paper in the context of accountancy ethics. (Is it unthinking obedience that causes accountants to act unlawfully on behalf of clients?) Outside the academy, Dannie Abse published an anti-Milgram play, *The Dogs of Pavlov,* in 1973, and two years later, in America, CBS broadcast a television movie, *The Tenth Level,* that made awkward melodrama out of the obedience experiments, and starred William Shatner as a spookily obsessed and romantically disengaged version of Professor Milgram. ("You may know your social psychology, Professor, but you have a lot to learn about the varieties of massage.") Peter Gabriel sang "We Do What We're Told (Milgram's 37)" in 1986. And there would be more than a whiff of Milgram in the 1990 episode of *The Simpsons,* "There's No Disgrace Like Home," in which the family members repeatedly electrocute one another until the lights across Springfield flicker and dim. Last year, "The Stanley Milgram Experiment"—a comedy sketch duo—made its off-off-Broadway debut in New York. Robbie Chafitz, one of the pair, had been startled and amused by the Milgram film as a teenager, and had always vowed to use the name one way or another. Besides, as he told me, "anything with electricity and people is funny."

6   But however celebrated the experiments became, there was a question they could never shake off. It was an ethical issue: had Stanley Milgram mistreated his subjects? Milgram must have seen the storm coming, at least from the moment when Herbert Winer marched into his office, talking of heart attacks. In the summer of 1962, other subjects recorded their feelings about the experiment in response to a questionnaire sent out by Milgram along with a report explaining the true purpose of the experiment. Replies were transferred on to index cards and are now held—unpublished and anonymous—at Yale. "Since taking part in the experiment," reads one card, "I have suffered a mild heart attack. The one thing my doctor tells me that I must avoid is any form of tension." Another card: "Right now I'm in group therapy. Would it be OK if I showed this report to [the] group and the doctors at the clinic?"

7   Since then, the experiment has been widely attacked from within the profession and from outside. To many, Milgram became a social psychological demon; Alan Elms has met people at parties who have recoiled at the news that he was a Milgram lieutenant. The psychologist Bruno Bettelheim described Milgram's work as "vile" and "in line with the human experiments of the Nazis." In his defense, Milgram would always highlight the results of post-experimental psychological studies—which had reported "no evidence of any traumatic reactions"—and the fact of the debriefings in Linsly-Chittenden Hall, in which care had been taken to give obedient subjects reasons not to feel bad about themselves. They were told to remember, for example, that doctors routinely hurt people in a thoroughly good cause. (Alan Elms wonders if this debriefing was

too effective, and that subjects should have been obliged to confront their actions more fully.)

8   But Milgram never quite won the ethical argument. And the controversy was immediately damaging to his career. Someone—perhaps a Yale colleague, according to Thomas Blass—quickly brought the experiment to the attention of the American Psychological Association, and Milgram's application for APA membership was delayed while the case against him was considered. Today, although the APA is happy to include Milgram's shock generator in a traveling psychology exhibition, it is careful to describe the experiments as "controversial" in its accompanying literature. As the APA points out, modern ethical guidelines (in part inspired by Milgram) would prevent the obedience studies from being repeated today.

9   The controversy followed him. In 1963 Milgram left Yale for Harvard. He was happy there. This is where his two children were born. And when a tenured job came up, he applied. But he needed the unanimous support of his colleagues, and could not secure it. He was blackballed by enemies of the obedience work. (According to Alexandra Milgram, her husband once devised a board game based on the tenure of university professors.) The late Roger Brown, a prominent Harvard psychologist, told Thomas Blass that there had been those in the department who thought of Milgram as "sort of manipulative, or the mad doctor. They felt uneasy about him."

10   So in 1967 Stanley Milgram left Harvard to become head of the social psychology programme in the psychology department in the Graduate Center of the City University of New York (CUNY). In one sense, it was a promotion; he was a full professor at thirty-three. "But after Yale and Harvard, it was the pits," said Milgram's friend and fellow social psychologist, Philip Zimbardo. "Most people I know who didn't get tenure, it had a permanent effect on their lives. You don't get to Yale or Harvard unless you've been number one from kindergarten on, you've been top—so there's this discontinuity. It's the first time in your life you've failed. You're Stanley Milgram, and people all over the world are talking about your research, and you've failed." Milgram was the most cited man in social psychology—Roger Brown, for example, considered his research to be of "profound importance and originality"—yet in later life, he was able to tell Zimbardo that he felt under-appreciated.

11   The ethical furor preyed on Milgram's mind—in the opinion of Arthur G. Miller, it may have contributed to his premature death—but one of its curious side effects was to reinforce the authenticity of his studies in the world outside psychology departments. Among those with a glancing knowledge of Milgram, mistreatment of experimental subjects became the only Milgram controversy. The studies remained intellectually sound, a minor building block of Western thought, a smart conversational gambit at cocktail parties. "People identified the problem with Milgram as just a question of ethics," says Henderikus Stam, of the University of Calgary in Canada, who trained as a social psychologist, but who lost faith and is now a psychological theoretician and historian. "So in a way people never got beyond that. Whereas there's a deeper epistemological question, which is: what can we actually know when we've done an

experiment like that, what are we left with? What have we learned about obedience?"

12   Within the academy, there was another, quieter, line of criticism against Milgram: this was methodological. In a paper in 1968 the social psychologists Martin Orne and Charles Holland raised the issue of incongruity, pointing out that Milgram's subjects had been given two key pieces of information: a man in apparent danger, and another man—a man in a lab coat—whose lack of evident concern suggested there was no danger. It seemed possible that obedient subjects had believed in the more plausible piece of information (no danger), and thus concluded, at some conscious or semi-conscious level, that the experiment was a fake, and—in a "pact of ignorance"—been generous enough to role-play for the sake of science. In other words, they were only obeying the demands of amateur dramatics.

13   Perhaps forgetting that people weep in the theatre, Milgram's response was to argue that the subjects' signs of distress or tension—the twitching and stuttering and racing heartbeats—could be taken as evidence that they had accepted the experiment's reality. He also drew upon the questionnaire he had sent out in 1962, in which his volunteers—now entirely in the know—had been asked to agree with one of five propositions, running from, "I fully believed the learner was getting painful shocks" to "I was certain the learner was not getting the shocks." Milgram was pleased to note that three-quarters of the subjects said they believed the learner was definitely or probably getting the shocks. (He added, reasonably, "It would have been an easy out at this point to deny that the hoax had been accepted.")

14   Herbert Winer reports that he was fully duped, and Alan Elms told me that, watching through the mirror during the summer of 1961, he saw very little evidence of widespread disbelief. But it is worth pointing out that Milgram could have reported his questionnaire statistics rather differently. He could have said that only fifty-six per cent accepted his first proposition: "I fully believed the learner was getting painful shocks." Forty-four per cent of Milgram's subjects claimed to be at least partially unpersuaded. (Indeed, on his own questionnaire, Winer said he had some doubts.) These people do not have much of a presence in Milgram's writings, but you catch a glimpse of them in the Yale Library index cards. One reads: "I was quite sure 'grunts and screams' were electrically reproduced from a speaker mounted in [the] students' room." (They were.) "If [the learner] was making the sounds I should have heard the screams from under the door—which was a poorly fit [*sic*] thin door. I'm sorry that I didn't have enough something to get up and open this door. Which was not locked. To see if student was still there." On another card: "I think that one of the main reasons I continued to the end was that . . . I just couldn't believe that Yale would concoct anything that would be [as] dangerous as the shocks were supposed to be." Another subject had noticed how the experimenter was watching him rather than the learner. Another hadn't understood why he was not allowed to volunteer to be the learner. And another wrote, "I had difficulty describing the experiment to my wife as I was so overcome with laughter—haven't had such a good laugh since the first time I saw the 4 Marx Bros—some 25 years ago."

15   For an experiment supposed to involve the undeserved torture of an innocent Irish-American man, there was a lot of laughter in Yale's Interaction
Laboratory. Frequently, Milgram's subjects could barely contain themselves as
they moved up the shock board. ("On one occasion," Milgram later wrote, "we
observed a seizure so violently convulsive that it was necessary to call a halt to
the experiment.") Behind their one-way mirror, Milgram and Elms were at times
highly amused. And when students are shown the Milgram film today, there
tends to be loud laughter in the room. People laugh, and—despite the alleged
revelation of a universal heart of darkness—they go home having lost little faith
in their friends and their families.

16   According to Henderikus Stam, the laughter of the students, and perhaps that
of the subjects, is a reasonable response to an absurd situation. It's a reaction
to the notion that serious and complex moral issues, and the subtleties of
human behaviour, can reasonably be illuminated through play-acting in a university laboratory. The experiment does nothing but illuminate itself. "What it
does is it says, 'Aren't we clever?' If you wanted to demonstrate obedience to
authority wouldn't you be better showing a film about the Holocaust, or news
clips about Kosovo? Why do you need an experiment, that's the question? What
does the experiment do? The experiment says that if we really want to know
about obedience to authority we need an abstract representation of that obedience, removed from all real forms of the abuse of authority. But what we then
do is to use that representation to refer back to the real historical examples."

17   What happens when we refer back to historical examples? Readers of *Hitler's
Willing Executioners,* Daniel Jonah Goldhagen's study of the complicity of ordinary German citizens in the Holocaust, will learn within one paragraph of a
German policeman, Captain Wolfgang Hoffmann, a "zealous executioner of
Jews," who "once stridently disobeyed a superior order that he deemed morally objectionable." The order was that he and members of his company should
sign a declaration agreeing not to steal from Poles. Hoffmann was affronted that
anyone would think the declaration necessary, that anyone would imagine his
men capable of stealing. "I feel injured," he wrote to his superiors, "in my sense
of honour." The genocidal killing of thousands of Jews was one thing, but plun-
dering from Poles was another. Here was an order to which he was opposed,
and which he felt able to disobey.

18   Goldhagen is impatient with what he calls "the paradigm of external compul-
sion," which sets the actions of the Holocaust's perpetrators in the context of
social-psychological or totalitarian state forces. His book aims to show how the
crimes of the Holocaust were carried out by people obeying their own consciences, not blindly or fearfully obeying orders. "If you think that certain people
are evil," he told me, "and that it's necessary to do away with them—if you hate
them—and then someone orders you to kill them, you're not carrying out the
deed only because of the order. You're carrying it out because you think it's right.
So in all those instances where people are killing people they hate—their enemies
or their perceived enemies—then Milgram is just completely inapplicable."

19   Goldhagen wonders if the Milgram take on the Holocaust met a particular
need, during the Cold War, for America's new German allies "to be thought well
of." He also wonders if, by robbing people of their agency, "of the fact that they're

moral beings," the experiment tapped into the kind of reductive universalism by which, he says, Americans are easily seduced—the belief that all men are created equal, and in this case equally obedient. Goldhagen has no confidence in the idea that Milgram was measuring obedience at all. The experimental conditions did not properly control for other variables, such as trust, nor did they allow for the way decisions are made in the real world—over time, after consultation. Besides, said Goldhagen, in a tone close to exasperation, "people disobey all the time! Look around the world. Do people always pay all their taxes? Do what their bosses tell them? Or quietly accept what any government decides? Even with all kinds of sanctions available, one of the greatest problems that institutions face is to get their members to comply with rules and orders." Milgram's findings, he says, "are roundly, repeatedly and glaringly falsified by life."

20   In the opinion of Professor Stam, this comes close to defining the problems of social psychology itself. It is a discipline, he says, that makes the peculiar claim that "if you want to ask questions about the social world, you have to turn them into abstract technical questions." The Milgram experiment, he says, "has the air of scientificity about it. But it's not scientific, it's . . . *scientistic.*"

21   And there is Milgram's problem: he devised an intensely powerful piece of tragicomic laboratory theatre, and then had to smuggle it into the faculty of social science. His most famous work—which had something to say about trust, embarrassment, low-level sadism, willingness to please, exaggerated post-war respect for scientific research, the sleepy, heavy-lidded pleasure of being asked to *take part,* and, perhaps, too, the desire of a rather awkward young academic to secure attention and respect—had to pass itself off as an event with a single, steady meaning. And that disguise has not always been convincing. It's odd to hear Arthur G. Miller—one of the world's leading Milgram scholars—acknowledge that there have been times when he has wondered, just for a moment, if the experiments perhaps mean nothing at all.

22   But the faculty of social psychology is not ready to let Milgram go. And there may be a new way to rescue the experiments from their ungainly ambiguity. This is the route taken by Professors Lee Ross and Richard E. Nisbett (at Stanford and the University of Michigan respectively), whose recent synthesis of social psychological thinking aims to give the subject new power. According to Professor Ross, the experiments may be "performance," but they still have social psychological news to deliver. If that is true, then we can do something that the late professor was not always able to do himself: we can make a kind of reconciliation between the artist and the scientist in Stanley Milgram.

23   Ross and Nisbett find a seat for Stanley Milgram at social psychology's high table. They do this slyly, by taking the idea of obedience—Milgram's big idea—and putting it quietly to one side. When Ross teaches Milgram at Stanford, he makes a point of giving his students detailed instructions on how to prepare for the classes—instructions that he knows will be thoroughly ignored. He is then able to stand in front of his students and examine their disobedience. "I asked you to do something that's good for you rather than bad for you," he tells them. "And I'm a legitimate authority rather than an illegitimate one, and I actually have power that the Milgram experimenter doesn't have. And yet you didn't obey. So the study can't just be about obedience." What it is primarily about, Ross tells his students—

and it may be about other things too—is the extreme power of a situation that has been built without obvious escape routes. (As Herbert Winer said: "At no time was there a pause or a break when anything could be raised. . . . ") "There was really no exit," Ross told me, "there was no channel for disobedience. People who were discomforted, who wanted to disobey, didn't quite know how to do it. They made some timid attempts, and it got them nowhere. In order to disobey they have to step out of the whole situation, and say to the experimenter, 'Go to hell! You can't tell me what to do!' As long as they continue to function within that relationship, they're asking the experimenter for permission not to give shocks, and as long as the experimenter denies them that permission, they're stuck. They don't know how to get out of it." Ross suspects that things would have turned out very differently given one change to the situation. It's a fairly big change: the addition of a prominent red button in the middle of the table, combined with a clearly displayed notice signed by the "Human Subjects' Committee" explaining that the button could be pressed "by any subject in any experiment at any time if he or she absolutely refuses to continue."

24   According to Ross and Nisbett (who are saying something that Milgram surely knew, but something he allowed to become obscured), the Obedience Experiments point us towards a great social psychological truth, perhaps *the* great truth, which is this: people tend to do things because of where they are, not who they are, and we are slow to see it. We look for character traits to explain a person's actions—he is clever, shy, generous, arrogant—and we stubbornly underestimate the influence of the situation, the way things *happened to be* at that moment. So, if circumstances had been even only subtly different (if she hadn't been running late; if he'd been *told* the film was a comedy), the behaviour might have been radically different. Under certain controlled circumstances, then, people can be induced to behave unkindly: to that extent, Milgram may have something to say about a kind of destructive obedience. But under other circumstances, Professor Ross promised me, the same people would be nice. Given the correct situation, he said, we could be led to do "terrifically altruistic and self-sacrificing things that we would never have agreed to before we started."

25   So the experiment that has troubled us for nearly forty years (that buzzing and howling), and which caused Milgram to have dark thoughts about America's vulnerability to fascism, suddenly has a new complexion. Now, it is about the influence of *any* situation on behaviour, good or bad: "You stop on the highway to help someone," Professor Ross said, "and then the help you try to give doesn't prove to be enough, so you give the person a ride, and then you end up lending them money or letting them stay in your house. It wasn't because that was the person in the world you cared about the most, it was just one thing led to another. Step by step."

26   That's the Milgram situation. "We can take ordinary people," Ross said, "and make them show a degree of obedience or conformity—or for that matter altruism or bravery, whatever—to a degree that we would normally assume you would only see in the rare few. And that's relevant to telling us what we're capable of making people do, but it also tells us that when we observe the world, we are often going to be making an attribution error, because lots of times, the

situational factors have been opaque to us, and therefore we are making erroneous inferences about people. The South African government says, 'Can we deal with this fellow Mandela?' and the answer is, 'No, he's a terrorist.' But a social psychologist would say, 'Mandela, in *one* context, given *one* set of situations, was a terrorist.'" According to Ross, that's the key lesson of social psychology; that's how the discipline can be useful in education, the work place, and law. "Our emphasis," he says, "should be on creating situations that promote what we want to promote, rather than searching endlessly for the right person. Don't assume that people who commit atrocities are atrocious people, or people who do heroic things are heroic. Don't get overly carried away; don't think, because you observed someone under one set of discrete situational factors, that you know *what they're like,* and therefore can predict what they would do in a very different set of circumstances."

27   It's hard not to think of Stanley Milgram in another set of circumstances—to imagine the careers he did not have in films or in the theatre, and to wonder how things would have turned out if his work had appeared at another time, or had been read a little differently. It may now be possible to place the Obedience Experiments somewhere near the center of the social psychological project, but that's not how it felt in the last years of Milgram's life. He had failed to secure tenure at Harvard. Disappointed, he moved to New York, assuming he would soon be leaving again, to take up a post at a more glamorous institution. But he was still at CUNY seventeen years later, at the time of his premature death. "He had hoped it would be just for five years," Alexandra Milgram told me, "But things got much more difficult to move on to other places. You were glad to have what you had. And he was happy to do the work that he did. I don't think he was as happy at the university as he was at, say, Harvard, but he was a very independent person: he had his ideas, he had his research."

28   The research pushed Milgram into a kind of internal exile. Confirming his reputation as social psychology's renegade, he pursued work that, although often brilliantly conceived and elegantly reported, could look eccentric and old-fashioned to colleagues, and that ran the risk of appearing to place method ahead of meaning. "It would flash and then burn out," says Professor Miller, "and then he'd go on to something else." He sent his (young, able-bodied) students on to the New York subway to ask people to give up their seats. He co-wrote a paper about *Candid Camera*'s virtues as an archive for students of human behaviour. Pre-empting the play *Six Degrees of Separation,* he studied the "small world" phenomenon, investigating the chains of acquaintance that link two strangers. He took photographs of rail commuters and showed them to those who travelled on the same route, to explore the notion of the "familiar stranger." In an expensive, elaborate, and ultimately inconclusive experiment in 1971, he explored the links between antisocial acts seen on television and similar acts in real life by getting CBS to produce and air two versions of a hit hospital drama, *Medical Center.* He asked students to try to give away money on the street. He tested how easy it was for people to walk between a pavement photographer and his subject. And when he was recuperating from one of a series of heart attacks, he made an informal study of the social psychology of being a hospital patient. He was only fifty-one when he died.

29   Once, shortly before the Obedience Experiments had begun, Milgram had written from Yale about his fear of having made the wrong career move. "Of course," he told a friend, "I am glad that the present job sometimes engages my genuine interests, or at least, a part of my interests, but there is another part that remains submerged and somehow, perhaps because it is not expressed, seems most important." He described his routine: pulling himself out of bed, dragging himself to the lecture room "where I misrepresent myself for two hours as an efficient and persevering man of science . . . I should not be here, but in Greece shooting films under a Mediterranean sun, hopping about in a small boat from one Aegean isle to the next." He added, in a spirit of comic self-laceration, "Fool!"

Review Questions

1. Why was Milgram's article rejected when it was first submitted for publication? What did Milgram do to ensure its professional acceptability?

2. What does Parker mean when he says (paragraph 5) that "Milgram returned to ordinary Nazis their Nuremberg defense, nicely polished in an American laboratory"?

3. In what sense did his obedience experiments ruin Milgram's career?

4. Based on what you have read about Daniel Jonah Goldhagen, explain the meaning of the title of his book, *Hitler's Willing Executioners*.

5. What does Henderikus Stam mean when he charges that Milgram's experiment is "not scientific, it's . . . scientistic"?

Discussion and Writing Suggestions

1. Parker charts the course of the Milgram experiments working their way into popular consciousness—from magazine articles to TV dramas, to episodes of *The Simpsons*. Why do you think that the obedience experiments, more than thousands of other social science experiments, performed during the 1960s, made such an indelible impact, even outside the profession of social psychology?

2. Parker focuses in part upon the ethical problems with Milgram's experiments. To what extent do you believe that these experiments were unethical? To what extent does Milgram's chief rejoinder— that his surveys taken after the fact show that the vast majority of his subjects suffered no permanent ill effects—effectively rebut the ethical objections?

3. One theory about why many of Milgram's subjects behaved as they did—going all the way to the top of the shock register—is that they

did not really believe that the subjects were being shocked; they simply went along with the experimenter because they did not think it possible that a prestigious institution like Yale would be a party to inflicting harm on people. To what extent do you find this theory plausible?

4. Parker notes that not only did many of Milgram's subjects laugh during the experiments and later, in recounting it to others, but many students also laugh when they watch Milgram's film ("Obedience") in class. If you saw the film, did you laugh when you saw it? Did others? Attempt to account for this apparently incongruous reaction.

5. How necessary was Milgram's experiment? Parker notes that many have argued that if we want to learn about the power of authority to compel obedience, all we need do is study the numerous historical examples (the Holocaust being the one most often cited) of obedience to malign authority. To what extent do the results of Milgram's experiments add anything to what we already know about obedience from actual historical events?

6. Parker includes the following quotation from Daniel Jonah Goldhagen, author of *Hitler's Willing Executioners:* "If you think that certain people are evil . . . and that it's necessary to do away with them—if you hate them—and then someone orders you to kill them, you're not carrying out the deed only because of the order. You're carrying it out because you think it's right" (paragraph 18) In other words, people who commit evil acts do so less because they feel compelled to obey external authority figures than because they are following their own consciences, their own sense of who is the enemy. To what extent do you find that this theory accounts for many of the evil acts in the world?

7. Parker cites Ross's theory that an important reason that so many of Milgram's subjects were fully obedient is that they had no "escape route"—the experimenter never gave them time or opportunity to call a halt to the experimental procedure. To what extent do you find this theory plausible? Would a "red button" to stop the experiment likely have led to a different set of results?

8. Lee Ross and Richard E. Nisbet believe that the main factor determining the obedience of Milgram's subjects was not the *character* of the subjects, but rather the *situation*—that given a different situation (i.e., a situation not involving a carefully controlled laboratory experiment), the same subjects who were so obedient might have behaved very differently. To what extent do you find this theory plausible? Can you think of examples in which people will behave in different ways in different situations?

The Stanford Prison Experiment
Philip G. Zimbardo

As well known—and as controversial—as the Milgram obedience experiments, the Stanford Prison Experiment (1973) raises troubling questions about the ability of individuals to resist authoritarian or obedient roles, if the social setting requires these roles. Philip G. Zimbardo, professor of psychology at Stanford University, set out to study the process by which prisoners and guards "learn" to become compliant and authoritarian, respectively. To find subjects for the experiment, Zimbardo placed an advertisement in a local newspaper:

Male college students needed for psychological study of prison life. $15 per day for 1–2 weeks beginning Aug. 14. For further information & applications, come to Room 248, Jordan Hall, Stanford U.

The ad drew seventy-five responses. From these Zimbardo and his colleagues selected twenty-one college-age men, ten of whom would become "prisoners" in the experiment, the other eleven "guards." The elaborate role-playing scenario, planned for two weeks, had to be cut short due to the intensity of subjects' responses. This article first appeared in the New York Times Magazine *(8 April 1973).*

In prison, those things withheld from and denied to the prisoner become precisely what he wants most of all.
> —Eldridge Cleaver, "Soul on Ice"

Our sense of power is more vivid when we break a man's spirit than when we win his heart.
> —Eric Hoffer, "The Passionate State of Mind"

Every prison that men build / Is built with bricks of shame, / And bound with bars lest Christ should see / How men their brothers maim.
> —Oscar Wilde, "The Ballad of Reading Gaol"

Wherever anyone is against his will that is to him a prison.
> —Epictetus, "Discourses"

1   The quiet of a summer morning in Palo Alto, Calif., was shattered by a screeching squad car siren as police swept through the city picking up college students in a surprise mass arrest. Each suspect was charged with a felony, warned of his constitutional rights, spread-eagled against the car, searched, handcuffed, and carted off in the back seat of the squad car to the police station for booking.

2   After fingerprinting and the preparation of identification forms for his "jacket" (central information file), each prisoner was left isolated in a detention cell to wonder what he had done to get himself into this mess. After a while, he was

---

blindfolded and transported to the "Stanford County Prison." Here he began the process of becoming a prisoner—stripped naked, skin-searched, deloused, and issued a uniform, bedding, soup, and towel.

3   The warden offered an impromptu welcome:

4   "As you probably know, I'm your warden. All of you have shown that you are unable to function outside in the real world for one reason or another—that somehow you lack the responsibility of good citizens of this great country. We of this prison, your correctional staff, are going to help you learn what your responsibilities as citizens of this country are. Here are the rules. Sometime in the near future there will be a copy of the rules posted in each of the cells. We expect you to know them and to be able to recite them by number. If you follow all of these rules and keep your hands clean, repent for your misdeeds, and show a proper attitude of penitence, you and I will get along just fine."

5   There followed a reading of the 16 basic rules of prisoner conduct, "Rule Number One: Prisoners must remain silent during rest periods, after lights are out, during meals, and whenever they are outside the prison yard. Two: Prisoners must eat at mealtimes and only at mealtimes. Three: Prisoners must not move, tamper, deface, or damage walls, ceilings, windows, doors, or other prison property. . . . Seven: Prisoners must address each other by their ID number only. Eight: Prisoners must address the guards as 'Mr. Correctional Officer.' . . . Sixteen: Failure to obey any of the above rules may result in punishment."

6   By late afternoon these youthful "first offenders" sat in dazed silence on the cots in their barren cells trying to make sense of the events that had transformed their lives so dramatically.

7   If the police arrests and processing were executed with customary detachment, however, there were some things that didn't fit. For these men were now part of a very unusual kind of prison, an experimental mock prison, created by social psychologists to study the effects of imprisonment upon volunteer research subjects. When we planned our two-week-long simulation of prison life, we sought to understand more about the process by which people called "prisoners" lose their liberty, civil rights, independence, and privacy, while those called "guards" gain social power by accepting the responsibility for controlling and managing the lives of their dependent charges.

8   Why didn't we pursue this research in a real prison? First, prison systems are fortresses of secrecy, closed to impartial observation, and thereby immune to critical analysis from anyone not already part of the correctional authority. Second, in any real prison, it is impossible to separate what each individual brings into the prison from what the prison brings out in each person.

9   We populated our mock prison with a homogeneous group of people who could be considered "normal-average" on the basis of clinical interviews and personality tests. Our participants (10 prisoners and 11 guards) were selected from more than 75 volunteers recruited through ads in the city and campus newspapers. The applicants were mostly college students from all over the United States and Canada who happened to be in the Stanford area during the summer and were attracted by the lure of earning $15 a day for participating in a study of prison life. We selected only those judged to be emotionally stable, physically healthy, mature, law-abiding citizens.

10   The sample of average, middle-class, Caucasian, college-age males (plus one Oriental student) was arbitrarily divided by the flip of a coin. Half were randomly assigned to play the role of guards, the others of prisoners. There were no measurable differences between the guards and the prisoners at the start of the experiment. Although initially warned that as prisoners their privacy and other civil rights would be violated and that they might be subjected to harassment, every subject was completely confident of his ability to endure whatever the prison had to offer for the full two-week experimental period. Each subject unhesitatingly agreed to give his "informed consent" to participate.

11   The prison was constructed in the basement of Stanford University's psychology building, which was deserted after the end of the summer-school session. A long corridor was converted into the prison "yard" by partitioning off both ends. Three small laboratory rooms opening onto this corridor were made into cells by installing metal barred doors and replacing existing furniture with cots, three to a cell. Adjacent offices were refurnished as guards' quarters, interview-testing rooms, and bedrooms for the "warden" (Jaffe) and the "superintendent" (Zimbardo). A concealed video camera and hidden microphones recorded much of the activity and conversation of guards and prisoners. The physical environment was one in which prisoners could always be observed by the staff, the only exception being when they were secluded in solitary confinement (a small, dark storage closet, labeled "The Hole").

12   Our mock prison represented an attempt to simulate the psychological state of imprisonment in certain ways. We based our experiment on an in-depth analysis of the prison situation, developed after hundreds of hours of discussion with Carlo Prescott (our ex-con consultant), parole officers, and correctional personnel, and after reviewing much of the existing literature on prisons and concentration camps.

13   "Real" prisoners typically report feeling powerless, arbitrarily controlled, dependent, frustrated, hopeless, anonymous, dehumanized, and emasculated. It was not possible, pragmatically or ethically, to create such chronic states in volunteer subjects who realize that they are in an experiment for only a short time. Racism, physical brutality, indefinite confinement, and enforced homosexuality were not features of our mock prison. But we did try to reproduce those elements of the prison experience that seemed most fundamental.

14   We promoted anonymity by seeking to minimize each prisoner's sense of uniqueness and prior identity. The prisoners wore smocks and nylon stocking caps; they had to use their ID numbers; their personal effects were removed and they were housed in barren cells. All of this made them appear similar to each other and indistinguishable to observers. Their smocks, which were like dresses, were worn without undergarments, causing the prisoners to be restrained in their physical actions and to move in ways that were more feminine than masculine. The prisoners were forced to obtain permission from the guard for routine and simple activities such as writing letters, smoking a cigarette, or even going to the toilet; this elicited from them a childlike dependency.

15   Their quarters, though clean and neat, were small, stark, and without esthetic appeal. The lack of windows resulted in poor air circulation, and persistent odors arose from the unwashed bodies of the prisoners. After 10 P.M. lockup, toilet priv-

ileges were denied, so prisoners who had to relieve themselves would have to urinate and defecate in buckets provided by the guards. Sometimes the guards refused permission to have them cleaned out, and this made the prison smell.

16 Above all, "real" prisons are machines for playing tricks with the human conception of time. In our windowless prison, the prisoners often did not even know whether it was day or night. A few hours after falling asleep, they were roused by shrill whistles for their "count." The ostensible purpose of the count was to provide a public test of the prisoners' knowledge of the rules and of their ID numbers. But more important, the count, which occurred at least once on each of the three different guard shifts, provided a regular occasion for the guards to relate to the prisoners. Over the course of the study, the duration of the counts was spontaneously increased by the guards from their initial perfunctory 10 minutes to a seemingly interminable several hours. During these confrontations, guards who were bored could find ways to amuse themselves, ridiculing recalcitrant prisoners, enforcing arbitrary rules, and openly exaggerating any dissension among the prisoners.

17 The guards were also "deindividualized": They wore identical khaki uniforms and silver reflector sunglasses that made eye contact with them impossible. Their symbols of power were billy clubs, whistles, handcuffs, and the keys to the cells and the "main gate." Although our guards received no formal training from us in how to be guards, for the most part they moved with apparent ease into their roles. The media had already provided them with ample models of prison guards to emulate.

18 Because we were as interested in the guards' behavior as in the prisoners', they were given considerable latitude to improvise and to develop strategies and tactics of prisoner management. Our guards were told that they must maintain "law and order" in this prison, that they were responsible for handling any trouble that might break out, and they were cautioned about the seriousness and potential dangers of the situation they were about to enter. Surprisingly, in most prison systems, "real" guards are not given much more psychological preparation or adequate training than this for what is one of the most complex, demanding, and dangerous jobs our society has to offer. They are expected to learn how to adjust to their new employment mostly from on-the-job experience, and from contacts with the "old bulls" during a survival of-the-fittest orientation period. According to an orientation manual for correctional officers at San Quentin, "the only way you really get to know San Quentin is through experience and time. Some of us take more time and must go through more experiences than others to accomplish this; some really never do get there."

19 You cannot be a prisoner if no one will be your guard, and you cannot be a prison guard if no one takes you or your prison seriously. Therefore, over time a perverted symbiotic relationship developed. As the guards became more aggressive, prisoners became more passive; assertion by the guards led to dependency in the prisoners; self-aggrandizement was met with self-deprecation, authority with helplessness, and the counterpart of the guards' sense of mastery and control was the depression and hopelessness witnessed in the prisoners. As these differences in behavior, mood, and perception became more evident to all, the need for the now "righteously" powerful guards to rule

the obviously inferior and powerless inmates became a sufficient reason to support almost any further indignity of man against man:

20 Guard K: "During the inspection, I went to cell 2 to mess up a bed which the prisoner had made and he grabbed me, screaming that he had just made it, and he wasn't going to let me mess it up. He grabbed my throat, and although he was laughing I was pretty scared. . . . I lashed out with my stick and hit him in the chin (although not very hard), and when I freed myself I became angry. I wanted to get back in the cell and have a go with him, since he attacked me when I was not ready."

21 Guard M: "I was surprised at myself . . . I made them call each other names and clean the toilets out with their bare hands. I practically considered the prisoners cattle, and I kept thinking: 'I have to watch out for them in case they try something.' "

22 Guard A: "I was tired of seeing the prisoners in their rags and smelling the strong odors of their bodies that filled the cells. I watched them tear at each other on orders given by us. They didn't see it as an experiment. It was real and they were fighting to keep their identity. But we were always there to show them who was boss."

23 Because the first day passed without incident, we were surprised and totally unprepared for the rebellion that broke out on the morning of the second day. The prisoners removed their stocking caps, ripped off their numbers, and barricaded themselves inside the cells by putting their beds against the doors. What should we do? The guards were very much upset because the prisoners also began to taunt and curse them to their faces. When the morning shift of guards came on, they were upset at the night shift who, they felt, must have been too permissive and too lenient. The guards had to handle the rebellion themselves, and what they did was startling to behold.

24 At first they insisted that reinforcements be called in. The two guards who were waiting on stand-by call at home came in, and the night shift of guards voluntarily remained on duty (without extra pay) to bolster the morning shift. The guards met and decided to treat force with force. They got a fire extinguisher that shot a stream of skin-chilling carbon dioxide and forced the prisoners away from the doors; they broke into each cell, stripped the prisoners naked, took the beds out, forced the prisoners who were the ringleaders into solitary confinement, and generally began to harass and intimidate the prisoners.

25 After crushing the riot, the guards decided to head off further unrest by creating a privileged cell for those who were "good prisoners" and then, without explanation, switching some of the troublemakers into it and some of the good prisoners out into the other cells. The prisoner ringleaders could not trust these new cellmates because they had not joined in the riot and might even be "snitches." The prisoners never again acted in unity against the system. One of the leaders of the prisoner revolt later confided:

26 "If we had gotten together then, I think we could have taken over the place. But when I saw the revolt wasn't working, I decided to toe the line. Everyone settled into the same pattern. From then on, we were really controlled by the guards."

27   It was after this episode that the guards really began to demonstrate their inventiveness in the application of arbitrary power. They made the prisoners obey petty, meaningless, and often inconsistent rules, forced them to engage in tedious, useless work, such as moving cartons back and forth between closets and picking thorns out of their blankets for hours on end. (The guards had previously dragged the blankets through thorny bushes to create this disagreeable task.) Not only did the prisoners have to sing songs or laugh or refrain from smiling on command; they were also encouraged to curse and vilify each other publicly during some of the counts. They sounded off their numbers endlessly and were repeatedly made to do pushups, on occasion with a guard stepping on them or a prisoner sitting on them.

28   Slowly the prisoners became resigned to their fate and even behaved in ways that actually helped to justify their dehumanizing treatment at the hands of the guards. Analysis of the tape-recorded private conversations between prisoners and of remarks made by them to interviewers revealed that fully half could be classified as nonsupportive of other prisoners. More dramatic, 85 percent of the evaluative statements by prisoners about their fellow prisoners were uncomplimentary and deprecating.

29   This should be taken in the context of an even more surprising result. What do you imagine the prisoners talked about when they were alone in their cells with each other, given a temporary respite from the continual harassment and surveillance by the guards? Girl friends, career plans, hobbies or politics?

30   No, their concerns were almost exclusively riveted to prison topics. Their monitored conversations revealed that only 10 percent of the time was devoted to "outside" topics, while 90 percent of the time they discussed escape plans, the awful food, grievances or ingratiating tactics to use with specific guards in order to get a cigarette, permission to go to the toilet, or some other favor. Their obsession with these immediate survival concerns made talk about the past and future an idle luxury.

31   And this was not a minor point. So long as the prisoners did not get to know each other as people, they only extended the oppressiveness and reality of their life as prisoners. For the most part, each prisoner observed his fellow prisoners allowing the guards to humiliate them, acting like compliant sheep, carrying out mindless orders with total obedience, and even being cursed by fellow prisoners (at a guard's command). Under such circumstances, how could a prisoner have respect for his fellows, or any self-respect for what *he* obviously was becoming in the eyes of all those evaluating him?

32   The combination of realism and symbolism in this experiment had fused to create a vivid illusion of imprisonment. The illusion merged inextricably with reality for at least some of the time for every individual in the situation. It was remarkable how readily we all slipped into our roles, temporarily gave up our identities, and allowed these assigned roles and the social forces in the situation to guide, shape, and eventually to control our freedom of thought and action.

33   But precisely where does one's "identity" end and one's "role" begin? When the private self and the public role behavior clash, what direction will attempts to impose consistency take? Consider the reactions of the parents, relatives, and

friends of the prisoners who visited their forlorn sons, brothers, and lovers during two scheduled visitors' hours. They were taught in short order that they were our guests, allowed the privilege of visiting only by complying with the regulations of the institution. They had to register, were made to wait half an hour, were told that only two visitors could see any one prisoner; the total visiting time was cut from an hour to only 10 minutes, they had to be under the surveillance of a guard, and before any parents could enter the visiting area, they had to discuss their son's case with the warden. Of course they complained about these arbitrary rules, but their conditioned, middle-class reaction was to work within the system to appeal privately to the superintendent to make conditions better for their prisoners.

34   In less than 36 hours, we were forced to release prisoner 8612 because of extreme depression, disorganized thinking, uncontrollable crying, and fits of rage. We did so reluctantly because we believed he was trying to "con" us—it was unimaginable that a volunteer prisoner in a mock prison could legitimately be suffering and disturbed to that extent. But then on each of the next three days another prisoner reacted with similar anxiety symptoms, and we were forced to terminate them, too. In a fifth case, a prisoner was released after developing a psychosomatic rash over his entire body (triggered by rejection of his parole appeal by the mock parole board). These men were simply unable to make an adequate adjustment to prison life. Those who endured the prison experience to the end could be distinguished from those who broke down and were released early in only one dimension—authoritarianism. On a psychological test designed to reveal a person's authoritarianism, those prisoners who had the highest scores were best able to function in this authoritarian prison environment.

35   If the authoritarian situation became a serious matter for the prisoners, it became even more serious—and sinister—for the guards. Typically, the guards insulted the prisoners, threatened them, were physically aggressive, used instruments (night sticks, fire extinguishers, etc.) to keep the prisoners in line, and referred to them in impersonal, anonymous, deprecating ways: "Hey, you," or "You [obscenity], 5401, come here." From the first to the last day, there was a significant increase in the guards' use of most of these domineering, abusive tactics.

36   Everyone and everything in the prison was defined by power. To be a guard who did not take advantage of this institutionally sanctioned use of power was to appear "weak," "out of it," "wired up by the prisoners," or simply a deviant from the established norms of appropriate guard behavior. Using Erich Fromm's definition of sadism, as "the wish for absolute control over another living being," all of the mock guards at one time or another during this study behaved sadistically toward the prisoners. Many of them reported—in their diaries, on critical-incident report forms, and during post-experimental interviews—being delighted in the new-found power and control they exercised and sorry to see it relinquished at the end of the study.

37   Some of the guards reacted to the situation in the extreme and behaved with great hostility and cruelty in the forms of degradation they invented for the prisoners. But others were kinder; they occasionally did little favors for the prisoners, were reluctant to punish them, and avoided situations where prisoners were being harassed. The torment experienced by one of these good guards is obvious in his perceptive analysis of what if felt like to be responded to as a "guard":

38   "What made the experience most depressing for me was the fact that we were continually called upon to act in a way that just was contrary to what I really feel inside. I don't feel like I'm the type of person that would be a guard, just constantly giving out [orders] . . . and forcing people to do things, and pushing and lying—it just didn't seem like me, and to continually keep up and put on a face like that is just really one of the most oppressive things you can do. It's almost like a prison that you create yourself—you get into it, and it becomes almost the definition you make of yourself, it almost becomes like walls, and you want to break out and you want just to be able to tell everyone that 'this isn't really me at all, and I'm not the person that's confined in there—I'm a person who wants to get out and show you that I am free, and I do have my own will, and I'm not the sadistic type of person that enjoys this kind of thing.'"

39   Still, the behavior of these good guards seemed more motivated by a desire to be liked by everyone in the system than by a concern for the inmates' welfare. No guard ever intervened in any direct way on behalf of the prisoners, ever interfered with the orders of the cruelest guards, or ever openly complained about the subhuman quality of life that characterized this prison.

40   Perhaps the most devastating impact of the more hostile guards was their creation of a capricious, arbitrary environment. Over time the prisoners began to react passively. When our mock prisoners asked questions, they got answers about half the time, but the rest of the time they were insulted and punished—and it was not possible for them to predict which would be the outcome. As they began to "toe the line," they stopped resisting, questioning and, indeed, almost ceased responding altogether. There was a general decrease in all categories of response as they learned the safest strategy to use in an unpredictable, threatening environment from which there is no physical escape—do nothing, except what is required. Act not, want not, feel not, and you will not get into trouble in prisonlike situations.

41   Can it really be, you wonder, that intelligent, educated volunteers could have lost sight of the reality that they were merely acting a part in an elaborate game that would eventually end? There are many indications not only that they did, but that, in addition, so did we and so did other apparently sensible, responsible adults.

42   Prisoner 819, who had gone into an uncontrollable crying fit, was about to be prematurely released from the prison when a guard lined up the prisoners and had them chant in unison, "819 is a bad prisoner. Because of what 819 did to prison property we all must suffer. 819 is a bad prisoner." Over and over again. When we realized 819 might be overhearing this, we rushed into the room where 819 was supposed to be resting, only to find him in tears, prepared to go back into the prison because he could not leave as long as the others thought he was a "bad prisoner." Sick as he felt, he had to prove to them he was not a "bad" prisoner. He had to be persuaded that he was not a prisoner at all, that the others were also just students, that this was just an experiment and not a prison and the prison staff were only research psychologists. A report from the warden notes, "While I believe that it was necessary for *staff* [me] to enact the warden role, at least some of the time, I am startled by the ease with which I could turn off my sensitivity and concern for others for 'a good cause.'"

43   Consider our overreaction to the rumor of a mass escape plot that one of the guards claimed to have overheard. It went as follows: Prisoner 8612, previously released for emotional disturbance, was only faking. He was going to round up a bunch of his friends, and they would storm the prison right after visiting hours. Instead of collecting data on the pattern of rumor transmission, we made plans to maintain the security of our institution. After putting a confederate informer into the cell 8612 had occupied to get specific information about the escape plans, the superintendent went back to the Palo Alto Police Department to request transfer of our prisoners to the old city jail. His impassioned plea was only turned down at the last minute when the problem of insurance and city liability for our prisoners was raised by a city official. Angered at this lack of cooperation, the staff formulated another plan. Our jail was dismantled, the prisoners, chained and blindfolded, were carted off to a remote storage room. When the conspirators arrived, they would be told the study was over, their friends had been sent home, there was nothing left to liberate. After they left, we would redouble the security features of our prison making any future escape attempts futile. We even planned to lure ex-prisoner 8612 back on some pretext and imprison him again, because he had been released on false pretenses! The rumor turned out to be just that—a full day had passed in which we collected little or no data, worked incredibly hard to tear down and then rebuilt our prison. Our reaction, however, was as much one of relief and joy as of exhaustion and frustration.

44   When a former prison chaplain was invited to talk with the prisoners (the grievance committee had requested church services), he puzzled everyone by disparaging each inmate for not having taken any constructive action in order to get released. "Don't you know you must have a lawyer in order to get bail, or to appeal the charges against you?" Several of them accepted his invitation to contact their parents in order to secure the services of an attorney. The next night one of the parents stopped at the superintendent's office before visiting time and handed him the name and phone number of her cousin who was a public defender. She said that a priest had called her and suggested the need for a lawyer's services! We called the lawyer. He came, interviewed the prisoners, discussed sources of bail money, and promised to return again after the weekend.

45   But perhaps the most telling account of the insidious development of this new reality, of the gradual Kafkaesque metamorphosis of good into evil, appears in excerpts from the diary of one of the guards, Guard A:

46   *Prior to start of experiment:* "As I am a pacifist and nonaggressive individual. I cannot see a time when I might guard and/or maltreat other living things."

47   *After an orientation meeting:* "Buying uniforms at the end of the meeting confirms the gamelike atmosphere of this thing. I doubt whether many of us share the expectations of 'seriousness' that the experimenters seem to have."

48   *First Day:* "Feel sure that the prisoners will make fun of my appearance and I evolve my first basic strategy—mainly not to smile at anything they say or do which would be admitting it's all only a game. . . . At cell 3 I stop and setting my voice hard and low say to 5486, 'What are you smiling at?' 'Nothing, Mr. Correctional Officer.' 'Well, see that you don't.' (As I walk off I feel stupid.)"

49   *Second Day:* "5704 asked for a cigarette and I ignored him—because I am a non-smoker and could not empathize. . . . Meanwhile since I was feeling empathetic towards 1037, I determined not to talk with him. . . . After we had count and lights out [Guard D] and I held a loud conversation about going home to our girl friends and what we were going to do to them."

50   *Third Day (preparing for the first visitors' night):* "After warning the prisoners not to make any complaints unless they wanted the visit terminated fast, we finally brought in the first parents. I made sure I was one of the guards on the yard, because this was my first chance for the type of manipulative power that I really like—being a very noticed figure with almost complete control over what is said or not. While the parents and prisoners sat in chairs, I sat on the end of the table dangling my feet and contradicting anything I felt like. This was the first part of the experiment I was really enjoying. . . . 817 is being obnoxious and bears watching."

51   *Fourth Day:* ". . . The psychologist rebukes me for handcuffing and blindfolding a prisoner before leaving the [counseling] office, and I resentfully reply that it is both necessary security and my business anyway."

52   *Fifth Day:* "I harass 'Sarge' who continues to stubbornly overrespond to all commands. I have singled him out for the special abuse both because he begs for it and because I simply don't like him. The real trouble starts at dinner. The new prisoner (416) refuses to eat his sausage . . . we throw him into the Hole ordering him to hold sausages in each hand. We have a crisis of authority; this rebellious conduct potentially undermines the complete control we have over the others. We decide to play upon prisoner solidarity and tell the new one that all the others will be deprived of visitors if he does not eat his dinner. . . . I walk by and slam my stick into the Hole door. . . . I am very angry at this prisoner for causing discomfort and trouble for the others. I decided to force-feed him, but he wouldn't eat. I let the food slide down his face. I didn't believe it was me doing it. I hated myself for making him eat but I hated him more for not eating."

53   *Sixth Day:* "The experiment is over. I feel elated but am shocked to find some other guards disappointed somewhat because of the loss of money and some because they are enjoying themselves."

54   We were no longer dealing with an intellectual exercise in which a hypothesis was being evaluated in the dispassionate manner dictated by the canons of the scientific method. We were caught up in the passion of the present, the suffering, the need to control people, not variables, the escalation of power, and all the unexpected things that were erupting around and within us. We had to end this experiment: So our planned two-week simulation was aborted after only six (was it only six?) days and nights.

55   Was it worth all the suffering just to prove what everybody knows—that some people are sadistic, others weak, and prisons are not beds of roses? If that is all we demonstrated in this research, then it was certainly not worth the anguish. We believe there are many significant implications to be derived from this experience, only a few of which can be suggested here.

56   The potential social value of this study derives precisely from the fact that normal, healthy, educated young men could be so radically transformed under

the institutional pressures of a "prison environment." If this could happen in so short a time, without the excesses that are possible in real prisons, and if it could happen to the "cream-of-the-crop of American youth," then one can only shudder to imagine what society is doing both to the actual guards and prisoners who are at this very moment participating in that unnatural "social experiment."

57   The pathology observed in this study cannot be reasonably attributed in pre-existing personality differences of the subjects, that option being eliminated by our selection procedures and random assignment. Rather, the subjects' abnormal social and personal reactions are best seen as a product of their transaction with an environment that supported the behavior that would be pathological in other settings, but was "appropriate" in this prison. Had we observed comparable reactions in a real prison, the psychiatrist undoubtedly would have been able to attribute any prisoner's behavior to character defects or personality maladjustment, while critics of the prison system would have been quick to label the guards as "psychopathic." This tendency to locate the source of behavior disorders inside a particular person or group underestimates the power of situational forces.

58   Our colleague, David Rosenhan, has very convincingly shown that once a sane person (pretending to be insane) gets labeled as insane and committed to a mental hospital, it is the label that is the reality which is treated and not the person. This dehumanizing tendency to respond to other people according to socially determined labels and often arbitrarily assigned roles is also apparent in a recent "mock hospital" study designed by Norma Jean Orlando to extend the ideas in our research.

59   Personnel from the staff of Elgin State Hospital in Illinois role-played either mental patients or staff in a weekend simulation on a ward in the hospital. The mock mental patients soon displayed behavior indistinguishable from that we usually associate with the chronic pathological syndromes of acute mental patients: Incessant pacing, uncontrollable weeping, depression, hostility, fights, stealing from each other, complaining. Many of the "mock staff" took advantage of their power to act in ways comparable to our mock guards by dehumanizing their powerless victims.

60   During a series of encounter debriefing sessions immediately after our experiment, we all had an opportunity to vent our strong feelings and to reflect upon the moral and ethical issues each of us faced, and we considered how we might react more morally in future "real-life" analogues to this situation. Year-long follow-ups with our subjects via questionnaires, personal interviews, and group reunions indicate that their mental anguish was transient and situationally specific, but the self-knowledge gained has persisted.

61   By far the most disturbing implication of our research comes from the parallels between what occurred in that basement mock prison and daily experiences in our own lives—and we presume yours. The physical institution of prison is but a concrete and steel metaphor for the existence of more pervasive, albeit less obvious, prisons of the mind that all of us daily create, populate, and perpetuate. We speak here of the prisons of racism, sexism, despair, shyness, "neurotic hang-ups," and the like. The social convention of marriage, as

one example, becomes for many couples a state of imprisonment in which one partner agrees to be prisoner or guard, forcing or allowing the other to play the reciprocal role—invariably without making the contract explicit.

62   To what extent do we allow ourselves to become imprisoned by docilely accepting the roles others assign us or, indeed, choose to remain prisoners because being passive and dependent frees us from the need to act and be responsible for our actions? The prison of fear constructed in the delusions of the paranoid is no less confining or less real than the cell that every shy person erects to limit his own freedom in anxious anticipation of being ridiculed and rejected by his guards—often guards of his own making.

Review Questions

1. What was Zimbardo's primary goal in undertaking the prison experiment?

2. What was the profile of the subjects in the experiments? Why is this profile significant?

3. Zimbardo claims that there is a "process" (paragraphs 2, 7) of becoming a prisoner. What is this process?

4. What inverse psychological relationships developed between prisoners and guards?

5. What was the result of the prison "riot"?

6. Why did prisoners have no respect for each other or for themselves?

7. How does the journal of Guard A illustrate what Zimbardo calls the "gradual Kafkaesque metamorphosis of good into evil"? (See paragraphs 45–54.)

8. What are the reasons people would voluntarily become prisoners?

9. How can the mind keep people in jail?

Discussion and Writing Suggestions

1. Reread the four epigraphs to this article. Write a paragraph of response to any one of them, in light of Zimbardo's discussion of the prison experiment.

2. You may have thought, before reading this article, that being a prisoner is a physical fact, not a psychological state. What are the differences between these two views?

3. In paragraph 8, Zimbardo explains his reasons for not pursuing his research in a real prison. He writes that "it is impossible to separate what each individual brings into the prison from what the prison brings out in each person." What does he mean? And how does this distinction prove important later in the article? (See paragraph 58.)

4. Zimbardo reports that at the beginning of the experiment each of the "prisoner" subjects "was completely confident of his ability to endure whatever the prison had to offer for the full two-week experimental period" (paragraph 10). Had you been a subject, would you have been so confident, prior to the experiment? Given what you've learned of the experiment, do you think you would have psychologically "become" a prisoner or guard if you had been selected for these roles? (And if not, what makes you so sure?)

5. Identify two passages in this article: one that surprised you relating to the prisoners and one that surprised you relating to the guards. Write a paragraph explaining your response to each. Now read the two passages in light of each other. Do you see any patterns underlying your responses?

6. Zimbardo claims that the implications of his research matter deeply—that the mock prison he created is a metaphor for prisons of the mind "that all of us daily create, populate, and perpetuate" (paragraph 61). Zimbardo mentions the prisons of "racism, sexism, despair, [and] shyness." Choose any one of these and discuss how it might be viewed as a mental prison.

7. Reread paragraphs 61 and 62. Zimbardo makes a metaphorical jump from his experiment to the psychological realities of your daily life. Prisons—the artificial one he created and actual prisons— stand for something: social systems in which there are those who give orders and those who obey. All metaphors break down at some point. Where does this one break down?

8. Zimbardo suggests that we might "choose to remain prisoners because being passive and dependent frees us from the need to act and be responsible for our actions" (paragraph 62). Do you agree? What are the burdens of being disobedient?

Disobedience as a Psychological and Moral Problem
Erich Fromm

Erich Fromm (1900–1980) was one of the twentieth century's distinguished writers and thinkers. Psychoanalyst and philosopher, historian and sociologist, he ranged widely in his interests and defied easy characterization. Fromm studied the works of Freud and Marx closely, and published on them both, but he was not aligned strictly with either. In much of his voluminous writing, he struggled to articulate a view that could help bridge ideological and personal conflicts and bring dignity to those who struggled with isolation in the industrial world. Author of more than thirty books and contributor to numerous edited collections and journals, Fromm is best known for Escape from Freedom *(1941),* The Art of Loving *(1956), and* To Have or To Be? *(1976).*

In the essay that follows, first published in 1963, Fromm discusses the seductive comforts of obedience, and he makes distinctions among varieties of obedience, some of which he believes are destructive, and others, life affirming. His thoughts on nuclear annihilation may seem dated in these days of post–Cold War cooperation, but it is worth remembering that Fromm wrote his essay just after the Cuban missile crisis, when fears of a third world war ran high. (We might note that despite the welcome reductions of nuclear stockpiles, the United States and Russia still possess, and retain battle plans for, thousands of warheads.) And in the wake of the 9/11 attacks, the threat of terrorists acquiring and using nuclear weapons against the United States seems very real. On the major points of his essay, concerning the psychological and moral problems of obedience, Fromm remains as pertinent today as when he wrote some forty years ago.

1 For centuries kings, priests, feudal lords, industrial bosses, and parents have insisted that *obedience is a virtue* and that *disobedience is a vice.* In order to introduce another point of view, let us set against this position the following statement: *human history began with an act of disobedience, and it is not unlikely that it will be terminated by an act of obedience.*

2   Human history was ushered in by an act of disobedience according to the Hebrew and Greek myths. Adam and Eve, living in the Garden of Eden, were part of nature; they were in harmony with it, yet did not transcend it. They were in nature as the fetus is in the womb of the mother. They were human, and at the same time not yet human. All this changed when they disobeyed an order. By breaking the ties with earth and mother, by cutting the umbilical cord, man emerged from a prehuman harmony and was able to take the first step into independence and freedom. The act of disobedience set Adam and Eve free and opened their eyes. They recognized each other as strangers and the world outside them as strange and even hostile. Their act of disobedience broke the primary bond with nature and made them individuals. "Original sin," far from corrupting man, set him free; it was the beginning of history. Man had to leave the Garden of Eden in order to learn to rely on his own powers and to become fully human.

3   The prophets, in their messianic concept, confirmed the idea that man had been right in disobeying; that he had not been corrupted by his "sin," but freed from the fetters of pre-human harmony. For the prophets, *history* is the place where man becomes human; during its unfolding he develops his powers of reason and of love until he creates a new harmony between himself, his fellow man, and nature. This new harmony is described as "the end of days," that period of history in which there is peace between man and man, between man and nature. It is a "new" paradise created by man himself, and one which he alone could create because he was forced to leave the "old" paradise as a result of his disobedience.

4   Just as the Hebrew myth of Adam and Eve, so the Greek myth of Prometheus sees all human civilization based on an act of disobedience. Prometheus, in stealing the fire from the gods, lays the foundation for the evolution of man. There would be no human history were it not for Prometheus' "crime." He, like Adam and Eve, is punished for his disobedience. But he does not repent and ask for forgiveness. On the contrary, he proudly says: "I would rather be chained to this rock than be the obedient servant of the gods."

5 Man has continued to evolve by acts of disobedience. Not only was his spiritual development possible only because there were men who dared to say no to the powers that be in the name of their conscience or their faith, but also his intellectual development was dependent on the capacity for being disobedient—disobedient to authorities who tried to muzzle new thoughts and to the authority of long-established opinions which declared a change to be nonsense.

6 If the capacity for disobedience constituted the beginning of human history, obedience might very well, as I have said, cause the end of human history. I am not speaking symbolically or poetically. There is the possibility, or even the probability, that the human race will destroy civilization and even all life upon earth within the next five to ten years. There is no rationality or sense in it. But the fact is that, while we are living technically in the Atomic Age, the majority of men—including most of those who are in power—still live emotionally in the Stone Age; that while our mathematics, astronomy, and the natural sciences are of the twentieth century, most of our ideas about politics, the state, and society lag far behind the age of science. If mankind commits suicide it will be because people will obey those who command them to push the deadly buttons; because they will obey the archaic passions of fear, hate, and greed; because they will obey obsolete clichés of State sovereignty and national honor. The Soviet leaders talk much about revolutions, and we in the "free world" talk much about freedom. Yet they and we discourage disobedience—in the Soviet Union explicitly and by force, in the free world implicitly and by the more subtle methods of persuasion.

7 But I do not mean to say that all disobedience is a virtue and all obedience is a vice. Such a view would ignore the dialectical relationship between obedience and disobedience. Whenever the principles which are obeyed and those which are disobeyed are irreconcilable, an act of obedience to one principle is necessarily an act of disobedience to its counterpart and vice versa. Antigone is the classic example of this dichotomy. By obeying the inhuman laws of the State, Antigone necessarily would disobey the laws of humanity. By obeying the latter, she must disobey the former. All martyrs of religious faiths, of freedom, and of science have had to disobey those who wanted to muzzle them in order to obey their own consciences, the laws of humanity, and of reason. If a man can only obey and not disobey, he is a slave; if he can only disobey and not obey, he is a rebel (not a revolutionary); he acts out of anger, disappointment, resentment, yet not in the name of a conviction or a principle.

8 However, in order to prevent a confusion of terms an important qualification must be made. Obedience to a person, institution, or power (heteronomous obedience) is submission; it implies the abdication of my autonomy and the acceptance of a foreign will or judgment in place of my own. Obedience to my own reason or conviction (autonomous obedience) is not an act of submission but one of affirmation. My conviction and my judgment, if authentically mine, are part of me. If I follow them rather than the judgment of others, I am being myself; hence the word *obey* can be applied only in a metaphorical sense and with a meaning which is fundamentally different from the one in the case of "heteronomous obedience."

9 But this distinction still needs two further qualifications, one with regard to the concept of conscience and the other with regard to the concept of authority.

10   The word *conscience* is used to express two phenomena which are quite distinct from each other. One is the "authoritarian conscience" which is the internalized voice of an authority whom we are eager to please and afraid of displeasing. This authoritarian conscience is what most people experience when they obey their conscience. It is also the conscience which Freud speaks of, and which he called "Super-Ego." This Super-Ego represents the internalized commands and prohibitions of father, accepted by the son out of fear. Different from the authoritarian conscience is the "humanistic conscience"; this is the voice present in every human being and independent from external sanctions and rewards. Humanistic conscience is based on the fact that as human beings we have an intuitive knowledge of what is human and inhuman, what is conducive of life and what is destructive of life. This conscience serves our functioning as human beings. It is the voice which calls us back to ourselves, to our humanity.

11   Authoritarian conscience (Super-Ego) is still obedience to a power outside of myself, even though this power has been internalized. Consciously I believe that I am following *my* conscience; in effect, however, I have swallowed the principles of *power;* just because of the illusion that humanistic conscience and Super-Ego are identical, internalized authority is so much more effective than the authority which is clearly experienced as not being part of me. Obedience to the "authoritarian conscience," like all obedience to outside thoughts and power, tends to debilitate "humanistic conscience," the ability to be and to judge oneself.

12   The statement, on the other hand, that obedience to another person is *ipso facto* submission needs also to be qualified by distinguishing "irrational" from "rational" authority. An example of rational authority is to be found in the relationship between student and teacher; one of irrational authority in the relationship between slave and master. Both relationships are based on the fact that the authority of the person in command is accepted. Dynamically, however, they are of a different nature. The interests of the teacher and the student, in the ideal case, lie in the same direction. The teacher is satisfied if he succeeds in furthering the student; if he has failed to do so, the failure is his and the student's. The slave owner, on the other hand, wants to exploit the slave as much as possible. The more he gets out of him the more satisfied he is. At the same time, the slave tries to defend as best he can his claims for a minimum of happiness. The interests of slave and master are antagonistic, because what is advantageous to the one is detrimental to the other. The superiority of the one over the other has a different function in each case; in the first it is the condition for the furtherance of the person subjected to the authority, and in the second it is the condition for his exploitation. Another distinction runs parallel to this: rational authority is rational because the authority, whether it is held by a teacher or a captain of a ship giving orders in an emergency, acts in the name of reason which, being universal, I can accept without submitting. Irrational authority has to use force or suggestion, because no one would let himself be exploited if he were free to prevent it.

13   Why is man so prone to obey and why is it so difficult for him to disobey? As long as I am obedient to the power of the State, the Church, or public opinion, I feel safe and protected. In fact it makes little difference what power it is that I am obedient to. It is always an institution, or men, who use force in one form

or another and who fraudulently claim omniscience and omnipotence. My obedience makes me part of the power I worship, and hence I feel strong. I can make no error, since it decides for me; I cannot be alone, because it watches over me; I cannot commit a sin, because it does not let me do so, and even if I do sin, the punishment is only the way of returning to the almighty power.

14   In order to disobey, one must have the courage to be alone, to err, and to sin. But courage is not enough. The capacity for courage depends on a person's state of development. Only if a person has emerged from mother's lap and father's commands, only if he has emerged as a fully developed individual and thus has acquired the capacity to think and feel for himself, only then can he have the courage to say "no" to power, to disobey.

15   A person can become free through acts of disobedience by learning to say no to power. But not only is the capacity for disobedience the condition for freedom; freedom is also the condition for disobedience. If I am afraid of freedom, I cannot dare to say "no," I cannot have the courage to be disobedient. Indeed, freedom and the capacity for disobedience are inseparable; hence any social, political, and religious system which proclaims freedom, yet stamps out disobedience, cannot speak the truth.

16   There is another reason why it is so difficult to dare to disobey, to say "no" to power. During most of human history obedience has been identified with virtue and disobedience with sin. The reason is simple: thus far throughout most of history a minority has ruled over the majority. This rule was made necessary by the fact that there was only enough of the good things of life for the few, and only the crumbs remained for the many. If the few wanted to enjoy the good things and, beyond that, to have the many serve them and work for them, one condition was necessary: the many had to learn obedience. To be sure, obedience can be established by sheer force. But this method has many disadvantages. It constitutes a constant threat that one day the many might have the means to overthrow the few by force; furthermore there are many kinds of work which cannot be done properly if nothing but fear is behind the obedience. Hence the obedience which is only rooted in the fear of force must be transformed into one rooted in man's heart. Man must want and even need to obey, instead of only fearing to disobey. If this is to be achieved, power must assume the qualities of the All Good, of the All Wise; it must become All Knowing. If this happens, power can proclaim that disobedience is sin and obedience virtue; and once this has been proclaimed, the many can accept obedience because it is good and detest disobedience because it is bad, rather than to detest themselves for being cowards. From Luther to the nineteenth century one was concerned with overt and explicit authorities. Luther, the pope, the princes, wanted to uphold it; the middle class, the workers, the philosophers, tried to uproot it. The fight against authority in the State as well as in the family was often the very basis for the development of an independent and daring person. The fight against authority was inseparable from the intellectual mood which characterized the philosophers of the enlightenment and the scientists. This "critical mood" was one of faith in reason, and at the same time of doubt in everything which is said or thought, inasmuch as it is based on tradition, superstition, custom, power. The principles *sapere aude* and *de omnibus est dubitandum*—"dare to be wise" and "of

all one must doubt"—were characteristic of the attitude which permitted and furthered the capacity to say "no."

17   The case of Adolf Eichmann [see note, page 190] is symbolic of our situation and has a significance far beyond the one in which his accusers in the courtroom in Jerusalem were concerned with. Eichmann is a symbol of the organization man, of the alienated bureaucrat for whom men, women and children have become numbers. He is a symbol of all of us. We can see ourselves in Eichmann. But the most frightening thing about him is that after the entire story was told in terms of his own admissions, he was able in perfect good faith to plead his innocence. It is clear that if he were once more in the same situation he would do it again. And so would we—and so do we.

18   The organization man has lost the capacity to disobey, he is not even aware of the fact that he obeys. At this point in history the capacity to doubt, to criticize, and to disobey may be all that stands between a future for mankind and the end of civilization.

Review Questions

1. What does Fromm mean when he writes that disobedience is "the first step into independence and freedom"?

2. Fromm writes that history began with an act of disobedience and will likely end with an act of obedience. What does he mean?

3. What is the difference between "heteronomous obedience" and "autonomous obedience"?

4. How does Fromm distinguish between "authoritarian conscience" and "humanistic conscience"?

5. When is obedience to another person *not* submission?

6. What are the psychological comforts of obedience, and why would authorities rather have people obey out of love than out of fear?

Discussion and Writing Suggestions

1. Fromm suggests that scientifically we live in the twentieth century but that politically and emotionally we live in the Stone Age. As you observe events in the world, both near and far, would you agree? Why?

2. Fromm writes: "If a man can only obey and not disobey, he is a slave; if he can only disobey and not obey, he is a rebel (not a revolutionary)" (paragraph 7). Explain Fromm's meaning here. Explain, as well, the implication that to be fully human one must have the freedom to both obey and disobey.

3. Fromm writes that "obedience makes me part of the power I worship, and hence I feel strong" (paragraph 13). Does this statement

ring true for you? Discuss, in writing, an occasion in which you felt powerful because you obeyed a group norm.

4. In paragraphs 15 and 16, Fromm equates obedience with cowardice. Can you identify a situation in which you were obedient but, now that you reflect on it, were also cowardly? That is, can you recall a time when you caved in to a group but now wish you hadn't? Explain.

5. Fromm says that we can see ourselves in Adolf Eichmann—that as an organization man he "has lost the capacity to disobey, he is not even aware of the fact that he obeys." To what extent do you recognize yourself in this portrait?

The Genocidal Killer in the Mirror
Crispin Sartwell

Upon first learning of such experiments as those conducted by Asch, Milgram, and Zimbardo, many of us are apt to shake our heads at the obedient participants, confident that we would behave differently—that is, independently and ethically—under the same circumstances. But how can we be so sure? In this essay on the phenomenon that novelist Joseph Conrad called the "heart of darkness," Crispin Sartwell reviews recent history to help persuade us that we should not be so smug about our own capacity to resist corrupt authority and to commit heinous acts. Among Sartwell's books are The Art of Living: Aesthetics of the Ordinary in World Spiritual Traditions *(1995),* Obscenity, Anarchy, Reality *(1996),* Act Like You Know: African-American Autobiography and White Identity *(1998), and* Extreme Virtue: Truth and Leadership in Five Great American Lives *(2003). The following essay appeared as an op-ed column in the* Los Angeles Times *on 11 April 2004.*

1   Ten years ago this month, the Hutu government of Rwanda mobilized its citizenry into a killing machine and started stacking corpses toward the sky. It's been 30 years since the Cambodian killing fields, 40 since the start of the Cultural Revolution, 60 since the height of the Nazi Holocaust, 100 since the Belgians started murdering Congolese, 500 since the beginnings of the African slave trade and the systematic annihilation of the native peoples of the Western Hemisphere.

2   There are various things we ought to have learned from the history of genocide. One, surely, is that no problem is as profound and no evil as prevalent as state power: The rise of genocide coincides with the rise of the modern political state, and every single one of these events is inconceivable without the bland bureaucracy of death.

3   But another is this: We—and by this I mean you and I—are deeply evil. I would like to believe that I am too good, too smart, too decent to hop on the genocide bandwagon. But I know better. It's obvious, and it's a familiar point, that average Germans, average Hutus, average Americans have been mobilized for genocide. I am not profoundly different than these people, and

if you think you are, then you are either a moral hero or you are prof
self-deluded.

4   Are you a moral hero? The qualities that are needed to recruit a pe
genocide are widely shared.

- *Deference to authority.* This would be the state, the experts—under normal
  conditions. Ponder, perhaps, how you react to a school principal or a police
  officer or a president. Do you often believe what the authorities tell you just
  because they are authorities?
- *Response to social consensus.* People are herd animals; they seek to associate themselves with a consensus of their acquaintances. If you hate being
  excluded by a clique, or dress in terms of trends, you are responding in this
  way.
- *Willingness to respond to people as members of groups, and to expect
  groups, overall, to display certain qualities.* I might not want to do this, but
  I do. I know a lot about gay people, for example: How they talk, where they
  live, what they do.
- *Desire for your own security and that of your family and friends, to the
  extent you are willing to make moral compromises to preserve it.* These are
  qualities found in greater or lesser degree in everyone, and they're more
  than enough. You, like me, are a genocidal killer, only you (probably), like
  me, haven't had the opportunity to display your enthusiasm. Your goodness,
  like mine, has little to do with who you are and everything to do with the
  social conditions you happen to find yourself in.

5   In Rwanda, the Hutu government claimed falsely that it was under attack
from Tutsis—a claim repeated incessantly on the state-run radio—and mobilized
the population into "civilian self-defense forces." It created squads dedicated
to "obligatory labor for the public good" and armed them with firearms or
machetes. It rewarded those who were zealous killers with houses or cars, punished those who hesitated and killed those who sheltered the intended victims.
Just two months later, 800,000 people were dead.

6   Hitler didn't kill 6 million Jews, or King Leopold 10 million Africans. They used
a bureaucracy and a media machine and, finally, people just like me and you.
They mobilized a society. I remember staring at Rwanda on my television, reading about Cambodia in my newspaper as the killing continued. I shook my head
and did absolutely nothing—basically the same approach taken by the world in
each instance. I fear that if the same thing were happening in my town to
people "not like me" in some identifiable way, I would take the same approach.

7   Many decent people have.

Review Questions

1. What links the historical events cited by Sartwell in the first paragraph of this column?

According to Sartwell, what two main things should we have learned from the history of genocide?

3. By what institutional means did leaders and governments accomplish their genocidal purposes, according to Sartwell?

Discussion and Writing Suggestions

1. To what extent do you agree with Sartwell that "no problem is as profound and no evil as prevalent as state power"?

2. Sartwell asks, "Are you a moral hero?" and then invites us to answer the bulleted questions that follow. Did you attempt to address such questions? Discuss your provisional responses. To what extent do you agree with Sartwell's assumption that "we . . . are deeply evil"? To what extent to you take issue with it?

3. Sartwell makes the following, radical claim: "Your goodness, like mine, has little to do with who you are and everything to do with the social conditions you happen to find yourself in." In other words, goodness is not an innate quality. It is a social, learned quality. Do you agree?

Just Do What the Pilot Tells You
Theodore Dalrymple

Most of the readings in this chapter have illustrated the dangers of unthinking obedience to either individual or group authority. But we don't mean to suggest that disobedience is always the best, the wisest, the most moral, or the most logical choice. As even Stanley Milgram acknowledged at the beginning of his article, "Some system of authority is a requirement of all communal living, and it is only the person living in isolation who is not forced to respond, with defiance or submission, to the commands of others" (page 184). Were we to routinely defy the authority of parents, teachers, police officers, employers, clients, etc., what we call civilization could not continue to function. We would be living in a Darwinian world where only the strong would survive. The law would not provide authority, but it would also not provide protection. In fact, we need to obey most orders that we are given for our own safety and welfare.

In the following article first published in the July 5, 1999, New Statesman, Theodore Dalrymple, a British physician, reminds us of those occasions when we should do what we are told. "Blind disobedience to authority," he observes, "is no more to be encouraged than blind obedience." In the course of his discussion Dalrymple attempts to find a reasonable balance between these two poles.

1 Some people think a determined opposition to authority is principled and romantic.

2   It is a quarter of a century since the psychologist Stanley Milgram published his masterpiece, *Obedience to Authority.* It is one of the few books of academic psychological research that can be read with as much pleasure as a novel and which suggest almost as much about the human condition as great literature. Only someone who had no interest whatever in the genocidal upheavals of our century could fail to be gripped, and horrified, by it.

3   Milgram asked ordinary people to come to the psychology laboratories of Yale University to take part in an experiment to determine the effects of punishment on learning. The subjects were told to deliver electric shocks of increasing severity, from 15 to 450 volts, whenever a man who was supposed to learn pairs of words made a mistake. In fact the man was an actor who received no shocks at all, but who simply acted as if he had.

4   Milgram discovered that about two-thirds of his subjects (who were probably representative of the population as a whole) were quite prepared to give a complete stranger electric shocks that they believed to be painful, dangerous and even possibly fatal, despite the stranger's screams of protest, simply because they were told by someone apparently in authority—the psychologist overseeing the experiment—that the test had to go on.

5   By a series of clever manipulations, Milgram proved that it was obedience to authority that led people to behave in this fashion, rather than, say, the unleashing of a latent sadistic urge to inflict pain on people. Although Milgram was restrained in his discussion of the significance of his findings, he nevertheless suggested that they helped to explain how, in certain circumstances, even decent people might become torturers and killers.

6   It is not difficult to see how someone might draw anarchist or anti-authority conclusions from Milgram's horrifying experimental results. Indeed the title alone sometimes seems to produce this effect. As I was re-reading it, after an interval of 20 years, on a plane to Dublin, the woman next to me—a social worker in a Dublin hospital—said: "I've always been against all authority."

7   "All?" I asked.

8   "All," she replied. "We've suffered a lot in Ireland from the authority of the Catholic Church."

9   "What about the pilot of this aircraft?" I asked. "I assume you would prefer him to continue to fly it, rather than, say, for me to take over, and that were I to attempt to do so, he should exert his authority over me as captain?"

10   She readily agreed that in this instance his authority was necessary, though only for a short time, and was legitimate because she had granted it to him. I pointed out that even the brief authority that she had been so kind as to bestow upon him actually depended upon a whole chain, or network, of other authority, such as licensing boards, medical examiners and so forth, upon whose competence, honesty and diligence she could not possibly pronounce. She was not against all authority, therefore: on the contrary, she trusted much of it implicitly, even blindly. And necessarily so in a complex, technologically advanced society.

11   But her initial response to the question of obedience to authority was far from unusual. She probably thought a blanket opposition to authority was a heroic moral stance, indeed the only possible decent attitude towards it. To oppose authority is always romantic and principled, to uphold it prosaic and cowardly.

12   Yet civilization requires a delicate balance between stability and change. Neither mulish support for what exists simply because it already exists nor Bukharinite opposition* to it for much the same reason is a sufficient guide to action. Disobedience to authority is not inherently more glorious than obedience. It rather depends on the nature of the orders given or the behaviour demanded. As Milgram himself wrote, "Some system of authority is a requirement of all communal living. . . . "

13   The psychological advantage to a person of decrying authority altogether and of adopting a mental attitude of invariant opposition is that it allows him to think himself virtuous without having to engage with the necessary, messy compromises of real life.

14   Like many another young doctor, I came across the problem of authority early in my career. I worked for a physician who was far more dedicated to the welfare of her patients than I knew that I should ever be, and whom I esteemed greatly both as a doctor and as a person; yet it seemed to me that in her zeal to help her patients, to leave no stone unturned on their behalf, she often carried the investigation and treatment of moribund patients far beyond what common sense dictated. Alas, this entailed suffering, for medical investigations are often uncomfortable or painful. In my opinion, unnecessary and fruitless hardship was inflicted upon patients in their last days of life; and it fell to my lot to inflict it.

15   I was, of course, only obeying orders. I sometimes questioned those orders, but in the end I obeyed them. I was a young and inexperienced man; I knew a fiftieth as much medicine as my superior and had a thousandth of her experience. She was haunted by the fear of not doing all that could be done to save a life, while I was haunted by the unpleasantness of taking another useless blood test from a dying patient. I was never sure in any individual case that she, not I, was right.

16   Besides, I believed that the interests of patients were served by the existence of a hierarchy among doctors. Someone had to take ultimate responsibility for the care of patients, and if junior doctors were to disobey their superiors every time they disagreed with them, the system would fall apart. Clearly a point might be reached in which it was a junior doctor's duty to disobey, but there was no general rule to guide him in the estimation of when that point had come. The exercise of judgement was, and will always remain, necessary.

17   The social worker's attitude towards authority was, in practice, far more nuanced than she admitted, but there is nevertheless a danger in the disjunction between her attitude in theory and her attitude in practice. For the idea that revolt against authority is everywhere and always a noble stance is one that can soon be communicated to people who are prepared to take it literally.

18   For example, teachers tell me that if they mention to parents that their children are misbehaving, sometimes in grotesquely antisocial ways, the parents will turn unpleasant—towards the teachers, who in this instance represent authority. Recently I met a stepfather who was sent to prison for attacking a

---

*Nikolai Bukharin, a theoretician of the Russian Revolution of 1917, became the editor of the official revolutionary newspaper *Pravda* and subsequently, a member of the ruling Politboro. Originally allied with Stalin, Bukharin differed with the Stalinist majority on the pace of agricultural collectivization and industrialization; his position became that of the "right oppsition." Dismissed from his posts, Bukharin was eventually tried for treason and executed.

teacher who complained about his stepson. The security men in my hospital tell me that when they catch a boy stealing a car in the hospital grounds and return him to his parents, the parents start shouting—at the security men, who again represent authority. Indeed some security men now refuse to take the car thieves home, for fear of parental violence directed at them.

19   Blind disobedience to authority is no more to be encouraged than blind obedience. It is far from pleasant when encountered. Among my patients are quite a number who admit to having always had "a problem with authority." They confess it coyly, as if it were a sign of spiritual election, when it is no such thing: it is, rather, a sign of unbridled egotism. Unable to apply themselves at school, they are unable to take orders at work, and their personal relationships are almost always stormy and violent. They accept no rules, not even the informal ones that grow up between people who live closely together. For people who have a problem with authority, their whim is law. The only consideration that moderates their conduct is the threat of superior, but essentially arbitrary, violence by others.

20   It is not difficult to guess the kind of parental upbringing that results in a problem with authority. Discipline in the home is without principle or consistency, but is rather experienced by the child as the arbitrary expression of the brute power of others over himself. The conduct that on one occasion results in a slap results on another occasion in a Mars bar. The child therefore learns that discipline is an expression not of a rule that has a social purpose, but of a stronger person's momentary emotional state. He therefore comes to the conclusion that the important determinants of a relationship with others are first how you feel, and second what you can get away with by virtue of your comparative strength. Nothing else is involved.

21   To such a person, all human relationships are essentially expressions of power. An order given by another person is thus a threat to his ego, because following orders is submission to power and nothing else: there can be no other reason for it. The distinction between service and slavery collapses. To obey is to extinguish your existence as an autonomous being.

22   While obedience to authority has its dangers—as this century above all others testifies—disobedience to authority likewise has its dangers. There are hidden ironies in Milgram's great work, a work that has generally been taken as a tract against obedience to authority.

23   His experimental design depended upon deceiving his experimental subjects, upon his not asking for their informed consent to take part in his experiments. Had Milgram applied modern ethical standards to the conduct of his experiments, they could never have been performed at all, and we should never have been horrified by their results.

24   Against this, Milgram might urge two considerations. First, that the experimental subjects retrospectively approved of their participation, once they had been fully informed of the experiment's purpose and design. But this does not in the least answer the ethical objection.

25   Second, that the knowledge gained from the experiments was so important that it was worth a little light deception of the subjects to obtain it. This argument turns upon the estimation by somebody—in this case, Milgram himself—that the light was worth the candle: in short, it depends upon our old friend, authority.

Review Questions

1. As a young physician, how did Dalrymple find himself conflicted over obeying authority?

2. What kind of problems does Dalrymple find with "[b]lind disobedience to authority"?

3. What, theorizes Dalrymple, is the usual cause of some people's problem with authority figures?

Discussion and Writing Suggestions

1. To what extent do you agree with Dalrymple about the dangers of routine disobedience to authority? Support your response with examples from your reading, or from your own observation or experience.

2. On the one hand, Dalrymple suggests, one should always defer to the authority of an airline pilot. On the other hand, it was immoral for subjects to obey the authority figure in the Milgram experiment. In less obvious cases than these, is it possible to suggest guidelines for people to use in determining whether particular orders, or orders from particular types of people, should be obeyed or disobeyed? What kinds of orders require the exercise of moral or logical judgment on the part of the person receiving the orders? Is it possible to devise a test—perhaps a series of steps ("If . . . then . . .) that would help people to determine whether it is rational and/or moral to obey authority? (Test these guidelines against some of the experimental procedures reported in this chapter. Test them also against the personal anecdote that Dalrymple tells about the time that he worked with a more experienced physician.)

3. To what extent do you agree with Dalrymple that people who have problems with authority are likely to have been subject to arbitrary discipline from parents or parental figures during their childhoods? To what extent do you agree that people who routinely defy authority are displaying "unbridled egotism"?

SYNTHESIS ACTIVITIES

1. Compare and contrast the Asch and the Milgram experiments, considering their separate (1) objectives, (2) experimental designs and procedures, (3) results, and (4) conclusions. To what extent do the findings of these two experiments reinforce one another? To what extent do they highlight different, if related, social phenomena? To what extent do their results reinforce those of Zimbardo's prison experiment?

2. Milgram writes that "perhaps the most fundamental lesson of our study [is that] ordinary people, simply doing their jobs, and without any particular hostility on their part, can become agents in a terrible destructive process." Using this statement as a principle, analyze several situations recounted in this chapter, and perhaps some outside this chapter, of which you are aware because of your studies, your reading, and possibly even your own experience. Draw upon not only Milgram himself, but also Asch, Zimbardo, Fromm, and Sartwell.

3. The writer Doris Lessing has argued that children need to be taught how to disobey so they can recognize and avoid situations that give rise to harmful obedience. If you were the curriculum coordinator for your local school system, how would you teach children to disobey responsibly? What would be your curriculum? What homework would you assign? What class projects? What field trips? One complicated part of your job would be to train children to understand the difference between *responsible* disobedience and anarchy. What is the difference?

   Take up these questions in a paper that draws on both your experiences as a student and your understanding of the selections in this chapter. Points that you might want to consider in developing the paper: defining overly obedient children; appropriate classroom behavior for responsibly disobedient children (as opposed to inappropriate behavior); reading lists; homework assignments; field trips; class projects.

4. A certain amount of obedience is a given in society. Stanley Milgram and others observe that social order, civilization itself, would not be possible unless individuals were willing to surrender a portion of their autonomy to the state. Allowing that we all are obedient (we must be), define the point at which obedience to a figure of authority becomes dangerous.

   As you develop your definition, consider the ways you might use the work of authors in this chapter and their definitions of acceptable and unacceptable levels of obedience. Do you agree with the ways in which others have drawn the line between reasonable and dangerous obedience? What examples from current stories in the news or from your own experience can you draw on to test various definitions?

5. Describe a situation in which you were faced with a moral dilemma of whether or not to obey a figure of authority. After describing the situation and the action you took (or didn't take), discuss your behavior in light of any two readings in this chapter. You might consider a straightforward, four-part structure for your paper: (1) your description; (2) your discussion, in light of source A; (3) your discussion, in light of source B; and (4) your conclusion—an overall appraisal of your behavior.

6. Erich Fromm equates disobedience with courage: "In order to disobey, one must have the courage to be alone, to err, and to sin."
Novelist Doris Lessing makes much the same statement by equating obedience with shame: "among our most shameful memories is
this, how often we said black was white because other people were
saying it." Using such statements as principles for analysis, examine an act of obedience or disobedience in your own life and determine the extent to which, following Fromm or Lessing, you now
consider it courageous or shameful. Having completed this part of
your analysis, conclude by reassessing your behavior. Write one or
more paragraphs on whether or not you would behave similarly if
given a second chance in the same situation.

7. Discuss the critical reaction to the Milgram experiments. Draw upon
Baumrind and Parker, as well as Milgram himself, in summarizing
both the ethical and procedural objections to the experiments.
Following these summaries, develop your own critique, positive or
negative, bringing in Milgram himself, where appropriate.

8. In his response to Diana Baumrind, Stanley Milgram makes a point
of insisting that follow-up interviews with subjects in his experiments show that a large majority were pleased, in the long run, to
have participated. (See Table 1 in the footnote to Baumrind, page
201.) Writing on his own postexperiment surveys and interviews,
Philip Zimbardo writes that his subjects believed their "mental
anguish was transient and situationally specific, but the self-
knowledge gained has persisted" (paragraph 60). Why might they
and the experimenters nonetheless have been eager to accept a positive, final judgment of the experiments? Develop a paper in
response to this question, drawing on the selections by Milgram,
Zimbardo, and Baumrind.

9. Develop a synthesis in which you extend Baumrind's critique of
Milgram (and possibly, the critiques of others, as discussed by
Parker) to the Stanford Prison Experiment. This assignment
requires that you understand the core elements of Baumrind's critique; that you have a clear understanding of Zimbardo's experiment; and that you systematically apply elements of the critique(s),
as you see fit, to Zimbardo's work. In your conclusion, offer your
overall assessment of the Stanford Prison Experiment. To do this,
you might answer Zimbardo's own question in paragraph 55: "Was
[the experiment] worth all the suffering?" Or you might respond to
another question: Do you agree that Zimbardo is warranted in
extending the conclusions of his experiment to the general
population?

10. In response to the question "Why is man so prone to obey and why
is it so difficult for him to disobey?" Erich Fromm suggests that
obedience lets people identify with the powerful and invites feel-

ings of safety. Disobedience is psychologically more difficult and requires an act of courage (see paragraphs 13 and 14). Solomon Asch notes that the tendency to conformity is generally stronger than the tendency to independence. And in his final paragraph, Philip Zimbardo writes that a "prison of fear" keeps people compliant and frees them of the need to take responsibility for their own actions. In a synthesis that draws on these three sources (and perhaps others, such as Sartwell), explore the interplay of *fear* and its opposite, *courage,* in relation to obedience. To prevent the paper from becoming too abstract, direct your attention repeatedly to a single case, the details of which will help to keep your focus. This case may be based upon a particular event from your own life or the life of someone you know.

11. To what extent are young people particularly prone to obedience? In developing your response, draw on Zimbardo, Brooks, and Szegedy-Maszak (several of the soldiers implicated in the Abu Ghraib scandal were college-age), as well as on your own outside reading, observations, and experience. If the Zimbardo experiment were conducted today, do you think that the results would be about the same as they were in the early 1970s?

12. Theodore Dalrymple writes that "civilisation requires a delicate balance between stability and change"—between (he implies) obedience, which maintains the status quo, and disobedience, which promotes change. Use this statement as an analytical principle to examine issues of stability and change in one small, contained example of a civilization: a group to which you have belonged and know intimately. This group could be a school-based or church-based club, a musical collaboration, a sports team, or a collection of employees at a workplace. In your analysis, examine the interplay of members' obedience and disobedience in the progress or dissolution of the group. The fruits of your examination will be a thesis by which you organize your subsequent writing.

13. How different are the American soldiers involved in the Abu Ghraib abuse from ordinary Americans? (Another way to pose the question: how likely would you or your neighbor be, under the same circumstances the soldiers faced, to commit similar acts?) Do you regard these soldiers as President Bush did, as a "disgraceful . . . few . . . who dishonored our country and disregarded our values"? To what extent do you see them as more representative of ordinary Americans? In a well-developed paper that draws on the Szegedy-Maszak article about Abu Ghraib and on the selections by Asch, Zimbardo, Milgram, and Fromm, argue that the soldiers who committed the abuses were a "disgraceful few" or, by contrast, more typical of other Americans than we feel comfortable admitting. The heart of your response will turn on your

understanding of "where" morality is located: within individuals, who carry and apply a consistent moral code wherever they go; or within the situations in which individuals find themselves and must make decisions.

RESEARCH ACTIVITIES

1. When Milgram's results were first published in book form in 1974, they generated heated controversy. The reactions reprinted here (by Baumrind and Parker) represent only a very small portion of that controversy. Research other reactions to the Milgram experiments and discuss your findings. Begin with the reviews listed and excerpted in the *Book Review Digest;* also use the *Social Science Index,* the *Readers' Guide to Periodical Literature,* and newspaper indexes to locate articles, editorials, and letters to the editor on the experiments. (Note that editorials and letters are not always indexed. Letters appear within two to four weeks of the weekly magazine articles to which they refer, and within one to two weeks of newspaper articles.) What were the chief types of reactions? To what extent were the reactions favorable?

2. Milgram begins his article "Obedience to Authority" with a reference to Nazi Germany. The purpose of his experiment, in fact, was to help throw light on how the Nazi atrocities could have happened. Research the Nuremberg war crimes tribunals following World War II. Drawing specifically on the statements of those who testified at Nuremberg, as well as those who have written about it, show how Milgram's experiments do help explain the Holocaust and other Nazi crimes. In addition to relevant articles, see Telford Taylor, *Nuremberg and Vietnam: An American Tragedy* (1970); Hannah Arendt, *Eichmann in Jerusalem: A Report on the Banality of Evil* (1963); Richard A. Falk, Gabriel Kolko, and Robert J. Lifton (eds.), *Crimes of War* (1971).

3. Obtain a copy of the transcript of the trial of Adolf Eichmann—the Nazi official who carried out Hitler's "final solution" for the extermination of the Jews. Read also Hannah Arendt's *Eichmann in Jerusalem: A Report on the Banality of Evil,* along with the reviews of this book. Write a critique both of Arendt's book and of the reviews it received.

4. The My Lai massacre in Vietnam in 1969 was a particularly egregious case of overobedience to military authority in wartime. Show the connections between this event and Milgram's experiments. Note that Milgram himself treated the My Lai massacre in the epilogue to his *Obedience to Authority: An Experimental View* (1974).

5. Investigate the court-martial of Lt. William Calley, convicted for his role in the My Lai massacre. Discuss the question of whether President Nixon was justified in commuting his sentence. Examine

in detail the dilemmas the jury must have faced when presented with Calley's defense that he was only following orders.

6. Research the Watergate break-in of 1972 and the subsequent cover-up by Richard Nixon and members of his administration, as an example of overobedience to authority. Focus on one particular aspect of Watergate (e.g., the role of the counsel to the president, John Dean, or why the crisis was allowed to proceed to the point where it actually toppled a presidency). In addition to relevant articles, see Robert Woodward and Carl Bernstein, *All the President's Men* (1974); Leon Jaworski, *The Right and the Power: The Prosecution of Watergate* (1976); *RN: The Memoirs of Richard Nixon* (1978); John Dean, *Blind Ambition* (1976); John Sirica, *To Set the Record Straight: The Break-in, the Tapes, the Conspirators, the Pardon* (1979); Sam Ervin, *The Whole Truth: The Watergate Conspiracy* (1980); John Ehrlichman, *Witness to Power: The Nixon Years* (1982).

7. In April 2004, news broke of the systematic abuse, including beatings and sexual humiliation, by American military police, of Iraqi "detainees" at Baghdad's Abu Ghraib prison. The scandal was intensified—as was outrage in the Muslim world—by graphic photographs that the soldiers had taken of these activities. A high-level American inquiry uncovered some of the following abuses:

> Punching, slapping, and kicking detainees; jumping on their naked feet . . . positioning a naked detainee on a MRE Box, with a sandbag on his head, and attaching wires to his fingers, toes, and penis to simulate electric torture . . . having sex with a female detainee. . . . Using military working dogs (without muzzles) to intimidate and frighten detainees, and in at least one case biting and severely injuring a detainee. . . . Breaking chemical lights and pouring the phosphoric liquid on detainees. . . . Beating detainees with a broom handle and a chair. . . . Sodomizing a detainee with a chemical light and perhaps a broom stick.

In the days following, many commentators noted the similarities between the Abu Ghraib's guards' behavior and the behavior of some of the subjects in the Milgram and Zimbardo experiments. Zimbardo himself, in an op-ed piece in the *Boston Globe*, wrote:

> The terrible things my guards [at Stanford] did to their prisoners were comparable to the horrors inflicted on the Iraqi detainees. My guards repeatedly stripped their prisoners naked, hooded them, chained them, denied them food or bedding privileges, put them into solitary confinement, and made them clean toilet bowls with their bare hands. . . . Over time, these amusements took a sexual turn, such as having the prisoners simulate sodomy on each other. . . . Human behavior is much more under the control of situational forces than most of us recognize or want to acknowledge. In a situation that implicitly gives permission for suspending moral values, many of us can be morphed into creatures alien to our usual natures.

Research the Abu Ghraib scandal; then write a paper comparing and contrasting what happened in the Baghdad prison with what happened in Zimbardo's Stanford prison experiment—and possibly also in Milgram's electric shock experiments. Focus not only on what happened, but also on *why* it may have happened.

8. Examine conformity as a social phenomenon (and a particular manifestation of obedience to group authority) in some particular area. For example, you may choose to study conformity as it exists among school children, adolescent peer groups, social clubs or associations, or businesspeople. You may want to draw upon your sociology or social psychology textbooks and such classic studies as William H. Whyte's *The Organization Man* (1956) or David Riesman's *The Lonely Crowd* (1950), or focus upon more recent books and articles, such as Rosabeth Moss Kantor's *A Tale of "O": On Being Different in an Organization* (1980) and John Goldhammer's 1996 book *Under the Influence: The Destructive Effects of Group Dynamics* (1996). You may also find enlightening some fictional treatments of conformity, such as Sinclair Lewis's *Babbitt* (1922), Sloan Wilson's *The Man in the Gray Flannel Suit* (1950), and Herman Wouk's *The Caine Mutiny: A Novel of World War II* (1951). What are the main factors creating the urge to conform among the particular group you are examining? What kind of forces may be able to counteract conformity?

9. At the outset of his article, Stanley Milgram refers to imaginative works revolving around the issue of obedience to authority: the story of Abraham and Isaac; three of Plato's dialogues, "Apology," "Crito," and "Phaedo"; and the story of Antigone (dramatized by both the fifth-century B.C. Athenian Sophocles and the twentieth-century Frenchman Jean Anouilh). Many other fictional works deal with obedience to authority—for example, George Orwell's *1984* (1949), Herman Wouk's novel *The Caine Mutiny* (and his subsequent play *The Caine Mutiny Court Martial*), and Shirley Jackson's "The Lottery." Check with your instructor, with a librarian, and with such sources as the *Short Story Index* to locate other imaginative works on this theme. Write a paper discussing the various ways in which the subject has been treated in fiction and drama. To ensure coherence, draw comparisons and contrasts among works showing the connections and the variations on the theme of obedience to authority.

What's Happening at the Mall?

Perhaps you think the answer to this chapter's opening question is obvious. After all, we Americans frequent shopping centers more than we do houses of worship. Each month of the year 2001, nearly 200 million of us shopped at a mall and bought fully one-half of the nation's consumer goods (excluding cars and car parts), some $1.8 trillion worth. So what's happening at the mall? We shop, which is hardly news. Yet if leading scholars and cultural critics can be believed, we do much, much more, often unaware of a larger drama being staged in which we play a significant part. As the historian and American Studies scholar James J. Farrell observes:

> Shopping centers are constructed of steel and concrete, bricks and mortar, but they are also made of culture. Indeed, culture is about the only thing they *can* be made of. . . . They're a place where we answer important questions: What does it mean to be human? What are people for? What is the meaning of things? Why do we work? What do we work for? And what, in fact, are we shopping for? Like colleges and churches, malls provide answers to these critical questions.

So we may go to malls to buy designer jeans or the latest electronic gear, but because malls are where we also go to see and be seen, to judge, to learn, and to buy both what we want as well as what we need, in visiting the mall we are participating in a larger cultural phenomenon—likely without realizing it.

Geographers describe shopping centers as "built environments" in which the engine of mass production capitalism meets you, the end-consumer. Consider the matchup: on entering the mall, you come face-to-face with billions of dollars invested in product design, manufacturing, advertising, and distribution—not to mention additional millions devoted to making the mall itself an appealing space in which to shop. Management knows that, on average, you will spend $71.04 on your 3.2 visits per month and devotes considerable energy to tuning your experience. From employing broad strategies like corridor designs that direct pedestrian flow past the maximum number of stores, to narrow ones like selecting background music to create just the right ambience for your visit, mall owners strive to provide a satisfying, stimulating experience—and they employ retail science to aid the process: Have you ever considered why the metal chairs in most food courts lack padding? Management has. Comfortable chairs encourage leisurely meals and discourage shopping. Make chairs *un*comfortable and customers will return to the stores more quickly. Whether or not you recognize these strategies, they exist and management employs them.

The shopping mall has become so commonplace a fixture on the retail landscape that we overlook its relatively new arrival as a building type. In the post–World War II years, the Eisenhower administration initiated the construction of thousands of miles of highways to promote interstate commerce just as automobiles became widely available. By the millions, Americans followed the highways out of town, abandoning the city and its problems for homes in the safer, cleaner, less-expensive suburbs. Visionary architect Victor Gruen understood that the rapidly expanding suburbs lacked not only opportunities for shopping but also spaces that fostered the spirited give and take of community life. A carefully designed structure might achieve both, Gruen reasoned, a place in which to meet, stroll, and talk—as people had in markets for thousands of years—as well as a place in which to shop. Gruen set to work. Mindful of the way that automobiles choked traditional shopping districts, he relegated cars to parking lots, away from the stores, thereby creating inside his shopping centers pedestrian promenades reminiscent of the grand arcades of nineteenth-century Europe. He also improved the shopping experience by carefully controlling the mix of retail tenants. Because the center was (and continues to be) private property, management could exclude bars and pool halls and other businesses that, in its view, detracted from its image of upbeat consumerism. Gone, too, were vagrants and the homeless, who may have enjoyed constitutional protections on Main Street but who were considered trespassers at the mall. And finally, implementing a technical solution that had been impractical before the 1950s, Gruen enclosed his centers to protect shoppers from the elements. His centrally heated and cooled buildings created a spring–like shopping environment, year-round.

One-half of Gruen's vision proved prophetic. In the fifty years following the debut of his innovative Southdale Center in Edina, Minnesota, developers opened 45,000 other centers across the country (the number includes open air, enclosed, and strip malls). However, developers eventually abandoned Gruen's call to merge community and commercial functions in a single, town-like shopping environment. If the appearance of community could enhance sales, mall management would offer community services. But if the noisy and sometimes rude exercise of community threatened business, management would protect its profits by barring, for example, picketers. Court cases followed that raised questions of how free free-speech ought to be in America's new public (though legally private) gathering places. Thus the mall emerged on the American scene with a mixed identity as both a commercial and a community space, an identity that remains fractured to this day. Victor Gruen lived long enough to see the profit motive overtake the needs of community in the design and management of shopping centers, and he left America for Europe deeply disappointed.

Meanwhile malls have grown ever larger and more extravagant, with especially ambitious ones offering lavish entertainment. Restaurants, movie theaters, amusement parks, and water parks attract and *keep* crowds for extended periods. As a building type, the mall has become so dominant that public venues have begun incorporating mall-like features. Attend a special exhibit at your local museum and the exit will likely funnel you into a gift shop. Catch a plane to visit a friend, and you will find the airport looking every bit like a mall, with wide pedestrian boulevards opening onto store-fronts. Malls, and elements of mall design, are everywhere.

Historians, geographers, religious studies experts, architects, psychologists, anthropologists, sociologists, and cultural critics all study what goes on (and does not go on) in shopping centers, and all have something to say about their significance in our lives. Some lament how the rise of malls correlates with a loss of authentic human interaction in our marketplaces; some celebrate the business savvy—the confluence of big money, design expertise, and management know-how—needed to make shopping dependably safe and pleasant; some see in mostly white suburban malls evidence of a troubling segregation; some warn that the shift of town centers from public to private spaces endangers our democracy; some savor the excitement of the modern market; and some see in our malls a new, "sacred" space where we gather to find order in an otherwise chaotic world.

In reading the nine selections that follow, you will learn more about these perspectives. And because you have almost certainly shopped in malls, you will bring direct experience to your reading and writing on the topic. The chapter opens with a selection from *One Nation Under Goods*, in which American Studies scholar James J. Farrell asks, "why should we think about malls" in the first place, aside from their obvious function as places to shop. (His answer: malls attract crowds, and if we want to understand American culture, we must go where the people are.) The next two selections set the emergence of shopping centers in a broad historical context. Laura Paquet provides a social history of shopping from ancient times to the present. Geographer Richard Francaviglia then suggests the ways in which Walt Disney's Main Street USA, his idealized recreation of late nineteenth- and early twentieth-century small-town Main Streets, became a prototype for modern mall design.

The readings continue with Victor Gruen's "Shopping Towns USA." One of the most influential shopping mall developers of the twentieth century, Gruen explains how the expanding automobile culture after World War II gave rise to the American suburb and the need for shopping centers that would provide "in modern community life [what] the ancient Greek Agora, the Medieval Market Place and our own Town Squares provided in the past." Writing in 1960, he envisioned shopping malls becoming important social as well as commercial centers. Writing thirty-three years later on the opening of the Mall of America, the nation's largest, David Guterson delivers grim news (as far as Gruen is concerned): Today, malls offer "only a desolate sub-stitute for the rich, communal lifeblood of the traditional marketplace." But Ira Zepp, Jr., a professor of religious studies, regards malls in a more posi-tive light, seeing in them a "sacred space" that fulfills "our need for order and orientation," much as houses of worship have in earlier times. His thesis that we can find spiritual comfort in shopping malls may seem a stretch for some, but the argument is well reasoned.

The chapter ends with historical, sociological, and psychological analyses of malls. Historian Lizabeth Cohen explores the ways in which mall development has perpetuated America's class and racial divisions. In recounting the battles of developers to exclude undesirable elements (for example, political protesters and the homeless) from malls, Cohen finds a threat to the "shared public sphere upon which our democracy depends." Sociologist George Lewis, writing in the *Journal of Popular Culture,* claims that management may publicly promote the *idea* of the mall as a community space but privately discourages the emergence of real communities. Even so, authentic communities of elders and teens manage to form at the mall, their priority being to socialize, not shop. Finally, in a chapter from his classic book *The Malling of America,* William Kowinski writes humorously but pointedly on "mallaise," a zombielike mental state that can overtake unwary shoppers.

Some authors in this chapter indict mall culture; others celebrate it. Your goal in reading and writing on this topic will be to challenge and clarify your own thinking. And you may, after working with this material, come to regard the most ordinary of activities, shopping at the mall, in a strange, new light.

Shopping for American Culture
James J. Farrell

Our discussion of malls and their place in American culture opens with "Shopping for American Culture," the introduction to James J. Farrell's One Nation Under Goods: Malls and the Seductions of American Shopping *(Smithsonian Books, 2003). Farrell, a historian, directs the American Studies program at St. Olaf College. Unapologetic in his enjoyment of malls (unlike several others in the chapter), he writes: "I love malls. I love them for all the obvious reasons. I love the color and the crowds. . . . I love people watching: seeing the wonder of children's eyes and the animated conversations of teenagers." If we want to understand American culture, says Farrell, we must study life at America's shopping malls, for malls express our consumer culture, revealing us to ourselves.*

1   Malls are an American cultural phenomenon. The United States now has more shopping centers than high schools, and in the last forty years, shopping center space has increased by a factor of twelve. By 2000, there were more than forty-five thousand shopping malls with 5.47 billion square feet of gross leasable space in the United States. Currently, America's shopping centers (most of which are strip malls) generate more than a trillion dollars in annual sales. Not counting sales of cars and gasoline, that's slightly more than half of the nation's retail activity. The International Council of Shopping Centers (ICSC) reported that in 2000, America's shopping centers served 196 million Americans a month and employed more than 10.6 million workers, about 8 percent of the nonfarm workforce in the country. We go to malls 3.2 times a month and spend an average of $71.04 each time (a one-third increase in

TABLE 7.1   Shopping Centers in the United States

	1970	1980	1990	
Number of shopping centers	11,000	22,100	36,500	
Total leasable sales area (billions of square feet)	1.49	2.96	4.39	5.57
Retail sales in shopping centers (billions of dollars)	82.0	305.4	681.4	1,136.0
Employment in shopping centers (millions of people)	2.49	5.28	8.60	10.69

Source: Data from ICSC, *Scope.* (*Scope* is a publication of the International Council of Shopping Centers, Inc., New York, N.Y.; reprinted by permission.)

spending from 1995 to 2000). Shopping centers also support our state and city governments, generating $46.6 billion in sales taxes, almost half of all state tax revenue (see Table 7.1).[1]

2   Shopping is such a common part of America's pursuit of happiness that we usually take shopping centers for granted. But although malls are usually places of consumer forgetfulness, they can inspire a sense of thoughtfulness. It's no particular problem if we come back from the mall empty-handed, but it should be a deep disappointment if we come back empty-headed.[2]

3   But why should we think about malls?

4   Quite simply, because Americans go to malls. We may not like the malling of America, but if we want to understand Americans, we have to look for them where they are, not where we think they ought to be. We need to follow Americans to the mall and see what they're doing because shopping centers can reveal cultural patterns that we don't usually see. In some ways, culture is what happens when we are not paying attention. When we are fully conscious of our choices, they are likely to express our individual values and preferences, but when we're going about our daily business with little thought about what we're doing, we act according to the habits of our hearts, and those habits are shaped as much by culture as by character.[3]

5   Malls are a great place for the pleasures of shopping, but they're an even better place for the pleasures of thinking, in part because they help us think about the cultural contours of shopping. Shopping is, etymologically, the process of going to shops to purchase goods and services. According to Webster, a shop is a small retail store; the word comes from a root that denoted the booths or stalls of the marketplace. The verb *to shop* appeared in the late eighteenth century; by the late twentieth century, shopping had become a way of life. Measured in constant dollars, the average American of today consumes twice as many goods and services as the average American of 1950 and ten times as much as a counterpart from 1928. On average, we each consume more than one hundred pounds of materials a day. Shopping, it seems, might be more American than apple pie.[4]

6   Sometimes shopping is a utilitarian act. We need a shirt or a suitcase, and we go to the mall to get it. Sometimes, though, shopping is intrinsically pleasurable,

and we go to the mall to just do it. Shopping itself can be therapeutic, even fun, whether or not anything ends up in the shopping bag. So an exploration of malls can help us think about what we have in mind—as well as what we don't have in mind—when we are shopping.[5]

7   When we get home from the mall, we tell the family, "I was shopping." It sounds simple. Yet shopping is a complex act, or, more precisely, a complex interaction. It's not just a matter of choosing items and paying for them, it's an act of desire that is shaped individually and culturally, an interaction with shops and with a complex infrastructure of production and distribution. It's an act of conscience in which our own values interact with commercial and cultural values. Shopping requires a biological being to enter an architectural space outfitted with commercial art and designed to sell artifacts manufactured and distributed in a market economy. Shopping centers are built of solid materials, but the spaces are also socially constructed and regulated by political entities. Our malls reflect and affect personal perceptions, social norms, religious beliefs, ethical values, cultural geography, domestic architecture, foreign policy, and social psychology. And the artifacts within shopping centers are equally complex, synthesizing material form and symbolic meaning. Shopping is no simple task.

malls reflect →

8   Malls are a good place to think about retailing and retail culture, an important subset of American commercial culture. Because we are consumers, we think we know how consumption works, but we don't usually pay attention to how consumption is *produced.* In malls of America, consumption is not just happenstance. It's carefully planned and programmed. To be informed consumers, therefore, we need information not just about the products we buy but also about the spaces—architectural and social—where we buy them.

9   Malls are America's public architecture, a primary form of public space, the town halls of the twentieth and twenty-first centuries. Sociologist Mark Gottdiener contends that the mall "has become the most successful form of environmental design in contemporary settlement space." The late nineteenth century was known for its train stations and department stores. In the early twentieth century it was skyscrapers and subways. Mid-twentieth-century Americans created suburban forms, including subdivisions, malls, and office parks. The late twentieth century was an era of malls and airports, and the airports increasingly looked like malls.[6]

10   Malls are also art galleries, carefully crafted collections of commercial art. To the connoisseur, they offer an unending display of artful design, including product design, package design, retail design, visual merchandising, sculpture, and architecture. The artists we find in museums often challenge our conceptions of ourselves and unsettle our sense of society. The artists who exhibit their skills in the museums we call malls, on the other hand, tend to reinforce our sense of ourselves, producing a commercial art that makes malls more popular than museums in American culture. But even people who have taken courses in art appreciation don't always take time to appreciate the creativity of commercial art.

11   Malls are also outstanding museums of contemporary American material culture. In them, we find a huge collection of the artifacts that help us make sense of our world. And as in most museums, reading these artifacts can help us read the culture.

12   Indeed, as cultural institutions, malls perform what Paul Lauter (
al work," a term that describes "the ways in which a book or other ki
a movie, a Supreme Court decision, an advertisement, an an
international treaty, a material object—helps construct the framew(
the metaphors, create the very language by which people comp
experience and think about their world." In short, malls help teach us the
common sense of our culture. If we look closely at malls, we will soon be looking inside our own heads. So it is partly the purpose of this book to explain
this social construction of common sense—the way we teach each other, both
explicitly and implicitly, the common sense of our culture.[7]

13   Understanding a single act of shopping means understanding the culture in
which it occurs. When we go to the mall looking for jeans, we find ourselves
embedded in a cultural fabric that fits us like a pair of jeans. Shopping centers
are constructed of steel and concrete, bricks and mortar, but they are also made
of culture. Indeed, culture is about the only thing they *can* be made of. Retailers
routinely use our cultural values to stimulate sales. Shopping centers reinforce
these values even as they distract us from other American values—justice, equal-
ity, democracy, and spirituality—that might also animate our lives.[8]

14   As this suggests, malls are a manifestation of popular philosophy. They're a
place where we answer important questions: What does it mean to be human?
What are people for? What is the meaning of things? Why do we work? What do
we work for? And what, in fact, are we shopping for? Like colleges and churches, malls provide answers to these critical questions. Like colleges, malls are
places where we make statements about the good, the true, and the beautiful. Like churches, they are places where we decide what is ultimately valuable
and how we will value it. And malls are places where we act out, and institu-
tionalize, our values.[9]

15   As the local outlet of the new world order, malls can teach us a great deal
about the central institutions of our American lives. Malls are the intersection of
manufacturing and merchandising, nature and culture, home and away, love and
money. At the mall, we can see the market at work, and we can contemplate
what it means to live in a society shaped by the powerful institutions of commercial capitalism. American individualism often makes it hard for Americans to
understand institutions and the prescriptions and patterns that structure our lives.
We forget that when we walk into a mall, we walk into a market full of *cultural*
questions and controversies. Anthropologists Mary Douglas and Baron Isherwood
contend that "consumption is the very arena in which culture is fought over and
licked into shape." Malls, therefore, are one place where we make significant decisions both as individuals and as a society.[10]

16   Yet if we want to understand malls, we must examine them within a broader framework. The mall makes sense in the flow of our whole lives, as we compare and contrast it to what we experience every day. The mall, for example,
tells us immediately that it's not home and it's not work. It's an architecture of
pleasure, not of comfort or efficiency. Shopping is what academics would call
an "intertextual experience," an activity that only makes sense if we know how
to read many different cultural "texts": ads, stores, mannequins, clothes, logos,
race, class, gender, and sexuality. And the mall's complexities are multiplied by
its customers.

17   There are many malls in America, and each mall is many things to many people. Architecturally, a mall is singular, but sociologically, psychologically, and culturally, it's plural. Each store is a variety store, not just because it sells a variety of products but because it evokes different responses from a variety of people. Each of us brings our own cognitive map to the mall, so it's a different place to a mother and her child, to a mall worker and a mall walker. It's different if we're different in any way—and we all are. Malls mean different things to women and men, to blacks and whites, to gay people and their heterosexual friends, to teenagers and senior citizens. The mall looks and feels different to poor people than it does to the affluent. Although the mall may try to be all things to all people, it succeeds mainly by being different things to different people. It's possible to speak truthfully about an American consumer culture, but if we look closely, we'll see that we are a consumption society with many different and interconnected consumer cultures.[11]

. . .

18   . . . We often go to malls to buy things we don't have—a pair of pants, a toaster, a new lamp, a book, or a CD. Yet we also go to buy more important things—an identity, a secure sense of self, a set of social relationships, a deeper sense of community, an expression of who we are and who we would like to be. We go to shopping centers with the unfulfilled needs of our American lives, so the mall's attractions are one way of studying the deficiencies of American life. We can use the things we carry *at* the mall to help us understand the things we carry *to* the mall. We can use the mall to make sense of our everyday life.

19   This book is the story of the stories we tell at the mall. Whatever else they may be, shopping centers are places where we tell stories about ourselves—about who we are and what we value. In the plot to separate us from our money, malls are also plotted. They tell stories—about business, about shoppers, about work and leisure, about good and evil, about American culture(s). Stores, and not just bookstores, are full of stories. Victoria's Secret is a romance novel about sex, seduction, and desire, about bodies and beauty, about femininity and masculinity. Sportsmart is the sports page of the mall, telling stories about striving and success. Abercrombie & Fitch combines adventure stories with coming-of-age stories. The Gap started by telling stories about the generation gap, but now their stories are about "cool" characters and their "casual" lives. The stories of progress at Radio Shack are often futuristic fantasies, and Hot Topic tells stories about individualism and conformity, dissent and deviance. The Rainforest Café spins adventure yarns and nature stories. The department stores tell stories about abundance and choice. All of the retailers tell stories about "the good life" and about America. All of the *things* in the mall also have a story. Each artifact is a story of nature becoming culture, of raw material (com)modified to make it meaningful to Americans. At the mall, it's always story time, and, at least according to the publicity, there's almost always a happy ending.

20   This book is the story of all those stories. It's a storybook.

21   It's also my story. It's a story by me, of course, but it's also a story about me, because I'm one of the people I'm writing about. I'm not a power shop-

per, but I love malls. I love them for all the obvious reasons. I lov
and the crowds. I love looking at commercial art, because it is, ir
tiful. I love people watching: seeing the wonder of children's eyes
mated conversations of teenagers. I like the oasis of pedestrian
culture: I like walking, and I like to walk in malls. But I also love m
in them, as geographer Jon Goss says, "I have learned a great deal about
myself: about my humanity, the values and beliefs of 'my' culture, and my
intimate desires."[12]

22   I appreciate malls more now than I did at the beginning of my research.
When you look closely at their complexity, especially the intricate coordination
needed to produce each day's consumption, it's a miracle that they work as well
as they do. I have come to understand that shopping centers are part of a huge
conspiracy, a conspiracy of customer satisfaction. The people who work in malls
genuinely want to please the people who shop in malls. So I appreciate the
ways that shopping center professionals study Americans to see just what, in
fact, will please us, and I appreciate the many pleasures that are to be found
at the mall, whether or not we ever buy anything.

23   But I also appreciate the ways that a shopping center can be a "social trap,"
an institution in which the sum total of perfectly good behavior is not so good.
Still, my main complaint is not primarily with malls but with a larger commercial
culture that characterizes us mainly as consumers. My main argument is with
an America that sells itself short by buying into the cluster of values expressed
so powerfully in our malls.[13]

Notes

1. International Council of Shopping Centers (ICSC), "Scope USA," at the ICSC web site, www.icsc.org; John Fetto, "Mall Rats," *American Demographics* 24 (March 2002). 10; Judith Ann Coady, "The Concrete Dream: A Sociological Look at the Shopping Mall" (Ph.D. diss., Boston University, 1987), 720; Ira G. Zepp Jr., *The New Religious Image of Urban America: The Shopping Mall as Ceremonial Center,* 2d ed. (Niwot: University Press of Colorado, 1997), 10.

2. As my colleague Eric Nelson says, malls "are the last place anyone would go to think seriously. There is nothing, however, that demands more serious thought." Eric Nelson, *Mall of America: Reflections of a Virtual Community* (Lakeville, Minn.: Galde Press, 1998), 152.

3. Zepp, *New Religious Image,* 10.

4. John C. Ryan and Alan Durning, *Stuff: The Secret Lives of Everyday Things* (Seattle: Northwest Environment Watch, 1997), 4–5.

5. Barry J. Babin, William R. Darden, and Mitch Griffin, "Work and/or Fun: Measuring Hedonic and Utilitarian Shopping Value," *Journal of Consumer Research* 20 (March 1994): 646–47.

6. Mark Gottdiener, "Recapturing the Center: A Semiotic Analysis of Shopping Malls," in *The City and the Sign: An Introduction to Urban Semiotics,* ed. Mark Gottdiener and Alexandros Ph. Lagopoulos (New York: Columbia University Press, 1986), 291.

7. Paul Lauter, *From Walden Pond to Jurassic Park: Activism, Culture, and American Studies* (Durham N.C.: Duke University Press, 2001), 11.

8. Leon G. Schiffman and Leslie Lazar Kanuk, *Consumer Behavior*, 5th ed. (Englewood Cliffs, N.J.: Prentice Hall, 1994), 437.

9. Jon Goss, "Once-upon-a-Time in the Commodity World: An Unofficial Guide to Mall of America," *Annals of the Association of American Geographers* 89 (March 1999): 47.

10. Mary Douglas and Baron Isherwood, *The World of Goods* (New York: Basic Books, 1979), 57.

11. Elizabeth Chin, *Purchasing Power: Black Kids and American Consumer Culture* (Minneapolis: University of Minnesota Press, 2001), 12–13.

12. Goss, "Once-upon-a-Time," 49.

13. David Orr, *Ecological Literacy: Education and the Transition to a Postmodern World* (Albany: State University of New York Press, 1992), 5.

Review Questions

1. According to Farrell, why should anyone think seriously about shopping centers?

2. In what ways can malls be understood as "cultural institutions"?

3. Farrell claims that the mall is "a place where we answer important questions." What are these questions?

4. How do shopping malls "tell stories"?

5. Why does Farrell appreciate malls?

Discussion and Writing Suggestions

1. Of the statistics concerning shopping centers that Farrell cites in paragraph 1 and Table 7.1, which do you find most striking? Why?

2. In paragraph 7 Farrell makes a series of provocative claims in developing the assertion that "shopping is a complex act, or, more precisely, a complex interaction." Choose any of the sentences in paragraph 7 that follow this assertion and then write for five minutes in response. Share your insights with others who have read the selection.

3. Reread paragraph 14 and select one of the questions that Farrell claims is raised by mall culture. Write two paragraphs in response: First, explain what you think Farrell means in posing the question. (For example, explain how malls help us to investigate "What does it mean to be human?") Second, discuss the validity of the question in relation to malls. (For instance, discuss how reasonable it seems to contemplate what it means to be human in a shopping mall.)

4. Farrell writes (paragraph 14): "Like churches, [malls] are places we decide what is ultimately valuable and how we will value it." Your comments?

5. Farrell suggests (in paragraph 16) that elements of shopping malls can be "read" like a "text" for meaning. How can one find clues to understanding American culture in advertisements? Store layouts? Mannequins? Clothes? Logos?

6. Do you agree with Farrell (paragraph 18) that we go to malls in search of "an identity, a secure sense of self, a set of social relationships, a deeper sense of community, an expression of who we are and who we would like to be"? How can these things be bought?

A Social History of Shopping
Laura Paquet

In the selection that follows, Laura Paquet presents an overview of shopping from ancient times to modern, opening with a little-known fact: The first street dedicated to shopping that could be closed off from a town at night appeared not in twentieth-century America but 3,600 years ago in the Mesopotamian city of Ur. Paquet is a Canadian journalist and travel writer who has published in numerous publications in Canada, the United States, and Europe, including National Geographic Traveler *and* Travel Canada. *The following selection first appeared in her book* The Urge to Splurge: A Social History of Shopping *(ECW Press, 2003).*

If you were looking for an analogy for the modern mall you would have to go back to the walled cities of Italy and France. Like San Gimignano or Les Baux de Provence, the mall offers the ancient trifecta of enclosure, protection, and control. The analogy is not with a well-policed downtown but with a small, thoroughly fascist medieval city-state.
— James B. Twitchell, *Lead Us Into Temptation,* 1999

1   We tend to think of malls as modern creations, spawned by the same post-war wave that gave us Levittown, transistor radios, and Tang.* And, yes, America's first fully enclosed, climate-controlled shopping mall *was* an invention of the Eisenhower era: the Southdale Shopping Center opened in suburban Minneapolis in 1956. However, it wasn't the world's first building to shelter a number of retailers under one weatherproof roof—not by a long shot.

---

* Shopping malls as we know them today came of age in the same era as *Levittown, transistor radios,* and *Tang,* products of America's economic boom following World War II when the ingenuity and science that had been channeled to the military was turned to the civilian sector. In 1947 in *Levittown,* NY, and 1951 in Levittown, PA, the Levitt brothers built inexpensive, pre-fabricated housing on as assembly-line basis in huge, suburban tracts. In 1954, Texas Instruments and Regency Electronics invented mass-market electronics with the release of the first *transistor radios.* What made the radios so appealing was that (unlike vacuum tube models) they were portable. In the 1960s, *Tang,* an instant, citrus-based beverage (add water and stir) that had accompanied astronauts on every Gemini and Apollo mission, became a heavily marketed drink to a consumer market fascinated with space travel.

2   Like so many things about city life, the mall as we know it evolved in stages. By about 1600 BC, in the Mesopotamian city of Ur, someone had come up with the idea of separating a street of shops from the rest of town with doors that were closed at night. Historians think that shoppers may have been able to take shelter from the elements under a series of awnings as well.

3   That's pretty much as far as the enclosed shopping promenade evolved for more than a millennium. But then the ancient Greeks came along, with their penchant for marketplaces. Unlike today's malls, where political rabble-rousing is very strongly discouraged, these marketplaces were centers of debate and discussion. In fact, one of the major Greek schools of philosophy, stoicism, was named for the *stoa,* a large roofed structure that was open to an outdoor square on one side but walled on the other three. Stoas served various functions, but many were used as marketplaces. By the fifth century BC, the Greek city of Miletus (now in Turkey) boasted an L-shaped market stoa fronting on the harbor, its prominent placement proof of the importance residents and visitors placed on trade.

4   Flash forward 500 years to the days when Trajan was emperor of the Roman Empire (AD 98–117). In a move that sounds eerily like the activities of the urban renewal zealots of the 1960s, Trajan decided that Rome's crowded jumble of streets and small buildings should be replaced with grand buildings and a more formal plan. Down came thousands of homes and shops, and up went the massive Forum.

5   Just as shopping malls and major sports stadiums tend to sprout next to each other today, a series of markets was built next to the Forum. The ones nearest the stadium were multi-story buildings terraced into the side of the Quirinal hill. But just beyond them was the Aula Traiana, a two-story market with a vaulted roof. The ruins today look oddly familiar, with large square shop doorways marching methodically down each side of a central corridor, and a second story of shops lining a gallery that runs the length of the hall. Add a Sunglass Hut kiosk and a food court, and you could be in a very early prototype of your local shopping center.

That's, Like, Totally Bazaar, Dude

6 The next move in "mall" development would take place in the Middle East, where some unremembered shopkeeper hit on the idea of building a roof between his shop and the one across the street. Others followed suit, sometimes covering multiple connected streets. The result was called a bazaar or souk.

7   One twelfth-century observer described a Jerusalem souk known as the Street of Herbs, which had divided itself into sections by commodity. "At the top of the street is a place where they sell fish. And behind the market where they sell the fish is a very large place on the left hand where cheese, chicken and eggs are sold. On the right hand of this market are the shops of the Syrian gold workers."[1]

8   These souks shared a few traits with their modern, enclosed counterparts, such as a labyrinthine floor plan, and diverse but segregated uses. In the fif-

teenth century, builders in Constantinople (today's Istanbul) would begin build-ing the mega-souk, the Mall of America of its day: the Grand Bazaar, also known as the Covered Market.

9   The bazaar started as a small warehouse in the 1400s and evolved along a series of actual streets, which were gradually roofed. Today, more than 3,300 shops line the 60-odd "streets" of the Grand Bazaar. While some of the historic divisions of individual streets have been superseded by new types of commerce (I doubt that souvenir t-shirts, for example, were a big seller during the reign of Suleyman the Magnificent in the 1500s), you can still find gemstones on Jewelers' Street, and silver teakettles, carpets, and leather goods in their own domains.

10   Even though the bazaar is now a massive tourist trap, alive with touts and pickpockets, I discovered on a trip in 1999 that it has a charm the average North American mall can't match.

11   The vaulted roof shimmers in jewel tones of blue, red, and gold through the rather gloomy lighting. An old man sits cross-legged in a courtyard in front of his carpets. Stall after stall displays open bowls of fragrant cardamom and cinna-mon. And instead of neon signs and blaring loudspeakers, most shops have a personable young man (and they are almost always men) whose sole job is to engage shoppers in conversation, using some of the most transparent ruses ever devised.

12   "You are going the wrong way!" one cried out as I passed him. I stopped, startled. It was entirely possible that he was right. I'd been wandering the twisty interior streets for half an hour, fascinated and utterly lost.

13   Seeing that he had caught my attention, he crowed, "This is the right way for you!" Delightedly, he pointed toward his small shop, and I couldn't resist taking a peek. Years later, it occurred to me that I could have used the services of someone like him when I was trying to funnel people to my book signing. Maybe there is something to this Wal-Mart greeter business, after all.

Throwing Good Shillings After Bad

14 For centuries, the vast majority of customers shopped on streets that were by turns muddy, windy, rainy, and dirty. But retailers across Europe were beginning to discover the advantages of setting up shop inside large buildings that already attracted crowds of the wealthy and powerful, such as castles, palaces and mer-chants' exchange buildings. In the 1500s, the nave of St. Paul's Cathedral in London was home to a number of small entrepreneurs, and it was a popular place for wealthy townspeople to show off their new clothes. Visitors to such public buildings could usually buy toys, books, sewing supplies, and other small items from makeshift stalls.

15   More established shopkeepers were initially wary of setting up business in communal buildings. When Sir Thomas Gresham, a London financier, built the Royal Exchange in 1568, he designed it as a facility for both traders (on the main floor) and shopkeepers (in the two upper galleries). However, shop-keepers who were used to living above their stores—where they could keep a close eye on the premises and thwart attempted burglaries—were not thrilled

about the idea of shops they couldn't guard overnight. Moreover, the thought of sharing the same building with so many competitors made them nervous.

16   The retail areas of the building were virtually empty for three years, until Gresham offered tenants a year's free rent if they agreed to move in. The shopkeepers who took him up on his offer wouldn't regret it; once it was full, the exchange prospered and spurred many other rich men to open similar enterprises. In 1676, the Exeter Exchange on the Strand in London was built solely to house market stalls.

The Palais Royal: Flush with Shopping

17 These seventeenth-century market buildings had some things in common with the modern mall, but shopping trends would soon take another turn that would send shoppers back outdoors.

18   Glazing techniques in the eighteenth century allowed shopkeepers to build large store windows, where they could set up elaborate displays that customers could not easily disturb (unlike a pile of goods on a market stall table). London streets such as Pall Mall and the Strand, with their spacious sidewalks, were soon lined with bow-fronted shops, which shoppers found much more enticing than simple stalls.

19   By the late 1700s, visitors from all over the world were marvelling at the pleasant, organized nature of London's shopping streets. "A stranger . . . appreciates the sidewalks made of broad stones, running down both sides of the streets, whereon he is safe from the terrifying rush of carts and coaches as if he were in his own room; for no wheel dares to encroach even a finger's breadth upon the footpath," wrote Carl Philip Moritz, a German who visited England in the 1780s. "Especially in the Strand, where one shop jostles another and people of very different trades often live in the same house, it is surprising to see how from bottom to top the various houses often display large signboards with painted letters."

20   However, one problem remained: shoppers didn't like browsing in the wind, rain, and hot sun. The solution to that problem would come from a city that had more pressing reasons than most others to solve it: Paris.

21   Unlike London, late eighteenth-century Paris was not a pleasant place to stroll. The streets—long before Baron Haussmann would develop the city's famous boulevards—were narrow, and few had sidewalks. Window shopping was a muddy and rather dangerous pursuit.

22   Then, in 1780, the Duke of Chartres had an inspired idea. Like modern English lords, who open their homes to tourists in order to pay their taxes, the duke needed money and decided to commercialize his residence. Luckily, he lived in the Palais Royal, so he had a prime bit of real estate to play with.

23   On the surface, his plan wasn't terribly revolutionary: he decided to enclose the palace's back garden on three sides with residential buildings, each with a colonnaded row of shops on the ground floor.

24   Similar squares existed throughout Europe, from the Piazza San Marco in Venice to Covent Garden in London. But the Palais Royal—with its prestigious location in the heart of Paris, and its use of the latest building materials and techniques—brought together the right elements at the right, prosperous time.

25   Instead of market stalls, the colonnades sheltered permanent, elegant shops. Each shop had a glazed window, perfect for displaying the luxury goods that the growing middle class coveted and the rich upper class could afford. The covered walkway in front of the shops opened not to a square full of traffic, as in Covent Garden, but to a festive park.

26   Like the Greeks' L-shaped stoa overlooking the harbor at Miletus, the colonnade of the Palais Royal allowed shoppers to move easily from outdoor space to enclosed space. It protected them from rain and snow, while allowing breezes to cool them in the heat of summer. In the garden court, fountains, trees, and concerts provided diversion for weary buyers.

27   The place was an immediate hit.

28   Like today's largest malls, the Palais Royal boasted many amenities besides shops, including cafés, social clubs, a currency exchange, hotels, concert rooms, theaters, and a waxworks. The three stories of apartments above the shops attracted the equivalent of today's loft owners—artists and single men—as well as a fair number of prostitutes, who had the sense to live where society gathered.

Sex and Bloody Revolution: At a Mall Near You!

29 The Palais Royal was not a cheap place to shop, which only added to its allure. Unlike people who browsed for ribbons and toys in the makeshift stalls of the previous century's exchanges, shoppers in the purpose-built Palais Royal chose largely from luxuries: jewelry, finely tailored clothes, marble objects, furniture, paintings, and similar items. In addition, they could avoid the hassle of bargaining, since the shopkeepers were the first in Paris to adopt fixed prices for their goods. Perhaps because the resulting prices were so high, the fixed-price trend wouldn't take wide hold in Paris for another six or seven decades.

30   The high prices didn't stop the crowds from coming. The Palais was *the* place to shop, flirt, gamble, and discuss big ideas. In fact, in a bit of brutal irony for the Palais' noble developer, the complex was one of the flashpoints for the French Revolution. On July 12, 1789, a riot against the city's royal troops began in the Palais' gardens and engulfed the city; two days later, a mob stormed the Bastille.

31   But even the intrigues and danger of the Revolution couldn't shake the hold the Palais had on the people of Paris. It remained a hotbed of gossip and social life. In 1790 a Russian visitor, N. M. Karamzin, observed:

> Everything that can be found in Paris (and what cannot be found in Paris) is in the Palais Royal . . . Here are assembled all the remedies for boredom and all the sweet banes for spiritual and physical health, every method of swindling those with money and tormenting those without it, all means of enjoying and killing time. One could spend an entire life, even the longest, in the Palais Royal, and as in an enchanting dream, dying, say "I have seen and known all."[2]

32   What wouldn't the developers of today's malls give for that kind of press?

33   However, success was a double-edged sword for the Palais Royal. During and after the Napoleonic Wars, its colonnades were magnets for off-duty soldiers looking for amusement. Customers became more interested in gambling and amorous liaisons, and less interested in buying goods. When the Duke of

Chartres's son, Louis Philippe, outlawed both prostitution and gambling on his property in 1837, the Palais' fortunes tumbled.

Arcades Uneaten by Pac-Man Machines

34 What the duke and his son had failed to foresee was the advantages of a completely enclosed shopping space. Colonnades let in light and fresh air, but they also admitted bugs and snow. Future developers would solve these problems with an innovation that was at once both obvious and ingenious.

35   In London and Milan, in Naples and in Paris itself, architects simply replaced the outer pillars of the colonnade with a solid wall or with a second row of facing shops. By doing so, they cut off the colonnade's extensive, permeable access to the outdoors. But while that meant that shoppers had fewer entry points, it also meant better protection from the elements—and better control over the resulting space. The result was the instantly popular shopping arcade.

36   English architectural critic Ralph Redivivus, writing in 1839, was as excited about the arcade concept as Karamzin had been about the Palais Royal half a century earlier:

> As far as possible convenience is concerned most assuredly nothing could be devised more suitable to such a climate as ours . . . than a covered street which bids defiance to the humours of the atmosphere, and where one may lounge and look at shopwindows, though the rain should come down in torrents, or though an August sun should broil people as they walk along in the open streets.[3]

37   Generally, in these days before electric light, arcades had glass roofs or skylights to decrease the need for candles or gaslight—a design element that caused maintenance headaches for the arcades' owners until the glass technology improved in the late nineteenth century.

38   Some arcades, following the pattern of the Grand Bazaar in Istanbul, were merely roofed versions of existing streets. Many others, such as London's Burlington Arcade, were enclosed spaces from their inception. Like the colonnades that had preceded them, these planned arcades drew heavily on classical ideas of regularity and order. Unlike the typically chaotic city street, they presented shoppers with a tidy environment of uniform windows and doors. And although they were enclosed, they were conceived as "streets" of a sort, often built between existing buildings and giving pedestrians an additional route between two other thoroughfares.

Snooty Shopping, U.K. Edition

39 Arcades were the last major form of enclosed, multiple-vendor shopping space to take root before the climate-controlled mall burst onto the scene in the twentieth century. But both arcades and their cousins, the colonnades, continued to evolve in the intervening years.

40   The fortunes of arcades rose or fell based on the fortunes of the streets that surrounded them. Closed off as they were, they usually withered if commerce moved elsewhere. Some of those that survived, such as the Burlington Arcade, pinned their hopes on the carriage trade.

41   From the day it opened in 1819, the Burlington Arcade has positioned itself as an elegant and exclusive shopping destination. Critics, of course, have always found its wares foolish. As journalist Augustus Sala noted dryly in 1859: "I don't think there is a shop in its *enceinte** where they sell anything that we could not do without. Boots and shoes are sold there, to be sure, but what boots and shoes? Varnished and embroidered and be-ribboned figments, fitter for a fancy ball or a lady's chamber, there to caper to the jingling melody of a lute, than for serious pedestrianism."[4] Harsh words from a man whose love of fine china and rare books often led him into debt.

42   In the intervening years since Sala's era, the arcade has maintained its image as an upscale destination. In early 2003, its Web site fairly radiated snooty class.

43   "The Burlington Arcade provides a fashionable destination for wealthy domestic and overseas visitors to London and is a focal point amongst some of London's most famous retailing names," it proclaimed. "Fortnum and Mason, Simpsons and Aspreys together with an exciting selection of restaurant, café and food emporiums are all within close proximity providing a rare opportunity for retailers in Burlington Arcade to access a broad range of affluent custom."[5]

44   Hey, it takes a lot of profit to maintain a Grade II heritage property.

Snooty Shopping, U.S. Edition

45 The Burlington Arcade is neither the first nor the last shopping enclave to appeal to customers' sense of status. But the next buildings to do so successfully would not be built in the old world. For the next stage in the mall's evolution, it's time to cross the Atlantic.

46   The first planned shopping area in the United States was Market Square, built in the Chicago suburb of Lake Forest, Illinois, in 1916. Like the Palais Royal, it consisted of three low buildings surrounding a central park, although in this case streets rather than colonnaded walkways fronted the buildings.

47   Six years later, a developer in Kansas City, Missouri, took this idea one step further. Country Club Plaza was billed as the first major shopping development in the world to focus specifically on shoppers arriving by car. Developer J.C. Nichols didn't have much choice: the city's rail line didn't reach as far as his site on a largely undeveloped swamp.

48   Locals called the place "Nichols' Folly," but the developer had the last laugh— he had correctly hedged his bets on America's burgeoning love for the automobile. Rather than a park, the Spanish-themed plaza with its red-tile roofs was built around a series of parking lots. But, like Market Square, it was a three-sided structure of low-slung buildings, and each shop had an external entrance.

49   Similar structures sprang up across the United States in subsequent decades, particularly in California. Efforts to promote the centers grew more flamboyant as the competition increased. In 1950, the Campus Drive-In shopping center in San Diego opened with a 50-foot neon majorette marking its entrance; the previous year, the new Town & Country Shopping Center in suburban Columbus, Ohio, had promoted night-time shopping by hiring a woman named Grandma Carver to dive 90 feet into a four-foot pool of flaming water set up in the parking lot.

---

* "An encircling fortification around a fort, castle, or town." [*American Heritage Dictionary*]

50   While they often offered drivers advantages over congested downtown shopping streets, these early malls shared one major disadvantage with their more traditional competitors: exposure to the elements. However, builders didn't have easy access to the technology needed to easily heat and cool a large, enclosed mall until the 1950s.

Oofta, by Golly! Cold-Weather Shopping in Minnesota

51 Weather wasn't such a major problem in sunny California and Texas, but in the cities of the Midwest, humid summers and icy winters discouraged shoppers from coming out to spend. It's no accident that America's first fully enclosed, climate-controlled shopping mall sprang up from the prairie in suburban Minneapolis.

52   To avoid building boilers for the 800,000-square-foot Southdale Shopping Center, architect Victor Gruen's Los Angeles-based firm developed a new kind of heat pump to heat and cool the mall, which opened in 1956. Like the developers of European arcades a century earlier, Southdale's builders realized that their enclosed space gave them a major advantage over their competitors, an advantage they promoted in a fact sheet published for the mall's opening:

> In a region which is often beset by inclement weather, the fact that Southdale [shoppers] will enjoy a perpetual springtime looms as an important drawing card. Every foot of the Center, including all shops, arcades and public areas, will be air-conditioned, completely free of snow, soot, or wilting heat.[6]

53   Another advantage the center had over many older malls was the fact that it boasted two department stores, Dayton's and Donaldsons. In a situation reminiscent of Thomas Gresham's struggles with the Royal Exchange four centuries earlier, it took the developer more than a year of negotiations before the two companies agreed to open under the same roof.

Malls, Kudzu, and Other Creeping Menaces

54 In less than half a century since Southdale was built, malls have changed and expanded beyond most developers' wildest dreams—and most critics' direst nightmares.

55   Eight years after Southdale opened, the U.S. boasted 7,600 malls. By 1972, the total had jumped to 13,174. But it was the greedy 1980s that were the golden age of the mall developer: 16,000 malls were built in that decade.

56   By the end of 2001, there were more than 45,000 malls in America—6,086 in California alone. And even though 95 percent of these centers were strip malls—structures in which a line of stores opens onto a street or parking lot—it was clear that Americans had embraced the concept of planned shopping centers with a vengeance.

57   However, the statistics hide another story: the bloom had started to fade from the shopping center rose, at least in the United States. The savings and loan crisis knocked the development industry for a loop in the early 1990s, and analysts began muttering nervously that many areas of the country had more retail space than they needed.

58   As a result, many developers changed their approach in the 1990s. Instead of building "ordinary" new malls, they either built over-the-top extravaganzas, or focused on upgrading and expanding their existing properties.

Mega-Oofta: The Mall of America and Its Canadian Cousin

59 Southdale's original 800,000 square feet—considered enormous at the time—would make the complex simply an average "regional center" these days, according to definitions published by the International Council of Shopping Centers. Perhaps that's why Southdale has ballooned to 1.7 million square feet—the most recent expansion added restaurants, a 16-screen movie theater, and a third-floor wing of teenybopper stores called Trendz on Top.

60   Of course, Southdale is in a peculiar situation. It's competing for customers with the Godzilla* of U.S. shopping centers: the 4.3-million-square-foot Mall of America, which opened in 1992 just six miles to the east. So much ink has been spilled on that complex that I won't add much to it here. You probably already know most of the mind-boggling details, such as the fact that the mall logs 600,000 to 900,000 visits *every week,* and that over a third of its customers come from more than 150 miles away. More than 2,500 couples have been married here. And apparently, if you took off the roof, nine Eiffel Towers could be crammed inside.

61   Even those facts pale beside the vital statistics of Mall of America's mother ship, the West Edmonton Mall. Built in four phases (so far), between 1981 and 1998, the 5.2-million-square-foot mall is home to more than 800 stores, a bungee-jumping facility, a submarine, an ice rink, a chapel, several aquariums, a hotel, the world's biggest indoor theme park . . . when you have a reputation to uphold as the world's largest mall, the list of attractions just keeps growing.

62   My first and last visit to WEM, as its developers call it, took place in the summer of 1986, just after the third phase opened. Along with other attractions, that expansion added the water park and two "theme streets," Bourbon Street and Europa Boulevard.

63   I was in Edmonton for a wedding. As the bride-to-be and I floated in the wave pool, waiting for the next artificial roller to crest over us, I thought about the place and what it all meant. Of course, I was only 21 at the time, so I didn't think terribly hard.

64   I remember being both fascinated and appalled by the sheer size of the place. As a third-year university student in the middle of acquiring a traditional liberal arts education, I felt compelled to be at least somewhat appalled. But as a young woman with a little money saved up from a summer job, I couldn't help but be transfixed by the number of opportunities to splurge.

65   What sticks with me to this day, however, was the unabashed artificiality of WEM. The developers had no compunctions about claiming that a visit to their

---

* *Godzilla,* star of 22 sci-fi movies from the Toho film company of Japan, is a skyscraper-sized, Tyrannosaurus-rex look-alike monster with atomic-fire breathing powers that periodically wrecks havoc on Japanese cities. At least one Godzilla film a few years back was made in America; all of the prior ones were known for their cheesy (albeit serviceable) special effects. "Godzilla" has entered the language to signify any large, overpowering force.

Bourbon Street was just as good—or better—than a trip to the real New Orleans. Better, of course, because it was safer, more predictable, and climate controlled.

The Theme Park Mall

66 Safety and artificiality have come to be the defining qualities of malls around the world. As city cores fell into scary disrepair, mall managers around the world touted the fact that their spaces were enclosed, patrolled, and secure. Look around any mall today, and within minutes you'll likely spot a security guard in quasi-police garb. Read promotional materials and you'll see frequent references to well-lit parking lots. Some shopping centers have capitalized on this aura of security to bring formerly public events, such as Halloween trick or treat-ing—now known as "Malloween" in some malls—into their sanitized confines.

67   This focus on control annoys critics of shopping centers, and even makes shoppers who appreciate safety slightly uneasy. As I did at West Edmonton Mall, many others wonder whether this theme park atmosphere is healthy for us. As Daniel Miller and his British co-authors put it:

> When people yearn for a return to "personal service" or support current trends for opening up enclosed shopping centers to "natural light," we sug-gest that they are at least as concerned about the increasing artificiality of their social relationships (and in particular the perceived materialism of their children) as they are about the physical environment itself.[7]

68   If this sort of artifice is enough to bring people into the mall, getting them to stay requires an array of psychological trickery that would have amazed the Duke of Chartres.

You Can Head for the Check-out, But You Can Never Leave

69 Have you ever wondered why most malls have no windows to the outside world? That's easy. The architects want you to forget any other world even exists. The sight of trees, sunshine, and birds might encourage you to *leave the mall.* And, not surprisingly, shopping mall owners don't want you to do that.

70   Instead, they want you to stay inside as long as possible. The idea is to repli-cate the artificial feeling of a theater or a Hollywood sound stage, where shop-pers can be the stars of their own show. The shopping center industry has even coined a term for the idea of shopping as theater—the "retail drama"—which William Severini Kowinski popularized in his fascinating 1985 book, *The Malling of America.**

71   In the retail drama, we are all indebted actors treading the shopping mall boards. The sales clerks and the other shoppers are all part of the cast. In the mall, the large rectangular doorways of each store, shaped like the prosceni-um arches of a traditional stage, add to the fantasy. We can enter a variety of stages, try on new "costumes" and touch new "props," which we can ultimate-ly buy to fulfill our fantasies of who we are and who we want to become.

---

* A selection from Kowinski's *Malling of America* appears later in this chapter.

72   Blank, windowless walls aren't the only technique developers use to keep us immersed in our fantasies. Builders also do their best to ensure that we can't find our way out. Most of today's successful malls are designed more like ancient labyrinths than the long, straight corridor of the Burlington Arcade.

73   If you've ever become hopelessly lost in a mall, take comfort in the fact that you've been purposely led astray. It's known as the "Gruen effect," named after Southdale's architect. Basically, the intent is to force serious shoppers—the blinkered, intent folks who come to the mall with a shopping list and attitude—to see stores they wouldn't otherwise visit. Straight hallways and clear sightlines make it too easy to find your store, buy what you came for, and get out.

74   It's a peculiar concept. Many shoppers—like my husband, for example—find the idea of trolling through endless, confusing corridors so annoying that they avoid malls completely. Others, like me, spend half their time sighing in frustration as they try to decipher the rare mall maps.

75   I remember the first time I learned that the confusing nature of malls was no accident. I was taking a press tour of Bayshore—the very mall where, 16 years later, I'd be doing [a] book signing—and I noticed an escalator that ran from the ground floor directly up to the new third story. I naively asked why there weren't two sets of escalators: an up-and-down set between the first and second floors, and a second pair between the upper two stories.

76   The PR person giving the tour explained, without shame, that the one-way express escalator was designed to keep shoppers moving around the mall, even if they didn't really intend to.

77   I can testify that the escalator fulfils that function admirably. I've lost count of the times I've stepped onto it by mistake and watched the second-floor store I had hoped to reach pass me by like a desert mirage. As a result, I have to hike across half the mall to find a staircase, escalator, or elevator that will actually take me where I want to go.

78   This design strategy seems counterproductive. Yes, it makes me pass stores I didn't plan to see. But, trust me, I'm in no frame of mind to buy. Usually, I'm muttering unpleasant words under my breath as I hotfoot it down the corridors. Until, of course, I sprint by a display of discount books and something catches my eye.

79   All right, I admit it. I'm annoyed, but I still buy.

80   But with luck, this mall-as-maze idea will be one of the design trends to lose favor among shopping center architects. Such miracles do happen.

81   There are encouraging signs that change is in the wind. For instance, the wisdom of sealing off shoppers from the real world is now being questioned in Broomfield, Colorado. There, a new mall called FlatIron Crossing features "window walls" of clear glass that can even be rolled back to let in light and air when the weather permits. "We're trying to blur the lines of where outdoor and indoors start and stop," David School, one of the mall's developers, told a newspaper reporter in 1999.[8]

82   The builders of the stoa at Miletus, and the Duke of Chartres's architect at the Palais Royal, would recognize this idea. Just like the fashions sold in mall stores throughout the world, everything old eventually becomes new again in the world of shopping center design. And if bell-bottoms and platform shoes can be revived, nothing's impossible.

Notes

Particularly useful references for this chapter included Spiro Kostof's *A History of Architecture: Settings and Rituals,* Margaret MacKeith's *The History and Conservation of Shopping Arcades,* and Mark Girouard's *Cities and People.* The International Council of Shopping Centers provided valuable information on the history of the development of the modern American shopping center, as did the Web page of Steven Schoenherr, a history professor at the University of San Diego <history.sandiego.edu/gen/filmnotes/shoppingcenter.html>.

1. "At the top of the street," Arieh Sharon, *Planning Jerusalem,* London, Weidenfeld & Nicolson, 1973, quoted in Margaret MacKeith, *The History and Conservation of Shopping Arcades,* 9.

2. "Everything that can be found in Paris," N.M. Karamzin, *Letters of a Russian Traveler,* New York and Oxford, 1957, 215, quoted in Mark Girouard, *Cities and People,* 204.

3. "As far as possible convenience," Ralph Redivivus, *Civil Engineer and Architect's Journal,* March 1839, quoted in Margaret MacKeith, *The History and Conservation of Shopping Arcades,* 1.

4. "I don't think there is a shop," Augustus Sala, quoted in Alison Adburgham, *Shopping in Style,* 102.

5. "The Burlington Arcade provides," <http://www.burlington-arcade.co.uk>.

6. "In a region which is often beset," Southdale Shopping Center fact sheet, 1956, <http://www.southdale.com>.

7. "When people yearn for a return," Daniel Miller, Peter Jackson, Nigel Thrift, Beverley Holbrook, and Michael Rowlands, *Shopping, Place and Identity,* xi.

8. "We're trying to blur the lines," David Scholl, quoted in Jeanie Straub, "Regional shopping mall's design banks on meshing indoors, outdoors," *Boulder County Business Report,* December 17, 1999.

Review Questions

1. Laura Paquet both explains and argues in this selection. Review her work and note where she uses each approach.

2. Trace the evolution of shopping malls, from ancient times to present.

3. Which of the shopping centers Paquet discusses was initially built in the 1400s and has remained in use until the present day?

4. How did glazing techniques for producing glass and the construction of sidewalks affect London's shopkeepers in the late eighteenth century?

5. Architecturally, what were the main differences and similarities among the Palais Royal, the Burlington Arcade, and Southdale Center (the first modern mall)?

6. In the 1990s, what motivation did mall developers have to upgrade new and existing properties? Why was building an "ordinary" mall no longer an appealing prospect?

7. How do mall developers attempt to keep customers in the mall for as long as possible?

Discussion and Writing Suggestions

1. Reread the epigraph to this selection, by James B. Twitchell, comparing the modern mall to a fascistic medieval city-state. In your view, does the comparison hold?

2. Characterize the tone of Paquet's writing in this selection and offer quotations to support your view.

3. Is there any sense in which you view shopping malls differently, having read Paquet's selection? Does your learning that the origins of the modern mall can be traced back thousands of years affect your view of malls and what people do in them today? Explain.

4. In paragraph 31, reread N. M. Karamzin's account of the Palais Royal, the exclusive shopping district in Paris. Apply Karamzin's description, part-by-part, to a modern mall. How well does his account describe what one finds today?

5. Paquet writes that both the Palais Royal in Paris (1780) and the Burlington Arcade in London (1839) sold luxury items that appealed to relatively wealthy customers. These earlier forms of the shopping center aimed to attract an upscale clientele. In your experience with modern malls, to what extent do you find a similar targeting of customers? Are some malls geared especially to the wealthy? To the middle class? To the poor? How can you tell?

6. Paquet concludes with this statement: "Just like the fashions sold in mall stores throughout the world, everything old eventually becomes new again in the world of shopping center design." What does she mean?

Main Street Revisited
Richard Francaviglia

What models did developers turn to when creating the modern American shopping mall? In this next selection, Richard Francaviglia argues that Walt Disney played a key role. His romanticized "Main Street USA," a re-creation of small-town America's shopping district for his new theme park, Disneyland, set the standard for carefully designed and managed shopping environments. Main Street USA, moved indoors to a climate-controlled environment, became the modern shopping mall. A geographer and historian, Francaviglia directs the Center for Greater Southwestern Studies and the History of Cartography at the University of Texas, Arlington. This selection appeared in his book Main Street Revisited: Time, Space, and Image-

Building in Small-Town America *(University of Iowa Press, 1996), which won the J. B. Jackson Prize for conveying "the insights of professional geography in language that is interesting and attractive to a lay audience."*

1   Main Street USA . . . fits into the genre of intensely designed and orchestrated space/place. On every inch of Disney's Main Street USA, from the public square to the Plaza, architecture, street furniture, and all aspects of the streetscape are historically themed and carefully engineered. It is this sense of "history" that nearly overwhelms the visitor. All of the street lights are patterned after the "whiteway" lights that lined Main Streets in the early twentieth century. The park benches, wrought iron railings, plantings—everything on Main Street is carefully designed to convey a feeling of the late Victorian period. Even the trees and bushes are carefully sculpted and tended. On Main Street USA, most visitors imbibe the ambience of the past, but they are in fact participating in something far more elementary; their attitudes and perceptions are being shaped through a type of social engineering. This leads to the fourteenth axiom of Main Street development.* *Main Street is essentially a stage upon which several types of human dramas are performed simultaneously, each character or actor in the drama having a designated role that is dependent on his or her relationship to the "set."* Whether one stands behind the counter or in front of a store window brings with it different expectations. Disney was the ultimate merchant on Main Street, and visitors to Main Street USA are the ultimate customers.

2   In Disney's Main Street USA, architecture becomes the façade that creates the impression that all was right with the world in the small town at the turn of the century; it implies that commerce (and merchants) thrive along Main Street, and that society and a community are working together in harmony. Of course, Disney's Main Street does not feature those inevitable services that indicate the other, or darker, side of life. There are no funeral parlors, pool halls, or bars. It should come as no surprise that Disney created small-town America as it *should* have been. His Main Street mirrors a pre-adolescent period free from the change and turmoil that characterizes much of life. . . .

3   What concerns, even infuriates, historians and scholars most about Walt Disney is that he created an abstracted image that it is so tempting to confuse with reality. Disney masterfully abstracted his experiences in [one of his hometowns] *Marceline* and worked with his designers to capture the essences of other towns to produce a small-town image that has nearly universal appeal. In so doing, Disney intuitively knew that *all* planned townscapes—including those Main Streets created in the eighteenth and nineteenth centuries—were in a sense engineered to create effects. Even the vistas down Main Street USA were carefully designed to have significant features (the Railroad Station and Sleeping Beauty's Castle), or, as Disney himself is reported to have said, there should be a "wienie at the end of every street.". . .

---

* Throughout the book from which this selection was taken, Francaviglia draws broad lessons, what he sees as fundamental truths, about the evolution of Main Streets across America during the 19th and 20th centuries. Main Street's being a "stage upon which . . . human dramas are performed" is one such axiom. You will notice that James Farrell uses much the same language to discuss what goes on in shopping malls, earlier in the chapter.

4   At symbolic levels, Disney's engineering of the small-town environment in Main Street USA is revealing because he so beautifully captured the essence of the romanticism of the small town. Disney himself was moved by the originals, and shaped them into an icon that affects the way we will view its "real" counterparts. To the general public, Main Street USA in Disneyland was very credible in that it featured towers and architectural turrets where they seemed logical, and even though the trim was fairly lavish, it was subdued enough to remind one of Main Streets in the relatively prosperous period during the "McKinley Era"* at about the turn of the century.

5   Students of urban design know that Disney possessed an element of genius in that he carefully designed this Main Street to have an intersection about halfway between the public square and the plaza. That intersection provides a node of activity where merchants have materials on display outside and where towers can form visual exclamation points for the architecture. Looking down one of these side streets, one sees trees that convey the feeling that the commercial streetscape is yielding to a residential area. But in reality, the trees seen behind that intersection on Main Street are the trees of Jungleland, so close is the juxtaposition between one "world" of Disneyland and another. The entire Disneyland theme park is magnificently engineered into only about ninety-six acres of space, which is smaller than the area encompassed within the city limits of most American towns! In world history, few places this small have had such a powerful effect on so many people.

6   In keeping with his ability to create magic through place, Disney used night to his advantage. Because Main Street USA is experienced at night as well as during the daytime, Disney provided marvelous rim-lighting on the buildings. Incandescent bulbs were strung along all of the cornices to convey a very stylized and ornate appearance, enabling the architecture and the streetscape to "shine" at night as well as in the daytime. The Main Street electrical parade runs through the area at night, and Main Street at night provides a kind of visual excitement that was rarely, perhaps never, actually seen in the small towns of America. Rim-lighting of this kind was, however, common in pavilions and the grand buildings of expositions. Like many of Disney's creations, rim-lighting in this context brings a touch of the exotic or even whimsical to Main Street, rather reminding one more of the festive environments of parks and fairs than the Main Street of the typical American small town. Historian and social critic Jon Weiner recently noted that "Disneyland's Main Street is a fiction; the real Main Streets of real small towns at the turn of the century were not so nice"[1]—an understatement borne out by architectural historians and historical geographers. And yet, as architect Paul Goldberger accurately noted, Disney produced "a kind of universally true Main Street—it's better than the real Main Street of the turn of the century ever could be."[2] That Disney's Main Street seems so universally beautiful comes as less of a surprise when one realizes that Walt Disney was rather sophisticated and widely travelled: in fact, Tivoli Gardens in Copenhagen, Denmark, was said to have greatly impressed Walt Disney in 1952—a seminal year in the early designs of

---

* William McKinley (1843–1901), the 25th President of the United States (1897–1901), was assassinated while in office.

Disneyland.[3] Disney and his designers reportedly were impressed by an exhibit called "Yesteryear's Main Street" at the Museum of Science and Industry in Chicago, which was sponsored by General Motors.[4] Disney's Main Street, which, according to WED (which stands for Walter Elias Disney) imagineering historian David Mumford, "is actually a typical representation of a Walt Disney imagineering project, since it represents a collaborative effort by many creative people,"[5] was thus inspired by many places. . . .

7   If this description of [Main Street USA] sounds familiar, and it should indeed, that is because it has in fact become the model of the typical American shopping mall, where the visitor or shopper leaves the car in the parking lot and enters an environment that is climatically controlled, and where the real world is left outside. In malls, as in Disney's Main Streets, every aspect of design and circulation is carefully orchestrated (Fig. 7.1). This should come as no surprise, for many of the designers of shopping centers and malls in the United States

FIGURE 7.1 The Mall as Main Street. This diagram of the South Coast Plaza Shopping Center, a mall in Costa Mesa, California, reveals many of the same design elements seen in Disneyland's Main Street USA—notably an important intersection of four radiating axes (bottom) and a linear thoroughfare running into another point of decision-making where a carousel is positioned (upper center). The similarities are more than coincidental, as many shopping center designers have studied Disney's Main Street. Computer graphic based on a 1975 map in a kiosk at the mall.

have visited Disney's parks in order to develop a much better understanding of how people move through, appreciate, and patronize a retail environment.[6]

8   It is ironic that Walt Disney, who was politically conservative and espoused rugged individualism, actually produced an environment that embodies such nearly total social engineering and control. According to architectural critic Jane Holtz Kay, Disney's Main Street and shopping malls embody both "public persona" and "private autocracy."[7] The autocratic control of theme parks, of course, is linked to safety and security, and is perhaps one reason why shopping centers are highly successful, and highly criticized by those who feel that such places are "contrived." Malls, too, are able to control behavior using their "private" status. As William Kowinski succinctly stated in his classic article entitled "The Malling of America":

> Malls are designed for Disney's children. Stores are pressed close together; they have small low façades. In fact, everything about malls is minimized . . . the mall is laid out with few corners and no unused space along store rows so that there are no decisions to make—you just flow on.[8] *

9   Few can deny the attractiveness of mall environments to a generation of retail shoppers drawn to the relative serenity and the climate control of the shopping center. That such malls are a current incarnation of Main Street is borne out by the flourishing social life and the persistence of marketing and craft fairs within today's shopping centers. The relative visual uniformity of shopping centers from coast to coast should not be particularly surprising; they, like Disney's Main Street, are archetypal environments of popular culture. This has caused architectural critics to blast the lack of "imagination" of their creators while, ironically, reflecting nostalgically on the days of the *real* American town in, perhaps, the 1880s when, critics contend, there was far greater "individuality."

10   In reality, of course, this was not the case; as we have seen, by the 1880s Victorian era Main Streets had developed into highly standardized forms. Their major architectural components could—like McDonald's—be found from coast to coast. That scholars lament the standardization of the mall while praising the architectural integrity of historic Main Streets reveals the power of nostalgia in affecting even the most educated of our citizens. Whatever else one may say about the typical shopping center, it is an abstracted reincarnation of Main Street, where pedestrians have the right of way over vehicular traffic, where *all* store façades are attractive and where all of the merchants agree to maintain regular hours and carefully control their signage and sales pitches—techniques which avoid the appearance of haphazard or eccentric individualism.

11   Sociologists have long known that people visit shopping centers for far more than commercial reasons. More than twenty years ago, when Edward Tauber insightfully stated that "not all shopping motives, by any means, are even related to the product,"[9] he introduced the concept of "sociorecreational shopping." Several very revealing articles over the last dozen or more years have shown that shopping centers are important places of social interaction where people may wind up meeting future spouses and friends; where families go simply to stroll, to see people and to be seen by them; where young people go to "hang

---

* A selection from Kowinski's *Malling of America* appears later in this chapter.

out" and socialize. Whereas academicians may condemn this type of behavior as manipulated or inauthentic, it is in fact one of the major reasons why commercial and marketing towns have existed for centuries. This may be stated as the fifteenth axiom of Main Street development: *Despite its market-driven businesses, Main Street is primarily a social environment.* Main Street is an integral element in the "collective consciousness," as geographer Alan Baker used the term, to refer to landscape creation and perception that is linked to a national identity.[10]

Notes

1. Jon Weiner, "Tall Tales and True," *Nation* 258, no. 4: 134.
2. Paul Goldberger, in Judith Adams, *The American Amusement Park Industry:* 98.
3. Arline Chambers, "The Architecture of Reassurance: Designing the Disney Theme Parks," "Disney Chronology" (unpublished paper), p. 5.
4. Andrew Lainsbury, personal communication with author, July 13, 1995.
5. Letter from David Mumford to Jack and Leon Janzen, November 13, 1992, reproduced in Jack E. Janzen, "MAIN STREET . . . Walt's Perfect Introduction to Disneyland": 30.
6. Richard Francaviglia, "Main Street Revisited."
7. Jane Holtz Kay, "When You Stimulate a Star," *Landscape Architecture,* June 1990: 54.
8. *New Times,* May 1, 1978: 33.
9. Edward Tauber, "Sociorecreational Shopping," *Human Behavior* 2, no. 4; reproduced in *Intellectual Digest* 4, no. 3 (November 1973): 38.
10. Alan R. H. Baker, "Collective Consciousness and the Last Landscape: National Ideology and the Commune Council of Mesland (Loir-et-Cher) as Landscape Architect during the 19th Century," chapter 12 in *Ideology and Landscape in Historical Perspective,* edited by Alan Baker and Gideon Biger: 255–88.

Review Questions

1. Describe the ways in which Disney's Main Street USA is a carefully controlled environment.
2. What impression does Disney's street create for the visitor, according to Francaviglia?
3. What is the critics' chief complaint about this street?
4. In what ways does mall design borrow from Disney's Main Street USA?
5. Why is the placement of an intersection important to the success of Main Street USA as well as to the typical shopping mall?

Discussion and Writing Suggestions

1. If you have visited Disneyland or Disney World, describe your experiences on Main Street USA. Did the street impress you as it did

Francaviglia? To what extent do you find shopping mall design similar in key respects to the design of Main Street USA?

2. "Whatever else one may say about the typical shopping center, it is an abstracted reincarnation of Main Street, where pedestrians have the right of way over vehicular traffic, where *all* store facades are attractive and where all of the merchants agree to maintain regular hours and carefully control their signage and sales pitches—techniques which avoid the appearance of haphazard or eccentric individualism" (paragraph 10). To what extent do you agree that these aims are desirable?

3. In paragraph 11, quoting another author, Francaviglia introduces the term "sociorecreational shopping." Define the term and relate it to your own experiences as a mall shopper.

4. This selection is excerpted from a book-length study of America's Main Streets. Throughout the longer work, Francaviglia offers a number of "axioms" regarding his subject. You find two of these axioms in this selection. See paragraph 1: "Main Street is essentially a stage upon which several types of human dramas are performed simultaneously." An *axiom* is a statement that is universally recognized as true. Do you agree that Francaviglia's statement is beyond dispute?

5. Following question 4, Francaviglia offers a second axiom in this selection. See paragraph 11: "Despite its market-driven businesses, Main street is primarily a social environment." Do you agree that Francaviglia's statement is beyond dispute?

Shopping Towns USA
Victor Gruen and Larry Smith

Victor Gruen (born Viktor Grüenbaum, 1903–1980) is the American architect credited with creating the modern shopping mall. Born and trained In Vienna, he fled the Nazi occupation and moved to New York in 1938, where he worked as an architect before opening his own firm in 1951 in Los Angeles. Gruen believed that shopping centers would promote the interests not only of businesses but also of suburbanites, who lived in vast, culturally isolated developments that lacked the community focus of urban neighborhoods. Shopping centers could become community centers, argued Gruen, and in the process promote American values. Gruen is credited with building the first fully enclosed, air-conditioned shopping mall in Edina, Minnesota, in 1956. Ultimately, he returned to Europe, disappointed that other mall developers pursued profits more than they did community development. The following selection, in which Gruen articulates his vision for shopping centers, appears as the "Prologue" in Shopping Towns USA *(Reinhold Publishing, 1960).*

1 Buying and selling is as old as mankind. Prehistoric man exchanged the deer he had slain for a necklace of pretty shells. The modern housewife acquires a package of frozen food in exchange for some round pieces of metal. Gratification of

needs and desires motivates both transactions. Only the conditions under which they take place have changed.

2   A condition of most important consequence, of course, was the introduction of the middleman—the merchant—who turned barter into commerce. He carried the work produced by others from place to place, established trade routes and trading posts, founded country stores and merchant states. Wherever he settled he became an integral, invigorating part of urban life.

3   In the Greece of antiquity the merchant spread his wares under the colonnades of the *Stoa,* a building especially designated for his activity. The *Stoa* was as important in the *Agora,* or city square, as the *Bouleuterion* where the political representatives met, or the *Ecclesiasterion,* designed for public meetings. The Temple was nearby. Citizens strolling in the square discussed the topics of the day, transacted their business, did their marketing, while philosophers, poets, and entertainers argued, recited and performed. Court trials were held there. Banquets were spread. The *Agora* was the center of city life, and in this colorful, lively, dynamic environment commerce had its share.

4   This integration of human activities was a universal pattern. Its existence was guaranteed in ancient Rome where wheeled traffic was banished from the city's forum when vehicles threatened to crowd out the humans.

5   The medieval city market square was the city's center, not only geographically but socially and commercially, religiously and culturally. The City Hall and Guild Halls were placed there. The Cathedral, the merchants' and craftsmen's stalls and stores surrounded it. The open center area became in turn the market place, the fair ground and the entertainment center for the citizenry.

6   That genius of the Renaissance, Leonardo da Vinci, recognized the threat to human values of life when they become isolated. He designed a City Center for the convenience and pleasure of the people, confining wheeled vehicles to an underground road.

7   Our own New England and Midwest towns are witness to the basic town square concept which our forefathers brought with them from Europe. It persisted here well into the nineteenth century.

8   The advent of the Industrial Revolution radically changed the organization and character of cities. Thousands of factories were built in the midst of towns and cities. The city grew into a crazy quilt of packed humanity. The industrial slum became the new pattern of the city.

9   Life in the city soon became intolerable and those who could afford it led the march to the suburbs. The exodus increased its tempo with the advent of the interurban, elevated and subway trains and became a rout with the emergence of the automobile.

10   The automobile was the means by which the last vestige of community coherence was destroyed. So long as suburban dwellers traveled in vehicles that ran on tracks, new communities had a central point—the railway stop—to build around. As the cities stretched out along the tentacles of railroad lines, shops, churches, and community buildings sprang up around the railroad station; the size of residential areas was automatically controlled by the walking distance from the station. Such subcenters are still clearly recognizable in the Greater London Area.

11   When the automobile emerged as a means of private mass transportation, the final urban explosion took place. Automobiles, free of steel rails or overhead

wires, could move at will in every direction. They provided complete freedom of movement to the individual driver and made him independent of public transportation. So, with the automobile came a dispersal of population that followed no pattern whatever.

12   To accommodate the flood of humans seeking escape from the intolerable conditions of the city, mass housing builders tore up the ground, chopped down the trees, and removed swiftly and cynically every vestige of what the people had come to find. Modern suburbia was born, in which there were neither the values of a rural community nor those of an urban environment.

13   But people must live somewhere and suburbia grew. According to a report of the United States Census Bureau, suburbs grew seven times as fast as central cities in the years 1950 to 1954. The population of metropolitan areas in 1950 was 83,796,000; 95,304,000, in 1954. Within incorporated city areas an increase of 3.8 percent occurred; 27.8 percent in suburban communities of the metropolitan area. In 1957 a population census was taken in New York City in an attempt to obtain additional state aid by proving increased population. To the great surprise of city government it was found that the combined total population of the five boroughs had decreased from 7,891,957 in 1950 to 7,795,417—or 1.2 percent—at a time when the population of the Greater Metropolitan Area was increasing dramatically.

14   As the spreading continued with increasing speed, distances between places of residence and the central city grew by leaps and bounds.

15   In spite of this, public transportation faced the threat of annihilation. The inroads that private automobile traffic had made on public transportation is indicated by figures of a study made by the Westchester County Association. It showed that despite a population increase during the years 1949 to 1954 of 15.5 percent, the number of railroad commuters decreased during the same period by 16.3 percent.

16   Throughout the United States, the growth was so fast and frenzied that purely practical matters—construction of roads, highways, drainage and sewage, power and gas lines—lagged years behind; but any serious attempt at adequate planning of properly situated schools, shopping facilities, community centers and churches was nonexistent. Row upon row of identical houses set in an empty countryside proved to be less than the Heaven its settlers had bargained for. Suburbia had become an arid land inhabited during the day almost entirely by women and children and strictly compartmentalized by family income, social, religious, and racial background.

17   A psychiatrist of the United States Department of Health, Leonard J. Duhl, believes that this matriarchal pattern of suburbia sets up mental health hazards. Labeling it a "Feminine World," he describes it as a place where people are keeping up with the Joneses, where conformity is considered a necessity and where children have only limited experiences and are not exposed to broader environmental influences.*

---

* For more on the "Feminine World" of the suburbs that Gruen introduces here, see Lizabeth Cohen, "From Town Center to Shopping Center: The Reconfiguration of Community Market Places in Postwar America" in the *American Historical Review,* 101 (4), October 1996, particularly pp. 1072–1077. A portion of Cohen's article appears later in this chapter.

18   Critics of City Planning are equally concerned. Christopher Tunnard and Henry Hope Reed, in their book *American Skyline,* have this to say about suburbia:

> How different this is from our earlier American tradition which allowed people of all classes to mingle together as they still do in communities where people live as well as work. Something of this mixture is healthier for democracy which will surely suffer if residential suburbs continue to refuse public housing projects, business firms, industry and rest camps. Without these they will remain smug, lacklustre backwaters.

19   Many others, trained to apprehend the private and public dangers inherent in our unplanned suburban growth, are increasingly concerned. Charles Abrams, Chairman of the New York State Commission Against Discrimination, points out that: "The suburbs and their quest for status are shaping the American personality of the future as the frontier once shaped the American personality of the past."

20   Since suburbia is undoubtedly having a serious effect on the personality of our entire urban life, it is natural that its influence should be felt by the segment of human activity that is of primary concern to us here: the marketing of goods for the gratification of human needs and desires. In this amorphous conglomeration—suburbia—the merchant has had difficulty in finding a logical way to integrate his activities with the local scene.

21   Stores, which followed their customers into the suburbs, were no longer provided with obvious predetermined locations such as near railway stations. For the customer no longer emerged at defined points; he and his automobile were everywhere.

22   Under these circumstances the best bet seemed to be store locations on highways over which shoppers would have to travel on their way back and forth to the city. As the number of highway stores increased, more people stopped their cars along the curb and parking space became available only for a cash premium—a new type of hitching post, the parking meter, had made its appearance. Because the shortage and cost of curb parking tended to slow down sales, merchants arranged for off-street car storage areas, at first behind and later on in front of their stores.

23   Business grew and so did automobile traffic. Consequently, serious traffic congestion appeared on the highways, so serious that drivers began to avoid them by using alternate routes. When these roads inevitably attracted new stores and new congestion, super highways and freeways were constructed at tremendous cost in order to promote an easy flow of traffic.

24   In the meantime, residential areas surrounding congested traffic carriers, or facing the unsightly service facilities of stores, became undesirable. The original owners and tenants moved out and only those who could not afford or were not permitted to live in the more desirable places moved in. Soon stores found themselves surrounded by residential areas of reduced buying power.

25   As customers were siphoned off from the roads along which merchants had settled, partly by neighborhood deterioration, partly by the use of new freeways, a wild scramble for new locations started. Merchandising outlets were built in freshly created suburban areas still farther removed. Here, within a few years,

merchants encountered a repetition of the undesirable conditions from which they had tried to escape. The need for farsighted, comprehensive planning finally became urgently apparent.

26 Planning is needed not only to bring order, stability, and meaning to chaotic suburbia; it is necessary in order to establish a strong logical framework within which individual merchandising enterprises can flourish and provide crystallization points for suburbia's community life.

27 Some members of the business community have, in the past, resisted the concept of comprehensive planning. They regarded it as interference with individual initiative and free enterprise. It has been labeled by some as "undemocratic." But planning, properly understood and exercised, does not result in fixed patterns, in authoritarianism, in regimentation, or in the suppression of individualism.

28 No democratic society can flourish without law and order which, when applied to the physical environment, necessitates planning. In a complex and highly mechanized society environmental planning safeguards the basic human rights. By providing the best conditions for physical and mental health, it protects *life.* By establishing barriers against anarchy and the infringements of hostile natural and man-made forces, it protects *liberty.* By the creation of a humane environment it invites and encourages the *pursuit of happiness.*

29 When environmental planning is applied to the designing of new commercial facilities, many conditions must be analyzed, criteria weighed, requirements met, and problems solved. These all involve in various ways and to varying degrees the needs and desires of the shopper. It is deeply significant that the term is "shopping center," not "selling center." This indicates clearly that the wishes and desires of the shopper take priority over those of the seller. (An earlier term, "parking center," failed to catch on.)

30 The basic need of the suburban shopper is for a conveniently accessible, amply stocked shopping area with plentiful and free parking. This is the purely practical need for which the shopping center was originally conceived and which many centers most adequately fulfill. Good planning, however, will create additional attractions for shoppers by meeting other needs which are inherent in the psychological climate peculiar to suburbia. By affording opportunities for social life and recreation in a protected pedestrian environment, by incorporating civic and educational facilities, shopping centers can fill an existing void. They can provide the needed place and opportunity for participation in modern community life that the ancient Greek *Agora,* the Medieval Market Place and our own Town Squares provided in the past.

31 That the shopping center can fulfill this perhaps subconscious but nonetheless urgent need of suburbanites for the amenities of urban living, is convincingly proved in a large number of centers. In such centers, pedestrian areas are filled with teeming life not only during normal shopping hours, but on Sundays and holidays when people windowshop, promenade, relax in the garden courts, view exhibits and patronize the restaurants.

32 All age groups are provided for. Auditoriums are booked to capacity. Meeting rooms are busy with civic and cultural affairs. Dance schools, music schools, and ice skating rinks attract teen-agers; amusement centers are popular with children.

33 Such a planning concept also results in an upgrading of the residential area surrounding the center. It not only protects surrounding communities from

blight but actually raises their desirability and consequently their property values.

34   If the shopping center becomes a place that not only provides suburbanites with their physical living requirements, but simultaneously serves their civic, cultural and social community needs, it will make a most significant contribution to the enrichment of our lives.

Review Questions

1. How did the increased use of the automobile contribute to the need for shopping centers?

2. Why did some merchants initially resist the concept of a carefully planned shopping center?

3. Aside from providing access to well-stocked stores and plenty of free parking, what attractions do shopping centers offer suburban communities?

4. In what ways did the rapid growth of suburbia in the 1950s fail to create for new suburbanites the promised "Heaven" they were hoping for?

5. In what ways had suburbia become a "Feminine World," according to Gruen?

Discussion and Writing Suggestions

1. In paragraph 28, Gruen offers a vigorous defense of centrally planned shopping centers, arguing that retail development, just like democracy, demands law and order. We gain the free exercise of life, liberty, and happiness, he suggests, through maintaining order. How convinced are you by Gruen's defense of centralized shopping center design?

2. In what sense can it be said that Gruen believed his shopping centers could save America from the curse of suburbia? In developing an answer, see especially paragraphs 16–20.

3. Gruen states (in paragraph 31) that "the shopping center can fulfill [a] subconscious but nonetheless urgent need of suburbanites for the amenities or urban living." What are these needs? To what extent do you believe that people living in the suburbs have them?

4. Reread the final paragraph of this selection. Gruen was a visionary who believed that shopping centers could meet "civic, cultural, and social community needs," as well as the commercial needs of suburbanites. Are you sympathetic to this vision? In your experience, to what extent do shopping centers today meet his standards?

5. In the first five paragraphs, Gruen conducts a very brief historical tour of shopping. In the context of the overall selection, why does

he begin in this way? In developing your answer, pay close attention to his conclusion.

Enclosed. Encyclopedic. Endured:
One Week at the Mall of America
David Guterson

In 1993 journalist and novelist David Guterson, on assignment for Harper's *magazine, spent a week in the recently opened Mall of America. As you will discover, Guterson approached the mall with a skeptical eye, both fascinated with and wary of its massive scale. Guterson agrees with James Farrell that one can take the pulse of American culture by spending time in malls. But what Guterson sees is cause for alarm. A contributing editor to* Harper's, *Guterson has most notably written a collection of short stories,* The Country Ahead of Us, *the Country Behind (Vintage, 1996) and the novel* Snow Falling on Cedars, *which won the 1995 PEN/Faulkner Award.*

1   Last April, on a visit to the new Mall of America near Minneapolis, I carried with me the public-relations press kit provided for the benefit of reporters. It included an assortment of "fun facts" about the mall: 140,000 hot dogs sold each week, 10,000 permanent jobs, 44 escalators and 17 elevators, 12,750 parking places, 13,300 short tons of steel, $1 million in cash disbursed weekly from 8 automatic-teller machines. Opened in the summer of 1992, the mall was built on the 78-acre site of the former Metropolitan Stadium, a five-minute drive from the Minneapolis–St. Paul International Airport. With 4.2 million square feet of floor space—including twenty-two times the retail footage of the average American shopping center—the Mall of America was "the largest fully enclosed combination retail and family entertainment complex in the United States."

2   Eleven thousand articles, the press kit warned me, had already been written on the mall. Four hundred trees had been planted in its gardens, $625 million had been spent to build it, 350 stores had been leased. Three thousand bus tours were anticipated each year along with a half-million Canadian visitors and 200,000 Japanese tourists. Sales were projected at $650 million for 1993 and at $1 billion for 1996. Donny and Marie Osmond had visited the mall, as had Janet Jackson and Sally Jessy Raphael, Arnold Schwarzenegger, and the 1994 Winter Olympic Committee.* The mall was five times larger than Red Square† and twenty times larger than St. Peter's Basilica;‡ it incorporated 2.3 miles of hallways and

---

* Celebrities Donny and Marie Osmond, part of a Salt Lake City based family entertainment team, were best known for three television variety shows that aired on prime time between 1976 and 1981. Sally Jessy Raphael is a talk show host whose programs aired between 1985 and 2002. Arnold Schwarzenegger needs no introduction.

† *Red Square* is the central square in the ancient center of Moscow, near the Kremlin, where during the Communist Soviet era military parades were held on May 1st.

‡ Built in the 16th century in the Italian Renaissance style, *St. Peter's Basilica* is the great church of Vatican City.

almost twice as much steel as the Eiffel Tower. It was also home to the nation's largest indoor theme park, a place called Knott's Camp Snoopy.

3   On the night I arrived, a Saturday, the mall was spotlit dramatically in the manner of a Las Vegas casino. It resembled, from the outside, a castle or fort, the Emerald City or Never-Never Land,* impossibly large and vaguely unreal, an unbroken, windowless multi-storied edifice the size of an airport terminal. Surrounded by parking lots and new freeway ramps, monolithic and imposing in the manner of a walled city, it loomed brightly against the Minnesota night sky with the disturbing magnetism of a mirage.

4   I knew already that the Mall of America had been imagined by its creators not merely as a marketplace but as a national tourist attraction, an immense zone of entertainments. Such a conceit raised provocative questions, for our architecture testifies to our view of ourselves and to the condition of our souls. Large buildings stand as markers in the lives of nations and in the stream of a people's history. Thus I could only ask myself: Here was a new structure that had cost more than half a billion dollars to erect—what might it tell us about ourselves? If the Mall of America was part of America, what was that going to mean?

5   I passed through one of the mall's enormous entranceways and took myself inside. Although from a distance the Mall of America had appeared menacing— exuding the ambience of a monstrous hallucination—within it turned out to be simply a shopping mall, certainly more vast than other malls but in tone and aspect, design and feel, not readily distinguishable from them. Its nuances were instantly familiar as the generic features of the American shopping mall at the tail end of the twentieth century: polished stone, polished tile, shiny chrome and brass, terrazzo floors, gazebos. From third-floor vistas, across vaulted spaces, the Mall of America felt endlessly textured—glass-enclosed elevators, neon-tube lighting, bridges, balconies, gas lamps, vaulted skylights—and densely crowded with hordes of people circumambulating in an endless promenade. Yet despite the mall's expansiveness, it elicited claustrophobia, sensory deprivation, and an unnerving disorientation. Everywhere I went I spied other pilgrims who had found, like me, that the straight way was lost and that the YOU ARE HERE landmarks on the map kiosks referred to nothing in particular.

6   Getting lost, feeling lost, being lost—these states of mind are intentional features of the mall's psychological terrain. There are, one notices, no clocks or windows, nothing to distract the shopper's psyche from the alternate reality the mall conjures. Here we are free to wander endlessly and to furtively watch our fellow wanderers, thousands upon thousands of milling strangers who have come with the intent of losing themselves in the mall's grand, stimulating design. For a few hours we share some common ground—a fantasy of infinite commodities and comforts—and then we drift apart forever. The mall exploits our acquisitive instincts without honoring our communal requirements, our eternal desire for discourse and intimacy, needs that until the twentieth century were traditionally met in our marketplaces but that are not met at all in giant shopping malls.

---

* The *Emerald City* and *Never-Never Land* are the exotic, imaginary destinations featured in *The Wizard of Oz* and *Peter Pan,* respectively.

7 On this evening a few thousand young people had descended on the mall in pursuit of alcohol and entertainment. They had come to Gators, Hooters, and Knuckleheads, Puzzles, Fat Tuesday, and Ltl Ditty's. At Players, a sports bar, the woman beside me introduced herself as "the pregnant wife of an Iowa pig farmer" and explained that she had driven five hours with friends to "do the mall party scene together." She left and was replaced by Kathleen from Minnetonka, who claimed to have "a real shopping thing—I can't go a week without buying new clothes. I'm not fulfilled until I buy something."

8   Later a woman named Laura arrived, with whom Kathleen was acquainted. "I *am* the mall," she announced ecstatically upon discovering I was a reporter. "I'd move in here if I could bring my dog," she added. "This place is heaven, it's a *mecca.*"

9   "We egg each other on," explained Kathleen, calmly puffing on a cigarette. "It's like, sort of, an addiction."

10   "You want the truth?" Laura asked. "I'm constantly suffering from megamall withdrawal. I come here all the time."

11   Kathleen: "It's a sickness, It's like cocaine or something; it's a drug."

12   Laura: "Kathleen's got this thing about buying, but I just need to *be* here. If I buy something it's an added bonus."

13   Kathleen: "She buys stuff all the time; don't listen."

14   Laura: "Seriously, I feel sorry for other malls. They're so small and *boring.*"

15   Kathleen seemed to think about this: "Richdale Mall," she blurted finally. She rolled her eyes and gestured with her cigarette. "Oh, my God, Laura. Why did we even *go* there?"

16 There is, of course, nothing naturally abhorrent in the human impulse to dwell in marketplaces or the urge to buy, sell, and trade. Rural Americans traditionally looked forward to the excitement and sensuality of market day; Native Americans traveled long distances to barter and trade at sprawling, festive encampments. In Persian bazaars and in the ancient Greek agoras the very soul of the community was preserved and could be seen, felt, heard, and smelled as it might be nowhere else. All over the planet the humblest of people have always gone to market with hope in their hearts and in expectation of something beyond mere goods—seeking a place where humanity is temporarily in ascendance, a palette for the senses, one another.

17   But the illicit possibilities of the marketplace also have long been acknowledged. The Persian bazaar was closed at sundown; the Greek agora was off-limits to those who had been charged with certain crimes. One myth of the Old West we still carry with us is that market day presupposes danger; the faithful were advised to make purchases quickly and repair without delay to the farm, lest their attraction to the pleasures of the marketplace erode their purity of spirit.

18   In our collective discourse the shopping mall appears with the tract house, the freeway, and the backyard barbecue as a product of the American postwar years, a testament to contemporary necessities and desires and an invention not only peculiarly American but peculiarly of our own era too. Yet the mall's varied and far-flung predecessors—the covered bazaars of the Middle East, the stately arcades of Victorian England, Italy's vaulted and skylit gallerias, Asia's

monsoon-protected urban markets—all suggest that the rituals of indoor shopping, although in their nuances not often like our own, are nevertheless broadly known. The late twentieth-century American contribution has been to transform the enclosed bazaar into an economic institution that is vastly profitable yet socially enervated, one that redefines in fundamental ways the human relationship to the marketplace. At the Mall of America—an extreme example—we discover ourselves thoroughly lost among strangers in a marketplace intentionally designed to serve no community needs.

19   In the strict sense the Mall of America is not a marketplace at all—the soul of a community expressed as a *place*—but rather a tourist attraction. Its promoters have peddled it to the world at large as something more profound than a local marketplace and as a destination with deep implications. "I believe we can make Mall of America stand for all of America," asserted the mall's general manager, John Wheeler, in a promotional video entitled *There's a Place for Fun in Your Life.* "I believe there's a shopper in all of us," added the director of marketing, Maureen Hooley. The mall has memorialized its opening-day proceedings by producing a celebratory videotape: Ray Charles singing "America the Beautiful," a laser show followed by fireworks, "The Star-Spangled Banner" and "The Stars and Stripes Forever," the Gatlin Brothers, and Peter Graves. "Mall of America . . . ," its narrator intoned. "The name alone conjures up images of greatness, of a retail complex so magnificent it could only happen in America."

20   Indeed, on the day the mall opened, Miss America visited. The mall's logo—a red, white, and blue star bisected by a red, white, and blue ribbon—decorated everything from the mall itself to coffee mugs and the flanks of buses. The idea, director of tourism Colleen Hayes told me, was to position America's largest mall as an institution on the scale of Disneyland or the Grand Canyon, a place simultaneously iconic and totemic, a revered symbol of the United States and a mecca to which the faithful would flock in pursuit of all things purchasable.

21 On Sunday I wandered the hallways of the pleasure dome with the sensation that I had entered an M.C. Escher drawing*—there was no such thing as up or down, and the escalators all ran backward. A 1993 Ford Probe GT was displayed as if popping out of a giant packing box; a full-size home, complete with artificial lawn, had been built in the mall's rotunda. At the Michael Ricker Pewter Gallery I came across a miniature tableau of a pewter dog peeing on a pewter man's leg; at Hologram Land I pondered 3-D hallucinations of the Medusa and Marilyn Monroe. I passed a kiosk called The Sportsman's Wife; I stood beside a life-size statue of the Hamm's Bear, carved out of pine and available for $1,395 at a store called Minnesot-ah! At Pueblo Spirit I examined a "dream catcher"— a small hoop made from deer sinew and willow twigs and designed to be hung over its owner's bed as a tactic for filtering bad dreams. For a while I sat in front of Glamour Shots and watched while women were groomed and brushed for photo sessions yielding high-fashion self-portraits at $34.95 each. There was no

---

* *M.C. Escher* (1898–1972) was a printmaker famous for images that confused viewers' perceptions of geometric space, making (for instance) finite walkways into infinite loops from which people could never exit. For examples of his work, go to <http://www.mcescher.com/> and select "Gallery."

stopping, no slowing down. I passed Mug Me, Queen for a Day, and Barnyard Buddies, and stood in the Brookstone store examining a catalogue: a gopher "eliminator" for $40 (it's a vibrating, anodized-aluminum stake), a "no-stoop" shoehorn for $10, a nose-hair trimmer for $18. At the arcade inside Knott's Camp Snoopy I watched while teenagers played Guardians of the 'Hood, Total Carnage, Final Fight, and Varth Operation Thunderstorm; a small crowd of them had gathered around a lean, cool character who stood calmly shooting video cowpokes in a game called Mad Dog McCree. Left thumb on his silver belt buckle, biceps pulsing, he banged away without remorse while dozens of his enemies crumpled and died in alleyways and dusty streets.

22   At Amazing Pictures a teenage boy had his photograph taken as a body-builder—his face smoothly grafted onto a rippling body—then proceeded to purchase this pleasing image on a poster, a sweatshirt, and a coffee mug. At Painted Tipi there was wild rice for sale, hand-harvested from Leech Lake, Minnesota. At Animalia I, came across a polyresin figurine of a turtle retailing for $3,200. At Bloomingdale's I pondered a denim shirt with its sleeves ripped away, the sort of thing available at used-clothing stores (the "grunge look," a Bloomingdale's employee explained), on sale for $125. Finally, at a gift shop in Knott's Camp Snoopy, I came across a game called Electronic Mall Madness, put out by Milton Bradley. On the box, three twelve-year-old girls with good features happily vied to beat one another to the game-board mall's best sales.

23   At last I achieved an enforced self-arrest, anchoring myself against a bench while the mall tilted on its axis. Two pubescent girls in retainers and braces sat beside me sipping coffees topped with whipped cream and chocolate sprinkles, their shopping bags gathered tightly around their legs, their eyes fixed on the passing crowds. They came, they said, from Shakopee—"It's nowhere," one of them explained. The megamall, she added, was "a buzz at first, but now it seems pretty normal. 'Cept my parents are like Twenty Questions every time I want to come here. 'Specially since the shooting."

24   On a Sunday night, she elaborated, three people had been wounded when shots were fired in a dispute over a San Jose Sharks jacket. "In the *mall*," her friend reminded me. "Right here at megamall. A shooting."

25   "It's like nowhere's safe," the first added.

26   They sipped their coffees and explicated for me the plot of a film they saw as relevant, a horror movie called *Dawn of the Dead,* which they had each viewed a half-dozen times. In the film, they explained, apocalypse had come, and the survivors had repaired to a shopping mall as the most likely place to make their last stand in a poisoned, impossible world. And this would have been perfectly all right, they insisted, except that the place had also attracted hordes of the infamous living dead—sentient corpses who had not relinquished their attraction to indoor shopping.

27   I moved on and contemplated a computerized cash register in the infant's section of the Nordstrom store: "The Answer Is Yes!!!" its monitor reminded clerks. "Customer Service Is Our Number One Priority!" Then back at Bloomingdale's I contemplated a bank of televisions playing incessantly an advertisement for Egoïste, a men's cologne from Chanel. In the ad a woman on a wrought-iron balcony tossed her black hair about and screamed long and passionately; then there were many women screaming passionately, too, and

throwing balcony shutters open and closed, and this was all followed by a bottle of the cologne displayed where I could get a good look at it. The brief, strange drama repeated itself until I could no longer stand it.

. . .

28 On Valentine's Day last February—cashing in on the promotional scheme of a local radio station—ninety-two couples were married en masse in a ceremony at the Mall of America. They rode the roller coaster and the Screaming Yellow Eagle and were photographed beside a frolicking Snoopy, who wore an immaculate tuxedo. "As we stand here together at the Mall of America," presiding district judge Richard Spicer declared, "we are reminded that there is a place for fun in your life and you have found it in each other." Six months earlier, the Reverend Leith Anderson of the Wooddale Church in Eden Prairie conducted services in the mall's rotunda. Six thousand people had congregated by 10:00 A.M., and Reverend Anderson delivered a sermon entitled "The Unknown God of the Mall." Characterizing the mall as a "direct descendant" of the ancient Greek agoras, the reverend pointed out that, like the Greeks before us, we Americans have many gods. Afterward, of course, the flock went shopping, much to the chagrin of Reverend Delton Krueger, president of the Mall Area Religious Council, who told the *Minneapolis Star Tribune* that as a site for church services, the mall may trivialize religion. "A good many people in the churches," said Krueger, "feel a lot of the trouble in the world is because of materialism."

29 But a good many people in the mall business today apparently think the trouble lies elsewhere. They are moving forward aggressively on the premise that the dawning era of electronic shopping does not preclude the building of shopping-and-pleasure palaces all around the globe. Japanese developers, in a joint venture with the [developers of Canada's West Edmonton Mall], are planning a $400 million Mall of Japan, with an ice rink, a water park, a fantasy-theme hotel, three breweries, waterfalls, and a sports center. We might shortly predict, too, a Mall of Europe, a Mall of New England, a Mall of California, and perhaps even a Mall of the World. The concept of shopping in a frivolous atmosphere, concocted to loosen consumers' wallets, is poised to proliferate globally. We will soon see monster malls everywhere, rooted in the soil of every nation and offering a preposterous, impossible variety of commodities and entertainments.

30   The new malls will be planets unto themselves, closed off from this world in the manner of space stations or of science fiction's underground cities. Like the Mall of America and West Edmonton Mall—prototypes for a new generation of shopping centers—they will project a separate and distinct reality in which an "outdoor café" is not outdoors, a "bubbling brook" is a concrete watercourse, and a "serpentine street" is a hallway. Safe, surreal, and outside of time and space, they will offer the mind a potent dreamscape from which there is no present waking. This carefully controlled fantasy—now operable in Minnesota—is so powerful as to inspire psychological addiction or to elicit in visitors a catatonic obsession with the mall's various hallucinations. The new malls will be theatrical, high-tech illusions capable of attracting enormous crowds from distant points and foreign ports.

Their psychology has not yet been tried pervasively on the scale of the Mall of America, nor has it been perfected. But in time our marketplaces, all over the world, will be in essential ways interchangeable, so thoroughly divorced from the communities in which they sit that they will appear to rest like permanently docked spaceships against the landscape, windowless and turned in upon their own affairs. The affluent will travel as tourists to each, visiting the holy sites and taking photographs in the catacombs of far-flung temples.

31   Just as Victorian England is acutely revealed beneath the grandiose domes of its overwrought train stations, so is contemporary America well understood from the upper vistas of its shopping malls, places without either windows or clocks where the temperature is forever seventy degrees. It is facile to believe, from this vantage point, that the endless circumambulations of tens of thousands of strangers—all loaded down with the detritus of commerce—resemble anything akin to community. The shopping mall is not, as the architecture critic Witold Rybczynski has concluded, "poised to become a real urban place" with "a variety of commercial and noncommercial functions." On the contrary, it is poised to multiply around the world as an institution offering only a desolate substitute for the rich, communal lifeblood of the traditional marketplace, which will not survive its onslaught.

32   Standing on the Mall of America's roof, where I had ventured to inspect its massive ventilation units, I finally achieved a full sense of its vastness, of how it overwhelmed the surrounding terrain—the last sheep farm in sight, the Mississippi River incidental in the distance. Then I peered through the skylights down into Camp Snoopy, where throngs of my fellow citizens caroused happily in the vast entrails of the beast.

Review Questions

1. According to Guterson, what is one key difference between shopping places of old and modern malls?
2. What is the difference between a marketplace and a tourist attraction?
3. What has been America's "contribution" to the closed bazaar, according to Guterson?
4. Reread paragraphs 7–15, in which Guterson reports on an interview he conducted with several mall patrons. Characterize these interviewees. Why does Guterson include these conversations in the article? What point is he making (indirectly)?
5. Reread paragraphs 21–22, in which Guterson relates his experiences wandering "the hallways of the pleasure dome." By the end of paragraph 22, what impression has he created?
6. What predictions does Guterson make concerning modern mega-malls?

Discussion and Writing Suggestions

1. Having read Guterson's article, reflect for a moment on his title: "Enclosed. Encyclopedic. Endured." What do each of these words mean in relation to the article?

2. Guterson opens this article by citing some of the Mall of America's vital statistics. What effect do these statistics have on you?

3. Guterson makes a judgment in this selection about the Mall of America and, more broadly, about American culture. What is this judgment? As evidence for your answer, cite three or four sentences.

4. In paragraph 4, Guterson writes that the building of the Mall of America as a tourist attraction "raise[s] provocative questions, for our architecture testifies to our view of ourselves and to the condition of our souls." In paragraph 31 he makes a similar point, referring to Victorian England's nineteenth-century train stations. Explain Guterson's connection between architecture and the broader culture.

5. In paragraph 5, Guterson refers to fellow shoppers at the Mall of America as "other pilgrims." Speculate on his use of "pilgrims." Why does he not simply refer to these people as "shoppers"?

6. In paragraph 16, Guterson writes: "All over the planet the humblest of people have always gone to market with hope in their hearts and in expectation of something beyond mere goods—seeking a place where humanity is temporarily in ascendance." What does he mean? Is this your hope in going to the mall?

7. Guterson devotes paragraph 26 to a summary of the movie *Dawn of the Dead.* Speculate on his reasons for including the summary in this article.

**The Shopping Mall
as Sacred Space**
Ira Zepp, Jr.

A professor emeritus of Religious Studies at Western Maryland College, Ira Zepp, Jr. has written what a book reviewer for the Los Angeles Times *calls a "profound and refreshing work that allows us to see a common place of contemporary life in an utterly unexpected way."* The New Religious Image of Urban America: The Shopping Mall as Ceremonial Center *(2nd ed., University Press of Colorado, 1997) examines the mall as a type of architecturally spiritual place that "centers" and orders the world, much as cathedrals do. It will be a stretch for some to regard the mall as a place to go to restore spiritual order; but Zepp is persuasive, grounding his argument in scholarship and in a rich, cross-cultural understanding of spiritual practices. You just may find yourself convinced.*

1 I believe one of the reasons malls have grown rapidly and their popularity increased is that they fulfill our need for order and orientation. Malling means centering. Yin-Fu Tuan, professor of geography at the University of Minnesota, says that "to be livable, nature and society must show order and display a harmonious relationship."[1] Or as philosopher of religion Paul Tillich said, we seek to "unify multiplicity."

The Nature of the Center

2 A theoretical framework from religious studies helps explain people's fondness for centeredness.* Human beings have always tried to center their lives and their world. Returning to the center has been a universal tendency, whether that center be a family reunion, a hometown, a native land, or a religious center such as Rome or Jerusalem.

3   This human propensity to design centers is illustrated by the prevalence of both circular construction and construction using such related shapes as hexagons, octagons, squares, and crosses. These geometric expressions reflect that same reality and have the same purpose: to incorporate all the dimensions of the earth—north, south, east, and west—the four corners of the world and the cardinal points of the compass.

4   The number four, incidentally, was a sacred number for many Native Americans precisely because of its all-embracing nature. The Native American shaman, Black Elk, observed that much of Indian activity—from drawing to dancing, to building their homes, whether tepee, hogan, or igloo—was done in a circle. The social and religious meeting place for the Navaho, a structure which connects this world with its place of origin, is the round ceremonial center called *kiva*.

5   This circular and cyclical activity was a reflection of the "power of the world" which worked in circles also; for example, the wind whirls, the seasons cycle, birds often fly concentrically, the sun and moon (both round) go and come in a circle. Everything tries to be round. The circularity of space for the Native American is also symbolized in the sacred hoop and the desire of every tribal member is to keep the hoop unbroken.

6   The inclusiveness of circular design echoes how we experience the world and perceive reality. These circles, squares, and crosses are a way of saying that the universe and, finally, our lives are symmetrical, well regulated, ordered, and under control.

7   The quadrilateral symbol, in whatever form, is a miniaturization of the world, a microcosm, a small picture of how we understand the larger universe to be. By this propensity to center, we are telling ourselves life is integrated and whole.

8   Centers are not only measured spatially and mathematically, they can be existential as well. The Quakers begin their silent meditation with the phrase "centering down"—that is, becoming stable, anchored, "together," to more easily get in touch with the cosmic center, the sources of stability and peace.

---

* It will be obvious to many readers that the following discussion is dependent on the seminal works of Mircea Eliade and Paul Wheatley. Their contributions to the history of religions and human geography, respectively, are indispensable.

9   Communities have always centered themselves. Sometimes they have a functional center, as in many towns and villages laid out in the nineteenth-century, where there is a literal meeting of the quadrants at the town center. For example, you cannot avoid them if you drive through Harvard Square in Cambridge, Massachusetts or Gettysburg, Pennsylvania.

10   Other communities have ritual or ceremonial centers, such as parks, groves, or recreational areas. In religious studies we call such an area an axis mundi, the axle or pole around which our world turns and without which our world would collapse. These areas are indispensable to our personal and communal life. These centers are either built as a result of a hierophany (manifestation of the holy) or by ritual construction. Shopping malls are examples of the latter—what Mircea Eliade, the renowned religious historian at the University of Chicago, calls "mythic geometry."

11   The geometric designs in the mall also tell a story about how we ultimately understand the world to be; they are a replication of the larger planet. We have said by this paradigmatic structure that our experience of the world is one of balance and harmony. We have traveled to the "center" and discovered unity.

12   Carl Jung, the famous Swiss psychologist, calls the circle an archetype, an original image found in the collective unconscious of humankind. The pictures precede obviously the formulation and foundation of the living religions, but have appropriated these designs for their symbolic art and much of the architecture of their house of worship; for example, Buddhist stupas, Islamic mosques, Christian cathedrals, and Jewish temples and synagogues. Secular versions would be the Athenian agora, the Roman forum, the Mexican zocala, and the Middle Eastern bazaar.

13   The nature of the center gives us a clue to why so much human activity, from children's games to religious art and architecture to shopping malls, is expressed by circularity.

14   By applying the typology of Wheatley's and Eliade's "mythic geometry" to malls, we find a remarkable conformity and similarity between the design of the average mall and their models of sacred space.

Center as Source of Power

15 The number of people who gravitate to them indicate that centers are places of empowerment. Travelers, pilgrims, tourists, and shoppers departing from a center, find themselves renewed and strengthened as a result of the energy found there. Even if physically exhausted, their spirits are uplifted.

16   The axis mundi—whether it be a state capital, a religious shrine, or a mall as the social and shopping center of a community—becomes, to paraphrase Wheatley, "the pivot of ontological transition at which divine power enters the world and diffuses through wider territory."[2]

17   In this reduced version of the world, in this cosmos on a small scale where all life—human and natural—meet, you experience power coming from six directions: the four cardinal points of the compass and the zenith and nadir. To use Wheatley's graphic phrase, it is "an architectural evocation of an axis mundi."

18   Wheatley suggests that it is through such a center of the world that cosmic power enters and is spread throughout the country. This diffusion of energy binds "periphery and center, province and capital, dependencies and metropolitan territory."[3] This dissemination of power also established a unity of time and space. A community sense was created and maintained.

19   Paul Wheatley has abundant evidence in his *Pivot of the Four Quarters* that one reason gateways to traditional communities were large and ostentatious, out of all proportion to their function, was that power flowed out of the center through these entrances at the cardinal points.

20   Mall entrances, reflecting other significant centers of power, are often quite impressive. Their distinctiveness serves more than aesthetic, decorative, or functional purposes.

21   It is also interesting to watch the mall's capacity to balance centripetal and centrifugal forces. People are obviously drawn to this center and, just as effectively, the center delivers them back to the world with newly acquired treasures and relationships, if not a new sense of well-being.

22   When we are at the center, we can get our bearing, orient ourselves again, and find our way out of life's disorders. We discover at the center a source of power; this mirror of the universe concentrates the generally available dynamism.

23   Even in the midst of crowds, people are aware that a degree of renewal is taking place. Malls, at their centers, strive to be places of vitality and energy.

24   Consequently, it is not accidental that most places we call centers attempt to re-invigorate or recharge human energy. At both the personal and social levels, we find communities making such sources of power available.

25   This idea is ingrained in our language: New Windsor Conference Center, Baltimore Civic Center, Washington Heights Medical Center, Carroll County Agricultural Center, Aberdeen Shopping Center, Adams County Senior Center, Harford Recreational Center, Hagerstown Counseling Center, any number of college student centers, and religious worship centers. And so it goes. We find the concept of "center" an appropriate description for a place of human empowerment, a group of people who deliver social services, and an organization whose purpose is to help, heal, or otherwise improve the world.

26   This is undoubtedly what mall developer James Rouse* has in mind when he uses the concept of center. His speeches and essays are replete with references to "center." He refers to the "design of the center," the "quality of the center," "little details of the center," and to "our center." Whatever else Rouse intends to convey, it is the human aspect of the center he wants to emphasize.

27   The center was originally understood to be where God and people and heaven and earth were connected. And power was generated there. We all know examples of these centers: the sacred mountains of Sinai and Zion, the cities of Benares and Mecca, the temples of St. Peter's in Rome and the

---

* Developer *James Rouse* (1915–1986) ranks as a legendary figure among 20th-century American urban planners. At various points in his career, he built shopping malls; a comprehensively planned suburban community (Columbia, MD) that he hoped would correct the "sterility" of the suburbs; and festival marketplaces (including Fanueil Hall in Boston and South Street Sea Port in New York) in an effort to revive depressed urban areas. He later created a foundation to address problems of affordable housing.

Mormons in Salt Lake City, Utah. Church altars, dining room tables, and scholars' desks can also be center of the sacred.

28   Such centers act as magnets. Their attractiveness is in direct proportion to the power and meaning we find there. We make regular pilgrimages to these special places to regain our identity, and to be reconnected, which, as I mentioned earlier, is the meaning of *re-ligare* (religion).

Center as Celestial Echo

29 Primitive people from Polynesia to Egypt to the British Isles were very careful in the construction of their centers. They found it extremely important to have, as a base for their center, a celestial or transcendent reference point and pattern. Eliade stresses there was usually some celestial archetype which provided a model for our earthly building and temporal construction, which would act as an axis mundi. And this other-worldly or heavenly counterpart would represent the true and authentic world. The heavenly Jerusalem, the historical Jerusalem, and the coming Jerusalem are all reflections of a city already found in the mind of God.

30   Eliade summarizes the inclination we have to reflect transcendent patterns in the construction of centers:

> Man constructs according to an archetype. Not only do his city and his temple have celestial models, the same is true of the entire region that he inhabits, with the rivers that water it, the fields that give him his food, etc. The map of Babylon shows the city at the center of a vast circular territory bordered by a river, precisely as the Sumerian envisaged Paradise. This participation by urban culture in an archetypal model is what gives them their reality and validity.[4]

In one form or another, heavenly models are reflected in earthly circularity.

31   Even the political centers of Paris, Washington, D.C., and the centers (circuses) of London are further examples. It is true, as well, of Dante's celestial rose, the thousand-petaled Lotus of Buddhism, and the Tibetan Mandala.*

32   The design and layout of most modern shopping malls is a "secular" version of this ancient prototype. Many malls are built in the form of a cross, with all paths leading to the center. The cross here is, of course, not the Christian cross or a sectarian image. It is fundamentally a human image, for it is another way of drawing a circle.

---

* *Dante's celestial rose, the thousand-petaled Lotus of Buddhism,* and *the Tibetan Mandala* are all religious symbols involving circles and "centeredness," as Zepp puts it. In the third book of Dante's *Divine Comedy, The Paradiso,* Dante ascends to the tenth and final heaven and, in a mystical vision, encounters an emanation of God's love represented in a series of circles in the center of which is a cross--and in the cross, a blooming rose. The *Lotus* in *Buddhism* is said to symbolize a person seeking enlightenment. With roots that grow in murky water (self-ignorance), the Lotus plant sends a shoot upward, through darkness, toward the light (enlightenment)--at which point, nourished by the sun and air, it blossoms. Seen from above, the Lotus blossom appears as a series of nested cups, or circles, of petals at the center of which can be found the seeds. Each part of the flower, and plant, is related to a teaching in the Buddhist tradition. The *Tibetan Mandala* is a form of impermanent religious art that serves as part of Tibetan Buddhist meditation practice. Sometimes made of colored sand, they are arranged as a series of intersecting circles along a central axis.

FIGURE 7.2   Rose Window. Painton Cowen says that "every rose window is a symbol and image of the Creation and the created universe." Chartres' famous rose window is a triumph of geometry—an idealized model of the universe— circles within circles. Periphery and center are clearly depicted here. Dante's celestial rose and Buddha's thousand-petaled lotus are variations of this pattern. Photo of South Rose Window at Chartres, Paul Almasy/Corbis.

33   Knowing the frequency of circular patterns is more important than whether we know the engineer or architect's conscious and unconscious motivations for them. Circles in public buildings are symbols of welcome and inclusiveness, a way to make our non-private space more humanly accessible. The function of cardinal axiology, says Wheatley, is to assimilate and bring together all the surrounding ter- ritory—which is to say that the entire world meets in the center of every mall.

34   This sacred geometry can be seen in a representative sample of mall floor plans, gathered from across the country. And even in the malls which do not have a symmetrical design, a balance and harmony can be discerned in spite of the offcenteredness. White Flint Mall in Rockville, Maryland, is an example of this.

35   If there is not a pronounced interaction at the center of the mall as in Lancaster, Pennsylvania's Park City and Long Island's Smith Haven Mall, there may be a long corridor between rows of shops. In the center of the corridor may be a series of pools or flower gardens surrounded by trees and benches. Tampa Bay Center in Florida is a good illustration of this pattern. Or, in the absence of a large visible center, smaller centers (crosses or circles) may be placed inter- mittently along the walkway.

FIGURE 7.3 Park City, *Lancaster, PA.* This mall reflects the many circles of a rose window, the quadrilateral design of a mandala, and the floor plan of typical cathedral or basilica. The center in this mall is inescapable.

Center as Sign of Order

36 As humans we have a profound need to repudiate, if not escape, the disorder and brokenness of life, and to establish islands of stability as a counterpoint to chaos. The creation of a center is usually the way people resist disorder. We always seem to be in the process of ordering (cosmicizing)—that is, making a whole (cosmos) out of disintegration (chaos). Indeed, the words for world in Latin (*cosmos*) and in German (*Welt*) suggest that in this place life is ordered by meaning and purpose. It is a uni-verse.

37 Practical activities, even the routine operation of a shopping mall, take second place to our need to see ourselves related appropriately to our environment. The so-called practical activities may offend the gods or spirits of nature unless they are perceived to have their roles in a coherent world system.[5]

38 We could not live long in an asymmetrical, chaotic community. Jung wrote an excellent monograph entitled *The Mandala. Mandala* is the Sanskrit word for a circle, divided into four separate, equal sections. It is really a symbol of the universe and Jung said that it is also a picture of the self. He discovered, in his

clinical practice, that people of all ages who were emotionally disturbed or who were undergoing a certain degree of trauma, would often draw circular designs, presumably to reassure themselves that life is not radically ruptured. The innocent activity of our doodling often takes the shape of circles. At every level of human experience, the center must hold.

39   The re-creation of a center establishes order amidst chaos, serenity in turbulence, unity out of disparity, wholeness out of brokenness. The center, with all the paths leading to the middle, is a replication of the primordial world in all its harmony and pristine order.

40   Out of the disorder of the city and the disease of the suburbs arises the shopping mall and its perceived symmetry and tranquility. People come to this center feeling isolated, lonely, and anonymous. They need to be at ease, to belong, to center themselves again. Chaos will be cosmicized. Disorder will be ordered.

41   Again, the mathematical balance, so frequently found in malls, is a way of reinforcing that the world is ultimately safe. The enclosure, combined with architectural balance, engenders the sense of safety many people claim they find in the mall.

42   Wheatley, in his extraordinary study on urban communities—construction from Mexico to Burma—has shown how order integrates space at several significant levels, e.g., global (cosmic), state (political), capital (ceremonial), and temple (ritual).[6] I want to add to this list of levels the shopping mall, a combination of the ceremonial and the ritual. As a result of their centered nature, their capacity to reveal and to communicate stability, malls juxtapose themselves to the mundane world outside. The outside world's profane dimension, according to Eliade, has no mythical meaning, is not invested with prestige, and lacks an exemplary model.[7] Or as John E. Smith, head of the philosophy department of Yale University, says, "The profane stands over against the holy, not because it is sordid or 'unclean,' but because it is ordinary and harbors no mystery, nor calls forth the sense that beyond and beneath our life is a holy ground."

43   To the extent that the mall is space discontinuous from the trivial, ordinary world, it is understood to be potentially sacred. The sacred is always more real than the profane and therefore more powerful than the ordinary world. As Eliade says in his *Sacred and Profane,* whatever is designated as sacred participates in and releases power. This power, in turn, puts us next to reality, which is tantamount to Being itself. This archaic ontology is reflected in the design of most malls and experienced by those for whom the mall is "more than" a collection of shops. There is a sense in which the mall is a space thought to be more real, vital, and energizing than the run-of-the-mill pragmatic world beyond it.

44   Perhaps this is why there is within us a "nostalgia for paradise" (Eliade), a longing for the village, a yearning for home or hometown, where life was more real and animated. This "more than" characteristic is perceived in malls and presents us with a sense of welcome, stability, and centeredness in which we can share vicariously.

45   Many shopping malls, as the foregoing reveals, are designed to repeat a cosmogony, that is, to re-create an ordered world. This is not to be taken lightly. As intellectual and social historian Eric Voegelin says, "The analogical repetition is not an act of futile imitation, for in repeating the cosmos man participates, in the measure allowed to his existential limitations, in the creation of cosmic order itself."[8]

46   So the mall attempts to make the world a whole, to have it integrated, habitable, safe, and balanced. Eliade, from a lifetime of studying the human fascination with the sacred, concludes: "To the degree that ancient holy places, temples or altars lose their religious efficacy, people discover and apply other geomantic architecture or iconographic formulas which, in the end, sometimes astonishingly enough represent the same symbolism of the 'Center.'"[9]

47   I contend that the mall represents, for many contemporary people, a substitute for those ancient sacred centers. If churches, schools, and families (our three major institutions) fail us, we will seek other places to fulfill basic human needs. It is not accidental, therefore, that malls contain the same structures, objects, and symbols which gave ancient centers their rich human meaning. For, as Eliade emphasizes, "images, symbols, and myths are not irresponsible creations of the psyche; they respond to a need and fulfill a function, that of bringing to light the most hidden modalities of being. Consequently, the study of them enables us to reach a better understanding of man—of man 'as he is.'"[10]

Notes

1. Tuan, Yi-Fu, *Space and Place: The Perspective of Experience,* Minneapolis: University of Minnesota Press, 1977, p. 88.

2. Wheatley, Paul, *The Pivot of the Four Quarters,* Chicago: Aldine Publishing Co., 1972, p. 434.

3. *Ibid.,* p. 68.

4. Eliade, Mircea, *Cosmos and History: The Myth of the Eternal Return.* Trans. by William R. Trask. New York: Harper and Row Torchbook, 1959, p. 10.

5. Tuan, p. 88.

6. Wheatley, p. 53.

7. Eliade, p. 28.

8. Quoted in Wheatley, p. 57.

9. Eliade, Mircea, *Images and Symbols: Studies in Religious Symbolism,* New York: Sheed and Ward, 1969, p. 52.

10. Eliade, p. 12.

Review Questions

1. What is a "center" in the sacred sense that Zepp uses it?
2. Where do we find examples of centers both in religious and nonreligious settings?
3. What is the *axis mundi?*
4. Why, in the view of religious historian Paul Wheatley, are centers powerful places?
5. Why are malls often laid out as a cross?

6. According to Zepp, how can structures transmit the power of a center even if their architects do not consciously conceive of their designs as having cosmic significance?

7. Why do we seek out centers? In what sense can the mall as a cent be considered sacred space?

Discussion and Writing Suggestions

1. Does the fact that shopping malls, like cathedrals, mosques, and synagogues, have centers persuade you that the purpose of "the center" in each setting is the same?

2. In paragraph 22, Zepp writes: "When we are at the center, we can get our bearing, orient ourselves again, and find our way out of life's disorders. We discover at the center a source of power." Have you ever felt energized or uplifted as a result of visiting the mall? Put another way, does the prospect of going to a mall excite you? At the mall is there any sense in which you find your bearings or renew your energy?

3. Trace how Zepp uses the work of religious scholars Wheatley and Eliade to advance his analysis that malls are sacred space.

4. In his final paragraph, Zepp writes: "I contend that the mall represents, for many contemporary people, a substitute for . . . ancient sacred centers." Read the rest of paragraph 47 and determine the extent to which you feel Zepp has made a compelling case. Are you convinced that shopping centers, quite aside from their status as places where you can buy things, meet a fundamental human need?

5. Write a dialogue between you and an adult relative about your going to the mall to hang out with friends. Your relative prefers that you don't. Try using Zepp's arguments in the dialogue. What will be your relative's response?

From Town Center to Shopping Center
Lizabeth Cohen

In the following article, which appeared in the American Historical Review *(October 1996), Lizabeth Cohen traces the "restructuring of the consumer marketplace" that followed America's population shift to the suburbs after World War II. Millions of people who had lived in the cities, walking to the corner store, faced an entirely new experience as shoppers once they moved to the suburbs. In their new homes, a trip to the store meant a ride in the car, likely to a shopping center where relations between store owner and customer had fundamentally changed. Cohen, a professor of history at New York University, studies the effects*

that the new mass-consumption society had on America. You will see that she identifies two developments, relating to segregation and free speech, that threaten our general welfare.

1   When the editors of *Time* Magazine set out to tell readers in an early January 1965 cover story why the American economy had flourished during the previous year, they explained it in terms that had become the conventional wisdom of postwar America. The most prosperous twelve months ever, capping the country's fourth straight year of economic expansion, were attributable to the American consumer, "who continued spending as if there were no tomorrow." According to *Time*'s economics lesson, consumers, business, and government "created a nonvicious circle: spending created more production, production created wealth, wealth created more spending." In this simplified Keynesian* model of economic growth, "the consumer is the key to our economy." As R. H. Macy's board chair Jack Straus explained to *Time*'s readers, "When the country has a recession, it suffers not so much from problems of production as from problems of consumption." And in prosperous times like today, "Our economy keeps growing because our ability to consume is endless. The consumer goes on spending regardless of how many possessions he has. The luxuries of today are the necessities of tomorrow." A demand economy built on mass consumption had brought the United States out of the doldrums of the Great Depression and World War II, and its strength in the postwar period continued to impress those like retail magnate Straus whose own financial future depended on it.[1]

2   Although Straus and his peers invested great energy and resources in developing new strategies for doing business in this mass-consumption economy, historians have paid far less attention to the restructuring of American commercial life in the postwar period than to the transformation of residential experience. An impressive literature documents the way the expansion of a mass consumer society encouraged a larger and broader spectrum of Americans to move into suburban communities after the war.[2] Between 1947 and 1953 alone, the suburban population increased by 43 percent, in contrast to a general population increase of only 11 percent.[3] At an astonishing pace, the futuristic highways and mass-built, appliance-equipped, single-family homes that had been previewed at the New York World's Fair in 1939–1940 seemed to become a reality. Thanks to a shortage in urban housing, government subsidies in highway building and home construction or purchase, and pent-up consumer demand and savings, a new residential landscape began to take shape in metropolitan areas, with large numbers of people commuting into cities for work and then back to homes in the suburbs. (Increasingly as the postwar era progressed, suburbanites worked, not just lived, outside cities.)

3   Less explored by historians and slower to develop historically was the restructuring of the consumer marketplace that accompanied the suburbanization of residential life. New suburbanites who had themselves grown up in urban

---

* *John Maynard Keynes* (1883–1946) was an influential British economist for whom a school of economics (Keynesian) was named. Keynes advocated government intervention in the boom-and-bust business cycles of capitalism—especially in downturns, when government stimulus packages can lessen the effects of unemployment.

neighborhoods walki
downtown were nov
ambitious suburban t
stores into their plans. In t
district at the core of the reside
war planned community of Radbu
centers, such as Kansas City's Country
dents, and their descendents in early pos
Illinois, Levittown, New York, and Bergenfield, N
ture of the old-style urban community, where shop
space at the settlement's core and residences spread ou
most new suburban home developers made no effort to pro
commercial needs. Rather, suburbanites were expected to fend fo
by driving to the existing "market towns," which often offered the on
merce for miles, or by returning to the city to shop. Faced with slim retail o
ings nearby, many new suburbanites of the 1940s and 1950s continued to
depend on the city for major purchases, making do with the small, locally
owned commercial outlets in neighboring towns only for minor needs.

4   It would not be until the mid-1950s that a new market structure appropriate
to this suburbanized, mass-consumption society prevailed. Important precedents existed in the branch department stores and prototypical shopping centers constructed between the 1920s and 1940s in outlying city neighborhoods
and in older suburban communities, which began the process of decentralizing
retail dollars away from downtown. But now the scale was much larger. Even
more significant, the absence or inadequacy of town centers at a time of enormous suburban population growth offered commercial developers a unique
opportunity to reimagine community life with their private projects at its heart.[5]

5   By the early 1950s, large merchandisers were aggressively reaching out to
the new suburbanites, whose buying power was even greater than their numbers.[6] The 30 million people that *Fortune* magazine counted as suburban residents in 1953 represented 19 percent of the U.S. population but 29 percent
of its income. They had higher median incomes and homeownership rates, as
well as more children fourteen and under than the rest of the metropolitan
population, all indicators of high consumption.

6   Merchandisers also realized that postwar suburbanites were finally living the
motorized existence that had been predicted for American society since the
1920s. As consumers became dependent on, virtually inseparable from, their
cars, traffic congestion and parking problems discouraged commercial expansion in central business districts of cities and smaller market towns, already hin-
dered by a short supply of developable space.[7] Reaching out to suburbanites
where they lived, merchandisers at first built stores along the new highways,
in commercial "strips" that consumers could easily reach by car. By the mid-
1950s, however, commercial developers—many of whom owned department
stores—were constructing a new kind of marketplace, the regional shopping
center aimed at satisfying suburbanites' consumption *and* community needs.
Strategically located at highway intersections or along the busiest thoroughfares,
the regional shopping center attracted patrons living within half an hour's drive,

dant lots provided, and then proceed ~~~ ome bus service as well). Here was the ~~~ on of how community space should be con- ~~~ ciety built on mass consumption. Well-designed ~~~ would provide the ideal core for a settlement that ~~~ nodes off of major roadways rather than concentric ~~~ as in cities and earlier suburban communities. After ~~~ months in the late 1950s visiting these "modern-day down- ~~~ 's Wear Daily columnist Samuel Feinberg was moved to invoke ~~~ ens's proclamation on his return from the Soviet Union in the ~~~ have seen the future and it works." [8]

ıs essay will analyze the larger social and political implications of the shift community marketplace from town center to shopping center. Although I draw on national evidence, I pay special attention to the case of Paramus, New Jersey, a postwar suburb seven miles from the George Washington Bridge that sprouted virtually overnight in the vegetable fields of Bergen County and became the home of the largest shopping complex in the country by the end of 1957.[9] Within six months, R. H. Macy's Garden State Plaza and Allied Stores Corporation's Bergen Mall opened three quarters of a mile from each other at the intersection of Routes 4, 17, and the soon-to-be-completed Garden State Parkway. Both department store managements had independently recognized the enormous commercial potential of Bergen and Passaic counties; although the George Washington Bridge connected the area to Manhattan in 1931, the Depression and the war postponed major housing construction until the late 1940s. By 1960, each shopping center had two to three department stores as anchors (distinguishing it from many pre-war projects built around a single anchor), surrounded by fifty to seventy smaller stores. Attracting half a million patrons a week, these shopping centers dominated retail trade in the region.[10]

8   The Paramus malls have special significance because of their location adjacent to the wealthiest and busiest central business district in the nation. If these malls could prosper in the shadow of Manhattan, the success of their counterparts elsewhere should come as no surprise. Moreover, the Paramus case illuminates [two] major effects of shifting marketplaces on postwar American community life: in commercializing public space, they brought to community life the market segmentation that increasingly shaped commerce; [and] in privatizing public space, they privileged the rights of private property owners over citizens' traditional rights of free speech in community forums.

. . .

9   When planners and shopping-center developers envisioned [a] new kind of consumption-oriented community center in the 1950s, they set out to perfect the concept of downtown, not to obliterate it, even though their projects directly challenged the viability of existing commercial centers such as Hackensack, the political and commercial seat of Bergen County. It is easy to overlook this visionary dimension and focus only on the obvious commercial motives developers and investors shared. Of course, developers, department stores, and big investors such as insurance companies (who leapt at the promise of a huge return on the vast amounts of capital they controlled) were pursuing the enormous potential for profit in shopping-center development.[11] But they also

believed that they were participating in a rationalization of consumption community no less significant than the way highways were improving portation or tract developments were delivering mass housing.

10   The ideal was still the creation of centrally located public space that brought together commercial and civic activity. Victor Gruen, one of the most prominent and articulate shopping-center developers, spoke for many others when he argued that shopping centers offered to dispersed suburban populations "crystallization points for suburbia's community life." "By affording opportunities for social life and recreation in a protected pedestrian environment, by incorporating civic and educational facilities, shopping centers can fill an existing void."[12] Not only did Gruen and others promote the construction of community centers in the atomized landscape of suburbia, but in appearance their earliest shopping centers idealized—almost romanticized—the physical plan of the traditional downtown shopping street, with stores lining both sides of an open-air pedestrian walkway that was landscaped and equipped with benches.[13]

11   While bringing many of the best qualities of urban life to the suburbs, these new "shopping towns," as Gruen called them, also sought to overcome the "anarchy and ugliness" characteristic of many American cities. A centrally owned and managed Garden State Plaza or Bergen Mall, it was argued, offered an alternative model to the inefficiencies, visual chaos, and provinciality of traditional downtown districts. A centralized administration made possible the perfect mix and "scientific" placement of stores, meeting customers' diverse needs and maximizing store owners' profits. Management kept control visually by standardizing all architectural and graphic design and politically by requiring all tenants to participate in the tenants' association. Common complaints of downtown shoppers were directly addressed: parking was plentiful, safety was ensured by hired security guards, delivery tunnels and loading courts kept truck traffic away from shoppers, canopied walks and air-conditioned stores made shopping comfortable year 'round, piped-in background music replaced the cacophony of the street. The preponderance of chains and franchises over local stores, required by big investors such as insurance companies, brought shoppers the latest national trends in products and merchandising techniques. B. Earl Puckett, Allied Stores' board chair, boasted that Paramus's model shopping centers were making it "one of the first preplanned major cities in America."[14] What made this new market structure so unique and appealing to businessmen like Puckett was that it encouraged social innovation while maximizing profit.

12   Garden State Plaza and Bergen Mall provide good models for how shopping centers of the 1950s followed Gruen's prescription and became more than miscellaneous collections of stores. As central sites of consumption, they offered the full range of businesses and services that one would previously have sought downtown. They not only sold the usual clothing and shoes in their specialty and department stores—Sterns and J. J. Newberry at Bergen Mall, Bamberger's (Macy's New Jersey division), J. C. Penney's and Gimbels at Garden State Plaza—but also featured stores specifically devoted to furniture, hardware, appliances, groceries, gifts, drugs, books, toys, records, bakery goods, candy, jewelry, garden supplies, hearing aids, tires, even religious objects. Services grew to include restaurants, a post office, laundromat, cleaners, key store, shoe repair, bank, loan company, stock brokerage houses, barber shop, travel agency, real

estate office, "slenderizing salon," and Catholic chapel. Recreational facilities ranged from a 550-seat movie theater, bowling alley, and ice-skating rink to a children's gymnasium and playground.

13   Both shopping centers made meeting rooms and auditoriums available to community organizations and scheduled a full range of cultural and educational activities to legitimize these sites as civic centers, which also attracted customers. Well-attended programs and exhibitions taught shoppers about such "hot" topics of the 1950s and 1960s as space exploration, color television, modern art, and civics. Evening concerts and plays, ethnic entertainment, dances and classes for teenagers, campaign appearances by electoral candidates, community outreach for local charities: these were some of the ways that the Bergen Mall and Garden State Plaza made themselves indispensable to life in Bergen County. In sum, it was hard to think of consumer items or community events that could not be found at one or the other of these two shopping centers. (In the 1970s, a cynical reporter cracked that "the only institution that had not yet invaded" the modern shopping mall was the funeral home.) Furthermore, stores and services were more accessible than those downtown, as the centers were open to patrons from 10 a.m. to 9:30 p.m., at first four nights a week and by the 1960s, six nights a week. To a regional planner such as Ernest Erber, these postwar shopping centers helped construct a new kind of urbanism appropriate to the automobile age: the "City of Bergen," he named the area in 1960. The *New York Times* agreed, remarking of the Paramus commercial complex, "It lives a night as well as a day existence, glittering like a city when the sun goes down."[15]

14   When developers and store owners set out to make the shopping center a more perfect downtown, they aimed to exclude from this public space unwanted urban groups such as vagrants, prostitutes, racial minorities, and poor people. Market segmentation became the guiding principle of this mix of commercial and civic activity, as the shopping center sought perhaps contradictorily to legitimize itself as a true community center and to define that community in exclusionary socioeconomic and racial terms. The simple demographics of postwar America helped: when nine of the ten largest cities in the United States lost population between 1950 and 1960 while all metropolitan areas grew, three whites were moving out for every two non-whites who moved in, laying the groundwork for the racially polarized metropolitan populations of today.[16] In this way, suburbanization must be seen as a new form of racial segregation in the face of a huge wave of African-American migration from the South to the North during the 1950s.

15   Shopping centers did not exclude inadvertently by virtue of their suburban location. Rather, developers deliberately defined their communities through a combination of marketing and policing. Macy's reminded its stockholders in 1955 as it was building its first shopping center, the Garden State Plaza, "We are a type of organization that caters primarily to middle-income groups, and our stores reflect this in the merchandise they carry and in their physical surroundings."[17] It was this concern for "physical surroundings" that made the setting of the suburban shopping center appealing to retailers—and ultimately to customers. As Baltimore's Planning Council explained more explicitly than merchants ever would, "Greater numbers of low-income, Negro shoppers in Central Business District stores, coming at the same time as middle and upper income

white shoppers traveling to . . . segregated suburban centers, have had tunate implications [for downtown shopping]."[18]

16   Store selection, merchandise, prices, and carefully controlled access t(urban shopping centers supported the class and color line. A survey o. ---. sumer expenditures in northern New Jersey in 1960–1961 revealed that while 79 percent of all families owned cars, fewer than one-third of those with incomes below $3,000 did, and the low-income population included a higher percentage of non-white families than the average for the whole sample.[19] Although bus service was available for shoppers without cars, only a tiny proportion arrived that way (in 1966, a daily average of only 600 people came to the Garden State Plaza by bus compared to a mid-week daily average of 18,000 cars and a holiday peak of 31,000 cars, many carrying more than one passenger), and bus routes were carefully planned to serve non-driving customers—particularly women—from neighboring suburbs, not low-income consumers from cities such as Passaic, Paterson, and Newark.[20] Whereas individual department stores had long targeted particular markets defined by class and race, selling, for example, to "the carriage trade" at the upper end, shopping centers applied market segmentation on the scale of a downtown. In promoting an idealized downtown, shopping centers like Garden State Plaza and Bergen Mall tried to filter out not only the inefficiencies and inconveniences of the city but also the undesirable people who lived there.

. . .

17 Whereas, at first, developers had sought to legitimize the new shopping centers by arguing for their centrality to both commerce and community, over time they discovered that those two commitments could be in conflict. The rights of free speech and assembly traditionally safeguarded in the public forums of democratic communities were not always good for business, and they could conflict with the rights of private property owners—the shopping centers—to control entry to their land. Beginning in the 1960s, American courts all the way up to the Supreme Court struggled with the political consequences of having moved public life off the street and into the privately owned shopping center. Shopping centers, in turn, began to reconsider the desirable balance between commerce and community in what had become the major sites where suburbanites congregated.[21]

18   Once regional shopping centers like the Paramus malls had opened in the 1950s, people began to recognize them as public spaces and to use them to reach out to the community. When the Red Cross held blood drives, when labor unions picketed stores in organizing campaigns, when political candidates campaigned for office, when anti-war and anti-nuclear activists gathered signatures for petitions, they all viewed the shopping center as the obvious place to reach masses of people. Although shopping centers varied in their responses—from tolerating political activists to monitoring their actions to prohibiting them outright—in general, they were wary of any activity that might offend customers. A long, complex series of court tests resulted, culminating in several key Supreme Court decisions that sought to sort out the conflict between two basic rights in a free society: free speech and private property. Not surprisingly, the cases hinged on arguments about the extent to which the shopping center had displaced the traditional "town square" as a legitimate public forum.[22]

19   The first ruling by the Supreme Court was *Amalgamated Food Employees Union Local 590 vs. Logan Valley Plaza, Inc.* (1968), in which Justice Thurgood Marshall, writing for the majority, argued that refusing to let union members picket the Weis Markets in the Logan Valley Plaza in Altoona, Pennsylvania, violated the workers' First Amendment rights, since shopping centers had become the "functional equivalent" of a sidewalk in a public business district. Because peaceful picketing and leaflet distribution on "streets, sidewalks, parks, and other similar public places are so historically associated with the exercise of First Amendment rights," he wrote, it should also be protected in the public thoroughfare of a shopping center, even if privately owned. The Logan Valley Plaza decision likened the shopping center to a company town, which had been the subject of an important Supreme Court decision in *Marsh vs. Alabama* (1946), upholding the First Amendment rights of a Jehovah's Witness to proselytize in the company town of Chickasaw, Alabama, despite the fact that the Gulf Shipbuilding Corporation owned all the property in town. The "Marsh Doctrine" affirmed First Amendment rights over private property rights when an owner opened up his or her property for use by the public.[23] The stance taken in Logan Valley began to unravel, however, as the Supreme Court became more conservative under President Richard Nixon's appointees. In *Lloyd Corp. vs. Tanner* (1972), Justice Lewis F. Powell, Jr., wrote for the majority that allowing anti-war advocates to pass out leaflets at the Lloyd Center in Portland, Oregon, would be an unwarranted infringement of property rights "without significantly enhancing the asserted right of free speech." Anti-war leaflets, he argued, could be effectively distributed elsewhere, without undermining the shopping center's appeal to customers with litter and distraction.[24]

20   The reigning Supreme Court decision today is *PruneYard Shopping Center vs. Robbins* (1980). The Supreme Court upheld a California State Supreme Court ruling that the state constitution granted a group of high school students the right to gather petitions against the U.N. resolution "Zionism Is Racism." The court decided that this action did not violate the San Jose mall owner's rights under the U.S. Constitution. But, at the same time, the court reaffirmed its earlier decisions in *Lloyd vs. Tanner* and *Scott Hudgens vs. National Labor Relations Board* (1976) that the First Amendment did not guarantee access to shopping malls, and it left it to the states to decide for themselves whether their own constitutions protected such access.

21   Since *PruneYard,* state appellate courts have been struggling with the issue, and mall owners have been winning in many more states than they have lost. Only in six states, California, Oregon, Massachusetts, Colorado, Washington, and most recently New Jersey, have state supreme courts protected citizens' right of free speech in privately owned shopping centers. In New Jersey, the courts have been involved for some time in adjudicating free speech in shopping centers. In 1983, the Bergen Mall was the setting of a suit between its owners and a political candidate who wanted to distribute campaign materials there. When a Paramus Municipal Court judge ruled in favor of the mall, the candidate's attorney successfully appealed on the familiar grounds that "there is no real downtown Paramus. Areas of the mall outside the stores are the town's public sidewalks." He further noted that the mall hosted community events and contained a meeting hall, post office, and Roman Catholic chapel. In this case, and

in another one the following year over the right of nuclear-freeze advocates to distribute literature at the Bergen Mall, free speech was protected on the grounds that the mall was equivalent to a town center.[25]

22   Such suits should be unnecessary (at least for a while) in New Jersey, because in a historic decision in December 1994 the New Jersey Supreme Court affirmed that the state constitution guaranteed free speech to opponents of the Persian Gulf War who wanted to distribute leaflets at ten regional malls throughout the state. Writing for the majority, Chief Justice Robert N. Wilentz confirmed how extensively public space has been transformed in postwar New Jersey:

> The economic lifeblood once found downtown has moved to suburban shopping centers, which have substantially displaced the downtown business districts as the centers of commercial and social activity . . . Found at these malls are most of the uses and activities citizens engage in outside their homes . . . This is the new, the improved, the more attractive downtown business district—the new community—and no use is more closely associated with the old downtown than leafletting. Defendants have taken that old downtown away from its former home and moved all of it, except free speech, to the suburbs.

Despite the New Jersey Supreme Court's commitment to free speech, it nonetheless put limits on it, reaffirming the regional mall owners' property rights. Its ruling allowed only the distribution of leaflets—no speeches, bullhorns, pickets, parades, demonstrations, or solicitation of funds. Moreover, the court granted owners broad powers to regulate leaflet distribution by specifying days, hours, and areas in or outside the mall permissible for political activity. Thus, although shopping centers in New Jersey and five other states have been forced to accommodate some political activity, they have retained authority to regulate it and are even finding ways of preventing legal leafletters from exercising their constitutional rights, such as by requiring them to have million-dollar liability policies, which are often unobtainable or prohibitively expensive. In many other states, shopping centers have been able to prohibit political action outright, much as they control the economic and social behavior of shoppers and store owners.[26]

23   An unintended consequence of the American shift in orientation from public town center to private shopping center, then, has been the narrowing of the ground where constitutionally protected free speech and free assembly can legally take place.

. . .

24 Mass consumption in postwar America created a new landscape, where public space was more commercialized [and] more privatized within the regional shopping center than it had been in the traditional downtown center. This is not to romanticize the city and its central business district. Certainly, urban commercial property owners pursued their own economic interests, [and] political activity in public spaces was sometimes limited. . . . Nonetheless, the legal distinction between public and private space remained significant; urban loitering and vagrancy laws directed against undesirables in public places have repeatedly been struck down by the courts, while privately owned shopping centers have been able to enforce trespassing laws.[27] Overall, an important shift from one kind of social order to another took place between 1950 and 1980, with

major consequences for Americans. A free commercial market attached to a relatively free public sphere (for whites) underwent a transformation to a more
regulated commercial marketplace (where mall management controlled access,
favoring chains over local independents, for example) and a more circumscribed public sphere of limited rights. Economic and social liberalism went
hand in hand and declined together.

25   Not by accident, public space was restructured and segmented by class and
race in New Jersey, as in the nation, just as African Americans gained new protections for their right of equal access to public accommodations. Although civil
rights laws had been on the books in New Jersey since the late nineteenth century, comprehensive legislation with mechanisms for enforcement did not pass
until the 1940s. With the "Freeman Bill" of 1949, African Americans were finally guaranteed equal access to schools, restaurants, taverns, retail stores, hotels,
public transportation, and facilities of commercial leisure such as movie theaters,
skating rinks, amusement parks, swimming pools, and beaches, with violators
subject to fines and jail terms. Throughout the 1940s and 1950s, African-
American citizens of New Jersey—and other northern states—vigilantly challenged discrimination by private property owners. Yet larger structural changes
in community marketplaces were under way, financed by private commercial
interests committed to socioeconomic and racial segmentation. While African
Americans and their supporters were prodding courts and legislatures to eliminate legal segregation in public places, real-estate developers, retailers, and
consumers were collaborating to shift economic resources to new kinds of segregated spaces.[28]

26   The landscape of mass consumption created a metropolitan society in which
people were no longer brought together in central marketplaces and the parks,
streets, and public buildings that surrounded them but, rather, were separated
by class and race in differentiated commercial sub-centers. Moreover, all commercial sub-centers were not created equal. Over time, shopping centers
became increasingly class stratified, with some like the Bergen Mall marketing
themselves to the lower middle class, while others like the Garden State Plaza
went upscale to attract upper middle-class consumers. If tied to international
capital, some central business districts—such as New York and San Francisco—
have prospered, although they have not been left unscarred from recent retail
mergers and leveraged buy-outs. Other downtowns, such as Hackensack and
Elizabeth, New Jersey, have become "Cheap John Bargain Centers" serving customers too poor and deprived of transportation to shop at malls. Even in larger
American cities, poor urban populations shop downtown on weekends while
the white-collar workers who commute in to offices during the week patronize
the suburban malls closer to where they live. Some commercial districts have
been taken over by enterprising, often newly arrived, ethnic groups, who have
breathed new life into what would otherwise have been in decay, but they
nonetheless serve a segmented market. Worst off are cities like Newark, once
the largest shopping district in the state, which saw every one of its major
department stores close between 1964 and 1992 and much of its retail space
remain abandoned, leaving residents such as Raymond Mungin to wonder, "I
don't have a car to drive out to the malls. What can I do?" Mass consumption
was supposed to bring standardization in merchandise and consumption pat-

terns. Instead, diverse social groups are no longer integrated into central consumer marketplaces but rather are consigned to differentiated retail institutions,
segmented markets, and new hierarchies.[29]

27   Finally, the dependence on private spaces for public activity and the more
recent privatization of public space gravely threaten the government's constitutional obligations to its citizens. Not only freedom of speech and public
assembly in shopping centers are at issue. Just recently, Amtrack's Pennsylvania
Station in New York City tried to stave off two suits requiring it to respect constitutional rights guaranteed in public places: an effort by artist Michael Lebron
to display a political message on the gigantic curved and lighted billboard that
he had rented for two months, and a case brought by the Center for
Constitutional Rights to force Amtrak to stop ejecting people from the station
because they are homeless. When Jürgen Habermas theorized about the rise
and fall of a rational public sphere, he recognized the centrality in the eighteenth
and nineteenth centuries of accessible urban places—cafés, taverns, coffee-
houses, clubs, meeting houses, concert and lecture halls, theaters, and museums—to the emergence and maintenance of a democratic political culture. Over
the last half-century, transformations in America's economy and metropolitan
landscape have expanded the ability of many people to participate in the mass
market. But the commercializing, privatizing, and segmenting of physical gathering places that has accompanied mass consumption has made more pre-
carious the shared public sphere upon which our democracy depends.[30]

Notes

I would like to acknowledge the skill and imagination of two research assistants, Deb
Steinbach and Susan Spaet. My research was supported by grants from the National
Endowment for the Humanities (1993), the American Council of Learned Societies
(1994), and New York University (1993–1994). I am also grateful to several audiences
who shared helpful reactions to versions of this article: the international conference
"Gender and Modernity in the Era of Rationalization," Columbia University, September
1994; the conference "Significant Locales: Business, Labor, and Industry in the Mid-Atlantic
Region," sponsored by the Center for the History of Business, Technology, and Society,
Hagley Museum and Library, October 1994; the history department at George Washington
University, February 1995; Tricia Rose's American Studies Colloquium, New York University,
February 1995; the Historians of Greater Cleveland, May 1995; and my audience at Vassar
College, November 1995. Individuals whose readings have especially helped me include
Herrick Chapman, Michael Ebner, Ken Jackson, Richard Longstreth, Tricia Rose, Phil
Scranton, David Schuyler, Sylvie Schweitzer, and two anonymous readers for the *AHR*.

1. "The Economy: The Great Shopping Spree," *Time* (January 8, 1965): 58–62 (and
   cover).

2. See Kenneth T. Jackson, *Crabgrass Frontier: The Suburbanization of the United
   States* (New York, 1985); Robert Fishman, *Bourgeois Utopias: The Rise and Fall of
   Suburbia* (New York, 1987); Joel Garreau, *Edge City: Life on the New Frontier*
   (Garden City, N.Y., 1991); William Sharpe and Leonard Wallock, "Bold New City or
   Built-Up 'Burb? Redefining Contemporary Suburbia," with comments by Robert
   Bruegmann, Robert Fishman, Margaret Marsh, and June Manning Thomas, *American
   Quarterly* 46 (March 1994): 1–61; Carol O'Connor, "Sorting Out Suburbia,"
   American Quarterly 37 (Summer 1985): 382–94.

3. The Editors of *Fortune, The Changing American Market* (Garden City, N.Y., 1995), 76.

4. Ann Durkin Keating and Ruth Eckdish Knack, "Shopping in the Planned Community: Evolution of the Park Forest Town Center," unpublished paper in possession of author; Howard Gillette, Jr., "The Evolution of the Planned Shopping Center in Suburb and City," *American Planning Association Journal* 51 (Autumn 1985): 449–60; Daniel Prosser, "The New Downtowns: Commercial Architecture in Suburban New Jersey, 1920–1970," in Joel Schwartz and Daniel Prosser, *Cities of the Garden State: Essays in the Urban and Suburban History of New Jersey* (Dubuque, Iowa, 1977), 113–15; "Park Forest Moves into '52," *House and Home: The Magazine of Building* 1 (March 1952): 115–16; William S. Worley, *J. C. Nichols and the Shaping of Kansas City: Innovation in Planned Residential Communities* (Columbia, Mo., 1990); Richard Longstreth, "J. C. Nichols, the Country Club Plaza, and Notions of Modernity," *The Harvard Architecture Review, Vol. 5: Precedent and Invention* (New York, 1986), 121–32; William H. Whyte, Jr., "The Outgoing Life," *Fortune* 47 (July 1953): 85; Michael Birkner, *A Country Place No More: The Transformation of Bergenfield, New Jersey, 1894–1994* (Rutherford, N.J., 1994), 174–77; *Bergen Evening Record,* Special Foster Village Edition, August 10, 1949.

5. Jackson, *Crabgrass Frontier,* 255–61. On precedents in the pre–World War II period, see Richard Longstreth, "Silver Spring: Georgia Avenue, Colesville Road, and the Creation of an Alternative 'Downtown' for Metropolitan Washington," in *Streets: Critical Perspectives on Public Space,* Zeynep Celik, Diane Favro, and Richard Ingersoll, eds. (Berkeley, Calif., 1994), 247–57; Longstreth, "The Neighborhood Shopping Center in Washington, D.C., 1930–1941," *Journal of the Society of Architectural Historians* 51 (March 1992): 5–33; Longstreth, "The Perils of a Parkless Town," in *The Car and the City: The Automobile, the Built Environment, and Daily Urban Life,* Martin Wachs and Margaret Crawford, eds. (Ann Arbor, Mich., 1992), 141–53.

6. Editors of *Fortune, Changing American Market,* 78–80, 90. Also see "New Need Cited on Store Centers," *New York Times* (February 13, 1955): 7.

7. Richard Longstreth, "The Mixed Blessings of Success: The Hecht Company and Department Store Branch Development after World War II," Occasional Paper No. 14, January 1995, Center for Washington Area Studies, George Washington University.

8. Samuel Feinberg, "Story of Shopping Centers," *What Makes Shopping Centers Tick,* reprinted from *Women's Wear Daily* (New York, 1960), 1. For useful background on the development of regional shopping centers, see William Severini Kowinski, *The Malling of America: An Inside Look at the Great Consumer Paradise* (New York, 1985); Neil Harris, *Cultural Excursions: Marketing Appetites and Cultural Tastes in Modern America* (Chicago, 1990), 7, 76–77, 278–88; Margaret Crawford, "The World in a Shopping Mall," in Michael Sorkin, ed., *Variations on a Theme Park: The New American City and the End of Public Space* (New York, 1992), 3–30; Gillette, "Evolution of the Planned Shopping Center."

9. On the postwar growth of Paramus and Bergen County, see Raymond M. Ralph, *Farmland to Suburbia, 1920–1960,* Vol. 6, Bergen County, New Jersey History and Heritage Series (Hackensack, N.J., 1983), 62–71, 76–90; Catherine M. Fogarty, John E. O'Connor, and Charles F. Cummings, *Bergen County: A Pictorial History* (Norfolk, Va., 1985), 182–93; *Beautiful Bergen: The Story of Bergen County, New Jersey,* 1962; Patricia M. Ryle, *An Economic Profile of Bergen County, New Jersey* (Office of Economic Research, Division of Planning and Research, New Jersey Department of Labor and Industry, March 1980); League of Women Voters of Bergen County, *Where Can I Live in Bergen County: Factors Affecting Housing Supply* (Closter, N.J., 1972).

10. Feinberg, *What Makes Shopping Centers Tick,* 2, 94–102; Ralph, *Farmland to Suburbia,* 70–71, 84–85; Mark A. Stuart, *Our Era, 1960–Present,* Vol. 7, Bergen County, New Jersey History and Heritage Series (Hackensack, N.J., 1983), 19–22; Prosser, "New Downtowns," 119–20; Edward T. Thompson, "The Suburb That Macy's Built," *Fortune* 61 (February 1960): 195–200; "Garden State Plaza Merchant's Manual," May 1, 1957, and certain pages revised in 1959, 1960, 1962, 1963, 1965, 1969, Garden State Plaza Historical Collection.

11. On the financing of shopping centers and the great profits involved, see Jerry Jacobs, *The Mall: An Attempted Escape from Everyday Life* (Prospect Heights, Ill., 1984), 52.

12. Victor Gruen, "Introverted Architecture," *Progressive Architecture* 38, no. 5 (1957): 204–08; Victor Gruen and Larry Smith, *Shopping Towns USA: The Planning of Shopping Centers* (New York, 1960), 22–24; both quoted in Gillette, "Evolution of the Planned Shopping Center." For more on Gruen, see Kowinski, *Malling of America,* 118–20, 210–14; "Exhibit of Shopping Centers," *New York Times* (October 19, 1954): 42. Paul Goldberger recently profiled shopping-center builder Martin Bucksbaum in "Settling the Suburban Frontier," *New York Times Magazine* (December 31, 1995): 34–35.

13. Robert Bruegmann made the same point about the way the earliest design of suburban shopping centers resembled downtown shopping streets in a talk to the Urban History Seminar of the Chicago Historical Society, February 17, 1994.

14. Quoted in Feinberg, *What Makes Shopping Centers Tick,* 101. In addition to sources already cited on the control possible in a shopping center versus a downtown, see "Shopping Centers Get 'Personality,'" *New York Times* (June 29, 1958): 1.

15. Ernest Erber, "Notes on the 'City of Bergen,'" September 14, 1960, Box B, Ernest Erber Papers (hereafter, Erber), Newark Public Library (hereafter, NPL), Newark; "Paramus Booms as a Store Center," *New York Times* (February 5, 1962): 33–34; "The Mall the Merrier, or Is It?" *New York Times* (November 21, 1976): 62. For details on particular stores and activities at Bergen Mall and Garden State Plaza, see Feinberg, *What Makes Shopping Centers Tick,* 97–100; Fogarty, et al., *Bergen County,* 189; Prosser, "New Downtowns," 119. Almost every issue of the *Bergen Evening Record* from 1957 and thereafter yields valuable material (in articles and advertisements) on mall stores, services, and activities. The discussion here is based particularly on issues from November 8, 13, and 19, 1957, January 8, 1958, June 10, 1959, and March 2, 1960. Also see "Shoppers! Mass Today on Level 1," *New York Times,* June 14, 1994; press release on Garden State Plaza's opening in the Historical Collection of Garden State Plaza, folder "GSP history"; "It Won't Be Long Now . . . Bamberger's, New Jersey's Greatest Store, Comes to Paramus Soon," promotional leaflet, stamped August 22, 1956, file "Bergen County Shopping Centers," Johnson Free Public Library, Hackensack, N.J.; "The Shopping Center," *New York Times* (February 1, 1976): 6–7.

    For data on the allocation of shopping-center space in ten regional shopping centers in 1957, see William Applebaum and S. O. Kaylin, *Case Studies in Shopping Center Development and Operation* (New York, 1974), 101. For evidence of the community orientation of shopping centers nationwide, see Arthur Herzog, "Shops, Culture, Centers—and More," *New York Times Magazine* (November 18, 1962): 34–35, 109–10, 112–14; in the *New York Times:* "A Shopping Mall in Suffolk Offering More Than Goods," June 22, 1970: 39; "Supermarkets Hub of Suburbs," February 7, 1971: 58; "Busy Day in a Busy Mall," April 12, 1972: 55. On the community-relations efforts of branch stores, see Clinton L. Oaks, *Managing Suburban Branches of Department Stores* (Stanford, Calif., 1957), 81–83.

16. George Sternlieb, *The Future of the Downtown Department Store* (Cambridge, Mass., 1962), 10.

17. R. H. Macy & Company, *Annual Report* (New York, 1955). The *Times-Advocate,* March 14, 1976, argues that Bamberger's, Macy's store at the Garden State Plaza, was at the forefront of the chain's appeal to the middle to upper-income shopper. On market segmentation of shopping centers, also see William H. Whyte, Jr., *The Organization Man* (New York, 1956), 316–17; Jacobs, *The Mall,* 5, 12; and Albert Bills and Lois Pratt, "Personality Differences among Shopping Centers," *Fairleigh Dickinson University Business Review* 1 (Winter 1961), which distinguishes between the customers of the Bergen Mall and Garden State Plaza in socioeconomic terms. Crawford's "World in a Shopping Mall," in Sorkin, *Variations on a Theme Park,* discusses the sophisticated strategies that market researchers use to analyze trade areas and pitch stores to different kinds of customers, 8–9.

18. George Sternlieb, "The Future of Retailing in the Downtown Core," *AIP Journal* 24 (May 1963), as reprinted in Howard A. Schretter, *Downtown Revitalization* (Athens, Ga., 1967), 95, and quoted in Jon C. Teaford, *The Rough Road to Renaissance: Urban Revitalization in America, 1940–1985* (Baltimore, Md., 1990), 129.

19. United States Department of Labor, Bureau of Labor Statistics, "Consumer Expenditures and Income, Northern New Jersey, 1960–61," BLS Report No. 237–63, December 1963, Schomburg Center, New York Public Library, Clipping File "Consumer Expenses & Income-NJ."

20. "The Wonder on Routes 4 and 17: Garden State Plaza," brochure, file "Bergen County Shopping Centers," Johnson Free Public Library, Hackensack, New Jersey; "Notes on Discussion Dealing with Regional (Intermunicipal) Planning Program for Passaic Valley Area (Lower Portion of Passaic Co. and South Bergen," n.d., Box A, Folder 3, Erber, NPL; "Memorandum to DAJ and WBS from EE," November 22, 1966, Box B, Erber, NPL; National Center for Telephone Research (A Division of Louis Harris and Associates), "A Study of Shoppers' Attitudes toward the Proposed Shopping Mall in the Hudson County Meadowlands Area," conducted for Hartz Mountain Industries, February 1979, Special Collections, Rutgers University, New Brunswick, New Jersey.

21. Shopping centers retreated from promoting themselves as central squares and street corners not only because of the free speech issue but also to limit the loitering of young people. *New York Times:* "Supermarkets Hub of Suburbs," February 7, 1971: 58; "Coping with Shopping-Center Crises, Dilemma: How Tough to Get If Young Are Unruly," March 7, 1971: sect. 3, p. 1; "Shopping Centers Change and Grow," May 23, 1971: sect. 7, p. 1.

22. For a useful summary of the relevant court cases and legal issues involved, see Curtis J. Berger, "*PruneYard* Revisited: Political Activity on Private Lands," *New York University Law Review* 66 (June 1991): 633–94; also "Shopping Centers Change and Grow," *New York Times* (May 23, 1971): sect. 7, p. 1. The corporate shopping center's antagonism to free political expression and social action is discussed in Herbert I. Schiller, *Culture Inc.: The Corporate Takeover of Public Expression* (New York, 1989), 98–101.

23. On *Amalgamated vs. Logan Valley Plaza,* see "Property Rights vs. Free Speech," *New York Times* (July 9, 1972): sect. 7, p. 9; "Amalgamated Food Employees Union Local 590 v. Logan Valley Plaza," 88 S.Ct. 1601 (1968), *Supreme Court Reporter,* 1601–20; 391 US 308, U.S. Supreme Court Recording Briefs 1967, No. 478, microfiche; "Free Speech: Peaceful Picketing on Quasi-Public Property," *Minnesota Law Review* 53 (March 1969): 873–82. On *Marsh vs. State of Alabama,* see 66 S.Ct.

276, *Supreme Court Reporter,* 276–84. Other relevant cases between *Marsh vs. Alabama* and *Amalgamated vs. Logan Valley Plaza* are *Nahas vs. Local 905, Retail Clerks International Assoc.* (1956), *Amalgamated Clothing Workers of America vs. Wonderland Shopping Center, Inc.* (1963), *Schwartz-Torrance Investment Corp. vs. Bakery and Confectionary Workers' Union, Local No. 31* (1964); with each case, the Warren court was moving closer to a recognition that the shopping center was becoming a new kind of public forum.

24. "4 Nixon Appointees End Court's School Unanimity, Shopping Centers' Right to Ban Pamphleteering Is Upheld, 5 to 4," *New York Times* (June 23, 1972): 1; "Shopping-Center Industry Hails Court," *New York Times* (July 2, 1972): sect. 3, p. 7; "Lloyd Corporation, Ltd. v. Donald M. Tanner (1972)," 92 S.Ct. 2219 (1972), *Supreme Court Reporter,* 2219–37. The American Civil Liberties Union brief went to great lengths to document the extent to which shopping centers have replaced traditional business districts; see "Brief for Respondents," U.S. Supreme Court Record, microfiche, 20–29. See also People's Lobby Brief, U.S. Supreme Court Record, microfiche, 5.

   The Supreme Court majority wanted to make it clear that in finding in favor of the Lloyd Center, it was not reversing the Logan Valley decision, arguing for a distinction based on the fact that anti-war leafletting was "unrelated" to the shopping center, while the labor union was picketing an employer. The four dissenting justices, however, were less sure that the distinction was valid and that the Logan Valley decision was not seriously weakened by Lloyd. The important court cases between *Amalgamated vs. Logan Valley Plaza* and *Lloyd vs. Tanner* included *Blue Ridge Shopping Center vs. Schleininger* (1968), *Sutherland vs. Southcenter Shopping Center* (1971), and *Diamond vs. Bland* (1970, 1974).

25. Berger, "*PruneYard* Revisited"; Kowinski, *Malling of America,* 196–202, 355–59; "Shopping Malls Protest Intrusion by Protesters," *New York Times* (July 19, 1983): B1; "Opening of Malls Fought," *New York Times* (May 13, 1984): sect. 11 (New Jersey), 7; "Michael Robins v. PruneYard Shopping Center (1979)," 592 P. 2nd 341, *Pacific Reporter,* 341–51; "PruneYard Shopping Center v. Michael Robins," 100 S.Ct. 2035 (1980), *Supreme Court Reporter,* 2035–51; U.S. Supreme Court Record, *PruneYard Shopping Center vs. Robins* (1980), microfiche. The most important Supreme Court case between *Lloyd vs. Tanner* and *PruneYard* was *Scott Hudgens vs. National Labor Relations Board* (1976), where the majority decision backed further away from Logan Valley Plaza and refused to see the mall as the functional equivalent of downtown. "Scott Hudgens v. National Labor Relations Board," 96 S.Ct. 1029 (1976), *Supreme Court Reporter,* 1029–47.

26. "Court Protects Speech in Malls," *New York Times* (December 21, 1994): A1; "Big Malls Ordered to Allow Leafletting," *Star-Ledger* (December 21, 1994): 1; "Now, Public Rights in Private Domains," *New York Times* (December 25, 1994): E3; "Free Speech in the Mall," *New York Times* (December 26, 1994): 38; Frank Askin, "Shopping for Free Speech at the Malls," 1995, unpublished ms. in possession of the author.

27. "Amtrak Is Ordered Not to Eject the Homeless from Penn Station," *New York Times* (February 22, 1995): A1.

28. Article on passage of New Jersey Civil Rights Bill, *New York Times,* March 24, 1949; Marion Thompson Wright, "Extending Civil Rights in New Jersey through the Division Against Discrimination," *Journal of Negro History* 38 (1953): 96–107; State of New Jersey, Governor's Committee on Civil Liberties, "Memorandum on Behalf of Joint Council for Civil Rights in Support of a Proposed Comprehensive Civil Rights Act for New Jersey," 1948, II, B 8, Folder "Civil Rights, New Jersey, 1941–48," NAACP Papers, Library of Congress, Washington, D.C.; "Report of Legislative Committee, NJ State Conference of NAACP Branches," March 26, 1949, II, B 8, Folder "Civil Rights, New

Jersey, 1941–48," NAACP Papers. Other NAACP files on discrimination document the actual experiences of African Americans in New Jersey during the 1940s and 1950s.

29. "Closing of 'Last' Department Store Stirs Debate on Downtown Trenton," *Star-Ledger,* June 5, 1983; "Urban Areas Crave Return of Big Markets," *Star-Ledger,* July 17, 1984; "Elizabeth Clothier Mourns Demise of Century-Old Customized Service," *Sunday Star-Ledger,* January 10, 1988; "President's Report to the Annual Meeting Passaic Valley Citizens Planning Association." Box A, Folder 3.

30. Jürgen Habermas, *The Structural Transformation of the Public Sphere: An Inquiry into a Category of Bourgeois Society,* Thomas Burger trans., with Frederick Lawrence (Cambridge, Mass., 1989); Geoff Eley, "Nations, Publics, and Political Cultures: Placing Habermas in the Nineteenth Century," in Nicholas B. Dirks, Geoff Eley, and Sherry B. Ortner, eds., *Culture/Power/History: A Reader in Contemporary Social Theory* (Princeton, N.J., 1994), 297–335.

Review Questions

1. As people moved from cities to the suburbs, what changes occurred in their shopping patterns?

2. In the 1950s, how did the people who developed regional shopping centers plan to meet the needs of customers?

3. What two major effects followed from markets moving from town centers to shopping centers?

4. In what sense could the earliest developers of shopping centers be called visionaries?

5. In what sense was suburbanization a new form of racial segregation, according to Cohen?

6. How did developers seek to create in their shopping centers an "idealized downtown"?

7. Explain the legal battles that arose in connection with shopping centers.

8. The rise of the shopping center over the last 50 years has given many people access to the mass market, says Cohen. But this access has come at a price. What is that price?

Discussion and Writing Suggestions

1. Cohen argues that shopping centers gave rise to a new form of racial segregation in this country. In your own experience, have you observed or experienced segregation at a shopping center?

2. Reread paragraph 14 and explain the this passage: "Market segmentation became the guiding principle of [the shopping center's] mix of commercial and civic activity, as the shopping center sought perhaps contradictorily to legitimize itself as a true community center and to define that community in exclusionary socioeconomic

and racial terms." What was the mix of commercial and civic activity? What was contradictory about shopping center management's calling their centers "community centers"?

3. Reread paragraph 25 and comment on this passage: "While African Americans and their supporters were prodding courts and legislatures to eliminate legal segregation in public places, real-estate developers, retailers, and consumers were collaborating to shift economic resources to new kinds of segregated spaces." To what extent do you agree that suburban shopping malls constitute "segregated spaces"?

4. What evidence do you find from your own experience that shopping centers are "class stratified"—that is, some centers cater to the upper-middle class, some to the lower-middle class?

5. Have you seen any evidence that political activity (for instance, protesting or gathering of signatures for petitions) is any less welcome in a shopping center than it is on a city street? Write a descriptive paragraph or two describing the experience.

6. Interview an older acquaintance or relative, perhaps a grandparent, on how shopping has changed over the years. Does this person recall a time before the rise of shopping centers? What was better about shopping in the middle of the twentieth century versus shopping at the beginning of the twenty-first? What was worse?

Community Through Exclusion and Illusion
George Lewis

In this article, which first appeared in the Journal of Popular Culture *(Fall 1990), George Lewis investigates the extent to which shopping malls "really act as [a] social magnet, bringing people together in a true sense of community." Through public service programs and promotions, mall management would have us believe that its facilities function as town centers in the spirit that Victor Gruen had envisioned. But Lewis, a sociologist at the University of the Pacific, challenges that view, concluding that the groups that congregate in malls "seldom share the common ties and engage in the sort of social interactions necessary to forge a sense of 'we-ness.'" Lewis bases his insights on a study of two groups—elders and teenagers—at a New England shopping center.*

1 Everyday life in America, in the past three decades, has been critically affected by the evolution and spread of the shopping mall as the central concept in American retailing. These economic monoliths, evolving from the earlier retail form of the suburban shopping center, are now about far more than just shopping. People go to the modern mall for professional services, such as legal, medical or optical aid. There are fashion shows, art shows and musical performances in these climate controlled, air conditioned spaces. Restaurants, video arcades, movie theatres and even ice skating rinks and sand beaches with tanning lights focused upon them

are found in the contemporary enclosed mall. In a word, the regional shopping mall has become a kind of civic center, a point of attraction for millions of Americans, whether they choose to buy something there regularly or not.

. . .

Community in the Mall: Manufactured Illusion or Social Reality?

2   With all its promotions and public service programs, does the mall really act as this sort of social magnet, bringing people together in a true sense of community? The answer, if one is to define community as more than just the bringing together of demographically similar persons in one locale, is more apt to be negative than it is positive. Malls can, and do, lure and assemble *collectivities* and *crowds* of shoppers, but these groups seldom share the common ties and engage in the sort of social interactions necessary to forge a sense of "we-ness"—of community—from the raw social material of a crowd.

3   Jessie Bernard makes a crucial conceptual distinction here between "the community," which emphasizes *locale* as its most important and fundamental criterion, and "community," which emphasizes *common ties* and *interaction* as significant criteria in its conceptualization. "Community," then, is characterized not by locale, but by the *gemeinschaften* spirit of communal and primary relationships in which intimacy, sentiment, and a sense of belonging exist among individuals.[1]

4   Thomas Bender agrees, further defining community as characterized by close, usually face to face relationships. "Individuals are bound together by affective or emotional ties rather than by a perception of individual self-interest. There is a 'we-ness' in a community; one is a member."[2]

5   If this is the sort of social relationship one means by community, than it is difficult to find among customers at most shopping malls. Physically, malls are geared for high turnover. Chairs and benches in rest areas and food courts are unpadded in the seat—designed to be uncomfortable if sat in too long. The architecture of the mall itself, behind the colorful neon store logos and displays, is anonymous, uniform, predictable and plain. The corridors are wide and filled with hurrying customers. Security guards discourage loiterers and help to move foot traffic along. The muzak, if it exists, reinforces the image of the mall as a public space—a place where strangers encounter one another en route to their desired locations.

6   Most shoppers who frequent the mall, even if lured there by some promotional scheme, come alone or in small groups of two or three.[3] They are intent upon their business, focusing upon shopping and not upon interaction with other mall customers. For the most part, they do not know each other and they don't come to the mall on any regular, day-to-day basis. In short, the high turnover, volume of persons, and transiency that is a designed part of most malls works *against* the development and emergence of community within their walls.

7   This is understood by mall managers and developers. As one put it: "Having the *perception* of a community feeling does not mean that it actually exists. It is not the same thing. Perception is not necessarily reality."[4] So the important thing, from a marketing perspective, is to create the warm *illusion* of community, while at the same time quietly stacking the deck against its actual development. "We don't want the mall to be a community in any real sense, because

we'll attract people we don't want to. People who are not here to shop b
coming for some other purpose. It would upset our tenants who want to
money. We don't want anything to upset our tenants."

8   And yet, within this illusion, this false setting of community, the see
community have been planted. Ironically, among the very sorts of persons the
managers and developers do not want to see attracted to the mall—the non-
shoppers—have arisen fledgling forms of community, characterized by primary
ties, face to face interaction, daily meeting and the development of social networks. These developing communities, or social worlds—one comprised mainly
of retired persons and others over 65, and the other of teenagers—are the
empirical focus of this paper. The data presented here were collected in June
and July of 1988 in a series of unstructured interviews conducted in a large
shopping center in New England. The interviews, which total over 200 hours of
material, are one portion of a research effort undertaken by the Salt Center For
Cultural Studies, in examining various facets of the impact of popular and mass
culture on regional cultural forms.[5]

. . .

The Elderly

9   The mall is a central life setting for many elderly persons who frequent it on a
regular basis. They walk back and forth, up and down the common area of the
older wing of the mall (the "old mall"), greeting friends and acquaintances and
sitting with them, visiting, in the sunken circular seating areas they have named
the "north hole," "south hole," or "center hole." Some visit the mall every day,
arriving when the doors are opened in the morning. Many stay all day, leaving
in mid to late afternoon. A few will have a light dinner at one of the mall cater-
ies before going home for the evening.

10   Many of these persons are retired, many widowed. They feel they have little
else to fill their days. Their time in the mall usually conforms to set routines. They
will be found in a specific seating area at a regular time, have coffee at the same
restaurant at the same time, and leave the mall each day within 15 or 20 minutes
of their leaving time the day before. This patterning of behavior is pervasive among
the elderly and characterizes the nature of their social interaction at the mall.

11   Bert, for example, a 78-year-old retiree, comes to the mall every day of the
week. "I come here at quarter of eleven and I leave at twenty minutes past
one," he says matter-of-factly, as he sneaks a glance at his watch. "I do this every
day. Every day except. . . ."

12   His two companions finish for him; "Five days a week. He's missed one day
this year."

13   Bert resumes his own account. "And I have my lunch here at noontime." This
is Bert's eleven o'clock stop, outside of Porteous, one of the large department-
style anchor stores of the mall. He won't be here at eleven-thirty.

14   "I move every half hour. I go from here down to where the clock is. Then
where the clock is, I go down in front of Woolworth's, then I come back again
and go up there and take my bus by the front of JC Penney."

15   Linda, a mall custodian, noted that the elderly "would rather be at the mall
than anywhere else. They probably know more about the place than I do.

Probably know more than security does, too. I know 'cause my father-in-law is one of 'em. He comes in twice a day, every day. Ya, he sets over in the old mall, then he comes down and sets by Porteous for a while, then over by McDonalds."

16   The controlled environment of the mall offers another benefit to the elderly—it is a safe and comfortable place to walk for exercise. As Jacobs has pointed[6] out, many malls have instituted some form of walking program for the elderly—though the impetus for these programs usually comes from outside the mall itself, as the elderly are most often perceived by mall management as a group who does very little, if any, buying and thus contributes quite minimally in proportion to their presence, to the economic life of the mall.

17   "We really don't want them to come here if they're not going to shop," a mall manager remarked. "They take up seats we would like to have available for shoppers." However, from a public relations standpoint, it is difficult for mall management to overtly discourage the elderly from using the mall for their own purposes. Conversely, management can sometimes be talked into the minimal support of programs such as walking-for-health, in hopes it shows off to the community of shoppers they do want to attract, the degree of social consciousness and responsibility they supposedly feel.

18   The mall studied here is no exception to this pattern. A local doctor and the YMCA spearheaded the senior walking program, which opened in the spring of 1987 and which is now jointly sponsored by the doctor, the Y and the mall. The program encourages the elderly to walk laps and to record their own progress. To date, there are over 300 walkers signed into this program.

19   For those participating, entrance to the mall can be as early as 6:00 a.m., when security unlocks the doors—a full 3 or 4 hours prior to the opening of most commercial establishments inside the mall.

20   Pat, a regular "miler" in the program, usually arrives by car a few minutes before six and waits until the glass doors are unlocked.

21   "Age first," Pat insists as he holds a door for his two companions. Inside the mall, silent mannequins observe the three men begin their daily laps. Pat, now eighty years old, decides to take a short cut.

22   "You cheated," accuses the security guard.

23   "No, *you're* cheatin'," Pat accuses. "You're supposed to unlock all these doors and you're talkin' instead. I gotta bum hip, and when you get to my age, you won't be walkin'!" He smiles and disappears down the corridor. Two women call out to him in disbelief.

24   "You were here before us!"

25   "That's right," Pat laughs. "You're gettin' lazy."

26   After his five miles of walking laps, Pat sits down at his favorite restaurant, just now opening for business. Coming to the mall, he says, "gets me out of the house. I wish they opened at five. Pretty soon I'll be meeting six or seven fellas I know. We talk, shoot the breeze. I just come out here to kill a little time, that's all. What am I going to do at home?"

27   He leans back to prop his elbow on the back of his chair. His eyes follow a woman in red high heels taking choppy steps past a boutique. "I was in business 65 years. Was in the meat business. Gave it to my son, my son gave it to his son. I don't know whether you ever heard of it—Pat's Meat Mart?"

28   Two elderly ladies in cotton skirts and sneakers walk past and wave "Morning," he answers. These women he identifies as past customers of he jokes with them. "I have a lot of customers, really I do . . . people kn ya know."

29   He looks down and then away, as if he doesn't want to talk anymore. Then: "I was going to show you my darlin's picture." He pulls out his wallet and unfolds a fragile, yellowed newspaper clipping. "She was the nicest. Everybody loved her. They only make one like her. . . . I miss this one, I tell ya. I do, I really do. Oh, we were inseparable. I had her for 34 years. She died when she was 51, so—God wanted her. There's nothing I could do, ya know. That's the story of my life." A tight little smile.

30   "Where do ya want me to send the bill?" he asks, snapping back to the present.

31   Retired and living alone, many of these elderly seek the mall as a safe and neutral ground to keep up old job contacts—not just the more surface relationships with old customers, but more primary ties with workmates themselves. George, who worked for a large electrical plant until they "closed out" in 1983 and forced him into retirement, meets his work buddies every Friday in the mall for lunch. Over the five years he has done this, he notes, fewer and fewer are alive to attend. "Every month," he says, "the faces we used to see, they're thinnin' out, . . . thinnin' out. . . ."

32   Charlie comes to the mall to meet people and to avoid heat in the summer and cold in the winter. "Some people I meet here," he says, "I've known for forty years." The elderly congregate in knots and clusters, laughing and joking among themselves. Charlie flags down Bob and Irene in the crowd and gives them two coupons from the previous day's paper, good for money off at a mall fast food stand.

33   Connie complains of telephone sales people to the group—especially a seller of cemetery plots. "I told him I have my plot all picked out. I'm just sitting here waiting to go. He didn't call back." She continues, "Here (in the mall) we sit and talk about our illnesses, medications, diets. We have a lot of fun."

34   More than most social worlds, the world of the elderly in the mall takes its shape and character from the face to face relationships of the people who regularly are a part of it. For these elderly—most of whom are retired, who live alone, and are most probably widowed there is now little or no need to expend energy, concern and time in the areas of career, job development, self-improvement, spousal relations, or even in family and community activities. Cut off from these concerns and ties, their status and power position in the larger society lowered, they find meaning in the construction and maintenance of networks of personal relationships with others like themselves.[7] These "personal communities," then, are not defined by a bounded area so much as they are a web-like network of personal relationships in which each person is selectively attached to a definite number of discrete persons. At the edges of this network are those persons, such as the servers in the restaurants, the custodians, and the security personnel, with whom relationships are affectively neutral, of a surface level, and usually joking in nature.

35   Harry sums it up. "It's hard being a senior citizen. Very hard. It's a monotonous life. You know, when you're constructive for a good many years and then you have to relax and do nothing—and you're alone—that's worse."

36   Tom, sitting beside Harry, points out that he has some pretty good friends at the mall. He continues; "Girls down in the food court. They all look for us. We don't come in, they ask everybody where we are. They think we're sick, or something."

37   Harry and Bert tip their heads in agreement. "They look out for us. We kid a lot with them and everything."

38   Harry takes it from there. "Well, you're seeing a face, you know. If you stayed at home and you're alone, you see nothing. No matter where you'd live, you'd see a car go by. But people, you don't see." Silence. Then, "So you come out here to see the living, more or less." He looks to his friends for reinforcement. "Am I right? I think so."

39   Tom jumps in. "But you make everything sound so *sad,* Harry. My Lord, it's not *that* bad. I come out here to see my friends. To get out of the house. That's all."

The Teens

40   Teenagers visit the mall on an almost daily basis. They arrive in groups or individually to meet their friends. A number work in the mall, usually at minimum wage, in the fast food establishments located, for the most part, in the "new wing" of the mall, built just three years ago. When they are off work, they "hang out" with other youths, who use the mall as a place for social gathering.

41   The mall is one of the few places teenagers can go in this society where they are—albeit reluctantly—allowed to stay without being asked to leave.[8] Many who frequent the mall don't go to school. Some also try to stay away from their homes, but they really don't have anywhere else they can be on their own. As Millison concluded, malls are much the suburban equivalent to the urban street corners where inner city kids congregate.[9] Suburban kids come to malls to look around, meet and make friends, stay away from home, and hang out—because there is nowhere else to go.

42   Paul, a security guard, explains. "We aren't allowed to harass the kids, and I know they gotta hang out somewhere. But we tell them to keep moving, especially around the seats and tables in the food service area. They know they have to keep moving. If they get too loud, or talk back, or are creating any kind of disturbance like that, then we clear them out. Troublemakers we identify, and we don't let them back in."

43   Calling themselves "mall rats" (males) and "mall bunnies" (female), the teens congregate in the new wing of the mall, the largest number of them arriving in the late afternoon. They wander around the different shops, playing video games in the arcade, smoking cigarettes, showing off their latest hair, makeup and clothing styles, and waiting for something, anything, to happen. Most of them will stay until nine-thirty or ten, when the stores close and the mall shuts down.

44   Derick, 15, his hands jammed into the pockets of his frayed cutoff jean shorts, admits that the mall is "a place to go before I have to go to work. I only work right across the street. I have nowhere else to hang out. Most of my friends hang out here."

45   Looking at the arcade in the adjacent wing of the mall, he gestures towards it with a quick nod of his head. "Go over there to play video games. Spend all my money. I don't like spending all my money, but it's there." He shrugs. "Fuck it."

46   Standing near Derick in the small knot of teenagers, Ed, 16, takes a long drag off his cigarette and exhales out the corner of his mouth. "I just s coming on almost a daily basis last year, because it was something to d says. "You can come here anytime. It's pretty good, but if we didn't have any you'd probably get in more trouble than we would if we came here, so it kinda works out, you know. It's something to do and it kinda keeps you outa trouble."

47   As he says this, he scans the familiar row of neon lit food stalls. Shoppers rush by, but he appears calm and undisturbed, like his four friends standing nearby. They chatter noisily among themselves, making jokes, and playfully pushing each other around, only half aware, seemingly, of the bustle and motion of other people.

48   Nodding toward his friends, Ed goes on to explain the social networking that takes place in the mall. "I met all these people here. I've met lots of other people, too. One place where you can always find someone. If you know somebody, they know somebody else, they'll probably see 'em here, and you'll know them, then they'll know someone who is walking around and you know that person. So when you come here, you kinda build on people."

49   Some teens spend a great deal of time networking in the mall. For them, it is practically a second home. Tammy, age 14, says, "I used to come here every Saturday from eleven o'clock to nine-thirty, and just walk around with my friends, like Gina here, just walk around and check out the guys."

50   When roaming from shop to shop, playing video games, or cruising the strip becomes tiresome, teens usually migrate to the food court. Here they sit, talk, bum change, smoke cigarettes and try to avoid the attention of the security people, even as most of the activities they are engaged in will inevitably attract it.

51   The group gathers around a table, some standing, others sitting and talking. One of the girls breaks from her conversation to announce that Bob is coming. Bob has been kicked out of the mall for boisterous behavior and is not allowed in for another two months.

52   "Just about all of us have gotten kicked out at one time or another," Tony says in a matter of fact manner. "I was sitting down without anything to eat once, and like I didn't know the policy and he said, 'Move,' and I go, 'Why?' I ran my mouth a little too much. What I basically did was stand up for myself, but he didn't like that, so he just booted me for a couple months."

53   "Actually, I'm not supposed to be even in here. He said he's kicked me out forever, but I mean like I changed my hair style so he doesn't recognize me anymore."

54   Ed nods. "I changed mine and I changed my jacket. I used to wear a big leather jacket. I used to wear that all the time. That gave me away. But I've started wearing this jacket now with all my KISS pins on. And as long as I don't act up or do anything, they don't really care. See, I like it here so much I hafta come back."

55   Liz, 15, discusses relationships with the security guards in general. "Some days they can really get on us and other days they just won't come and like we'll be sitting down at the table and on busy days or on days they're not in a really good mood, they'll come over and tell us to move."

56   "They have no respect for mall rats," a boy standing on the edge of the group adds. "It's just days like that they can be real dinks."

57   And yet the mild harassment of the security guards is easily borne, especially when changing one's costume or haircut can many times be enough to erase identity in their eyes. Indeed, such treatment is better, for most, than the treatment they can expect elsewhere. And this relatively light scrutiny given them by the security guards also allows some teens to get away with minor interpersonal drug transactions, especially when the mall is crowded and busy.

58   "Other than The Beach, which is just like, 'deal it out on the streets,' I mean ya can get just about anything out here—pot, acid, hash, right here on Saturdays, when it is crowded."

59   "If you know the right people, you can pick up anything."

60   "And we pretty much know everybody here."

61   For some teens, the mall—with or without drugs—is an escape from home or school. Heather, 16, explains that she comes here "to get away from home, get away from problems 'cause I can't stay at home. Because of my nephew and my sister. They bother me. So I come to the mall." Slouching in her seat, she flips open the top of her red Marlboro box and counts her cigarettes. "School is no better. I go through a year of school, and they still put me through the next grade even if I'm failing. I like it, but it's not gonna get me through college if I do that. I don't care about partying. I just wanna get through school."

62   For Tiffany the mall has become a second home of sorts. At the age of thirteen she lives with Tony, another of the mall rats, and one other mall friend. "My mom kicked me out when I was eleven," she says with an edge of anger in her voice. "She's a bitch. I call her every day and she's just. . . ." Tiffany stops short as she shakes her head and rolls her eyes.

63   "I started going to foster homes and everything and I just quit. Now, I'm in State custody and I just. . . ." She stops again and laughs nervously and blushes. "Sorry about that," she says, apologizing to her friends, seeming to imply that she has become too personal, too emotional. Abruptly, she continues, "I don't do anything that they want me to do." She lets out a quick triumphant laugh.

64   "I swear to God if they came up to me and dragged me where I didn't want to go, I'd beat the crap right out of them. I would kill 'em. I got 'em twisted around my little finger. They don't mess with me." She growls, as she clenches her teeth and curls her small fist, pounding it lightly on the table.

65   Tony leans back and shakes his head slightly to part his long hair from his face. "I left home and I quit school and moved from, like, hotel to hotel for awhile with a Navy buddy and that wasn't a really good situation, 'cause we were getting kicked outta hotels and motels. We didn't have anywhere to go. So we went up to The Beach and when I went up there it's like there's a Burger King and an auto parts store and a Shop and Save and it's like . . . there was no mall. I was real glad to get back down here, 'cause it was, like, up there, it was boring the hell out of me."

66   The social world of these teens revolves around their contacts and time at the mall. Indeed, this world of the teenager is, in its larger sense, one of segregation from adults and the assumption of adult sexual, economic, and social roles. This segregation, and the relative lack of any clearly defined and socially supported roles for youth, help define the mall community of "rats and bunnies," especially those who have opted out, or been driven from, socially acceptable school and family settings.

67   These youths, disallowed entrance into the social world of adulthoo
attempting to forge meaning and community from their shifting networks
to face peer relationships in the mall. And yet, unlike the elderly, theirs is
tively unstable social system. Teens come and go and, more importantly, they
grow up. As a consequence, relationships rest almost entirely in present time and
revolve around present circumstances. The past is seldom spoken of, or shared.
"Best friends" at the mall may part ways next month, and not see each other
again. This fluidity and change in social relationships is a socially uncertain part
of the teen years which, for mall rats and bunnies, is also characterized by a lin-
gering malaise concerning the world outside their fragile community—a malaise
in which jealousy, mistrust and despair are prominent features. As Tony says:

68   "We are the mall rats. We are the mall. What the fuck else can I say?"

Conclusion: Community in the Mall

69 The American shopping mall has been bemoaned by critics for its impersonal-
ity, its uniformity, its total focus on meaningful interaction as rational and economic in nature. Where are the primary relations, the face to face interactions,
the social networks that exist along with the economic transactions of the traditional marketplace, the local community, or even the urban village? This case
study of one American mall suggests that, for shoppers in the mall, one does
indeed need to look elsewhere for the primary interactive ties of community,
no matter how cleverly mall management creates the *illusion* of community at
the mall. In the end, it seems, this is a shared illusion—neither management nor
shoppers are fooled by it, but both can *pretend* that they are creating or engaging in the meaningful and socially necessary relations of community.

70   Ironically, then, the real community ties that do exist in the mall have little to
do with its economic function. The elder and the teen spend very little money
there and do not frequent the mall for economic reasons. They are there, each
day, to greet friends, to create and strengthen their meaningful, face to face primary relationships, to define themselves as a social world, whether it be one of
"milers" or of "mall rats"—a community of kind to which they can give emotional
support and from which they can draw a sense of self and group identity.

71   Mall management does not like to see such groups develop. They use mall
space for other than economic purposes. These warm knots of community can
and do disrupt the cool smooth flow of economic transaction. Group members
take seats designed for shoppers. They create a focus in the mall that is not economic in nature.

72   Politically, however, it is hard—especially with the elderly—to ban, or even to
overtly discourage their presence. But it can be contained and monitored by
security personnel. And, especially with the teens, if it becomes too socially visible and disruptive, some members of the group can be ejected.

73   Why, then, under these less than ideal circumstances, do the elderly and
teenagers use the mall as their locus of community? It seems likely there are at
least five general social reasons for this choice. First, and probably most important, elders and teens both represent social groupings for whom our society provides little social space. The elderly, once they are retired especially, are cut off
from the familiar and fulfilling world of work. Their income drops sharply. They

are likely to be treated more and more as children by both their families and their non-elderly acquaintances. If they are widowed and live at home, they have lost most of the primary face to face support they have relied on for most of their adult lives.[10]

74   Consequently, they have a need to seek out others in similar situations. The mall is a central, safe place to get to, and there is usually regularly scheduled mass transportation available for the benefit of the shoppers (when it most likely would *not* be available on any regular basis for, say, transport to a non-economically oriented center or meeting place, such as a park or activities center).

75   For the teens, caught as they are between the statuses of childhood and adulthood, there are few social spaces or physical places open where they can congregate and develop their own contacts and social networks.[11] Most often, their activity is too closely defined, monitored, and circumscribed for them to see it as their own (in institutions such as the family and the school). Or, if they do find a niche of their own—such as cruising Main Street or hanging out in a park or fast food parking lot—they are usually dispersed by the authorities, or caught in curfews, or both.

76   And when school and family settings become nonviable alternatives, teens really have very few places to go. Once again, the mall offers its lure. It is centrally located, easy to get to for those with or without their own transportation, seen as a "safe" place by parents, and may, for some, also be the location of their full- or part-time job (usually for minimum wage—but that is another bit of discrimination teens have to bear).

77   Second, the elderly and teens are, to a great extent, faceless persons to adult American society. They are categorized as "old people" or "kids," and, because of the unimportance of their marginal status, they tend to be overlooked as individuals, though they are stereotypically reacted to as members of groups. For both of these groups, this social reaction increases their need to affirm identity and to create meaningful community for themselves.[12]

78   It also means that, in the mall setting, the elderly are usually overlooked, are nearly invisible to the shoppers hurrying on their way. Being socially invisible, the elderly cannot get much in the way of shoppers and thus their presence, as disruption, is less likely to be an issue requiring action on the part of mall management.

79   For the teens, even the security guards who keep them under surveillance can easily be fooled by a simple change of hair style or jacket. The boisterous teen who is ejected from the mall easily "slips out" of his or her public identity and is back the next day or week, a unique *person* returning to his or her community, invisible in return even to the watching security guards.

80   Third, as alluded to in point one above, the mall is centrally located, easy to get to, safe and climate controlled. The amenities that exist there for the shoppers—restaurants, rest rooms, benches and seats—can also be used by the non-shopper, as long as mall management does not actively discourage such usage.

81   Fourth, for the elderly, discouragement could be dangerous, in a public relations sense. Conversely, the elderly can be used to advantage to further the mall's illusion of community by publicizing their support of community

programs such as that of walking-for-health. For the teens, many of them work in the fast food stores and do leave money in the video arcade and the record stores. Therefore they do have some economic links to some of the business-es operating in the mall. The mall rats and bunnies also provide a visually excit-ing and socially validating backdrop for these youth oriented businesses, for other youths and young adults who come to shop.

82   Finally, these communities seem, in general, to police themselves quite well. They are aware of their status in the eyes of mall management and attempt, each in their own distinctive way, to keep a low enough profile so their pres-ence is tolerated.[13]

83   Ironically, then, and for these reasons, deep within the impersonal and con-crete structure of the mall, cultural chains of belonging seem to have been forged. The sense of community, to such an extent denied these groupings of the elderly and the young, in the larger society, is being created and shared in the mall, while shoppers rush blindly past under lights of cold neon, across the polished sheen of endless tiled floors.

Notes

1. Jessie Bernard, *The Sociology of Community* (Glenview, Ill: Scott, Foresman, 1973), p. 3.

2. Thomas Bender, *Community and Social Change in America* (Baltimore: Johns Hopkins University Press, 1978), p. 7.

3. Chain Store Age Executive, "Why They Shop Some Centers," 1987, 54, 33.

4. Interview with mall marketing director, 1986.

5. The author served as Director of Research for this study. Interviews quoted in this paper were conducted by himself, SALT staff members Pamela Wood and Hugh French, and students Brett Jenks, Edite Pedrosa, Amy Rowe, Julie Maurer, Peter Lancia, Harry Brown, Amy Schnerr and Lou Brown. Original tapes and transcripts are on file at SALT CENTER, Kennebunkport, ME 04609.

6. Jerry Jacobs, *The Mall: An Attempted Escape From Every Day Life* (Prospect Heights, Ill: Waveland Press, 1984), pp. 27–32.

7. Robert Atchley, *Social Forces and Aging* (Belmont, CA: Wadsworth, 1985), pp. 56–58.

8. Bob Greene, "Fifteen: Young Men Cruising Shopping Malls," *Esquire*, 1982, 98, pp. 17–18; Kowinski, *op. cit.*, pp. 68–73.

9. Martin Millison, *Teenage Behavior In Shopping Centers,* International Council of Shopping Centers, 1976, p. 11.

10. Peggy Eastman, "Elders Under Siege," *Psychology Today,* 1984, January, p. 30.

11. Richard Flacks, *Youth and Social Change* (Chicago: Markham, 1971), p. 17.

12. *loc. cit.,* p. 223.

13. This includes relations between the two groups. The elderly mainly frequent the old wing of the mall, while the teens frequent the new wing. The elderly arrive very early and usually leave by late afternoon. The teens usually arrive in mid to late afternoon and stay until the mall closes.

Review Questions

1. In what sense have modern malls become "civic centers"?

2. What are the differences between "the community" and "community," according to Lewis? Why does he introduce this distinction early in the article?

3. What conditions at malls inhibit the growth of community?

4. For what reasons do elders come to the mall? How does mall management react to their presence?

5. Why do teenagers visit the mall?

6. What characteristics do the teenage community and the elderly community share when at the mall?

7. In what sense is the world of the mall a "shared illusion," according to Lewis?

8. What five reasons does Lewis give for teens and elders seeking out the mall as a place to build their communities?

Discussion and Writing Suggestions

1. Lewis quotes a mall manager saying: "Having the *perception* of a community feeling does not mean that it actually exists. It is not the same thing." Why would mall managers take the trouble to create an illusion that malls encourage community ties?

2. Why is it "ironic," according the Lewis, that malls have become the meeting place for actual communities?

3. In shopping malls you have visited, what evidence do you find of an elder's community similar to the one Lewis describes?

4. Read the account of Pat, a mall regular (paragraphs 20–29). What is your response to Pat's story?

5. Reread paragraphs 43–57. Based on your experience, how accurate is Lewis's description of what teenagers do at the mall?

6. One of the key investigative tools for a sociologist like Lewis is the personal interview. Reread those portions of the article devoted to interviews of the elderly and teenagers. How important are these interviews to the success of Lewis's argument? What, in your view, do they add to the selection?

7. Write several paragraphs describing one of your experiences as a "mall rat" or "mall bunny." Include an account of the teenagers who gather at the mall as well as a description of the mall itself (for example, discuss its location, its appearance, the type of customers it attracts). In a final paragraph describe the extent to which you think the people you have described form a community.

Mallaise: How to Know If You Have It
William Kowinski

William Kowinski's The Malling of America: An Inside Look at the Great Consumer Paradise *(William Morrow, 1985) has become a classic in the literature on the cultural impact of shopping centers. The following selection, which forms a chapter in* Malling, *is representative of Kowinski's tone throughout: ironic, playful, and pointed in its critique of malls and their effects. "Mallaise" is his attempt to name the disease that some people feel on being absorbed by the totality of the mall's environment. Perhaps you will recognize one or more of the symptoms.*

1   Malls make some people sick. Literally, sometimes. They feel feverish, their eyes glaze, their stomachs tumble, they fall down, they throw up.

2   Some people are just annoyed by one or another aspect of a mall, or a non-specific quality of a particular mall, or malls in general. "That mall makes me *sick!*" they say. Or "I don't like malls—I *hate* them." Malls make people angry. Some of these people are shoppers, but some are people who work in malls or even own mall stores.

3   Malls affect people. They're designed to. But in some ways, either by their nature or by a side effect caused by their main ingredients, they do things to people that people are unaware of or don't understand, but if they knew or understood, they probably wouldn't like it.

4   There are other more obvious things that happen to people in malls that they don't or wouldn't like. Crime, for instance.

5   This section of *The Malling of America* is about some of the negative aspects of malls that affect people and that people perceive. Does the mall make you tired? Set your nerves on edge? Do you find it difficult to concentrate? Do you feel the absence of certain phenomena—weather, for example, or civil liberties? Do you sometimes wonder if you are really as safe as mall management would like you to believe?

6   If you're a parent, do you fear for your children's ability to survive outside comfort control because they spend so much time in the mall? And if you're an adolescent, do you feel your horizons becoming limited to a hundred chain store outlets and three anchor department stores? Or are you worried that this is precisely the world your parents do live in, and where they want you always to remain?

7   These are some of the symptoms of mallaise. Perhaps you have one or two, or know someone who does, or perhaps you want to be prepared, just in case. Then perhaps you should read on.

8   I had my first attack of *mal de mall* in Columbia, Maryland. I was in a restaurant in the Columbia Mall having coffee. The attack was characterized by feverishness, sudden fatigue, and high anxiety, all recurring whenever I glanced out at the mall itself. The thought of going out there again made me sweat and swoon, and I had to fight the hallucinatory certainty that when I left the restaurant I would be in Greengate mall, or maybe Woodfield, or Tysons Corner. Or *all* of them.

9 *Mal de mall,* or mall sickness, is one of the classifications of mallaise, the general term for physical and psychological disturbances caused by mall contact. I know because I made them all up. Among the symptoms I have personally observed or heard about from their victims are these:

10 *Dismallcumbobulation:* "I don't like to go to malls because I always get lost," a woman told me, "and that's embarrassing. I feel stupid. It makes me mad." The hyped-up overabundance of similar products plus the bland sameness of many mall environments make people feel lost even when they aren't. Even familiar malls relocate stores and reconfigure themselves, which adds to the feeling of a continuous featureless space. And the similarity of one mall to another is disorienting. You walk out of the Stuft Potato and you not only don't remember which way your car is, you might not remember what mall this is. There are other kinds of dismallcumbobulation: the loss of a sense of time as well as place, and forgetting one's purpose in coming to the mall— all of which can lead to apathy and hopelessness, loss of consciousness, or fainting. Some victims recommend deep-breathing exercises every fifteen minutes while at the mall.

11 *Inability to Relate to Others:* "It's impossible to talk to someone when you're shopping at the mall," a friend told me, explaining why she prefers to shop alone. "I notice it at the mall all the time—you see two people together but they aren't really talking to each other. They're talking, but they're staring off in different directions, and pretty soon they just wander away from each other." Among the possible effects of this symptom are disenchantment and divorce.

12 *Plastiphobia,* or the fear of being enclosed in a cocoon of blandness. "Suddenly I just stood still and looked around," a young man said. "I saw all the people and what we were all doing there, what we were spending our day doing, and I suddenly just couldn't wait to get out. I was in a plastic place with plastic people buying plastic products with plastic charge cards. I had to escape." Sometimes this reaction is accompanied by severe anxiety, alienation from the human race, and in at least one very severe case I know of, by all the usual manifestations of a drug overdose.

13 All of these, and their variations, are unfortunate side effects (or perhaps just extreme cases) of the main psychological effects that the mall intends. Excitement may become overstimulation; relaxation may drift into confusion and torpor. The combination is what I call the Zombie Effect.

14 There is, in fact, a fine line between the ideal mall shopper and the dismayed mall shopper, between mall bliss and mallaise, between the captivated shopper and the Zombie Effect. The best description of the Zombie Effect I've heard was Barbara Lambert's, which she imparted while we toured the malls of Chicagoland.

15 It hits you, Barbara said, when you're standing there naked, looking in the mirror of the dressing room. Your clothes are in a pile on the floor or draped over a chair. Maybe it's just a little cubicle with a curtain, and you can still hear the hum and buzz of the mall and the tiny timbres of Muzak. You're about to try something on, in an effortless repetition of what you've been doing since you came to the mall. And suddenly you realize *you've been here all day.* Time has in fact been passing while you've been gliding through store after store in

a tender fuzz of soft lights and soft music. The plash of fountains, the glow of people, but almost no intrusive sound has broken your floating—no telephone, no demands, nothing to dodge or particularly watch out for. Just a gentle visual parade of clothes, fabric tags, and washing instructions. Racks, displays, cosmetics, brisk signs, flowing greenery, and spasms of color in the dream light. An ice-cream cone, a cup of coffee. Other figures have glided by: walking models of the mall's products, or walking models of the weird. An old man who reminds you of your grandfather, sitting on a blond-wood bench under a potted palm. A woman who may or may not have been your best friend's other best friend in high school, striding by on strange shoes—or maybe that's a new style and yours are strange? You're looking at your naked image in a bare little room, and a little breeze touches you. Whatever you actually came here for is in the distant past. You've been floating here . . . for hours.

16 But that's the whole idea of this psychological structure: to turn off your mind and let you float; to create a direct and unfettered connection between eyeing and buying; and the more you do, the easier it becomes. Malls make for great eye/hand-on-credit-card co-ordination.

17 The way it's done is with a combination of peacefulness and stimulation. The environment bathes you in sweet neutrality with soft light, candied music, and all the amenities that reassure and please without grabbing too much individual attention. At the same time, the stores and products dance for you with friendly smiles and colorful costumes. The sheer number of products and experiences you pay for and their apparent variety are in themselves factors that excite and focus.

18 Once again, it's all a lot like television. TV lulls and stimulates simultaneously. The medium itself is familiar and comfortable and friendly; the programs can be interesting but it is not really by accident that they are not as compact, colorful, dramatic, or insistent as the commercials. Watching television we are everywhere and nowhere in particular, just as at the mall. Suddenly you might realize that you've been watching it all day, just floating for hours. And if you look at people watching television—especially their eyes—they look pretty much like mall shoppers: the Zombie Effect.

19 But these effects are all supposed to be pleasant and unconscious. When either the lulling or stimulating quality—or especially the combination and conflict between them—is strongly felt, then it's no longer pleasant. Overstimulation causes anxiety, and sometimes an intense focus on heavy-duty, no-nonsense, get-out-of-my-way shopping, or else a frenzied need to get out of there, fast and forever. The lulling and sense deprivation cause listlessness and confusion, and occasionally rebellion at being Muzaked into implacable mushy madness. The conflict of both going on at the same time can cause the sense of dislocation and exhaustion that is the clearest indicator of the Zombie Effect. The victim shuffles and mumbles, is distant or unduly preoccupied, doesn't listen, acts automatically, and not only can't remember where the car is parked but often doesn't care.

20 There are ancilliary symptoms and causes as well: headaches caused by guilt at buying too much; depression at not being able to buy everything; the walking emptiness caused by consistently emphasized, endless greed.

21   The cure for all forms of mallaise is theoretically simple: The victim leaves the mall. There are no laws requiring people to stay in the mall, or even to go there in the first place. It isn't anyone's civic, moral, spiritual, or intellectual duty. The mall may be the best place—or even the only place—to shop for certain products, but that doesn't mean the shopper has to stay there for hours. Nevertheless, it isn't always easy to leave.

22   For that is another aspect of the Zombie Effect: Victims stay for no good or apparent reason, and even beyond their conscious desire to be there. Shoppers mallinger partly because of the mall's psychological apparatus, its implicit promise of safety, sanctuary, and salvation. Of Nirvana! The Crystal City! A New Heaven on a New Earth! The mall hasn't become the most successful artificial environment in America for nothing.

23   With its real walls and psychological illusions, the mall protects against so many hazards and uncertainties that the mallaise sufferer may well mallinger a little longer to ponder the consequences of walking out. Such a person may fear trading the malladies of the Zombie Effect for the perils of mall withdrawal, which is characterized by shaking in downtown areas, fear of crossing streets, inordinate terror in the presence of rain or sunshine, confusion when actual travel is required between purchases, and the feeling of estrangement when wearing a coat.

24   I wish I could say that medical science is on top of this new set of malladies, but the truth is that it is scandalously behind the times. Right now, there may be many thousands of Zombie Effect sufferers, untreated and undiagnosed. If you find this hard to believe—well, have you been to the mall lately?

25   There is one more form of mallaise that is especially frustrating because it is not so simply cured, even theoretically. It is the state of being malcontented with what the mall offers and how it offers it. Sufferers will rail on about the same limited clothing styles reproduced in a hundred mall shops, or the same five movies shown in two dozen mall theaters—the only cinemas around. They will complain endlessly about fast-print outlets masquerading as bookstores, where clerks don't know anything more about books than what appears on the computer stock list. They will raise angry fists against the screening boxes calling themselves cinemas, with their dark and blurry unwatchable images on the screen, and cold and tinny sound.

26   These unfortunate mallcontents really have a problem, because in many places they don't have any alternative: If they want to shop for clothes, see a first-run movie, buy a new book or record, it's the mall or nothing.

27   They flail away at the promises the mall implies but does not keep. They are in a sense prisoners of the mall, if only because the mall's predominance has destroyed the alternatives they miss, even the imaginary ones.

Discussion and Writing Suggestions

1. At what point in this selection did you realize that Kowinski has a sense of humor? Work through the piece and mark what in your view are the funniest lines.

2. Through humor, Kowinski makes a number of penetrating observations about mall culture. Of the various maladies he catalogs (with
tongue in cheek), which one seems the most insightful? Why?

3. Have you observed in yourself, a friend, or family member any
symptoms of *mal de mall?* Describe your experience.

4. Kowinski compares mall shopping to television watching (see paragraph 18). Is the comparison apt, in your view?

5. In paragraph 16, Kowinski writes that the "whole idea of [the
mall's] psychological structure [is] to turn off your mind and let
you float; to create a direct and unfettered connection between
eyeing and buying." Have you ever noticed that malls are designed
to have a "psychological structure"? Explain.

6. In introducing the Zombie Effect (see paragraph 18), Kowinski
writes: "Watching television we are everywhere and nowhere in
particular, just as at the mall." Do you agree?

7. Kowinski gives the feeling of being lost in a mall a funny name:
dismallcumbobulation. But he is making a serious point in noting the
essential sameness of malls. Have you noticed how one mall often
looks like others—with the same chain stores and repeating architectural features? One could shop at a mall in Louisville or in
Buffalo and not be able to tell them apart. How do you respond to
these similarities? Have you ever been dismallcumbobulated?

8. In paragraph 25, Kowinski may come closest to expressing his
underlying view of malls than at any other point in the selection.
Reread the paragraph and summarize what you take to be his general attitude toward malls.

SYNTHESIS ACTIVITIES

1. In an explanatory paper that draws on several selections in this
chapter, explain to a time traveler from the sixteenth century, or a
visitor from the remotest regions on present-day Earth, the phenomenon of shopping malls. Answer basic questions, such as: What
is a mall? When did malls appear? Why? How are malls organized
and managed? Discuss important factors that gave rise to malls:
weather; transportation (development of cars and highways); and
the growth of suburbs. Finally, without taking sides, explain the
controversies sparked by malls.

2. In an exploratory paper, one in which you speculate more than
argue, attempt to define the deep-seated appeal that shopping centers hold for many people. The selections by Zepp and Francaviglia
should be helpful. In paragraph 44, Zepp suggests that we feel a
nostalgia in shopping malls—a longing for home, for a simplified
version of the world. In writing about Main Street USA (which

became a model design for malls), Francaviglia describes how Walt Disney re-created Main Street as it should have been, as simpler and more ordered than Main Streets actually were. Both authors attempt to explain the attraction of shopping malls. Working with these and one or two other authors in this chapter, explore the psychological (and if Zepp is to be believed, even spiritual) changes that can come over shoppers as they enter a mall.

3. James Farrell (paragraph 14) writes: "Like churches, [malls] are places where we decide what is ultimately valuable and how we will value it." Ira Zepp devotes considerable effort to understanding malls as sacred spaces. Working with these two authors and any others in the chapter who can contribute to the discussion, write an argument on the spiritual or religious dimensions of shopping malls. In this argument, you could discount the connection entirely, accept it, or accept it in part.

4. Lizabeth Cohen argues that malls built in the suburbs effectively shut out people who lived in the city and who could not afford a car—a development Cohen regards as a new expression of an old problem: racial and economic segregation. In your experience with shopping malls, what evidence do you find of either or both types of segregation? In developing a response, draw on the selections by Farrell (and his notion that malls tell "stories"); and Paquet (with her history of shopping centers in the eighteenth and nineteenth centuries appealing to wealthy clientele). Descriptions of your own experiences in malls could figure heavily into your paper.

5. Richard Francaviglia writes that "Sociologists have long known that people visit shopping centers for far more than commercial reasons" (paragraph 11). In a paper that draws on the work of Francaviglia, Gruen, Zepp, and Lewis as well as on your own experience, explain these noncommercial reasons for going to the mall.

6. Laura Paquet begins her selection by quoting an author who compares the modern mall to a fascistic medieval city-state. Francaviglia characterizes mall management as "autocratic." In a paper that draws on these two authors and also on Cohen and Guterson, answer this question: For customers, store owners, and mall management, what is gained and what is lost in rigorously controlling activities at the mall? Note that Victor Gruen, writing in 1960, argued (in paragraph 27) that carefully planning and controlling the retail space need *not* result in "authoritarianism, regimentation, or in the suppression of individualism."

7. Several authors in this chapter write on the layout of malls. Paquet relates the experience of getting lost. Francaviglia writes on the importance of intersections. Zepp writes about the significance of key design elements (such as circles). For Guterson, the mall feels like a giant prison. Given the work of these authors and

your experience at malls, write a paper examining the importance of mall design.

8. Use William Kowinski's concept of "mallaise" to analyze one or more of your visits to a mall. As independent evidence for mallaise, you might refer to the selections by Guterson (especially paragraph 5) and Paquet (especially paragraphs 59–82). The test of your analysis will be how successfully Kowinski's vocabulary helps you to see your shopping experience(s) in new and interesting ways.

9. Gruen (paragraphs 1–5) and Guterson (paragraphs 6, 16–18) fondly recall the bazaars and market places of old in which people came not only to buy but also to engage in the give and take of community life. Guterson (see especially paragraph 31) and Lewis (see paragraphs 1–7), particularly, claim that authentic community is difficult to find in modern shopping centers. If one finds community at all, it exists in spite of, not because of, management's efforts. What is your sense of shopping malls as a center of community life? Drawing on the views of authors in this chapter, develop your answer into an argument.

10. Guterson, Kowinski, Cohen, Lewis, and Paquet have found much to be critical of in shopping malls. By contrast, Farrell, Zepp, Francaviglia, and Gruen find much to recommend in malls. Given your experiences in malls, with which set of authors do you tend to agree? Do malls please you more than they disturb you, or vice versa? Draw on the authors in this chapter as you develop your answer in an argument.

11. In *Shopping Towns USA*, Victor Gruen envisioned shopping centers becoming the hub of suburban life. Centers would combine commercial space with public, civic space into "crystallization points" that would free suburbanites from traveling to the city to make major purchases. Moreover, shopping centers with their tightly controlled programs for design and management would make rational the previously haphazard method of locating stores in suburbia. Gruen did not live to see his vision fulfilled. Was his plan naive? Do you think the community function of shopping centers could coexist with the commercial function? Is there still hope for such a combination, or is the mall's effort best left to making money?

12. In the introduction to this chapter you will find a block quotation from James J. Farrell's book, *One Nation Under Goods*. Farrell claims that shopping centers are places where the culture answers fundamental questions about itself, such as: What does it mean to be human? What are people for? Reread the full list of questions, select *one*, and write a synthesis in which you argue that it is possible, or impossible, to answer such a question by studying shopping centers. In addition to using Farrell's selection, you might draw on the work of Paquet, Francaviglia, Gruen, Lewis, and Cohen.

13. Relate an experience you've had in a shopping center and analyze it in light of any of the reading selections in this chapter. How can the insights of one (or more) of the chapter's authors help you to understand your experience?

RESEARCH ACTIVITIES

1. Devote some time to viewing movies that are set, at least partially, in malls: You might consider the horror classic, George Romero's *Dawn of the Dead* (a sequel to *Night of the Living Dead*), *Mall Rats*, *Scenes from a Mall*, and *Fast Times at Ridgemont High*. Watch one or more of the movies several times, and then write a paper in which you "read" the director's vision of modern American life as it is expressed in shopping malls. As part of your research, you might draw on movie reviews. More ambitious projects will involve a comparative treatment of two or more movies.

2. Investigate and report on the types of data that social scientists collect in their efforts to help store owners boost sales. You might begin with a book like *Why We Buy: The Science of Shopping*, in which Paco Underhill (an anthropologist) relates how he conducts field studies of shoppers in the act of shopping. Others who investigate the purchasing habits of shoppers include sociologists, psychologists, and economists. The general topic, the "science of shopping," is very broad, and you will want to narrow the focus. Some possibilities: the design of store displays, the training of sales staff, the choice of background music, or the routing of customers through a retail space. This assignment stresses information, so you will be writing an explanatory synthesis.

3. Read William Kowinski's *Malling of America*, from which one selection in this chapter ("Mallaise") was excerpted. *Malling* has become something of a classic. After you read it, gather book reviews from around the country (check the *Book Review Digest*) and report on the book's reception.

4. Identify one shopping mall project about which you would like to learn more. The project may be a national destination mall, like the Mall of America, or a regional mall near your home. Based on newspaper and magazine articles, trace for readers the mall's progress from the permit process to the opening. How involved was the community in the process? Were there protests? Did the town or city government provide incentives for mall development? Did the developers rely on union labor? These are just of a few of the many questions you might explore in your research. Your goal is to tell the mall's story, from conception to design to building to occupancy.

5. Research the phenomenon of "dead" or "ghost" malls: facilities that are twenty years or older that have been left vacant. What are the

forces that drive malls to failure? (Possibilities: population trends; an anchor store's not renewing its lease; competition from new or neighboring malls.) How great a problem are vacant malls? How have communities repurposed them? In writing your paper, gather enough research to point out broad, industrywide trends and then, as a case study, illustrate these trends by relating the demise of a *particular* shopping mall.

6. Choose a shopping mall to visit three or four times over the course of several weeks. On your first visit, spend one hour watching people shop, and take notes. Later, review your notes and decide on a particular question you would like to explore on return visits. Pose that question as precisely as possible: it may concern a particular population at the mall (seniors, mothers with kids, fathers with kids, couples, teens, etc); a particular aspect of mall management (perhaps security, janitorial, or food services); mall architecture; traffic flow. Any of the readings in this chapter will help you to identify a particular question to pursue. Having framed the question, return to the mall for a series of one-hour visits in which you make and record observations. (Avoid shopping! Your focus is on gathering information.) Write a paper in which you report on your research. Include a description of the mall studied, a context for your question (a discussion of why the question is interesting), data that you recorded (albeit informally), and a discussion of what you discovered.

7. Research one of the predecessors of the modern mall, taking as your starting point the article in this chapter by Laura Paquet. Paquet discusses the Greek stoa, the Roman Forum, the Middle Eastern bazaar or souk, the Grand Bazaar of Constantinople, the Royal Exchange (London), the Palais Royal (Paris), or the arcades of London or Milan. The research paper that you write will be explanatory in nature. Assume that your audience is familiar with shopping malls but unfamiliar with the shopping venues throughout history that preceded the mall.

8. Reread paragraphs 17–23 in Lizabeth Cohen's article, "From Town Center to Shopping Center," and select for further research one of the Supreme Court cases she discusses concerning the limits to free speech in privately owned shopping centers. Locate the Supreme Court opinion and summarize it. Re-create for readers the conflict that led to the court case, and discuss (after your summary) the implications of the Court's decision on future protests at shopping centers. You might try conducting your research on the Internet, particularly if you have access to the LexisNexis database. Select "Federal Case Law" and, within this area, "Supreme Court" cases. Choose "Guided Search," as opposed to "Basic Search," so that you can use more keywords and combinations of keywords. Try such keywords as "free speech" OR "freedom of speech" AND "mall"

OR "privately owned shopping center*" and other such terms; and search for "all available dates." If you have the citation number for a case (like "485 U.S. 112"), you can directly input the citation (without the need for keywords) to retrieve the case.

9. Research differences in shopping patterns between men and women. You might focus on one or more of the following questions: Do men and women shop with different expectations about the speed of making purchases? Do either tend to shop for the sake of (that is, the pleasure of) shopping? Do women "look" more than men? Do either tend to regard shopping more as a social as opposed to functional, or necessary, activity? Do men more than women tend to be impulse shoppers? Locate carefully controlled studies when conducting your research.

Weight Debate

You may have heard of (or may be fighting!) the "Freshman 15"—the extra weight that first-year students gain when they settle down to endless helpings of high-calorie cafeteria food. More calories in than out (no time for exercise with all that studying—right?) is the basic equation for weight gain. And in record numbers, Americans—college students included—are packing on the pounds. The most recent figures indicate that 64 percent of American adults are overweight or obese and that 13 percent of children are overweight. By 2005, the poor diet and sedentary lifestyles associated with obesity may lead to more preventable deaths than tobacco use, according to one recently published study. At the same time that the majority of Americans are gaining unprecedented amounts of weight, an alarmingly high number of girls and young women are voluntarily starving themselves (sometimes to death) in an effort to achieve an idealized image of slenderness promoted by the media. Too many pounds and too few: America has a weight problem.

Open most newspapers or magazines and the chances are excellent that you will find advertisements featuring images of underweight models. The entertainment and advertising industries bombard us with streams of fit, toned actors who remind us, whether we agree or not, that thin is in. Whole industries have emerged to help us achieve this lean and hungry look, but recent statistics show that fewer and fewer of us are succeeding.

According to the Centers for Disease Control and the *Journal of the American Medical Association,* the number of Americans who are overweight or obese has reached epidemic proportions.* One in two American adults is overweight; one in five is obese. In this country we spend $75 billion annually in obesity-related medical expenses and lose another $42 billion in diminished productivity. Add to these amounts the $33 billion Americans spend trying to *lose* weight each year, and the magnitude of the problem begins to take shape. Lest you think being overweight or obese poses a problem only to those immediately concerned, think again: Medicaid and Medicare, funded by *your* tax dollars, paid $39 billion dollars in 2003 for people suffering from obesity-related illnesses: diabetes, heart disease, certain cancers, and gallbladder disease. That's federal money *not* spent on providing student loans, for instance.

Monetary losses associated with weight gain represent only the measurable portion of the problem. In a culture infatuated with youthful athleticism, the obese too often suffer from profound lack of self-esteem as friends, family, coworkers, and strangers unfairly equate being fat with flaws of character. And it is not as if the overweight and obese don't try to lose weight. Dieting is one of America's urgent pastimes: at any given moment, 29 percent of men and 44 percent of American

---

* In 2001, the U.S. Surgeon General published a "Call to Action to Prevent and Decrease Overweight and Obesity." You can find the full report along with comprehensive statistics on the state of America's weight at <http://www.surgeongeneral.gov/topics/obesity/>.

women are trying to lose weight. But diets—95 percent of them—do *not* work, according to recent studies; and so those who have every intention of thinning down find themselves doomed to a cycle of losing weight and, within months or a few years, gaining all or most of it back. At the other end of the scale, literally and figuratively, the psychological costs of monitoring one's weight are equally overwhelming to the nation's 7 to 10 million anorexics and bulimics. For well over a decade, physicians and therapists have sought to help their patients get the nutrition they need to thrive, but their conditions remain stubbornly resistant to change.

On the one hand, then, our culture pressures us to be thin, exacting a heavy price in self-esteem if we are not. On the other, competitive forces have led the food industry to invest millions in manipulating the flavors and textures of their goods so that we will buy and eat more. Couple this effort with clever advertising campaigns, super-sized portions, and bright packaging, and one wonders why every American isn't either overweight or terrified to eat anything at all.* Our culture makes us the object of a strange tug-of-war, urging us to consume while at the same time warning us to show no visible signs of consumption. As a result, some choose self-starvation; record numbers move in the other direction, eating all that good food even as they look miserably each morning at the bathroom scale. Whether too fat or too thin, at the end of the day Americans think constantly, even obsessively, about weight.

This chapter gathers some provocative articles and essays on being overweight and obese—that is, on being *fat*. We use this politically incorrect word neutrally, not pejoratively, following the usage of several authors whose work appears in the pages that follow.† The readings divide into two sections, the first a gathering of facts and figures, the second a series of commentaries. We open with a February 2004 cover story, "Rethinking Weight," from *U.S. News and World Report* in which senior writer Amanda Spake presents an overview of America's weight debate, calling our attention particularly to a question occupying many researchers: Should we consider obesity a disease, as we do alcoholism? (In July 2004, Medicare announced that it would cover the expenses related to obesity treatments. These include stomach surgery, diet programs, and behavioral and psychological counseling.) Following this overview, you will find an editorial by physicians Jeffrey P. Koplan and William H. Dietz from the the *Journal of the American Medical Association*, which begins with the claim that "Obesity is epidemic in the United States." Next we offer two tables summarizing data from a recent study by the Centers for Disease Control and Prevention on the prevalence of obesity among U.S. adults.

The second part of the chapter consists of readings that comment on our culture's preoccupation with thinness. We begin with an op-ed piece for the

---

* In early 2004, McDonald's decided to stop offering a "Supersize" option at its restaurants.

† The literature on anorexia nervosa and bulimia is so extensive that we could not represent it with any reasonably comprehensive coverage here. If you have an interest in these subjects, you will find many books and articles readily available in community as well as academic libraries, and also on the Web.

Los Angeles Times by Greg Critser, who argues that in order to reduce weight-related problems in this country we should stigmatize the behavior of unhealthy overeating, teaching children (especially) that "[e]ating too much food is a bad thing." Next comes a policy statement from the National Association to Advance Fat Acceptance (NAAFA) on the subject of "Dieting and the Diet Industry." Mary Ray Worley, a NAAFA member, writes of the debilitating self-hatred among fat people and of her life-changing decision to join "a growing number of people [who] believe it's possible to be happy with your body even if it happens to be fat." Roberta Seid follows with "Too 'Close to the Bone': The Historical Context for Women's Obsession with Slenderness." In a startlingly original critique, Seid examines the spiritual dimensions of our obsession with thinness as well as the historical changes that led to a new—and thinner—body ideal. Next, Hillel Schwartz argues that our culture is caught in the grip of a "despotism of slenderness." He imagines a fat "utopia" in which fat people accept themselves and are accepted by the culture at large. In an editorial that appeared in the journal *Science,* Marion Nestle, a professor in the Department of Nutrition and Food Studies at New York University, then offers insights into the politics of obesity. We conclude the chapter with a selection by Atul Gawande, writing in the *New Yorker.* A surgeon who assisted on a gastric-bypass, Gawande tells the story of Vincent Caselli, a Boston-area contractor whose efforts to lose weight proved so futile that he submitted to an increasingly popular surgical procedure that reduced his stomach to a one-ounce-sized pouch.

A note on statistics: Monthly, it seems, researchers are updating data on the incidence of overweight and obesity, and you will find discrepancies among articles on such basic information as the percentage of the U.S. adult population that is overweight or obese (the correct number, as of March 2004, is 64 percent). When citing statistics in your work, use those found in the most recent of this chapter's articles: the selection from *U.S. News and World Report* (February 2004) and the tables from the Centers for Disease Control (November 2003). If you can find even more current data (check the CDC website, <www.cdc.gov>, and type "obesity statistics" into the search box), so much the better. Changing statistics aside, the arguments you will find in this chapter on how we should be thinking about America's weight problems remain current.

Rethinking Weight
Amanda Spake

One sure sign that the obesity epidemic has caught the nation's attention is the increased number of articles devoted to the subject in the popular press. The following selection appeared as a cover story in the 9 February 2004 edition of U.S. News and World Report. *Amanda Spake is a senior writer for the magazine and has served both as a contributor to* Salon.com *and as an editor to the* Washington Post *magazine and* Mother Jones. *In this piece, Spake directs our attention to a central debate among obesity researchers: whether or not to classify obesity as a disease (just as alcoholism is classified as a disease). The ultimate positions of the government and insurance companies in this debate will determine for tens of millions the levels of support they will receive in fighting to achieve a healthy weight.*

1 Maria Pfisterer has never in her life been skinny. The Arlington, Texas, mother of three was at her slimmest at age 18, when she married Fred, an Air Force sergeant. But she was plump, not seriously fat. She first became seriously overweight at age 21, when she gained about 70 pounds during her first pregnancy. By the time she delivered her daughter Jordan, now 14, she was carrying over 200 pounds on her 5-foot, 2-inch frame.

2 Over the past 14 years, Pfisterer has tried every weight-loss strategy imaginable: She has taken the (now banned) appetite-suppressing drug combo fen-phen (she lost 60 pounds only to regain it during her second pregnancy). She went on a doctor-prescribed and -supervised low-calorie diet (she lost 10 pounds but regained it). She has been enrolled in Jenny Craig, Weight Watchers, Curves, and a variety of quick-weight-loss fads. All resulted in a little lost and more regained. She has taken antidepressants, reputed to have weight loss as a side effect. They didn't for her. She would love to get into one of those intensive medical weight-loss programs, but she can't afford the $4,000-plus price tag. So she does what she can. "If I lose weight, it seems like I always go back up to that same 197 to 202 range," she says. "I just don't know how to keep it off."

3 Pfisterer isn't alone. A majority of Americans—now 64 percent—are overweight or obese and struggling to conquer their expanding waistlines before their fat overtakes their health and makes them sick or kills them. At the heart of this obesity epidemic is a debate over whether obesity is a biological "disease" and should be treated like any other life-threatening illness—cancer, heart disease—or whether it is simply a risk factor for those killers. The stakes are high because the answer may determine who gets treated for obesity, what treatments are available, who pays for treatment, and, ultimately, who stays healthy.

4 New understandings of the biology of obesity are driving the debate. "I think there's enough data now relating to mechanisms of food intake regulation that suggest obesity is a biologically determined process," says Xavier Pi-Sunyer, director of the Obesity Research Center at St. Luke's-Roosevelt Hospital in New York City. And many national and international health organizations—from the National Institutes of Health (NIH) to the World Health Organization—agree. The WHO has listed obesity as a disease in its International Classification of Diseases since 1979. In fact, the organization recently called on member states to adopt programs to encourage a reduction of fat and sugar in the global diet. The recommendation did not sit well with the U.S. food industry or with some within the Bush administration, who still maintain the obesity epidemic can be reversed by individuals taking more personal responsibility and making better lifestyle choices. Many health insurers agree. "For a wide number of people in this country the question is: How do you motivate people to make changes in diet and increase physical activity?" says Susan Pisano of the Health Insurance Association of America.

5 The reason governments, insurance companies, and others still take such positions, says Pi-Sunyer, is that "they are worried they will have to reimburse doctors and patients for treatment. And now, you have such a huge number

of people needing treatment." On any given day, about 29 percent of men and 44 percent of women are trying to lose weight, and presumably a large percentage of those would love to be offered medically supervised treatment if it were covered in their health insurance plan.

6   Instead, they pay out of pocket for a $33 billion commercial diet industry—and keep getting fatter. The number of people who are severely obese—that is, those with a body mass index of 40 or above or who are more than 100 pounds overweight—is growing two times as fast as is obesity generally. From 1986 to 2000, the prevalence of Americans reporting a BMI of 40 or above quadrupled, from about 1 in 200 adults to 1 in 50. People who are severely obese generally have more weight-related illnesses and require more expensive treatments than do those who are merely "too fat."

7   **Fat's High Price** A new study by RTI International and the Centers for Disease Control and Prevention, published this month in the journal *Obesity Research,* shows that the nation is spending about $75 billion a year on weight-related disease. Type II diabetes, heart disease, hypertension, high cholesterol, gallbladder disease, osteoarthritis merely top the list. Almost 80 percent of obese adults have one of these conditions, and nearly 40 percent have two or more.

8   Healthcare costs for illnesses resulting from obesity now exceed those related to both smoking and problem drinking. About 325,000 deaths a year are attributed to obesity. The trend lines are only expected to get worse, since childhood obesity is also increasing rapidly.

9   Researchers are encouraged by the stance taken by the WHO and NIH, as well as the American Medical Association, the National Academy of Sciences, and the CDC. Says Yale psychologist Kelly Brownell: "The ramifications could be enormous—for opening up better treatments, and to some extent for social attitudes toward people with this problem. When alcoholism was declared a disease, it changed attitudes and reduced the stigma of blame."

10   And to be sure, there is no shortage of stigma and blame when it comes to obesity. Weight discrimination dates back to the early Christian church, which included "gluttony" as one of the seven deadly sins. Obesity was viewed as the outward manifestation of the "sin" of overindulgence. Most overweight adults have suffered ridicule, self-consciousness, or depression, particularly if they were obese as children or adolescents. Severely obese patients frequently report workplace discrimination. One woman told researchers: "They put my desk in the back office where no one could see me."

11   Prejudice against the obese stems from the widely held belief that getting fat—and certainly staying fat—results from a failure of willpower, a condition that could be remedied if obese people simply made a personal choice to eat less. But to most obesity experts this notion of personal choice is downright nutty. "Who would choose to be obese?" asks Rudolph Leibel, a Columbia University geneticist and a noted obesity researcher. "Telling someone they've decided to become obese is like saying, 'You've decided to give yourself a brain tumor.'"

12   Increasingly, researchers are demonstrating that obesity is controlled by a powerful biological system of hormones, proteins, neurotransmitters, and genes that regulate fat storage and body weight and tell the brain when, what, and how much to eat. "This is not debatable," says Louis Aronne, director of the

Comprehensive Weight Control Program at New York-Presbyterian Hospital and president-elect of the North American Association for the Study of Obesity.* "Once people gain weight, then these biological mechanisms, which we're beginning to understand, develop to prevent people from losing weight. It's not someone fighting 'willpower.' The body resists weight loss."

13   This wonder of natural chemical engineering evolved over centuries to protect humans against famine and assure reproduction of the species. "The idea that nature would leave this system to a matter of 'choice' is naive," says Arthur Frank, director of George Washington University's Weight Management Program. "Eating is largely driven by signals from fat tissue, from the gastrointestinal tract, the liver. All those organs are sending information to the brain to eat or not to eat. So, saying to an obese person who wants to lose weight, 'All you have to do is eat less,' is like saying to a person suffering from asthma, 'All you have to do is breathe better.' "

14   When Maria Pfisterer looks at her family, she sees her future—and it is frightening. Her father, a diabetic with congestive heart failure and hypertension, weighs nearly 400 pounds, and at age 60 he can scarcely move. Her older sister is also obese and suffers from hypertension. Both Maria and her sister worry they will eventually develop diabetes like their dad.

15   "My daughter Jordan is very heavy. She's struggling already with weight, and if she gets any more sedentary, I worry what will happen to her," says Pfisterer. "I'm trying to teach her to eat better and keep active. She's into dance, but she'll say, 'I'm the fattest kid there.' It breaks my heart."

16   Pfisterer herself says she does not eat a lot and is always on the go. "I don't eat half gallons of ice cream or bags of chips. But if I lose a little, I regain. I think genetics have a lot to do with it."

17 **Studies of Twins** Leibel, director of the division of molecular genetics at Columbia University College of Physicians and Surgeons, has spent a career documenting what Pfisterer knows intuitively. He says, "I believe there are strong genetic factors that determine susceptibility to obesity." Obesity does not result from a single gene, he explains, but rather a variety of genes that interact with environmental influences to increase one's chance of becoming obese. In studies of adult twins, who share many or all of the same genes, BMI,[†] body composition, and other measures of fatness appear to be 20 to 70 percent inherited.

18   Still, biology is not destiny. Overweight results from one thing: eating more food than one burns in physical activity. Genes simply facilitate becoming fat. "I think the primary problem is on the food intake side," Leibel adds. "There are multiple genes involved in that intake process, and there is good reason to believe that nature and evolution have selected for ingestion of large amounts of food."

19   But even when limitless food is available, not everyone gets fat. In a series of studies of adult twins in Quebec who ate a high-calorie diet designed to produce weight gain, results between sets of twins were vastly different. Some twin

---

* *The North American Association for the Study of Obesity* is later referred to by its acronym *NAASO*. See the organization's Web site at <http://www.naaso.org/>.

† *BMI*, or Body Mass Index, is a ratio of weight in relation to height and one measure of fatness. See page 348 for a BMI chart.

pairs gained three times as much weight and fat as others. "We know there are genetic factors," says Jules Hirsch, professor emeritus at Rockefeller University, "but obesity may be a multistep process." Hirsch says an overabundance of fat cells leading to obesity may be the result of gene-environmental interactions that occur in infancy or in utero, leading to vastly different responses to food in adulthood. The story of the offspring of women who survived the Dutch winter famine of 1944–45 may be a case in point. Babies born to women who suffered severe undernutrition early in their pregnancies tended to have more fat and become obese more readily as adults. But the offspring of women who were undernourished late in pregnancy tended to be leaner and have less fat as adults. Clearly, says Hirsch, there is a great deal more to learn about how obesity develops.

20   Even scientists who basically accept that obesity is a sophisticated biological problem feel that treatment has to consider the powerful roles of social organization and psychology. Take the case of the bottomless soup bowls.

21   University of Illinois nutrition and marketing professor Brian Wansink sat student volunteers in front of bowls of tomato soup in his lab and told them they were involved in a "taste test." Some of the students' bowls were normal. The others had bowls that automatically refilled from a hidden tube in the bottom. The students with the bottomless bowls ate an average of about 40 percent more soup before their brain told them they were full. "Biology has made us efficient at storing fat," says Wansink. "But obesity is not just biology; it's psychology. We're not good at tracking how much we eat. So we use cues—we eat until the plate is empty, or the soup is gone, or the TV show is over."

22   Indeed, research shows that people eat more in groups and with friends than they do when dining alone. Simply eating with one other person increases the average amount eaten at meals by 44 percent. Meals eaten with large groups of friends tend to be longer in duration and are as much as 75 percent bigger that those eaten alone. Eating with someone, suggests John DeCastro, the author of these studies, probably leads to relaxation and a "disinhibition of restraint."

23   Viewing obesity principally as a biological disease worries Wansink because he fears it will remove personal control and shift blame to someone else. But doctors who treat overweight patients say that thinking of obesity as a disease would simply make more treatment available. Most obesity programs rely on personal responsibility to put into action behavioral techniques designed to achieve greater control over biology. "Most of our treatment is still based on modifying choice," says GWU's Frank. "But underneath it all you've got to recognize why it is so difficult to eat less and lose weight. It doesn't make it easier, but it takes it out of the world of willful misconduct."

24 **Frauds** The biggest dilemma overweight people face is the world of largely mediocre, misleading, useless, or downright dangerous devices, diet programs, supplements, and drugs promoted to reduce fat. "The treatment of obesity is littered with a history of abuses," says NAASO's Aronne. "Every infomercial out there about weight is damaging people because it's giving them an unrealistic view of what can be done." Most university- and hospital-based weight-loss programs produce a 10 percent loss of body weight in six months. This is more than enough to reduce the incidence of Type II diabetes by 58 percent and

lower blood pressure in borderline hypertensives. But it is not enough to make a fat person as thin as a Hollywood celebrity. Coverage of obesity by health insurers might bring science and sanity to the chaos of weight loss, where, as Aronne puts it, "ethical treatments are competing in an unethical marketplace."

25   But clinicians acknowledge that weight-loss successes are modest. "To be frank, a lot of the treatment has not been very effective," says Pi-Sunyer. He points out that there are currently two drugs approved for long-term treatment of obesity, sibutramine and orlistat. Their effect is modest, and their cost is high, about $100 a month. "So for people to pay that amount, they would like to see more impressive results." Two drugs approved for treating epilepsy, topiramate and zonisamide, are being tested to treat obesity, but the jury is still out on them. "So that's an out for the insurers," says Pi-Sunyer. They can say, 'Unless you have a treatment that takes weight off and keeps it off, then why pay for it?' It would be a much stronger argument if we had a more proven treatment."

26   What's standing in the way? Basically funding for research. The American Obesity Association reports that NIH funding for research on obesity is less than one sixth that spent on AIDS. "Given the nature of the problem and the side effects," says Pi-Sunyer, "we're spending a pittance."

27   The health insurance industry argues that obesity treatments can't be covered because there is no evidence of effectiveness. Critics counter that the same argument could apply to a lot of complicated diseases. "We don't have a good way of treating Alzheimer's disease," says GWU's Frank, "and we don't have a particularly good way of treating AIDS either. We have a health insurance system based on illness, not treatment effectiveness. Why should obesity be the one disease that's subjected to this cost-effectiveness standard?"

28   About half of the $75 billion yearly price tag for obesity is covered by taxpayers in Medicare and Medicaid funds. These government health plans are debating right now whether the plans should cover obesity treatment. Currently, only in cases of severe obesity will government and some private insurers reimburse doctors for surgery to reduce girth.

29   But not always. Samantha Moore, a 26-year-old Maine woman who weighs nearly 400 pounds, was recently turned down a third time for gastric bypass surgery. Even though she has been dieting all her life, her insurer denied surgery because she has not made enough "medically supervised" attempts at weight loss. Does the insurer pay for medically supervised weight loss? "No," says Moore. "It's shocking to me that the insurance company keeps saying, essentially, 'You're not sick enough to get this surgery.' I think they're putting off a decision because if I wait much longer, I'll be too sick to get the surgery."

30 **Fat or Fit?** Not all scientists agree that labeling obesity "a disease" will improve the situation for people like Pfisterer or Moore. Stephen Ball, an exercise physiologist at the University of Missouri, says, "If we call obesity a disease, then anything that reduces one's fatness or lowers BMI would be a successful treatment, such as liposuction or a very low-calorie diet, where we know these are not healthy. By the same token, if you don't lose weight with an exercise program but your blood glucose becomes normal, cholesterol improves, then that could

be considered a failure, because it didn't reduce weight. Fitness is a more important indicator of health outcomes than fatness."

31   Indeed, Steven Blair at the Cooper Institute in Dallas has shown that cardio-vascular fitness as measured on a treadmill test is a better predictor of mortality and illness than BMI. "I'm convinced . . . that people who are active or fit but in a high BMI group have lower death rates from all causes—cancer, heart disease, diabetes—than the sedentary and unfit in the normal or lean BMI category. Even among women in our study with BMIs of 37, 20 percent did well enough on the treadmill test to be considered fit. We're obsessed with weight, but where has that gotten us?"

32   Ultimately, if better and more accessible treatments are not offered to obese Americans, the cost not only of obesity but of treatment and health insurance will escalate. The number of people undergoing surgery doubled from 2001 to 2003, in part because people are becoming more obese but also because many want medical help with weight loss and can't find any other treatment health insurers will cover.

33   Frustrated with her options and limited ability to pay for treatment, about six months ago Maria Pfisterer began to explore the possibility of gastric bypass surgery. She is not 100 pounds overweight, and her BMI is not over 40—generally the criteria physicians use for evaluating candidates who would benefit from surgery. Gastric bypass surgery is an irreversible procedure in which the size of the stomach is reduced and the small intestine is bypassed to produce rapid weight loss in people whose fat is putting their lives in danger. Recovery is long, complication rates are high, side effects are bothersome, and it's major surgery—people die from it. But Pfisterer learned through obesity-help.com, a Web site offering advice to the obese, that her insurer might pay for surgery, given her family history.

34   "For people like me, who are considered on the low end for surgery, there are other options that might be better," she says. "But I can't take advantage of them unless health insurance starts to pay for them."

Review Questions

1. What debate lies at the center of the obesity epidemic, and what is its significance?

2. Why did the Bush administration object to the World Health Organization's classification of obesity as a "disease" and recommendation that people eat less fat and sugar?

3. What motivation do insurers have for *not* regarding obesity as a disease? Currently, what is the insurance industry's response to coverage for weight-loss treatments?

4. Identify some of the more important obesity-related statistics that Spake cites in this article.

5. What do obesity researchers believe about the claim that obese people lack the willpower to lose weight?

6. What adaptive use has storing fat had in human history?

7. What do studies of twins suggest about the interplay between genetic makeup and environment in causing obesity?

8. What roles do social organization and psychology play in gaining weight, according to obesity studies?

9. In what ways can consumers be confused by the various treatments for obesity, some medically approved, some not?

10. Summarize the argument that it is possible to be fat but fit.

Discussion and Writing Suggestions

1. Did any of the obesity related statistics in this article surprise you? Which ones? Why?

2. "'Who would choose to be obese?' asks Rudolph Leibel, a Columbia University geneticist and a noted obesity researcher. 'Telling someone they've decided to become obese is like saying, "You've decided to give yourself a brain tumor." ' " Your response?

3. Reread paragraphs 30 and 31. How difficult would it be for you, considering cultural stereotypes, to regard an active but obese person as "fit"? Explain your response.

4. Spake writes: "Weight discrimination dates back to the early Christian church, which included 'gluttony' as one of the seven deadly sins. Obesity was viewed as the outward manifestation of the 'sin' of overindulgence." What evidence of this "early Christian" thinking do you see in evidence today? Do you detect any sense in which obese people are regarded as morally flawed?

5. To what extent are Spake's remarks concerning weight discrimination and prejudice against the obese (see paragraphs 10–11) applicable to those who are overweight (but not obese)?

6. Discuss evidence you have seen of weight discrimination and prejudice.

7. Review the references to Maria Pfisterer throughout the article, in paragraphs 1–3, 14–16, and 33–34. To what use is Spake putting these references in the article?

Caloric Imbalance and Public Health Policy
Jeffrey P. Koplan, MD, MPH and
William H. Dietz, MD, PhD

On 27 October 1999, the Journal of the American Medical Association (JAMA), *one of the country's most prestigious medical journals, devoted an entire issue to obesity—a publication decision that demanded the attention of the American public. Articles in this issue reported on the increased mortality and disease risk associated with obesity. Working with data that had been recently gathered by the Centers for Disease Control and Prevention (CDC) in Atlanta, Koplan and Dietz open their editorial with a brief, dramatic statement. In 2001, the U.S. Surgeon General, David Satcher, amplified the urgency of their editorial in his* Call to Action to Prevent and Decrease Overweight and Obesity. *It is now commonplace to see the words* obesity *and* epidemic *in the same sentence.*

1   Obesity is epidemic in the United States. More than 50% of U.S. adults are now overweight, based on a body mass index (BMI)[1] of 25 kg/m² or more.[2] Furthermore, 22% of the U.S. adult population is obese, based on a BMI of 30 kg/m² or more, equivalent to approximately 13.5 kg (30 lb) overweight. Three percent of U.S. adults have a BMI of 40 kg/m² or more, which represents a weight excess of approximately 45 kg (100 lb). Blacks and Hispanics are disproportionately affected. As the study by Mokdad and colleagues in this issue of *The Journal*[3] clearly demonstrates, the increase in the prevalence of obesity has been rapid. No area of the country has been spared.

2   Obesity is not simply a cosmetic disorder. Approximately 60% of overweight 5- to 10-year-old children already have 1 associated biochemical or clinical cardiovascular risk factor, such as hyperlipidemia, elevated blood pressure, or increased insulin levels, and 25% have 2 or more.[4] As Must and colleagues[5] demonstrate in their article, the risk factors observed in children will become chronic diseases in adults. Almost 80% of obese adults have diabetes, high blood cholesterol levels, high blood pressure, coronary artery disease, gallbladder disease, or osteoarthritis, and almost 40% have 2 or more

---

[1] Your Body Mass Index is your weight in kilograms divided by the square of your height in meters. See the BMI chart immediately following this editorial. [editors]

[2] Flegal KM, Carroll MD, Kuczmarski RJ, Johnson CL. Overweight and obesity in the United States: prevalence and trends, 1960–1994. *Int J Obesity,* 1998;22:39–47.

[3] Mokdad AH, Serdula MK, Dietz WH, Bowman BA, Marks JS, Koplan JP. The spread of the obesity epidemic in the United States, 1991–1998. *JAMA.* 1999;282:1519–1522.

[4] Freedman DS, Dietz WH, Srinivasan SR, Berenson GS. The relation of overweight to cardiovascular risk factors among children and adolescents: the Bogalusa Heart Study. *Pediatrics.* 1999;103:1175–1182.

[5] Must A, Spadano J, Coakley EH, Field AE, Colditz G, Dietz WH. The disease burden associated with overweight and obesity. *JAMA.* 1999;282:1523–1529.

[handwritten margin notes: smoking, #1 leader in preventable death]

of these comorbidities. Based on the study by Allison and colleagues,[6] only smoking exceeds obesity in its contribution to total mortality rates in the United States. A recent estimate suggesting that the direct and indirect costs of obesity in the United States approximated 10% of the national health care budget[7] underscores why the nation can no longer afford to ignore obesity as a major medical problem.

[handwritten margin note: Genes are not solely to blame.]

3   Genes related to obesity are clearly not responsible for the epidemic of obesity because the gene pool in the United States did not change significantly between 1980 and 1994. However, comparison of the differences in BMI in children and adolescents on a percentile by percentile basis indicates that the changes in BMI were limited to the upper half of the BMI distribution; the mean BMI increased by substantially more than the median.[8] These observations suggest either that 50% of children and adolescents had obesity susceptibility genes that were acted on by environmental changes, or that environmental changes only affected 50% of the population.

4   The human body, like any system, obeys the laws of thermodynamics. An excess of energy intake over expenditure leads to storage of energy in the form of fat. What may have developed as an evolutionary response to periods of famine and sparse foodstuffs has become a burden with negative health consequences in contemporary society. Only during the last several decades has an imbalance of energy intake and output occurred for a large proportion of the American population.

5   Between surveys conducted from 1977 through 1978 and 1994 through 1996, reported daily energy intakes increased from 9404 (2239) to 10 311 kJ (2455 kcal) in men and from 6443 (1534) to 6913 kJ (1646 kcal) in women.[9,10] Innumerable environmental changes that foster eating more frequently have occurred: the availability of more food and foods with higher energy content, the growth of the fast food industry, the increased numbers and marketing of snack foods, and an increased time for socializing along with a custom of socializing with food and drink. In a parallel development, opportunities in daily life to burn energy have diminished: children watch more television daily, physical education has been markedly reduced in our schools, many neighborhoods lack sidewalks for safe walking, the workplace has become

[6] Allison DB, Fontaine KR, Manson JE, Stevens J, VanItallie TB. Annual deaths attributable to obesity in the United States. *JAMA*. 1999;282:1530–1538.

[7] Wolf AM, Colditz GA. Current estimates of the economic costs of obesity in the United States. *Obesity Res*. 1998;6:97–106.

[8] Troiano RP, Flegal KM. Overweight children and adolescents: description, epidemiology, and demographics. *Pediatrics*. 1998;101(suppl):497–504.

[9] Federation of American Societies for Experimental Biology, Life Sciences Research Office. *Third Report on Nutrition Monitoring in the United States*. Vol 2. Washington, DC: U.S. Government Printing Office; 1995.

[10] Frazao E. *America's Eating Habits: Changes and Consequences*. Washington, DC: U.S. Dept of Agriculture; 1999. Information Bulletin AIB–750.

increasingly automated, household chores are assisted by labor saving machinery, and walking or bicycling has been replaced by automobile travel for all but the shortest distances. *← important → (how we've become obese)*

6   Public health and clinical strategies to address the obesity epidemic must begin with weight maintenance for the adult population, weight loss for the obese, and increased physical activity for all. Weight maintenance for the obese as well as the nonobese will prevent further increases in the prevalence and the severity of obesity and also will prevent new cases of obesity in those who currently have weights within the healthy range. Modest weight losses of 5% to 10% of body weight improve glucose tolerance, hyperlipidemia, and blood pressure in obese adults.[11] Because physical activity may prevent obesity, improve obesity-associated comorbidities,[12] reduce mortality,[13,14] and have beneficial effects on a variety of other chronic diseases,[15] strategies to increase physical activity must be implemented for the entire population. Implementation *should increase physical activity* of these strategies will require a shift in emphasis from a cosmetic ideal weight for height to an acceptable weight for health.

7   The time has come to develop a national comprehensive obesity prevention strategy that incorporates educational, behavioral, and environmental components analogous to those already in place for tobacco use. For example, the decline in tobacco use not only reflects an increased awareness of the health consequences of its use but also reflects a broad social strategy to reduce exposure. Prevention *After we viewed tobacco as a health hazard PPL. stopped using it. Will PPL do that with obesity.* of tobacco use includes health warnings on cigarette packages, creation of tobacco-free spaces in restaurants and public buildings, enforcement of laws that prohibit tobacco sales to minors, and taxes that make cigarettes expensive.

8   Solutions to the obesity epidemic will differ from those that have reduced tobacco use. In contrast to tobacco use, energy intake derives from multiple foods rather than a single product. Furthermore, people can choose not to smoke, whereas they cannot easily choose not to eat without adverse health consequences. As in the case of tobacco users, obese individuals must not become the target of discrimination but should be seen as persons with a chronic health condition in need of support and treatment. Nonetheless, without comprehensive population-based efforts to prevent and treat obesity, the prevalence of obesity and its expensive associated diseases and mortality are likely to continue to

[11] National Institutes of Health. *Clinical Guidelines on the Identification, Evaluation, and Treatment of Overweight and Obesity in Adults.* Bethesda, Md: National Institutes of Health; 1998. Publication 98–4083.

[12] U.S. Department of Health and Human Services. *Physical Activity and Health: A Report of the Surgeon General.* Atlanta, Ga: Centers for Disease Control and Prevention; 1996.

[13] Lee CD, Blair SN, Jackson AS. Cardiorespiratory fitness, body composition, and all-cause and cardiovascular disease mortality in men. *Am J Clin Nutr.* 1999;69:373–380.

[14] Wei M, Kampert JB, Barlow CE, et al. Relationship between low cardiorespiratory fitness and mortality in normal-weight, overweight, and obese men. *JAMA.* 1999;282:1547–1553.

[15] Powell KE, Carperson CJ, Koplan JP, Ford ES. Physical activity and chronic disease. *Am J Clin Nutr.* 1989;49:999–1006.

increase. Like rickets, pellagra, goiter, and dental caries, the most effective solutions to the obesity epidemic are likely environmental. However, in contrast to single-nutrient deficiency diseases, which can be addressed by nutrient fortification, environmental solutions to obesity will be more complex.

9   Because obesity has not been the focus of major preventive efforts, a desperate need exists for research to identify effective interventions and programs to prevent obesity. Several promising directions are already apparent. As Robinson[16] demonstrates in this issue of *The Journal,* reduced television viewing by children slows rates of weight gain. A recent school-based intervention that focused on increased physical activity, increased fruit and vegetable consumption, reduced consumption of high-fat foods, and reduced inactivity significantly reduced obesity prevalence in preadolescent girls.[17] One successful experimental approach to make fruits and vegetables or other nutritious foods more competitive is to offer more diverse, attractive, and less-expensive alternatives to high energy value foods in vending machines and cafeteria lines.[18] Schools also provide one of the few supervised locations where children can be physically active. The significant health benefits associated with physical activity and the reduced opportunities for children to be active make restoration of daily physical education in schools a priority. Nonetheless, some communities lack the facilities or have chosen not to support physical education programs.

10   In response to the high costs of health care associated with obesity and inactivity, a number of major corporations have initiated effective programs that include weight loss and increased physical activity.[19] However, given the economics and dynamics of the small- to medium-sized workplaces in which 50% of the U.S. workforce is employed, broader dissemination of such programs may be limited. With relatively high turnover of members in managed care plans and uncertain cost recovery of investments in diet and exercise programs whose benefits may not be apparent for a year or two, managed care plans may be less motivated to institute such health promotion programs. The health and financial benefits, such as reduced workdays lost to illness or reduced health care costs, are increasingly supported by data but will require wide acceptance by employers and health plans before workers become the focus of activities promoting healthful diets and levels of physical activity.

11   Because work-site physical activity programs will not be an option for many adults, changes in the community environment to promote physical activity may offer the most practical approach to prevent obesity or reduce its comorbidities.

---

[16] Robinson TN. Reducing children's television viewing to prevent obesity: a randomized controlled trial. *JAMA.* 1999;282:1561–1567.

[17] Gortmaker SL, Peterson K, Wiecha J, et al. Reducing obesity via a school-based interdisciplinary intervention among youth: Planet Health. *Arch Pediatr Adolesc Med.* 1999;153:409–418.

[18] French SA, Story M, Jeffery RW, et al. Pricing strategy to promote fruit and vegetable purchase in high school cafeterias: *J Am Diet Assoc.* 1997;97:1008–1010.

[19] Tully S. America's healthiest companies. *Fortune.* 1995;131:98–106.

Restoration of physical activity as part of the daily routine represents a critical goal. As recent studies have shown, physical activity need not be vigorous or continuous to produce health benefits.[20,21,22] Changes that promote physical activity may be as mundane as improving the location and appearance of stairwells or as complex as the redesign of communities. In many parts of the United States, community infrastructure to support physical activity already exists, such as sidewalks and bicycle trails, and work-sites, schools, and shopping areas in close proximity to residential areas. Such infrastructure makes walking or bicycling to school, to work, or to shop part of daily physical activity. In these areas, strategies to promote physical activity may be easier to implement than in communities that lack such infrastructure.

12   Automobile trips that can be safely replaced by walking or bicycling offer the first target for increased physical activity in communities. Recent data indicate that approximately 25% of all trips are less than 1 mile, and 75% of these are by car[23] (Paul Schimek, oral communication, September 14, 1999). Reliance on physical activity as an alternative to car use is less likely to occur in many cities and towns unless they are designed or retro-fitted to permit walking or bicycling. The location of schools, work sites, and shopping areas near residential areas will require substantial changes in community or regional design. Several incentives may promote such changes. Alternatives to automobiles will reduce air pollution as well as increase physical activity. Community recreation areas or facilities may promote physical activity during leisure time. Such facilities clearly improve the desirability of communities. For example, a recent survey of new home buyers indicated that almost all of the amenities that made communities desirable places to live were features that promoted physical activity, such as walking and jogging trails, outdoor swimming pools, playgrounds, and parks.[24]

13   People in the United States are proud of the nation's magnificent geography and enjoy exploration of and adventures in it. U.S. mythology is filled with images of vigorous physicality and glorified hard work—cowboys, farmers, longshoremen, miners, and athletes. Most U.S. citizens value the image of physically active presidents—from the boxing and hunting of Teddy Roosevelt to the swimming of Franklin Delano Roosevelt, the touch football of John Kennedy,

[20] Dunn AL, Marcus BH, Kampert JB, Garcla ME, Kohl HW III, Blair SN. Comparisons of lifestyle and structured interventions to increase physical activity and cardiorespiratory fitness. *JAMA.* 1999;281:327–334.

[21] Andersen RE, Wadden TA, Bartlett SJ, Zemel B, Verde TJ, Franckowiak SC. Effects of lifestyle activity vs. structured aerobic exercise in obese women. *JAMA.* 1999;281:335–340.

[22] Manson JE, Hu FB, Rich-Edwards JW, et al. A prospective study of walking as compared with vigorous exercise in the prevention of coronary heart disease in women. *N Engl J Med.* 1999;341:650–658.

[23] Schimek P. Unpublished calculations from 1995 Nationwide Personal Transportation Survey. U.S. Department of Transportation, Federal Highway Administration, Research and Technical Support Center. Lanham, Md: Federal Highway Administration; 1997.

[24] Fletcher J. Is this Disneyland? no, the new suburbs. *Wall Street Journal.* June 4, 1999:W12.

TABLE 8.1 Body Mass Index Chart

	19	20	21	22	23	24	25	26	27	28	29	30	31	32	33	34	35	36
Height (inches)							**Body Weight (pounds)**											
58	91	96	100	105	110	115	119	124	129	134	138	143	148	153	158	162	167	172
59	94	99	104	109	114	119	124	128	133	138	143	148	153	158	163	168	173	178
60	97	102	107	112	118	123	128	133	138	143	148	153	158	163	168	174	179	184
61	100	106	111	116	122	127	132	137	143	148	153	158	164	169	174	180	185	190
62	104	109	115	120	126	131	136	142	147	153	158	164	169	175	180	186	191	196
63	107	113	118	124	130	135	141	146	152	158	163	169	175	180	186	191	197	203
64	110	116	122	128	134	140	145	151	157	163	169	174	180	186	192	197	204	209
65	114	120	126	132	138	144	150	156	162	168	174	180	186	192	198	204	210	216
66	118	124	130	136	142	148	155	161	167	173	179	186	192	198	204	210	216	223
67	121	127	134	140	146	153	159	166	172	178	185	191	198	204	211	217	223	230
68	125	131	138	144	151	158	164	171	177	184	190	197	203	210	216	223	230	236
69	128	135	142	149	155	162	169	176	182	189	196	203	209	216	223	230	236	243
70	132	139	146	153	160	167	174	181	188	195	202	209	216	222	229	236	243	250
71	136	143	150	157	165	172	179	186	193	200	208	215	222	229	236	243	250	257
72	140	147	154	162	169	177	184	191	199	206	213	221	228	235	242	250	258	265
73	144	151	159	166	174	182	189	197	204	212	219	227	235	242	250	257	265	272
74	148	155	163	171	179	186	194	202	210	218	225	233	241	249	256	264	272	280
75	152	160	168	176	184	192	200	208	216	224	232	240	248	256	264	272	279	287
76	156	164	172	180	189	197	205	213	221	230	238	246	254	263	271	279	287	295

TABLE 8.2 Body Mass Index Chart

	37	38	39	40	41	42	43	44	45	46	47	48	49	50	51	52	53	54
Height (inches)							**Body Weight (pounds)**											
58	177	181	186	191	196	201	205	210	215	220	224	229	234	239	244	248	253	258
59	183	188	193	198	203	208	212	217	222	227	232	237	242	247	252	257	262	267
60	189	194	199	204	209	215	220	225	230	235	240	245	250	255	261	266	271	276
61	195	201	206	211	217	222	227	232	238	243	248	254	259	264	269	275	280	285
62	202	207	213	218	224	229	235	240	246	251	256	262	267	273	278	284	289	295
63	208	214	220	225	231	237	242	248	254	259	265	270	278	282	287	293	299	304
64	215	221	227	232	238	244	250	256	262	267	273	279	285	291	296	302	308	314
65	222	228	234	240	246	252	258	264	270	276	282	288	294	300	306	312	318	324
66	229	235	241	247	253	260	266	272	278	284	291	297	303	309	315	322	328	334
67	236	242	249	255	261	268	274	280	287	293	299	306	312	319	325	331	338	344
68	243	249	256	262	269	276	282	289	295	302	308	315	322	328	335	341	348	354
69	250	257	263	270	277	284	291	297	304	311	318	324	331	338	345	351	358	365
70	257	264	271	278	285	292	299	306	313	320	327	334	341	348	355	362	369	376
71	265	272	279	286	293	301	308	315	322	329	338	343	351	358	365	372	379	386
72	272	279	287	294	302	309	316	324	331	338	346	353	361	368	375	383	390	397
73	280	288	295	302	310	318	325	333	340	348	355	363	371	378	386	393	401	408
74	287	295	303	311	319	326	334	342	350	358	365	373	381	389	396	404	412	420
75	295	303	311	319	327	335	343	351	359	367	375	383	391	399	407	415	423	431
76	304	312	320	328	336	344	353	361	369	377	385	394	402	410	418	426	435	443

BMI Tables. To use these tables, find your height in the left-hand column. Move across to a given weight. The number at the top of the column is your BMI.

the jogging of Jimmy Carter and Bill Clinton, the wood-splitting and horseback riding of Ronald Reagan, and the golf and horseshoe tossing of George Bush. Similar role models are needed for women and minorities.

14   However, despite the pervasive conceptual preference for being lean and active, the environments and behaviors that have been developed make both characteristics difficult to achieve. Far too many people appear to have accepted the determinants of the problems of overweight and inactivity, and rely on "treatments" in the forms of myriad ineffective diet remedies and nostrums. As with many health issues, it is essential to emphasize prevention as the only effective and cost-effective approach. There is a particular need to focus on children and adolescents whose excess weight and sedentary lifestyle will form the basis for a lifetime of preventable morbidity and increased premature mortality.

15   Obesity, overweight, and a sedentary lifestyle are serious health issues now and will only worsen without thoughtful and scientifically based interventions that address societal and individual attitudes and behaviors and their environmental context. Physicians and other health care professionals, elected officials, educators, employers, and parents need to recognize the magnitude and impact of this major health problem and provide the will and energy to correct it through preventive approaches. In the past 25 years, several newer areas have been incorporated as targets for clinical and public health concern, such as tobacco control and injury prevention. It is now time to promote weight control and physical activity.[25]

Review Questions

1. What percentage of Americans is overweight, and what percentage is obese? What is the source of these data?

2. What is the relationship between obesity and general health, according to the authors?

3. Why, according to the authors, can the United States "no longer afford to ignore obesity as a major medical problem"?

4. What causes obesity?

5. What are the authors' recommendations for combating the epidemic of obesity?

6. Why will environmental strategies play an especially important role in the fight against obesity, and in what ways will these strategies prove complex?

7. The authors urge readers to accept prevention as an approach to obesity, as opposed to treatment. Why?

[25] Acknowledgments: We thank Martha Katz, MA, Steve Gortmaker, PhD, and Tom Robinson, MD, for their comments and suggestions.

Discussion and Writing Suggestions

1. Scan the footnotes of this article from the *Journal of the American Medical Association.* For what sorts of statements do the authors cite sources? Generally, how dependable do you find the information in this editorial?

2. What elements of the editorial identify it *as* an editorial? (You might reflect on the editorials you read in newspapers.) To what extent does the piece by Koplan and Dietz fit the same genre of writing?

3. The authors review a good deal of information in their discussion of "caloric imbalance." Do you find that the authors are *not* discussing any elements of being overweight or obese that you consider to be important?

4. Koplan and Dietz use the highly charged word "epidemic" in their article. Physicians use this word to denote a specific set of circumstances. Look up "epidemic" in a dictionary and discuss the ways in which the rising incidence of obesity compels the authors to use this word.

5. The authors state that their recommendations for reducing obesity "will require a shift in emphasis from a cosmetic ideal weight for height to an acceptable weight for health" (paragraph 6). What forces are at work in the culture that help to define and promote a cosmetically ideal weight? What success do you envision for moving Americans away from such an ideal?

6. The authors are calling for a major national mobilization against obesity that is reminiscent of the mobilization against tobacco use. To what extent do you feel that the authors have made the case in this editorial for such a broadscale, expensive, and extended campaign? Have they convinced you that obesity poses a major health risk to the well-being of the nation?

Prevalence of Obesity Among U.S. Adults, by Characteristics and by State
Centers for Disease Control and Prevention

The Centers for Disease Control and Prevention (CDC) published a report entitled "U.S. Obesity Trends in Adults from 1991–2001," from which a broad conclusion emerged: "The prevalence of obesity among U.S. adults increased to 20.9 percent in 2001, a 5.6 percent increase in 1 year and a 74 percent increase since 1991." On its Web site, the CDC describes itself as "the lead federal agency for protecting the health and safety of people—at home and abroad, providing credible information to enhance health decisions, and promoting health through strong partnerships." As such, the CDC is charged *with devising and implementing strategies for preventing disease. The first stage in developing a strategy, of course, is to understand the extent of a problem, which the CDC attempted to do with its study. Note that Dr. Jeffrey Koplan, lead author of the JAMA editorial immediately preceding these tables, was a former director of the CDC. The two tables below are from the 2002 study. To see complete data, go to the CDC Web site at <http://www.cdc.gov/nccdphp/dnpa/obesity/>.*

Prevalence of Obesity Among U.S. Adults, by Characteristics

1   In 2000, the prevalence of obesity among U.S. adults was 19.8 percent, which reflects a 61 percent increase since 1991.

2   In 2000, 38.8 million American adults met the classification of obesity, defined as having a body mass index, BMI score of 30 or more.

3   Between 2000 and 2001 obesity prevalence climbed from 19.8 percent of American adults to 20.9 percent of American adults.

TABLE 8.3   1991–2001 Prevalence of Obesity Among U.S. Adults, by Characteristics

Characteristics	Percent Obese BRFSS data by year:[*]					
	1991	1995	1998	1999	2000	2001
Total	12.0	15.3	17.9	18.9	19.8	20.9
Gender						
Men	11.7	15.6	17.7	19.1	20.2	21.0
Women	12.2	15.0	18.1	18.6	19.4	20.8
Age groups						
18–29	7.1	10.1	12.1	12.1	13.5	14.0
30–39	11.3	14.4	16.9	18.6	20.2	20.5
40–49	15.8	17.9	21.2	22.4	22.9	24.7
50–59	16.1	21.6	23.8	24.2	25.6	26.1
60–69	14.7	19.4	21.3	22.3	22.9	25.3
<70	11.4	12.1	14.6	16.1	15.5	17.1
Race, ethnicity						
White, non Hispanic	11.3	14.5	16.6	17.7	18.5	19.6
Black, non Hispanic	19.3	22.6	26.9	27.3	29.3	31.1
Hispanic	11.6	16.8	20.8	21.5	23.4	23.7
Other	7.3	9.6	11.9	12.4	12.0	15.7
Educational Level						
Less than high school	16.5	20.1	24.1	25.3	26.1	27.4
High school degree	13.3	16.7	19.4	20.6	21.7	23.2
Some college	10.7	15.1	17.8	18.1	19.5	21.0
College or above	8.0	11.0	13.1	14.3	15.2	15.7
Smoking status						
Never smoked	12.0	15.2	17.9	19.0	19.9	20.9
Ex-smoker	14.0	17.9	20.9	21.5	22.7	23.9
Current smoker	9.9	12.3	14.8	15.7	16.3	17.8

[*]Behavioral Risk Factor Surveillance System.

TABLE 8.4   Obesity Prevalence Among U.S. Adults by State. BRFSS Data by Year*

State Obesity	1991	1995	1998	1999	2000	2001
Alabama	13.2	18.3	20.7	21.8	23.5	23.4
Alaska	13.1	19.2	20.7	19.2	20.5	21.0
Arizona	11.0	12.8	12.7	11.6	18.8	17.9
Arkansas	12.7	17.3	19.2	21.9	22.6	21.7
California	10.0	14.4	16.8	19.6	19.2	20.9
Colorado	8.4	10.00	14.0	14.3	13.8	14.4
Connecticut	10.9	11.9	14.7	14.5	16.9	17.3
Delaware	14.9	16.2	16.6	17.1	16.2	20.0
District of Columbia	15.2	n/a	19.9	17.9	21.2	19.9
Florida	10.1	16.5	17.4	17.9	18.1	18.4
Georgia	9.2	12.6	18.7	20.7	20.9	22.1
Hawaii	10.4	10.4	15.3	15.3	15.1	17.6
Idaho	11.7	13.8	16.0	19.5	18.4	20.0
Illinois	12.7	16.4	17.9	20.2	20.9	20.5
Indiana	14.8	19.6	19.5	19.4	21.3	24.0
Iowa	14.4	17.2	19.3	20.9	20.8	21.8
Kansas	n/a	15.8	17.3	18.5	20.1	21.0
Kentucky	12.7	16.6	19.9	21.1	22.3	24.2
Louisiana	15.7	17.4	21.3	21.5	22.8	23.3
Maine	12.1	13.7	17.0	18.9	19.7	19.0
Maryland	11.2	15.8	19.8	17.6	19.5	19.8
Massachusetts	8.8	11.1	13.8	14.3	16.4	16.1
Michigan	15.2	17.7	20.7	22.1	21.8	24.4
Minnesota	10.6	15.0	15.7	15.0	16.8	19.2
Mississippi	15.7	18.6	22.0	22.8	24.3	25.9
Missouri	12.0	18.0	19.8	20.8	21.6	22.5
Montana	9.5	12.6	1.7	14.7	15.2	18.2
Nebraska	12.5	15.7	17.5	20.2	20.6	20.1
Nevada	n/a	13.3	13.4	15.3	17.2	19.1
New Hampshire	10.4	14.7	14.7	13.8	17.1	19.0
New Jersey	9.7	14.2	15.2	16.8	17.6	19.0
New Mexico	7.8	12.7	14.7	17.3	17.8	18.8
New York	12.8	13.3	15.9	16.9	17.2	19.7
North Carolina	13.0	16.5	19.0	21.0	21.3	22.4
North Dakota	12.9	15.6	18.7	21.2	19.8	19.9
Ohio	14.9	17.2	19.5	19.8	21.0	21.8
Oklahoma	11.9	13.0	18.7	20.2	19.0	22.1
Oregon	11.2	14.7	17.8	19.6	21.0	20.7
Pennsylvania	14.4	16.1	19.0	19.0	20.7	21.4
Rhode Island	9.1	12.9	16.2	16.01	16.8	17.3
South Carolina	13.8	16.1	20.2	20.2	21.5	21.7
South Dakota	12.8	13.6	15.4	19.0	19.2	20.6
Tennessee	12.1	18.0	18.5	20.1	22.7	22.6
Texas	12.7	15.0	19.9	21.1	22.7	23.8
Utah	9.7	12.6	15.3	16.3	18.5	18.4
Vermont	10.0	14.2	14.4	17.2	17.7	17.1
Virginia	10.1	15.2	18.2	18.6	17.5	20.0
Washington	9.9	13.5	17.6	17.7	18.5	18.9
West Virginia	15.2	17.8	22.9	23.9	22.8	24.6
Wisconsin	12.7	15.3	17.9	19.3	19.4	21.9
Wyoming	n/a	13.9	14.5	16.4	17.6	19.2

*Behavioral Risk Factor Surveillance System.

4   Currently, more than 44 million Americans are considered obese by BMI index; that is, have a Body Mass Index (Kg/m^2) greater than or equal to 30. This reflects an increase of 74 percent since 1991.

5   This table reflects the percentages of individuals who are obese within specific categories such as, gender, age, race, education, and smoking status.

Prevalence of Obesity Among U.S. Adults, by State

6   [There is an] obesity epidemic within the U.S. . . . [In] 1991, only 4 of 45 participating states had obesity prevalence rates of 15 to 19 percent and none had prevalence greater than 20 percent.

7   By the year 2000, all of the 50 states except Colorado had prevalences of 15 percent or greater, with 22 of the 50 states having obesity prevalence as high as 20 percent or greater.

8   In 2001, 20 states had obesity prevalence of 15–19 percent; 29 states had prevalences of 20–24 percent; and one state reported a prevalence more than 25 percent. The prevalence of obesity among U.S. adults increased to 20.9 percent in 2001, a 5.6 percent increase in 1 year and a 74 percent increase since 1991.

References

Mokdad AH, Serdula M, Dietz W, et al. The spread of the obesity epidemic in the United States, 1991–1998. *JAMA* 1999;282:1519–1522.

Mokdad AH, Serdula M, Dietz W, et al. The continuing obesity epidemic in the United States. *JAMA* 2000;284.1050–1651

Mokdad AH, Bowman BA, Ford ES, et al. The continuing epidemics of obesity and diabetes in the United States. *JAMA* 2001;286(10):1195–1200.

Mokdad AH, Bowman BA, Ford ES, et al. Prevalence of obesity, diabetes, and obesity related health risk factors, 2001. *JAMA* 2003:289;76–79.

Review Questions

1. As you study the Characteristics table, what correlation do you find between race/ethnicity and obesity?

2. In the Characteristics table, what correlation do you find between level of education and incidence of obesity?

3. Review both CDC tables and summarize the general trend in incidence of obesity.

4. According to the "Obesity Prevalence . . . by State" table, which are the least obese and most obese areas of the country?

Discussion and Writing Suggestions

1. Select your age group, race/ethnicity, educational level, and smoking status in the Characteristics table. To what extent do the percentages reported reflect what you have observed about the prevalence of obesity?

2. Select your state in the "Obesity Prevalence . . . by State" table. Do the percentages reported reflect what you have observed about the prevalence of obesity?

3. Focus on the 1991 through 2001 percentages of obesity among people who have smoked and quit, never smoked, or presently smoke. What inferences can you draw between smoking status and obesity?

4. Speculate on possible explanations for the relationship between obesity and level of education.

5. To what extent are you surprised to find differences among states in levels of obesity? Identify one such difference and speculate on the causes of the difference.

6. Why might those older than 70 tend to be less obese than those aged 30–69?

7. Do you find any surprises in the CDC data? Discuss.

8. Write a paragraph summarizing what for you are the key findings in one of the two tables.

Too Much of a Good Thing
Greg Critser

In an op-ed essay for the Los Angeles Times *(22 July 2001), Greg Critser argues that, faced with a rising obesity epidemic, we should stigmatize overeating. Critser is careful to distinguish between stigmatizing the person and the act, but he makes no apologies for urging that we teach children that "[e]ating too much food is a bad thing." Critser has written a book on the obesity epidemic:* Supersize *(Houghton Mifflin, 2002).*

1   Sometime over the next month or so, United Nations health and nutrition experts will convene in New York to begin discussing what many consider to be the pivotal medical issue of our day: obesity and its impact on children. For the U.N., traditionally concerned with starvation and malnutrition, it is a historic first, following up on an alarm it sounded about obese adults in 1999. "Obesity," the U.N. proclaimed, "is the dominant unmet global health issue, with Westernized countries topping the list."

2   Solid epidemiological data drives the effort. In Canada, Great Britain, Japan, Australia—even coastal China and Southeast Asia—the rate of childhood obesity has been soaring for more than a decade. Closer to home, at least 25% of all Americans under age nineteen are overweight or obese, a figure that has doubled over the last 30 years and a figure that moved the surgeon general to declare childhood obesity an epidemic. The cost in health care dollars to treat obesity's medical consequences—from diabetes to coronary heart disease to a variety of crippling bone conditions—will eventually make the battle against HIV/AIDS seem inexpensive. Yet in the U.S., the most important foot soldiers against obesity are increasingly paralyzed by years of media-induced food hysteria, over-generalized and outdated nutritional wisdom, and, truth be told, an unwillingness to set firm and sometimes unpopular food parameters. That infantry is the much-strained American family and its increasingly harried commandant, *Parentis americanus.* What it needs to promulgate is dietary restraint, something our ancestors knew simply as avoiding gluttony.

3   This is not to say that parents should be blamed for the nation's growing dietary permissiveness. They are wary of confronting their children's eating habits for a reason: For years, conventional wisdom held that food should never become a dinner table battleground. "Pressure causes tension," write Harvey and Marilyn Diamond, authors of the classic *Fit for Life,* which has sold more than 3 million copies. "Where food is concerned, tension is always to be avoided." The operative notion is that a child restrained from overeating will either rebel by secretly gorging when away from the table or, worse, will suffer such a loss of self-esteem that a lifetime of disastrous eating behavior will follow.

4   Of course, no one should be stigmatized for being overweight. But stigmatizing the unhealthful behaviors that cause obesity would conform with what we know about effective health messages. In both the campaign against unsafe sex and the campaign against smoking, stigmatizing such behaviors proved highly effective in reducing risk and harm. It's true, smokers—and homosexuals—may have experienced a modicum of stereotyping in the short run, but such is the price of every public health advance: short-term pain for long-term gain.

5   Another inhibition to imposing dietary restraint is the belief, promoted in handbook after handbook of parental advice, that "kids know when they are full." But perhaps not. In fact, new research suggests just the opposite: Kids don't know when they are full.

6   In a recent study, Pennsylvania State University nutritional scholar Barbara Rolls and her associates examined the eating habits of two groups of kids, one

of three-year-olds, another of five-year-olds. The children were presented with a series of plates of macaroni and cheese. The first plate was a normal serving built around baseline nutritional needs; the second was slightly larger; the third was what might be called "supersized."

7   What the researchers found is that the younger children consistently ate the same baseline amount, leaving more food on the plates with larger servings. The 5-year-olds, though, altered their eating behavior dramatically depending on the amount they were served, devouring whatever was on the plate. Something had happened. The mere presence of an oversized portion had induced exaggerated eating. The authors concluded that "these early years may provide a unique opportunity for interventions that reduce the risk of developing overweight." Those interventions "should include clear information on appropriate portion sizes for children."

8   Theorizing aside, our disinclination to restrain eating flies in the face of overwhelming evidence that, of all age groups, children seem to be the ones who respond most positively to dietary advice. In four randomized studies of obese 6- to 12-year-olds, those who were offered frequent, simple behavioral advice were substantially less overweight 10 years later than kids who did not get the advice. In fact, 30% of those studied were no longer obese at all.

9   The case for early intervention has been further buttressed by new studies on another age-old medical injunction: never put a kid on a diet. (The concern was that under-nutrition could lead to stunted growth.) But as the authors of a study of 1,062 kids under age three concluded in the journal *Pediatrics,* "a supervised, low-saturated-fat and low-cholesterol diet has no influence on growth during the first three years of life." Overweight kids who were put on such a diet ended up with better, more moderate eating habits.

10   Changing the eating habits of children, though, is antithetical to some notions many parents hold dear. And to some it seems a relic of an earlier, more religious era of moral certainties when gluttony was vilified as one of the seven deadly sins. Many boomer parents believe, as one parent and nutritionist said at a recent summit on childhood obesity, that "kids have the right to make bad nutrition decisions." That may be true. But ours is a world where at least a billion dollars a year is spent by just one fast-food chain to convince families to visit a crazy-looking clown with his own playground and purchase a thousand supersize calories for a mere $2.50. McDonald's official line today is that three meals a week at its restaurants are perfectly acceptable for an average kid. That's three meals a week of grease, refined flour, and a jumbo shot of sugar.

11   Given today's bounty of cheap and unhealthful food alternatives, and given the inconvenience that goes with making good nutritional choices, one might wonder if a campaign against over-consumption, a campaign advocating restraint, could work. On this point, we might take a cue from the French. In the early 20th century France, in response to its first experiences with widespread child obesity, launched the puericulture movement, which focused on excessive weight gain in early childhood and adolescence. Its prescription: All meals should be adult-supervised; all portions should be moderate, with "seconds" a rare treat. All but an occasional small snack were forbidden. As its historian Peter

N. Stearns writes in *Fat History,* puericulture's message was simple: Eating too much food is a bad thing.

12   Therein lies at least part of the explanation for the legendary leanness of the French: They were taught in childhood not to overeat. And it didn't seem to do much harm to their self-esteem.

Review Questions

1. With what particular problem is Critser concerned in this essay?

2. According to conventional wisdom, how should parents set limits with respect to their children's intake of food?

3. Notwithstanding conventional wisdom, what are the three arguments (two supported by research studies) that Critser makes for curtailing the food intake of children?

4. What objections does Critser anticipate to his proposals, and how does he rebut these objections?

Discussion and Writing Suggestions

1. Critser advocates that we teach children that "[e]ating too much food is a bad thing." Do you agree? In your view, what are a parent's responsibilities in teaching children about eating and overeating?

2. Some parents and nutritionists have objected to Critser's proposed instruction of children and they maintain that children "have the right to make bad nutrition decisions." Who is more persuasive on this point (discussed in paragraph 10), Critser or those who argue for a child's nutritional autonomy?

3. Reread paragraph 4, which Critser begins: "Of course, no one should be stigmatized for being overweight." In fact, is Critser advocating stigmatization? What is the difference between stigmatizing an act (that is, overeating) and stigmatizing an actor (the person who overeats)?

4. Notwithstanding Critser's assertion that "no one should be stigmatized for being overweight," to what extent do you find him to be morally intolerant in this essay? Of whom does he disapprove—children who overeat, their parents, the broader culture that fosters overeating? Or do you find that his objection is to overeating itself?

5. What assumptions does Critser make about the origins of overeating? In considering this question, you might think about the roles of individual willpower, genes, parental and institutional authority, and a child's autonomy.

NAAFA Policy on Dieting and the Diet Industry
National Association to Advance Fat Acceptance

The National Association to Advance Fat Acceptance (NAAFA) was founded in 1969 as a "non-profit human rights organization dedicated to improving the quality of life for fat people." NAAFA is both an advocacy group, publishing and advocating for positions on issues that affect fat people, like the following policy statement on dieting, and a support group that offers members "tools for self empowerment." You can visit the NAAFA Web site at http://www.naafa.org for a closer look at the organization's official documents, informational brochures, book service, and more. What you will find consistently is a content and a tone that promotes fat acceptance.

History/Existing Condition

1   The term "diet" within this policy refers exclusively to weight reduction diets. "Dieting" is defined as any attempt to achieve or maintain lower body weight by intentionally limiting or manipulating the amount or type of food intake. Weight reduction diets include medically supervised diets; self-administered diets; commercial diet organizations and centers; weight-loss support groups or behavior modification programs; "fad" diets; "sensible, well-balanced" diets; in-hospital fasts; very-low-calorie diets (VLCDs); prepackaged food plans; and diets supplemented by drugs or artificial food products or supplements.

2   "Dieting" does not refer to attempts to lower fat, sugar, salt, or cholesterol intake, increase fiber intake, exercise or pursue a medically mandated nutritional regimen prescribed for specific medical conditions. Weight-loss diets have long been promoted as a permanent cure for "obesity," although they rarely produce long-lasting or permanent results. According to existing medical research, fewer than five percent of all dieters succeed in losing a significant amount of weight and maintaining that weight loss over a five-year period. Ninety percent of all dieters regain some or all of the weight originally lost and at least one-third gain more. In recent years, an increasing body of research has substantiated this diet failure rate and acknowledged genetic and physiological factors in the determination of body size.

3   Although these statistics apply to all types of diets, even those considered "sensible," physicians continue to prescribe weight-loss diets as a viable treatment for fat patients; and researchers, the media, and the diet industry continue to urge fat people to resist their body's natural predisposition and struggle harder to lose weight. As diet failure rates become widely publicized, some "experts" pretend to abandon "dieting" and encourage their clients to "just eat less and exercise more."

4   Promoting diets and diet products is a major industry in the United States. According to Marketdata Enterprises, the annual revenue for the diet industry was over $30 billion dollars in 1990. This figure includes money spent on diet centers and programs, group and individual weight-loss, diet camps, prepackaged foods; over-the-counter and prescription diet drugs; weight-loss books and magazines; and physicians, nurses, nutritionists, and other health professionals specializing in weight-loss (total 1990 revenue—$8 billion); commercial and

residential exercise clubs with weight-loss programs (total 1990 revenue—$8 billion); and sugar-free, fat-free, and reduced calorie ("lite") food products, imitation fats and sugar substitutes (total 1990 revenue—$14 billion).

5   The diet industry's advertising and marketing strategy is based on the creation and perpetuation of fear, biases, and stereotypes. Fat people are portrayed as unhealthy, unattractive, asexual, weak-willed, lazy, and gluttonous. Weight loss or a thin figure are equated with virtue, health, and success. Failure to participate in dieting or lack of success in losing weight are blamed on a lack of willpower or determination and a lack of moral values. Fat people are taught to feel guilty and blame themselves for the failures of weight-loss programs, and to expect and accept rejection, mistreatment, and discrimination regarding their weight. This negative media campaign has a devastating impact on millions of fat people. These messages lower fat people's self-esteem and foster discontent, self-doubt, and self-hatred, especially during the weight regain state of the dieting "yo-yo" cycle.

6   Diet promoters also emphasize dieting's supposed health benefits and minimize risks related to dieting. People of all sizes are misled about the extent and severity of the health risks associated with being fat and are told that being thin is the only way to good health, and that dieting makes people thin. Many health problems traditionally attributed to "obesity," such as high blood pressure, heart problems, high cholesterol, and gallbladder problems, are often caused by the dieting process itself. Recent studies indicate that repeated "yo yo" dieting may actually reduce one's life span rather than increase longevity.

7   Currently there are very few controls or regulations to inform and protect the dieting consumer. Weight loss "success" is only vaguely defined using short-term results, and weight loss "failure is always blamed on the consumer, and health risks are not disclosed. The few regulations that do exist are rarely, or at most, loosely enforced.

NAAFA's Official Position

8 Since reducing diets rarely achieve permanent weight loss and can result in negative health consequences, since laws and regulations protecting the consumer are nonexistent or remain unenforced, and since people undertaking diets are rarely given sufficient information to allow them to give true informed consent, the National Association to Advance Fat Acceptance strongly discourages participation in weight-reduction dieting. Further, NAAFA strongly condemns any diet marketing strategy based on guilt and fear. Such approaches cause untold suffering to fat people by ruining their self-esteem and by perpetuating negative stereotypes. NAAFA demands that local, state, and federal governments regulate the diet industry to protect the consumer from misleading claims regarding safety and long-term effectiveness.

NAAFA Advocates:

- That local, state, and federal legislatures introduce, pass, enact, and enforce legislation which protects consumers against dangerous or ineffective diets and misleading diet advertising.
- That state and federal regulatory agencies, such as the Food and Drug Administration (FDA) and the Federal Trade Commission (FTC), adopt

regulations based on NAAFA's "Guidelines for the Diet Industry" and closely monitor and control all aspects of the multi-billion-dollar diet industry.

- That all commercials for weight-loss diets and diet products be banned from radio and television because of lack of product success, negative health consequences, and the extreme negative impact of anti-fat propaganda on the self-esteem and quality of life of fat people.
- That federal regulations require all diets and weight-loss products to clearly display a health warning (similar to those found on cigarettes) regarding possible hazards and side effects.
- That regulations be adopted that require the diet industry to publish five-year (minimum) follow-up studies and "success" rates. All such statistics must be verifiable by objective outside researchers and clearly displayed on all diet products and advertising.
- That the Centers for Disease Control track morbidity and mortality caused by dieting and make the findings available to the public.
- That the National Institutes of Health (NIH) include input from consumer advocacy groups in establishing public health policy about dieting and obesity.
- That consumer protection agencies, such as Consumers Union, conduct biannual studies on the efficacy of diet products and programs.
- That institutions such as the military, hospitals, schools, mental institutions, or prisons provide adequate food and not force anyone to diet against their will.
- That employers, schools, and judges never use weight loss or dieting as a condition for employment, promotion, admission, or avoiding incarceration.
- That health care professionals and medical institutions never deny other medical treatment to patients who choose not to diet.
- That the diet industry refrain from creating or perpetuating negative stereotypes about fat people in its marketing strategies.
- That diet companies and diet industry trade organizations voluntarily comply with NAAFA's "Guidelines for the Diet Industry."
- That individuals considering dieting study available literature on long-term results and side effects and carefully weigh dieting's possible benefits and risks.
- That dieters refuse to feel guilty or blame themselves for presumed lack of willpower if a diet fails.
- That no one allow themselves to be coerced into dieting against their will.
- That no one make assumptions or judge another person on the basis of body size or dietary preferences.

NAAFA Resolves to:

- Educate the public, the media, and potential dieters as to the low long-term success rates and possible negative health consequences of weight reduction dieting.
- Discourage the diet industry from basing their product advertising on fear and guilt and from using and perpetuating negative stereotypes of fat people.
- Promote alternatives to weight-loss diets in a manner which is sensitive to the emotional and financial investment which many fat people have made in repeated weight-loss attempts.

- Provide advice and emotional support to individuals who have dieted unsuccessfully and blame themselves, rather than the product, for the diet's failure.
- Alert consumers to diets or weight-loss schemes which have been determined to be dangerous or fraudulent, have lawsuits pending against them, or are being investigated by government agencies.
- Assist plaintiffs and/or their attorneys engaged in litigation involving diet fraud and ill effects of dieting, by providing them with referrals to expert witnesses who might testify on their behalf.
- Advocate for the safety and emotional and physical well-being of consumers by attempting to influence public policy about dieting, obesity, and diet industry regulation.

Review Questions

1. How does NAAFA define "dieting"?
2. What percentage of dieters lose weight and keep it off five years after beginning their diet?
3. How much money was spent on the diet industry in 1990? (In 2004, the amount was $33 billion.)
4. What are the risks of dieting, according to NAAFA?
5. What is NAAFA's official position on dieting, and what action does it want taken regarding the dieting industry?

Discussion and Writing Suggestions

1. NAAFA states that "[t]he diet industry's advertising and marketing strategy is based on the creation and perpetuation of fear, biases, and stereotypes." Locate a print, television, or radio ad for a diet program and analyze its content for "fear, biases, and stereotypes." Discuss the ways in which NAAFA's assertion is or is not validated by your research.

2. How does NAAFA summarize the stereotypes of fat people? What stereotypes about fat people have you encountered in your experience? List these and compare your list with those of others in your class.

3. Do you believe that the regulation of weight-loss diets is feasible? How do you imagine this regulation would be accomplished?

4. Explore the NAAFA Web site at <http://www.naafa.org>. What are your reactions to the content on the Web site? How would you describe its tone? To what extent does NAAFA present itself as a well-run organization?

5. Review the positions that NAAFA advocates. Which strike you as most workable? Least workable? Why?

Fat and Happy: In Defense of Fat Acceptance
Mary Ray Worley

Mary Ray Worley is a member of NAAFA, the National Association to Advance Fat Acceptance. Hers is the only first-person account you will read in this chapter of the social and psychological pressures that fat people can experience. She does much to elucidate anti-fat stereotypes and, through her spirited writing, does much to dispel them. As you read, you might bear in mind the contrasts between Worley's position on obesity and that of Greg Critser, who argues that we should stigmatize the act of overeating.

1 If you've grown up in twentieth-century American society, you probably believe that being fat is a serious personal, social, and medical liability. Many Americans would rather die or cut off a limb than be fat, many believe that fatness is a serious health risk, and many are convinced that it is a simple matter to reduce one's body size and are so offended by body fat that they believe it is acceptable to shun fat people and make them the butt of cruel jokes. Those who are fat quickly learn to be deeply ashamed of their bodies and spend their lives trying to become what they are not and hide what cannot be hidden. Our society believes that thinness signals self-discipline and self-respect, whereas fatness signals self-contempt and lack of resolve. We're so accustomed to this way of thinking that many of us have never considered that there might be an alternative.

2   Nevertheless, a growing number of people believe it's possible to be happy with your body even if it happens to be fat. In August 2000 I attended the annual convention of the National Association to Advance Fat Acceptance (NAAFA) in San Diego, and it was like visiting another planet altogether. I hadn't realized how deeply my body shame affected my life until I spent a glorious week without it. I'll never be the same again.

3   The first time I had that "different planet" feeling was at the pool party on the first night of the convention. Here were all these fat people in stylish swimsuits and cover-ups, and whereas on my home planet a fat person was expected to feel apologetic and embarrassed about her body—especially in a swimsuit—here were a hundred or so fat people who were enjoying being in their bodies without a shred of self-consciousness. They were having so much fun it was infectious. I felt light-headed and giddy. I kept noticing how great everyone looked. They were confident and radiant and happy—and all sizes of fat. Definitely not my planet.

4   One of the features of NAAFA's conventions is that they invite vendors who sell stylish large-size clothing. So whereas on my home planet, you're lucky if you can find a swimsuit that fits at all, on this planet you have choices and can find a swimsuit that's made from beautiful fabric and looks absolutely smash-

ing on you. Where I come from, you're grateful if you can find clothes that you can actually get on, and forget finding clothes that really fit you. But on this planet there were play clothes, dress-up clothes, you name it. Choices galore. Beautiful fabrics with an elegant drape and a certain panache. I'd never before had so many choices. The clothes I tried on (and bought) not only fit me but looked terrific. As the week wore on and everyone had visited the vendors' booths, we all looked snazzier and snazzier, and the ones who had been to past conventions looked snazzy from the get-go.

5   The next night at the talent show those of us who didn't get a part in the high school musical because we were too fat had a chance to play the lead for five minutes. (I sang a snappy little number by Stephen Sondheim called "The Ladies Who Lunch," from *Company,* and hammed it up big time. I had a blast!) Top billing was given to a troupe of belly dancers called the Fatimas. Now, I had read about this attraction in the literature I received about the convention, and I have to admit that I thought it would be some kind of a spoof or a joke. I just couldn't conceive of a group of fat women doing serious belly dancing, but it was no joke. These women were indeed serious—and excellent—belly dancers. They wore the full belly-dancing regalia—that is, gauze and bangles and beads and not much else. When they first looped and bobbed their way out into the middle of the room, I think my chin must have dropped through the floor. They were exquisitely beautiful and voluptuous and graceful and serene. I thought that anyone, no matter how acculturated to my home planet, would have to be just about dead not to recognize how beautiful they were. And they were all so different from each other. We are accustomed to seeing mostly thin bodies that look more or less the same, but these bodies showed an amazing degree of delightful diversity. Body fat does not distribute itself on every fat person in the same way, so there's lots of variety. Plus they weren't all young. A couple of them had to have been past fifty, and they were so beautiful. And exotic, and mesmerizing. I had always assumed that as a fat woman I could never do that, and especially not as a fat woman past fifty. Wrong, wrong, wrong. I felt a jolt as my old assumptions were jettisoned out into space. Bag that old paradigm. This one is definitely a lot more fun.

6   One of the featured speakers at the convention was Dr. Diane Budd, who spoke about the medical and scientific communities' take on fatness. Although the data gathered for most current studies indicate that body size is primarily determined by one's genetic makeup, most researchers con- clude—in spite of their own findings—that fat individuals should try to lose weight anyway. There are no data that indicate (a) that such efforts are likely to be effective (in fact, more than 90 percent of those who lose weight gain it back), (b) that a person's overall health would be improved by losing weight, or (c) that the effort to lose weight won't in fact turn out to have last- ing harmful effects on one's appetite, metabolism, and self-esteem. Our assumptions about the desirability of thinness are so deeply ingrained that sci- entists find it next to impossible to align their recommendations with their findings; apparently they cannot bring themselves to say that since body size is largely a result of one's genetic makeup it's best to get on with the business of learning to live in the body you have, whatever its size.

7   Moreover, none of the studies take into account the physical implications of the social ostracism and body hate that are a regular part of most fat people's lives. Fat people are often taunted in public and are pressured by family members to lose weight. Complete strangers feel they are not out of line to criticize the contents of a fat person's grocery cart, and family members may evaluate everything a fat person puts on her plate. Fat people need to be active and strong enough to carry their body weight comfortably, but they may feel ill at ease exercising in public because of unkind stares and comments. They may feel that they can't wear shorts or sleeveless t-shirts or swimsuits for fear of offending the delicate sensibilities of others and inviting rude comments, and so they will be too hot and too embarrassed and will give up on regular exercise because they don't have the support they need to continue. Now *that* is a health risk.

8   Moreover, fat people are often reluctant to seek medical attention because health professionals are among the most prejudiced people around. Regardless of the ailment you are seeking treatment for, if you are fat, your doctor may put you on a diet before she treats your cough, and attribute whatever complaint you have to your weight. Pressures like these must certainly contribute to the shortening of many fat people's lives, quite apart from any physical risk resulting from a preponderance of body fat.

9   The upshot is that it's very likely that the health risks of being fat have been highly overestimated. In combination with other risk factors, being fat may occasionally contribute to compromised health, but not nearly to the degree that many people think. When a fat person goes to a weight-loss clinic, the goal is usually to lose weight as quickly as possible, as though to snatch the poor fat soul out of the jaws of imminent death. And often the harsh methods used to effect that weight loss are in and of themselves much more harmful than being fat is. In fact, it is my understanding that statistically a person is much less likely to regain weight that is lost very slowly. So what's the big rush? The big rush is that we hate fat and want to put as much distance between ourselves and it as quickly as possible. Quick and dramatic weight loss sells; slow and gradual weight loss does not. There's nothing compassionate, rational, or scientific about it. We just hate fat.

10   Many fat people have made numerous efforts and spent thousands of dollars throughout their lives to lose weight and each time regained the lost pounds plus a few more. Have this happen to you enough times and you will be apprehensive at the prospect of losing weight for fear of gaining back more than you lose. On my own account, there's no way I want to diet again, because it will just make me fatter in the long run. Help like that I don't need, and I sure as spitfire don't need to pay through the nose for it.

11   After years and years of dieting it slowly dawned on me that my body rebelled when I tried to restrict my food intake. All those years I figured that it was me who was failing, and then I began to realize that it was the method that was failing. I began to wonder whether the problem itself was being incorrectly defined. I began raising new questions just about the time that researchers were discovering that, rather than being a simple intake-outtake equation, body weight resulted from a complex interplay of set point (the body's tendency to stay within a certain narrow weight range), appetite and satiety cues, metabo-

lism, and genes. Moreover, our bodies are designed to protect us from starvation and have some powerful defenses against it. They react to dieting just as they do to starving. They don't know there is a McDonald's around every corner. For all they know, we're still living in the Ice Age, when the next meal may be hours or days or miles away. So when we decrease the amount of food we eat, our bodies slow the metabolic rate to fend off possible starvation. It's a great system, really. In my case I'm convinced that as determined as I have been to become thin, my body has always been more determined to save me from starvation. My body is more stubborn than I am. Amazing.

12   So I stopped dieting and began to make peace with food and with my body. I slowly stopped being afraid of food. In 1999 I became a vegetarian, and somehow that change—and the culture that seems to go with it—put food in a new light for me. Food was no longer the enemy; it was a gift and a source of joy. I began to slow down and relish my meals, to enjoy food and be grateful for all the ways that it nourishes me.

13   Over the last fifteen years or so I've made many attempts to become more active on a regular basis with varying degrees of success. I often would go swimming three or four times a week for two, three, or four months followed by a hiatus of several weeks or months. About two years ago, I realized that I always felt better when I was being active. So why the long hiatuses? Because I was exercising in hopes of losing weight. After months of dogged discipline with what I considered to be meager results at best, I would naturally become discouraged and stop. Within a few weeks I would stop feeling the surge of energy and well-being that comes with regular exercise.

14   So what would happen if I just exercised because I felt better when I did? How about moving just for the fun of it? So I gave up the notion of losing weight and consequently gave up feeling hopeless, and as a result the hiatuses have become fewer and shorter in duration. I began to vary my workouts more, so that I got less bored and enjoyed myself more. Who knew that moving, even in a large body, could be this much fun? I'd never allowed myself to have this kind of fun in my body before.

15   I discovered to my delight that the more physically competent I became, the better I felt about my body. My husband, Tom, and I go for long hikes in the woods, and some of those hikes have been challenging for me—not too challenging, but just enough. Two years ago we visited Yosemite National Park, and we hiked partway up to the top of Vernal Fall. It was a demanding hike, and pretty much everybody was huffing and puffing. We made it up to the bridge that's just shy of halfway to the top. It was good to know when to stop, but it rankled me that I didn't have the energy or stamina to make it all the way. So I decided that next time I will. Next spring we're planning another trip to Yosemite, and I'm going to make it to the top of Vernal Fall. I don't care how long it takes me or how much I have to huff and puff. My only stipulation is that I have to be strong enough to have fun doing it. I don't want it to be a torture session.

16   I've been training with that goal in mind for months now. Instead of avoiding stairs, I look for them. I'm no longer ashamed of huffing and puffing—I'm proud. I'm pushing myself just enough so that I'm becoming stronger and have more endurance all the time. This summer I discovered that I can hike all day long. What

a thrill! In July, Tom and I hiked in Copper Falls State Park from 12 noon until 8 P.M. (we stopped to rest three times). And in August I traipsed around the San Diego Wild Animal Park from 9 A.M. until 8 P.M. (again with three rests). How wonderful to have a body that will carry me through an entire day of fun! I never realized before what a miracle my body is, its glorious ability to build muscle and save me from starvation. I'm only beginning to discover what a marvelous gift it is.

17   After years of fighting our set points, our metabolism, our genes, and our hunger, after decades of being ashamed, hating our bodies, and trying to manipulate them into being something they're not, after spending mountains of money and energy trying to conform to someone else's ideal, it isn't surprising that some of us question whether this is the best way to for us to live. A few of us brave adventurers have found another way, and it involves much less agony, costs much less money, and is much more fun.

18   We're not giving up, and we're not letting ourselves go. Rather we're forging a new relationship with our bodies, one that doesn't involve self-loathing, one that appreciates the miraculous bodies we have, one that brings joy. There's plenty of room on this new planet, and here you needn't apologize for your size. You're entitled to the space you take up. You can find clothes that show off the gorgeous person you are, you can play and dance without self-consciousness, you can be proud of yourself and never dread unwanted attention, you can be a brave pioneer and a friend to those who have suffered on planets less kind and less joyous than this one.

Discussion and Writing Suggestions

1. How would you characterize Worley's point of view in this essay? Distilled to a single statement, what is she arguing? To what extent do you find yourself sympathetic to her point of view?

2. Worley writes: "Our society believes that thinness signals self-discipline and self-respect, whereas fatness signals self-contempt and lack of resolve" (paragraph 1). To what extent do you find this statement a fair and accurate representation of how our society views fat people? How do you define "society" in this case? Who (or what) are its agents?

3. What role has NAAFA played in helping Worley think and feel differently about herself?

4. Is Worley's self-acceptance the same thing as complacency about her obesity? Explain your answer.

5. Writing an editorial in the *Journal of the American Medical Association,* Koplan and Dietz claim that "[g]enes related to obesity are clearly not responsible for the epidemic of obesity" (page 344). To what extent does their claim negate the force of Worley's argument (paragraph 6) that "it's best to get on with the business of learning to live in the body you have, whatever its size"?

6. Reread paragraphs 7 and 8 on "the social ostracism and body hate that are a regular part of most fat people's lives." Even if one allows that, in light of new research, Worley is wrong about the causes and medical impact of being fat, to what extent do the points she makes about the social, psychological, and emotional costs of obesity still have force?

7. What are the differences between exercising to lose weight and exercising to feel better? (See paragraphs 13–16.) What lessons are embedded in this distinction?

8. Comment on the "old planet"/"new planet" distinction that Worley develops in paragraphs 2, 3, and 18.

Too "Close to the Bone": The Historical Context for Women's Obsession with Slenderness
Roberta Seid

Roberta Seid critiques our culture's "religion" of thinness and explains how Americans have come to be adherents of this religion, as well of the psychological and even spiritual costs of adherence. You will find in Seid's essay an excellent example of how scholarship—historical and cultural scholarship, in this case—can shine a light on complex problems, helping us to view them in entirely new ways. When she wrote this piece in 1994, Seid was a lecturer in the Program for the Study of Women and Men in Society at the University of Southern California, Los Angeles.

1 Why have Americans, particularly American women, become fatphobic? Why and how have they come to behave as though the shape of their lives depends on the shape of their bodies? Why have they clung to these beliefs despite the toll they take on private lives, and especially despite their most extreme and dangerous manifestation, eating disorders? This chapter addresses these questions by placing the phenomenon in a broad historical context, with particular focus on fashion and the unique and dangerous twist it has taken in our era.

2 Although current explanations for our thinness mania are valuable, they often leave many questions unanswered. Feminists have often blamed fashion for oppressing and subordinating women, but fashion has rarely had the destructive effects we see today. Moreover, the fashion for thinness, which has prevailed only for the past 40 years or so, requires explanation itself. The eating disorders literature, often focused on individual psychopathology, has found neither a consistent etiological profile nor a universally accepted explanation for why eating disorders have swelled into a social disease. Nor does it explain why millions of women without clinical eating disorders mimic the behavior and mind set of affected women. Finally, a much weaker body of literature attributes the phenomenon to the mass media's influence. Although the media's power to shape our perceptions cannot be underestimated, this explanation also begs the question. Why would the media necessarily promote slenderness?

3   A more comprehensive explanation emerges when we stand back and, employing a broad historical perspective, look at the underlying cultural beliefs that affect both genders. Our culture is swept up in a web of peculiar and distorted beliefs about beauty, health, virtue, eating, and appetite. We have elevated the pursuit of a lean, fat-free body into a new religion. It has a creed: "I eat right, watch my weight, and exercise." Indeed, anorexia nervosa could be called the paradigm of our age, for our creed encourages us all to adopt the behavior and attitudes of the anorexic. The difference is one of degree, not of kind. Like any religion worthy of the name, ours also has its damnation. Failure to follow the creed—and the corporeal stigmata of that failure, fatness and flabbiness—produce a hell on earth. The fat and flabby are damned to failure, regardless of professional and personal successes. Our religion also has its rewards, its salvation. In following the creed, one is guaranteed beauty, energy, health, and a long successful life. Followers are even promised self-transformation: The "thin person within," waiting to burst through the fat, is somehow a more exciting, sexy, competent, successful self. Virtue can be quantified by the numbers on the scale, the lean-to-fat ratio, clothing size, and body measurements. And, in a curious inversion of capitalist values, less is always better.

Body Ideals Before the 20th Century

4   The creed of thinness is composed of prejudices, and they have a history. A cursory review of Western civilization's aesthetic and health ideals indicates the novelty and arbitrariness of current beliefs. The female body has not altered for thousands of years; the range of body types in the past does not differ from the range we know today. What has changed is the body type (or types) regarded as ideal, as well as the effort put into meeting this ideal and the methods used to do so. Although styles of dress have tended to change at an ever-quickening tempo since the 12th century, body ideals have changed slowly. By looking at the visual evidence provided by paintings of dressed people and of the nude, we can see that never before have men or women desired a body so "close to the bone."

5   There have been, of course, other periods when slenderness was admired. During the 15th century, paintings of long-limbed ladies reverberated with the vaulting reaches of Gothic cathedrals. Sixteenth-century Mannerists in northern Europe painted elongated nudes, such as the nymphs in Cranach the Elder's *The Judgment of Paris.* More recently, the Romantic vogue for slenderness in the 1830s–1850s encouraged young ladies to strive for the tiny waist favored by fashion—an effort later immortalized in *Gone with the Wind* when Scarlett O'Hara's stays are tightened to achieve a 17-inch waist.[1]

6   Nonetheless, it would be misleading to assume that these eras resembled our own. Gothic and Mannerist nudes had not a bone or muscle showing; they

---

[1] For a fuller discussion of past body ideals, see Roberta P. Seid, *Never Too Thin: Why Women Are at War with Their Bodies* (New York: Prentice-Hall Press, 1989), 37–81. The best sources for a general overview are Francois Boucher, *20,000 Years of Fashion: The History of Costume and Personal Adornment,* expanded edition (New York: Harry N. Abrams, 1987) and Kenneth Clark, *The Nude: A Study in Ideal Form* (Princeton, NJ: Princeton University Press, 1956).

were sweetly and fully fleshed. Women of the Romantic period may have wanted tiny waists, but they also wanted their shoulders, arms, calves, and bosoms ample, indicating an "amorous plenitude."[2] Indeed, thinness was considered ugly, a woman's misfortune. The French epicure J. A. Brillat-Savarin defined thinness as those of his epoch typically did—as "the condition of the individual whose muscular flesh, not being filled with fat, reveals the forms and angles of the bony structure." Thinness in women was, he observed, "a terrible misfortune. . . . The most painstaking toilette, the sublimest costume, cannot hide certain absences, or disguise certain angles."[3] Nor did the Romantic lady equate slenderness with health and energy as we do today; health was not part of her aesthetic ideal. Rather, slenderness signified delicacy and fragility, the qualities she sought.

7   Just a century ago, body ideals and ideas were the reverse of our own, underscoring the fact that there was no folk wisdom about the value of slenderness that science has recently confirmed. Indeed, the female ideal was Junoesque: tall, full-busted, full-figured, mature. Dimpled flesh—what we today shudderingly call "cellulite"—was considered desirable. Sinewy, "close to the bone" women "no bigger than a whipping post" suffered disdain, not those with amply fleshed curves properly distributed and disciplined only by the corset.[4] The undergarment industry even came to the aid of the slighted thin woman with inflatable rubber garments (replete with dimples) for her back, calves, shoulders, and hips. They may have provided meager comfort, for they could deflate at unexpected moments.[5]

8   Fat was seen as a "silken layer" that graced the frames of elegant ladies. It was regarded as "stored-up force," equated with reserves of energy and strength. Plumpness was deemed a sign of emotional well-being; it was identified with a good temperament, with a clean conscience, with temperate and disciplined habits, and above all with good health. Today, of course, we have totally inverted these associations.[6]

9   In the mid-19th century, the prolific writer Catherine Beecher described healthy weight. If you felt heavy and got on the scale (a rare experience in the 19th century), and weighed either heavy or light, you were in bad health. But if you felt light and weighed heavy, then you were in excellent health; weighing heavy was good. More importantly, Beecher distinguished between feelings

---

[2] See the excellent discussion of this ideal in Valerie Steele, *Fashion and Eroticism: Ideals of Feminine Beauty from the Victorian Era to the Jazz Age* (New York: Oxford University Press, 1985), 108–110.

[3] Jean Anthelme Brillat-Savarin, *The Physiology of Taste or Meditations on Transcendental Gastronomy* (New York: Doubleday, 1926 [orig. 1826]), 172, 187.

[4] Steele, 1985, 218–223; Hillel Schwartz, *Never Satisfied: A Cultural History of Diets, Fantasies, and Fat* (New York: Free Press, 1986), Illustration 5 (1857 cartoon from *Harper's Weekly*).

[5] David Kunzle, "The Corset as Erotic Alchemy: From Rococo Galanterie to Montaut's Physiologies," in Thomas Hess and Linda Nochlin, eds., *Art News Annual*, vol. 38, *Woman as Sex Object: Erotic Art, 1730–1970* (1972); Steele, 1985, 128, 221.

[6] Seid, 1989, 70–80.

and actual weight—a distinction lost to many today, who determine how they feel by the numbers on the scale.[7]

Development of the Obsession with Thinness

10 The transformation of these values began at about the turn of the present century, when slenderness came into fashion. This occurred for a variety of reasons, among them the modernist aesthetic with its idealization of speed and motion, and its penchant for stripping things down to their essential forms. (Some called it the revenge of the thin who for so long had been slighted.) But "slim" is a relative term, and the women who boasted the new form would by contemporary standards be called overweight. In addition, in the first half of this century, the belief that plumpness signaled robust health remained strong.

11   The culture of slimming as we know it is really a post–World War II phenomenon.[8] Fashion continued to value a slender (if curving) form, and the health industry, finally convinced by insurance companies, launched massive campaigns to persuade Americans to lose weight. Key ideas that would take full force in subsequent decades began to emerge. Chief among these was "fat-phobia," the conviction that animal fat of any kind—on the body, in the blood, on the plate—was dangerous. The perception developed that Americans were too fat and getting fatter; that they ate too much, ate the wrong foods, and were sedentary and therefore flabby. Americans' self-perception shifted to that of a diseased, unhealthy group, even though they enjoyed the best health and greatest longevity ever known in American society. These pronouncements did not abate, even though average life expectancy continued to improve. Most important was the growing fear that Americans were getting physically and *morally* soft. For at the heart of all the campaign literature was a moral concern about how Americans would react to postwar plenty and leisure—how they would handle modernization.

12   In subsequent decades, these ideas intensified. Weight loss techniques began to be seen as life-prolonging in and of themselves. The fitness ethic emerged from these beliefs and fueled obsession with exercise. But the new emphasis on fitness was just a variation on the theme of slenderness. The ideal remained a fat-free body. The "health food" craze played on the same dynamic, growing out of and then later helping to fuel and dignify diet obsessions. In addition, the standards of slenderness grew more extreme, both in charts of ideal weight and in fashion. The famous 1960s model Twiggy, at 5 feet 7 inches and 98 pounds, represented the boundary beyond which no ambulatory person could go; however, her image became one that women thereafter aspired to meet. Female beauty had come to be represented by a gawky, bare-boned adolescent. Simultaneously, definitions of "overweight" and "obesity" began to include normal-sized Americans.

---

[7] Beecher's standards are quoted by Harvey Green, *Fit for America: Health–Fitness–Sport and American Society* (New York: Pantheon Books, 1986), 64.

[8] For a fuller discussion with citations of sources, see Seid, 1989, Chapters 12 and 13.

13   More compelling, however, were the principles underlying fatphobia, which turned it into a national obsession. The health industry embraced the questionable concept of "ideal weight"—the idea that the weight associated with optimum health and longevity could be determined by height. It was then decreed that everyone of the same height and bone structure should meet this ideal. But this injunction assumed that body weight and the ratios of fat to lean tissue were direct functions of exercise and eating habits. The obvious corollary was that everybody should reduce to ideal weight and that everybody could easily do so—if they exerted enough willpower. In short, these decrees blamed the victim: if you were fat, it was your fault. This is the most powerful and pernicious aspect of fatphobia; indeed, in modern America, being fat is as shameful as being dirty. We seem to believe that slenderness is as attainable as cleanliness, and as crucial to respectable grooming. We can easily embrace these ideas because they fit so well with America's self-help-oriented, democratic ideology. We can all be body aristocrats, we believe, if we just try hard enough. This set of beliefs fuels prejudices against fat and has allowed the thinness mania to spiral into a religion.

14   More and more evidence is emerging that discredits this whole ideology and shows that its premises are empirically flawed. The thinner are not necessarily healthier, nor are they more fit. Our fundamental beliefs—that people of the same height should have the same weight, and that people can exercise absolute control over their body weights—are also flawed. Numerous studies demonstrate that the majority of the "fat" cannot slim down permanently. The problem is not their lack of willpower, but the unreasonable expectation placed on them to weigh a certain amount. Animal breeders have long known that nature did not intend everyone to be the same size, but modern science seems to have temporarily forgotten.

15   Sadly, efforts to squeeze into the ideal size are often useless and destructive—not only because they can exacerbate the problem they are designed to cure, but because they trigger psychological, physiological, and behavioral consequences, including binge eating, food obsessions, and, in susceptible individuals, eating disorders. Even worse, dieters pay a price in sense of well-being, in health, and in the ability to lead rich and productive lives. The contemporary and historical literature on famine describes ennui, tension, irritability, preoccupation with food, loss of libido, and lassitude created by diets equivalent to those advised for weight loss. The United Nations World Health Organization has established a daily intake of 1000 calories as the border of semistarvation; modern diets often recommend less. The famine literature attributes these symptoms to hunger and undernourishment; the literature on overweight attributes them to lack of willpower or to psychopathology.

16   Laboring under perverse notions about food and appetite, we believe that permanent dieting and chronic hunger are healthy and energy-giving; we are convinced that food does not nourish, but rather kills. If we find ourselves eating with unbridled appetite, we believe that there is either something wrong with us or with the food itself, which must be "addictive." In truth, the well-nourished, not the undernourished, grow strong, healthy, and productive. Poor appetite is a sign of the depressed and the ill; indeed, women are often grateful for an illness—it makes dieting easier.

17   It is hard to resist the parallel between Victorian attributes toward sex and modern attitudes toward food. In the 19th century, the control of sexual instincts was the acme of virtue; sexual behavior was the yardstick of goodness. Today, eating habits and body weights have become the yardsticks of virtue, and food rules have become as dour and inhibitory as the sex rules of the 19th century. Perhaps cultures require some kind of instinctual control to feel that they qualify as "civilized."

Why Women More Than Men?

18 Given that this belief system pervades our culture, why does it affect women so much more than men? Why do more women than men suffer from eating disorders, obesity, and distorted body image? Why are women, not men, at war with their bodies? There are many reasons, some more obvious than others.

19   One reason is biological. Standards for males simply are not as extreme or as inimical to normal masculine body builds as are women's standards. Indeed, our female ideal violates the anthropomorphic reality of the average female body. The ideal female weight, represented by actresses, models, and Miss Americas, has progressively decreased to that of the thinnest 5–10% of American women. Consequently, 90–95% of American women feel that they don't "measure up."[9] Societies have never been kind to deviants, but in America a statistical deviation has been normalized, leading millions of women to believe that they are abnormal.

20   In addition, the taut, lean, muscled body—the "fit" form so many strive to achieve—is more like the body of a male than of a female. The goal is to suppress female secondary sexual characteristics, from dimpled flesh to plumpness in thighs, behinds, hips, and bosom. Women consequently are pitted in a war against their own biologies to meet the standard.

21   It is not just biology that confounds women. They strive to meet this unreasonable standard because it has become a moral imperative in our society, and because, despite a quarter-century of feminism, the quest for physical beauty

---

[9] Although exact figures on this subject remain elusive, many sources confirm this general trend. This percentage was suggested by Rita Freedman, *Beauty Bound* (Lexington, Mass.: Lexington Books, 1986), 149, but it is corroborated by other sources. I studied statistics of Miss America contenders with data for the earlier periods from Frank Deford, *There She Is: The Life and Times of Miss America* (New York: Viking Press, 1971), 313–316, and from Miss America Pageant Yearbooks, 1972–1983, and found a dramatic slenderizing trend. For more details, see Seid, 1989, Chapter 10. For a study of a similar development in the *Playboy* centerfolds, whose average weights dropped from 11% below the national average in 1970 to 17% below it in 1978, see Paul E. Garfinkel and David M. Garner, *Anorexia Nervosa: A Multidimensional Perspective* (New York: Brunner/Mazel, 1982), 108–109, and D. M. Garner, P. E. Garfinkel, D. Schwartz, and M. Thompson, "Cultural Expectations of Thinness in Women," *Psychological Reports* 47 (1980): 483–491. On the rise of an emaciated ideal in the ballet subculture, see L. M. Vincent, *Competing with the Sylph* (New York: Andrews & McMeel, 1979). Jennifer Brenner, professor of psychology at Brandeis University, and Dr. Joseph Cunningham recently reported the results of their study comparing the weights of New York fashion models and Brandeis students. "Female models are 9 percent taller and 16 percent thinner than average women," Brenner reported in an article by Lena Williams, "Girl's Self-Image Is Mother of the Woman," *New York Times* (National Edition), February 6, 1992, A1, A12.

remains deeply powerful. On even a practical level, women's self-image, their social and economic success, and even their survival can still be determined largely by their beauty and by the men it allows them to attract, while for men these are based largely on how they act and what they accomplish. Looks simply are of secondary importance for male success.

22   But the impulse toward beauty runs much deeper than the desire for social acceptance and success. Beauty and fashion are intertwined, and women try to meet unreasonable weight standards also because fashion—our system of dress—requires them to do so. Though many have castigated fashion as a shallow and frivolous vanity, it is propelled by profound impulses, which it shares with all dress systems. Dress and adornment are basic to all human cultures. Even the most primitive tribes find ways to decorate the body. The overwhelming importance of dress is underscored by the fact that from the moment we slip out of the womb to the moment of our deaths, we alter our natural appearance. How we choose to dress is a complex cultural phenomenon. Clothing and adornment are simultaneously a material object, a social signal, a ritual, and a form of art. Every facet of a society—from its economic base to its social structure, from its values about human beings and their bodies to its loftiest spiritual and aesthetic ideals—influences the forms and rules of dress. Each culture sets up its own rules, and in following them, people defer to and perpetuate fundamental social values and norms.

23   In obeying fashion's dictates, we are bowing to powerful constraints about self-presentation and about how others should interpret our attitudes, behavior, and identity. The enormous time and energy women (and men) devote to it is simply another of civilization's many demands and, possibly, pleasures. For in dressing, in following fashion, we are engaged in a game, a plastic art, a process whereby we partially create ourselves. We are involved in social and private play of the profoundest type—trying to transcend our uncivilized, animal state, to make ourselves human. Friedrich Nietzsche, in *The Birth of Tragedy,* argued that "We derive such dignity as we possess from our status as art works." Fun, fantasy, humor, artistic creativity, and our deepest aspirations exist in the dress constraints of everyday life.[10]

24   Fashion, the dress system of the West, has, however, taken a rather peculiar twist in recent decades—one that helps explain our body obsessions. Fashionable beauty is no longer about the clothes covering the body, but about the naked body itself. This has not been true before in the history of fashion. Fashion is, as we have seen, a plastic art. Although it would be foolhardy to describe the past as Edenic, it nonetheless is true that fashion has traditionally been a handmaiden to beauty. It allowed people to approach the reigning ideal by manipulating cosmetics and clothing—that is, by manipulating what they put *on* themselves, not what they *were* underneath those clothes, stays, girdles, and so forth.

---

[10] Nietzsche's statement is quoted in Steele, 1985, 245. For a fuller theoretical discussion and bibliography on the role of dress and adornment in human culture, see Roberta P. Seid, *The Dissolution of Traditional Rural Culture in Nineteenth-Century France: A Study of the Bethmale Costume* (New York: Garland Press, 1987), 1–45.

25   By the late 20th century, however, women's bodies, which heretofore had never been exposed to the public eye, virtually became wholly exposed. With the introduction of the miniskirt and teeny tops, women's legs, thighs, and upper bodies were suddenly revealed, bereft of the aid of body-shaping undergarments. The fitness craze and the growing liberalization in censorship and in acceptable norms of nudity intensified the trend.

26   By the 1980s, even fashion magazines showed naked or leotarded bodies more than they showed clothing. The undressed body—the bare bones of being, celebrated as liberating and "natural"—had become the focus of fashion. No longer did a woman have the luxury of manipulating only what was outside her body, the "not me"; now she had to manipulate her self, the once private stretches of the body.

27   This new, "natural" look could not really be liberating, because fashion is antithetical (almost by definition) to nature, so stringent standards began being set for the now-exposed form. Suddenly, the average American woman became aware of flaws she never knew existed; pronouncements were made about how every private crevice of her anatomy was to look. Women consequently ran smack into a dilemma between the naked and the nude.

28   The art historian Sir Kenneth Clark argued that the nude is a form of art; the naked is merely the human body undressed, replete with all its flaws and blemishes. The naked becomes the nude through art, with the artist transforming that humble and flawed form into an ideal of beauty.[11] Yet today, bombarded by verbal and visual commercial images of the nude, women have been seduced into believing that they should—and could, with enough effort—have one of those perfect bodies. They expect the image reflected in their mirrors to look like the nude. It almost never does. And so they renew their battle against their recalcitrant bodies.

29   Changes in the structure of fashion contributed further to the battle: No authorities put brakes on the urge to meet the slender ideal. This, too, was new in fashion's history. Although there has always been considerable harmony among standards of feminine beauty, health, and the gestalt of an era, excesses of fashion were heretofore severely criticized by social authorities, including doctors, teachers, and clergy, parents, and, since the 19th century, feminists. The clergy and moralists, in particular, stressed that there were values more important than outward appearance; that the soul and one's deeds mattered, not fashion standards; that, in the words of the old adage, "Pretty is as pretty does." In the late 20th century—at least until alarm about eating disorders spread—all these authorities, especially physicians, seemed to agree that one could never be too thin. This unholy alliance between societal and fashion authorities allowed the vogue for thinness to go to extremes.

30   Even contemporary feminists have been slow to resist the slenderness fashion. They were initially seduced, perhaps, by its underlying message that biology is not destiny. Even more, the rhetoric of the slenderness ideal—that health

---

[11] Clark, 1956, 3–9.

is beauty and beauty health, and both are fit and thin—may have persuaded them. They applauded the fact that physical strength and health were now feminine ideals. It took a while for them to realize that what was sought, what had become ideal, was merely the *appearance* of health and vigor—and that dangerous means were being used to achieve it.

31   Despite the historical uniqueness of these developments, some rather cruel historical consistencies remain. More stringent bodily controls are still required of the female than of the male. Animal-like functions, such as belching, nose wiping, urinating, sweating, scratching, spitting, masturbating, farting, and even body odor, remain less permissible for women than for men. In the male subculture, unlike female subcultures, there is an acceptance of and a certain humor about these behaviors, which sometimes become the subject of good-natured contests. Men simply are permitted to be more comfortable about natural functions and to exhibit them to a greater extent in public. They do not compromise masculinity; rather, they often confirm it. Women, on the other hand, compromise their femininity if they do not control these behaviors. The same discrepancy applies to diet and body size: Women are expected to manage these even more stringently than men. Similarly, as long as control of appetite and body weight is regarded as virtuous, women must exercise this control more than men. Once again, women are expected to be the custodians and embodiments of virtue for the culture.

Thinness and Our Cultural and Spiritual Values

32 What remains puzzling about this unique fashion for bare-boned skinniness is what it suggests about our aesthetic ideals—and, even more importantly, about our values, our gestalt. If we step back a moment and look at our ideal of beauty from a more distant perspective (perhaps that of a future historian or anthropologist), we can perhaps see how peculiar it is that we celebrate the living version of Giacometti sculptures, anorexics with barbells.

33   Future historians might conjecture that Americans had fallen in love with death, or at least with mortification of the flesh. They might speculate that terror of nuclear destruction had made fashion play with cadavers and turn them into images of beauty. Or they might argue that we had been so influenced by modern art, Bauhaus aesthetics, and contemporary steel architecture that our ideal human body also had come to consist only of the scaffolding that held it up and of the machinery that made it move. Or they might suggest that we had come to see technology, not human beings, as the prime force in history, and so had chosen to resemble our conquerors.

34   Alternatively, they might argue that our fascination with the unconscious, and our new awareness that scientific reality was concealed from us—that the universe was made up of particles we could not see and governed by laws that defied the logic of our senses—led us to strip the outer body of any meaning or significance and of any possible beauty. Or, more simply, they might conjecture that in an era of population density, it was more practical and economical to have skinny people. Thin people would need less room, so more of them could be squeezed into the spaces on mass transit and into workplaces, and they

could live in smaller houses. It certainly also might be interpreted as democratic. No one had the right to take up more space than another or to command respect through the imposing grandeur of body size.

35   They might also conjecture that late 20th-century America had so confused its image of women that what looked female could no longer be considered beautiful. Even more, they might contend that we had dehumanized, not just masculinized, the human form. We had reduced it to its smallest, least imposing form. They might argue that we had come to idealize technology, and also (befitting our secular age) to distinguish humans from other animals and the civilized from the uncivilized not by the presence of consciousness, a soul, and a conscience, but by the suppression of animal fat. They might even suggest that we had become so terrified of what made us human—especially our passions and our vulnerability—that we didn't want our bodies to betray any softness, curves, or idiosyncrasies. Or they might think that we had suppressed tender flesh because we no longer saw human beings as sources of comfort and nurture.

36   From a purely aesthetic perspective, our fat-free beauties might come out no better. Indeed, even unprejudiced present-day observers may be taken aback. Faces are gaunt and angular; necks are steeples of bones. Unfleshed arms and legs, full of sharp angles, look gangly and disproportionately long. Indeed, dieted women look as though the life and color have been sucked out of them. Nor, for all the paeans to strength, do these scrawny, narrow women look strong or stable, or as if they have a stature to be reckoned with. Indeed, the lean body looks as repressed and controlled as the spirit that must have gotten it that way.

37   It is odd, too, that we have developed an erotic ideal that suppresses flesh and minimizes sexual characteristics. There is little to linger over, to explore, to discover. When the body has been efficiently reduced to a flat surface, it offers no softness, no warmth, no tenderness, no mysteries—qualities once integral to images of sexuality. Our erotic ideal has become as hard and unyielding, perhaps, as the love relationships that dominate social life.

38   In criticizing our new religion, I am not suggesting that we gorge wantonly or that we ignore our health and our physical appearance. This would be a surrender to the treacherous polarities that dominate our thinking: Our choices seem to be thinness or fatness, gluttony or starvation, vigorous exercise or lethargy, ascetic rituals or self-indulgence, youthfulness or old age, beauty or ugliness. I am suggesting that we recultivate our tastes and find a saner middle ground where our bodies can round out with more life, flesh, and health; where we can relish the fruits of our prosperity without self-punishment; and where we understand that the nourishment that is one of life's greatest pleasures is also one of its most basic necessities.

39   It would be a tragedy, after 25 years of the women's movement, if women did not rebel against this "religion" that threatens to sabotage their hard-won victories. Is the "liberated woman," supposedly at ease in the boardroom, really consumed with self-loathing and obsessed with tallying calories, exercise, and the vital statistics of the body (weight, muscle-to-fat ratio, inches of breast, hip, and thigh)? Never measuring quite right, she may be as victimized by biology as her predecessors.

40   I am not suggesting, as many past and present feminists have, that we do away with beauty and fashion standards altogether. It would be a bleak world if we did not celebrate beauty and if we did not encourage the imagination and play involved in bedecking ourselves and molding our own images. The impulses toward adornment and self-beautification run deep in human culture and are connected to its noblest aspirations. Nor am I suggesting that fashion standards of the past were always benign. Each era has exacted its own price for beauty, though our era is unique in producing a standard based exclusively on the bare bones of being, which can be disastrous for human health, happiness, and productivity.

41   But I am urging that we dismantle this new religion, because it is misguided and destructive. It does not provide reasonable guidelines by which to live. Our bodies, our fitness, and our food should not be our paramount concerns. They have nothing to do with ethics, or relationships, or community responsibilities, or with the soul. They have nothing to say about the purpose of life, except that we should survive as well and as long and as beautifully as we can. They give us no purpose beyond ourselves. This is a religion appropriate only for a people whose ideals do not extend beyond their physical existence, and whose vision of the future and of the past is strangely empty. Surely Americans can produce a worthier creed.

42   In making the denial of hunger and its physical manifestations, thinness, into a primary virtue, our "religion" is unique among the major world religions. Although there is a long history of fasting for spiritual cleansing or purity, no religion has set it up as a virtue; indeed, most have condemned it. Buddha rejected fasting because he did not find it a way to enlightenment. Judaism prescribes only a few fast days a year. Otherwise, it proscribes such deprivation: According to the Talmud, people must be well nourished so they can do what is important in life—follow God's commandments and perform *mitzvot* (good deeds). The early fathers of the Christian Church, too, condemned fasting, and the Church exacted higher penances for the sin of not eating than it did for the sin of gluttony. The Muslims, even during their great fast of Ramadan, do not abstain from food. They are merely proscribed from eating during certain hours, and the other hours are given to feasting. In these religions, food has not been seen as a temptation put in humanity's path, but as vital for people to carry out their larger spiritual tasks.

43   It is one thing to follow a rigid dietary code and rituals of behavior in accordance with the laws of a God or gods we worship. The faithful are trying to fulfill God's or the gods' commandments, not only for their own salvation, but also to hasten the arrival of a more perfect world. It is quite another thing to follow rigid dietary and behavior codes only to improve our physical selves. Such actions are not part of a larger system of morals. They have no vision of a higher good or of a better future that their rituals might help create. This is a solipsistic religion in the narrowest and strictest sense, in that it is only about the bare bones of being. If avoiding fatness and possible disease is the main preoccupation of our lives, then what are we living for?

44   Our new religion bankrupts us. Historically unprecedented numbers of us are healthy—able to enjoy sex without fear of unwanted pregnancy, to go

through childbirth without the once omnipresent threat of death, to treat once-fatal infectious diseases easily, and to alleviate the minor aches and pains that caused discomfort to our forebears (from toothaches to earaches to headaches to skin eruptions to upset stomachs). Advances in technology, medicine, and food production, wrought by painstaking human efforts, have given us a well-being virtually unknown in previous centuries. We should be grateful, but instead we hate our bodies because they bulge here or are flabby there or fail to respond to our most rigorous diets. Surely this is the worst form of hubris—to despise our bodies because they are not perfect. Our new religion neither puts checks on this kind of vanity nor underscores how trivial is the accomplishment of weight loss and of physical perfection. Instead, it seduces us into believing that this quest is the worthiest of human goals.

45   We must abandon our new religion because it trivializes human life itself. We must restore a humanistic vision in which self-improvement means cultivating the mind and enlarging the soul; developing generosity, humor, dignity, and humility; living more graciously with biology, aging, and death; living with our limitations. We need a concept of self-improvement that reminds us to learn from the past, to build on it, and to bequeath wisdom to future generations. We stand poised between a past for which we have lost respect and a future we must now struggle to envision.

Review Questions

1. According to Seid, what is our "new religion," and what is its creed?

2. In what ways is the 20th- and 21st-century ideal of beauty arbitrary?

3. To what does "close to the bone" of Seid's title refer?

4. In what ways has the ideal of female beauty changed in the last 100 years?

5. Why did the current "fatphobia" take hold?

6. What, according to Seid, is the "most . . . pernicious aspect of fat-phobia" (paragraph 13)?

7. In what ways is the blame-the-victim logic directed against fat people flawed, according to Seid?

8. In paragraph 18, Seid asks: "Why do more women than men suffer from eating disorders, obesity, and distorted body image?" What is her answer?

9. After launching her extended critique against the "religion" of dieting and the "close to the bone" ideal of beauty, what recommendation does Seid make?

Discussion and Writing Suggestions

1. In paragraph 3, Seid challenges the reader with a daring assertion: "[A]norexia nervosa could be called the paradigm of our age, for our creed encourages us all to adopt the behavior and attitudes of the anorexic. The difference is one of degree, not of kind." Two questions: First, if you have followed the logic of Seid's argument, does this assertion follow? Second, to what extent do you agree?

2. In paragraphs 13–14, Seid explains the logic by which Americans come to blame fat people for being fat. Summarize that logic—and then comment on it. For instance, have you ever encountered this type of blame-the-victim thinking? Is it reasonable, in your view, to regard fat people as victims?

3. In your experience, or in the experience of people you know, to what extent is it true that "dieters pay a price in sense of well-being, in health, and in the ability to lead rich and productive lives" (paragraph 15)?

4. In paragraph 15, Seid juxtaposes the "contemporary and historical literature on famine" with the messages implied in and stated directly by our dieting culture. What is your response?

5. How do you respond to Seid's assertion in paragraph 17 comparing our culture's preoccupation with weight to Victorian culture's preoccupation with sex?

6. Seid argues that in the twentieth century the world of fashion has focused not only on clothes but on the body, the result being that a woman who wants to dress fashionably must attend to the body beneath the clothes as well as to the clothes themselves (see paragraphs 24–27). How consciously aware are you of having to "manipulate" yourself—that is your body—in order to be fashionably correct? After you have answered this question, meet in a group of four or more classmates, with equal numbers of men and women. Compare answers.

7. In paragraph 29, Seid speaks of an "unholy alliance between societal and fashion authorities." What, in her view, is so unholy? Do you agree?

8. Seid writes in paragraph 41: "Our bodies, our fitness, and our food . . . have nothing to do with ethics, or relationships, or community responsibilities, or with the soul." In paragraph 43 she writes that severe dieting for the sake of thinness, alone, is a "solipsistic religion" and contributes nothing to the greater good of society. Seid makes a strong and cogent argument in this essay against the "religion" of thinness and the ways in which it "trivializes human life itself." Discuss her conclusions and recommendations. Do you

agree? Could you imagine yourself or others agreeing and *still* wanting to diet?

9. Notwithstanding Seid's arguments, statistical trends are clear (see the selections in this chapter from the *Journal of the American Medical Association* and the Centers for Disease Control) that the number of overweight and obese people is rising, which in turn is leading to increased levels of illness and death. In what ways do these scientific reports affect your reading of Seid?

Fat and Happy?
Hillel Schwartz

"Fat and Happy?" forms the final chapter of historian Hillel Schwartz's book-length study of dieting, Never Satisfied *(Free Press, 1986). Like Seid, who critiques what she terms a "religion" of thinness, Schwartz critiques what he calls a "despotism of slenderness." The selection has a satiric feel to it, but underlying all satire—this included—are points seriously made. Indeed, much of the logic presented here you will find shared by other writers, such as Seid and Worley. In the two sections of the chapter reproduced here, Schwartz presents a "Vindication of Fat" and an image of "The Fat Society: A Utopia."*

Recently there has been a growing protest against the despotism of slenderness, and a scientific debate over the dangers of a moderate fatness. Underlying the protest and the debate is a utopian vision of a Fat Society where neither overweight nor obesity stands in the way of social freedom or personal happiness.

The Vindication of Fat

1 Fatness is fine.

2   If fat people are unhappy people, blame not their fat but their fellow citizens who bill them as clowns, clodhoppers, cannibals, or criminals; who spread such commercial rumors as "To be fat is the end of life"; who sport bumper stickers on their vans, "No fat chicks"; who print posters which read, "It's in to be thin. It's out to be stout."[1] Blame the kindergarten teachers, the coaches, the friends and physicians who goad fat people into a maze of diets from which they may never return. Dieting makes everything worse, for the chances are high that fat people will fail. They will be saddened and frustrated by their failures, and they will come to agree with everyone else that they are failures in all of life. Because they have failed they are fat, and because they are fat they fail.

3   It is the taking off and the putting on of weight that endangers the body. Not the fat or the pounds but the dieting itself, the frustration, and the constant

[1] Marvin Grosswirth, *Fat Pride* (NY, 1971) 161, D-Zerta ad, and American Physical Fitness Research Institute poster, "Fit to Quote" (Santa Monica, Calif., 1969).

hunger. No one has been able to prove that fatness *per se* cuts life short. If left alone, 99 percent of human beings will reach a plateau weight, a set point at which their metabolisms will be satisfied and their bodies healthy. It is the dieting, the anxiety, and the perpetual scrimmaging with food that lead to illness. "What causes the most damage is not the actual weight itself, but the fear of weight." People who drive their weights down and up through a series of diets are those most likely to become fatter and unhappier than before, for they upset the natural equilibrium of their bodies. In self-defense, their bodies stock-pile fat whenever and wherever possible, hedging as they may against the next (self-imposed) privation. Meanwhile hearts suffer through cycles of feast and famine, strained at each new feast, shocked at each new famine. "To fat, to starve—/Perchance to die of it! Ah, there's the rub." Pokeberry, dinitrophenol, rainbow pills, liquid protein—there is no end to death by dieting.[2]

4   And still the dieting goes on, as fat people are compromised and persecut-ed. Like other minorities, fat people are treated like children, given silly nick-names, considered socially and sexually immature. The "Diet Conscience," an electronic guardian, sneers when the refrigerator door is opened, "Are you eating again? Shame on you! No wonder you look the way you do! Ha! Ha! Ha! You'll be sorry, fatty. Do yourself a favor; *shut the door!*"[3]

5   Like other minorities, fat people are seen as throwbacks to a more primitive time. Neanderthals in museum dioramas are squat and fat; cannibals stirring pots are fat; Oriental despots are fat; harems are full of slothful fat women and

---

[2] Louis I. Dublin believed that he had demonstrated that weight-reducing decreased mortality: "Overweight shortens life," *MLIC* 32 (Oct 1951) 1–4, and idem, "Relation of obesity to longevity," *NEJM* 248 (1953) 971–74. But see Public Health Service, *Obesity and Health* (Washington, D.C., 1966) 59; George V. Mann, "Obesity, the national spook," *AJPH* 61 (1971) 1491–98; idem, "Influence of obesi-ty on health," *NEJM* 291 (1974) 178–85, 226–32; and William Bennett and Joel Gurin, *The Dieter's Dilemma* (NY, 1982) 134–35.

On the absence of a causal relationship between fatness or overweight and increased mortality, see Ancel Keys et al., "Coronary heart disease: overweight and obesity as risk factors," *AIM* 77 (1972) 15–27; Tavia Gordon and William B. Kannel, "Obesity and cardiovascular disease: the Framingham study," *Clinics in Endocrinology and Metabolism* 5 (1976) 367–75; Susan C. Wooley et al., "Obesity and women—I. A closer look at the facts," *Women's Studies Int Q* 2 (1979) 74; Reubin Andres, "Effect of obesity on total mortality," *IJO* 4 (1980) 381–86; Kelly D. Brownell, "Obesity," *J of Consulting and Clinical Psych* 50 (1982) 820; and Carol Sternhill, "We'll always be fat, but fat can be fit," *Ms.* (May 1985) 142. On the dan-gers of a weight-loss/weight-gain cycle, see Vinne Young, *It's Fun to Be Fat* (NY, 1953) 10, 26 and quote on 23; Nick Lyons, *Locked Jaws* (NY, 1979) 13 quote; and Sharon G. Patton, "Why dieting can make you fat," *New Woman* (Aug 1984) 34.

On deaths from dieting, see Roland C. Curtin, "The heart and its danger in the treatment of obesi-ty," *J of Balneology and Climatology* 12 (1908) 223 on pokeberry; Chapter Seven on dinitrophenol and amphetamines; House of Representatives Subcommittee on Health and the Environment, *Hearing . . . on the Most Popular Diet in America Today, Liquid Protein, Dec 28, 1977* (Washington, D.C., 1978) 3–7; Centers for Disease Control, "Follow-up on deaths associated with liquid protein diets," *Morbidity and Mortality Weekly Report* 27 (1978) 223–24; Harold E. Sours et al., "Sudden death associated with very low calorie weight reduction regimens," *AJCN* 34 (1981) 453–61, and see also 1639–40, 2855–57.

[3] Ann M. Lingg, "A plump girl talks back," *Amer Mercury* 78 (March 1954) 30, an early reference to minority status; Lew Louderback, "More people should be fat," *SEP* 240 (Nov 4, 1967) 10; Grosswirth, *Fat Pride*, 40; and Mildred Klingman, *Secret Lives of Fat People* (Boston, 1981) 72 on Diet Conscience. See also Lisa Schoenfielder and Barb Wieser, eds., *Shadow on a Tightrope: Writings by Women on Fat Oppression* (Iowa City, Ia., 1983).

supervised by fat eunuchs. The modern world is passing them by. Fat people are stuck in the past, so much so that modern businessmen and scientists prefer an employee who has been in jail or in a mental ward to one who is fat. Criminality and insanity seem less intransigent, less rooted, than obesity.[4]

6   If fat people are not such atavisms, why do they do so poorly in school and in business? The same vicious circle surrounding other minorities surrounds fat people, who have more difficulty getting into the best colleges and who are not promoted as quickly as their leaner rivals. How they look is more important than how well they do their jobs. The New York City Traffic Department in 1965 dismissed six meter maids for being overweight; National Airlines fired a stewardess for being 4 lbs overweight. As of 1982 only Michigan had a law specifically banning discrimination on account of weight. In 1980 a *New Yorker* cartoon depicted a judge sentencing a defendant: "It is the Court's opinion that, although innocent, you are dangerously overweight." This comedy had already been played out in Miami, where a woman being sentenced for a misdemeanor assault explained that at 315 lbs she was too heavy to work. The judge gave her three years' probation on the condition that she lose 65 lbs at 3 lbs per week; if she went off her diet, she would go to prison.[5]

7   Physicians are equally unsympathetic. They find fat patients distasteful. Fat people seem more difficult to examine, less likely to cooperate. Fat people are waddling reminders of the failure of medicine to come up with a safe, workable program for long-term weight reduction, just as poor people and homeless people are stark reminders of the failure of the economic system. Like politicians, physicians blame the victims. It is not the doctor's fault if fat people are weak, dishonest, lazy, and childish. All one can do with such people is to threaten them with disease and death, play on their fears. "If, knowing these dangers—as you now do—you continue to overeat, it must be obvious that you are acting in a childish fashion. You are immature. This *alone* will prove to you that you are acting *like a child* if you continue to be fat. Now it is up to you. . . . Be childish and die, or grow up and live!"[6]

---

[4] Robert J. Homant and Daniel B. Kennedy, "Attitudes toward ex-offenders: a comparison of social stigmas," *J of Criminal Justice* 10 (1982) 383–91.

[5] Peter L. Benson et al., "Social costs of obesity," *Social Behavior and Personality* 8 (1980) 91–96 on colleges; Llewellyn Louderback, *Fat Power* (NY, 1970) 47, 52, 53, 55; Chris Chase, *The Great American Waistline* (NY, 1981) 196 on stewardesses; *New Yorker* (Sept 29, 1980) 49; and "Better than prison," *Time* 97 (June 7, 1971) 39. Concerning weight discrimination at law, see David H. Tucker for the Maryland Commission on Human Relations, *Report on the Study of Weight and Size Discrimination,* typescript (Baltimore, 1980); Jane O. Baker, "The Rehabilitation Act of 1973: protection for victims of weight discrimination?" *UCLA Law R* 29 (April 1982) 947–71; David Berreby, "Is being fat a handicap? Courts differ," *National Law J* 4 (Aug 30, 1982) 3:1; Lynne Reaves, "Fat folks' rights: weight bias issues emerging," *Amer Bar Assoc J* 69 (1983) 878; and Lauren R. Reskin, "Employers must give obese job applicants a fat chance," *Amer Bar Assoc J* 71 (Sept 1985) 104.

[6] George L. Maddox et al., "Overweight as a problem of medical management in a public outpatient clinic," *AJMS* 252 (Oct 1966) 394–402; Hilde Bruch, *The Importance of Overweight* (NY, 1957) 318–24; Howard D. Kurland, "Obesity: an unfashionable problem," *Psychiatric Opinion* 7,6 (1970) 20–24; and Alfred J. Cantor, *How to Lose Weight the Doctor's Way* (NY, 1959) quote on 40.

8   Yet nearly half of all dieters get their dieting information from such patronizing doctors, doctors who until recently have had no specific training in nutrition. In 1970, three-quarters of doctors surveyed found obesity and overweight to be very frequent among their patients, yet few have pursued the study of obesity (bariatrics) in order to improve their courses of treatment. Nor have they been in particularly good shape themselves; the Scarsdale diet doctor Herman Tarnower was 15 lbs overweight according to his own charts. Physicians are no better than gamblers playing "statistical roulette with the lives of fat people," prescribing diet pills that affect blood pressure and kidneys, dictating diets that are subtle forms of sadism, calling for a "grim, dour self-punishment. If we submit we become miserable, if not actually neurotic."[7]

9   And then? "Then you are told that your frustrations, your worries, your inhibitions, and your insecurities turn into fat." Tranquilizers will not work; they make you fatter. You need psychological help. A woman in the 1950s was given the name of a psychiatrist because she was fat. She wrote to Dear Abby, "Now Abby, I am not *crazy*, I am just a little overweight. Have you ever heard of anything so insulting?" Abby thought a psychiatrist might do her a world of good, but Abby had no statistics to support such a claim, and there are none now. Psychiatrists are as inept with fat people as they are, still, with the schizophrenics whom they often use as a model for the obese. Perhaps because they are so inept, they demand much more of their fat patients. "Goddammit!" cried one fat woman at her psychiatrist, "You call *me* insatiable; you're the one who's never satisfied."[8]

10   Society itself will not be satisfied until all fat people are gone. Aldebaran, a member of the Los Angeles Fat Underground, wrote an open letter to a doctor in 1977: "You see fat as suicide, I see weight-loss as murder—genocide, to be precise—the systematic murder of a biological minority by organized medicine." But not just by organized medicine. By society as a whole. In the United States, a fat person's prior identification is with fatness; as a status, fatness comes before religion, race, sexual preference, income, gender. Only in a society intent on doing away with fat people could fatness become so distinct and so negative a stigma. George Nathan Blomberg, fat hero of the 1978 novel by Mark Dintenfass, *The Case Against Org*, becomes defiant in the face of such genocide: "Listen, one must choose to be obese: it is an act of courage." Near the

---

[7] Ruth Adams, *Did You Ever See a Fat Squirrel?* (Emmaus, Pa., 1972) 197; Tillie Lewis Tasti Diet ad in *Supermarket News* (March 29, 1976) on "Where Do Diet Food Customers Get Their Information?"; Louis Harris and Associates, *Harris Survey Yearbook* (NY, 1971) 203, 213; Diana Trilling, *Mrs. Harris: The Death of the Scarsdale Diet Doctor* (NY, 1981) 85 and cf. Peter Wyden and Barbara Wyden, *How the Doctors Diet* (NY, 1968); interview with Dr. Frederick J. Stare, Sept 27, 1984, concerning physician education in nutrition; and Martin Lederman, *The Slim Gourmet* (NY, 1955) quote on 8.

[8] Vinne Young, "Don't get ill getting thin," *Science Digest* 36 (Aug 1954) 1 (quote); Abigail van Buren (= Pauline Phillips), *Dear Abby* (Englewood Cliffs, N.J., 1958) 121; Walter W. Hamburger, "Psychology of dietary change," *AJPH* 48 (1958) 1342–48; Robert M. Lindner, *The Fifty-Minute Hour* (NY, 1955) 133 (quote); Albert J. Stunkard and A. J. Rush, "Dieting and depression reexamined," *AIM* 81 (1974) 526–33; and Colleen S. W. Rand, "Treatment of obese patients in psychoanalysis," *Psychiatric Clinics of North Amer* 1 (1978) 661–72.

end he knows, "There is no skinny guy inside me struggling to get out. I am Org forever." And on the last page he imagines "I and the world and a chocolate cherry all melting together, becoming one and everything."[9]

The Fat Society: A Utopia

11 If the tables could be turned, if this were a fat society, a society that admired and rewarded fatness—a society that has never existed in this country for both sexes at the same time—things would be very much different and very much better. It would be like Servia, Indiana, in 1899, "A Town of Fat People," population 206, temperate, quiet, and affluent. Or like Roseto, Pennsylvania, in the 1960s, population 1,700, nearly all of the residents obese and hardly a heart murmur among them.[10]

12 In a fat society, dinners would be scrumptious, sociable, and warm. No Mixed Gelatinoids as hors d'oeuvres, no Strained Nitrogen Gumbo for the soup, no Grilled Proteids with Globulin Patties for the entrée, no Compôte of Assorted Vitamins for dessert. There would be 101 Things To Do With Cottage Cheese—use it as a facial, take it out on a leash for a walk, build a snowman—but no one would have to eat it.[11]

13 In a fat society, children would be fed and fed well when hungry. When they were fed, they would be satisfied, because there would be no snares laid around food. Feeding would be calm and loving, always sufficient, never forced. Children as they grew into adolescence would acquire no eating disorders, since fat people and thin people would be on equal terms and there would be none of that anxious dieting which so often starts off the career of an anorectic or bulimic. No one would be obsessed with food because all people would have the opportunity to be powerful and expressive beyond the dining table.[12]

14 In a fat society, fat people would dress expressively. Their fashions would no longer be called "oversize" or "halfsize," and they would have the same choice of fabrics and designs as everyone else. Not just pantyhose but all clothes would be "Just my Size." Full-size models would be featured in the salons of *haute couture;* full-size fiberglass mannequins would pose with others in the most elite shop-windows. Fat people would no longer need to buy their clothes at specialty shops like The Forgotten Woman and Catherine Stout, or discreetly through the mails from Lane Bryant, Roaman's, and King-Size. A fat woman

---

[9] Aldebaran, "Fat liberation—a luxury?" *State and Mind* 5 (June–July 1977) 34; Stuart Byron, "The unmaking of a fattie," *Village Voice* (Dec 17, 1970) 10; and Mark Dintenfass, *The Case Against Org* (Boston, 1978) 5, 189, 246, quoted with permission from Little, Brown & Co.

[10] *NYDT* (Sept 3, 1899) illus, supp. 20:3; Louderback, *Fat Power,* 167.

[11] Irvin S. Cobb, *At His Best* (Garden City, N.Y., 1929) 244 on gelatinoids, and Totie Fields, *I Think I'll Start on Monday: The Official 8 1/2 Oz Mashed Potato Diet* (NY, 1972) 32 on cottage cheese. On conviviality and its suppression by dieters, see James A. Pike and Howard A. Johnson, *Man in the Middle* (Greenwich, Conn., 1956) 53; Robert Waithman, "Plea to the joyless eaters," *NYT Mag* (Feb 12, 1956) 19, 62; and Jean Kerr, *Please Don't Eat the Daisies* (NY, 1957) 172.

[12] Cf. Margaret Atwood, *Lady Oracle* (NY, 1976) esp. 74, 321; Susan C. Wooley and Orland W. Wooley, "Should obesity be treated at all?" in *Eating and Its Disorders,* eds. A. J. Stunkard and E. Stellar (NY, 1984) 185–92.

could wear dramatic colors and horizontal stripes when the fancy struck; a fat man could indulge a secret desire to wear a large-checked light gray suit.[13]

15   A fat society would be forthright about the body beneath the clothes. It would be relaxed about bodily functions, assured about sensuality, confident with sexuality. Compulsive weighing would disappear; no longer would the scale (always described as a male) lord it over anyone's body. The prudery of weight-watching, the overzealous guardianship of the body, would vanish. Beauty and sexuality would be independent of pounds and of calipers. The fat person would be a "strikingly *unavoidable* creature," and neither the fat man nor the fat woman would be typed as nonsexual or sexually corrupt. "I am touchable," fat people would say to themselves, and they would think of their pounds as "voluptuous planes." Like Sarah Fay Cohen Campbell in the novel *Fat People* (1982), they would accept their bodies as loving instruments and learn to play them in an open tuning.[14]

16   Women in particular would wear their weight with new conviction. They would affirm their physiological gifts, their genetic and cultural tendencies to put on flesh, their extra layering of body fat. Fat women would not live in the future conditional, suspended between what they are and who they will be when they are finally thin. Fat women would not have to invent fantasy selves a quarter their bulk and four times as lovely. "I've earned my wrinkles and padding," women would say with Ruthanne Olds. "They represent a lot of rewarding life experience." So everyone would at last welcome back the Earth Mother, the Venus of Willendorf, the female colossus, the grand diva, "La Stupenda," and divinity would once more be nurturant rather than vindictive.[15]

17   A fat society would be a comforting society, less harried, more caring. It would favor the gourmet over the glutton, slow food over fast food, matriarchy and communal affection over patriarchy and self-hate, eroticism over pornography, philanthropy and art over greed and blind technology. It would mean

---

[13] Margaret Dana, *Behind the Label* (Boston, 1938) 117–20; Marya Mannes, "Juno in limbo: the trauma of size 16," *Harper's Mag* (July 1964) 37–40; Grosswirth, *Fat Pride*, 69, Susie Orbach, *Fat Is a Feminist Issue* (NY, 1979) 90–91; Jean DuCoffe and Sherry Suib Cohen, *Making It Big* (NY, 1980) 12, 22, 25–31; Evelyn Roaman and Dee Ratienee, *The Evelyn Roaman Book: An Expert Shows You How Heavy Can Be Happy* (NY, 1980); Dale Godey, *Your Guide to Dressing Thin* (NY, 1981) 12–27; Ann Harper and Glenn Lewis, *The Big Beauty Book* (NY, 1982) 104; and William Johnston, "The fun of being a fat man," *Amer Mag* 94 (July 1922) 54–55.

[14] Lila Austin, "I'm fat, and I like it!" *GH* III (Sept 1940) 48; Nora S. Kinzer, *Put Down and Ripped Off* (NY, 1977) 34, 49–50; Marcia Millman, *Such a Pretty Face: Being Fat in America* (NY, 1980) 106, 162–63; Harper and Lewis, *Big Beauty Book*, quote on 3; DuCoffe and Cohen, *Making It Big*, 258 (quote), 260–63; David Newman and Robert Benton, "Fat power," *Esquire* 66 (Dec 1966) 212–15 on visual grandeur of fat men; Carol S. Smith, *Fat People* (NY, 1978); and see "Fatso" film (20th-Century Fox, 1980).

[15] Charlotte C. Rowett, "Success, avoirdupois, and clothes," *Woman Beautiful* 4 (June 1910) 40–41; DuCoffe and Cohen, *Making It Big*, 334; Anne Scott Beller, *Fat and Thin* (NY, 1977) esp. ch. 7; Kim Chernin, *The Obsession: Reflections on the Tyranny of Slenderness* (NY, 1981) esp. 133, 139; Jean Stafford, "The echo and the nemesis," *Children Are Bored on Sunday* (NY, 1953) 10–39, a fantasy self; Ruthanne Olds, *Big and Beautiful: Overcoming Fat Phobia* (Washington, D.C., 1982) 13; Stella J. Reichman, *Great Big Beautiful Doll* (NY, 1977) 26–28; and Marion Woodman, *The Owl Was a Baker's Daughter* (Toronto, 1980) 10, 18.

therefore an end to narcotics and narcissism. In a fat society, there would be no "flight from feelings," no need to resort to a form of privacy that kills as it protects. No one would have such stingy personal boundaries that the self would seem always under siege. Mirrors would neither frighten nor enchant. There would be more to the person than a mercurial reflection from shopwindows. "Sizing up" a person would be a wonderfully complex experience; tape measures and scales would have nothing to do with it.[16]

18   A fat society would be less harshly competitive, less devouring. People could be assertive without seeming aggressive or threatening. There would be no cannibalism, no fear of swallowing or being swallowed up. Accepting one's own bulk, one need not consume others or gnaw at one's self. Dieting is cannibalism. Dieters eat off their own bodies: "You start to get thin when you begin to *live on your own fat.*" Dieters are encouraged to be cannibals: "If your body-republic doesn't get enough food to support all the citizens, some will die and be cannibalized to feed the others. . . . In this body-politic of cell-citizens, you can fool all of the people all of the time, and if you want to *get* thin and *stay* thin, that's what you must do." Dieters have no recourse but to be cannibals: "To reduce weight, an obese person must burn his own body fat. It's as simple as that. He must eat himself up! A bit cannibalistic? I'm afraid so. But it's the only way to lose weight." That legendary diet drug which was nothing but a live tapeworm was the folkloric representation of such cannibalism. In a fat society, no one would be eaten up from within and no one would be eaten alive. Fat people, weighted, solid, would not fear the desires of others or their own desires. If fat people now lie or steal or hide, that is because they are always trying to save face ("such a pretty face") and disguise their needs. They must act surreptitiously, with the night and the bathroom as their refuge. In a fat society, no one would be forced to such humiliating secrecy. All hunger would be honest hunger.[17]

Review Questions

1. What is the "vicious circle" that affects fat people and "other minorities," according to Schwartz?

2. Schwartz asserts that physicians play an important, and largely negative, role in the lives of fat people. What is this role?

---

[16] See Donald B. Meyer, *The Positive Thinkers* (Garden City, N.Y., 1965) 120 on the "flight from feelings"; Véronique Nahoum, "La belle femme ou le stade du miroir en histoire," *Communications* 31 (1979) 22–32 on mirrors; and Susan Griffin, *Pornography and Silence* (NY, 1981) esp. 60–62.

[17] Nina W. Putnam, *Tomorrow We Diet* (NY, 1922) 89; Phillip W. Haberman, Jr., "How to diet if you have no character at all," *Vogue* 135 (June 1960) 148; and Thyra S. Winslow, *Think Yourself Thin* (NY, 1951) 113. On tapeworms, Ronald L. Baker, *Hoosier Folk Legends* (Bloomington, Ind., 1982) 226, and Jane Fonda, *Workout Book* (NY, 1981) 10.

3. In the section titled "The Fat Society: A Utopia" (paragraphs 11–18), what attributes of our current culture does Schwartz link to slenderness?

4. List any three of Schwartz's especially strong assertions, what you would consider to be his "zingers"—his most highly charged, argumentative statements. Quote carefully, cite paragraph numbers, and explain in a sentence or two what makes each statement argumentative.

Discussion and Writing Suggestions

1. In his introduction to "Fat and Happy?"—the final chapter in his book *Never Satisfied*—Hillel Schwartz observes that "[r]ecently there has been a growing protest against the despotism of slenderness." In what sense can the culture of slenderness be said to be despotic?

2. To what extent does modern medical evidence contradict Schwartz's assertion that "[no] one has been able to prove that fatness *per se* cuts life short"? (See Gawande, the editorial in the *Journal of the American Medical Association*, and the Surgeon General's "Call to Action" at <http://www.surgeongeneral.gov/topics/obesity/default.htm>.) If medical evidence invalidates Schwartz's assertion about fatness and duration of life, does this same evidence also invalidate Schwartz's other points about being fat and happy?

3. In paragraph 10, Schwartz makes an extreme assertion, quoting a fat activist to suggest that weight-loss regimes are a species of "murder" by organized medicine and the larger society. Your response?

4. Schwartz observes that in "the United States, . . . fatness comes before religion, race, sexual preference, income, [and] gender" (paragraph 10). Is Schwartz's observation accurate? Do you find yourself ordering your initial impressions of people by weight first? How might you argue against Schwartz on this point?

5. To what extent does Schwartz's "fat utopia" appeal to you? Would it, in fact, be a more enjoyable world than our currently "despotic" world of slenderness? What problems can you anticipate in Schwartz's utopia?

6. Schwartz has carefully cited evidence for many of his claims, even the seemingly extreme ones. Locate one such footnoted claim (perhaps, "a fat man could indulge a secret desire to wear a large-checked light gray suit") and then locate and read some of the cited sources. Report to your class on what you find.

7. Schwartz wrote the book *Never Satisfied*, in which this selection appears, in 1986. In the two decades that have elapsed, how well

does his critique of slim culture and his imagined utopia of fat culture hold up for you?

The Ironic Politics of Obesity
Marion Nestle

In this editorial, which appeared in the journal Science *(7 February 2003), Marion Nestle identifies several ironies relating to the obesity epidemic, including the sources of a "leadership vacuum" that compromises our government's ability to fight the problem. A professor in the Department of Nutrition and Food Sciences at New York University, Nestle is the author of* The Food Pushers: How the Food Industry Influences Nutrition and Health *(University of California Press, 2002) and* Safe Food: Bacteria, Biotechnology, and Bioterrorism *(University of California Press, Berkeley, 2003). She has worked with the U.S. Surgeon General and the Food and Drug Administration on dietary issues and consults with the food industry.*

1   Here is a great irony of 21st-century global public health: While many hundreds of millions of people lack adequate food as a result of economic inequities, political corruption, or warfare, many hundreds of millions more are overweight to the point of increased risk for diet-related chronic diseases. Obesity is a worldwide phenomenon, affecting children as well as adults and forcing all but the poorest countries to divert scarce resources away from food security to take care of people with preventable heart disease and diabetes.

2   To reverse the obesity epidemic, we must address fundamental causes. Overweight comes from consuming more food energy than is expended in activity. The cause of this imbalance also is ironic: improved prosperity. People use extra income to eat more and be less active. Market economies encourage this. They turn people with expendable income into consumers of aggressively marketed foods that are high in energy but low in nutritional value, and of cars, television sets, and computers that promote sedentary behavior. Gaining weight is good for business. Food is particularly big business because everyone eats.

3   Moreover, food is so overproduced that many countries, especially the rich ones, have far more than they need—another irony. In the United States, to take an extreme example, most adults—of all ages, incomes, educational levels, and census categories—are overweight. The U.S. food supply provides 3800 kilocalories per person per day, nearly twice as much as required by many adults. Overabundant food forces companies to compete for sales through advertising, health claims, new products, larger portions, and campaigns directed toward children. Food marketing promotes weight gain. Indeed, it is difficult to think of any major industry that might benefit if people ate less food; certainly not the agriculture, food product, grocery, restaurant, diet, or drug industries. All flourish when people eat more, and all employ armies of lobbyists to discourage governments from doing anything to inhibit overeating.

4   Food companies are well aware of the economic implications of reversing the obesity epidemic, as are government agencies. Economists at the U.S.

Department of Agriculture (USDA) calculate that "large adjustments" would occur in the agriculture and processed food industries if people ate more healthfully. That threat is one reason why food producers contribute generously to congressional campaigns, and why federal agencies have failed to take the obvious first step: a national obesity-prevention campaign in response to the Surgeon General's 2001 *Call to Action.*[*] Such a campaign would have to address dietary aspects and include messages to eat less as well as the far less controversial "be more active." No other federal health agency has stepped in to lead the nation on dietary issues, which explains why USDA is left in charge of national nutrition policy. USDA's primary mission is to promote U.S. agricultural products ("eat more"), but it also issues advice about diet and health (sometimes meaning "eat less"). This notorious conflict accounts for the ambiguity of federal dietary guidelines ("aim for a healthy weight," "choose beverages and foods to moderate your intake of sugars") and the confusing nature of USDA's food guide pyramid.

5　If campaigns to promote more healthful eating are not in the best interest of industry, and government agencies are caught in conflicts of interest, how can any society address its obesity epidemic? The leadership vacuum in the United States leaves much room for litigation against the obesity-promoting practices of food companies. Whatever their legal merits, the current lawsuits engage the food industry's rapt attention and encourage scrutiny of their current products and practices. The vacuum also creates an opportunity for scientists and public interest groups to advocate better policies. Existing food policies could be tweaked to improve the environment of food choice through small taxes on junk foods and soft drinks (to raise funds for anti-obesity campaigns); restrictions on food marketing to children, especially in schools and on television; calorie labels on fast foods; and changes in farm subsidies to promote the consumption of fruits and vegetables. The politics of obesity demand that we revisit campaign contribution laws and advocate for a government agency—independent of industry—with clear responsibility for matters pertaining to food, nutrition, and health.

Review Questions

1. What are some of the "ironies" Nestle calls your attention to in this editorial?

2. Why have federal agencies not responded with plans to combat obesity response to the Surgeon General's *Call to Action* (against unhealthy weight gain)?

3. The U.S. Department of Agriculture faces a conflict of interest, according to Nestle. What is it? Nestle believes that the current

---

[*] The *Surgeon General's Call to Action to Prevent and Decrease Overweight and Obesity* (2001) can be found at <http://www.surgeongeneral.gov/topics/obesity/>.

"leadership vacuum" in the United States with regard to fighting the obesity epidemic has created opportunities. What are they?

4. What solution does Nestle offer to resolve the ironies that she points to in this editorial?

Discussion and Writing Suggestions

1. Before reading this editorial, to what extent were you aware of the "politics" associated with obesity? What is especially political about the topic? What are the origins of the politics?

2. Do you think it a good idea for the government to create a new agency—and bureaucracy—to coordinate a response to the obesity epidemic? Explain your response.

3. Reflect on the amount of advertising in various media devoted to food. List the number and types of food-related ads you encounter during a typical day.

4. Dwell for a moment on the first irony to which Nestle points: the existence of obesity and obesity-related illnesses alongside malnutrition and its related illnesses. Devote five minutes to writing out your thoughts. Sometime after you've finished, return to what you've written and circle a line or two that you think might be developed into a paper.

The Man Who Couldn't Stop Eating
Atul Gawande

Atul Gawande tells the story of Vincent Caselli, who underwent a gastric bypass to lose weight by surgically reducing the size of his stomach, thus making him physically unable to eat and absorb the nutrients from more than an ounce of food at a sitting. The statistics on the gastric-bypass procedure, the last resort of people who cannot shed weight in other ways, confirm the sharp rise of obesity in this country. According to the American Society for Bariatric Surgery, in 1992 surgeons performed 16,200 of the procedures. In 2002, the number jumped to 63,100 and one year later to 103,200. Gawande, who assisted on the surgery, calls this "among the strangest operations surgeons perform" in that it "is intended to control a person's will—to manipulate his innards so that he does not overeat." Those who, like Caselli, are morbidly obese and whose weight profoundly reduces their quality of life are turning to the gastric bypass more frequently. Gawande, a surgical resident and also a staff writer for the New Yorker, uses the story of Caselli to "contemplate the human appetite." As such, he provides a fitting and compelling end to the selections in this chapter on obesity. The essay appeared originally in the 9 July 2001 issue of the New Yorker. Gawande is the author of Complications: A Surgeon's Notes on an Imperfect Science (Picador, 2002).

1 At 7:30 A.M. on September 13, 1999, an anesthesiologist and two orderlies rolled our patient, whom I will call Vincent Caselli, into the operating room,

where his attending surgeon and I awaited him. Caselli was a short man of middle age—five feet seven, fifty-four years old. The son of Italian immigrants, he had worked as a heavy-machine operator and road-construction contractor. (He and his men had paved a rotary in my own neighborhood.) He had been married for thirty-five years; he and his wife had three girls, all grown now. And he weighed four hundred and twenty-eight pounds. Housebound, his health failing, he no longer had anything resembling a normal life. And so, although he was afraid of surgery, he had come for a Roux-en-Y gastric-bypass operation. It is the most drastic treatment we have for obesity. It is also among the strangest operations surgeons perform. It removes no disease, repairs no defect or injury. It is an operation that is intended to control a person's will—to manipulate his innards so that he does not overeat—and it is soaring in popularity. Some forty-five thousand patients underwent obesity surgery in 1999, and the number is expected to double by 2003.

2   For the very obese, general anesthesia alone is a dangerous undertaking; major abdominal surgery can easily become a disaster. Obesity substantially increases the risk of respiratory failure, heart attacks, wound infections, hernias—almost every complication possible, including death. Nevertheless, Dr. Sheldon Randall, the attending surgeon, was relaxed, having done more than a thousand of these operations. I, the assisting resident, remained anxious. Watching Caselli struggle to shift himself from the stretcher onto the operating table and then stop halfway to catch his breath, I was afraid that he would fall in between. Once he was on the table, his haunches rolled off the sides, and I double-checked the padding that protected him from the table's sharp edges. He was naked except for his "universal"–size johnny, which covered him like a napkin, and a nurse put a blanket over his lower body for the sake of modesty. When we tried to lay him down, he lost his breath and started to turn blue, and the anesthesiologist had to put him to sleep sitting up. Only with the breathing tube and a mechanical ventilator in place were we able to lay him flat.

3   He was a mountain on the table. I am six feet two, but even with the table as low as it goes I had to stand on a step stool; Dr. Randall stood on two stools stacked together. He nodded to me, and I cut down the middle of our patient's belly, through skin and then dense inches of glistening yellow fat, and we opened the abdomen. Inside, his liver was streaked with fat, too, and his bowel was covered by a thick apron of it, but his stomach looked ordinary—a smooth, grayish-pink bag the size of two fists. We put metal retractors in place to hold the wound open and keep the liver and the slithering loops of bowel out of the way. Working elbow deep, we stapled his stomach down to the size of an ounce. Before the operation, it could accommodate a quart of food and drink; now it would hold no more than a shot glass. We then sewed the opening of this little pouch to a portion of bowel two feet past his duodenum—past the initial portion of the small bowel, where bile and pancreatic juices break food down. This was the bypass part of the operation, and it meant that what food the stomach could accommodate would be less readily absorbed.

4   The operation took us a little over two hours. Caselli was stable throughout, but his recovery was difficult. Patients are usually ready to go home three days after surgery; it was two days before Caselli even knew where he was. His kidneys failed for twenty-four hours, and fluid built up in his lungs. He became

5   delirious, seeing things on the walls, pulling off his oxygen mask, his chest leads for the monitors, even yanking out the I.V. We were worried, and his wife and daughters were terrified, but gradually he pulled through.

5   By the third day after surgery, he was well enough to take sips of clear liquids (water, apple juice, ginger ale), up to one ounce every four hours. On my afternoon rounds, I asked him how he'd done. "O.K.," he said. We began giving him four-ounce servings of Carnation Instant Breakfast for protein and modest calories. He could finish only half, and that took him an hour. It filled him up and, when it did, he felt a sharp, unpleasant pain. This was to be expected, Dr. Randall told him. It would be a few days before he was ready for solid food. But he was doing well. He no longer needed I. V. fluids. And, after he'd had a short stay in a rehabilitation facility, we sent him home.

6   A couple of weeks later, I asked Dr. Randall how Caselli was getting on. "Just fine," the surgeon said. Although I had done a few of these cases with him, I had not seen how the patients progressed afterward. Would he really lose all that weight? I asked. And how much could he eat? Randall suggested that I see Caselli for myself. So one day that October, I gave him a call, and he invited me to stop by.

7   Vincent Caselli and his wife live in an unassuming saltbox house not far outside Boston. To get there, I took Route 1, past four Dunkin' Donuts, four pizzerias, three steak houses, two McDonald's, two Ground Rounds, a Taco Bell, a Friendly's, and an International House of Pancakes. (A familiar roadside vista, but that day it seemed a sad tour of our self-destructiveness.) I rang the doorbell, and a long minute passed. I heard a slow footfall coming toward the door, and Caselli, visibly winded, opened it. But he smiled broadly when he saw me and gave my hand a warm squeeze. He led me—his hand on table, wall, doorjamb for support—to a seat at a breakfast table in his flowered-wallpaper kitchen.

8   I asked him how things were going. "Real good," he said. He had no more pain from the operation, the incision had healed, and, though it had been only three weeks, he'd already lost forty pounds. But, at three hundred and ninety, and still stretching his size-64 slacks and size-XXXXXXL T-shirts (the largest he could find at the local big-and-tall store), he did not yet feel different. Sitting, he had to keep his legs apart to let his abdomen sag between them, and the weight of his body on the wooden chair forced him to shift every minute or two because his buttocks would fall asleep. Sweat rimmed the folds of his forehead and made his thin salt-and-pepper hair stick to his pate. His brown eyes were rheumy, above dark bags. He breathed with a disconcerting wheeze.

9   We talked about his arrival home from the hospital. The first solid food he had tried was a spoonful of scrambled eggs. Just that much, he said, made him so full it hurt, "like something was ripping," and he threw it up. He was afraid that nothing solid would ever go down. But he gradually found that he could tolerate small amounts of soft foods—mashed potatoes, macaroni, even chicken if it was finely chopped and moist. Breads and dry meats, he found, got "stuck," and he'd have to put a finger down his throat and make himself vomit.

10   Caselli's battle with obesity, he explained, began in his late twenties. "I always had some weight on me," he said—he was two hundred pounds at nineteen,

when he married Teresa (as I'll call her), and a decade later he reached three hundred. He would diet and lose seventy-five pounds, then put a hundred back on. By 1985, he weighed four hundred pounds. On one diet, he got down to a hundred and ninety, but he gained it all back. "I must have gained and lost a thousand pounds," he told me. He developed high blood pressure, high cholesterol, and diabetes. His knees and his back ached all the time, and he had limited mobility. He used to get season tickets to Boston Bruins games, and go out regularly to the track at Seekonk every summer to see the auto racing. Years ago, he drove in races himself. Now he could barely walk to his pickup truck. He hadn't been on an airplane since 1983, and it had been two years since he had been to the second floor of his own house, because he couldn't negotiate the stairs. "Teresa bought a computer a year ago for her office upstairs, and I've never seen it," he told me. He had to move out of their bedroom, upstairs, to a small room off the kitchen. Unable to lie down, he had slept in a recliner ever since. Even so, he could doze only in snatches, because of sleep apnea, which is a common syndrome among the obese and is thought to be related to excessive fat in the tongue and in the soft tissues of the upper airway. Every thirty minutes, his breathing would stop, and he'd wake up asphyxiating. He was perpetually exhausted.

11   There were other troubles, too, the kind that few people speak about. Good hygiene, he said, was nearly impossible. He could no longer stand up to urinate, and after moving his bowels he often had to shower in order to get clean. Skin folds would become chafed and red, and sometimes develop boils and infections. And, he reported, "Sex life is nonexistent. I have real hopes for it." For him, though, the worst part was his diminishing ability to earn a livelihood.

12   Vincent Caselli's father had come to Boston from Italy in 1914 to work in construction, and he soon established his own firm. In 1979, Vincent went into business for himself. He was skilled at operating heavy equipment—his specialty was running a Gradall, a thirty-ton, three-hundred-thousand-dollar hydraulic excavator—and he employed a team of men year-round to build roads and sidewalks. Eventually, he owned his own Gradall, a ten-wheel Mack dump truck, a backhoe, and a fleet of pickup trucks. But in the past three years he had become too big to operate the Gradall or keep up with the daily maintenance of the equipment. He had to run the business from his house, and pay others to do the heavy work; he enlisted a nephew to help manage the men and the contracts. Expenses rose, and since he could no longer go around to city halls himself, he found contracts harder to get. If Teresa hadn't had a job—she is the business manager for an assisted-living facility in Boston—they would have gone bankrupt.

13   Teresa, a freckled redhead, had been pushing him for a long time to diet and exercise. He, too, wanted desperately to lose weight, but the task of controlling himself, day to day, meal to meal, seemed beyond him. "I'm a man of habits," he told me. "I'm very prone to habits." And eating, he said, was his worst habit. But, then, eating is everyone's habit. What was different about *his* habit? I asked. Well, the portions he took were too big, and he could never leave a crumb on his plate. If there was pasta left in the pot, he'd eat that, too. But why, I wanted to know. Was it that he just loved food? He pondered this question for

a moment. It wasn't love, he decided. "Eating felt good instantaneously," he said, "but it only felt good instantaneously." Was it excessive hunger that drove him? "I was never hungry," he said.

14 As far as I could tell, Caselli ate for the same reasons that everyone eats: because food tasted good, because it was seven o'clock and time for dinner, because a nice meal had been set out on the table. And he stopped eating for the same reason everyone stops: because he was full and eating was no longer pleasurable. The main difference seemed to be that it took an unusual quantity of food to make him full. (He could eat a large pizza as if it were a canapé.) To lose weight, he faced the same difficult task that every dieter faces—to stop eating before he felt full, while the food still tasted good, and to exercise. These were things that he could do for a little while, and, with some reminding and coaching, for perhaps a bit longer, but they were not, he had found, things that he could do for long. "I am not strong," he said.

15 In the spring of 1999, Caselli developed serious infections in both legs: as his weight increased, and varicosities appeared, the skin thinned and broke down, producing open, purulent ulcers. Despite fevers and searing pain, it was only after persistent coaxing from his wife that he finally agreed to see his doctor. The doctor diagnosed a serious case of cellulitis, and he spent a week in the hospital receiving intravenous antibiotics.

16 At the hospital, he was given an ultrasound scan to check whether blood clots had formed in the deep veins of his legs. A radiologist came to give him the results. Caselli recounted the conversation to me. "He says, 'You don't have blood clots, and I'm really surprised. A guy like you, in the situation you're in, the odds are you're gonna have blood clots. That tells me you're a pretty healthy guy'"—but only, he went on, if Caselli did something about his weight. A little later, the infectious-disease specialist came by to inspect his wounds. "I'm going to tell you something," Caselli recalls the man saying. "I've been reading your whole file— where you were, what you were, how you were. You take that weight off—and I'm not telling you this to bust your ass—you take that weight off and you're a very healthy guy. Your heart is good. Your lungs are good. You're strong."

17 "I took that seriously," Caselli said. "You know, there are two different doctors telling me this. They don't know me other than what they're reading from their records. They had no reason to tell me this. But they knew the weight was a problem. And if I could get it down somewhere near reality . . ."

18 When he got home, he remained sick in bed for another two weeks. Meanwhile, his business collapsed. Contracts stopped coming in entirely, and he knew that when his men finished the existing jobs he would have to let them go. Months before, his internist had suggested that he consider surgery and he had dismissed the notion. But he didn't now. He went to see Dr. Randall, who spoke with him frankly about the risks involved. There was a one-in-two-hundred chance of death and a one-in-ten chance of a significant complication, such as bleeding, infection, gastric ulceration, blood clots, or leakage into the abdomen. The doctor also told him that it would change how he ate forever. Unable to work, humiliated, ill, and in pain, Vincent Caselli decided that surgery was his only hope.

19 It is hard to contemplate the human appetite without wondering if we have any say over our lives at all. We believe in will—in the notion that we have a

choice over such simple matters as whether to sit still or stand up, to talk or not talk, to have a slice of pie or not. Yet very few people, whether heavy or slim, can voluntarily reduce their weight for long. The history of weight-loss treatment is one of nearly unremitting failure. Whatever the regimen—liquid diets, high-protein diets, or grapefruit diets, the Zone, Atkins, or Dean Ornish diet—people lose weight quite readily, but they do not keep it off. A 1993 National Institutes of Health expert panel reviewed decades of diet studies and found that between ninety and ninety-five percent of people regained one-third to two-thirds of any weight lost within a year—and all of it within five years. Doctors have wired patients' jaws closed, inflated plastic balloons inside their stomachs, performed massive excisions of body fat, prescribed amphetamines and large amounts of thyroid hormone, even performed neurosurgery to destroy the hunger centers in the brain's hypothalamus—and still people do not keep the weight off. Jaw wiring, for example, can produce substantial weight loss, and patients who ask for the procedure are highly motivated; yet some still take in enough liquid calories through their closed jaws to gain weight, and the others regain it once the wires are removed. We are a species that has evolved to survive starvation, not to resist abundance.

20   Children are the surprising exception to this history of failure. Nobody would argue that children have more self-control than adults; yet in four randomized studies of obese children between the ages of six and twelve, those who received simple behavioral teaching (weekly lessons for eight to twelve weeks, followed by monthly meetings for up to a year) ended up markedly less over-weight ten years later than those who didn't; thirty percent were no longer obese. Apparently, children's appetites are malleable. Those of adults are not.

21   There are at least two ways that humans can eat more than they ought to at a sitting. One is by eating slowly but steadily for far too long. This is what people with Prader-Willi syndrome do. Afflicted with a rare inherited dysfunction of the hypothalamus, they are incapable of experiencing satiety. And though they eat only half as quickly as most people, they do not stop. Unless their access to food is strictly controlled (some will eat garbage or pet food if they find nothing else), they become mortally obese.

22   The more common pattern, however, relies on rapid intake. Human beings are subject to what scientists call a "fat paradox." When food enters your stomach and duodenum (the upper portion of the small intestine), it triggers stretch receptors, protein receptors, and fat receptors that signal the hypothalamus to induce satiety. Nothing stimulates the reaction more quickly than fat. Even a small amount, once it reaches the duodenum, will cause a person to stop eating. Still we eat too much fat. How can this be? It turns out that foods can trigger receptors in the mouth which get the hypothalamus to *accelerate* our intake—and, again, the most potent stimulant is fat. A little bit on the tongue, and the receptors push us to eat fast, before the gut signals shut us down. The tastier the food, the faster we eat—a phenomenon called "the appetizer effect." (This is accomplished, in case you were wondering, not by chewing faster but by chewing less. French researchers have discovered that, in order to eat more and eat it faster, people shorten their "chewing time"—they take fewer "chews per standard food unit" before swallowing. In other words, we gulp.)

23   Apparently, how heavy one becomes is determined, in part, by how the hypothalamus and the brain stem adjudicate the conflicting signals from the mouth and the gut. Some people feel full quite early in a meal; others, like Vincent Caselli, experience the appetizer effect for much longer. In the past several years, much has been discovered about the mechanisms of this control. We now know, for instance, that hormones, like leptin and neuropeptide Y, rise and fall with fat levels and adjust the appetite accordingly. But our knowledge of these mechanisms is still crude at best.

24   Consider a 1998 report concerning two men, "BR" and "RH," who suffered from profound amnesia. Like the protagonist in the movie *Memento,* they could carry on a coherent conversation with you, but, once they had been distracted, they recalled nothing from as recently as a minute before, not even that they were talking to you. (BR had had a bout of viral encephalitis; RH had had a severe seizure disorder for twenty years.) Paul Rozin, a professor of psychology at the University of Pennsylvania, thought of using them in an experiment that would explore the relationship between memory and eating. On three consecutive days, he and his team brought each subject his typical lunch (BR got meat loaf, barley soup, tomatoes, potatoes, beans, bread, butter, peaches, and tea; RH got veal parmigiana with pasta, string beans, juice, and apple crumb cake). Each day, BR ate all his lunch, and RH could not quite finish. Their plates were then taken away. Ten to thirty minutes later, the researchers would reappear with the same meal. "Here's lunch," they would announce. The men ate just as much as before. Another ten to thirty minutes later, the researchers again appeared with the same meal. "Here's lunch," they would say, and again the men would eat. On a couple of occasions, the researchers even offered RH a fourth lunch. Only then did he decline, saying that his "stomach was a little tight." Stomach stretch receptors weren't completely ineffectual. Yet, in the absence of a memory of having eaten, social context alone—someone walking in with lunch—was enough to re-create appetite.

25   You can imagine forces in the brain vying to make you feel hungry or full. You have mouth receptors, smell receptors, visions of tiramisu pushing one way and gut receptors another. You have leptins and neuropeptides saying you have either too much fat stored or too little. And you have your own social and personal sense of whether eating more is a good idea. If one mechanism is thrown out of whack, there's trouble.

26   Given the complexity of appetite and our imperfect understanding of it, we shouldn't be surprised that appetite-altering drugs have had only meager success in making people eat less. (The drug combination of fenfluramine and phentermine, or "fen-phen," had the most success, but it was linked to heart-valve abnormalities and was withdrawn from the market.) University researchers and pharmaceutical companies are searching intensively for a drug that will effectively treat serious obesity. So far, no such drug exists. Nonetheless, one treatment has been found to be effective, and, oddly enough, it turns out to be an operation.

27   At my hospital, there is a recovery-room nurse who is forty-eight years old and just over five feet tall, with boyish sandy hair and an almost athletic physique. Over coffee one day at the hospital café, not long after my visit with

Vincent Caselli, she revealed that she once weighed more than two hundred and fifty pounds. Carla (as I'll call her) explained that she had had gastric-bypass surgery some fifteen years ago.

28   She had been obese since she was five years old. She started going on diets and taking diet pills—laxatives, diuretics, amphetamines—in junior high school. "It was never a problem losing weight," she said. "It was a problem keeping it off." She remembers how upset she was when, on a trip with friends to Disneyland, she found that she couldn't fit through the entrance turnstile. At the age of thirty-three, she reached two hundred and sixty-five pounds. One day, accompanying her partner, a physician, to a New Orleans medical convention, she found that she was too short of breath to walk down Bourbon Street. For the first time, she said, "I became fearful for my life—not just the quality of it but the longevity of it."

29   This was 1985. Doctors were experimenting with radical obesity surgery, but there was dwindling enthusiasm for it. Two operations had held considerable promise. One, known as jejunoileal bypass—in which nearly all the small intestine was bypassed, so that only a minimum amount of food could be absorbed—was killing people. The other, stomach stapling, was proving not to be very effective over time; people tended to adapt to the tiny stomach, eating densely caloric foods more and more frequently.

30   Working in the hospital, however, Carla heard encouraging reports about the gastric-bypass operation—stomach stapling plus a rerouting of the intestine so that food bypassed only the duodenum. She knew that the data about its success was still sketchy, that other operations had failed, but in May of 1986, after a year of thinking about it, she had the surgery.

31   "For the first time in my life, I experienced fullness," she told me. Six months after the operation, she was down to a hundred and eighty-five pounds. Six months after that, she weighed a hundred and thirty pounds. She lost so much weight that she had to have surgery to remove the aprons of skin that hung from her belly and thighs down to her knees. She was unrecognizable to anyone who had known her before, and even to herself. "I went to bars to see if I could get picked up—and I did," she said. "I always said no," she quickly added, laughing. "But I did it anyway."

32   The changes weren't just physical, though. She said she felt a profound and unfamiliar sense of will power. She no longer *had* to eat anything: "Whenever I eat, somewhere in the course of that time I end up asking myself, 'Is this good for you? Are you going to put on weight if you eat too much of this?' And I can just stop." She knew, intellectually, that the surgery was why she no longer ate as much as she used to. Yet she felt as if she were choosing not to do it.

33   Studies report this to be a typical experience of a successful gastric-bypass patient. "I do get hungry, but I tend to think about it more," another woman who had had the operation told me, and she described an internal dialogue very much like Carla's: "I ask myself, 'Do I really need this?' I watch myself." For many, this feeling of control extends beyond eating. They become more confident, even assertive—sometimes to the point of conflict. Divorce rates, for example, have been found to increase significantly after the surgery. Indeed, a few months after her operation, Carla and her partner broke up.

34   Carla's dramatic weight loss has proved to be no aberration. Published case series now show that most patients undergoing gastric bypass lose at least two-thirds of their excess weight (generally more than a hundred pounds) within a year. They keep it off, too: ten-year follow-up studies find an average regain of only ten to twenty pounds. And the health benefits are striking: patients are less likely to have heart failure, asthma, or arthritis; eighty percent of those with diabetes are completely cured of it.

35   I stopped in to see Vincent Caselli one morning in January of 2000, about four months after his operation. He didn't quite spring to the door, but he wasn't winded this time. The bags under his eyes had shrunk. His face was more defined. Although his midriff was vast, it seemed smaller, less of a sack.

36   He told me that he weighed three hundred and forty-eight pounds—still far too much for a man who was only five feet seven inches tall, but ninety pounds less than he weighed on the operating table. And it had already made a difference in his life. Back in October, he told me, he missed his youngest daughter's wedding because he couldn't manage the walking required to get to the church. But by December he had lost enough weight to resume going to his East Dedham garage every morning. "Yesterday, I unloaded three tires off the truck," he said. "For me to do that three months ago? There's no way." He had climbed the stairs of his house for the first time since 1997. "One day around Christmastime, I say to myself, 'Let me try this. I gotta try this.' I went very slow, one foot at a time." The second floor was nearly unrecognizable to him. The bathroom had been renovated since he last saw it, and Teresa had, naturally, taken over the bedroom, including the closets. He would move back up eventually, he said, though it might be a while. He still had to sleep sitting up in a recliner, but he was sleeping in four-hour stretches now—"Thank God," he said. His diabetes was gone. And although he was still unable to stand up longer than twenty minutes, his leg ulcers were gone, too. He lifted his pants legs to show me. I noticed that he was wearing regular Red Wing work boots—in the past, he had to cut slits along the sides of his shoes in order to fit into them.

37   "I've got to lose at least another hundred pounds," he said. He wanted to be able to work, pick up his grandchildren, buy clothes off the rack at Filenes, go places without having to ask himself, "Are there stairs? Will I fit in the seats? Will I run out of breath?" He was still eating like a bird. The previous day, he'd had nothing all morning, a morsel of chicken with some cooked carrots and a small roast potato for lunch, and for dinner one fried shrimp, one teriyaki chicken strip, and two forkfuls of chicken-and-vegetable lo mein from a Chinese restaurant. He was starting up the business again, and, he told me, he'd gone out for a business lunch one day recently. It was at a new restaurant in Hyde Park—"beautiful"—and he couldn't help ordering a giant burger and a plate of fries. Just two bites into the burger, though, he had to stop. "One of the fellas says to me, 'Is that all you're going to eat?' And I say, 'I can't eat any more.' 'Really?' I say, 'Yeah, I can't eat any more. That's the truth.'"

38   I noticed, however, that the way he spoke about eating was not the way Carla had spoken. He did not speak of stopping because he wanted to. He spoke of stopping because he had to. You want to eat more, he explained, but "you start to get that feeling in your insides that one more bite is going to

push you over the top." Still, he often took that bite. Overcome by waves of nausea, pain, and bloating—the so-called dumping syndrome—he'd have to vomit. If there were a way to eat more, he would. This scared him, he admitted. "It's not right," he said.

39   Three months later, in April, Caselli invited me and my son to stop by his garage in East Dedham. My son was four years old and, as Vince remembered my once saying, fascinated with all things mechanical. The garage was huge, cavernous, with a two-story rollup door and metal walls painted yellow. There, in the shadows, was Vince's beloved Gradall, a handsome tank of a machine, as wide as a county road, painted yield-sign yellow, with shiny black tires that came up to my chest and his company name emblazoned in curlicue script along its flanks. On the chassis, six feet off the ground, was a glass-enclosed control cab and a thirty-foot telescoping boom, mounted on a three-hundred-and-sixty-degree swivel. Vince and a friend of his, a fellow heavy-equipment contractor I'll call Danny, were sitting on metal folding chairs in a sliver of sunlight, puffing fat Honduran cigars, silently enjoying the day. They both rose to greet us. Vince introduced me as "one of the doctors who did my stomach operation."

40   I let my son go off to explore the equipment and asked Vince how his business was going. Not well, he said. Except for a few jobs in late winter plowing snow for the city in his pickup truck, he had brought in no income since the previous August. He'd had to sell two of his three pickup trucks, his Mack dump truck, and most of the small equipment for road building. Danny came to his defense. "Well, he's been out of action," he said. "And you see we're just coming into the summer season. It's a seasonal business." But we all knew that wasn't the issue.

41   Vince told me that he weighed about three hundred and twenty pounds. This was about thirty pounds less than when I had last seen him, and he was proud of that. "He don't eat," Danny said. "He eats half of what I eat." But Vince was still unable to climb up into the Gradall and operate it. And he was beginning to wonder whether that would ever change. The rate of weight loss was slowing down, and he noticed that he was able to eat more. Before, he could eat only a couple of bites of a burger, but now he could sometimes eat half of one. And he still found himself eating more than he could handle. "Last week, Danny and this other fellow, we had to do some business," he said. "We had Chinese food. Lots of days, I don't eat the right stuff—I try to do what I can do, but I ate a little bit too much. I had to bring Danny back to Boston College, and before I left the parking lot there I just couldn't take it anymore. I had to vomit.

42   "I'm finding that I'm getting back into that pattern where I've always got to eat," he went on. His gut still stopped him, but he was worried. What if one day it didn't? He had heard about people whose staples gave way, returning their stomach to its original size, or who managed to put the weight back on in some other way.

43   I tried to reassure him. I told him what I knew Dr. Randall had already told him during a recent appointment: that a small increase in the capacity of his stomach pouch was to be expected, and that what he was experiencing seemed normal. But could something worse happen? I didn't want to say.

44   Among the gastric-bypass patients I had talked with was a man whose story remains a warning and a mystery to me. He was forty-two years old, married, and had two daughters, both of whom were single mothers with babies and still lived at home, and he had been the senior computer-systems manager for a large local company. At the age of thirty-eight, he had had to retire and go on disability because his weight—which had been above three hundred pounds since high school—had increased to more than four hundred and fifty pounds and was causing unmanageable back pain. He was soon confined to his home. He could not walk half a block. He could stand for only brief periods. He went out, on average, once a week, usually for medical appointments. In December, 1998, he had a gastric bypass. By June of the following year, he had lost a hundred pounds.

45   Then, as he put it, "I started eating again." Pizzas. Boxes of sugar cookies. Packages of doughnuts. He found it hard to say how, exactly. His stomach was still tiny and admitted only a small amount of food at a time, and he experienced the severe nausea and pain that gastric-bypass patients get whenever they eat sweet or rich things. Yet his drive was stronger than ever. "I'd eat right through pain—even to the point of throwing up," he told me. "If I threw up, it was just room for more. I would eat straight through the day." He did not pass a waking hour without eating something. "I'd just shut the bedroom door. The kids would be screaming. The babes would be crying. My wife would be at work. And I would be eating." His weight returned to four hundred and fifty pounds, and then more. The surgery had failed. And his life had been shrunk to the needs of pure appetite.

46   He is among the five to twenty percent of patients—the published reports conflict on the exact number—who regain weight despite gastric-bypass surgery. (When we spoke, he had recently submitted to another, more radical gastric bypass, in the desperate hope that something would work.) In these failures, one begins to grasp the power that one is up against. An operation that makes overeating both extremely difficult and extremely unpleasant—which, for more than eighty percent of patients, is finally sufficient to cause appetite to surrender and be transformed—can sometimes be defeated after all. Studies have yet to uncover a single consistent risk factor for this outcome. It could, apparently, happen to anyone.

47   It was a long time before I saw Vince Caselli again. Earlier this year, I called him to ask about getting together, and he suggested that we go out to see a Boston Bruins game. A few days later, he picked me up at the hospital in his rumbling Dodge Ram. For the first time, he looked almost small in the outsized truck. He was down to about two hundred and fifty pounds. "I'm still no Gregory Peck," he said, but he was now one of the crowd—chubby, in an ordinary way. The rolls beneath his chin were gone. His face had a shape. His middle no longer rested between his legs. And, almost a year and a half after the surgery, he was still losing weight. At the FleetCenter, where the Bruins play, he walked up the escalator without getting winded. Our tickets were taken at the gate—the Bruins were playing the Pittsburgh Penguins—and we walked through the turnstiles. Suddenly, he stopped and said, "Look at that. I went right through, no problem. I never would have made it through there before." It was the first time he'd gone to an event like this in years.

48   We took our seats about two dozen rows up from the ice, and he laughed a little about how easily he fit. The seats were as tight as coach class, but he was quite comfortable. (I, with my long legs, was the one who had trouble finding room.) Vince was right at home here. He had been a hockey fan his whole life, and could supply me with all the details: the Penguins' goalie Garth Snow was a local boy from Wrentham and a friend of one of Vince's cousins; Joe Thornton and Jason Allison were the Bruins' best forwards, but neither could hold a candle to the Penguins' Mario Lemieux. There were nearly twenty thousand people at the game, but within ten minutes Vince had found a friend from his barbershop sitting just a few rows away.

49   The Bruins won, and we left cheered and buzzing. Afterward, we went out to dinner at a grill near the hospital. Vince told me that his business was finally up and running. He could operate the Gradall without difficulty, and he'd had full-time Gradall work for the past three months. He was even thinking of buying a new model. At home, he had moved back upstairs. He and Teresa had taken a vacation in the Adirondacks; they were going out evenings, and visiting their grandchildren.

50   I asked him what had changed since I saw him the previous spring. He could not say precisely, but he gave me an example. "I used to love Italian cookies, and I still do," he said. A year ago, he would have eaten to the point of nausea. "But now they're, I don't know, they're too sweet. I eat one now, and after one or two bites I just don't want it." It was the same with pasta, which had always been a problem for him. "Now I can have a bite and I'm satisfied."

51   Partly, it appeared that his taste in food had changed. He pointed to the nachos and buffalo wings and hamburgers on the menu, and said that, to his surprise, he no longer felt like eating any of them. "It seems like I lean toward protein and vegetables nowadays," he said, and he ordered a chicken Caesar salad. But he also no longer felt the need to stuff himself. "I used to be real reluctant to push food away," he told me. "Now it's just—it's different." But when did this happen? And how? He shook his head. "I wish I could pinpoint it for you," he said. He paused to consider. "As a human, you adjust to conditions. You don't think you are. But you are."

52   These days, it isn't the failure of obesity surgery that is prompting concerns but its success. Physicians have gone from scorning it to encouraging, sometimes imploring, their most severely overweight patients to undergo a gastric-bypass operation. That's not a small group. More than five million adult Americans meet the strict definition of morbid obesity. (Their "body mass index"—that is, their weight in kilograms divided by the square of their height in metres—is forty or more, which for an average man is roughly a hundred pounds or more overweight.) Ten million more weigh just under the mark but may nevertheless have obesity-related health problems that are serious enough to warrant the surgery. There are ten times as many candidates for obesity surgery right now as there are for heart-bypass surgery in a year. So many patients are seeking the procedure that established surgeons cannot keep up. The American Society of Bariatric Surgery has only five hundred members nationwide who perform gastric-bypass operations, and their waiting lists are typically months long. Hence the too familiar troubles associated with new and

lucrative surgical techniques (the fee can be as much as twenty thousand dollars): newcomers are stampeding to the field, including many who have proper training but have not yet mastered the procedure, and others who have no training at all. Complicating matters further, individual surgeons are promoting a slew of variations on the standard operation which haven't been fully researched—the "duodenal switch," the "long limb" bypass, the laparoscopic bypass. And a few surgeons are pursuing new populations, such as adolescents and people who are only moderately obese.

53   Perhaps what's most unsettling about the soaring popularity of gastric-bypass surgery, however, is simply the world that surrounds it. Ours is a culture in which fatness is seen as tantamount to failure, and get-thin-quick promises—whatever the risks—can have an irresistible allure. Doctors may recommend the operation out of concern for their patients' health, but the stigma of obesity is clearly what drives many patients to the operating room. "How can you let yourself look like that?" is society's sneering, unspoken question, and often its spoken one as well. Women suffer even more than men from the social sanction, and it's no accident that seven times as many women as men have had the operation. (Women are only an eighth more likely to be obese.)

54   Indeed, deciding *not* to undergo the surgery, if you qualify, is at risk of being considered the unreasonable thing to do. A three-hundred-and-fifty-pound woman who did not want the operation told me of doctors browbeating her for her choice. And I have learned of at least one patient with heart disease being refused treatment by a doctor unless she had a gastric bypass. If you don't have the surgery, you will die, some doctors tell their patients. But we actually do not know this. Despite the striking improvements in weight and health, studies have not yet proved a corresponding reduction in mortality.

55   There are legitimate grounds for being wary of the procedure. As Paul Ernsberger, an obesity researcher at Case Western Reserve University, pointed out to me, many patients undergoing gastric bypass are in their twenties and thirties. "But is this really going to be effective and worthwhile over a forty-year span?" he asked. "No one can say." He was concerned about the possible long-term effects of nutritional deficiencies (for which patients are instructed to take a daily multivitamin). And he was concerned about evidence from rats that raises the possibility of an increased risk of bowel cancer.

56   We want progress in medicine to be clear and unequivocal, but of course it rarely is. Every new treatment has gaping unknowns—for both patients and society—and it can be hard to decide what to do about them. Perhaps a simpler, less radical operation will prove effective for obesity. Perhaps the long-sought satiety pill will be found. Nevertheless, the gastric bypass is the one thing we have now that works. Not all the questions have been answered, but there are more than a decade of studies behind it. And so we forge ahead. Hospitals everywhere are constructing obesity-surgery centers, ordering reinforced operating tables, training surgeons and staff. At the same time, everyone expects that, one day, something new and better will be discovered that will make what we're now doing obsolete.

57   Across from me, in our booth at the grill, Vince Caselli pushed his chicken Caesar salad aside only half eaten. "No taste for it," he said, and he told me

he was grateful for that. The operation, he said, had given him his life back. But, after one more round of drinks, it was clear that he still felt uneasy.

58   "I had a serious problem and I had to take serious measures," he said. "I think I had the best technology that is available at this point. But I do get concerned: Is this going to last my whole life? Someday, am I going to be right back to square one—or worse?" He fell silent for a moment, gazing into his glass. "Well, that's the cards that God gave me. I can't worry about stuff I can't control."

Review Questions

1. "The Man Who Couldn't Stop Eating" is a long article, which the author has broken into unlabeled sections. Identify these sections—and label them.

2. What made Vince Caselli a candidate for stomach bypass surgery?

3. What does the research show on the success of weight loss among adults? Among children?

4. Identify some of the ways that people can overeat.

5. What are some of the conflicting body signals regarding appetite that make the scientific understanding of obesity so complex and difficult to understand?

6. What are the positive and negative effects of the surgery?

7. Why is the stomach-bypass surgery beginning to concern physicians?

Discussion and Writing Suggestions

1. How would you describe Gawande's attitude toward gastric-bypass surgery? Toward obesity itself?

2. What evidence can you find—for instance, in the tone of his writing, in the questions that he poses, or in his choice of subject matter—that Gawande is a physician?

3. In paragraph 7, Gawande writes that on his way to Vince Caselli's house he passes several fast food restaurants. What effect does this paragraph have on you? Why do you think he includes it in the essay?

4. Discuss Gawande's use of Vincent Caselli's story as a structural backbone to this essay. Citing examples, show how Gawande builds the essay by retelling, and playing off, Vince's story. (Note that the essay is not about Vince Caselli, per se, but about obesity, obesity surgery, and the place of obesity in the larger culture.)

5. In paragraph 19, Gawande writes: "It is hard to contemplate the human appetite without wondering if we have any say over our lives at all." What does Gawande mean by this? What is your reaction to the statement?

6. Given the increasing incidence of obesity in America, how reasonable a solution do you think gastric-bypass surgery is? As a society, how much emphasis should we be placing on treating obesity, as opposed to preventing it?

SYNTHESIS ACTIVITIES

1. In the opening of "Fat and Happy?" Schwartz remarks that fat people are unhappy largely due to the pressures that the larger culture places on them to go on diets that inevitably fail. Worley makes a similar point about the futility of dieting. And medical specialists (see Gawande and also Koplan and Dietz, the authors of the editorial in the *Journal of the American Medical Association*) observe that most dieters are doomed to regain the weight they lose. Given such overwhelming agreement on the prospects for successful dieting, what then is an overweight or obese person to do? Drawing on the selections in this chapter, write an argument synthesis structured in a problem-solution format. Use your sources to define the problem: the apparent fact that diets don't work, and that we're facing a marked increase in overweight and obese people who need to lose weight. Use the remainder of your essay to formulate a sensible response to this problem.

2. For cultural reasons (see Seid, Schwartz, and Worley), women and men may feel the need to lose weight. But the scientific reality is that many should lose weight to maintain good health (see the CDC tables, Gawande, Spake, and the *JAMA*). Compare and contrast the argument that being overweight or obese is a social problem with the argument that excess weight is a medical condition. Recall that your comparison and contrast should lead to a central claim. That claim, your thesis, will help you to organize the synthesis.

3. Drawing primarily on the selections by Seid, Schwartz, Worley, and Spake, write an explanatory synthesis that presents the ways in which fat people are made to feel inadequate by the culture at large.

4. If, as several of the authors in this chapter report, diets are ineffective for the great majority of dieters, then one could conclude that dieters themselves are not to blame for their failure to lose weight. If there is no one to blame, if we can't point an accusing finger to a dieter's lack of willpower, how should we think about the problems of being overweight and obese? What evidence do you see, if any, that we as a culture are prepared to approach problems *without* laying blame? In preparing an argument synthesis that responds to this question,

reread the selections by Spake (who addresses the question of whether or not obesity ought to be regarded as a disease), Worley, Critser, Seid (especially paragraph 13), and Schwartz. Focus your reading on discussions of blame-making—of who takes or should take responsibility for the problems of being overweight or obese. What patterns emerge that you can discuss in your synthesis?

5. Hillel Schwartz writes that our culture promotes a "despotism of slenderness." First, do you agree that the ideal body type in our culture is slender? Second, do you agree that this slender ideal is despotic? Despotism requires a despot, does it not? Who—or what—in this case is the despot? Drawing on the selections by Schwartz and others in this chapter, write a synthesis that argues for or against a cultural "despotism of slenderness." In making your case, you might refer to sources outside this chapter—for instance, to the worlds of advertising, fashion, weight-loss products, and fast food.

6. Write an explanatory synthesis on the mixed messages that consumers receive concerning body weight from the medical community, the food industry, the clothing industry, and the entertainment industry. Draw on any observations you have made about the topic, based on your experiences with mass media (ads, TV, movies, billboards, radio, etc.). Also draw on the selections by Seid, Nestle, *JAMA*, Schwartz, and Worley.

7. In a synthesis that draws upon your own experiences or those of someone you know, explain the challenges of trying to maintain your weight in a culture that does not readily forgive being overweight or obese. In your synthesis, refer to the selections in this chapter that discuss the cultural pressures of being fat—including Seid, Schwartz, Critser, and Worley.

8. Compare and contrast Critser's belief that bad eating behaviors should be stigmatized with Worley's realization that she should accept being fat and forge "a new relationship" with her body. Alternatively, compare and contrast Critser's position with that of experts cited by Spake, who believe that obesity has more to do with genetic makeup than with willpower.

9. How extreme do you find the gastric-bypass surgery described by Gawande? Do you understand why morbidly obese people would elect to undergo the operation? Do you understand why "moderately obese" people would do so? Write a synthesis in which you discuss the various cultural pressures to be thin (see Seid and Schwartz) and the various remedies available to achieve this goal—including dieting, exercise, and surgery (see Spake, Koplan and Dietz, and Gawande). If you have no strongly held views on the topic, write an explanatory synthesis. If you do, write an argument synthesis. Either way, your synthesis should be governed by a carefully constructed thesis.

10. Nestle observes that there is no independent federal agency, outside the U.S. Department of Agriculture, that is responsible for forming a coordinated, national response to the epidemic of overweight and obesity. If you agree with Nestle that the USDA is hopelessly compromised in this matter (see paragraphs 4 and 5), do you advocate the creation of a new agency (and a new bureaucracy)? Do you believe the problem warrants an effort of that magnitude? (In establishing the extent of the problem in your paper, draw on the *JAMA* article and the CDC tables. Also, see the introduction to this chapter for current dollar figures relating to obesity expenditures.)

11. Using Nestle's notion of "ironic politics," analyze the mixed messages people receive concerning the incidence of obesity and overweight in this country. Recall that your success with an analysis (see Chapter 4) turns on your ability to state an analytical principle clearly (Nestle's "irony") and to use that principle to illuminate some phenomenon in the world. What are the ironies you see in our culture's confused interactions with food, weight, self-image, and health?

12. Reread Seid's "Too 'Close to the Bone'" and critique it as an example of analysis. Explain why her article is an analysis and then, step by step, *how* she goes about conducting this analysis. What is (are) the analytical principle(s) she draws on? (See paragraph 3, especially.) To what phenomena does she apply them? How do her analytical principles help to illuminate her subject? What are her conclusions—and how do you imagine a *different* analytical principle might be used to draw other conclusions? Conclude your critique with an overall assessment of Seid's article.

RESEARCH ACTIVITIES

1. Research the debate surrounding the creation of the U.S. government's "Food Pyramid." You will readily be able to locate official government publications online that describe the pyramid. Locate articles in the library and online describing the disagreements and compromises involved in designing the pyramid. You may want to consult Walter C. Willett's *Eat, Drink, and Be Healthy* (Simon and Schuster, 2001) for a critique of the pyramid on nutritional grounds. See also Marion Nestle's editorial in this chapter, discussing the U.S. Department of Agriculture's conflicts of interest in creating the pyramid.

2. According to some experts, pharmaceutical research may hold out the best hope for addressing the problems of obesity. Research the history of and present state-of-the-art regarding diet pills. When were they introduced? To date, how effective have they been? You may want to reserve special attention for the recent "fen-phen" diet

pill scare, in which a potent combination of appetite suppressants was found to cause heart-valve problems.

3. Conduct research into Body Mass Index (BMI), which you can find on page 348, and is discussed in the editorial by Koplan and Dietz. In your report, answer these basic questions: Why and when was the index developed? By whom? What did it replace? What medical assumptions underlie the index? How has it been used, and how is it being used today?

4. Hillel Schwartz's article contains extensive footnotes. Review the entries in his list and select several to track down and read, according to your interests. Based on your findings, devise a research question and conduct additional research. Write a paper in which you present your results.

5. Roberta Seid observes that the modern conception of being overweight and obese came into being at an identifiable historical moment—her point being that ideal body types have changed over time and that we live in a time in which the ideal is "close to the bone." Write a research paper that presents an explanatory overview of the changing conceptions of the ideal body type, from ancient times through the present. Take Seid's article as your starting point. As a next step, you might move outward from her footnotes. You may want to consult Peter Stearns's *Fat History* (New York University Press, 1997).

6. Identify a commercially successful dieting program. Collect the company's literature and then conduct an inquiry, over the Internet and in the library, on the effectiveness of that program. Locate, if you can, any complaints—you can try the local Better Business Bureau—and prepare a final report in which you assess the program's credibility. (You might also wish to investigate the effectiveness of a diet program as presented in a book, such as *The South Beach Diet*.)

7. Research the prevalence of obesity in other countries or cultures. You might begin with the World Health Organization's Web site <http://www.who.int/en/> and the International Association for the Study of Obesity <http://www.iaso.org>. You will need to narrow your focus, given the broadness of the topic. You might research obesity among the French, whom Greg Critser says are known for their "legendary leanness." You might investigate the Pima Indians or inhabitants of Nauru. Consider beginning your research with an article that appeared in the Boston *Globe* on 26 February 2002: "Developing Nations Taking on West's Flabby Look," by Stephen Smith. (You can access the *Globe*'s archives at http://www.globe.com.) Following an observation made by Marion Nestle, you might look at countries whose populations suffer simultaneously from malnutrition *and* obesity.

8. Research the various elective surgical techniques for managing weight, including liposuction and the gastric-bypass described by Gawande. Where were these procedures developed? By whom? What is their rate of success? The dangers associated with them? What new weight reduction surgeries are being developed?

9. Research the social and psychological effects of being overweight or obese. You might start with "Social, Educational, and Psychological Correlates of Weight Status in Adolescents" by Nicole H. Falkner et al. in *Obesity Research* (v. 9: pp. 32–42, 2001, available online at http://www.obesityresearch.org/). The references section should be very helpful in steering you to related articles.

10. Research the topic of obesity-related bias and discrimination. You might begin with "Bias, Discrimination, and Obesity" by Rebecca Puhl and Kelly Brownell in *Obesity Research* (v. 9, pp. 788–805, 2001, available online at http://www.obesityresearch.org/). The references section should be helpful in steering you to related articles.

New and Improved: Six Decades of Advertising

9

Possibly the most memorable ad campaign of the twentieth century (dating from the late 1920s) takes the form of a comic strip. A bully kicks sand into the face of a skinny man relaxing on the beach with his girlfriend. Humiliated, the skinny man vows to get even. "Don't bother, little boy!" huffs the scornful girlfriend, who promptly dumps him. At home, the skinny man kicks a chair in frustration, declares that he's sick of being a scarecrow, and says that if Charles Atlas (once a "97-lb. weakling" himself) can give him a "real body," he'll send for his FREE book. In the next frame, the once-skinny man, now transformed into a hunk, thanks to Atlas's "Dynamic Tension" fitness program, admires himself in front of the mirror: "Boy, it didn't take Atlas long to do this for me. Look, how those muscles bulge! . . . That big stiff won't dare insult me now!" Back on the beach, the bully is decked by the once-skinny man, as his adoring girlfriend looks on: "Oh Mac! You are a real man after all!"

Crude? Undoubtedly. But variations of this ad, which made Atlas a multimillionaire, ran for decades (his company is still in business). Like other successful ads, it draws its power from skillful appeals to almost primitive urges—in this particular case, the urge to gain dominance over a rival for the attention of the opposite sex. Of course, effective ads don't always work on such a primal level. Another famous ad of the 1920s appeals to our need to gain respect from others for higher accomplishments than punching out opponents. Headlined "They Laughed When I Sat Down at the Piano—But When I Started to Play. . . !" the text offers a first-person account of a man who sits down to play the piano at a party. As he does so, the guests make good-natured fun of him; but once he began to play, "a tense silence fell on the guests. The laughter died on their lips as if by magic. I played through the first bars of Liszt's immortal 'Liebenstraum.' I heard gasps of amazement. My friends sat breathless—spellbound." For sixteen additional paragraphs, the writer goes on to detail the effect of his playing upon the guests and to explain how "You, too, can now *teach yourself* to be an accomplished musician—right at home," by purchasing the program of the U.S. School of Music. Again, the reader is encouraged to send for the free booklet. And by the way, "Forget the old-fashioned idea that you need 'special talent'" to play an instrument.

The ubiquity of advertising is a fact of modern life. In fact, advertising can be traced as far back as ancient Roman times when pictures were inscribed on walls to

409

promote gladiatorial contests. In those days, however, the illiteracy of most of the population and the fact that goods were made by hand and could not be mass produced limited the need for more widespread advertising. One of the first American advertisers was Benjamin Franklin, who pioneered the use of large headlines and made strategic use of white space. But advertising as the mass phenomenon we know is a product of the twentieth century, when the United States became an industrial nation—and particularly of the post–World War II period, when a prosperous economy created our modern consumer society, marked by the middle-class acquisition of goods, the symbols of status, success, style, and social acceptance. Today, we are surrounded not only by a familiar array of billboards, print ads, and broadcast ads, but also by the Internet, which has given us "spam," the generic name for an entire category of digital pitches for debt reduction, low mortgage rates, and enhanced body parts—compared to which the average Buick ad in a glossy magazine reads like great literature.

Advertisements are more than just appeals to buy; they are windows into our psyches and our culture. They reveal our values, our (not-so-hidden) desires, our yearnings for a different lifestyle. For example, the Marlboro man, that quintessence of taciturn cowboy masculinity, at home only in the wide open spaces of Marlboro Country, is a mid-twentieth-century American tribute to (what is perceived as) nineteenth-century American values, popularized in hundreds of westerns. According to James Twitchell, a professor of English and advertising at the University of Florida, "He is what we have for royalty, distilled manhood. . . . The Marlboro Man needs to tell you nothing. He carries no scepter, no gun. He never even speaks. Doesn't need to." He is also the product of a bolt of advertising inspiration: previously, Marlboro had been marketed—unsuccessfully—as a woman's cigarette. Another example of how ads reveal culture is the memorable campaign for the Volkswagen Beetle in the 1960s. That campaign spoke to the counterculture mentality of the day: instead of appealing to the traditional automobile customer's desire for luxury, beauty, size, power, and comfort, Volkswagen emphasized how small, funny-looking, bare bones—but economical and sensible—their cars were. On the other hand, snob appeal—at an affordable price, of course—has generally been a winning strategy. In the 1980s and 1990s Grey Poupon mustard ran a successful campaign of TV commercials featuring one Rolls-Royce pulling up alongside another. A voice from one vehicle asks, "Pardon me; do you have any Grey Poupon?" "But of course!" replies a voice in the other car; and a hand with a jar of mustard reaches out from the window of the second car to pass to the unseen occupant of the first car. This campaign is a perfect illustration of what University of California at Davis history professor Roland Marchand calls the appeal of the democracy of goods: "the wonders of modern mass production and distribution enable . . . everyone to enjoy society's most desirable pleasures, conveniences, or benefits."

So pervasive and influential has advertising become that it has created a significant backlash among social critics. Among the most familiar charges against advertising: it fosters materialism, it psychologically manipulates people to buy things they don't need, it perpetuates gender and racial stereotypes (particularly in its illustrations), it is deceptive, it is offensive, it debases the language, and it is omnipresent—we cannot escape it. Although arguing the truth or falsity of these assertions (more fully covered in the selection by Bovée and Arens, pages 440–45) makes for lively debate, our focus in this chapter is not on the ethics of advertising, but rather on how it works. What makes for successful advertising? How do advertisers—and by advertisers we mean not only manufacturers but also the agencies they hire to produce their advertisements—pull our psychological levers to influence us to buy (or think favorably of) their products? What are the textual and graphic components of an effective advertisement—of an effective advertising campaign? How—if at all—has advertising evolved over the past several decades?

Advertising has seen significant changes in the six decades since the end of World War II. It is unlikely that the comic-strip Charles Atlas ad or the verbose "They Laughed When I Sat Down at the Piano" ad would succeed today. Both seem extremely dated. More representative of today's advertising style is the successful milk campaign; each ad features a celebrity such as Bernie Mac or Lauren Bacall with a milk mustache, a headline that says simply "got milk?", and a few short words of text supposedly spoken by the pictured celebrity. But the changes in advertising during the six decades covered in this chapter are more of style than of substance. On the whole, the similarities between an ad produced in the 1950s and one produced today are more significant than the differences. Of course, hair and clothing styles change with the times, message length recedes, and both text and graphics assume a lesser degree of apple-pie social consensus on values. But on the whole, the same psychological appeals, the same principles of headline and graphic design that worked sixty years ago, continue to work today. We choose one automobile over another, for instance, less because our vehicle of choice gets us from point A to point B, than because we invest it—or the advertiser does—with rich psychological and cultural values. In 1957 the French anthropologist and philosopher Roland Barthes wrote (in a review of a French automobile, the Citroën DS), "I think that cars today are almost the exact equivalent of the great Gothic cathedrals: I mean the supreme creation of an era, conceived with passion by unknown artists, and consumed in image if not in usage by a whole population which appropriates them as a purely magical object." It's not known whether Barthes ever considered a career as an advertising copywriter; but he probably would have been a good one.

How advertising works, then, is the subject of the present chapter. By applying a variety of theoretical and practical perspectives to a gallery of six decades of advertisements (and to other ads of your own choosing), you'll be able to practice your analytical skills upon one of the more fascinating areas of American mass culture. The main subjects of your analyses are represented later in this chapter by a portfolio of forty-two advertisements that originally appeared in such magazines as *Time, Newsweek, U.S. News and World Report*, and *Sunset*. For ease of comparison and contrast, most of the ads can be classified into a relatively few categories: cigarettes, alcohol, automobiles, and food, with a number of other ads in the "miscellaneous" category. These ads have been selected for their inherent interest, as well as for the variety of tools that have been employed to communicate the message, what some advertisers call the USP—the Unique Selling Proposition.

The first part of the chapter, however, consists of a number of articles or passages from books, each representing an analytical tool, a particular perspective from which one can view individual advertisements. In the first selection, "Advertising's Fifteen Basic Appeals," Jib Fowles offers a psychological perspective. Fowles identifies and discusses the most common needs to which advertisers attempt to appeal. Among these are the need for sex, the need for affiliation with other people, the need for dominance, and the need for autonomy. In "Making the Pitch in Print Advertising," Courtland L. Bovée et al. outline the key elements of the textual component of advertising—including headlines, subheadings, and body text. In "Elements of Effective Layout," Dorothy Cohen discusses the key components of advertising graphics: balance, proportion, movement, unity, clarity and simplicity, and emphasis. In "The Indictments Against Advertising" Courtland L. Bovée and William F. Arens consider and respond to some of the most frequent charges leveled against Madison Avenue.

Finally, as indicated above, the chapter continues and concludes with "A Portfolio of Advertisements: 1945–2003," a collection of forty-two ads for various products published in popular magazines in the United States and Great Britain during the last sixty years.

Charles O'Neill, an independent marketing consultant, has written, "Perhaps, by learning how advertising works, we can become better equipped to sort out content from hype, product values from emotions, and salesmanship from propaganda." We hope that the selections in this chapter will allow you to do just that, as well as to develop a greater understanding of one of the most pervasive components of American mass culture.

Advertising's Fifteen Basic Appeals
Jib Fowles

Our first selection provides what you will likely find the single most useful analytical tool for studying advertisements. Drawing upon studies of numerous ads and upon interviews with subjects conducted by Harvard psychologist Henry A. Murray, Fowles developed a set of fifteen basic appeals he believes to be at the heart of American advertising. These appeals, according to Fowles and to Murray, are directed primarily to the "lower brain," to those "unfulfilled urges and motives swirling in the bottom half of [our] minds," rather than to the part of the brain that processes our more rational thoughts and impulses. As you read Fowles's article and his descriptions of the individual appeals, other examples from contemporary print and broadcast ads may occur to you. You may find it useful to jot down these examples for later incorporation into your responses to the discussion and synthesis questions that follow.

Jib Fowles has written numerous articles and books on the popular media, including Mass Advertising as Social Forecast: A Method for Futures Research *(1976),* Why Viewers Watch: A Reappraisal of Television's Effects *(1992),* Advertising and Popular Culture *(1996), and* The Case for Television Violence *(1999). This selection first appeared in* Etc. 39.3 *(1982) and was reprinted in* Advertising and Popular Culture.

Emotional Appeals

1   The nature of effective advertisements was recognized full well by the late media philosopher Marshall McLuhan. In his *Understanding Media,* the first sentence of the section on advertising reads, "The continuous pressure is to create ads more and more in the image of audience motives and desires."

2   By giving form to people's deep-lying desires, and picturing states of being that individuals privately yearn for, advertisers have the best chance of arresting attention and affecting communication. And that is the immediate goal of advertising: to tug at our psychological shirtsleeves and slow us down long enough for a word or two about whatever is being sold. We glance at a picture of a solitary rancher at work, and "Marlboro" slips into our minds.

3   Advertisers (I'm using the term as a shorthand for both the products' manufacturers, who bring the ambition and money to the process, and the advertising agencies, who supply the know-how) are ever more compelled to invoke consumers' drives and longings; this is the "continuous pressure" McLuhan refers to. Over the past century, the American marketplace has grown increasingly congested as more and more products have entered into the frenzied competition after the public's dollars. The economies of other nations are quieter than ours since the volume of goods being hawked does not so greatly exceed demand. In some economies, consumer wares are scarce enough that no advertising at all is necessary. But in the United States, we go to the other extreme. In order to stay in business, an advertiser must strive to cut through the considerable commercial hub-bub by any means available—including the emotional appeals that some observers have held to be abhorrent and underhanded.

4   The use of subconscious appeals is a comment not only on conditions among sellers. As time has gone by, buyers have become stoutly resistant to advertisements. We live in a blizzard of these messages and have learned to turn up our collars and ward off most of them. A study done a few years ago at Harvard University's Graduate School of Business Administration ventured that the average American is exposed to some 500 ads daily from television, newspapers, magazines, radio, billboards, direct mail, and so on. If for no other reason than to preserve one's sanity, a filter must be developed in every mind to lower the number of ads a person is actually aware of—a number this particular study estimated at about seventy-five ads per day. (Of these, only twelve typically produced a reaction—nine positive and three negative, on the average.) To be among the few messages that do manage to gain access to minds, advertisers must be strategic, perhaps even a little underhanded at times.

5   There are assumptions about personality underlying advertisers' efforts to communicate via emotional appeals, and while these assumptions have stood the test of time, they still deserve to be aired. Human beings, it is presumed,

walk around with a variety of unfulfilled urges and motives swirling in the bottom half of their minds. Lusts, ambitions, tendernesses, vulnerabilities—they are constantly bubbling up, seeking resolution. These mental forces energize people, but they are too crude and irregular to be given excessive play in the real world. They must be capped with the competent, sensible behavior that permits individuals to get along well in society. However, this upper layer of mental activity, shot through with caution and rationality, is not receptive to advertising's pitches. Advertisers want to circumvent this shell of consciousness if they can, and latch on to one of the lurching, subconscious drives.

6   In effect, advertisers over the years have blindly felt their way around the underside of the American psyche, and by trial and error have discovered the softest points of entree, the places where their messages have the greatest likelihood of getting by consumers' defenses. As McLuhan says elsewhere, "Gouging away at the surface of public sales resistance, the ad men are constantly breaking through into the *Alice in Wonderland* territory behind the looking glass, which is the world of subrational impulses and appetites."

7   An advertisement communicates by making use of a specially selected image (of a supine female, say, or a curly-haired child, or a celebrity) which is designed to stimulate "subrational impulses and desires" even when they are at ebb, even if they are unacknowledged by their possessor. Some few ads have their emotional appeal in the text, but for the greater number by far the appeal is contained in the artwork. This makes sense, since visual communication better suits more primal levels of the brain. If the viewer of an advertisement actually has the importuned motive, and if the appeal is sufficiently well fashioned to call it up, then the person can be hooked. The product in the ad may then appear to take on the semblance of gratification for the summoned motive. Many ads seem to be saying, "If you have this need, then this product will help satisfy it." It is a primitive equation, but not an ineffective one for selling.

8   Thus, most advertisements appearing in national media can be understood as having two orders of content. The first is the appeal to deep-running drives in the minds of consumers. The second is information regarding the good[s] or service being sold: its name, its manufacturer, its picture, its packaging, its objective attributes, its functions. For example, the reader of a brassiere advertisement sees a partially undraped but blandly unperturbed woman standing in an otherwise commonplace public setting, and may experience certain sensations; the reader also sees the name "Maidenform," a particular brassiere style, and, in tiny print, words about the material, colors, price. Or, the viewer of a television commercial sees a demonstration with four small boxes labeled 650, 650, 650, and 800; something in the viewer's mind catches hold of this, as trivial as thoughtful consideration might reveal it to be. The viewer is also exposed to the name "Anacin," its bottle, and its purpose.

9   Sometimes there is an apparently logical link between an ad's emotional appeal and its product information. It does not violate common sense that Cadillac automobiles be photographed at country clubs, or that Japan Air Lines be associated with Orientalia. But there is no real need for the linkage to have a bit of reason behind it. Is there anything inherent to the connection between Salem cigarettes and mountains, Coke and a smile, Miller Beer and com-

radeship? The link being forged in minds between product and appeal is a pre-logical one.

10   People involved in the advertising industry do not necessarily talk in the terms being used here. They are stationed at the sending end of this communications channel, and may think they are up to any number of things—Unique Selling Propositions, explosive copywriting, the optimal use of demographics or psychographics, ideal media buys, high recall ratings, or whatever. But when attention shifts to the receiving end of the channel, and focuses on the instant of reception, then commentary becomes much more elemental: an advertising message contains something primary and primitive, an emotional appeal, that in effect is the thin end of the wedge, trying to find its way into a mind. Should this occur, the product information comes along behind.

11   When enough advertisements are examined in this light, it becomes clear that the emotional appeals fall into several distinguishable categories, and that every ad is a variation on one of a limited number of basic appeals. While there may be several ways of classifying these appeals, one particular list of fifteen has proven to be especially valuable.

     Advertisements can appeal to:

1. The need for sex
2. The need for affiliation
3. The need to nurture
4. The need for guidance
5. The need to aggress
6. The need to achieve
7. The need to dominate
8. The need for prominence
9. The need for attention
10. The need for autonomy
11. The need to escape
12. The need to feel safe
13. The need for aesthetic sensations
14. The need to satisfy curiosity
15. Physiological needs: food, drink, sleep, etc

Murray's List

12 Where does this list of advertising's fifteen basic appeals come from? Several years ago, I was involved in a research project which was to have as one segment an objective analysis of the changing appeals made in post-World War II American advertising. A sample of magazine ads would have their appeals coded into the categories of psychological needs they seemed aimed at. For this content analysis to happen, a complete roster of human motives would have to be found.

13   The first thing that came to mind was Abraham Maslow's famous four-part hierarchy of needs. But the briefest look at the range of appeals made in advertising was enough to reveal that they are more varied, and more profane, than Maslow had cared to account for. The search led on to the work of psychologist Henry A. Murray, who together with his colleagues at the Harvard Psychological

Clinic has constructed a full taxonomy of needs. As described in *Explorations in Personality,* Murray's team had conducted a lengthy series of in-depth interviews with a number of subjects in order to derive from scratch what they felt to be the essential variables of personality. Forty-four variables were distinguished by the Harvard group, of which twenty were motives. The need for achievement ("to overcome obstacles and obtain a high standard") was one, for instance; the need to defer was another; the need to aggress was a third; and so forth.

14   Murray's list had served as the groundwork for a number of subsequent projects. Perhaps the best-known of these was David C. McClelland's extensive study of the need for achievement, reported in his *The Achieving Society.* In the process of demonstrating that a people's high need for achievement is predictive of later economic growth, McClelland coded achievement imagery and references out of a nation's folklore, songs, legends, and children's tales.

15   Following McClelland, I too wanted to cull the motivational appeals from a culture's imaginative product—in this case, advertising. To develop categories expressly for this purpose, I took Murray's twenty motives and added to them others he had mentioned in passing in *Explorations in Personality* but not included on the final list. The extended list was tried out on a sample of advertisements, and motives which never seemed to be invoked were dropped. I ended up with eighteen of Murrays' motives, into which 770 print ads were coded. The resulting distribution is included in the 1976 book *Mass Advertising as Social Forecast.*

16   Since that time, the list of appeals has undergone refinements as a result of using it to analyze television commercials. A few more adjustments stemmed from the efforts of students in my advertising classes to decode appeals; tens of term papers surveying thousands of advertisements have caused some inconsistencies in the list to be hammered out. Fundamentally, though, the list remains the creation of Henry Murray. In developing a comprehensive, parsimonious inventory of human motives, he pinpointed the subsurface mental forces that are the least quiescent and most susceptible to advertising's entreaties.

Fifteen Appeals

17   **1. Need for Sex.**   Let's start with sex, because this is the appeal which seems to pop up first whenever the topic of advertising is raised. Whole books have been written about this one alone, to find a large audience of mildly titillated readers. Lately, due to campaigns to sell blue jeans, concern with sex in ads has redoubled.

18   The fascinating thing is not how much sex there is in advertising, but how little. Contrary to impressions, unambiguous sex is rare in these messages. Some of this surprising observation may be a matter of definition: the Jordache ads with the lithe, blouse-less female astride a similarly clad male is clearly an appeal to the audience's sexual drives, but the same cannot be said about Brooke Shields* in the Calvin Klein commercials. Directed at young women and

---

* *Brooke Shields* (b. 1965) is a model (at age 3 she was the Ivory Snow baby), as well as a stage (*Grease*), TV, and film actress; her most well known films are *Pretty Baby* (1978) and *Blue Lagoon* (1980).

their credit-card carrying mothers, the image of Miss Shields instead invokes the need to be looked at. Buy Calvins and you'll be the center of much attention, just as Brooke is, the ads imply; they do not primarily inveigle their target audience's need for sexual intercourse.

19   In the content analysis reported in *Mass Advertising as Social Forecast* only two percent of ads were found to pander to this motive. Even *Playboy* ads shy away from sexual appeals: a recent issue contained eighty-three full-page ads, and just four of them (or less than five percent) could be said to have sex on their minds.

20   The reason this appeal is so little used is that it is too blaring and tends to obliterate the product information. Nudity in advertising has the effect of reducing brand recall. The people who do remember the product may do so because they have been made indignant by the ad; this is not the response most advertisers seek.

21   To the extent that sexual imagery is used, it conventionally works better on men than women; typically a female figure is offered up to the male reader. A Black Velvet liquor advertisement displays an attractive woman wearing a tight black outfit, recumbent under the legend, "Feel the Velvet." The figure does not have to be horizontal, however, for the appeal to be present as National Airlines revealed in its "Fly me" campaign. Indeed, there does not even have to be a female in the ad; "Flick my Bic"* was sufficient to convey the idea to many.

22   As a rule, though, advertisers have found sex to be a tricky appeal, to be used sparingly. Less controversial and equally fetching are the appeals to our need for affectionate human contact.

23   **2. Need for Affiliation.**   American mythology upholds autonomous individuals, and social statistics suggest that people are ever more going it alone in their lives, yet the high frequency of affiliative appeals in ads belies this. Or maybe it does not: maybe all the images of companionship are compensation for what Americans privately lack. In any case, the need to associate with others is widely invoked in advertising and is probably the most prevalent appeal. All sorts of goods and services are sold by linking them to our unfulfilled desires to be in good company.

24   According to Henry Murray, the need for affiliation consists of desires "to draw near and enjoyably cooperate or reciprocate with another; to please and win affection of another; to adhere and remain loyal to a friend." The manifestations of this motive can be segmented into several different types of affiliation, beginning with romance.

25   Courtship may be swifter nowadays, but the desire for pair-bonding is far from satiated. Ads reaching for this need commonly depict a youngish male and female engrossed in each other. The head of the male is usually higher than the female's, even at this late date; she may be sitting or leaning while he is standing. They are not touching in the Smirnoff vodka ads, but obviously there is an intimacy, sometimes frolicsome, between them. The couple does touch

---

* *"Flick my Bic"* became a famous and successful slogan in advertisements for Bic cigarette lighters during the late 1970s and 1980s. Fowles hints at the not-too-subtle sexual implications of the line.

for Martell Cognac when "The moment was Martell." For Wind Song perfume they have touched, and "Your Wind Song stays on his mind."

26   Depending on the audience, the pair does not absolutely have to be young—just together. He gives her a DeBeers diamond, and there is a tear in her laugh lines. She takes Geritol* and preserves herself for him. And numbers of consumers, wanting affection too, follow suit.

27   Warm family feelings are fanned in ads when another generation is added to the pair. Hallmark Cards brings grandparents into the picture, and Johnson and Johnson Baby Powder has Dad, Mom, and baby, all fresh from the bath, encircled in arms and emblazoned with "Share the Feeling." A talc has been fused to familial love.

28   Friendship is yet another form of affiliation pursued by advertisers. Two women confide and drink Maxwell House coffee together; two men walk through the woods smoking Salem cigarettes. Miller Beer promises that afternoon "Miller Time" will be staffed with three or four good buddies. Drink Dr. Pepper, as Mickey Rooney is coaxed to do, and join in with all the other Peppers. Coca-Cola does not even need to portray the friendliness; it has reduced this appeal to "a Coke and a smile."

29   The warmth can be toned down and disguised, but it is the same affiliative need that is being fished for. The blonde has a direct gaze and her friends are firm businessmen in appearance, but with a glass of Old Bushmill you can sit down and fit right in. Or, for something more upbeat, sing along with the Pontiac choirboys.

30   As well as presenting positive images, advertisers can play to the need for affiliation in negative ways, by invoking the fear of rejection. If we don't use Scope, we'll have the "Ugh! Morning Breath" that causes the male and female models to avert their faces. Unless we apply Ultra Brite or Close-Up to our teeth, it's good-bye romance. Our family will be cursed with "House-a-tosis" if we don't take care. Without Dr. Scholl's antiperspirant foot spray, the bowling team will keel over. There go all the guests when the supply of Dorito's nacho cheese chips is exhausted. Still more rejection if our shirts have ring-around-the-collar, if our car needs to be Midasized. But make a few purchases, and we are back in the bosom of human contact.

31   As self-directed as Americans pretend to be, in the last analysis we remain social animals, hungering for the positive, endorsing feelings that only those around us can supply. Advertisers respond, urging us to "Reach out and touch someone," in the hopes our monthly [phone] bills will rise.

32   **3. Need to Nurture.**   Akin to affiliative needs is the need to take care of small, defenseless creatures—children and pets, largely. Reciprocity is of less consequence here, though; it is the giving that counts. Murray uses synonyms like "to feed, help, support, console, protect, comfort, nurse, heal." A strong need

---

* The original *Geritol* (a combination of the words "geriatric" and "tolerance") was an iron tonic and vitamin supplement marketed to people over forty between 1950 and 1979 with the slogan, "Do you have iron poor, tired blood?" Though today Geritol is the label on a group of health-related products, the name became famous—and, to some extent, funny—as a means of restoring energy and youthful vigor to middle-aged and elderly people.

it is, woven deep into our genetic fabric, for if it did not exist we could not successfully raise up our replacements. When advertisers put forth the image of something diminutive and furry, something that elicits the word "cute" or "precious," then they are trying to trigger this motive. We listen to the childish voice singing the Oscar Mayer weiner song, and our next hot-dog purchase is prescribed. Aren't those darling kittens something, and how did this Meow Mix get into our shopping cart?

33   This pitch is often directed at women, as Mother Nature's chief nurturers. "Make me some Kraft macaroni and cheese, please," says the elfin preschooler just in from the snowstorm, and mothers' hearts go out, and Kraft's sales go up. "We're cold, wet, and hungry," whine the husband and kids, and the little woman gets the Manwiches ready. A facsimile of this need can be hit without children or pets: the husband is ill and sleepless in the television commercial, and the wife grudgingly fetches the NyQuil.

34   But it is not women alone who can be touched by this appeal. The father nurses his son Eddie through adolescence while the John Deere lawn tractor survives the years. Another father counts pennies with his young son as the subject of New York Life Insurance comes up. And all over America are businessmen who don't know why they dial Qantas Airlines* when they have to take a trans-Pacific trip; the koala bear knows.

35   **4. Need for Guidance.**   The opposite of the need to nurture is the need to be nurtured: to be protected, shielded, guided. We may be loath to admit it, but the child lingers on inside every adult—and a good thing it does, or we would not be instructable in our advancing years. Who wants a nation of nothing but flinty personalities?

36   Parent-like figures can successfully call up this need. Robert Young† recommends Sanka coffee, and since we have experienced him for twenty-five years as television father and doctor, we take his word for it. Florence Henderson‡ as the expert mom knows a lot about the advantages of Wesson oil.

37   The parent-ness of the spokesperson need not be so salient; sometimes pure authoritativeness is better. When Orson Welles§ scowls and intones, "Paul Masson will sell no wine before its time," we may not know exactly what

---

* *Qantas Airlines* is an Australian airline whose ads during the 1980s and 1990s featured a cuddly koala bear standing in for both the airline and the exotic delights of Australia.

† *Robert Young* (1907–1988) acted in movies (including Alfred Hitchcock's *Secret Agent* (1936) and *Crossfire* (1947) and TV (starring in the long-running 1950s series *Father Knows Best* and the 1960s series *Marcus Welby, M.D.*). A classic father figure, in his later career he appeared in ads for Sanka coffee.

‡ *Florence Henderson* (b. 1934), acted on Broadway and TV (primarily, in musical and comedy roles). Her most famous TV show was *The Brady Bunch* (1968–1974), where she played a mother of three daughters who married a man with three sons.

§ *Orson Welles* (1915–1985) was a major American filmmaker and actor whose films include *Citizen Kane* (1941—generally considered the greatest American film of all time), *The Magnificent Ambersons* (1942), *The Lady from Shanghai* (1947), *Macbeth* (1948), and *Touch of Evil* (1958). Toward the end of his life—to the dismay of many who revered him—the magisterial but financially depleted Welles became a spokesman for Paul Masson wines.

he means, but we still take direction from him. There is little maternal about Brenda Vaccaro* when she speaks up for Tampax, but there is a certainty to her that many accept.

38   A celebrity is not a necessity in making a pitch to the need for guidance, since a fantasy figure can serve just as well. People accede to the Green Giant, or Betty Crocker, or Mr. Goodwrench.† Some advertisers can get by with no figure at all: "When E. F. Hutton‡ talks, people listen."

39   Often it is tradition or custom that advertisers point to and consumers take guidance from. Bits and pieces of American history are used to sell whiskeys like Old Crow, Southern Comfort, Jack Daniel's. We conform to traditional male/female roles and age-old social norms when we purchase Barclay cigarettes, which informs us "The pleasure is back."

40   The product itself, if it has been around for a long time, can constitute a tradition. All those old labels in the ad for Morton salt convince us that we should continue to buy it. Kool-Aid says "You loved it as a kid. You trust it as a mother," hoping to get yet more consumers to go along.

41   Even when the product has no history at all, our need to conform to tradition and to be guided are strong enough that they can be invoked through bogus nostalgia and older actors. Country-Time lemonade sells because consumers want to believe it has a past they can defer to.

42   So far the needs and the ways they can be invoked which have been looked at are largely warm and affiliative; they stand in contrast to the next set of needs, which are much more egoistic and assertive.

43   **5. Need to Aggress.**   The pressures of the real world create strong retaliatory feelings in every functioning human being. Since these impulses can come forth as bursts of anger and violence, their display is normally tabooed. Existing as harbored energy, aggressive drives present a large, tempting target for advertisers. It is not a target to be aimed at thoughtlessly, though, for few manufacturers want their products associated with destructive motives. There is always the danger that, as in the case of sex, if the appeal is too blatant, public opinion will turn against what is being sold.

44   Jack-in-the-Box sought to abruptly alter its marketing by going after older customers and forgetting the younger ones. Their television commercials had a seventy-ish lady command, "Waste him," and the Jack-in-the-Box clown exploded before our eyes. So did public reaction until the commercials were toned down. Print ads for Club cocktails carried the faces of octogenarians under the head-

---

* Brenda Vaccaro (b. 1939) is a stage, TV, and film actress; her films include *Midnight Cowboy* (1969), *Airport '77* (1977), *Supergirl* (1984), and *The Mirror Has Two Faces* (1996).

† *Mr. Goodwrench* (and the slogan "Looking for Mr. Goodwrench"), personified as an engaging and highly capable auto mechanic, is a product of the General Motors marketing department.

‡ *E. F. Hutton* (named after its founder Edward Francis Hutton) was a major brokerage firm that was brought down in the 1980s by corporate misconduct. Its most famous TV ad portrayed, typically, two well-dressed businesspeople in conversation in a crowded dining room or club room. The first man says to the other, "My broker says. . . . " The second man listens politely and responds, "Well, my broker is E. F. Hutton, and *he* says . . . ," and everyone else in the room strains to overhear the conversation. The tag line: "When E. F. Hutton talks, people listen."

line, "Hit me with a Club"; response was contrary enough to bring the campaign to a stop.

45   Better disguised aggressive appeals are less likely to backfire: Triumph cigarettes has models making a lewd gesture with their uplifted cigarettes, but the individuals are often laughing and usually in close company of others. When Exxon said, "There's a Tiger in your tank," the implausibility of it concealed the invocation of aggressive feelings.

46   Depicted arguments are a common way for advertisers to tap the audience's needs to aggress. Don Rickles* and Lynda Carter† trade gibes, and consumers take sides as the name of Seven-Up is stitched on minds. The Parkay [margarine] tub has a difference of opinion with the user; who can forget it, or who (or what) got the last word in?

47   **6. Need to Achieve.**   This is the drive that energizes people, causing them to strive in their lives and careers. According to Murray, the need for achievement is signalled by the desires "to accomplish something difficult. To overcome obstacles and attain a high standard. To excel one's self. To rival and surpass others." A prominent American trait, it is one that advertisers like to hook on to because it identifies their product with winning and success.

48   The Cutty Sark ad does not disclose that Ted Turner failed at his latest attempt at yachting's America Cup; here he is represented as a champion on the water as well as off in his television enterprises. If we drink this whiskey, we will be victorious alongside Turner. We can also succeed with O. J. Simpson‡ by renting Hertz cars, or with Reggie Jackson§ by bringing home some Panasonic equipment. Cathy Rigby‖ and Stayfree maxipads will put people out front.

49   Sports heroes are the most convenient means to snare consumers' needs to achieve, but they are not the only one. Role models can be established, ones which invite emulation, as with the profiles put forth by Dewar's scotch.

---

* *Don Rickles* (b. 1926) is a night-club comedian (who has also appeared in TV and films) famous for his caustic wit and for humorously insulting people in the audience.

† *Lynda Carter* (b. 1951) is an actress, whose most famous role was the heroine of the 1976 TV series *Wonder Woman*.

‡ *O. J. Simpson* (b. 1957) is a famous football player–turned film actor (*The Naked Gun*) and defendant in a notorious murder trial in the 1990s. In a highly controversial decision, Simpson was acquitted of killing his ex-wife Nicole Simpson and her friend Ron Goldman; but in a subsequent civil trial he was found liable for the two deaths. Before the trial, Simpson was well known for his TV commercials for Hertz rental cars, featuring him sprinting through airports to get to the gate to demonstrate what you *wouldn't* have to do if you rented a car through Hertz.

§ *Reggie Jackson* (b. 1946), a member of the Baseball Hall of fame, played as an outfielder between 1967 and 1987. Known as "Mr. October" for his dramatic game-winning at-bats during post-season play, he had more strikeouts (2,597) than any other player. He was the first baseball player to have a candy bar (the "Reggie Bar") named after him, and toward the end of his career was a pitchman for Panasonic televisions.

‖ *Cathy Rigby*, an Olympian, was the first American gymnast to win a medal (in 1970) at the World Championships. She went on to star in a Broadway revival of the musical *Peter Pan* (surpassing Mary Martin for the greatest number of performances). Subsequently, she became a sportscaster for ABC Sports.

Successful, tweedy individuals relate they have "graduated to the flavor of Myer's rum." Or the advertiser can establish a prize: two neighbors play one-on-one basketball for a Michelob beer in a television commercial, while in a print ad a bottle of Johnnie Walker Black Label has been gilded like a trophy.

50   Any product that advertises itself in superlatives—the best, the first, the finest—is trying to make contact with our needs to succeed. For many consumers, sales and bargains belong in this category of appeals, too; the person who manages to buy something at fifty percent off is seizing an opportunity and coming out ahead of others.

51   **7. Need to Dominate.**   This fundamental need is the craving to be powerful—perhaps omnipotent, as in the Xerox ad where Brother Dominic exhibits heavenly powers and creates miraculous copies. Most of us will settle for being just a regular potentate, though. We drink Budweiser because it is the King of Beers, and here comes the powerful Clydesdales to prove it. A taste of Wolfschmidt vodka and "The spirit of the Czar lives on."

52   The need to dominate and control one's environment is often thought of as being masculine, but as close students of human nature advertisers know, it is not so circumscribed. Women's aspirations for control are suggested in the campaign theme, "I like my men in English Leather, or nothing at all." The females in the Chanel No. 19 ads are "outspoken" and wrestle their men around.

53   Male and female, what we long for is clout; what we get in its place is Mastercard.

54   **8. Need for Prominence.**   Here comes the need to be admired and respected, to enjoy prestige and high social status. These times, it appears, are not so egalitarian after all. Many ads picture the trappings of high position; the Oldsmobile stands before a manorial doorway, the Volvo is parked beside a steeplechase. A book-lined study is the setting for Dewar's 12, and Lenox China is displayed in a dining room chock full of antiques.

55   Beefeater gin represents itself as "The Crown Jewel of England" and uses no illustrations of jewels or things British, for the words are sufficient indicators of distinction. Buy that gin and you will rise up the prestige hierarchy, or achieve the same effect on yourself with Seagram's 7 Crown, which ambiguously describes itself as "classy."

56   Being respected does not have to entail the usual accoutrements of wealth: "Do you know who I am?" the commercials ask, and we learn that the prominent person is not so prominent without his American Express card.

57   **9. Need for Attention.**   The previous need involved being *looked up to,* while this is the need to be *looked at.* The desire to exhibit ourselves in such a way as to make others look at us is a primitive, insuppressible instinct. The clothing and cosmetic industries exist just to serve this need, and this is the way they pitch their wares. Some of this effort is aimed at males, as the ads for Hathaway shirts and Jockey underclothes. But the greater bulk of such appeals is targeted singlemindedly at women.

58   To come back to Brooke Shields: this is where she fits into American marketing. If I buy Calvin Klein jeans, consumers infer, I'll be the object of fascination. The desire for exhibition has been most strikingly played to in a print

campaign of many years' duration, that of Maidenform lingerie. The woman exposes herself, and sales surge. "Gentlemen prefer Hanes" the ads dissemble, and women who want eyes upon them know what they should do. Peggy Fleming* flutters her legs for L'eggs, encouraging females who want to be the star in their own lives to purchase this product.

59   The same appeal works for cosmetics and lotions. For years, the little girl with the exposed backside sold gobs of Coppertone, but now the company has picked up the pace a little: as a female, you are supposed to "Flash 'em a Coppertone tan." Food can be sold the same way, especially to the diet-conscious; Angie Dickinson poses for California avocados and says, "Would this body lie to you?" Our eyes are too fixed on her for us to think to ask if she got that way by eating mounds of guacomole.

60   **10. Need for Autonomy.**   There are several ways to sell credit card services, as has been noted: Mastercard appeals to the need to dominate, and American Express to the need for prominence. When Visa claims, "You can have it the way you want it," yet another primary motive is being beckoned forward—the need to endorse the self. The focus here is upon the independence and integrity of the individual; this need is the antithesis of the need for guidance and is unlike any of the social needs. "If running with the herd isn't your style, try ours," says Rotan-Mosle, and many Americans feel they have finally found the right brokerage firm.

61   The photo is of a red-coated Mountie on his horse, posed on a snow-covered ledge; the copy reads, "Windsor—One Canadian stands alone." This epitome of the solitary and proud individual may work best with male customers, as may Winston's man in the red cap. But one-figure advertisements also strike the strong need for autonomy among American women. As Shelley Hack† strides for Charlie perfume, females respond to her obvious pride and flair; she is her own person. The Virginia Slims tale is of people who have come a long way from subservience to independence. Cachet perfume feels it does not need a solo figure to work this appeal, and uses three different faces in its ads; it insists, though, "It's different on every woman who wears it."

62   Like many psychological needs, this one can also be appealed to in a negative fashion, by invoking the loss of independence or self-regard. Guilt and regrets can be stimulated: "Gee, I could have had a V-8." Next time, get one and be good to yourself.

63   **11. Need to Escape.**   An appeal to the need for autonomy often co-occurs with one for the need to escape, since the desire to duck out of our social obligations, to seek rest or adventure, frequently takes the form of one-person flight. The dashing image of a pilot, in fact, is a standard way of quickening this need to get away from it all.

64   Freedom is the pitch here, the freedom that every individual yearns for whenever life becomes too oppressive. Many advertisers like appealing to the need for escape because the sensation of pleasure often accompanies escape, and what

---

* *Peggy Fleming* (b. 1948), an Olympic figure skater, and Gold Medal winner (1968), later became a TV sports commentator and a representative for UNICEF (the United Nations Children's Emergency Fund).

† *Shelley Hack* (b. 1952) portrayed Tiffany Welles in the 1970s TV show "Charlie's Angels."

nicer emotional nimbus could there be for a product? "You deserve a break today," says McDonald's, and Stouffer's frozen foods chime in, "Set yourself free."

65   For decades men have imaginatively bonded themselves to the Marlboro cowboy who dwells untarnished and unencumbered in Marlboro Country some distance from modern life; smokers' aching needs for autonomy and escape are personified by that cowpoke. Many women can identify with the lady ambling through the woods behind the words, "Benson and Hedges and mornings and me."

66   But escape does not have to be solitary. Other Benson and Hedges ads, part of the same campaign, contain two strolling figures. In Salem cigarette advertisements, it can be several people who escape together into the mountaintops. A commercial for Levi's pictured a cloudbank above a city through which ran a whole chain of young people.

67   There are varieties of escape, some wistful like the Boeing "Someday" campaign of dream vacations, some kinetic like the play and parties in soft drink ads. But in every instance, the consumer exposed to the advertisement is invited to momentarily depart his everyday life for a more carefree experience, preferably with the product in hand.

68   **12. Need to Feel Safe.**   Nobody in their right mind wants to be intimidated, menaced, battered, poisoned. We naturally want to do whatever it takes to stave off threats to our well-being, and to our families'. It is the instinct of self-preservation that makes us responsive to the ad of the St. Bernard with the keg of Chivas Regal. We pay attention to the stern talk of Karl Malden* and the plight of the vacationing couples who have lost all their funds in the American Express travelers cheques commercials. We want the omnipresent stag from Hartford Insurance to watch over us too.

69   In the interest of keeping failure and calamity from our lives, we like to see the durability of products demonstrated. Can we ever forget that Timex takes a licking and keeps on ticking? When the American Tourister suitcase bounces all over the highway and the egg inside doesn't break, the need to feel safe has been adroitly plucked.

70   We take precautions to diminish future threats. We buy Volkswagen Rabbits for the extraordinary mileage, and MONY insurance policies to avoid the tragedies depicted in their black-and-white ads of widows and orphans.

71   We are careful about our health. We consume Mazola margarine because it has "corn goodness" backed by the natural food traditions of the American Indians. In the medicine cabinet is Alka-Seltzer, the "home remedy"; having it, we are snug in our little cottage.

72   We want to be safe and secure; buy these products, advertisers are saying, and you'll be safer than you are without them.

---

* *Karl Malden* (b. 1912) with his familiar craggy face and outsized nose, was a stage and later a film actor. He was the original Mitch in the Broadway production of Tennessee Williams's *Streetcar Named Desire,* a role he reprised in the 1951 movie version. His films include *On the Waterfront* (1954), *Cheyenne Autumn* (1964), and *Patton* (1970), and he starred in the 1972 TV series *Streets of San Francisco.* Malden became famous to a later generation of viewers as a pitchman for the American Express card, with the slogan, "Don't leave home without it!"

73   **13. Need for Aesthetic Sensations.**   There is an undeniable aesthetic component to virtually every ad run in the national media: the photography or filming or drawing is near-perfect, the type style is well chosen, the layout could scarcely be improved upon. Advertisers know there is little chance of good communication occurring if an ad is not visually pleasing. Consumers may not be aware of the extent of their own sensitivity to artwork, but it is undeniably large.

74   Sometimes the aesthetic element is expanded and made into an ad's primary appeal. Charles Jordan shoes may or may not appear in the accompanying avant-grade photographs; Kohler plumbing fixtures catch attention through the high style of their desert settings. Beneath the slightly out of focus photograph, languid and sensuous in tone, General Electric feels called upon to explain, "This is an ad for the hair dryer."

75   This appeal is not limited to female consumers: J&B scotch says "It whispers" and shows a bucolic scene of lake and castle.

76   **14. Need to Satisfy Curiosity.**   It may seem odd to list a need for information among basic motives, but this need can be as primal and compelling as any of the others. Human beings are curious by nature, interested in the world around them, and intrigued by tidbits of knowledge and new developments. Trivia, percentages, observations counter to conventional wisdom—these items all help sell products. Any advertisement in a question-and-answer format is strumming this need.

77   A dog groomer has a question about long distance rates, and Bell Telephone has a chart with all the figures. An ad for Porsche 911 is replete with diagrams and schematics, numbers and arrows. Lo and behold, Anacin pills have 150 more milligrams than its competitors; should we wonder if this is better or worse for us?

78   **15. Physiological Needs.**   To the extent that sex is solely a biological need, we are now coming around full circle, back toward the start of the list. In this final category are clustered appeals to sleeping, eating, drinking. The art of photographing food and drink is so advanced, sometimes these temptations are wondrously caught in the camera's lens: the crab meat in the Red Lobster restaurant ads can start us salivating, the Quarterpounder can almost be smelled, the liquor in the glass glows invitingly. Imbibe, these ads scream.

Styles

79 Some common ingredients of advertisements were not singled out for separate mention in the list of fifteen because they are not appeals in and of themselves. They are stylistic features, influencing the way a basic appeal is presented. The use of humor is one, and the use of celebrities is another. A third is time imagery, past and future, which goes to several purposes.

80   For all of its employment in advertising, humor can be treacherous, because it can get out of hand and smother the product information. Supposedly, this is what Alka-Seltzer discovered with its comic commercials of the late sixties; "I can't believe I ate the whole thing," the sad-faced husband lamented, and the audience cackled so much it forgot the antacid. Or, did not take it seriously.

81   But used carefully, humor can punctuate some of the softer appeals and soften some of the harsher ones. When Emma says to the Fruit-of-the-Loom

fruits, "Hi, cuties. Whatcha doing in my laundry basket?" we smile as our curiosity is assuaged along with hers. Bill Cosby gets consumers tickled about the children in his Jell-O commercials, and strokes the need to nurture.

82   An insurance company wants to invoke the need to feel safe, but does not want to leave readers with an unpleasant aftertaste; cartoonist Rowland Wilson creates an avalanche about to crush a gentleman who is saying to another, "My insurance company? New England Life, of course. Why?" The same tactic of humor undercutting threat is used in the cartoon commercials for Safeco when the Pink Panther wanders from one disaster to another. Often humor masks aggression: comedian Bob Hope in the outfit of a boxer promises to knock out the knock-knocks with Texaco; Rodney Dangerfield, who "can't get no respect," invites aggression as the comic relief in Miller Lite commercials.

83   Roughly fifteen percent of all advertisements incorporate a celebrity, almost always from the fields of entertainment or sports. The approach can also prove troublesome for advertisers, for celebrities are human beings too, and fully capable of the most remarkable behavior. If anything distasteful about them emerges, it is likely to reflect on the product. The advertisers making use of Anita Bryant* and Billie Jean King† suffered several anxious moments. An untimely death can also react poorly on a product. But advertisers are willing to take risks because celebrities can be such a good link between producers and consumers, performing the social role of introducer.

84   There are several psychological needs these middlemen can play upon. Let's take the product class of cameras and see how different celebrities can hit different needs. The need for guidance can be invoked by Michael Landon, who plays such a wonderful dad on "Little House on the Prairie"; when he says to buy Kodak equipment, many people listen. James Garner for Polaroid cameras is put in a similar authoritative role, so defined by a mocking spouse. The need to achieve is summoned up by Tracy Austin and other tennis stars for Canon AE-1; the advertiser first makes sure we see these athletes playing to win. When Cheryl Tiegs‡ speaks up for Olympus cameras, it is the need for attention that is being targeted.

85   The past and future, being outside our grasp, are exploited by advertisers as locales for the projection of needs. History can offer up heroes (and call up

---

* *Anita Bryant* (b. 1940), a singer and entertainer (and as Miss Oklahoma, runner-up in the 1958 Miss America competition), became controversial during the late 1970s with her campaigns against homosexuality and AIDS. At the time, she was making ads and TV commercials for Florida orange juice, but was dropped by the sponsor after boycotts by activists.

† *Billie Jean King* (b. 1943) was a championship tennis player in the late 1960s and 1970s. In 1973 she was named *Sports Illustrated*'s "Sportsperson of the Year," the first woman to win this honor. She won four U.S. championships and six Wimbledon's single championships. In 1973, in a much publicized "Battle of the Sexes" match, King won all three sets against the 55-year-old Bobby Riggs (once ranked as the best tennis player in the world), who had claimed that "any half-decent male player could defeat even the best female players."

‡ *Cheryl Tiegs* (b. 1947) is a supermodel perhaps best known for her affiliation with the *Sports Illustrated Annual Swimsuit Issue*. A 1978 poster of Tiegs in a pink swimsuit became a cultural icon. Recently, she has entered the business world with an accessory and wig line for Revlon.

the need to achieve) or traditions (need for guidance) as well as art objects (need for aesthetic sensations). Nostalgia is a kindly version of personal history and is deployed by advertisers to rouse needs for affiliation and for guidance; the need to escape can come in here, too. The same need to escape is sometimes the point of futuristic appeals but picturing the avant-garde can also be a way to get at the need to achieve.

Analyzing Advertisements

86 When analyzing ads yourself for their emotional appeals, it takes a bit of practice to learn to ignore the product information (as well as one's own experience and feelings about the product). But that skill comes soon enough, as does the ability to quickly sort out from all the non-product aspects of an ad the chief element which is the most striking, the most likely to snag attention first and penetrate brains farthest. The key to the appeal, this element usually presents itself centrally and forwardly to the reader or viewer.

87   Another clue: the viewing angle which the audience has on the ad's subjects is informative. If the subjects are photographed or filmed from below and thus are looking down at you much as the Green Giant does, then the need to be guided is a good candidate for the ad's emotional appeal. If, on the other hand, the subjects are shot from above and appear deferential, as is often the case with children or female models, then other needs are being appealed to.

88   To figure out an ad's emotional appeal, it is wise to know (or have a good hunch about) who the targeted consumers are; this can often be inferred from the magazine or television show it appears in. This piece of information is a great help in determining the appeal and in deciding between two different interpretations. For example, if an ad features a partially undressed female, this would typically signal one appeal for readers of *Penthouse* (need for sex) and another for readers of *Cosmopolitan* (need for attention).

89   It would be convenient if every ad made just one appeal, were aimed at just one need. Unfortunately, things are often not that simple. A cigarette ad with a couple at the edge of a polo field is trying to hit both the need for affiliation and the need for prominence; depending on the attitude of the male, dominance could also be an ingredient in this. An ad for Chimere perfume incorporates two photos: in the top one the lady is being commanding at a business luncheon (need to dominate), but in the lower one she is being bussed (need for affiliation). Better ads, however, seem to avoid being too diffused; in the study of post-World War II advertising described earlier, appeals grew more focused as the decades passed. As a rule of thumb, about sixty percent have two conspicuous appeals; the last twenty percent have three or more. Rather than looking for the greatest number of appeals, decoding ads is most productive when the loudest one or two appeals are discerned, since those are the appeals with the best chance of grabbing people's attention.

90   Finally, analyzing ads does not have to be a solo activity and probably should not be. The greater number of people there are involved, the better chance there is of transcending individual biases and discerning the essential emotional lure built into an advertisement.

Do They or Don't They?

91 Do the emotional appeals made in advertisements add up to the sinister manipulation of consumers?

92   It is clear that these ads work. Attention is caught, communication occurs between producers and consumers, and sales result. It turns out to be difficult to detail the exact relationship between a specific ad and a specific purchase, or even between a campaign and subsequent sales figures, because advertising is only one of a host of influences upon consumption. Yet no one is fooled by this lack of perfect proof; everyone knows that advertising sells. If this were not the case, then tight-fisted American businesses would not spend a total of fifty billion dollars annually on these messages.

93   But before anyone despairs that advertisers have our number to the extent that they can marshal us at will and march us like automatons to the check-out counters, we should recall the resiliency and obduracy of the American consumer. Advertisers may have uncovered the softest spots in minds, but that does not mean they have found truly gaping apertures. There is no evidence that advertising can get people to do things contrary to their self-interests. Despite all the finesse of advertisements, and all the subtle emotional tugs, the public resists the vast majority of the petitions. According to the marketing division of the A. C. Nielsen Company, a whopping seventy-five percent of all new products die within a year in the marketplace, the victims of consumer disinterest which no amount of advertising could overcome. The appeals in advertising may be the most captivating there are to be had, but they are not enough to entrap the wily consumer.

94   The key to understanding the discrepancy between, on the one hand, the fact that advertising truly works, and, on the other, the fact that it hardly works, is to take into account the enormous numbers of people exposed to an ad. Modern-day communications permit an ad to be displayed to millions upon millions of individuals; if the smallest fraction of that audience can be moved to buy the product, then the ad has been successful. When one percent of the people exposed to a television advertising campaign reach for their wallets, that could be one million sales, which may be enough to keep the product in production and the advertisements coming.

95   In arriving at an evenhanded judgment about advertisements and their emotional appeals, it is good to keep in mind that many of the purchases which might be credited to these ads are experienced as genuinely gratifying to the consumer. We sincerely like the goods or service we have bought, and we may even like some of the emotional drapery that an ad suggests comes with it. It has sometimes been noted that the most avid students of advertisements are the people who have just bought the product; they want to steep themselves in the associated imagery. This may be the reason that Americans, when polled, are not negative about advertising and do not disclose any sense of being misused. The volume of advertising may be an irritant, but the product information as well as the imaginative material in ads are partial compensation.

96   A productive understanding is that advertising messages involve costs and benefits at both ends of the communications channel. For those few ads which do make contact, the consumer surrenders a moment of time, has the lower

brain curried, and receives notice of a product; the advertiser has given up money and has increased the chance of sales. In this sort of communications activity, neither party can be said to be the loser.

Review Questions

1. Why is advertising more common in highly industrialized countries like the United States than in countries with "quieter" economies?

2. How are advertisers' attempts to communicate their messages, and to break through customer resistance, keyed to their conception of human psychology, according to Fowles?

3. What are the "two orders of content" of most advertisements, according to Fowles?

4. How is Fowles indebted to Henry Murray?

5. Why must appeals to our need for sex and our need to aggress be handled carefully, according to Fowles?

6. How does the use of humor or the use of celebrities fit into Fowles's scheme?

Discussion and Writing Suggestions

1. In paragraph 4 Fowles cites a study indicating that only a fraction of the advertisements bombarding consumers every day are even noticed, much less acted upon. How do the results of this study square with your own experience? About how many of the commercial messages that you view and hear every day do you actually pay attention to? What kinds of messages draw your attention? What elicits positive reactions? Negative reactions? What kinds of appeals are most successful in making you want to actually purchase the advertised product?

2. What do you think of Fowles's analysis of "advertising's fifteen basic appeals"? Does this classification seem an accurate and useful way of accounting for how most advertising works upon us? Would you drop any of his categories, or perhaps incorporate one set into another set? Has Fowles neglected to consider other appeals that you believe to be equally important? If so, can you think of one or more advertisements that employ such appeals omitted by Fowles?

3. Categorize several of the ads in the ad portfolio later in the chapter (pages 448–92) using Fowles's schema. Explain how the headlines, body text, and graphics support your categorization choices.

4. Fowles asserts that "[c]ontrary to impressions, unambiguous sex is rare in [advertising] messages." This article first appeared in 1982. Does Fowles's statement still seem true today? To what extent do you believe that advertisers in recent years have increased their reliance on overt sexual appeals? Cite examples.

5. Fowles believes that "the need to associate with others [affiliation]. . . is probably the most prevalent appeal" in advertising. To what extent do you agree with this statement? Locate or cite print or broadcast ads that rely on the need for affiliation. How do the graphics and text of these ads work on what Fowles calls "the deep running drives" of our psyches or "the lower brain"?

6. Locate ads that rely upon the converse appeals to nurture and to guidance. Explain how the graphics and text in these ads work upon our human motivations. If possible further categorize the appeal: for example, are we provided with guidance from a parent-figure, some other authority figure, or from the force of tradition?

7. Conduct (perhaps with one or more teammates) your own analysis of a set of contemporary advertisements. Select a single issue of a particular magazine, such as *Time* or the *New Yorker*. Review all of the full-page ads, classifying each according to Fowles's categories. An ad may make more than one appeal (as Fowles points out in paragraph 89), but generally one will be primary. What do your findings show? Which appeals are the most frequent? The least frequent? Which are most effective? Why? You may find it interesting to compare the appeals of advertising in different magazines aimed at different audiences—for example, a general interest magazine, such as *Newsweek,* compared with a more specialized magazine, such as the *New Republic,* or *People,* or *Glamour,* or *Guns and Ammo.* To what extent do the types of appeals shift with the gender or interests of the target audience?

Making the Pitch in Print Advertising
Courtland L. Bovée, John V. Thill, George P. Dovel, Marian Burk Wood

No two ads are identical, but the vast majority employ a common set of textual features: headlines, body copy, and slogans. In the following selection, the authors discuss each of these features in turn, explaining their importance in attracting the potential customer's attention and selling the virtues of the product or service offered. You will find this discussion useful in making your own analyses of advertisements.

Courtland L. Bovée is the C. Allen Paul Distinguished Chair at Grossmont College. John V. Thill is CEO of Communication Specialists of America. George P. Dovel is president of the

Dovel Group. Marian Burk Wood is president of Wood and Wood Advertising. This passage originally appeared in the authors' textbook Advertising Excellence, *McGraw-Hill (1995).*

Copywriters and Copywriting

1 Given the importance of copy, it comes as no surprise that copywriters are key players in the advertising process. In fact, many of the most notable leaders and voices in the industry began their careers as copywriters, including Jane Maas, David Ogilvy, Rosser Reeves, Leo Burnett, and William Bernbach. As a profession, copywriting is somewhat unusual because so many of its top practitioners have been in their jobs for years, even decades (rather than moving up the management ranks as is usual in many professions). Copywriters can either work for agencies or set themselves up as free-lancers, selling their services to agencies and advertisers. Because it presents endless opportunities to be creative, copywriting is one of those rare jobs that can be fresh and challenging year after year.

2 Although successful copywriters share a love of language with novelists, poets, and other writers, copywriting is first and foremost a business function, not an artistic endeavor. The challenge isn't to create works of literary merit, but to meet advertising objectives. This doesn't mean that copywriting isn't an art, however; it's simply art in pursuit of a business goal. Nor is it easy. Such noted literary writers as Stephen Vincent Benét, George Bernard Shaw, and Ernest Hemingway tried to write ad copy and found themselves unable to do it effectively. It's the combined requirements of language skills, business acumen, and an ability to create under the pressure of tight deadlines and format restrictions (such as the limited number of words you have to work with) that make copywriting so challenging—and so endlessly rewarding.

3 Copywriters have many styles and approaches to writing, but most agree on one thing: copywriting is hard work. It can involve a great deal of planning and coordinating with clients, legal staffers, account executives, researchers, and art directors. In addition, it usually entails hammering away at your copy until it's as good as it can be. David Ogilvy talked about doing 19 drafts of a single piece of copy and writing 37 headlines for a Sears ad in order to get 3 possibilities to show to the client. Actually, the chance to write and rewrite that many times is a luxury that most copywriters don't have; they often must produce copy on tight schedules with unforgiving deadlines (such as magazine publication deadlines).

4 The task of copywriting is most often associated with the headlines and copy you see in an ad, but copywriters actually develop a wide variety of other materials, from posters to catalogs to press releases, as well as the words you hear in radio and television commercials.

Print Copy

5 Copywriters are responsible for every word you see in print ads, whether the words are in a catchy headline or in the fine print at the bottom of the page. The three major categories of copy are headlines, body copy, and slogans.

Headlines

6 The *headline,* also called a *heading* or a *head,* constitutes the dominant line or lines of copy in an ad. Headlines are typically set in larger type and appear at the top of the ad, although there are no hard-and-fast rules on headline layout. *Subheads* are secondary headlines, often written to move the reader from the main headline to the body copy. Even if there is a pageful of body copy and only a few words in the headline, the headline is the most important piece of copy for two reasons: First, it serves as the "come-on" to get people to stop turning the page and check out your ad. Second, as much as 80 percent of your audience may not bother to read the body copy, so whatever message these nonreaders carry away from the ad will have to come from the headline.

7 Copywriters can choose from a variety of headline types, each of which performs a particular function.

- *News headlines.* News headlines present information that's new to the audience, such as announcing a new store location, a new product, or lower prices. This approach is common because potential customers are often looking for new solutions, lower prices, and other relevant changes in the marketplace. For example, a newspaper ad from the Silo home electronics chain announced a recent sale using a news headline: "Everything on Sale! 4 Days Only! 5–20% Off Everything!" Headlines like this are typical in local newspaper advertising.

- *Emotional headlines.* The emotional appeal described earlier in the chapter is represented by emotional headlines. The quotation headline "I'm sick of her ruining our lives" was used in an ad for the American Mental Health Fund to echo the frustration some parents feel when they can't understand their teenagers' behavior. Combined with a photo of a sad and withdrawn teenage girl, the headline grabs any parent who has felt such frustration, and the body copy goes on to explain that families shouldn't get mad at people with mental illnesses but should help them get treatment for their conditions.

- *Benefit headlines.* The benefit headline is a statement of the key customer benefit. An ad for Quicken personal finance software used the question-form headline: "How do you know exactly where your money goes and how much you have?" followed by "It's this simple" above a photograph of the product package. The customer benefit is keeping better track of your money, and Quicken is the solution offered.

- *Directive headlines.* Headlines that direct the reader to do something, or at least suggest the reader do something, can motivate consumer action. Such headlines can be a hard sell, such as "Come in now and save," or they can be something more subtle, such as "Just feel the color in these black and whites," the headline in an ad for Ensoniq keyboards.

- *Offbeat and curiosity headlines.* Humor, wordplay, and mystery can be effective ways to draw readers into an ad. An ad promoting vacation travel to Spain used the headline "Si in the dark," with a photo of a lively nighttime scene. The word *Si* is catchy because it first looks like an error, until the reader reads the body copy to learn that the ad is talking about Spain (*si* is Spanish for "yes").

- *Hornblowing headlines.* The hornblowing headline, called "Brag and Boast" heads by the Gallup & Robinson research organization, should be used with care. Customers have seen it all and heard it all, and "We're the greatest" headlines tend to sound arrogant and self-centered. This isn't to say that you can't stress superiority; you just need to do it in a way that takes the customer's needs into account, and the headline must be honest. The headline "Neuberger & Berman Guardian Fund" followed by the subhead "#1 Performing Growth and Income Fund" blows the company's own horn but also conveys an important product benefit. Since investors look for top-performing mutual funds, the information about being number one is relevant.
- *Slogan, label, or logo headlines.* Some headlines show a company's slogan, a product label, or the organization's logo. Powerful slogans like Hallmark's "When you care enough to send the very best" can make great headlines because they click with the reader's emotions. Label and logo headlines can build product and company awareness, but they must be used with care. If the label or logo doesn't make some emotional or logical connection with the reader, the ad probably won't succeed.

8   Headlines often have maximum impact when coupled with a well-chosen graphic element, rather than trying to carry the message with words alone. In fact, the careful combination of the two can increase the audience's involvement with the ad, especially if one of the two says something ironic or unexpected that has to be resolved by considering the other element. A magazine ad for Easter Seals had the headline "After all we did for Pete, he walked out on us." At first, you think the birth-defects organization is complaining. Then you see a photo of Pete with new artificial legs, walking away from a medical facility. It's a powerful combination that makes the reader feel good about the things Easter Seals can do for people.

Body Copy

9   The second major category of copy is the *body copy,* which constitutes the words in the main body of the ad, apart from headlines, photo captions, and other blocks of text. The importance of body copy varies from ad to ad, and some ads have little or no body copy. Ads for easy-to-understand products, for instance, often rely on the headline and a visual such as a photograph to get their point across. In contrast, when the selling message needs a lot of supporting detail to be convincing, an ad can be packed full of body copy. Some advertisers have the impression that long body copy should be avoided, but that isn't always the case. The rule to apply here is to use the "right" number of words. You might not need many words in a perfume ad, but you might need a page or two to cover a complex industrial product.

10   As with headlines, body copy can be built around several different formats. *Straight-line copy* is copy that takes off from the headline and develops the selling points for the product. *Narrative copy,* in contrast, tells a story as it persuades; the same selling points may be covered, but in a different context. *Dialog/monolog copy* lets one or two characters in the ad do the selling

through what they are saying. *Picture-and-caption copy* relies on photographs or illustrations to tell the story, with support from their accompanying captions.

Slogans

11 The third major category of copy includes *slogans,* or *tag lines,* memorable sayings that convey a selling message. Over the years, Coca-Cola has used such slogans as "Coke is it," "It's the real thing," and "Always Coca-Cola." Slogans are sometimes used as headlines, but not always. Their importance lies in the fact they often become the most memorable result of an advertising campaign. You've probably got a few slogans stuck in your head. Ever heard of "Quality is job number 1," "Don't leave home without it," or "Melts in your mouth, not in your hand"?

12 The Korean automaker Hyundai recently switched back to the slogan "Cars that make sense," which is a great way of expressing its desired positioning as a lower-cost but still reliable alternative to Japanese and U.S. cars. For several years, the company had used "Hyundai. Yes, Hyundai," but "Cars that make sense" has proved to be a much more effective way to define the value it offers consumers.

Review Questions

1. What are the particular challenges of copywriting , as opposed to other types of writing?

2. How do the authors classify the main types of ad headlines?

CHECKLIST FOR PRODUCING EXCELLENT COPY

❑ A. Avoid clichés.
  • Create fresh, original phrases that vividly convey your message.
  • Remember that clever wordplay based on clichés can be quite effective.

❑ B. Watch out for borrowed interest.
  • Make sure you don't use inappropriate copy or graphics since they can steal the show from your basic sales message.
  • Be sure nothing draws attention from the message.

❑ C. Don't boast.
  • Be sure the ad's purpose isn't merely to pat the advertiser on the back.
  • Tout success when you must convince nonbuyers that lots of people just like them have purchased your product; this isn't the same as shouting "We're the best!"

3. What are the main types of body copy styles, according to the authors?

Discussion and Writing Suggestions

1. Apply the authors' criteria for effective headlines to three or four of the ads in the portfolio (pages 448–92)—or to three or four ads of your own choosing. To what extent do these headlines succeed in attracting attention, engaging the audience, and fulfilling the other requirements of effective headlines?

2. Imagine that you are a copywriter who has been assigned the account for a particular product (your choice). Develop three possible headlines for an advertisement for this product. Incorporate as many as possible of the criteria for effective headlines discussed by the authors (paragraphs 6–8).

3. Classify the *types* of headlines in a given product category in the ad portfolio (pages 448–92). Or classify the types of headlines in full-page ads in a single current magazine. Which type of headline appears to be the most common? Which type appears to be the most effective in gaining your attention and making you want to read the body copy?

4. Classify the *types* of body copy styles in a given product category in the ad portfolio. Or classify the types of body copy styles in full-page ads in a single current magazine. How effective is the copy in

---

❏ D. Make it personal, informal, and relevant.
  • Connect with the audience in a way that is personal and comfortable. Pompous, stiff, and overly "businesslike" tends to turn people away.
  • Avoid copy that sounds like it belongs in an ad, with too many overblown adjectives and unsupported claims of superiority.

❏ E. Keep it simple, specific, and concise.
  • Make your case quickly and stick to the point. This will help you get past all the barriers and filters that people put up to help them select which things they'll pay attention to and which they'll ignore.
  • Avoid copy that's confusing, meandering, too long, or too detailed.

❏ F. Give the audience a reason to read, listen, or watch.
  • Offer a solution to your audience's problems.
  • Entertain your audience.
  • Consider any means possible to get your audience to pay attention long enough to get your sales message across.

selling the virtues of the product or the institution or organization behind the product?

5. Assess the effectiveness of a given ad either in the ad portfolio or in a recent magazine or newspaper. Apply the criteria discussed by the authors in the box labeled "Checklist for Producing Excellent Copy." For example, to what extent is the copy fresh and original? To what extent does the copy make the message "personal, informal, and relevant" to the target audience? To what extent is the message "simple, specific, and concise"?

6. Write your own ad for a product that you like and use frequently. In composing the ad, apply the principles of effective headlines, subheads, body copy, and slogans discussed by the authors. Apply also the principles of "Checklist for Producing Excellent Copy." You will also need to think of (though not necessarily create) an effective graphic for the ad.

Elements of Effective Layout
Dorothy Cohen

In the previous selection, Courtland L. Bovée et al. discusses the chief textual features of print advertising. In the following passage Dorothy Cohen reviews the equally important (and perhaps more important, in terms of seizing the reader's attention) graphic components. Chief among these are balance, proportion, movement, unity, clarity and simplicity, and emphasis. After reading Cohen, you should be well equipped to work on the analysis assignments in this chapter and, more generally, to assess the graphic quality of the ads you regularly encounter in magazines and newspapers.

This selection originally appeared in Dorothy Cohen's textbook Advertising *(1988).*

1   Fundamentally a good layout should attract attention and interest and should provide some control over the manner in which the advertisement is read. The message to be communicated may be sincere, relevant, and important to the consumer, but because of the competitive "noise" in the communication channel, the opportunity to be heard may depend on the effectiveness of the layout. In addition to attracting attention, the most important requisites for an effective layout are balance, proportion, movement, unity, clarity and simplicity, and emphasis.

Balance

2   Balance is a fundamental law in nature and its application to layout design formulates one of the basic principles of this process. Balance is a matter of weight distribution; in layout it is keyed to the *optical center* of an advertisement, the point which the reader's eye designates as the center of an area. In an advertisement a vertical line which divides the area into right and left

halves contains the center; however the optical center is between one-tenth and one-third the distance above the mathematical horizontal center line. . . .

3   In order to provide good artistic composition, the elements in the layout must be in equilibrium. Equilibrium can be achieved through balance, and this process may be likened to the balancing of a seesaw. The optical center of the advertisement serves as the fulcrum or balancing point, and the elements may be balanced on both sides of this fulcrum through considerations of their size and tonal quality.

4   The simplest way to ensure *formal balance* between the elements to the right and left of the vertical line is to have all masses in the left duplicated on the right in size, weight, and distance from the center. . . . Formal balance imparts feelings of dignity, solidity, refinement, and reserve. It has been used for institutional advertising and suggests conservatism on the part of the advertiser. Its major deficiency is that it may present a static and somewhat unexciting appearance; however, formal balance presents material in an easy-to-follow order and works well for many ads.

5   To understand *informal balance,* think of children of unequal weight balanced on a seesaw; to ensure equilibrium it is necessary to place the smaller child far from the center and the larger child closer to the fulcrum. In informal balance the elements are balanced, but not evenly, because of different sizes and color contrast. This type of a symmetric balance requires care so that the various elements do not create a lopsided or top-heavy appearance. A knowledge or a sense of the composition can help create the feeling of symmetry in what is essentially asymmetric balance.

6   Informal balance presents a fresh, untraditional approach. It creates excitement, a sense of originality, forcefulness, and, to some extent, the element of surprise. Whereas formal balance may depend on the high interest value of the illustration to attract the reader, informal balance may attract attention through the design of the layout. . . .

Proportion

7 Proportion helps develop order and creates a pleasing impression. It is related to balance but is concerned primarily with the division of the space and the emphasis to be accorded each element. Proportion, to the advertising designer, is the relationship between the size of one element in the ad to another, the amount of space between elements, as well as the width of the total ad to its depth. Proportion also involves the tone of the ad: the amount of light area in relation to dark area and the amount of color and noncolor.

8   As a general rule unequal dimensions and distances make the most lively design in advertising. The designer also places the elements on the page so that each element is given space and position in proportion to its importance in the total advertisement and does not look like it stands alone.

Movement

9 If an advertisement is to appear dynamic rather than static, it must contain some movement. *Movement* (also called *sequence*) provides the directional flow for

the advertisement, gives it its follow-through, and provides coherence. It guides the reader's eye from one element to another and makes sure he or she does not miss anything.

10   Motion in layout is generally from left to right and from top to bottom—the direction established through the reading habits of speakers of Western language. The directional impetus should not disturb the natural visual flow but should favor the elements to be stressed, while care should be taken not to direct the reader's eye out of the advertisement. This can be done by the following:

- *Gaze motion* directs the reader's attention by directing the looks of the people or animals in an ad. If a subject is gazing at a unit in the layout, the natural tendency is for the reader to follow the direction of that gaze; if someone is looking directly out of the advertisement, the reader may stop to see who's staring.
- *Structural motion* incorporates the lines of direction and patterns of movement by mechanical means. An obvious way is to use an arrow or a pointed finger. . . .

Unity

11 Another important design principle is the unification of the layout. Although an advertisement is made up of many elements, all of these should be welded into a compact composition. Unity is achieved when the elements tie into one another by using the same basic shapes, sizes, textures, colors, and mood. In addition, the type should have the same character as the art.

12   A *border* surrounding an ad provides a method of achieving unity. Sets of borders may occur within an ad, and, when they are similar in thickness and tone, they provide a sense of unity.

13   Effective use of white space can help to establish unity. . . . *White space* is defined as that part of the advertising space which is not occupied by any other elements; in this definition, white space is not always white in color. White space may be used to feature an important element by setting it off, or to imply luxury and prestige by preventing a crowded appearance. It may be used to direct and control the reader's attention by tying elements together. If white space is used incorrectly, it may cause separation of the elements and create difficulty in viewing the advertisement as a whole.

Clarity and Simplicity

14 The good art director does not permit a layout to become too complicated or tricky. An advertisement should retain its clarity and be easy to read and easy to understand. The reader tends to see the total image of an advertisement; thus it should not appear fussy, contrived, or confusing. Color contrasts, including tones of gray, should be strong enough to be easily deciphered, and the various units should be clear and easy to understand. Type size and design should be selected for ease of reading, and lines of type should be a comfortable reading length. Too many units in an advertisement are distracting; therefore, any elements that can be eliminated without destroying the message should be. One way in which clarity can be achieved is by combining the logo, trademark, tag line, and company name into one compact group.

Emphasis

15 Although varying degrees of emphasis may be given to different elements, one unit should dominate. It is the designer's responsibility to determine how much emphasis is necessary, as well as how it is to be achieved. The important element may be placed in the optical center or removed from the clutter of other elements. Emphasis may also be achieved by contrasts in size, shape, and color, or the use of white space.

Review Questions

1. How does balance in an ad differ from proportion?
2. What two possible types of movement can be incorporated into an advertisement?
3. Cite some of the chief ways of achieving unity in an ad.

Discussion and Writing Suggestions

1. Select an advertisement either in the ad portfolio (pages 448–92) or in a current magazine or newspaper. Analyze the ad in terms of Cohen's discussion of effective layout. How well does the ad employ *balance, proportion, movement, unity, clarity and simplicity,* and *emphasis* to sell the product or communicate the main idea? Which of these elements are most important in accomplishing the task?

2. Cohen writes that "balance is a fundamental law in nature." What do you think she means by this? What natural examples of balance occur to you?

3. Select two ads, one demonstrating what Cohen calls "formal balance," one demonstrating "informal balance." Cohen writes that formal balance "imparts feelings of dignity, solidity, refinement, and reserve" and that it suggests "conservatism on the part of the advertiser." Informal balance, on the other hand, "presents a fresh, untraditional approach" and "creates a sense of originality, forcefulness, and, to some extent, the element of surprise." To what degree do the ads you have selected demonstrate the truth of Cohen's assertions?

4. Find an ad demonstrating unusual use of proportion among its graphic elements. How does the distinctive proportionality help communicate the advertiser's message?

5. Find an ad demonstrating striking use of movement, clarity and simplicity, or emphasis. How does the element you have chosen work to help communicate the ad's message?

6. Find an ad that violates one or more of the graphic principles that Cohen discusses. To what extent do such violations hurt (or even destroy) the ad's effectiveness? How would you fix the problem?

The Indictments Against Advertising
Courtland L. Bovée and William F. Arens

If we were completely rational beings, then advertisements would simply inform us that a particular product or service was available and explain its benefits—if not also its drawbacks. (Some ads still do this: If we wanted to sell a CD, for example, we might just post a "For Sale" notice on a bulletin board, giving the name of the CD and its price.) Since—for better or for worse—we're not completely rational beings, but subject to the sway of powerful emotional appeals (as Jib Fowles explains, in the first selection of this chapter), and since modern advertising is a multibillion-dollar enterprise involving market research, customer psychology, skillful copywriting, and sophisticated graphic arts, the typical magazine or broadcast ad aims to do much more than simply inform us of the availability of consumer products. In addition, the pervasiveness of contemporary advertising means that almost everywhere we turn, we are bombarded with appeals to buy—mostly under the guise of persuading us that buying will somehow improve our lives. The ubiquity and apparent power of advertising (it does work, to some degree, or why would companies continue to advertise?) have inevitably caused a backlash, not only among the general public, but also among social critics, who see advertising—the original spam—as more than just an annoyance, but also as a pernicious influence in contemporary society.

The following selection sums up the chief arguments against advertising and also attempts to respond to these arguments. As you read this passage, think of current ads, either print or broadcast, that may illustrate the points made by the authors.

Courtland L. Bovée is the author or coauthor of several textbooks on business and advertising, including Techniques of Writing Business Letters, Memos, and Reports *(1974),* Advertising Excellence *(1995), and* Contemporary Advertising *(1986), where the following selection first appeared. William F. Arens is coauthor of* Contemporary Advertising.

Social Criticism of Advertising

1   Advertising is the most visible activity of business. What a company may have been doing privately for many years suddenly becomes public the moment it starts to advertise. By publicly inviting people to try their products, companies invite public criticism and attack if their products do not live up to the promised benefits. Defenders of advertising say it is therefore safer to buy advertised than unadvertised products. By putting their names behind the goods, the makers of advertised articles stick their necks out and will try harder to fulfill their promises.

2   Because advertising is so public, it is widely criticized, not only for the role it plays in selling products but also for the way it influences our society. As a selling tool, advertising is attacked for its excesses. Some critics charge that, at its worst, advertising is downright untruthful and, at best, it presents only positive information about products. Others charge that advertising manipulates people psychologically to buy things they can't afford by promising greater sex appeal, improved social status, or other unrealistic expectations. Still others attack adver-

tising for being offensive or in bad taste. Many argue that there is just too much advertising and that this overwhelming quantity is one reason it has such an impact on our society.

3   As a social influence, advertising is often charged, on the one hand, with contributing to crime and violence and, on the other hand, with making people conform. Critics attack advertising for perpetuating stereotypes of people, for making people want things they don't need and can't afford, and for creating insecurity in order to sell goods. Advertising, they say, debases our language, takes unfair advantage of our children, makes us too materialistic, and encourages wastefulness. Finally, by influencing the media, critics charge, advertising interferes with freedom of the press. . . .

4   Let's examine some of the more common criticisms as they are usually expressed. . . .

Advertising Makes Us Too Materialistic

5 Critics claim that advertising adversely affects our value system because it suggests that the means to a happier life is the acquisition of more things instead of spiritual or intellectual enlightenment. Advertising, they say, encourages people to buy more automobiles, more clothing, and more appliances than they need, all with the promise of greater status, greater social acceptance, and greater sex appeal. For example, they point to the fact that millions of Americans own 20 or more pairs of shoes, several TV sets, and often more than one vehicle.

6   There is no doubt that we are the most materialistic society in the world. So the basic question concerning materialism is this: Is there a relationship between happiness and materialism? Does the acquisition of more goods and services contribute to contentment and the joy of living.

7   Philosophers and social scientists have debated the relationship between affluence and happiness for centuries, but they have reached no concrete conclusions. Defenders of advertising maintain that material comfort is necessary before a person can devote time to higher cultural and spiritual values. Therefore, they say, the stress on material things doesn't rule out spiritual and cultural values. In fact, they believe it may create a greater opportunity for it since the satisfaction of a person's higher desires is more likely when that person's lower, more basic desires have been met. They also like to point out that, through its support of the media, advertising has brought literature, opera, drama, and symphonies to millions who would never have seen them otherwise.

8   In reality, the first responsibility of advertising is to aid its sponsor by informing, persuading, and reminding the sponsor's customers and prospects. Most sponsors are frankly more interested in selling goods and making profits than in bringing about cultural changes or improvements. Sponsors find that advertising is most effective when it accurately reflects the society and the market to which it is targeted. Therefore, when culturally uplifting advertising copy sells goods, advertisers will use it. And some of them do. Likewise, if people want a more cultural approach to advertisements and respond to them, advertisers will probably be delighted to comply because it will be in their own best interest.

Ultimately, the bottom line will prevail. The profit and loss in dollars and cents determine the advertising approach.

Advertising Manipulates People Psychologically to Buy Things They Don't Need

9   Advertising is often criticized for its power to make people do irrational things. The following are some suggestions based on variations of this criticism:

1. Advertising should be informative but not persuasive.
2. Advertising should report only factual, functional information.
3. Advertising shouldn't play on people's desires, emotions, fears, or anxieties.
4. Advertising should deal only with people's functional needs for products not their psychological needs for status, appeal, security, sexual attractiveness, or health.

10   Underlying all these criticisms is (1) a belief in the power of advertising to control customers against their will, or (2) an attitude that consumers simply have no freedom of choice when confronted with advertising persuasion.

11   Apologists for advertising point out that persuasion is a fact of life and so is our need to confront persuasion on a daily basis. We see it in every avenue of our existence, not just in advertising. Teachers try to persuade students to study. Students try to persuade teachers to give them better grades. Girlfriends persuade boyfriends; preachers persuade congregations; charities persuade donors; borrowers persuade lenders; stockbrokers persuade investors; kids persuade parents; and advertising persuades people. In short, we are all busy persuading or being persuaded in one way or another.

12   Second, they point out that when we persuade, we usually use a variety of tactics depending on the subject matter and the response of the listener. Sometimes the simple facts of our case are overwhelmingly persuasive. Other times we appeal to some other need or motive of our listener because the facts alone aren't persuasive enough. Should we use emotional appeals in persuasion? If not, say the defenders, then we are all guilty because we all do it.

13   Frankly, all of us have needs and desires beyond the basics of food, clothing, and shelter. One benefit of a free society is that we can choose to what degree we wish to indulge our desires, needs, and fantasies. Some people prefer a simple life without mortgage payments, fancy cars, and trips abroad. Others enjoy the material pleasures of a modern, technological society. There are advertising sponsors at both ends of that spectrum. Food companies offer natural products as well as convenience packaged goods. Shoe companies offer simple sandals as well as formal footwear.

14   Perhaps, if we recognize that advertising is persuasive by definition, then we can become better consumers and critics of advertising. All companies attempt to persuade consumers to try their products. Not all are successful, though. In spite of the fact that advertising techniques have become far more effective and efficient in recent years, there is still no black magic. The final reality is that many more products fail than succeed in the marketplace. . . .

Advertising Is Offensive or in Bad Taste

15 Many people find advertising offensive to their religious convictions, morality, or political perspective. Others find the use of advertising techniques that emphasize sex, violence, or body functions to be in bad taste. Certainly this is one of the most controversial issues.

16   Taste is highly subjective. Apologists point out that what is good taste to some is bad taste to others. And tastes change. What is considered offensive today may not be offensive in the future. People were outraged when the first advertisement for underarm deodorant was published in the *Ladies Home Journal,* but today no one questions such an advertisement. Some people find liquor ads offensive, while others find them simply informative. There has been some experimentation with advertising birth control products on television. Some feel this advertising supplies badly needed consumer information. Others feel that birth control is not a proper subject for a mass medium.

17   In the not-so-distant past, nudity was rarely seen in print advertisements. Today it is often featured in ads for grooming and personal hygiene products. Where nudity is relevant to the product being advertised, people are less likely to regard it as obscene or offensive.

18   Often the products themselves are not offensive, but the way they are advertised may be open to criticism. Advertising frequently emphasizes the sensational aspects of a product, particularly a book or motion picture. Shock value may be used to gain attention, particularly by inexperienced copywriters. However, this sensationalism is often a reflection of the tastes and interests of the American people. If the advertisements don't attract the people they seek, the advertising campaign will falter and die. The audience, therefore, has the ultimate veto authority by ignoring offensive material.

19   It is unrealistic to assume that advertising, particularly mass advertising, will ever be free of this criticism. But reputable advertisers try to be aware of what the public considers to be tasteful advertising.

Advertising Perpetuates Stereotypes

20 Groups such as the National Organization for Women (NOW) protest that many of today's advertisements do not acknowledge the changing role of women in our society. One feminist says:

> Advertising is an insidious propaganda machine for a male supremacist society. It spews out images of women as sex mates, housekeepers, mothers, and menial workers—images that perhaps reflect the true status of women in society, but which also make it increasingly difficult for women to break out of the sexist stereotypes that imprison them.

21   Consumer charges of ethnic and racial bias and of animal abuse in advertising were made to federal and business regulatory agencies for some time. The targets of these complaints included ads that showed a Japanese gardener at work and floor wax commercials that featured a black scrubwoman. Charges of animal abuse were made against beer commercials in which a dray

horse was seen hauling a huge, old-fashioned brewery wagon. While none of these advertisements were illegal, all were objects of consumer efforts to halt their use, even to penalizing the advertisers.

22   Unfortunately, despite the efforts of many, there is still too much bias and sexism in advertising. The proper portrayal of women and minorities is still open to debate, however, and changes with the times.

23   Today it is especially important to portray women realistically, since they make so many important purchasing decisions. An area of vast change is the representation of minorities. Blacks, Hispanics, Italians, Chinese, American Indians, and others are now shown in favorable environments as a result of their upward mobility as well as organized pressure and threats of boycotts. New advertising agencies staffed with minority personnel are succeeding in reaching minority markets. Likewise, advertisers are taking special care to create advertisements that will neither offend nor alienate minority groups.

Advertising Is Deceptive

24 Perhaps the greatest attack on advertising has been and continues to be against the deceptive practices of some advertisers. This area has also received the greatest regulatory scrutiny . . .

25   Critics define deceptiveness not only as false and misleading statements but also as any false impression conveyed, whether intentional or unintentional. Advertising deception can take a number of forms, and many of these are highly controversial with no hard and fast rules. . . .

26   Advertising must have the confidence of consumers if it is to be effective. Continued deception is self-defeating because, in time, it causes consumers to turn against a product.

27   Advertising puts the advertiser on record for all who care to look. Because of greater scrutiny by consumers and the government, it is in the advertisers' own interest to avoid trouble by being honest. The company that wants to stay in business over the long term knows it can do so only with a reputation for honest dealing.

Defense of Advertising

28 Advertising professionals admit that advertising has often been used irresponsibly over the years. But they like to use the analogy of a high-powered automobile: if a drunk is at the wheel, there's going to be a lot of damage. The problem, though, is the drunk at the wheel, not the car.

29   In other words, they admit that advertising has been and sometimes still is misused. But they believe the abuse that has been heaped on advertising as a marketing tool and as a social influencer is no longer justified and is so excessive as to make all advertising appear bad. In support, they point out that of all the advertising reviewed by the Federal Trade Commission in a typical year, 97 percent is found to be satisfactory. Moreover, they say, the very critics who attack advertising's excesses use advertising techniques themselves to sell their books and further their points of view.

30   Frankly, the sins of the past still haunt advertising today. What was once an unchecked, free-swinging business activity is now a closely scrutinized and heavily regulated profession. The excesses with which advertising has been rightfully or wrongfully charged have created layer upon layer of laws, regulations, and regulatory bodies. These are used by consumer groups, government, special-interest groups, and even other advertisers to review, check, control, and change advertising.

Review Questions

1. How do defenders of advertising respond to the charge that advertising makes us too materialistic?

2. According to the authors, what are the main rebuttals to the charge that advertising manipulates us to buy things that we don't need?

3. What evidence is cited by those who charge that advertising perpetuates stereotypes?

4. What do the authors see as effective checks on deception in advertising?

Discussion and Writing Suggestions

1. Find an ad, either in the ad portfolio (pages 448–92), or in a newspaper or magazine, that might be charged with debasing our language. What specifically in this ad might provoke such a charge? To what extent could you defend the ad from the charge in the terms described by Bovée and Arens?

2. That advertising makes us more materialistic than we otherwise would be is one of the most common charges leveled against advertising. Find ads, either in the ad portfolio or in magazines or newspapers, that would lend credence to such a charge, and explain your conclusions with specific references to the text and graphics of the ad.

3. In general, to what extent do you think it is a good thing to encourage materialism—that is, to encourage people not only to buy products and services but also to encourage them to *want* to buy? What specific evidence do you find in contemporary American society of the benefits and problems of materialism?

4. Recall an advertising campaign—either print or broadcast—that seems to support the charge that "advertising manipulates people psychologically to buy things they don't need." What particular features of this advertising campaign are manipulative? To what extent do you believe that the rebuttals to such charges by the

"[a]pologists" for the advertisers (paragraph 16) effectively refute this charge? You might consider other social forces, besides advertising, that manipulate people to buy what they don't need.

5. Cite one or more examples of advertisements or advertising campaigns that you believe are in bad taste. What particular features of these ads are distasteful, and why? What evidence do you see that the distasteful campaign has either failed or been successful?

6. Select an ad, either in the ad portfolio or in a newspaper or magazine, that you believe perpetuates racial, gender, or other stereotypes. What features of the text and graphics in the ad encourage and perpetuate such stereotypes? How do you believe that such stereotyping might be considered, and perhaps even intended, by the sponsor of the ad as being necessary or desirable to help sell the product or service?

7. To what extent does the ad portfolio provide evidence of changing attitudes toward racial, gender, sexual, or other stereotyping from 1945 to the present? Discuss particular ads in developing your response.

8. Find an ad—either in the ad portfolio or in a newspaper or magazine, or on TV—that you believe to be deceptive, and explain the nature of the deception. Refer to particular features of the ad's language and/or graphics.

A Portfolio of Advertisements: 1945–2003

The following portfolio offers for your consideration and analysis a selection of forty-two full-page advertisements that appeared in American and British magazines between 1945 (shortly after the end of World War II) and 2003. In terms of products represented, the ads fall into several categories—cigarettes, alcohol (beer and liquor), automobiles, food and drink, household cleaners, lotions, and perfumes. The portfolio also includes a few miscellaneous ads for such diverse products as men's hats, telephones, and airlines. These ads originally appeared in such magazines as Time, Newsweek, U.S. News and World Report, Sports Illustrated, Ladies Home Journal, Ebony, *and* Ms. *A number of the ads were researched in the Advertising Archive, an online (and subscription) collection maintained by The Picture Desk <www.picture-desk.com>.*

The advertisements in this portfolio are not *representative of all ads that appeared during the last sixty years. We made our selection largely on the basis of how interesting, striking, provocative, and unusual these particular ads appeared to us. Admittedly, the selection process was biased. That said, the ads in this portfolio offer rich possibilities for analysis. With practice, and by applying principles for analysis that you will find in the earlier selections in this chapter, you will be able to "read" into these ads numerous messages about cultural attitudes toward gender relations, romance, smoking, and automobiles. The ads will prompt you* to consider why we buy products that we may not need or why we prefer one product over another when the two products are essentially identical. Each advertisement is a window into the culture. Through careful analysis, you will gain insights not only into the era in which the ads were produced but also into shifting cultural attitudes over the last sixty years.

Following the portfolio, we provide two or three specific questions for each ad (pages 493–502), questions designed to stimulate your thinking about the particular ways that the graphics and text are intended to work. As you review the ads, however, you may want to think about the more general questions about advertisements raised by the readings in this chapter:

1. What appears to be the target audience for the ad? If this ad was produced more than two decades ago, does its same target audience exist today? If so, how would this audience likely react today to the ad?
2. What is the primary appeal made by the ad, in terms of Fowles's categories? What, if any, are the secondary appeals?
3. What assumptions do the ad's sponsors make about such matters as (1) commonly accepted roles of women and men; (2) the relationship between the sexes; (3) the priorities of men and women?
4. What is the chief attention-getting device in the ad?
5. How does the headline and body text communicate the ad's essential appeals?
6. How do the ad's graphics communicate the ad's essential appeals?
7. How do the expressions, clothing, and postures of the models, as well as the physical objects in the illustration, help communicate the ad's message?
8. How do the graphic qualities of balance, proportion, movement, unity, clarity and simplicity, and emphasis help communicate the ad's message?

"...not a creature was stirring..."

(None, save the doctor going out on a call.)

You remember how it starts—that beloved old Christmas poem:

'Twas the night before Christmas, when all through the house Not a creature was stirring,—not even a mouse.

Well, that isn't always true for the doctor. Sometimes there's just no rest at all for him—even on Christmas Eve.

Blizzard or heat wave... December or July... night or day... near or far... early or late . . . no matter when you call, he comes!

According to a recent nationwide survey:

MORE DOCTORS SMOKE CAMELS THAN ANY OTHER CIGARETTE

YOUR "T-ZONE" WILL TELL YOU...

T for Taste...
T for Throat...

that's your proving ground for any cigarette. See if Camels don't suit your "T-Zone" to a "T."

R. J. Reynolds Tobacco Co.
Winston-Salem, N. C.

CAMEL
TURKISH & DOMESTIC BLEND CIGARETTES
CHOICE QUALITY

● Not a single branch of medicine was overlooked in this nationwide survey made by three leading independent research organizations. To 113,597 doctors from Canada to Mexico, from the Atlantic to the Pacific went the query—*What cigarette do you smoke, Doctor?*

The brand named most was Camel.

Like anyone else, a doctor smokes for pleasure. He appreciates rich, full flavor and cool mildness just as any other smoker. If you don't happen to be a Camel smoker now, try Camels. Let your "T-Zone" give you the answer.

Camels *Costlier Tobaccos*

Camels, 1947

The Christmas Gift
for Important Men

• Websters are being specially boxed and Christmas wrapped this year. Boxes of 25, as low as $3.75. Give Websters by the box. A luxurious gift to yourself and to men who are used to the best.

• There are five different sizes of Websters. Each is made of 100% long Havana, bound in top-quality Broadleaf and wrapped in finest Connecticut Shadegrown. Boxes of 25 and 50 in all sizes. Wherever fine cigars are smoked.

WEBSTER CIGARS
EXECUTIVE AMERICA'S TOP CIGAR

Golden Wedding, 15c	Chico, 15c	Queens, 18c	Fancy Tales, 25c	Directors, 35c
Box of 25—$3.75	Box of 25—$3.75	Box of 25—$4.50	Box of 25—$6.25	Box of 25—$8.75

A PRODUCT OF THE WEBSTER TOBACCO COMPANY, INC., NEW YORK

Webster Cigars, 1945

Gently Does It

GENTLENESS makes good friends in fun-making . . . and in a cigarette, where gentleness is one of the greatest requirements of modern taste. That's why today's Philip Morris, born gentle, refined to special gentleness in the making, makes so many friends among our young smokers. Enjoy the gentle pleasure, the fresh unfiltered flavor, of today's Philip Morris. In the convenient snap-open pack, regular or smart king-size.

Philip Morris

. . . gentle for modern taste

Philip Morris, 1950s

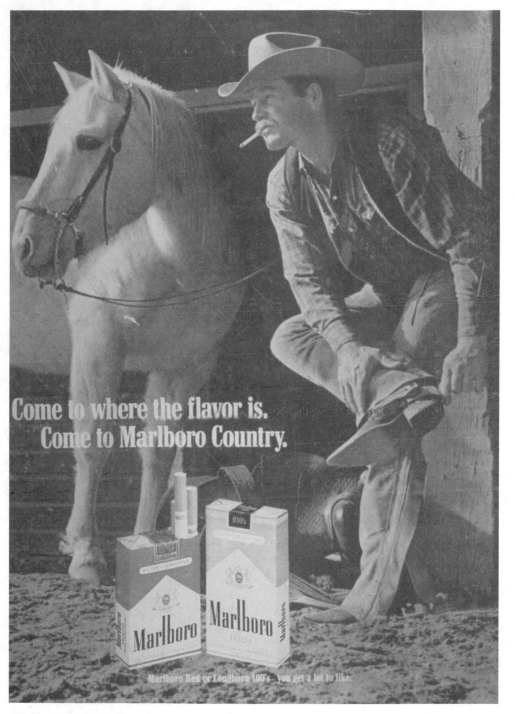

Marlboro, 1970s

Can you spot the Camel Filters smoker?

HARVE'S HEALTH FOOD HAVEN

©1972 R. J. Reynolds Tobacco Company, Winston-Salem, N. C.

In this picture everybody has a gimmick... almost everybody. Try picking the one who doesn't go along.

1. Nope. He's Lance Boyle. Gimmick: brags about wars he was never in. Yells "bombs away" as he flicks his French cigarette. **2.** Sorry. He's Harvey Dibble. His restaurant specializes in dried prunes. Gimmick: smokes wheat germ cigarettes. **3.** Eunice Trace, Starlet. Gimmick: restoring wholesomeness to movies. (Last film review: "At last, a movie the entire family can walk out on.") **4.** Smokey Stanhope, accountant. Gimmick: a guitar. Unfortunately makes the mistake of playing it. **5.** Right. He's just himself. And he sees through all the gimmicks. That's why he wants an honest, no-nonsense cigarette. Camel Filters. Easy and good tasting. Made from fine tobacco. **6.** Calls himself "Killer." Gimmick: thinks soccer uniform enhances his image. When he puffs out his chest, his pants fall down.

Camel Filters.
They're not for everybody
(but they could be for you).

CAMEL
FILTER CIGARETTES

Famous Camel Quality

20 mg. "tar;" 1.4 mg. nicotine av. per cigarette, FTC Report AUG.'72.

Camels, 1970s

Camels, 1979

More, 1980s

Camel Lights, 1992

Camels, 2000s

Pabst Blue Ribbon, 1940s

ERNEST HEMINGWAY, who has been called the greatest living American writer, is also internationally famous as a deep-sea fisherman. Since publication of *The Sun Also Rises* in 1926, his novels and short stories have enriched the literature of the English language consistently, year after year. His newest book is *The Old Man and the Sea.*

Ballantine Ale, 1953

America is returning to the genuine—in foods, fashions and tastes. Today's trend to Ballantine light Ale fits right into this modern picture. In all the world, no other beverage brewed has such extra excellence brewed into it. And "Brewer's Gold" is one big reason for Ballantine Ale's deep, rich, genuine flavor.

They all ask for ale **Ballantine** LIGHT **Ale !**

Ballantine Ale, 1950s

BACARDI. rum is so "mixable"...
It's a one-brand bar.

Big, bold highballs, sassy Daiquiris, cool tonics and colas—Bacardi rum is enjoyable always and *all* ways. Extra Special: our man Fernando is pouring very rare Bacardi Añejo rum (Ahn-YAY-ho), one of the fine rums from Bacardi. So incredibly smooth he enjoys it even in a snifter. Try it, too!

*BACARDI IMPORTS, INC., MIAMI, FLA. RUM, 80 PROOF.

Bacardi Rum, 1960s

AT THE PULITZER FOUNTAIN, N.Y.C.

In Fine Whiskey...

FLEISCHMANN'S
is the BIG buy!

The First Taste will tell you why!

Established 1870

BLENDED WHISKEY • 86 AND 90 PROOF • 65% GRAIN NEUTRAL SPIRITS
THE FLEISCHMANN DISTILLING CORPORATION, NEW YORK CITY

Fleischmann's Whiskey, 1964

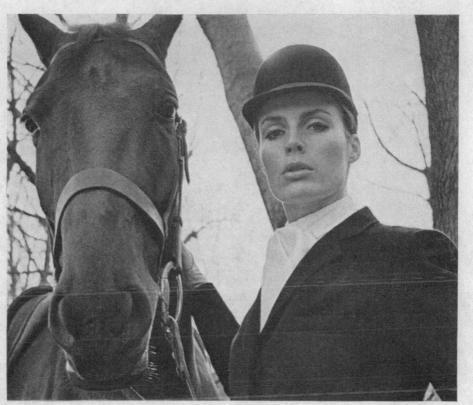

"I'll have a Hennessy Very Superior Old Pale Reserve Cognac, thank you."

The Taste of Success

Every drop of Hennessy V.S.O.P. Reserve is Grande Fine Champagne Cognac.
It's made solely from grapes grown in La Grande Champagne—the small district in
the Cognac region which is the source of the very greatest Cognac.
What's more, Hennessy is selected from the largest reserves of aged Cognacs in existence.
Enjoy a taste of success today...

Hennessy V.S.O.P. Reserve Cognac

Hennessy V.S.O.P. Grande Fine Champagne Cognac. 80 Proof. ©Schieffelin & Co., N.Y.

Hennessy Cognac, 1968

Smirnoff Vodka, 1970s

The morning after should be just as beautiful as the night before.
Pure clean Cossack Vodka.

WITH LIME, ORANGE, TOMATO JUICE, BITTER LEMON, TONIC, GINGER ALE, OR WITH ANYTHING YOU LIKE.

Cossack Vodka, 1970s

Miller Beer, 1979

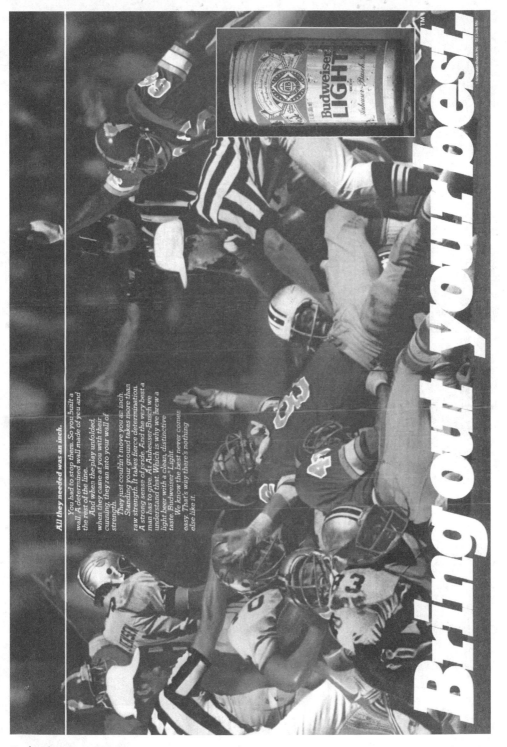

All they needed was an inch.

You had to stop them. So you built a wall. A determined wall made of you and the rest of the line.

And when the play unfolded, when they came at you with their cunning, they ran into your wall of strength.

They just couldn't move you an inch.

Standing your ground takes more than raw strength. It takes fierce determination. A strong sense of pride. At Anheuser-Busch we understand that. Which is why we brew a light beer with a clean, distinctive taste. Budweiser Light.

We know the best never comes easy. That's why there's nothing else like it.

Bring out your best.

Budweiser Beer, 1990s

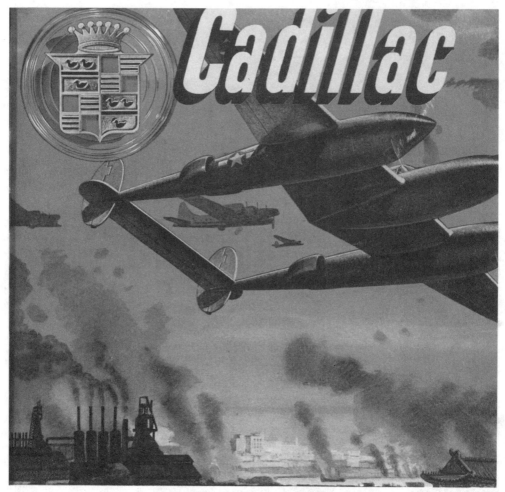

Pay-off for Pearl Harbor!

Three years ago, the sneak attack on Pearl Harbor found America unprepared to defend its rights. Yet, even at that early date, Cadillac was in its third year of building aircraft engine parts for military use. Today are look hopefully forward to the time when this important contribution to America's air power will pay off in such a scene as that illustrated above.

For more than five years we have been working toward that end. Back in 1939, we started building precision parts for Allison—America's famous liquid-cooled aircraft engine—used to power such potent fighters as the Lightning, the Warhawk, the Mustang, the Airacobra and the new Kingcobra.

In addition to our work for Allison, which has included more than 57,000,000 man-hours of precision production—we assisted Army Ordnance Engineers in designing the M-5 Light Tank and the M-8 Howitzer motor carriage, and have produced them in quantities. Both are powered by Cadillac engin equipped with Hydra-Matic transmission

We are now building other weapons whi utilize some of our Cadillac peacetime pr ucts. We can't talk about all of them yet—b we are confident they will prove significa additions to Allied armor.

Every Sunday Afternoon . . . GENERAL MOTORS SYMPHONY OF THE AIR—NBC Network

CADILLAC MOTOR CAR DIVISION   GENERAL MOTORS CORPORATION

LET'S ALL
BACK THE ATTACK
BUY WAR BONDS

Cadillac, 1945

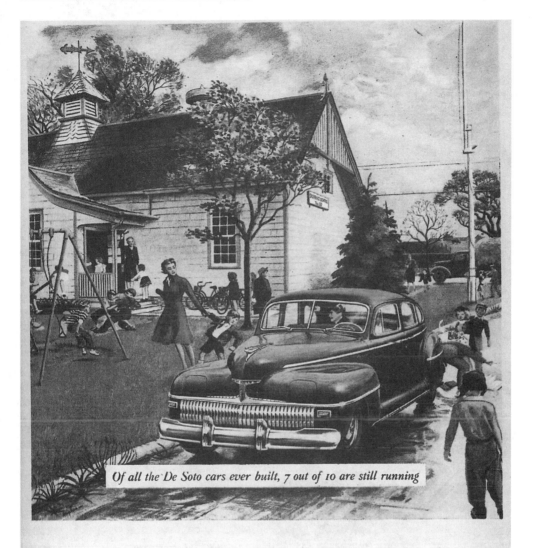

Of all the De Soto cars ever built, 7 out of 10 are still running

8 out of 10 owners say, "De Soto is the most satisfactory car I ever owned"*

*FROM A MAIL SURVEY AMONG THOUSANDS OF OWNERS
OF 1941 AND 1942 DE SOTO CARS

DE SOTO DIVISION OF CHRYSLER CORPORATION

DeSoto

DESIGNED TO ENDURE

De Soto, 1947

Worth Its Price

If a motorist wanted to make the move to Cadillac solely for the car's prestige—he would most certainly be justified in doing so. For the Cadillac car has never stood so high in public esteem as it does today—and the rewards which grow out of this unprecedented acceptance comprise the rarest and greatest satisfactions in all motordom.

There is, for instance, *the inescapable feeling of pride* that comes with ownership of so distinguished and beloved a possession . . . the wonderful *sense of well-being* that comes from having reached a point of achievement where you can enjoy one of the world's most sought-after manufactured products . . . and the *marvelous feeling of confidence and self-esteem* that is found

CADILLAC   MOTOR   CAR   DIVISION

Cadillac, 1954

in PRESTIGE !

in the respect and admiration universally accorded the owner of a Cadillac car. Those who presently enjoy these unique Cadillac virtues will tell you that they are, in themselves, worth the car's whole purchase price.

Of course, most motorists would hesitate to take such a step purely for their personal edification. But in Cadillac's case, this wonderful prestige is actually a "bonus", so to speak—an extra dividend that comes with every Cadillac car, in addition to its breath-taking styling, its magnificent performance, its superlative luxury and its remarkable economy.

Have you seen and driven the 1954 Cadillac? If you haven't, then you've a truly wonderful adventure awaiting you—and one that you should postpone no longer.

GENERAL MOTORS CORPORATION

"Ford's out Front from a Woman's Angle"

1. **"I don't know** synthetic enamel from a box of my children's paints... but if synthetic enamel is what it takes to make that beautiful, shiny Ford finish, I'm all for it!

2. **"My husband says** the brakes are self-centering and hydraulic—whatever that means! All I know is they're so easy that I can taxi the children all day without tiring out!

3. **"Peter, he's my teen-age son,** tells me that 'Ford is the only car in its price class with a choice of a 100-horsepower V-8 engine or a brilliant new Six.' He says no matter which engine people pick, they're out front with Ford!

4. **"The interior** of our Ford is strictly my department! It's tailored with the dreamiest broadcloth. Such a perfect fit! Mary Jane says women help design Ford interiors. There's certainly a woman's touch there!

5. **"Do you like** lovely silver, beautifully simple and chaste looking? That's what I always think of when I touch those smart Ford door handles and window openers.

6. **"Now here's another thing** women like and that's a blissfully comfortable ride—one that isn't bumpity-bump even on some of our completely forgotten roads."

Listen to the Ford Show starring Dinah Shore on Columbia Network Stations Wednesday Evenings.

There's a **Ford** in your future

Ford, 1947

This is your reward for the great Dodge advance—the daring new, dramatic new '56 Dodge.

The Magic Touch of Tomorrow!

The *look* of success! The *feel* of success! The *power* of success!
They come to you in a dramatically beautiful, dynamically powered new Dodge that introduces the ease and safety of push-button driving –the Magic Touch of Tomorrow! It is a truly great value.

New '56 DODGE

Dodge, 1955

Drive a Riviera home tonight. Who cares if people
think you're younger, richer and more romantic than you really are?

A Riviera has a strange effect on people. Simply looking at one makes your mouth water, your eyes
open wider and your heart beat faster. You grin admiringly when you notice the headlights, tucked
behind shields that open with the touch of the headlight switch. You breathe harder when you
turn loose some of those 325 horsepower. And that's just what happens to the driver. Wait till you see the
awe a Riviera inspires in passersby! Amazing. Also attainable, for considerably less than
you might suspect. (Before you fall headlong for a Riviera, ask yourself if a firmer suspension and
assorted other sporting touches give you a twinge of anticipation. Yes? Ask your dealer about
our new Riviera Gran Sport. The name alone is a hint of what's in it for you.) Check with your Buick dealer
soon. He may convince you you're younger, richer and more romantic than you thought you were.

Wouldn't you really rather have a Buick?

Buick, 1965

Corvette Sting Ray Sport Coupe with eight standard safety features, including outside rearview mirror. Use it always before passing.

The day she flew the coupe

What manner of woman is this, you ask, who stands in the midst of a mountain stream eating a peach?

Actually she's a normal everyday girl except that she and her husband own the Corvette Coupe in the background. (He's at work right now, wondering where he misplaced his car keys.)

The temptation, you see, was over-powering. They'd had the car a whole week now, and not once had he offered to let her drive. His excuse was that this, uh, was a big hairy sports car. Too much for a woman to handle: the trigger-quick steering, the independent rear suspension, the disc brakes—plus the 4-speed transmission and that 425-hp engine they had ordered—egad! He would

teach her to drive it some weekend. So he said.

That's why she hid the keys, forcing him to seek public transportation. Sure of his departure, she went to the garage, started the Corvette, and was off for the hills, soon upshifting and downshifting as smoothly as he. His car. Hard to drive. What propaganda!

'66 CORVETTE BY CHEVROLET
Chevrolet Division of General Motors, Detroit, Michigan

Corvette, 1966

The Turbo engine with the Family Pack.   The Diesel engine with

VOLVO GIVE THEIR BLESSING

When it comes to marriages Volvo like to put on a big spread.

That's why, with the 400 series, we're giving you a wider choice than any other manufacturer. You can pick a bigger engine with standard specification or a smaller engine with the luxury package.

In fact, with a total of five different engine sizes and six different interior packages on offer, you can mix and match as much as you like.

You could for instance, unite the 1.6 engine with the Luxury Pack, which features air-conditioning and leather upholstery.

With other manufacturers however, you don't get such a happy coupling. You'll find that the luxury package for example, only comes with the larger engine.

THE VOLVO 400 SERIES FROM £11,375 (1.6) EXCLUDING SUNROOF) TO £16,025 (TURBO SE INCLUDING SUNROOF). PRICE INCLUDES DELIVERY CHARGE OF £419, BUT EXCLUDES 6 MONTHS

Volvo, 1990s

the Business Pack.

The 1.6 engine with the Leather Interior.

TO ALL SORTS OF MARRIAGES.

Volvo's approach (which applies to the 440 hatchback and 460 saloon) means you not only get the car that suits your exact needs, but you decide exactly where your money goes.

And you don't have to wait any longer for

delivery of your specially built car. For information pack call 0800 400 430.

The Volvo 400 series. From £11,175 (w ribbons not included).

THE VOLVO 400 SERIES. A CAR YOU CAN BELIEV

ROAD FUND LICENCE £74.20. ALL PRICES AND PRODUCT INFORMATION CORRECT AT TIME OF GOING TO PRESS. *EXCLUDING TURBO DIESEL AND LUXURY PACK COMBINATION.

Jeep vehicle, 2003

Good School Day Lunches

make healthier, brighter youngsters

Many children do not get adequate lunches! And yet upon proper food depends not only their future health, but today's well-being, cheerfulness—and even report cards!

Lunch should include a hot dish, and be substantial but easy to digest. Good nourishing soup is a big help—and Campbell's Vegetable Soup is just right! Children love it, and it brings them all the sturdy goodness of 15 different garden vegetables combined with a rich, invigorating beef stock. No wonder mothers everywhere agree "It's almost a meal in itself!"

Campbell's VEGETABLE SOUP

OK FOR THE RED-AND-WHITE LABEL

A WEEK'S SCHOOL LUNCHES

MONDAY
Campbell's Vegetable Soup
Peanut Butter Sandwich
Baked Custard   Celery
Orange   Graham Crackers

TUESDAY
Campbell's Tomato Soup
Cottage Cheese and Orange Marmalade Sandwich
Carrot Sticks
Banana   Molasses Cookies

WEDNESDAY
Campbell's Scotch Broth
Lettuce and Hard-Cooked Egg Salad
Toasted Raisin Bread
Fresh Pear   Cocoa

THURSDAY
Campbell's Vegetable Soup
Cold Roast Veal Sandwich
Baked Apple   Celery
          Milk

FRIDAY
Campbell's Cream of Spinach Soup
Toasted Tuna Fish Salad Sandwich
Sliced Tomatoes
Stewed Peaches   Chocolate Milk

Campbell's, 1945

Coca-Cola, 1945

What's for dinner, Duchess?

Prediction: The new wives of 1947 are going to have more fun in the kitchen.

Previous cooking experience is desirable, perhaps, but not essential. There are so many new easy-to-use foods, so many new ways to prepare foods, so many interesting ways to serve foods, cooking will be a novel and exciting adventure.

Further prediction: Cheese dishes will be featured more often on their menus. They'll know that cheese gives tastiness and variety to meals. And cheese, like milk (nature's most nearly perfect food), is rich in protein, calcium, phosphorus, in vitamins A and G.

Yes, we have a personal interest in cheese. For Kraft, pioneer in cheese, is a unit of National Dairy. And what we've said about housewives using more cheese is entirely true.

It's also true that they're learning more about the whys and wherefores of food each year — just as the scientists in our laboratories are learning more about better ways to process, improve and supply it.

These men are backed by the resources of a great organization. They explore every field of dairy products, discover new ones. And the health of America benefits constantly by this National Dairy research.

Dedicated to the wider use and better understanding of dairy products as human food . . . as a base for the development of new products and materials . . . as a source of health and enduring progress on the farms and in the towns and cities of America.

NATIONAL DAIRY
PRODUCTS CORPORATION
AND AFFILIATED COMPANIES

National Dairy Products Corporation, 1947

MAY: # Heavens, Ann —
wish I could clean up quick as that!

ANN: You could, hon! Just use a cleanser that doesn't leave dirt-catching scratches.

MAY: Goodness! What in the world do scratches have to do with it?

ANN: A lot, silly! Those tiny scratches you get from gritty cleansers hold onto dirt and double your cleaning time.

MAY: Well, you old smartie! I'd never thought of *that* before.

ANN: I hadn't thought of it either—till I discovered Bon Ami! See how fine-textured and white it is. It just *slides* dirt off—and when you rinse it away, it doesn't leave any of that horrid grit in the tub.

MAY: Say no more, darling! From now on there's going to be a new cleaning team in our house—me and Bon Ami!

EASY ON YOUR HANDS, Bon Ami *Powder* is the ideal cleanser for kitchen sinks, as well as bathtubs. Also try Bon Ami *Cake* for cleaner windows, mirrors and windshields.

THE **SPEEDY** CLEANSER *that*
"hasn't scratched yet!"

Bon Ami, 1947

This is the story of Annie...

NOW ANNIE WAS...

AS BEAUTIFUL A GIRL...

AS EVER WAS PUT TOGETHER!

WHY, WHEN ANNIE WALKED DOWN THE STREET...

WOW!

YET ANNIE HAD HER BAD MOMENTS...LIKE ANY OTHER GAL.

AND YOU WANT TO KNOW WHY? ANNIE'S HANDS WERE A MESS. ALWAYS ROUGH AND DRY, LIKE SANDPAPER.

AND WHEN A MAN WANTS TO HOLD A GIRL'S HANDS... EVEN A GIRL LIKE ANNIE ...HE DOESN'T WANT TO WEAR GLOVES...

THEN, LUCKILY, FANNIE TOLD ANNIE ABOUT AN ENTIRELY NEW AND DIFFERENT HAND LOTION! THE **BEFOREHAND** LOTION...TRUSHAY!

SO ANNIE SMOOTHED CREAMY, FRAGRANT **TRUSHAY** ON HER HANDS <u>BEFORE</u> SHE DID DISHES...BECAUSE **TRUSHAY** GUARDS HANDS <u>EVEN</u> IN HOT, SOAPY WATER!

AND ANNIE PUT **TRUSHAY** ON HER HANDS <u>BEFORE</u> SHE TUBBED HER UNDIES...SO **TRUSHAY'S** SPECIAL "OIL-RICHNESS" COULD HELP PREVENT DRYNESS AND ROUGHNESS.

SO NOW ANNIE IS ABLE TO KEEP HER HANDS SOFT AND SMOOTH AND HOLDABLE... THANKS TO **TRUSHAY'S** WONDERFUL SOFTENING HELP.

TRUSHAY

The "Beforehand" Lotion

PRODUCT OF BRISTOL-MYERS

P. S. Trushay's grand for softening hands at *any* time. Wonderful, too, for rough, dry elbows and heels...before a powder base...before and after exposure to weather. Trushay contains no alcohol, is not sticky. Begin today to use Trushay.

Trushay, 1947

Mrs. Dorian Mehle of Morrisville, Pa., is all three: a housewife, a mother, and a very lovely lady.

"I wash 22,000 dishes a year... but I'm proud of my pretty hands!"

You and Dorian Mehle have something in common. Every year, you wash a stack of dishes a quarter-mile high!

Detergents make your job so much easier. They cut right into grease and grime. They get you through dishwashing in much less time, but while they dissolve grease, they also take away the natural oils and youthful softness of your hands!

Although Dorian hasn't given up detergents her hands are as soft, as smooth, as young-looking as a teenager's. Her secret is no secret at all. It's the world's best-known beauty routine. It's pure, white Jergens Lotion, after every chore.

When you smooth on Jergens Lotion, this liquid formula doesn't just "coat" your hands. It penetrates right away, to help *replace* that softening moisture your skin needs.

Jergens Lotion has two ingredients doctors recommend for softening. Women must be recommending it, too, for more women use it than any other hand care in the world. Dorian's husband is the best testimonial to Jergens Lotion care. Even after years of married life, he still loves to hold her pretty hands!

Use Jergens Lotion like a prescription: three times a day, after every meal!

Now—lotion dispenser FREE of extra cost with $1.00 size. Supply limited.

Use JERGENS LOTION – avoid detergent hands

Jergens Lotion, 1954

President Lee A. Potter Jr., *of the Young Presidents Organization Inc. and Forman, Ford & Co. "To be successful, look the part. That certain look of success attracts the confidence of important men."*

A man's hat speaks eloquently of his personal measure of authority. That's why Disney hats are so often considered part of a businessman's equipment. The rare skill of their handcraftsmanship, the executive character of their styling reflect the critical judgment and taste of the wearer.* Disney's uniquely impressive effect has made these hats the choice of prominent men for 65 years.

*Case in point, THE DISNEY CAPELLO. This marvelously light hat, styled with flattering tapered crown and narrow brim, is fashion at its finest. At fine stores, $20. Many other Disney hats from $10 to $40.
Free! Handsome booklet containing helpful hints by American business leaders. Ask your Disney dealer for "Guide Quotes to Success."

Disney

The Hat of Presidents

Disney Hats, 1954

Madam! Suppose you traded jobs with your husband?

You can just bet the first thing he'd ask for would be a telephone in the kitchen.

You wouldn't catch him dashing to another room every time the telephone rang, or he had to make a call.

He doesn't have to do it in his office in town. It would be mighty helpful if you didn't have to do it in your "office" at home.

That's in the kitchen where you do so much of your work. And it's right there that an additional telephone comes in so handy for so many things.

Along with a lot of convenience is that nice feeling of pride in having the best of everything—especially if it is one of those attractive new telephones in color.

 P.S. *Additional telephones in kitchen, bedroom and other convenient places around the house cost little. The service charge is just pennies a day.*

Bell Telephone System

Bell Telephone, 1956

The phone company wants more installers like Alana MacFarlane.

Alana MacFarlane is a 20-year-old from San Rafael, California. She's one of our first women telephone installers. She won't be the last.

We also have several hundred male telephone operators. And a policy that there are no all-male or all-female jobs at the phone company.

We want the men and women of the telephone company to do what they want to do, and do best.

For example, Alana likes working outdoors. "I don't go for office routine," she said. "But as an installer, I get plenty of variety and a chance to move around."

Some people like to work with their hands, or, like Alana, get a kick out of working 20 feet up in the air.

Others like to drive trucks. Some we're helping to develop into good managers.

Today, when openings exist, local Bell Companies are offering applicants and present employees some jobs they may never have thought about before. We want to help all advance to the best of their abilities.

AT&T and your local Bell Company are equal opportunity employers.

Bell Telephone, 1974

Think of her as your mother.

She only wants what's best for you.
A cool drink. A good dinner. A soft pillow and a warm blanket.
This is not just maternal instinct. It's the result of the longest
Stewardess training in the industry.
Training in service, not just a beauty course.
Service, after all, is what makes professional travelers prefer American.
And makes new travelers want to keep on flying with us.
So we see that every passenger gets the same professional treatment.
That's the American Way.

Fly the American Way
American Airlines.

American Airlines, 1968

Charlie, 1988

Shineaway 17 Lotion, 1980s

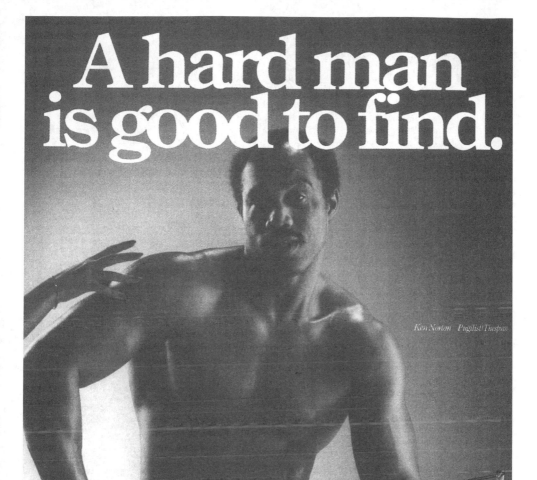

A hard man is good to find.

Ken Norton Pugilist/Thespian

To unlock your body's potential, we proudly offer Soloflex. Twenty-four old-fashioned iron pumping exercises, each correct in form and balance. All on a simple machine that fits in a corner of your home.

For a free Soloflex brochure, call anytime **1-800-453-9000.** In Canada, **1-800-543-1005.**

SOLOFLEX®
Weightlifting, Pure and Simple.

VHS Video Brochure™ available upon request. © 1985, Soloflex, Inc. Hillsboro, Oregon 97124

Soloflex, 1985

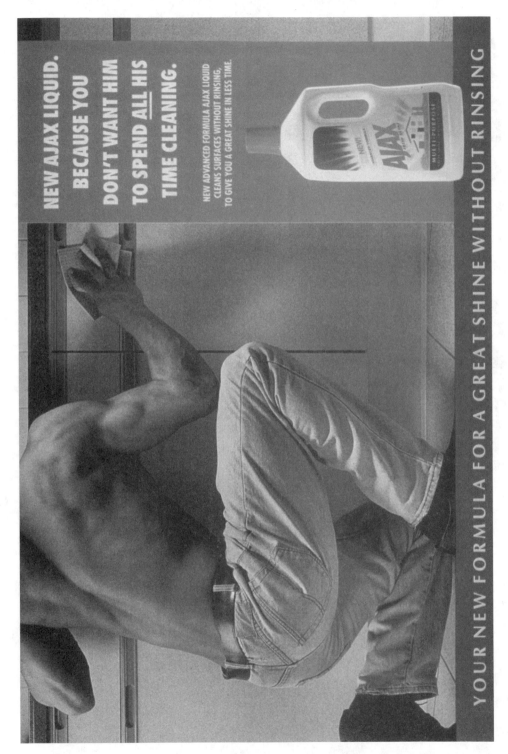

Ajax, 1990s

Discussion and Writing Suggestions

TOBACCO

Camels, 1947 (p. 448)

1. How does the intended appeal of this ad differ most dramatically from a comparable ad today?

2. What kind of psychological appeals are made by the picture in the top half of this ad and the text accompanying it? How does the image of a doctor out on a night call tie in, for selling purposes, with the ad's headline?

Webster Cigars, 1945 (p. 449)

1. How does the dress and general appearance of the people in the ad, as well as the setting depicted, communicate meaning, particularly as it applies to the appeal of the product?

2. To whom is this advertisement addressed? Cite headline and body text, as well as graphics, that support your response. What kind of ads today are addressed to a similar audience?

Philip Morris, 1950s (p. 450)

1. How do the placement, posture, and dress of the models in the ad help create its essential psychological appeal? Why do you suppose (in relation to the selling of cigarettes) the models' eyes are closed?

2. Discuss some of the messages communicated both by the graphic and the text of this ad. Focus in particular on the quality of "gentleness" emphasized in the ad.

Marlboro, 1970s (p. 451)

1. The Marlboro Man has become one of the most famous—and successful—icons of American advertising. What elements of the Marlboro Man (and his setting, Marlboro Country) do you notice, and what role do these elements play in the appeal being made by this ad?

2. This ad appeared during the 1970s. (The popularity of the Marlboro Man extended into the 1980s, however.) To what extent do you think it would have the same appeal today?

3. Comment on the elements of graphic design (balance, proportion, movement, unity, clarity and simplicity, emphasis) that help make this ad effective. Focus particularly on the element of movement.

Camel Filters, 1970s (p. 452)

1. How do the contrasts in appearance (including posture and facial expressions) between the Camel Filters smoker and the others in the graphic support the essential appeal made by this ad?

2. How does the body text—particularly the thumbnail descriptions of each of the five candidates for Camels Filters smoker—reinforce the ad's intended meaning?

Camels, 1979 (p. 453)

1. What do the relative positions and postures of the man and the woman in the ad indicate about the ad's basic appeal?
2. What roles do the props—particularly, the motorcycle and the models' outfits—and the setting play in helping to sell the product?
3. How do the design elements in the ad emphasize the product?
4. Compare the graphic elements of this ad to those of the Fleischmann's Whiskey ad (page 462).

More, 1980s (p. 454)

1. What qualities are conveyed by the couple depicted in the ad? Focus on their dress, posture, and facial expressions. How do these qualities contribute to the appeal of the product?
2. Compare and contrast the effect of this ad with earlier ads depicted for this product (Webster Cigars, Philip Morris) that also show two or more people enjoying tobacco products.
3. Comment on the effectiveness of the graphic elements of this advertisement.

Camel Lights, 1992 (p. 455)

1. During the early 1990s, Joe Camel (depicted here, shooting pool) became one of the most popular and recognized icons of contemporary marketing. The cartoon figure appeared not only on billboards and magazine ads, but also on T-shirts and baseball caps. Joe Camel's appeal, particularly to teenagers, was deemed so pernicious that a group of state attorneys general joined forces in 1997 to force R. J. Reynolds, manufacturer of Camels, to retire the offending dromedary. (The Marlboro Man was targeted in the same settlement, though one of the first models for the Marlboro Man had already died—of lung cancer.) Based on this advertisement, what appears to be the essential elements of Joe Camel's appeal?
2. Contrast this ad with the earlier Camels ad (the man on the motorcycle), as well as the earlier ads for tobacco products, such as Webster's, Philip Morris, and Marlboro. How does the appearance of Joe Camel indicate a major shift of cultural attitudes?

Camels, 2000s (p. 456)

1. This is an example of retro appeal. What elements make it so? What elements mark the ad, on the other hand, as a contemporary one?

How does the combination of retro and contemporary elements (including, for example, the posture and attitude of the model) contribute to create a particular type of appeal?

2. Compare and contrast the three Camels ads presented in this section of the portfolio. Focus on the psychological appeals, the cultural values implied in the ads, and the graphic and textual means used to persuade the buyer to smoke Camels.

BEER AND LIQUOR

Pabst Blue Ribbon, 1940s (p. 457)

1. Ads in the 1940s often took comic-book form. (See also the 1947 Trushay ad later in this portfolio, page 483.) To what kind of audience is this format most likely to appeal? What are some of the advantages and disadvantages of the comic-book format?

2. The problem/solution structure of the narrative in this ad is one of the oldest and still most frequently employed (particularly in TV commercials) in marketing. To what extent does it seem appropriate for the selling of beer? To what extent is it appropriate for other products and services? (Cite examples from contemporary or recent ads.)

3. To what extent do you find examples of outdated social attitudes in this ad?

Ballantine Ale, 1953 (pp. 458–59)

1. You may be surprised to find Ernest Hemingway selling ale. To what extent do you find celebrity endorsements an effective method of marketing? Why do you think that the creators of this ad might have believed that Hemingway (as opposed, say, to a professional athlete) might be an effective promoter of (or is qualified to address the need for guidance on) Ballantine Ale?

2. Comment on the apparent strategy behind the graphic and textual elements in this ad—particularly, the setting, Hemingway's posture, and his letter.

3. If you are familiar with any of Hemingway's stories or novels, do you notice any similarity of style or subject matter between what you have previously read and Hemingway's testimonial letter to Ballantine Ale?

Ballantine Ale, 1950s (p. 460)

1. This illustration, reminiscent of some of Norman Rockwell's paintings, is typical of many beer and ale ads in the 1950s, which depict a group of well-dressed young adults enjoying their brew at a social event. Comment on the distinctive graphic elements in this ad and speculate as to why these elements are seldom employed in

contemporary advertisements for beer and ale. Why, in other words, does this ad seem old-fashioned?

2. Contrast the appeal and graphics of this ad with the ads for Miller and Budweiser later in this portfolio.Contrast the appeal and graphics of this ad with the ads for Miller and Budweiser later in this portfolio.

3. Identify the adjectives in the body text and attempt to correlate them to the graphic in helping to construct the message of the ad.

Bacardi Rum, 1960s (p. 461)

1. What meaning is conveyed by the placement, posture, and expressions of the four models in this ad? How do you think this meaning is intended to help sell the product? (Does the picture remind you of a particular movie hero?)

2. Comment on the significance of the props in the photo.

3. How does the text ("Big, bold highballs, sassy Daiquiris, cool tonics . . . ") help reinforce the meaning created by the picture?

Fleischmann's Whiskey, 1964 (p. 462)

1. Comment on (1) the significance of the extra-large bottle of whiskey; (2) the stances of the two models in the ad; (3) the way the headline contributes to the ad's meaning.

2. Compare and contrast the graphic in this ad with that of the 1979 Camels ad earlier in this portfolio (the man on the motorcycle).

Hennessy Cognac, 1968 (p. 463)

1. What is the primary appeal of this ad? How do the woman, the horse, and the headline work to create and reinforce this appeal?

2. Compare and contrast this ad to the Webster Cigar ad in terms of their appeal and their graphics.

Smirnoff Vodka, 1970s (p. 464)

1. What meaning is conveyed by the two figures in this ad? How do the models' postures and the props help reinforce this meaning?

2. How do you interpret the headline? How does the headline—and the sub-headline ("You drink it for what it is")—tie in to the meaning created by the photo?

Cossack Vodka, 1970s (p. 465)

1. What is the essential appeal behind this ad?

2. The comic-book style of the drawing is reminiscent of the work of Roy Lichtenstein (1923–1997), an American painter who drew inspiration from advertisements and romance magazines, as well as

comic books, to depict and parody artifacts of pop culture. What is the effect of this particular style on creating—and perhaps commenting upon—the message in the text balloon and in the ad in which it appears?

3. How does the text at the bottom of the idea reinforce the message created by the graphic? In particular, how is this message intended to sell the product?

Miller Beer, 1979 (p. 466)

1. To what extent does this 1979 ad embody marketing techniques for beer that are still employed today?

2. Comment on the posture and expressions of the three models depicted in the ad. How do these elements help create the ad's essential appeal?

3. Compare and contrast this ad with the 1950s Ballantine Ale ad earlier in this portfolio (page 460).

Budweiser Beer, 1990s (p. 467)

1. To what extent is this ad based on a similar appeal as the preceding Miller ad? To what extent is it based on other appeals?

2. What's the advantage (in terms of effectiveness of appeal) of using the second person—"you"—in the body text? How does the text attempt to make the connection between the product advertised and the activities of the football players? To what extent do you think that this is an effective ad?

3. Comment on the workings and effectiveness of the graphic design elements in this ad.

AUTOMOBILES

Cadillac, 1945 (p. 468)

1. What is the essential strategy behind portraying a group of military aircraft on a bombing raid in an automobile ad? What, exactly, is this ad selling?

2. Explain how the graphic elements of this ad—and the interplay between the elements of the graphic and the text (headline and body text)—reinforce the ad's basic appeal.

De Soto, 1947 (p. 469)

1. How does the scene portrayed in the illustration help create the basic appeal of this ad? Focus on as many significant individual elements of the illustration as you can.

2. To what extent does the caption (in the illustration) and the headline support the message communicated by the graphic?

3. Explain why both this ad and the preceding Cadillac ad are products of their particular times.

Cadillac, 1954 (pp. 470–71)

1. What is the particular marketing strategy behind this ad? Based on the ad's text, compose a memo from the head of marketing to the chief copywriter proposing this particular ad and focusing on the strategy. The memo doesn't have to be cynical or to insult the prospective Cadillac buyers; it should just be straightforward and direct.

2. How do the ad's graphics reinforce the message in the text?

Ford, 1947 (p. 472)

1. Cite and discuss those textual elements in the ad that reflect a traditional conception of the American woman.

2. How do the visual elements of the ad reinforce the assumptions about traditional gender roles reflected in the ad?

Dodge, 1955 (p. 473)

1. Discuss the multiple appeals of this ad. How are these appeals reflected in the ad's text and graphics? For instance, discuss the angle from which the automobile is photographed.

2. Both this ad and the 1947 Ford ad (page 472) feature one or more women in the graphic. Compare and contrast the use of women in the two ads.

Buick, 1965 (p. 474)

1. Compare and contrast the appeal made in this ad to the appeal made in either the 1947 Ford ad (page 472) or the 1954 Cadillac ad (pages 470–71). Cite particular aspects of the text and graphics to support your comparison.

2. The text of the ad discusses two categories of the "people" mentioned in the first sentence. Discuss how the ad makes different, if related, appeals to these two categories of "people."

3. Discuss, in terms of their overall effect, the placement of the automobile and the woman in the ad, as well as the perspective from which both are viewed.

Corvette, 1966 (p. 475)

1. How do the graphic elements reinforce the message developed in the text of this ad?

2. Comment on the dress and the posture of the model, as these relate to the ad's essential appeal. What's the significance of the woman eating a peach in a mountain stream?

3. The body text in this ad tells a story. What kind of husband-wife dynamic is implied by this story? To what extent do you find similarities between the implied gender roles in this ad and those in the 1947 Ford ad ("Ford's out Front from a Woman's Angle," page 472)? To what extent do you find differences, ones that may be attributable to the twenty years between the two ads?

Volvo, 1990s (pp. 476–77)

1. What cultural phenomenon is being addressed in the graphic and the headline of this ad? To what extent do you believe that associating Volvo with this phenomenon is an effective way to market this particular automobile?

2. What is the connection between the three apparently ill-matched couples in the illustration and the ad's basic message and appeal?

3. How is humor used to enhance the ad's (and the message's) appeal? That is, how are the couples in the illustration presented as incongruous (if happy)?

Jeep vehicle, 2003 (p. 478)

1. Explain the meaning of the ad's headline.

2. Discuss the graphic, in terms of the ad's headline. Consider the significance of the viewing angle.

FOOD, CLEANSERS, BEAUTY PRODUCTS, AND OTHER

Campbell's, 1945 (p. 479)

1. What kind of appeal is being made in the first two sentences of the body text? How does the graphic in the top half of the ad support this appeal?

2. What kind of marketing strategy is behind the menu in the lower right portion of the ad?

Coca-Cola, 1945 (p. 480)

1. This ad appeared shortly after the conclusion of World War II. How do the text and the graphics of the ad take advantage of the international mood at the time? Comment on the appearance and arrangement of the men portrayed in the ad.

2. Compare the strategy of this Coca-Cola ad (text and graphics) with that of the 1950s Ballantine ad (page 460).

National Dairy Products Corporation, 1947 (p. 481)

1. How does the couple pictured in the ad illustrate gender expectations of the period? Comment on the dress, postures, and expressions of the models.

2. What, exactly is this ad *selling*? (It is presented more as a news-magazine article than as a conventional advertisement.) How is the appeal tied to contemporary developments by "scientists" and their "research," particularly as these relate to "the new wives of 1947"?

3. What does the text of this ad imply about the situation of young married couples in postwar households?

Bon Ami, 1947 (p. 482)

1. How do the text and graphics of this ad illustrate a bygone cultural attitude toward gender roles? Notice, in particular, the dress, postures, and expressions of the women pictured, as well as the style of the illustration. Focus also on the wording of the text.

2. In terms of Jib Fowles's categories, what kind of appeal is being made by the Bon Ami ad?

Trushay, 1947 (p. 483)

1. Retell the "story of Annie" in narrative form, in a paragraph. What does Annie's story tell us about gender relations in the 1940s? To what extent have gender relations changed on the particular issue covered by Annie's story?

2. Ads that resembled comic strips were not uncommon sixty years ago. Based on the impact made by this ad today, why do you think the comic strip format might have gone out of fashion?

3. Suppose you were a contemporary copywriter for a hand lotion product. Develop some ideas for an ad or a campaign that might be effective for today's potential customers.

Jergens Lotion, 1954 (p. 484)

1. Compare and contrast the appeals and the strategies of this Jergens Lotion ad and the Trushay ad preceding it. Are the ads intended to appeal to the same target audiences? To what extent are the psychological appeals of the two ads similar? Compare the illustrations of the two ads. How do they differ in basic strategy?

2. The model in the Jergens Lotion ad is immaculately dressed and groomed, and she is sitting among stacks of fine china (as opposed to everyday dishware). What do you think is the marketing strategy behind these graphic choices?

Disney Hats, 1954 (p. 485)

1. Point out specific language in the headline and body that helps create the basic appeal of this ad for Disney hats. How does the illustration—both the man in the hat and the background against which he is posed—reinforce this appeal?

2. Comment on how the connotations and significance of men's head-wear have changed—and not changed—over the years or how they help support the appeal of the product advertised. (Notice, for example, the hat-wearing models in the 1947 Camels ad, the 1954 Cadillac ad, the 1983 Marlboro ad, and the 1990s Camels ad.

Bell Telephone, 1956 (p. 486)

1. Discuss the attitude toward gender roles implicit in the 1956 Bell ad. How do the graphics, the headline, and the body text, reinforce this attitude? What is the significance of the quotation marks around "office" in the final sentence of the third paragraph?

2. Notice that the woman at the desk seems a lot more comfortable and at ease than the man holding the crying baby and the dishes. What does this fact tell us about the attitudes toward gender roles of those who created this ad?

Bell Telephone, 1974 (p. 487)

1. Compare and contrast the 1956 Bell ad with the 1974 Bell ad, in terms of their attitudes toward gender roles. How do the text and graphics reinforce the essential differences?

2. The 1956 Bell ad pictures a woman at a desk (a white-collar job); the 1974 ad pictures a woman working at a telephone pole (a blue-collar job). Would the 1974 ad have the same impact if "Alana MacFarlane" had, like her 1956 counterpart, been pictured at a desk?

3. Like the 1945 Cadillac ad (page 468) the 1974 Bell ad seems more of a public service announcement than a conventional advertisement. Compare and contrast these ads in terms of their messages to readers.

American Airlines, 1968 (p. 488)

1. Discuss the mixed messages (in terms of appeal) being transmitted by the American Airlines ad. To what extent do you think the apparently conflicting appeals make for an effective ad?

2. Comment on the dress, pose, and expression of the model in the ad, which appeared in *Ebony* magazine. How do these create a different impact than would an illustration, say, of a flight attendant serving a drink or giving a pillow to an airline passenger?

Charlie, 1988 (p. 489)

1. Notice the woman's outfit, as well as her briefcase, in the Charlie ad. How is appearance of this woman as significant as the appearance of the woman in the Smirnoff Vodka ad (page 464) for the ad's basic message?

2. The Charlie ad and the Bell 1974 ad (page 487) are as different as can be imagined from the Trushay ad. Yet, the Bell and the Charlie ads make quite different appeals. Explain. Consider, for example, how a woman—or a man—of the late 1940s might respond to the Bell ad, on the one hand, and the Charlie ad, on the other.

Shineaway 17 Lotion, 1980s (p. 490)

1. Account for the postures of the man and the woman, in terms of the essential message and appeal of this ad.

2. Both this and the preceding Charlie ad rely to some extent on sex appeal. Compare and contrast other aspects of these two ads.

Soloflex, 1985 (p. 491)

1. How does the illustration in this ad reinforce the basic appeal of the headline?

2. Ads are frequently criticized for the incongruity between illustration and product being advertised—for example, a scantily clad woman posed provocatively in front of a pickup truck. To what extent does the Soloflex ad present an appropriate fit between graphic and product advertised?

Ajax, 1990s (p. 492)

1. Why do you suppose the model's head is not pictured?

2. How does this ad play off shifting cultural attitudes toward gender roles? Would the ad be more objectionable if it pictured a female in a comparable state of undress?

3. Compare and contrast this ad to earlier ads for cleaners and cleansing lotions, such as Bon Ami and Jergens Lotion.

SYNTHESIS ACTIVITIES

1. Select one *category* of advertisements (cigarettes, alcohol, etc.) represented in the ad portfolio. Compare and contrast the types of appeals underlying these ads, as discussed by Fowles. To what extent do you notice significant shifts of appeal from the 1940s to the present? Which types of appeal seem to you most effective with particular product categories? Is it more likely, for example, that people will buy cigarettes because they want to feel autonomous or because the cigarettes will make them more attractive to the opposite sex?

2. Select a series of ads in different product categories that all appear to rely on the same primary appeal—perhaps the appeal to sex or the appeal to affiliation. Compare and contrast the overall strategies of these ads. Draw upon Fowles and other authors represented in

this chapter to develop your ideas. To what extent do your analyses support arguments often made by social critics (and advertising people) that what people are really buying is the image, rather than the product?

3. Discuss how a selection of ads reveals shifting cultural attitudes over the past six decades toward either (a) gender relations; (b) romance between men and women; (c) smoking; (d) automobiles. In the case of (a) or (b) above, the ads don't have to be for the same category of product. In terms of their underlying appeal, in terms of the implicit or explicit messages embodied both in the text and the graphics, how and to what extent do the ads reveal that attitudes of the target audiences have changed over the years?

4. Select a TV commercial or a TV ad campaign (for example, for Sprint phone service) and analyze the commercial(s) in terms of Fowles's categories, as well as the discussions of some of the authors in this chapter. To what extent do the principles discussed by these authors apply to broadcast, as well as to print ads? What are the special requirements of TV advertising?

5. Find a small group of ads that rely upon little or no body copy—just a graphic, perhaps a headline, and the product name. What common features underlie the marketing strategies of such ads? What kinds of appeal do they make? How do their graphic aspects compare? What makes the need for text superfluous?

6. As indicated in the introduction to this chapter, social critics have charged advertising with numerous offenses: "it fosters material-ism, it psychologically manipulates people to buy things they don't need, it perpetuates gender and racial stereotypes (particularly in its illustrations), it is deceptive, it is offensive, it debases the lan-guage." To what extent do some of the advertisements presented in the ad portfolio (and perhaps others of your own choosing) demon-strate the truth of one or more of these charges? In developing your response, draw upon Bovée and Arens as well as some of the ads in the portfolio (or elsewhere).

7. Read the textual content (headlines and body text) of several ads *without* paying attention (if possible) to the graphics. Compare the effectiveness of the headline and body text by themselves with the effectiveness of the ads, *including* the graphic elements. Focusing on a group of related ads (related by product category, by appeal, by decade, etc.), devise an explanation of how graphics work to effective-ly communicate the appeal and meaning of the products advertised.

8. Many ads employ humor—in the graphics, in the body copy, or both—to sell a product. Examine a group of advertisements that rely on humor to make their appeal and explain how they work. For example, do they play off an incongruity between one element of the ad and another (such as between the headline and the graphic), or between one element of the ad (or the basic message of

the ad) and what we know or assume to be the case in the "real world"? Do they employ wordplay or irony? Do they picture people doing funny things (funny because inappropriate or unrealistic)? What appeal underlines the humor? Aggression? Sex? Nurture? Based on your examination and analyses, what appear to be some of the more effective ways of employing humor?

9. Think of a new product that you have just invented. This product, in your opinion, will revolutionize the world of [fill in the blank]. Devise an advertisement to announce this product to the world. Consider (or reject) using a celebrity to help sell your product. Select the basic appeal of your product (see Fowles). Then, applying concepts and principles discussed by other authors in this chapter, write the headline, subhead, and body copy for the product. Sketch out (or at least describe) the graphic that will accompany the text. Show your proposed ad to one or more of your classmates, get reactions, and then revise the ad, taking into account your market feedback.

10. Imagine that you own a small business—perhaps an independent coffee shop (not Starbucks, Peet's, or Coffee Bean), a videogame company, or a pedicab service that conveys tourists around a chic beach town. Devise an ad that announces your services and extols its benefits. Apply the principles discussed by Fowles and other writers in this chapter.

11. Write a parody ad—one that would never ordinarily be written— applying the selling principles discussed by Fowles and other authors in this unit. For example, imagine you are the manager of the Globe Theatre in Elizabethan England and want to sell season tickets to this season's plays, including a couple of new tragedies by your playwright in residence, Will Shakespeare. Or imagine that you are trying to sell Remington typewriters in the age of computers (no software glitches!). Or—as long as people are selling bottled water—you have found a way to package and sell air. Advertisers can reportedly sell anything with the right message. Give it your best shot.

12. Based on the reading you have done in this chapter, discuss the extent to which you believe advertisements create needs in consumers, reflect existing needs, or some combination of both. In developing your paper, draw on both particular advertisements and on the more theoretical overviews of advertising developed in the chapter.

13. Select one advertisement and conduct two analyses of it, using two different analytical principles: perhaps one from Fowles's list of fifteen emotional appeals and one from Cohen's principles of effective layout. Having conducted your analyses and developed your insights, compare and contrast the strengths and weaknesses of the analytical principles you've employed. Conclude more

broadly with a discussion of how a single analytical principle can close down, as well as open up, understanding of an object under study.

14. As you have seen, advertisements change over time, both across product categories and within categories. And yet the advertisements remain a constant, their presence built on the assumption that consumers can be swayed both overtly and covertly in making purchasing decisions. In a paper drawing on the selections in this chapter, develop a theory on why ads change over time. Is it because people's needs have changed and, therefore, new ads are required? (Do the older ads appeal to the same needs as newer ads?) In developing your discussion, you might track the changes over time in one product category.

RESEARCH ACTIVITIES

1. Drawing upon contemporary magazines (or magazines from a given period), select a set of advertisements in a particular product category. Analyze these advertisements according to Fowles's categories, and assess their effectiveness in terms of the discussions of other authors in this chapter.

2. Select a particular product that has been selling for at least 25 years (e.g., Bayer aspirin, Tide detergent, IBM computers, Oldsmobile—as in "This is not your father's Oldsmobile") and trace the history of print advertising for this product over the years. To what extent has the advertising changed over the years? To what extent has the essential sales appeal remained the same? In addition to examining the ads themselves, you may want to research the company and its marketing practices. You will find two business databases particularly useful: ABI/INFORM and the academic version of LexisNexis.

3. One of the landmark campaigns in American advertising was Doyle, Dane, Bernbach's series of ads for the Volkswagen Beetle in the 1960s. In effect a rebellion against standard auto advertising, the VW ads' Unique Selling Proposition was that ugly is beautiful—an appeal that was overwhelmingly successful. Research the VW ad campaign for this period, setting it in the context of the agency's overall marketing strategy.

4. Among the great marketing debacles of recent decades was Coca-Cola's development in 1985 of a new formula for its soft drink which (at least temporarily) replaced the much beloved old formula. Research this major development in soft drink history, focusing on the marketing of New Coke and the attempt of the Atlanta-based Coca-Coca company to deal with the public reception of its new product.

5. Advertising agencies are hired not only by manufacturers and by service industries; they are also hired by political candidates. In fact, one of the common complaints about American politics is that candidates for public office are marketed just as if they were bars of soap. Select a particular presidential or gubernatorial election and research the print and broadcast advertising used by the rival candidates. You may want to examine the ads not only of the candidates of the major parties but also the candidates of the smaller parties, such as the Green and the Libertarian parties. How do the appeals and strategies used by product ads compare and contrast with those used in ads for political candidates?

6. Public service ads comprise another major category of advertising (in addition to product and service advertising and political advertising). Such ads have been used to recruit people to military service, to get citizens to buy war bonds, to contribute to charitable causes, to get people to support or oppose strikes, to persuade people to stop using (or not to start using) drugs, to prevent drunk driving, etc. Locate a group of public service ads, describe them, and assess their effectiveness. Draw upon Fowles, Bovée, *et al.*, and Cohen in developing your conclusions.

7. Research advertising in American magazines and newspapers before World War II. Focus on a limited number of product lines—for example, soft drinks, soap and beauty products, health-related products. What kind of differences do you see between ads in the first part of the twentieth century and more recent or contemporary advertising for the same types of products? In general, how have the predominant types of appeal used to sell products in the past changed (if they have) with the times? How are the graphics of early ads different from preferred graphics today? How has the body copy changed? (Hint: you may want to be on the alert for ads that make primarily negative appeals—i.e., what may happen to you if you don't use the product advertised.)

Credits

No. 4, October 1996. Reprinted by permission of The American Historical Association and the author.

Page 311: "Community Through Exclusion and Illusion: The Creation of Social Worlds in an American Shopping Mall," by George Lewis, *Journal of Popular Culture*, Vol. 24. No. 2. Fall 1990, pp. 121–36. Copyright © 1990 by George Lewis. Reprinted by permission of Blackwell Publishers.

Page 323: "Mallaise: How to Know If You Have It" from *The Malling of America: An Inside Look at the Great Consumer Paradise* by William Severini Kowinski. Copyright © 1985 by William Severini Kowinski. Reprinted by permission of the author.

CHAPTER 8

Page 335: "Rethinking Weight" by Amanda Spake, *U.S. News and World Report*, February 9, 2004, pp. 51–56. Copyright © 2004 U.S. News and World Report, L.P. Reprinted with permission.

Page 348: Reprinted with the permission of Simon & Schuster Adult Publishing Group from *Eat, Drink, and Be Healthy* by Walter C. Willert, M.D. as adapted from *Nutrition and Your Health: Dietary Guidelines for Americans* (1995). Copyright © 2001 President and Fellows of Harvard College.

Page 354: Excerpt from *Fat Land: How Americans Became the Fattest People in the World* by Greg Critser. Copyright © 2003 by Greg Critser. Reprinted by permission of Houghton Mifflin Company. All rights reserved. First appeared in *Los Angeles Times*, July 22, 2001.

Page 358: NAAFA (National Association to Advance Fat Acceptance) Policy on Dieting and the Diet Industry, *NAAFA Website*. Reprinted by permission of the NAAFA.

Page 362: "Fat and Happy: In Defense of Fat Acceptance" by Mary Ray Worley, *NAAFA Website*. Reprinted by permission of the NAAFA.

Page 367: "Too 'Close to the Bone': The Historical Context for Women's Obsession with Slenderness" by Roberta P. Seid from *Feminist Perspectives on Eating Disorders* edited by Patricia Fallon, Melanie A. Katzman, and Susan C. Wooley. Copyright © 1994 The Guilford Press. Reprinted by permission of The Guilford Press.

Page 380: Reprinted with the permission of Free Press, a division of Simon & Schuster Adult Publishing Group from *Never Satisfied: A Cultural History of Diets, Fantasies and Fat* by Hillel Schwartz. Copyright © 1996 by Hillel Schwartz. All rights reserved.

Page 388: Reprinted with permission from "The Ironic Politics of Obesity" by Marion Nestle, *Science*, February 7, 2003. Copyright © 2003 by The American Association for the Advancement of Science.

Page 390: "The Man Who Couldn't Stop Eating" from *Complications* by Atul Gawande. Copyright © 2002 by Atul Gawande. Reprinted by permission of Henry Holt and Company, LLC.

CHAPTER 9

Page 412: "Advertising's Fifteen Basic Appeals" from *Advertising and Popular Culture* by Jib Fowles. Copyright © 1996 by Jib Fowles. Reprinted by permission of the publisher Sage Publications, Inc.

Page 430: "Making the Pitch in Print Advertising" from *Advertising Excellence* by Courtland L. Bovée, John V. Thill, George P. Dovel, and Marian Burk Wood. Copyright © 1995 The McGraw-Hill Companies, Inc.

Page 436: "Elements of Effective Layout" from *Advertising* by Dorothy Cohen. Copyright © 1988 Dorothy Cohen. Reprinted by permission of Pearson Education, Inc.

Index

I'm confused. If you're critiquing Baumrinds article which is about Milgrims experiment don't you need to explain it.

CHECKLIST FOR WRITING SUMMARIES

- **Read the passage carefully.** Determine its structure. Identify the author's purpose in writing.
- **Reread.** *Label* each section or stage of thought. *Highlight* key ideas and terms.
- **Write one-sentence summaries** of each stage of thought.
- **Write a thesis:** a one- or two-sentence summary of the entire passage.
- **Write the first draft** of your summary.
- **Check your summary** against the original passage.
- **Revise** your summary.

CHECKLIST FOR WRITING CRITIQUES

- **Introduce** both the passage being critiqued and the author.
- **Summarize** the author's main points, making sure to state the author's purpose for writing.
- **Evaluate** the validity of the presentation.
- **Respond** to the presentation: agree and/or disagree.
- **Conclude** with your overall assessment.